OUT OF THE ASHES

Robert W. White is Professor and Chair of the Department of Sociology at Indiana University-Purdue University Indianapolis (IUPUI). He is the author of *Ruairí Ó Brádaigh, The Life and Politics of an Irish Revolutionary* (2006), *Provisional Irish Republicans: An Oral and Interpretive History* (1993), and co-editor of *Self, Identity, and Social Movements* (2000). He also produced the online (open access) documentary, *Unfinished Business: The Politics of 'Dissident' Irish Republicans* (2012):
http://www.ulib.iupui.edu/utility/video/unfinishedbusiness.html.

OUT OF THE ASHES

AN ORAL HISTORY OF THE PROVISIONAL IRISH REPUBLICAN MOVEMENT

(SOCIAL MOVEMENTS VS TERRORISM)

ROBERT W. WHITE

MERRION
PRESS

First published in 2017 by
Merrion Press
10 George's Street
Newbridge
Co. Kildare
Ireland
www.merrionpress.ie

978-1-78537-093-9 (paper)
978-1-78537-095-3 (Kindle)
978-1-78537-115-8 (Epub)
978-1-78537-096-0 (PDF)

British Library Cataloguing in Publication Data
An entry can be found on request

Library of Congress Cataloging in Publication Data
An entry can be found on request

Interior design by www.jminfotechindia.com
Typeset in Garamond 10.5/14
Cover design by Fiachra McCarthy

Printed by TJ International Ltd, Padstow, Cornwall.

CONTENTS

ABBREVIATIONS

AIA	Anglo-Irish Agreement
AICC	Anglo-Irish Intergovernmental Conference
CIRA	Continuity Irish Republican Army
CLMC	Combined Loyalist Military Command
C/S	Chief of Staff
32 CSM	32 County Sovereignty Movement
DAAD	Direct Actions Against Drugs
DUP	Democratic Unionist Party
EEC	European Economic Community
EOKA	Ethniki Organosis Kyprion Agoniston
FBI	Federal Bureau of Investigation
GFA	Good Friday Agreement
GHQ	General Headquarters
GOC	General Officer Commanding
GPO	General Post Office
ICJP	Irish Commission for Justice and Peace
IICD	Independent International Commission on Decommissioning
INLA	Irish National Liberation Army
IRA	Irish Republican Army
IRB	Irish Republican Brotherhood
IRSP	Irish Republican Socialist Party
LVF	Loyalist Volunteer Force
MLA	Member of the Legislative Assembly
NIAS	Northern Ireland Attitude Survey
NICRA	Northern Ireland Civil Rights Association
NILP	Northern Ireland Labour Party
NIO	Northern Ireland Office
NORAID	Irish Northern Aid Committee

ABBREVIATIONS

ONH	Óglaigh na hÉireann
PD	People's Democracy
PIRA	Provisional Irish Republican Army
PRO	Public relations officer
PSNI	Police Service of Northern Ireland
PTA	Prevention of Terrorism Act
PUP	Progressive Unionist Party
RAAD	Republican Action Against Drugs
RIC	Royal Irish Constabulary
RIR	Royal Irish Regiment
RNU	Republican Network for Unity
RSF	Republican Sinn Féin
RTÉ	Radió Teilifís Éireann
RUC	Royal Ulster Constabulary
SDLP	Social Democratic and Labour Party
SF	Sinn Féin
SIS	Secret Intelligence Service
SLR	self-loading rifle
TD	Teachta Dála
UDA	Ulster Defence Association
UDP	Ulster Democratic Party
UDR	Ulster Defence Regiment
UFF	Ulster Freedom Fighters
UKUP	UK Unionist Party
USC	Universal Social Charge
UUP	Ulster Unionist Party
UUUC	United Ulster Unionist Council
UVF	Ulster Volunteer Force

PREFACE

This oral history is the result of more than thirty years' worth of interviews and conversations with activists in the Irish Republican Movement. On the surface it is an updated version of my *Provisional Irish Republicans: An Oral and Interpretive History*. However, other than some quotations from respondents, a few of the figures and following the same general timeline into the 1990s, this is a completely new book.

In the late 1970s and early 1980s, I developed a general interest in the causes and consequences of small group political violence. Then came the 1981 hunger strike. The official view was that the hunger strikers were criminals being used by mafia-like godfathers. From a distance, that seemed off the mark since the typical criminal does not fast to the death for political status. Curiosity led me to J. Bowyer Bell's history, *The Secret Army: The IRA*. Bell had spoken with the Provisionals and offered a different and much more interesting story. In contrast to Bell, it seemed that there was an ever-increasing body of literature on 'terrorism' that was written by academics who had never met a 'terrorist'. Several of those scholars were associated with counter-terrorism institutes and think tanks.

The successful entré of Bell and others, the predominance of the English language and an interest in things Irish, led me to consider a case study of why people joined the Provisionals. With the support and encouragement of David Knoke, I entered the Irish field in January of 1984. The late J. Bowyer Bell, Edward Moxon-Browne, John McCarthy and Rob Robinson were also very kind and helpful in the early stages of this project.

It seems like I've never left the field and there have been interesting interviews and adventures along the way. In speaking about what makes someone a good guerrilla, Seán Mac Stiofáin commented, 'You wouldn't survive very long, would you?' He was correct. In discussing enthusiastic new recruits, I asked Ruairí Ó Brádaigh if they made him nervous. He looked me in the eye and replied, 'I'm suspicious of everyone.' I had known him almost twenty years; I took it as good advice.

Not everything reduces to an entertaining quip, though, and while this has not been participant observation research, at times the observer has gotten closer to the field than intended. I was among the crowd in Belfast in August 1984 when a plastic bullet killed John Downes. In the early 1990s, a senior Sinn Féiner suggested I get in touch with Denis Donaldson, then in New York, and gave him my contact information. I did not contact Donaldson but a Freedom of Information Act request would later reveal that US Customs investigated me. That might explain the wry smile on Donaldson's face when we did eventually meet, in Belfast. More recently, following an on the record interview with activists in a legal political organization, I was arrested by the Gardaí under Section 30 of the Offenses Against the State Act and accused of membership of an unlawful organization, namely Óglaigh na hÉireann. My time as a guest of the state only lasted a few hours, but it was an interesting experience that shed light on what others have experienced on a much more serious level. A couple of days later, while sitting in the Great Hall of the Northern Ireland Assembly watching Deputy First Minister Martin McGuinness have his photo taken with a group of students, it occurred to me that we now had something in common – being arrested by the Gardaí. That evening, while debriefing with an old friend, I was reminded of the old rumour that I was some kind of CIA agent.

Because reality can be quite boring, there is fiction. Contrary to the beliefs of some, I am not now, nor have I ever been, a member of Óglaigh na hÉireann (Provisional, Continuity, Real or any other version) or any other paramilitary organization (including the PLO and Mau Mau, whose activists I have also interviewed). The same holds for Irish Northern Aid, Friends of Sinn Féin, the CIA, the FBI and so on. I am, however, a member of the Sons of the American Revolution. What you see is pretty much what you get – an academic interested in the causes and consequences of small group political violence, in the pay of only Indiana University. All royalties from this book will go to the Barbara White Thoreson Scholarship in the IU School of Liberal Arts, IUPUI.

This research has been funded by a National Science Foundation Dissertation Research Grant (1984), the Harry Frank Guggenheim Foundation (1995), the Department of West European Studies (IU Bloomington), the Indiana University Graduate School (a Fellowship for Off-Campus Dissertation Research), an H.H. Powers Travel Grant (Oberlin College), two Indiana University New Frontiers in the Humanities awards, the IUPUI Office of Professional Development (several travel grants), the Office of the Vice President for International Affairs (IUB – several travel grants), the IU School of Liberal Arts (IUPUI) and the Department of Sociology (IUPUI).

There are so many people to thank for their help and advice that I will likely leave someone out. If so, please accept my apology. I first want to thank the respondents who were willing to share their experiences. I also want to thank again all of those people mentioned in the preface to *Provisional Irish Republicans: An Oral and Interpretive History*. Their help and assistance provided a foundation for what is presented here. Archbishop (now Cardinal) Joseph Tobin, who was in the leadership of the Redemptorist Congregation from 1984 to 1997, graciously provided background information on Father Alec Reid and his efforts at peace.

Some of those who have helped might be surprised to be listed here; none of them are responsible for errors, egregious or trivial: Bob Althauser, Annette Armstrong-Williams, Richard Behal, Erin Bethuram, Stefany Boleyn, Lorenzo Bosi, Líta Ní Chathmhaoil, Dean Tom Davis, Des Dalton, Tijen Demirel-Pegg, Danny Devenny, Ruth Dudley Edwards, Diana Embry, Richard English, Kay Epling, Jack and Bev Falkenberg, Niall Farrell, Sam Graves, Josephine Hayden, Sue Herrell, Kieran Hoare and Barry Houlihan of the James Hardiman Library (National University of Ireland, Galway), Shelby Hampton, Marissa Huth, Merle Illg, Shola Jhanji, Jenny Johnson, Joy Kramer, Sean Lamarr, Lori Langdoc, Libby Laux, John Leamnson, Brian Leon, M.D., Dean David Lewis, Val and Dolores Lynch and family, Mike Maitzen, Clark McCauley, Marisa

McGlinchey, Jim McIlmurray, Anthony McIntyre, Tommy McKearney, Ed Moloney, Seamus Murphy, Yvonne Murphy, Niall Ó Dochartaigh, Ricky O'Rawe, Liam O'Rourke, Erik Osburn, Kristi Palmer, Scott Pegg, Janelle Pivec, Shezad Qazi, David Rapoport, Dieter Reinisch, Mike Scott, Peter Seybold, Andy Smith, Elena Smith, Peter Seybold, Kelly Spurgeon, Nikki Strange, Dave Strong, Ling Tao, David Tharp, Carrie Twomey, Kayla Valdes, Louise Watkins, Jeff Wilson, Maya Youghbor, Conor Graham and Fiona Dunne of Merrion Press, Howard Christy White and Margaret Mary Hanrahan White. The help of Sara Benken, Adam Mills and Casey Mumaw of the Institutional Review Board is very much appreciated. Staff members of the *Belfast Telegraph*, the Linenhall Library and the Burns Library at Boston College have been very helpful. I also want to express how much I value the friendship of a few people who, for various reasons, will remain unidentified.

The following people were exceptionally helpful in responding to my arrest: Sara Benken (of the IRB), Dean William Blomquist, Susan Brouillette (of the office of Senator Richard Lugar), Associate Dean Phil Goff, and Vice President for International Affairs Patrick O'Meara. Fran Quigley's support, suggestions, and friendship are deeply appreciated.

I thank Taylor and Francis for permission to reprint information found in:

R.W. White and T.F. White, 'Revolution in the city: On the resources of urban guerrillas', *Terrorism and Political Violence* 3/4 (1991), pp. 100–32; and

R.W. White, 'The Provisional Irish Republican Army: An Assessment of Sectarianism', *Terrorism and Political Violence* 9/1 (1997), pp. 20–55.

Finally, I want to thank my family – Terry, Kerry and Claire, plus Neptune and Buttons – for their willingness to listen to endless this and thats over the years.

R.W.W.
Indianapolis, Indiana

PART 1

Introduction

1

SOCIAL MOVEMENTS VERSUS TERRORISM

There has never been a period of peace in Ireland. And they tell us that's because the fucking Irish are always causing the trouble ... They started it off. They formed a national army to take over Ireland, colonize it. They kept the army here over a period of a couple of hundred years after that, to hold it. They then planted it with Protestants ... They formed a very tight, close-knit society, where no Catholic or no Irish person, ethnic Irish, could join ... And they ruled Ireland with a mailed fist – literally – a grasp of iron and nobody stepped out of line. And it's only natural that a people are going to breed at some stage someone who says, 'I am not going to take that.' Now what does that make him? Does that make him a rabble-rouser? Does it make him a troublemaker? It ought to. Obviously if he stands up and hits back it makes him a combatant. A combatant, right? And it makes him, therefore, eventually a murderer and a terrorist. And if that's what a terrorist is, I want to be a terrorist.

– Provisional Irish republican 'Terrorist'[1]

More than 3,600 people were killed in the recent 'Irish Troubles' but other than general statements like that, there is little agreement about what happened.

A common interpretation is that the conflict was sectarian, Irish republican Catholics versus loyalist Protestants with the British caught in the middle. Padraig O'Malley, in *The Uncivil Wars: Ireland Today*, writes that, at its most basic level, 'the conflict pits one million-plus Protestants who believe "the maintenance of the Union with Great Britain is the only means of securing their future" against the one half million Catholics who believe "they can only secure their future in a united Ireland"'. Steve Bruce, in *The Red Hand: Protestant Paramilitaries in Northern Ireland*, writes that 'of those who are prepared to kill at all, many are quite happy to kill *anyone* of the other side' and states that the two sides were 'equally sectarian'.[2]

An interesting aspect of the conflict is how openly sectarian Protestant paramilitaries ('loyalists' – loyal to the Crown) were. In the summer of 1996, the RUC blocked a parade by the Orange Order at Drumcree Church, outside Portadown, in County Armagh. The Orange Order is a 'Protestant fraternity'.[3] A mid-Ulster loyalist described their response to the situation:

The initial plan was to hijack a number of Catholic-owned taxis in the Portadown area. They would then be taken to various locations where the cars would be burnt but

Twaddell Avenue protest against a ban on Orange marches showing the support of 'Ulster Protestant Voice', North Belfast, 2014. ©Robert White.

the drivers released unharmed. The idea was to send a clear message to the Catholic community in the Portadown and Lurgan areas: if the Orangemen can't walk down the Garvaghy Road then you won't be allowed to work in any of our areas.[4]

It was in this context that Catholic taxi driver Michael McGoldrick was shot dead outside Lurgan. Anti-Catholic sentiments and the view that defending Protestantism is part of the loyalist identity are common themes in loyalist commentary and literature. A banner for 'United Protestant Voice' was part of the ongoing Twaddell Avenue protest against a ban on Orange marches in North Belfast.

In contrast, Irish republicans deny that their struggle is sectarian. Instead, they claim they were (and in some cases still are) fighting a war of national liberation against the British. In 1985, a veteran of the Provisional IRA and a Sinn Féin activist from Derry was asked, 'Is the struggle in the North a sectarian struggle?' He replied:

No. Well, it depends what aspect you take on it. From a republican aspect it's not sectarian …no one can call themselves a republican and be sectarian at the same time. If there has been sectarianism it would have showed itself. And I think that an awful lot of people may have gotten involved in the Republican Movement for one reason or another but there's a self-weeding process which means that the more people mix with republicans and talk to republicans the more obvious it becomes that any notion of sectarianism hasn't got any place in the Republican Movement.[5]

The respondent claimed that sectarianism is contrary to the nature of Irish republicanism which, in the words of Wolfe Tone, seeks to unite 'Catholic, Protestant, and Dissenter'.[6]

The respondent is from Derry City, however, and Derry has an Irish nationalist/Catholic majority and does not have a history of sectarian conflict. Belfast, on the other hand, has a lengthy history of sectarian conflict. One of the more notorious events of the conflict was the Belfast IRA's attack on the Bayardo Bar in 1975 that left four people dead. The IRA claimed that loyalists paramilitaries frequented the bar. However, the deceased were Protestant civilians out for a drink at their neighbourhood tavern.[7] A Sinn Féiner from Belfast was asked to comment on the sectarian nature of the conflict. He responded by saying: '*Obviously I don't agree with it. I think that the reasons why there is a war in the six counties are based very firmly in the political structure of the six counties ...*' His account is similar to that of the Provisional from Derry. Both claim the conflict was political, not sectarian, but the Belfast Provisional also admitted that there were sectarian activists in the Irish Republican Movement. In August 1969, Protestant mobs attacked Catholic neighbourhoods in Belfast. The Belfast Sinn Féiner was asked if there were Catholics who just wanted to hit back at the Protestants in response. He commented:

> *I think that there are sectarian Catholics. And I think there are sectarian people in the Republican Movement. Now I don't think they're in a majority ... But I think that's a misdirected hatred. I think that what people should be doing is not looking at how they can get one up on Protestants but at how they can change the political situation. But, you're quite right – obviously in 1969 and 1971, after the pogroms, there was a blind wish to retaliate and to kill and shoot and burn and so on. But – and I think the media particularly like to cast the Republican Movement in the role of godfathers and those that organize sectarian reprisals, and so on ... it flies in the face of history ... what has happened in the North – the conflict in the North is not sectarian in that it has not originated for sectarian reasons. It's originated for political reasons.*[8]

These comments show some of the complexity of the conflict in Ireland and the Irish Republican Movement.[9] The Provisionals were influenced by sectarian attacks, but they were non-sectarian and their inspiration – at least from the perspective of members – is political.

What people say and what they do may be very different. Table 1 summarizes the groups that killed people and their victims from the summer of 1969 until the signing of the Good Friday Agreement in 1998.[10] Broadly, there were three actors: Irish republicans, Protestant paramilitaries and the security forces. The Provisional IRA was the most deadly organization, responsible for almost 1,800 fatalities. Protestant/loyalist paramilitaries, including the Ulster Volunteer Force (UVF), the Ulster Freedom Fighters (UFF) and the Loyalist Volunteer Force (LVF), killed almost a thousand people. The security forces, the Royal Ulster Constabulary (RUC), the Ulster Defence Regiment (UDR)/Royal Irish Regiment (RIR) and the British Army killed more than 350 people, about one-fifth as many victims as the Provisionals.

TABLE 1

Cross-tabulation of Perpetrators and Victims, Irish Conflict 1969–1998

Victim	Organization/Group Responsible						
	Provisional IRA	Official IRA/ INLA/Other Republican Groups	Protestant Paramilitaries (Loyalists)	British Army	RUC	UDR/ RIR	Other
British Army	469	28	1	3	2	0	3
RUC	271	16	7	2	1	0	3
UDR/RIR	191	7	3	2	0	0	1
Provisional IRA	123	3	19	108	11	2	3
Other Republicans	5	30	8	15	5	0	3
Protestant Paramilitaries	28	8	69	11	2	0	1
Catholic Civilians	164	30	661	135	24	6	31
Protestant Civilians	349	36	120	17	5	2	27
Political Activists	16	9	31	1	2	0	2
Prison Officers	21	2	2	0	0	0	0
Former Security Officers	58	6	0	0	0	0	0
Other	101	10	58	3	1	0	7
Total	**1,796**	**185**	**979**	**297**	**53**	**10**	**81**

The table shows that a little more than half of the Provisional IRA's victims were members of the security forces, including more than 450 British soldiers. These casualties are consistent with the argument that the IRA was fighting a war of national liberation. If the Provisional IRA was primarily motivated by sectarian hatred of Protestants, then why target a victim who will shoot back? The table also shows that the Provisional IRA was responsible for the deaths of almost 125 of its own members; several of them were killed in premature explosions. In contrast, the British Army killed more than a hundred Provisional IRA volunteers, but only eleven Protestant paramilitaries. The British Army was in a much more deadly conflict with the Provisional IRA than it was with loyalists.

Focusing on civilian casualties reveals some of the complexity of what happened. Each actor killed civilians, but not to the same degree. The Provisional IRA killed more than five hundred civilians, and approximately two-thirds of them were Protestant. Many of those civilians, Catholic and Protestant, were killed in accidental explosions, especially during the Provisional IRA's bombing campaign (1971–6). Overall, however, approximately 20 per cent of the Provisional IRA's victims were Protestant civilians. In contrast, the vast majority (80 per cent) of the victims of Protestant paramilitaries were civilians, and roughly two-thirds of loyalist victims were Catholic civilians. Loyalists targeted the Catholic community, and many of their victims were shot in individual incidents. In a relative sense, the Provisional IRA was much less sectarian than Protestant paramilitaries. This does not deny the fact that the Provisional IRA killed hundreds of Protestant civilians, many of whom were shot dead or killed in explosions where Protestant civilians were predominantly or exclusively the victims, and in no way is Table 1 meant to reduce victims to numbers.

The British Army's victims are especially interesting. Not only did the British Army kill more civilians than it killed paramilitaries, British soldiers killed almost eight times as many Irish nationalist/Catholic civilians as they did pro-union/Protestant civilians (unionists). The two communities had vastly different relationships with the British Army.[11]

Accounts from soldiers who served in Northern Ireland offer insight into those relationships. In *Bloody Belfast: An Oral History of the British Army's War Against the IRA*, a soldier describes having tea and cakes with a lady and her son in Sandy Row, a Protestant area in South Belfast. Her son asked, 'Can I have a look at your gun, mister?' The soldier unloaded the rifle and:

> I handed it to him and he then proceeded to strip the working part out and told me how they worked! I asked him how he knew so much about the SLR and had another soldier showed him? He replied, 'No; me daddy's got one but he won't let me play with it.' There followed a stunned silence but quickly broken by the mother who had turned bright red. She said: 'The little bugger is always joking; take no notice, it's only make believe.' We did not search that house which I suppose we should have done, so I shall never know if the 'little bugger' nearly gave the game away.[12]

Another soldier, who patrolled Andersonstown and Lenadoon in nationalist West Belfast, described his experience:

> If you stopped any time, you stopped adjacent to a door or window, because the Provos don't like shooting at you if there was a prospect of hitting their own; they preferred you out in the open or against a plain wall. If people were nearby, we stood close to them so they acted as a human shield. It may seem callous to use civilians as protection, but it was a battle of wits and using any means possible to outwit the gunman or sniper.[13]

In Protestant/loyalist Sandy Row, a soldier overlooked evidence of paramilitary activity and in Catholic/republican West Belfast, a soldier used civilians as a shield. British soldiers did much more than use nationalist civilians as shields, though. In 1972, soldiers in South Fermanagh stabbed to death two nationalists, Michael Naan and Andrew Murray – the 'Pitchfork Murders'.[14]

It is not a surprise that British soldiers viewed the two communities differently. The Provisional IRA was embedded in a community that wanted out of the United Kingdom. That community, through Irish republican paramilitaries, was killing British soldiers. Protestant paramilitaries were embedded in a community that wanted to remain a part of the United Kingdom – the British

Army was their army. Anne Cadwallader, in *Lethal Allies*, offers convincing evidence of collusion between the security forces and loyalist paramilitaries.[15] The 'Troubles' are not neatly summarized as a Catholic–Protestant sectarian conflict.

The conflict is not easily summarized as the British Army defending the liberal democracy of Northern Ireland from Provisional IRA terrorists, either. 'Democracy' in Northern Ireland was compromised as evidenced by the fact that, between 1971 and 1975, thousands of people were arrested, never charged and held indefinitely – internment. British soldiers who killed Catholic/nationalist civilians got away with it. The first British soldier prosecuted for killing an unarmed civilian was Corporal Francis Foxford, who shot dead 12-year-old Kevin Heatley on 28 February 1973. Kevin Heatley was the sixty-ninth Catholic civilian killed by the British Army in Northern Ireland. Foxford was charged with manslaughter and found guilty but the conviction was quashed on the grounds of irregular conduct by prosecuting personnel. The first British soldier convicted of murder while on duty during the conflict was Private Ian Thain, who killed Thomas Reilly on 9 August 1983. Reilly was the 106th Catholic civilian killed by the British Army in Northern Ireland. Thain was sentenced to life in prison but, after serving twenty-six months of the sentence, he was released and allowed to return to his British Army regiment.[16] The 'rule of law' that is essential to democracy was compromised in Northern Ireland.[17]

From 1970 onwards, it was routine to describe the Provisional IRA as an elite terrorist organization. Following the 1981 hunger strike, Paul Wilkinson offered the following:

> The Provisional IRA is one of the best equipped, and most experienced and ruthless terrorist organizations active in Western Europe today. In terms of experience it has been waging campaigns even longer than the Italian *Brigate Rosse* and the Basque *Euzkadi: ta Askatasuna*, and it is regarded very highly in international terrorist circles as an exemplar of organization and tactics against a highly professional and equally experienced adversary, the British security forces.[18]

In *Terrorist Group Profiles*, a report by the US Vice President's Task Force on Combatting Terrorism led by George H.W. Bush, the Provisional IRA is described as seeking to 'Undermine British support for Northern Ireland remaining in the United Kingdom through a campaign of attrition and terrorism'.[19]

The labels 'terrorist' and 'terrorism' are problematic and several scholars comment on the difficulties of defining terrorism. In fact, the problem is not with defining the term but with the selective application of the definition. Paul Wilkinson was co-editor of the influential journal *Terrorism and Political Violence* and was co-founder of the Centre for the Study of Terrorism and Political Violence at the University of St Andrews. In *Terrorism versus Democracy: The Liberal State Response*, he defined terrorism as: 'the systematic use of coercive intimidation, usually to service political ends. It is used to create and exploit a climate of fear among a wider target group than the immediate victims of the violence and to publicize a cause, as well as to coerce a target acceding to the terrorists' aims.' According to Wilkinson, terrorism 'can be employed by desperate and weak minorities, by states as a tool of domestic and foreign policy, or by belligerents as an accompaniment in all types and stages of warfare'.[20] Anti-state insurgents, pro-state vigilantes and state agents engage in terrorism.

Based on this definition, the Provisional IRA was a terrorist organization, but can the same be said of the British Army? In August 1971, in order to quell unrest, internment was introduced. Over a three-day period, British soldiers in the Parachute Regiment shot dead eleven civilians in West Belfast, including Revd Hugh Mullan, a Catholic priest on the way to give last rites to a victim, and Joan O'Connor, a 50-year-old housewife and mother of eight children. The 'Ballymurphy Massacre' was not an isolated incident. Six months later, soldiers, again in the Parachute Regiment, shot twenty-six Catholic civilians attending an anti-internment march in Derry; thirteen people died that day, a fourteenth victim died later. Some terrorism scholars point out that it was an illegal march, as if that somehow lessens the fact that British soldiers shot dead unarmed civilians with high-powered rifles.[21] Paul Wilkinson described 'Bloody Sunday' as an 'horrific aberration'.[22] An alternative explanation is that Bloody Sunday resulted from a policy that called for 'the systemic use of coercive intimidation' brought on by the failure of internment to quell dissent. The British Army killed well over a hundred Catholic civilians. That is an awful lot of 'aberrations'.[23]

Unfortunately, history is littered with examples of Western states using violence to intentionally target civilian populations and deliver a political message. During the night of 14–15 December 1940, the Luftwaffe destroyed Coventry. In retaliation, Prime Minister Winston Churchill ordered a plan 'for the most destructive possible bombing attacks against a selected German town'. According to the War Cabinet's plan, 'We should rely largely on fires, and should choose a closely built-up town, where bomb craters in the streets would impede the firefighter' and 'Since we aimed at affecting the enemy's morale, we should attempt to destroy the greater part of a particular town.' On 16 December 1940, the Royal Air Force bombed Mannheim and Churchill's goal for 1941 was to 'bomb every Hun corner of Europe'.[24]

Activists are aware that governments denounce terrorism while they kill people for their own political ends. Danny Morrison, then Sinn Féin's Director of Publicity, was interviewed in 1988. Morrison said *'the IRA is not a terrorist organization'* and he compared IRA violence with violence by the British and US governments: *'the British, for example, in order to break the German positions' power, during the second World War, bombed Hamburg, bombed Dresden, bombed Cologne, when they were packed with refugees – great firestorm, [thousands of] civilians burned to death in one night. What are we talking about in the IRA – eleven people getting killed? [the Enniskillen bomb, 1987].'* In April 1986, the La Belle Discotheque in West Berlin, a popular haunt for United States servicemen, was bombed. Three people were killed and, in retaliation, the United States launched air strikes on the Libyan cities of Tripoli and Benghazi. Danny Morrison drew further comparison:

> *Now, the IRA has never done anything like that. And that was in reprisal for one marine getting killed in a disco, in the La Belle disco in Berlin. And a government – [the] American government – goes out and kills … civilians, including babies, including women. Now, you give me an example where the IRA has killed half of that number? … there were twenty-one civilians killed in two bomb attacks in Birmingham in 1974. And warnings were passed on. And the warnings were not acted on. And in*

one case I think the warning was badly passed on ... Now that's the most people ever killed in a single instance by the IRA and it was not done deliberately. Now compare that with a premeditated act of aerial bombing.[25]

Even if it was Morrison's job to present his movement in the best possible light, academics cannot ignore the fact that Western states, as described above by Paul Wilkinson, engage in 'the systemic use of coercive intimidation'. In the 1950s, one of the categories of the 'nuclear target list' of the United States was 'Population'. If the 'shock and awe' bombing of Baghdad in 2003 was not 'the systematic use of coercive intimidation', then what is?[26]

Faced with the dilemma of state violence, some terrorism experts refine their definitions and intentionally exclude state activity. In *Inside Terrorism*, for example, Bruce Hoffman states that terrorism is 'perpetrated by a subnational group or non-state entity' and then defines it as 'the deliberate creation and exploitation of fear through violence or the threat of violence in pursuit of political change'.[27] Restricting terrorism to 'subnational' groups is problematic. As Jeff Goodwin notes, 'state terrorism has been much more deadly than oppositional terrorism'.[28] The restriction leads to using different terms to describe the same political behaviour. In their research on approaches to reducing 'terrorism', for example, Laura Dugan and Erica Chenoweth refer to Palestinian violence as 'terrorism' but Israeli state violence as 'repression', even though each involves 'the deliberate creation and exploitation of fear through violence'. A result is their ahistorical claim that, 'The modern terrorist environment can be traced to the Palestine Liberation Organization ...'[29] Referring to state terror as 'repression' undermines our understanding of complex political conflicts and contributes to what Marc Sageman has described as 'stagnation' in terrorism research.[30]

'Terrorists' are aware of the hypocrisy. Ruairí Ó Brádaigh, a former IRA Chief of Staff, was elected to the Dublin parliament while a political prisoner in the 1950s. When asked about being described as a terrorist, he laughed and commented:

Why do they never say that I was elected a parliamentary representative in the 1950s when I was elected to an all-Ireland parliament of the future? They won't say that because to say that would admit that there has been support and that there can be support in quantity in the future. So, it's one's terminology. Somebody said one person's freedom fighter is another person's terrorist. It depends what side you're on.[31]

Critics might dismiss Ó Brádaigh's view as self-serving, but scholars embark on a slippery slope when they ignore activists' self-definitions. Even a cursory reading of twentieth-century political history shows that Éamon de Valera, Menachem Begin and Nelson Mandela, along with Gerry Adams and Martin McGuinness, were 'terrorists' who became constitutional politicians. Chances are that being labelled a terrorist has not led anyone to reject political violence. More important, the labels 'terrorism' and 'terrorist' are pretty much useless for helping us understand why people engage in small-group political violence.

Instead of worrying about the definition of terrorism, scholars would be better off if they adopted a social movements approach and used the more neutral term 'political violence'.

Charles Tilly, a noted scholar of social movements, defines political violence as 'any observable interaction in the course of which persons or objects are seized or physically damaged in spite of resistance'.[32] A virtue of this definition is it acknowledges that state and non-state actors threaten and engage in political violence. This allows for examination of small group violence, large-scale violence by governments and everything in-between, without using labels that suggest some kinds of political violence are better or worse than others.

Another advantage of the social movements approach is that it is also more neutral when it comes to trying to understand and interpret people's behaviour. In some quarters, there is an assumption that politically violent behaviour is qualitatively different from non-violent political behaviour. Henry Patterson, for example, objects to describing Provisional IRA members as activists, stating:

> I do not think it useful to use the portmanteau term 'activist' to describe someone committed to the use of violence as a prime means of bringing about political change. The term is better suited to those who were involved in the civil rights movement and in organisations, movements, and parties that sought to bring change through popular mobilisation, not through violence.[33]

The assumption that non-violent and violent politics are distinct is untenable, however, since state actors, the police and soldiers, *and* non-state actors engage in violent and non-violent political behavior, as shown in Table 1. Donatella della Porta, in *Social Movements, Political Violence, and the State: A Comparative Analysis of Italy and Germany*, writes, 'We should not forget, however, that violent political actions were performed by normal activists, and that the members of the most radical organizations began their careers in normal organizations.'[34]

The social movement literature shows that state violence and insurgent violence are often connected. In their examination of collective violence in Europe, *The Rebellious Century, 1830– 1930*, Charles Tilly, Louise Tilly and Richard Tilly show that 'violence grows out of an *inter*action of organized groups which are carrying on sustained collective action' and that 'violent events did not begin much differently from the non-violent ones'.[35] States and their agents are not neutral. Political violence develops when one actor, whether it is a government or a political group, resists a claim from another actor to economic and social resources and/or political power. Because violence grows out of interaction, the initial intentions of actors 'provide shaky criteria for the distinction of violence from nonviolence'.[36] What may have started with the best of intentions, a non-violent civil rights protest, may end with political violence, as happened in Derry on Bloody Sunday.

Because violence grows out of interaction between political opponents and because we cannot assume that states are neutral actors, William Gamson, in *The Strategy of Social Protest*, argues that, 'In place of the old duality of extremist politics and pluralist politics, there is simply politics.' Gamson writes, 'Rebellion, in this view, is simply politics by other means.'[37] Peacefully marching on a street and flying a hijacked aeroplane into the World Trade Center may lie at different extremes of a continuum, but each is a *political* behaviour.

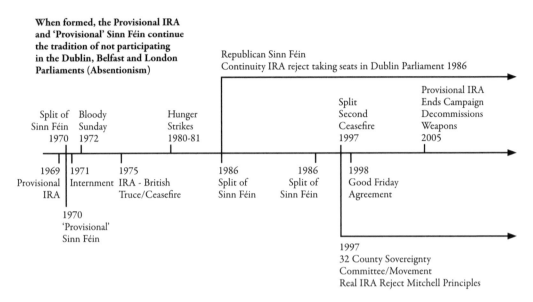

When formed, the Provisional IRA
and 'Provisional' Sinn Féin continue
the tradition of not participating
in the Dublin, Belfast and London
Parliaments (Absentionism)

Republican Sinn Féin
Continuity IRA reject taking seats in Dublin Parliament 1986

Split of   Bloody   Hunger   Split   Provisional IRA
Sinn Féin   Sunday   Strikes   Second   Ends Campaign
1970   1972   1980-81   Ceasefire   Decommissions
                                                                                1997   Weapons
                                                                                               2005

1969   1971   1975   1986   1986   1998
Provisional Internment IRA - British   Split of   Split of   Good Friday
IRA   Truce/Ceasefire   Sinn Féin   Sinn Féin   Agreement

1970
'Provisional'
Sinn Féin

1997
32 County Sovereignty
Committee/Movement
Real IRA Reject Mitchell Principles

FIGURE 1

Provisional Irish Republican Timeline (1969–2005)

This oral history examines the political choices that led people into two organizations of the Irish Republican Movement, namely the Provisional IRA and 'Provisional' Sinn Féin. The Provisionals, and the social and political changes that influenced their activism, are followed from their formation in 1969/70 through two splits (1986, 1997), the Good Friday Agreement (1998) and the transformation of Sinn Féin into a constitutional political party, including the formal end of the Provisional IRA campaign and the decommissioning of weapons in 2005.[38]

A unique feature of this oral history is that it is informed by accounts from activists that were collected over a thirty-year period. My intention is neither to praise nor to condemn the Provisionals, but rather to draw on their accounts to present what happened between 1969 and 2005 from their perspective. The end result, I hope, is an increased understanding of the social processes that lead people into and out of involvement in social movement organizations that engage in political violence. Underlying the approach is the conviction that if scholars want to understand why people do the things they do, then they should speak to them.

Some scholars question this approach since there is a tendency to assume that interaction with activists is an indicator of sympathy for the cause. As IRA historian J. Bowyer Bell writes: 'Such investigation based on access – achieved after an endless vigil in some largely uninhabited hotel at the back of the beyond – often assures that the orthodox assume sympathy with the rebel. Damned by hound for consorting with the hare.'[39] Because they don't like the message, some critics question the messenger. There is also a concern that accounts from activists cannot be trusted – that the Provisionals engage in 'Provo-speak'.[40]

It is widely established that scholars should not accept accounts from activists at face value, whether or not the activists embrace violent politics. Accounts from activists should not be dismissed out of hand, either. Although some social scientists are content to observe behaviour from a distance and then draw conclusions, we should not pursue what has been described as the 'sociology of the chicken yard'.[41] Unlike chickens, we can ask people about their motives, ask them to explain the meaning of events for them. Instead of condemning or condoning armed struggle – 'terrorism' for those who insist – social knowledge is better served if we only seek to understand the behaviour. Explaining social behaviour without even attempting to speak with those engaging in it is at best misguided but, more often, it reflects academic arrogance. When it comes to 'terrorism research', too many scholars observe the behaviour from a distance and end up with results that reflect the perspective of the governmental and non-governmental agencies that fund them.[42]

Those who remain convinced that the accounts of persons who endorse political violence cannot be trusted may want to consult the methodological procedures described in Appendix 1. Otherwise, I leave it to the reader to assess how much 'Provo-speak' invalidates what follows.

2

RESISTANCE (1170–1923)

In every generation the Irish people have asserted their right to national freedom and sovereignty; six times during the past three hundred years they have asserted it in arms.

– 1916 Proclamation of the Irish Republic[1]

The Provisional IRA and 'Provisional' Sinn Féin were created in December 1969 and January 1970. However, the roots of Irish resistance to English rule date from the Anglo-Normans of the twelfth century. Friedrich Engels described Ireland 'as England's first colony' and wrote that the country was 'completely ruined by the English wars of conquest from 1100 to 1850 …'[2] Irish Republicans constantly refer to this conquest, if selectively.

By the end of the seventeenth century, during which the Irish lost three wars, perhaps 90 per cent of Irish lands were under the control of a Protestant Ascendancy whose allegiance was to London. Protestant control was especially evident in Dublin, Ireland's capital, and in Ulster where the lands of Gaelic chiefs had been confiscated and given to colonists from Scotland and England. The colonists differed from the Irish in their religion, customs and language. The vast majority of the population was Catholic and had few social, political or economic rights.[3]

In the eighteenth century, the development of republican political philosophy and the inspiration of the American and French revolutions brought political change. In the 1790s, for example, suffrage was extended to Catholic landholders. Others wanted more radical change and progressives in the Church of Ireland and 'Dissenters' – Protestants in denominations that suffered discrimination at the hands of the established Church of Ireland – formed the Society of United Irishmen in Belfast. They were middle-class manufacturers, drapers and merchants, and they were disenchanted with English commerce laws designed to restrict Irish production. Catholics were attracted to the Society's political program, which espoused religious equality. The United Irishmen wanted to unite 'Catholic, Protestant, and Dissenter' and establish the 'rights of man' in Ireland but they were driven underground and into exile.[4]

Theobald Wolfe Tone, born in Dublin and a member of the Church of Ireland, was the most notable of the United Irishmen. The author of the influential pamphlet, 'An Argument on Behalf of the Catholics in Ireland', Tone was exiled in 1795. In the United States and in France he tried to convince republican governments to support Irish independence. Tone summarized his political philosophy with the following:

To subvert the tyranny of our execrable government, to break the connection with England, the never-failing source of all our political evils, and to assert the independence of my country – these were my objects. To unite the whole people of Ireland, to abolish the memory of all past dissensions, and to substitute the common name of Irishman in place of the denominations of Protestant, Catholic and Dissenter – these were my means.[5]

In 1798, Tone helped to organize a French invasion in support of an Irish rebellion. The rebellion failed and United Irishmen were executed, fled the country or went into hiding. Tone was captured aboard a French ship and asked to be treated as an officer of the French Army. The request was denied and he was found guilty of treason. He was scheduled for a public hanging but, instead, took his own life.[6]

The 1798 rebellion strengthened England's ties with Ireland. The Act of Union, effective from 1 January 1801, suppressed the Irish parliament in Dublin and created the United Kingdom of Great Britain and Ireland. At the same time, Tone became a martyr and his tomb, in Bodenstown, County Kildare, became a site for pilgrimage. The Act of Union did not solve the 'Anglo-Irish problem'. In 1803, Robert Emmet, a surviving United Irishman, organized an attack on Dublin Castle that failed. Emmet's oration from the dock has become part of Irish republican lore: 'When my country takes her place among the nations of the earth, then and not till then, let my epitaph be written.'[7] Emmet was hanged and then beheaded, and his supporters, fearing the authorities, buried him secretly, without epitaph.

In the 1840s, Daniel O'Connell mobilized the Catholic peasantry who worked the land but did not own it. He was a liberal, opposed to slavery and political violence as a matter of principle. A campaign by the Catholic Association, led by O'Connell, won Catholic emancipation (the right to take seats in parliament) in 1829. However, a campaign by the Repeal Association in the 1840s, also led by O'Connell, was unable to overturn the Act of Union. Members of Young Ireland, like William Smith O'Brien, John Mitchel and Fintan Lalor, supported O'Connell but were not opposed to the use of physical force.[8]

As it became clear that the Repeal Association would fail, the social and economic situation in Ireland was becoming desperate. In 1845, 1846 and 1847, blight struck the staple of Ireland's peasantry, the potato. Absentee landlords and British laissez-faire economics exacerbated the problem; the government did not intervene and Ireland continued to export food while hunger, typhus, dysentery and scurvy became pervasive. Between 1846 and 1851, famine and emigration reduced Ireland's population by more than two million people.[9]

The devastation caused by the famine led the Young Irelanders to break with Daniel O'Connell and agitate for rebellion. The government responded with arrests and habeas corpus was suspended. John Mitchel, for example, was arrested, found guilty of treason and exiled. Mitchel's *Jail Journal*, which chronicles his transportation to Bermuda and Van Dieman's Land, is a classic of prison literature. In 1848, William Smith O'Brien led a small rebellion that was quickly suppressed and, in 1849, another attempt at rebellion led by Fintan Lalor also failed.

The Young Ireland Movement is especially important because contemporary Irish Republicans claim direct descent from 1848. Veterans of 1848 established the secret Irish Republican Brotherhood (IRB) in Ireland and the open Fenian Brotherhood in the United States for immigrants who had fled famine and poverty.[10] By the 1860s, and with the help of Irish-American veterans of the US Civil War, the IRB and the Fenians were organizing a rebellion. The authorities again suspended habeas corpus and arrested prominent activists, including Jeremiah O'Donovan Rossa. In 1867, a disorganized rebellion was quickly suppressed.

As happened in 1848, this did not end the Irish Republican Movement. Throughout the 1870s and 1880s, the Fenians and the IRB carried out a dynamite war in England, but their legacy is more complex than a simple refusal to end political violence. Their prisoners suffered dearly and their supporters used that suffering to generate sympathy. In a letter smuggled from prison, O'Donovan Rossa described how his hands were shackled behind his back and he was forced to eat like a dog: 'I have already told you about the hypocrisy of these English masters who, after placing me in a position which forced me to get down on my knees and elbows to eat, are now depriving me of food and light and giving me chains and a Bible.'[11]

Karl Marx was one of many people who rejected Fenian violence but sympathized with Fenian prisoners.[12] In a by-election in Tipperary in 1869, O'Donovan Rossa was the first Irish Republican prisoner elected to the British parliament. The British, however, voided the election.[13]

Fenians were also involved in Land League agitation that won back from landlords much of what had been confiscated in the seventeenth century. Coupled with the Land League was the rise of the Home Rule Movement. Charles Stuart Parnell, a member of the Protestant Ascendancy, was the leader of the Irish Parliamentary Party at Westminster. In 1886, Parnell achieved a measure of success when Prime Minister William Gladstone introduced a Government of Ireland Act that would have re-established an Irish parliament in Dublin. However, the Unionist community, especially in Ulster, feared that 'Home Rule' meant 'Rome Rule' and thirty-two people were killed in sectarian riots in Belfast.[14] The Bill failed, but the fight between constitutional Irish nationalists pushing for Home Rule and Protestant and Conservative defenders of the Union dominated Irish politics up to the First World War. When Home Rule legislation was finally passed, in 1914, it was rescinded until after the War and then eclipsed by events.

During this time of political ferment, James Connolly, a socialist and labour organizer, helped found the Irish Citizen Army to defend workers in Dublin. In opposition to Home Rule and in defence of the Union, Sir Edward Carson and James Craig helped found the Ulster Volunteers (later, UVF).[15] In response to the UVF, the IRB helped organize the Irish National Volunteers. One of the IRB leaders was Tom Clarke, a Fenian who had spent fifteen years in English prisons. Clarke and his IRB comrades brought like-minded nationalists into their conspiracy, including Thomas McDonagh, Joseph Plunkett and Patrick Pearse.[16]

Pearse was special, a teacher and poet known for impassioned speeches. At the 1913 Wolfe Tone commemoration, Pearse described Tone's final resting place as 'the holiest place in Ireland'.[17] In 1915, Jeremiah O'Donovan Rossa died in New York and his body was returned to Dublin for burial. Pearse turned the funeral into a major political event, declaring at the graveside:

> The defenders of this realm have worked well in secret and in the open. They think that they have pacified Ireland. They think that they have purchased half of us and intimidated the other half. They think that they have foreseen everything, think that they have provided against everything; but the fools, the fools, the fools! – they have left us our Fenian dead, and, while Ireland holds these graves, Ireland unfree shall never be at peace.[18]

Irish Republicans still draw on Pearse's oration for inspiration.

At the outbreak of the First World War, Edward Carson urged the UVF to join the British Army. John Redmond, Parnell's successor as leader of the Irish Parliamentary Party, also encouraged the Irish Volunteers to enlist and it split the organization. A majority supported their

Chief of Staff, Eoin MacNeill, who was opposed to Irish soldiers fighting for Britain. Unknown to MacNeill, the IRB had decided that 'Ireland's honour would be tarnished if the war were allowed to pass, as the Boer War [1899–1902] had been, without a fight being made.'[19]

Their plan was to arm the Irish Volunteers with weapons from Germany and use a routine mobilization as a cover to launch a rebellion on Easter Sunday, 1916. One of the organizers was Sir Roger Casement, who was delivered to the Kerry coast by a German submarine a few days before Easter. However, Casement was arrested, charged with treason and ended up in the Tower of London. On Holy Saturday, the Royal Navy intercepted the *Aud*, loaded with German weapons. The ship was scuttled off the coast of Cork and when Eoin MacNeill discovered the IRB's plan, he issued an order cancelling Irish Volunteer parades on Easter Sunday. The Military Council considered the situation and went ahead with the rebellion.[20]

On 'Easter Monday' rebels seized the GPO in Dublin and Patrick Pearse, 'Commander-in-Chief of the Army of the Republic and President of the Provisional Government', proclaimed the Irish Republic: 'IRISHMEN AND IRISHWOMEN: In the name of God and of the dead generations from which she receives her old tradition of nationhood, Ireland, through us, summons her children to her flag and strikes for her freedom ...' The Proclamation was signed by Tom Clarke, P.H. Pearse, James Connolly, Seán MacDermott, Eamonn Kent, Thomas McDonagh and Joseph Plunkett.

Within a week, central Dublin was reduced to rubble and the Easter Rising suppressed. There was little support for the rebellion, but the British overreaction that followed generated sympathy for the republican cause. Early on the morning of 4 May 1916, Joseph Plunkett was allowed to marry Grace Gifford in the Kilmainham Prison Chapel; he was then shot by firing squad. James Connolly had been wounded in the GPO. He was carried on a stretcher to the prison yard, watched the execution of Seán MacDermott, and then strapped upright in a chair and shot. Willie Pearse played a minor role in the rebellion and was evidently executed because he was Patrick's brother; they were the only sons of a widowed mother. Casement's situation was complicated because he had been knighted for exposing colonial abuses in the Congo and Brazil. During the summer his reputation was smeared by the release of diaries detailing homosexual activity. Casement was found guilty of treason, hanged in Pentonville Prison and buried in a quicklime grave. Sixteen Irish Republicans were executed for their participation in the Rising, including all seven of the signers of the Proclamation. Their execution ensured they became martyrs for Ireland.[21]

When the 1916 prisoners were released, they reorganized the Irish Republican Army and the political party Sinn Féin (Ourselves or Ourselves Alone). Arthur Griffith, a Dublin journalist, had founded the party in 1905 and several of the rebels were members; the Rising was also referred to as the 'Sinn Féin Rebellion'. Sinn Féin became the political wing of the Irish Republican Movement and Éamon de Valera, the most senior of the surviving 1916 leaders, was elected the party's President. In a by-election in 1917, Count Plunkett, Joseph Plunkett's father and a Sinn Féin candidate, was elected to Westminster. He refused to take his seat and, instead, called for the creation of an independent Irish parliament. It was in this context, with the First World War still raging, that the British considered extending conscription to Ireland. The threat that Irish men would be compelled to serve in the British Army united nationalists. The British relented and Sinn Féin benefitted.

The First World War ended on 11 November 1918. The next month, Sinn Féin won 73 of the 105 Irish seats at Westminster; the Irish Parliamentary Party, representing constitutional Irish nationalists, won 6 seats and the Unionist Party, representing Protestant and Loyalist North-East Ireland, won 26 seats. On 21 January 1919, the elected Sinn Féin representatives who were available (several of them had been arrested) met at the Mansion House in Dublin, the official residence of the Lord Mayor of Dublin. They ratified the Easter Proclamation, declared Irish independence and formed a government, Dáil Éireann (Assembly of Ireland). A 'temporary ministry' was appointed that included 1916 veterans Cathal Brugha as Prime Minister and Michael ('Mick') Collins as Minister for Home Affairs. Count Plunkett was Minister for Foreign Affairs.[22] Following his escape from Lincoln Prison in England, Éamon de Valera was elected 'President of Dáil Éireann' and Brugha became Minister for Defence.[23]

On the day Dáil Éireann met, IRA Volunteers ambushed the Royal Irish Constabulary (RIC) in Limerick and began the war for Irish independence. The IRA that day, and for much of the war, acted on its own initiative, without the official sanction of the Irish people, the Catholic hierarchy or the revolutionary government. During 1920–22, there were as many as 15,000 IRA Volunteers with 3,000–5,000 of them active at any one time. To counter the IRA, the British hastily mustered an Auxiliary Division of ex-British soldiers, labelled Black and Tans because of their uniforms, to support the RIC. The combined RIC/British forces are estimated to have been 40,000.

The British Army, the RIC and the IRA waged campaigns of violence and counter-violence, and parts of Ireland became ungovernable. For example, in the spring of 1920, the RIC shot dead Tomás Mac Curtain, the Sinn Féin Lord Mayor of Cork, in front of his family. His successor, Terence MacSwiney, was arrested for possession of seditious documents and went on hunger strike. MacSwiney died in Brixton Prison, England, after seventy-four days. On a Sunday morning, 21 November 1920, agents of Michael Collins, the IRA's Director of Intelligence, shot dead eleven suspected British spies. In retaliation, the Black and Tans shot dead twelve people at a Dublin football match – 'Bloody Sunday'. At the end of November, Tom Barry's 'flying column' in West Cork killed eighteen Auxiliaries in an ambush at Kilmichael. In December, another Auxiliary was killed and eleven were wounded in Cork City. That night, Black and Tans looted and torched Cork.[24]

Michael Collins and Tom Barry were ruthless. Barry burned out two pro-British homes for every pro-republican home that was burned. In his memoir, *Guerilla Days in Ireland*, he writes, 'Sentiment has no place in stopping terror tactics, and only a ruthless counteraction can ever effectively halt it.'[25] A relative sense of the efficacy of the IRA is found in the casualty figures. In 1920, the IRA killed 176 police officers and 54 soldiers, and suffered 43 casualties.[26] The IRA was strongest in the South and West, in Longford in the midlands and in Dublin. In the northeast, the majority of the population was pro-Union and the Ulster Special Constabulary was organized to support the RIC; in time they would become the B Specials, an almost exclusively Protestant paramilitary reserve available for emergencies.[27]

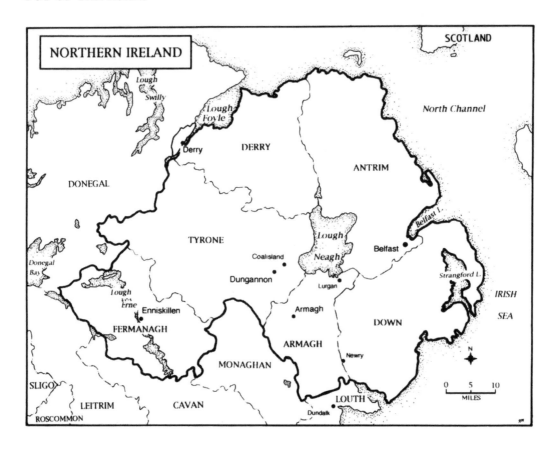

The widespread political unrest forced the British to partition Ireland. Under the Government of Ireland Act (1920), Northern Ireland was created out of the six north eastern counties of Ulster and the Irish Free State was created out of the remaining twenty-six counties. Northern Ireland had approximately one and a quarter million people, of whom about two-thirds were Protestant and pro-Union and about one-third were Catholic and Irish nationalist in politics. Unionists initially wanted all nine counties of Ulster, but the large number of Catholic/nationalists in the western counties of Cavan, Donegal and Monaghan would have threatened their majority status. In contrast, the Free State had almost three million citizens. The vast majority of them were Catholic (90–95 per cent) and Irish nationalist in politics.[28]

Elections were scheduled for 24 May 1921. In the North, Unionists won forty out of fifty-two seats and established the Northern Ireland parliament in Belfast. James Craig became the first Prime Minister. Elected Sinn Féiners and moderates in the Nationalist Party refused to participate. In the rest of Ireland, Sinn Féin won 124 out of 128 seats in an election to the all-Ireland Second Dáil Éireann.[29]

In July 1921, the British accepted the fact that they could not defeat the IRA or suppress the rebel government and agreed to a truce. The rebels formalized their position and De Valera was given the title 'President of the Irish Republic'. Elected representatives took an oath to 'support and defend the Irish Republic and the Government of the Irish Republic, which is Dáil Éireann, against all enemies, foreign and domestic'.[30] Then plenipotentiaries – including Arthur Griffith and Michael Collins – were sent to London to negotiate a treaty on behalf of the Irish Republic. After two long months, however, they were faced with an ultimatum from Prime Minister David Lloyd George: settle for less than the republic or 'war, and war within three days'. Without consulting Dáil Éireann, on 6 December 1921, they signed a treaty that secured a form of independence for a part of Ireland. Northern Ireland would remain a province of the United Kingdom and the twenty-six county Irish Free State would become a dominion of the British Commonwealth of Nations. Politicians who took their seats in the Dublin parliament would be required to sign an oath of allegiance to the British monarch.

The Treaty split Dáil Éireann with its supporters – Michael Collins, Arthur Griffith, William Cosgrave, Desmond Fitzgerald et al. – focusing on what they had won and arguing that it was a stepping-stone to the republic. Pearse Béaslaí summarized their perspective: 'We can make our own constitution, control our own finances, have our own schools and colleges, our own country, our own flag, our own coinage and stamps, our own police, aye, and last but not least, our own army ... Why, for what else but that have we been fighting for?'

The opposition – Éamon de Valera, Erskine Childers, Brian O'Higgins, Tom Maguire, Mary MacSwiney – stuck by the oath they had taken and refused to return to the Empire. Cathal Brugha summarized their perspective:

> Why, if instead of being so strong, our last cartridge had been fired, our last shilling had been spent and our last man were lying on the ground and his enemies howling round him and their bayonets raised, ready to plunge them into his body, that man would say – true to the traditions handed down – if they said to him: 'Now will you come into our Empire?' – he would say, and he should say: 'No, I will not.' This is the spirit that has lasted all through the centuries ...[31]

The Second Dáil Éireann ratified the Treaty by a vote of sixty-four to fifty-seven and this split Sinn Féin and the IRA. Éamon De Valera resigned as President of Dáil Éireann and was succeeded by Arthur Griffith. Griffith formed a pro-Treaty ministry that created a Provisional Government with Michael Collins as Chairman. The 'faithful' deputies in Sinn Féin rejected the Provisional Government and formed their own 'Emergency Government'.

The anti-Treaty IRA took up headquarters in the Four Courts, in Dublin. The Free State demanded their surrender, they refused and, on 28 June 1922, the government bombarded the Four Courts and started the Irish Civil War. The Free State forces, supported by the British, drove the anti-Treaty IRA from the cities and into the countryside. In July, Cathal Brugha was shot dead in central Dublin. In August, Arthur Griffith died of a heart attack and the IRA killed Michael Collins in Cork. William T. Cosgrave succeeded Griffith as Chairman of the Provisional Government and President of Dáil Éireann. The Catholic hierarchy condemned the anti-Treaty IRA. Undeterred, the IRA shot dead Seán Hales, a member of Dáil Éireann. In reprisal for killing Hales, on 8 December 1922, four prominent IRA commanders – Dick Barrett, Joe McKelvey,

Liam Mellows and Rory O'Connor – were executed. Between November 1922 and May 1923, seventy-seven anti-Treaty IRA prisoners were executed.

After Liam Lynch, the IRA's Chief of Staff (C/S), was killed in action in April 1923, the rebel government in exile met with the IRA Executive and called a ceasefire. Frank Aiken, the Chief of Staff, issued an order to dump arms and Éamon de Valera followed with a famous statement: 'Soldiers of the Republic. Legion of the Rearguard. The Republic can no longer be defended successfully by your arms … Other means must be sought to safeguard the nation's right.'[32] The Irish Civil War was over and, in its wake, there were bitter political divisions. Depending upon one's perspective, the Irish Republican Movement had achieved more than anyone could have expected in the aftermath of the Easter Rising. For others, the Irish Free State was much less than the all-Ireland republic proclaimed in 1916.

This division affected Irish politics for the rest of the century. On one side were former revolutionaries turned constitutional politicians who laid the foundation for parliamentary democracy in southern Ireland. William Cosgrave, Desmond Fitzgerald, Kevin O'Higgins and others organized the political party Cumann na Gaedheal and in the 1923 Free State general election they won more seats than any other party (63 out of 152). They did not win an overall majority, however, but went ahead and took their seats in what they claimed was the Third Dáil Éireann.[33] On the other side were those who refused to compromise – Éamon de Valera, Sinn Féin and the IRA. The Second Dáil Éireann was never formally dissolved and they claimed that the Emergency Government was the legal all-Ireland government. Sinn Féin won forty-four seats in 1923 but refused to participate in the Dublin government. The new government was 'Leinster House', the eighteenth-century estate in which it was located; it was not the Third Dáil Éireann. The choice between accepting the Treaty and participating in the Dublin and Belfast parliaments or rejecting the Treaty and those parliaments – abstentionism – still haunts Irish republicans.

When the Provisionals were formed in 1969/70, the Irish Republican Movement still had activists from the 1916–23 era who still refused to compromise. In 1916, Éamon de Valera was Joe Clarke's commanding officer. Clarke was also an official in the rebel Dáil Éireann. During the War of Independence, Tom Maguire was an IRA general in the Mayo South Brigade and a member of the Second Dáil Éireann. At the time of the Truce, Tony Ruane was a teenaged IRA volunteer in the Mayo North Brigade and Jimmy Steele was a teenaged member of Na Fianna Éireann, in Belfast. Clarke, Maguire, Ruane and Steele, along with others like them, would give legitimacy to the Provisionals' claim that they were the true heirs of 1916.[34]

PART 2

An Oral History

3

KEEPING THE FAITH (1923–1962)

One fellow lived up the road here ... He went through it all, took all the hard knocks and, in good times and in bad, he didn't change his views or his principles to suit the tide of the time. And, therefore, these people stood out and then they immediately attracted all the disenchanted, if you like. And that's how the Movement has reorganized ... they had active people and those like me, who were already ready-made for them.

– Ruairí Ó Brádaigh[1]

After the Irish Civil War, the anti-Treaty groups were in the political wilderness. Éamon de Valera suggested they start a campaign against the oath of allegiance. With the oath gone, Sinn Féin could enter Leinster House and pursue the republic through constitutional means. Delegates attending the 1926 Ard Fheis turned down the proposal, however. De Valera resigned as President of Sinn Féin and formed a new political party, Fianna Fáil (Soldiers of Destiny). He took with him much of Sinn Féin and the IRA. In the 1927 general election in the Free State, Fianna Fáil won 44 seats (out of 153) and replaced Sinn Féin (5 seats) as the alternative to Cumann na Gaedheal (47 seats). Fianna Fáil still refused to go into Leinster House and Cumann na Gaedheal formed a minority government.[2]

Many republicans were bitter about the Civil War executions and held Kevin O'Higgins, the Minister for Justice and External Affairs, responsible. On 10 July 1927, O'Higgins was gunned down on his way to mass by IRA veterans acting independently. In response, the government arrested known IRA activists and introduced repressive legislation that would hurt Sinn Féin, the IRA and Fianna Fáil. In order to stop the legislation, and in spite of promising they would never do it, de Valera and the other Fianna Fáil Teachta Dáila (TDs) signed the oath and took their seats in Leinster House/Dáil Éireann. They stopped the legislation but, in the process, became 'Treaty party number two'. Fianna Fáil was not yet in government and there was a peaceful but uneasy relationship between Fianna Fáil, the IRA and Sinn Féin, which were united in their opposition to Cumann na Gaedheal.[3]

By remembering the past and looking to the future, the anti-Treaty groups kept alive their dream of a reunited Irish republic. In 1920, Black and Tans had killed Paddy Dalton, Jerry Lyons and Paddy Walsh, in the Valley of Knockanure, in County Kerry. That same year, John Hunt was born in nearby Athea, County Limerick. In 1929, a commemoration was organized at

Glortageanna, County Kerry, in memory of Dalton, Lyons and Walsh. John Hunt attended the commemoration:

> *My father took me. We walked it. It's in Kerry. It's two miles from my house … to the Valley of Knockanure. And Paddy Dalton, as far as I know, was a cousin of my father's … The execution took place, the Black and Tan's murder, only nine years before that. So it was quite fresh in the memory of all the people there except me as a young fellow, nine years old. But I could feel it from the other people, the people that knew Dalton, Walsh and Lyons [were] brutally murdered by the Black and Tans and taken in and executed right inside the ditch.*[4]

Commemorations brought like-minded people together and kept them connected to events and each other. They also paved the way for younger people.

In the 1932 Irish Free State election, Fianna Fáil passed Cumann na Gaedheal (which would be reorganized as Fine Gael) and formed a coalition government with the Irish Labour Party. Éamon de Valera succeeded William Cosgrave as Taoiseach and would go on to become the most successful Irish politician of the twentieth century; his career included service as President of the Assembly of the League of Nations. For the next fifty years, former gunmen would dominate an Irish government that, at one time, they argued was illegitimate.

In power, de Valera and Fianna Fáil's actions reflected their credentials. The IRA was de-proscribed and the oath of allegiance was eliminated. De Valera also brought in a new constitution that claimed all of Ireland for the Dublin government. According to Article 2, 'The national territory consists of the whole island of Ireland, its islands and the territorial seas.' Article 3 claimed jurisdiction over the 'whole' terrortory, 'Pending the reintegration of the national territory …'.[5] The Constitution was Catholic and conservative. It recognized 'the special position of the Holy Catholic Apostolic and Roman Church' and the state would 'endeavour to ensure that mothers shall not be obliged by economic necessity to engage in labour to the neglect of their duties in the home'.[6] De Valera also met with Prime Minister Neville Chamberlain and negotiated the return of Irish ports that had remained under British control. As it would turn out, control of the ports was essential for Ireland remaining neutral during the Second World War, which was undeniable evidence of the Free State's independence.

Removing the trappings of British authority was not enough for Sinn Féin and the IRA. They wanted action to reunite the country and it was inevitable that there would be conflict with the Fianna Fáil government. In 1935, the IRA in Longford killed a landlord and the Dublin IRA supported striking tram and bus workers. In 1936, after being legal for only four years, the IRA was again proscribed. The Movement's newspaper, *An Phoblacht*, was suppressed and the annual parade to Tone's grave at Bodenstown was banned.[7]

While Fianna Fáil removed the symbols of Empire, in Northern Ireland, the Unionist Party secured its place in the United Kingdom. In 1922, a local government bill added a declaration of allegiance to the Crown for councillors. Through gerrymandering, Unionists took control of Fermanagh and Tyrone even though these two counties had Catholic/nationalist majorities. They also took control of predominately nationalist cities like Derry, Dungannon and Strabane. In 1934,

James Craig, Prime Minister of the Northern Ireland (Stormont) government in Belfast, stated proudly, 'I have always said that I am an Orangeman first and a politician and a member of this parliament afterwards ... All I boast is that we have a Protestant parliament and a Protestant state.'[8]

In Northern Ireland, the moderate Nationalist Party was in the permanent minority. The alternative to constitutional politics was the Republican Movement. Billy McKee, who was a teenager when he joined in 1936, described his background:

> From a very early age I was republican-minded, although I didn't know myself at the time what it was. My grandparent, my old grandmother, was very nationally-minded. And she was a tailoress and I, as a child, sometimes went to stay with her ... during what were known as the hungry thirties, the hungry twenties. And she sang all the songs about the '98 [Rising] and the Famine and Troubles in Ireland. And of course I was singing them with her. But I didn't understand at the time. But as time grew on, I had to start querying to my father and mother and different people, the lads I knocked about with ... what was this all about. So I finally found out and I realized the torture that the Irish people had been going through and the attitude of our fighting men or able men in the country ... I realized that a time would come that I would have to take my place among them.[9]

Billy McKee was not from a republican family. Joe Cahill was. He described his childhood experiences:

> Both my father and mother had been involved one way or another in the Republican Movement. And I think it was probably more from my mother that I got my republican education. She had been very progressive on Ireland, and always teach you to involve things Irish and get involved in things Irish. [My parents] would take me to commemorations. The type of thing I'd be taken to then would have been commemoration concerts, where you'd have Irish songs, Irish dance, Irish ceilidh. Commemorations, republican commemorations during my youth were banned. You weren't allowed to go to them. For instance, Milltown Cemetery in Belfast, it was illegal for any more than two people to assemble anywhere. The gates of the cemetery would have been closed for a week with a police guard on them, and you would have to satisfy the police that you were going to visit a relative's grave in order to get into the cemetery. This is at the Easter period ... people always resented this and they would hold the commemorations outside the cemetery. There'd be thousands of people outside the cemetery and ... [f]ive decades of the Rosary. But before they would be to the end of the Rosary, the police would baton charge and then it would develop into a riot. That was a regular thing every Easter Sunday in Belfast. Written up on the graffiti on the walls in Belfast, in nationalist areas, would be 'Attend Milltown Cemetery 3 pm Easter Sunday.' And I can see it definitely in my mind to this present day, where that would be chalked up on the walls ... People would come out in the thousands for this. And they never got into the cemetery, because as long as there was a ring of policemen around, the gates would be closed.[10]

Cahill explained why he joined Na Fianna Éireann in 1937:

> I suppose it was the environment that I grew up in. The thirties – poverty and unemployment, and that sort of thing. I felt that something had to be done about it. I became involved with various groups as a young

lad, but I soon came to the conclusion that the root of all the trouble in Ireland was British occupation. And I suppose education through reading about Tone and people like that [played a part]. The only way forward was to break the connection with England and the only people that I saw that could do it, or that had the will to do it, was the Republican Movement. By then, of course, the country had been divided. As far as the South was concerned I felt that they had deserted the North. They were concerned about the twenty-six county part of Ireland and had completely forgotten about the North. Whereas the Republican Movement operated generally in the North but it was an all-Ireland organization. And I felt that they were the only ones that could do something constructive about it. So, naturally, I headed towards them and I think that was my downfall [Laughs].[11]

Other young recruits who would help build the Provisionals in Belfast included Proinsias Mac Airt, Jimmy Drumm and Séamus Twomey.

The IRA's appeal extended far beyond Belfast. John Joe McGirl joined the IRA in Leitrim. Cathal Goulding, with a rebel pedigree that dated from the Fenians, joined in Dublin. Seán Keenan joined in Derry. Joe 'J.B.' O'Hagan grew up in Lurgan and left school at the age of seventeen. He was recruited in the late 1930s:

my mother had a republican background. There was a lot of historical books that would have come into the house, and, I suppose, reading those books and then, at that time, there was a Wolf Tone Annual that was written by Brian O'Higgins who had been active in the Republican Movement in 1916. So those books were coming into the house ... Also the very fact that two uncles of mine were involved in the Republican Movement in the twenties. One of them, my uncle Dan, fought in the First World War ... He came home and joined the Republican Movement – joined the IRA – was interned in the Argenta, a prison ship. And he remained very, very staunch to the Republican Movement. He refused the English pension for being gassed and, for the DCM [Distinguished Conduct Medal], he could have got an extra pension.[12]

Cahill, McKee, O'Hagan and the others joined a movement that was preparing for war.

At their 1938 Convention, the IRA delegates elected an Army Council that was committed to action. Seán Russell, a 1916 veteran, was elected Chief of Staff. Another member was George Plunkett, the brother of 1916 martyr Joseph Plunkett. Some leading republicans, including Tom Barry and Seán Mac Bride, questioned Russell's appointment and the wisdom of another campaign and withdrew. In their place, Russell brought back people who had drifted away, including Paddy McGrath, another 1916 veteran who still had a British bullet in his chest. Seamus O'Donovan, the former IRA Director of Chemicals, returned and drew up plans for a bombing campaign in England. Russell also approached the few remaining people who had continued to meet as the Second Dáil Éireann. Fifteen years removed from the Irish Civil War, they still regarded themselves as the legitimate government of Ireland.[13]

The seven members of the 'Executive Council of Dáil Éireann' included Brian O'Higgins, a past president of Sinn Féin (1931–3) and then editor of the *Wolfe Tone Weekly* (1937–9); Count Plunkett, the father of Joseph and George Plunkett; Mary MacSwiney, the sister of hunger-strike martyr Terrence MacSwiney; and Tom Maguire, whose brother was executed by the Free State in 1923. They had suffered deep personal losses that, without question, influenced their commitment. At Seán Russell's request, the Executive Council transferred to the Army Council the right to establish a republican government in Ireland. Whether or not anyone else agreed, the IRA became the de jure government of Ireland. In *The Secret Army: The IRA*, J. Bowyer Bell writes, this 'was not simply a totem but was taken very seriously in some quarters both as a moral basis for violence and also a real step toward the Republic'.[14]

In January 1939, the IRA formally declared war on Britain. A bombing campaign in English cities soon spread to Ireland, North and South. The London, Dublin and Belfast governments took a hard line. In the summer of 1939, an explosion in Coventry killed five people and injured sixty. British justice was swift. Peter Barnes and James McCormack were in the IRA but they were not responsible for the explosion. In spite of this they were arrested, found guilty of murder and hanged in February 1940. In Dublin, the Offences Against the State Act (1939) was passed and the government set up special criminal courts, military tribunals and introduced internment.[15]

Internees held in the Curragh Camp, in County Kildare, faced dreadful conditions and, on 14 December 1940, they set fire to their huts. In retaliation, Irish soldiers and military police rounded up the internees, beat them and then locked them in the remaining huts. A couple of days later, with the internees lined up to receive their first food since the fire, Irish soldiers fired without warning and killed Barney Casey of Longford. The internees who were considered leaders were handcuffed and marched to a small stone and brick building with a glass roof – the Glasshouse. The Camp Commandant was James Guiney. John Hunt who was twenty years old in 1940, was one of the prisoners. He recalled what happened next:

> And he [Guiney] says to me, 'What's your name?' And I said, 'Hunt.' He said, 'Hunt what?' I said, 'John Hunt is my name.' He said, 'In here you'll say sir.' I said, 'In here I will not say sir.' Then Guiney said to me, 'Does your father own a public house in Athea, a saloon in Athea?' I said, 'Yes.' He said, 'Well, I knew your father.' He said, 'When we were on the run we used to stay there.' But that did not make things easy for me. That made things harder for me, I think … Anyway, I did three months' solitary confinement in the Glasshouse from that night on …

Hunt described what life was like in the Glasshouse:

> I got many a beating in there. They'd come in; they'd think of some excuse; they'd punch you. And then you had to go for your meals. They tripped you and everything and knocked you down … When a man is a political prisoner, no matter where he is, he is a prisoner against the people who caught him and captivated him. He's their pawn. They're diving on him like a dog, every chance they get, so that when he gets out he'll remember and he won't come back again. A political prisoner is treated very, very, rough, in any country in the world. If he's a political prisoner he's dealt with by the heads of the government. They have supreme control over their prisoner. The Glasshouse was bad. But any time that you're a captive, any time that you're held by force, unless you're some kind of an individual that has no feeling, you are going to feel very, very degraded, because somebody has you by the collar of the neck all the time. That's

an awful thing to any man, to any human being. Any human being that's brutally forced to do something against his will, it's very, very, very hard on that individual. That's why you have a lot of these people who commit suicide in prisons and places like that – because they would sooner die than go through this humiliation.[16]

John Hunt was one of around two thousand internees, many of whom were mistreated by IRA veterans of the 1919–23 era who were now working for the Fianna Fáil government. Between 1940 and 1946, with Éamon de Valera as Taoiseach, the Irish government let three Irish republicans die on hunger strike and executed six more, including Paddy McGrath.[17]

In Northern Ireland, the Stormont government introduced internment and rounded up so many men that for five months some of them were held on the *Al Rawdah*, an old steamer moored in Strangford Lough; women were sent to Armagh Prison. At Easter 1942, an IRA unit in West Belfast fired shots at RUC officers and then ran to a safe house. Constable Patrick Murphy entered the house, shots were exchanged and Murphy was killed. The unit's O/C, Tom Williams, was seriously wounded and believed he was dying. Williams accepted responsibility for killing Murphy even though he had not fired the fatal shot. Again, justice was swift. Three months later, six members of the unit, including Joe Cahill, had been charged with murder, found guilty and sentenced to be hanged. Because executing six IRA volunteers for the death of one RUC constable seemed excessive, a reprieve campaign generated widespread support; three days before the scheduled execution five of the six were granted a reprieve. On 2 September 1942, nineteen-year-old Tom Williams was hanged and buried in an unmarked grave in Crumlin Road Jail. For the rest of his life, Joe Cahill would be associated with the death of Constable Patrick Murphy and the hanging of Tom Williams – a murderer for some; a patriot who escaped the hangman's noose for others.[18]

Because the Second World War was underway and because of censorship, most Irish people were distracted and unaware of the IRA campaign and the repression. Irish republicans, however, followed events closely. Rory Brady (to become Ruairí Ó Brádaigh) was born in Longford Town, the child of IRA and Cumann na mBan veterans. He remembered the 1940 hunger strike:

one of the hunger strikers who died in 1940, his funeral came through town … I was seven or eight, and so we were all brought out to it. And I couldn't understand this at all. I knew that the British left the town in 1921 or '22, but why were men dying on hunger strike in Dublin, in 1940? And at school it was quite bitter because some of the kids said it was suicide. And I suppose I was enough politically aware to say, 'Well, what about Terence MacSwiney?' They'd say, 'Ah, well, that's different.' Well how different? It's the principle of it. It's the same. And also there were two men hanged in England in that year [Peter Barnes and James McCormick]. Nineteen-forty, as well. And one of them [McCormick] was from near us. And, the morning that it happened, it was on Ash Wednesday. The Irish are great, too, on these things happening on a religious holiday. They mark it. Like, 8 December is the Feast of the Immaculate Conception, when Rory O'Connor, Liam Mellowes and the others who were executed without trial. So, you know, the calls and the ballads and the recitations. All this. Ash Wednesday, it was nine o'clock in the morning and before we went to school he [his father] was standing looking at the clock in the room and has his watch out. And when the clock struck nine he says, 'Kneel down and say your prayers. Two Irishmen now lie into quicklime graves, in Birmingham.' I suppose you move on and you kind of forget about those things, but then when the whole thing starts happening [again] you remember all that.[19]

Through their words and deeds, one generation was passing their values on to the next generation.

The 1940s campaign was a disaster for several reasons. Seán Russell left for the United States and then went to Germany seeking international support; Russell died on a U-boat while trying to return to Ireland. The campaign lost direction and never recovered and internees who spent years imprisoned without charge, trial or release date grew frustrated leading to inevitable splits and factions. In the North, the high point of the campaign was probably when Jimmy Steele and Hugh McAteer escaped from Crumlin Road Jail. McAteer became Chief of Staff, but only a few months later both of them were back in Crumlin Road.

There was no high point in the South. Charlie Kerrins, who took over as C/S when McAteer was rearrested, was hanged for the murder of a Dublin police officer whom he had not shot. Prisoners in Portlaoise Prison were kept naked and in solitary confinement because they refused to wear the prison uniform. One of them was Tomás Mac Curtain, who had been sentenced to death for killing a Detective Garda. Mac Curtain's life was spared because he was the son of the murdered Lord Mayor of Cork, a republican martyr. The government persisted even when it was clear that the IRA was finished. Seán McCaughey spent five years in Portlaoise with only a blanket to wear and, for at least a year of that time, he was held in solitary confinement. In the spring of 1946, with the campaign long over and the military court that sentenced him no longer operating, McCaughey went on hunger strike for his release. He refused food for nineteen days and then stopped taking liquid; he died after thirty-one days. Seán Mac Bride, representing the family at an inquest, asked the prison doctor, 'If you had a dog would you treat it in that fashion?' The reply was, 'No'. J. Bowyer Bell summarizes the government's approach: 'The Irish Minister of Justice, Gerald Boland, announced in pride that the IRA was dead and that he had killed it.' In 1923, future Minister Gerry Boland and future Chief of Staff Seán Russell had travelled together to Moscow seeking weapons for the IRA.[20]

As prisoners and internees were released, only a few were willing to pick up the pieces. They were led by Paddy McLogan, Tomás Mac Curtain and Tony Magan – the 'Three Macs'. McLogan had been involved since 1913 and is described as 'a second Tom Clarke' and 'ice cold in contention'. Mac Curtain was released from Portlaoise in 1947 and reported back, 'snatched from the gallows' to become Chairman of the Army Council. Magan, another 1940s internee, was elected Chief of Staff at the 1948 IRA Convention. He is described as a 'hard man, tightly disciplined and utterly painstaking'. In the thick of the reorganization were two young veterans, John Joe McGirl in Leitrim and Cathal Goulding in Dublin.[21]

Two important resolutions were passed at the IRA's 1948 Convention. First, they agreed that they were reorganizing for a campaign against the British in the North. Second, they agreed that there would be no aggressive military action in the South. They had personally experienced the wrath of the Dublin government and wanted to avoid a repeat. Slowly but surely they rebuilt the army. Joe Cahill was released from Crumlin Road in 1949 and reported back. The final releases

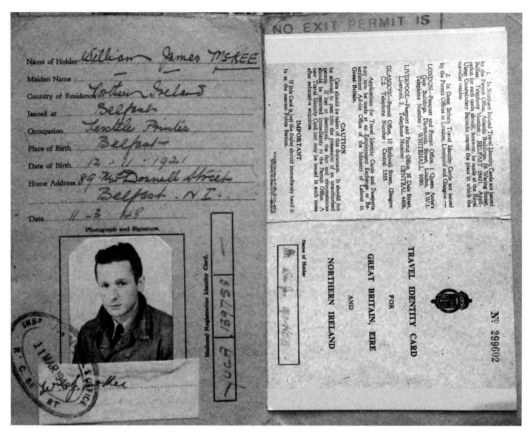

Billy McKee 'Travel Identity Card for Great Britain, Eire, and Northern Ireland', 1948. Courtesy of Billy McKee.

came in 1950 with Hugh McAteer and Liam Burke, and then Jimmy Steele. That year, Paddy McLogan was elected President of Sinn Féin.[22]

Magan, McLogan and Mac Curtain reorganized the IRA in a world that was changing. Following the Second World War, anti-colonial and anti-imperial liberation movements emerged in places like Algeria, Cuba and Vietnam. Many of these movements challenged a declining British Empire – Aden, Cyprus, India, Kenya and Palestine. In Northern Ireland, nationalists formed the Anti-Partition League and in southern Ireland, Seán Mac Bride organized the political party Clann na Poblachta.

Mac Bride is one of the most interesting persons in modern Irish history. His father was executed in 1916 and his mother was Yeats's muse. He was the IRA's Chief of Staff (1936), the Minister for External Affairs in Dublin (1948–51) and helped found Amnesty International (1961). His accolades include the Nobel Peace Prize (1974) and the Lenin Peace Prize (1977).[23]

Clann na Poblachta was progressive in its politics and republican in outlook. Following the 1948 Free State election, and after sixteen long years in power, Fianna Fáil was replaced by an inter-party government led by a Fine Gael–Labour coalition that included Clann na Poblachta. In 1949, Seán Mac Bride was the Minister for External Affairs when the Free State withdrew itself from the British Commonwealth and formally became the 'Republic of Ireland'. The Republic maintained its claim on all thirty-two Irish counties. The British, in reply, passed the Ireland Act (1949), which guaranteed that partition could not end without the consent of the Belfast parliament. While out of power, Éamon de Valera went on a world-wide anti-partition tour.[24]

The anti-colonial, anti-imperial and anti-partition environment helped bring recruits to the Irish Republican Movement. John Stephenson (to become *Seán Mac Stiofáin*), was born in England in 1928. He described his family background: 'My mother was Irish but my father was completely anti-Irish. He was a Tory and imperialist. A complete opposite of everything I stood for.'[25] In his memoir, *Revolutionary in Ireland*, Mac Stiofáin writes that his mother told him, 'I'm Irish, therefore you're Irish. You're half Irish anyway. Don't forget it.'[26] As the Second World War was ending, he faced compulsory national service and the possibility of ending up in the British Army fighting colonial insurgencies. He wanted 'no part in any of them'. Therefore, he volunteered and was able to choose service in the Royal Air Force, where he would be less likely to be involved in the fighting. Mac Stiofáin served in the RAF from 1945 to 1948 and, for part of that time, he was stationed in Jamaica, where he was struck by the racism and poverty. The experience strengthened his opposition to colonialism.

After completing his service, Mac Stiofáin married an Irish woman in London and he joined the IRA. In his own words:

> *I was convinced that the situation in Ireland morally justified an armed uprising, that the IRA was obviously the only organization that was going to organize an armed uprising. Prior to that, I joined a non-violent organization known as the Anti-Partition of Ireland League. I only stayed a few months and I discovered it was dominated by the political parties in Dublin and manipulated by them ... I joined the Republican Movement out of conviction, a conviction that there was a wrong to be righted in Ireland and a conviction that the only way to right that wrong, or at least the main way to right that wrong, was the use of the armed struggle.*[27]

Mac Stiofáin became the O/C (Commanding Officer) of the IRA's London unit.

The children of the 1920s activists were coming of age. A Donegal republican who joined in the late 1940s explained:

> *I was involved with the Republican Movement at a very early age because of my father being a member of the Republican Movement as well. From 1916 'til the Civil War, my home was a place for anybody who came on the run, or to seek help. It was always given to them. So I was sort of brought up within republican circles, my father being a republican.*

Like many recruits, the Donegal republican had straightforward politics inspired by the belief that his country had been wronged:

Republican ideals to me came very, very naturally because I resented British rule in Ireland – totally resented it. And I could see a grave injustice being done against our people. And I felt that I, as an Irishman, had the same right to my country and, not as a gratuity, but as a right to my country. And to have equal rights within my country – that is, a job, a way of life that gave me fulfillment and satisfaction. [I felt] that I had a right to the culture and the language which was denied me – the same right as any other country or any other nation. And I could see that right be denied to me by British occupation and by British rule.[28]

Others had a broader outlook. In the autumn of 1950, Rory Brady enrolled at University College, Dublin, and began using the Irish form of his name, Ruairí Ó Brádaigh. He also joined Sinn Féin. He described his politics at that time:

It was a particular period of time. Post-World War Two when anticolonial struggles were breaking out globally and the great anti-partition campaign by the establishment politicians was taking place. And I know that, during the seventies, journalists sometimes asked me about this type of thing, and I said it was my opinion that no matter where I was in the world I was likely to be involved in some type of similar national liberation struggle. And, as it happened, it was in Ireland and it was this unfinished business of the British government's presence in the six north eastern counties.

Like Mac Stiofáin, Ó Brádaigh saw the Irish struggle as part of a more general anti-colonial struggle:

We started it in 1916. We put the first crack in the British Empire. It was the start of the anti-colonial movement, and they all had their noses up for freedom – black men, yellow men and so on. We showed the way; [now] we're at the end of the queue. Why don't we finish the job? We were the indomitable Irish that started all this off, when they [the British] controlled a quarter of the world. And now our question isn't finished and all these people have passed us by.[29]

He joined the Dublin IRA and was then appointed the O/C of a reorganized unit in Longford. He finished college in 1954, took a job teaching secondary school in Roscommon and was also a Training Officer for the IRA.

In order to gain weapons, experience and publicity, the IRA raided British Army barracks. The results were mixed. In 1951, a raid on Ebrington Barracks in Derry brought in rifles, machine guns and ammunition. Two years later, Cathal Goulding, John Stephenson and Manus Canning were arrested after a raid on an Officers Training School in England. They were the first of another round of IRA prisoners in England. In Wakefield Prison, they met Cypriot guerrillas from Ethniki Organosis Kyprion Agoniston (EOKA) and Klaus Fuchs, the German-born spy who had passed nuclear secrets to the Soviets. Goulding was a working-class Dubliner and developed a relationship with Fuchs. Stephenson learned Irish and transitioned to Seán Stephenson and then Seán Mac Stiofáin. For a raid in 1954, Dubliner Seán Garland joined the British Army and then helped an IRA team sneak into Gough Barracks, in Armagh. They drove

Ruairí Ó Brádaigh's graduation from University College, Dublin, 1954. Ó Brádaigh family collection.

out with a truck-load of weapons. A few months later, two volunteers and five British soldiers were wounded, and eight volunteers were captured during a failed raid on Omagh Barracks. This raid had a long-term effect on the IRA.[30]

In the North, the security forces were placed on alert and the RUC raided activists' homes, which was expected. All the captured volunteers were from south of the border, however, and the IRA leadership knew that would catch the attention of the Dublin government. In December 1954, at a meeting of all O/Cs of local units, Tony Magan and Tómas MacCurtáin introduced General Army Order No. 8:

(a) Volunteers are strictly forbidden to take any military action against 26-County forces under any circumstances whatsoever. The importance of this order in present circumstances especially in the Border areas cannot be overemphasised.

(b) Minimum arms shall be used in training in the 26 county area. In the event of a raid, every effort shall be made to get the arms away safely. If this fails, the arms shall be rendered useless and abandoned.

(c) Maximum security precautions must be taken when training ...[31]

It was an extension and clarification of the 1948 policy of no aggression in the twenty-six counties. If there was a raid, volunteers were told to dump or destroy weapons instead of defending them. If they were arrested with weapons, they were told to point out that they were 'for use against the British forces of occupation only'. Ruairí Ó Brádaigh, O/C of the Longford Unit, attended the meeting. He spoke about the decisions made at the time:

The basic policy adopted in 1948, which is very important, was that the objective would be a successful military campaign against the British occupation forces – number one. Number two, that no aggressive or offensive action be taken against ... the twenty-six county area. Now, that did not specifically rule out defensive action where, if you like, an attempt would be made to grab the arms. But General Order Number 8 came in, in '54, because ... while it was generally acceptable that there'd be no aggressive action, there would have been strong feelings about letting arms go. Now, after Armagh and Omagh, the Army leadership's bona fides could not be questioned about the fact that it was going ahead with number one, because if there hadn't been the strikes substantially – against substantial targets in the six counties – perhaps there would have been people who would say, 'Ah, this leadership has gone soft'. They want to give up the arms and all that type of thing. But you can see from the way General Order Number 8 was drafted ... that every attempt be made to get the arms away; that diversionary action [was used] and so on and that ... if there were a possibility that the arms be neutralized or destroyed [they were]. There is a little thing called the H-piece in the Thompson gun which, if removed, the rest was useless.[32]

In 1955, Ó Brádaigh would lead a successful raid on Arborfield Barracks in England.

The raids generated publicity and brought in recruits. Phil O'Donoghue, a Dubliner, joined in 1954. He described his recruitment:

Well, I was just about seventeen, I'd say, and they had carried off some operations in England and Northern Ireland. And I suppose I was impressed at that time by some of the operations that they had carried out. So I started trying to make inquiries then when I came across the paper, The United Irishmen. *There was no strong belief in my family regarding the Republican Movement, you know?[33]*

In the 1955 Westminster election, Sinn Féin put forward candidates in all twelve constituencies in Northern Ireland. Half of them were in jail because of the Omagh raid. The party received more than 150,000 votes and elected two prisoners, Phil Clarke in Fermanagh/South Tyrone and Tom Mitchell in Mid-Ulster. Because Clarke was a felon, his Unionist Party opponent filed a petition and was declared the winner. Mitchell's situation was more complicated because his opponent did not file a petition. The seat was declared vacant and then Mitchell won the by-election with an increased majority. His second opponent filed a petition and was declared the winner.[34]

Sinn Féin was also growing in the South, if less dramatically. Seán Lynch, from North Longford, joined in the mid-1950s:

> *The reason why I decided to get involved in the Republican Movement was that I was born into the republican tradition, both on my father's and my mother's side ... [My father] was in the old Sinn Féin courts, which were set up by Austin Stack – First Dáil, Second Dáil and this sort of thing there. My mother was from a very strong republican family. The Tan War in Longford – we were very proud of the Longford part in the fight for freedom here – and, as a matter of fact, in '21, one of the [incidents in Longford, the Battle of Clonfin] would have been about ten miles [from here]. And I had two of those participating – a brother on my father's and a brother on my mother's – and two first cousins of my mother's.*[35]

Following the Westminster election, Sinn Féin contested the Southern local elections. Frank Glynn was a student at University College, Galway. He described the growing interest in the Republican Movement:

> *In the early fifties, there was this new republican fervour [that] was developing out of what had come down in the forties. And some of the people in '45 and that had come of out of jail and they were starting up the Republican Movement again ... And, at that time, I used to pal around with a fellow ... from North Leitrim, and he had a very republican fervour, too. And we started going to Sinn Féin meetings and gradually all this thing evolved from public meetings to indoor meetings. And then we decided – it was in '55. It was [my] second year in the university and there were County Council elections coming on, and Paddy Fox, who was one of the old republicans who had been in the Curragh [in the 1940s] ... said to us we should put up someone for the County Council. Well, even though it was coming to exam times, we decided to do that ... We nominated [Paddy Ruane] for the Council and went out and worked for him. And he was duly elected. And that was the beginning, I suppose.*[36]

Sinn Féin elected seven representatives to county and city councils. They were few in number, but it was a beginning. In a pragmatic move, it was decided that representatives could take seats at the local level without recognizing the authority of Leinster House.

The election results were welcome. So was the return to Ireland of Seán Cronin, a veteran of the Irish Free State Army who had been working as a journalist in the United States. Cronin joined the IRA and the leadership quickly realized that he was an experienced soldier and very bright. Everyone agreed that there would be a campaign, and Cronin was put in charge of drawing a battle plan – 'Operation Harvest'. The question was not if but when the campaign would start. Mac Curtain wanted to build on the election results and start a passive resistance campaign, with boycotts and protests, which would mobilize a support base for a military campaign. Others were tired of waiting. In the summer of 1956, Joe Christle criticized the leadership for being too conservative and was dismissed by Tony Magan. Christle took with him several members of the Dublin unit and they started their own mini-campaign.

Christle's actions forced the Army Council to take action. If they did nothing, there would be more defections. And, whether or not they started their campaign, when the authorities went after Christle's group they would also go after them. The Army Council brought together the best of the volunteers and created 'flying columns' that would operate in the North. And on the night of 12 December 1956, the campaign began with attacks across Northern Ireland, except Belfast. In response, the London and Belfast governments mobilized British troops, called up the B Specials to support the RUC, banned Sinn Féin and authorized internment.[37]

There is a well-publicized myth that Belfast was excluded because the IRA leadership feared that action there would lead to sectarian conflict. In reality, Belfast was excluded because Paddy Doyle, the O/C and a member of the Army Council, had been arrested and there were concerns about an informer. The leadership was so concerned about Belfast that it did not even tell people there when the campaign would start. Joe Cahill, Doyle's successor as Belfast O/C, was asked if he knew the campaign was starting. He replied, '*No, I wouldn't have at that stage, you know?*' Before the informer problem could be sorted out, most of the Belfast IRA was interned in Crumlin Road Jail, including Joe Cahill, Ivor Bell, Jimmy Drumm, Leo Martin, Billy McKee and Jimmy Steele. Cahill, his brother Frank and Leo Martin were among the last men released in the spring of 1961.[38]

The campaign was most successful along the border, especially in Fermanagh. A raid on Derrylin RUC barracks resulted in the first casualty – Constable John Scally. And in a New Year's Day 1957 raid on Brookeborough Barracks, the IRA suffered its first casualties – Seán South from Limerick and Fergal O'Hanlon from Monaghan. The wounded included Seán Garland, Dáithí O'Connell and Phil O'Donohue. On the surface, the Brookeborough raid was a disaster. The idealism of the deceased volunteers resonated with nationalist Ireland, however. Their funerals drew crowds in the thousands and they were immortalized in ballads – 'Sean South from Garryowen' and O'Hanlon in 'The Patriot Game'.

The reaction of the Irish public to the deaths of South and O'Hanlon helped restrain the coalition government in Dublin, led by Fine Gael. After the Derrylin and Brookeborough raids, for example, several volunteers were arrested on the Southern side of the border. Instead of facing years in jail for IRA membership, they were given six months for not answering questions. Prisoners took advantage of the lax conditions. Phil O'Donoghue offered an example: *I was brought into the hospital and, when we went to Dublin there, I got out of the ambulance and I cleared off, and I was one of the first to get away. And they were only in the hospital there a few weeks when some of them got out as well.*[39] O'Donoghue was rearrested a few months later at a training camp. The increased nationalist sentiment also led to votes. In a Leinster House/Dáil election in the spring of 1957, Sinn Féin received 65,000 votes and elected four abstentionist TDs. Two of them, Ruairí Ó Brádaigh and John Joe McGirl, were in Mountjoy Jail in Dublin and could not have taken their seats if they had wanted to. The election also returned Fianna Fáil to power with Éamon de Valera as Taoiseach.

The leadership should have anticipated that Fianna Fáil would introduce internment, but did not.[40] Tony Magan was picked up and, for the second time, became an internee in the Curragh Camp. A Sinn Féin meeting was raided and the leadership, including Paddy McLogan, was interned. When IRA prisoners completed their sentences, they were released, taken into custody and sent to the Curragh. De Valera and Fianna Fáil ignored the fact that Ruairí Ó Brádaigh had been elected to the Dublin parliament. Ó Brádaigh described his 'release':

We were due for release at half seven in the morning and, the last thing at night, the chief officer, the chief warder – he was just friendly as a person – he came down and he said, 'Ruairí, we got a phone call from the department.' He said, 'It's what you expect in the morning. The lot of you.' So we were just going to bed and we expected half seven in the morning and our relatives would be outside and all this kind of thing. Instead of that, we were awakened at half five, while it was still dark. It was the month of July, the middle of July. It appeared to be dark or just getting bright and they gave us some herbal tea and a slice of bread. Out to the gate and they had a number of lorries backed up to the gate. So they just let us out one at a time through a wicket gate and I was first out. And the minute I stepped out, Inspector McMahon was there of the Special Branch and he said, 'Ruairí'.[41]

That day, Ó Brádaigh was one of more than a dozen former prisoners who immediately became internees. The IRA never recovered from losing its leadership in the summer of 1957.

There is a tendency to assume that the 1950s IRA was filled with idealistic young men on a naïve mission to free Ireland. However, Irish republicanism has never been monolithic. The 1950s volunteers included future socialists like Seán Garland and Cathal Goulding. Prisoners in Crumlin Road and the Curragh discussed liberation movements in places like Cuba and Vietnam. But the IRA also had its right-wing conservatives, like Seán South. South's devotion to Irish culture is legendary. He was also a conservative Catholic and wrote letters to the *Limerick Leader* complaining about the communist influence in Hollywood.[42] Phil O'Donoghue described the mix of people in the Curragh:

Well, there was every type of individual. They had one certain rule there … It was anybody who promoted or advocated communism, there was a total ban on that. But when you got to know some of these lads, they had socialist leanings. You had fascist leanings. We had one camp when we were down at the Curragh, on one end it was socialists, at the other end was the fascists, and both of them singing their songs –we'll keep the red flag flying high on one end and we're all standing firm behind the Führer on the other end [laughs]. So you can imagine what it was like [laughing]. And in the middle you had extreme Catholics. There was that as well.[43]

In the autumn of 1958, Ruairí Ó Brádaigh and Dáithí O'Connell escaped from the Curragh and planned to rejoin the IRA as volunteers. Instead, the leadership ranks were so thin that they became Chief of Staff and Director of Operations, respectively.

By that point, the campaign had peaked. In 1957, there were 341 incidents in Northern Ireland. In 1959, there were twenty-seven incidents. There were also internal issues. Tomás Mac Curtain, the O/C in the Curragh, was furious because of an unauthorized escape. Then, in the 1959 Westminster election, Sinn Féin's vote fell to 64,000, with no candidates elected. The one thing the Movement did still have, though, was committed activists. Cathal Goulding and Seán Mac Stiofáin were released in 1959 and returned to Ireland. Seán Mac Stiofáin described his return: *'My wife and children had been in Ireland for five years before that, so I rejoined them. They were in Cork at that time. I reported back to the Movement. The day I arrived in Ireland, on 4 February 1959, I reported back to the Movement.'*[44] Mac Stiofáin was appointed O/C of Cork. Goulding would become Quartermaster.

There was little either of them could do to help turn the situation around, however. The level of activity had fallen so much and the Dublin government was confident enough that internment was ended and the Curragh closed. That allowed more volunteers to return to the field, but their return was often short-lived. That was the case for J.B. O'Hagan who recalled: *'58, I was interned in the Curragh. '59, I came out of the Curragh and back on active service, and was arrested in the North.*[45] In November 1959, O'Hagan, Dáithí O'Connell and Mark Devlin were out canvassing for support in Tyrone when they ran into a RUC/B Special patrol. O'Hagan and Devlin were arrested on the spot. O'Connell, who made a run for it, was shot several times and then arrested.

Seán Cronin was elected Chief of Staff at the 1960 Convention and then arrested as he travelled home. Ruairí Ó Brádaigh took over as C/S only for Cathal Goulding, Paddy Mulcahy and Paddy Ryan, all members of the Army Council, to get arrested. The good news was that, in the Southern local elections, Sinn Féin elected sixteen councillors, including John Joe McGirl, who was elected to the County Council in Leitrim. In the 1961 Leinster House election, however, the party's vote fell to 36,000 and the four winners of 1957 lost the seats they had never taken. The campaign had run its course. Ruairí Ó Brádaigh was the only person on the Army Council at the start and the end of the campaign. He described the situation:

> *Right through the summer of '61 – it's beginning to come back to me now as I am talking to you – I remember we took several initiatives where we hoped to shoot British soldiers, and we launched several operations in that regard, in the vicinity of British Army barracks in the North and so on that would maximize the situation. Kevin Mallon used to say, 'High yield targets' – in the sense of public support. And none of them, none of them came off. The personnel were there, the arms, and none of them came off ... [The] whole profile of the Army needed to be raised ... So the Army had to strike out and strike hard ... [My] aim was then double barreled ... Once I was convinced in my own mind that there was no longer a possibility, it was to end it to maximum advantage, to end it with dignity and, if you like, with honour.*

Others on the Council included: Paddy Fox, from Galway; Tom Mitchell, who had been released from Crumlin Road; and two young volunteers who had moved into the leadership, Denis McInerney and Seamus Costello. The Council met and agreed to end the campaign. A formal statement was issued in February 1962. Over a period of five years, the IRA had killed six members of the RUC but no British soldiers. Ten republicans had been killed: eight IRA members, one Sinn Féiner (James Crossan, evidently assassinated by the RUC) and one sympathizer killed in a premature explosion.

For some, the campaign's failure was less important than the fact that another generation of Irish rebels had taken up arms to try and break the connection with England. The formal statement was largely written by Ruairí Ó Brádaigh. It ended with:

> The Irish Resistance Movement renews its pledge of eternal hostility to the British Forces of Occupation in Ireland. It calls on the Irish people for increased support and looks forward with confidence – in co-operation with the other branches of the Republican

Movement – to a period of consolidation, expansion and preparation for the final and victorious phase of the struggle for the full freedom of Ireland.

There would be another campaign. In the meantime, another generation had gained experience as guerrillas and been exposed to revolutionary politics. Ruairí Ó Brádaigh summed it up:

> *So the end of a campaign didn't mean the end of the Army because there had been other campaigns. And if it had to be halted, the important thing was to halt it in such circumstances that there would be no splits or disunity and that ... the organization would be intact. An experienced organization [which] would provide a basis for re-engaging which occurred seven years later ...*[46]

4

CIVIL RIGHTS AND REVOLUTIONARY POLITICS
(1962–1969)

Goulding played a very clever game. He was openly in favour of certain things which didn't violate fundamental republican principles, but in later years it transpired that he was in favour of those things all along.

– Seán Mac Stiofáin[1]

The end of the campaign marked the beginning of several important changes that would lead to the creation of the Provisionals. What is not widely understood is that there was discontent in the Movement from the end of the campaign to the split in 1969/70.

Some volunteers wanted to continue and had to be persuaded otherwise. Tony Magan and Paddy McLogan were upset that they had not been consulted on ending the campaign and refused to let it drop. They were expelled and others drifted away. Seán Mac Stiofáin commented:

> *Some of them had washed up ... Tired. ... Disillusioned with the way things had gone with the campaign. [They] felt the Movement wasn't getting anywhere and wanted to reorganize their lives. Some of them had been either in prison or on active service for a period of about five years and that meant five years of going around without a penny in their pocket. And this kind of thing. Some of them wanted to get married and get employment and lead their lives at least – a normal life for at least some period of years. It was a bad period.[2]*

A small group of highly committed people picked up the pieces. Following the Army Convention in the autumn, Cathal Goulding reluctantly agreed to serve as Chief of Staff. Others on the Army Council included Seamus Costello, Tomás Mac Giolla, Paddy Mulcahy, Ruairí Ó Brádaigh and Mick Ryan; Mac Giolla was the Chairman.[3]

Mac Giolla, who was employed as an accountant with the Electricity Supply Board, was also elected President of Sinn Féin. The Ard Chomhairle (Executive) was a mix of younger people like Seán Ó Brádaigh (Ruairí's brother) and veterans like Larry Grogan who, as a member of the Army Council, had voted for war in 1938 and 1956, and Joe Clarke, the 1916 veteran. The Ard

Fheis followed the convention and that allowed the Army to make sure it was well represented in the Sinn Féin leadership. Army men on the Ard Chomhairle included Goulding, Mac Stiofáin and Dáithí O'Connell (who was still in Crumlin Road Jail).

It was obvious that no matter how deep their own commitment, they were few in number and had little influence in Ireland. Nineteen-sixty three was the 200th anniversary of the birth of Wolfe Tone, who had tried to unite 'Catholic, Protestant, and Dissenter'.The Movement had virtually no connection with the Protestant community, North or South. They established the Wolfe Tone Society to try and open things up through lectures, seminars and discussion groups.[4] As it turned out, they were part of the general political and social awakening that included the Second Vatican Council, the US Civil Rights Movement and the Beatles. In 1964, Harold Wilson became Britain's first Labour Prime Minister since Clement Attlee, in 1951. In Northern Ireland, Sir Basil Brooke retired after twenty years and Terence O'Neill became Prime Minister at Stormont. In Dungannon, middle-class nationalists established a Campaign for Social Justice to protest unfair housing allocations.[5]

Not everyone embraced change, however. To get around the ban on Sinn Féin, which dated from 1956, their candidates contested the 1964 Westminster elections as 'Republicans'. Billy McMillen, the candidate in West Belfast, opened an office and put an Irish tricolour in the window. Under the Flags and Emblems Act (1954), it was illegal to fly a flag that might cause a breach of the peace. Revd Ian Paisley was a young, fiery fundamentalist minister and the organizer of the Free Presbyterian Church of Ulster. When the tricolour appeared, he threatened to march up the Falls Road and seize it. The RUC removed the flag and Paisley called off his march. The flag was replaced, the RUC seized it and there was a riot. Fra McCann recalled the riot:

> My first recollections of any trouble was back in 1963 or 1964 and what became known as the Divis Street riots … Sinn Féin, at that time, were standing in the elections and there was an office in Divis Street and there was an Irish tricolour flying in the window. And the first time that I ever heard of Paisley, he had threatened to march down onto the Falls and – I think it was the day the RUC attacked the place. And that developed and there was a terrible lot of people injured and I remember my mother and my father being – my mother especially – being terrified, and most other mothers in the area being terrified at the RUC running about. They were firing tear gas and things like that there … That was my first experience … I was about ten at the time or eleven.[6]

In the election, none of the republican candidates won, but they received a total of 101,000 votes, indicating there was still support in the North. That autumn, the Ard Fheis approved the creation of Republican Clubs as a way to get around the ban on Sinn Féin.[7] As for Paisley, he became a thorn in the side of just about everyone. When Terence O'Neill visited Catholic schools and met with Seán Lemass, de Valera's successor as Taoiseach, Paisley accused O'Neill of 'treachery' and picketed his appearances. In 1966, Paisley was awarded an honorary doctorate from Bob Jones University, a conservative Christian university in South Carolina.[8]

The Movement's leadership had little choice but to embrace leftist politics since the alternative was irrelevancy. In moving to the left, they began interacting with new people. Tony Coughlan and Roy Johnston, for example, had been active in the Connolly Association in England, which had ties to the communist parties in Ireland and Britain. When they returned to Ireland in the early 1960s, Coughlan became a lecturer at Trinity College, Dublin and Johnston took a position as an operations research analyst with Aer Lingus. Both of them became active in the Wolfe Tone Society and Johnston, in particular, became very close to Cathal Goulding. In his memoir, *Century of Endeavour*, Johnston writes that Goulding wanted help in converting the IRA, 'from an illegal army into a democratically disciplined political movement reflecting the interests of the working people as a whole, broadly based on the socialist ideas of Marx, as adapted by Connolly to the Irish situation'.[9] Johnston became Goulding's 'Political Education Officer' in the IRA. He also joined Sinn Féin and would work with Seán Ó Brádaigh on a progressive social and economic programme.

Moving to the left and exploring revolutionary politics raised the fundamental question of whether or not they could realize their potential if they continued to reject participation in the Dublin, Belfast and London parliaments. Cathal Goulding may have been straightforward with Roy Johnston, but he was more careful with others. Seán Mac Stiofáin commented on this:

> *First of all, it took a couple of years before this change in the direction of the Movement appeared around the beginning of 1964. And I opposed it on the Council level. I was hopeful that we would retain a majority opposed to the policy changes that were being pushed. And I was confident about how to do it. Because Goulding played a very clever game. He was openly in favour of certain things which didn't violate fundamental republican principles but, in later years, it transpired that he was in favour of those things all along.*[10]

Goulding was walking a fine line and trying not to provoke a split.

Some people got upset and quit and, not long after the Divis Street riots, Billy McKee walked away. He explained:

> *[it was] a different atmosphere altogether. So I could not be part or partial of it … Cathal Goulding, was arrested in England and he got time, he done time in England. And when he was in England, he met up with a Professor [Klaus] Fuchs, and Fuchs is an ardent communist. And he started briefing Goulding on the proper way to bring about a united Ireland – to give up the guns, the physical force. And they get in and get in among the people and get your men into it and take over eventually. And it was a good idea all right, but not in Northern Ireland. But, I could not join the Orange Order. When they would ask me, 'Was I a Catholic?' – Out. To get into the Masons, you could be in a hundred years and you would never get in on their leadership. [It] was established. You had no chance of taking over that. The trade union – there was different branches in the trade union – and to get in there would've been all right, but they also were mostly left-wing people. So why would I want to get in there?… they were going out disbanding the gun.*[11]

Billy McKee left at approximately the same time that 16-year-old Gerry Adams joined Sinn Féin.[12] Joe Cahill resigned from the IRA in 1965 and he described the period:

I was interned in 1957 until 1961. And when I came out of internment, I felt that there were moves afoot to run down the military wing, to run down the IRA and to supersede the whole thing just into a purely political action. I felt at that time – I was in the IRA at that particular time – that it was taking the wrong road … it was going down the political lane rather than the military lane. I am a firm believer that the two must go together – politics and military struggle … I hadn't changed my thoughts on anything. I was probably more militant than ever at that particular time. And there's always the fear in Ireland of politics, that politicians are corrupt.[13]

Some republicans left Ireland altogether. In 1966, Phil O'Donoghue and his family moved to South Africa.[14]

Seán Mac Stiofáin was the most vocal of the 'traditionalists' – while Goulding and his supporters were trying to make the Movement politically relevant, Mac Stiofáin was rebuilding the IRA:

shortly after that [the end of the campaign] I was appointed in charge of the Movement for the whole of County Cork and most of County Kerry. And I initiated a recruitment campaign in those years that had amazing results. We set up a new unit in West Cork where there hadn't been one for maybe twenty-five years. And we got a new unit in South Kerry and got recruits everywhere. In fact, in those days, you had about 110 men in Belfast and 121, I think, in Cork-South Kerry, but very little in-between. That was literally the situation. We had small units, of maybe five or six, scattered around the country. I doubt if there was more than thirty in Dublin at the time.[15]

Because Mac Stiofáin spoke out, he caught the attention of the disenchanted and he was elected to the Army Council in 1965.

Seán Mac Stiofáin is often portrayed as a conservative Catholic. Seán Cronin would later describe him as 'something of an anti-communist zealot'.[16] Mac Stiofáin rejected the view that he was right wing. Instead, he described himself as *'radically left-wing in everything, except religion'*:

The only thing that differentiates between myself and Marxists is that I believe in God. I'm a practicing Christian; Marxists are not … don't make the mistake of condemning religion, instead of condemning the Catholic or any other church … [All] churches are institutions and will inevitably support the status quo, but religion itself is a very good thing … If the teachings of the founder of the Christian Church, that is Christ himself, were applied you'd have no need for revolutionary movements. So, I'm not right-wing. I'm very radically left-wing in everything, except religion. And I'm opposed to abortion. I reluctantly accept there's a case for divorce but the divorce should be controlled. I don't like the idea of people just being able to get a divorce on demand. And, as for contraception, I'd say, 'Well, that's a matter of conscience for the couples involved.' But I don't care what kind of label it would earn me, I'm utterly and completely opposed to abortion. It's a terrible crime. But because of that, I know that some people say, 'Well, that's enough.' But I say this back, I want a democratic socialist republic in Ireland … I oppose all the policies of the American government down through the years: the coup d'état in Chile; the overthrow of the legitimate government in Guatemala ... of course the terrible crime of Vietnam ... I just want a fair, square deal and rights for everybody. And you won't get that under a capitalist system.

Mac Stiofáin was open to leftist politics but bothered by the hypocrisy of communists:

Look at the Communist Party in Great Britain. They backed the armed struggle in places where it didn't have a hope for success – in Malaya, for example. They backed the armed struggle everywhere in the world except here in Ireland. The Communist Party of Ireland is much the same. They back the armed struggle of the ANC [African National Congress], they back the armed struggle of the PLO [Palestine Liberation Organization]. They won't back the armed struggle here in their own country. And they say not because they are pacifists but because they believe that the IRA hasn't the capacity to wage a proper military campaign. But that's all splittin' hairs. The fact is that the Communist Party of Ireland will always oppose an armed struggle in Ireland and the same with regard to the communist parties in Western Europe.[17]

At his first Army Council meeting, Mac Stiofáin reminded them of General Order No. 4, which barred communists from membership, and argued that Roy Johnston's membership should be withdrawn. Cathal Goulding replied that Johnston was the best thing to happen to the Movement in years and that if Johnston went, so would he. That ended that discussion.

On the Army Council, Goulding, Seán Garland and Seamus Costello pushed for more politics and were increasingly open-minded on ending abstentionism. On the other side, Mac Stiofáin and Ruairí Ó Brádaigh, and Paddy Mulcahy or Denis McInerney, depending on the year, were open to political agitation but totally opposed to dropping abstentionism. Tomás Mac Giolla, Chairman of the Council and President of Sinn Féin, was seen as a neutral on the issue.[18]

In the spring of 1966, nationalist Ireland celebrated the fiftieth anniversary of the Easter Rising. The Dublin government, led by Seán Lemass as Taoiseach and with Éamon de Valera as President, organized official events. Stormont tried to minimize the influence of the celebration by banning trains from the South, but events were not banned. A sense of the enthusiasm the anniversary generated is seen in the turnout for a commemoration in Coalisland, a small town in Tyrone with fewer than 5,000 inhabitants. Twenty thousand people attended the event and the increase in nationalism attracted recruits, including a fifteen-year-old student in Tyrone:

The first actual ... demonstration that I was at would have been the anniversary of the 1916 Rising. It was here right up the street and out through the Square [in Dungannon] ... And it was the first time for a number of years that an Easter Parade would've been held to that degree ... I was allowed to leave the school here and we went on an organized trip and part of it was a pageant of the 1916 Rising which was staged in Dublin.

The respondent was from a republican family:

My father and uncles on my father's side would be republicans. My mother's people wouldn't be actually involved in politics at all, but my father was actively involved in the Republican Movement. Although he had never been in jail or anything like that, he would have been involved in activities concerning Sinn Féin and other things throughout the 1930s and forties ... there was no television and very little radio even ... politics was really fought every night of the week. And, of course, Irish politics was the main [topic]. And the main type of issue was whether de Valera was right or whether the Treaty, which side of the Treaty and that sort of thing. So it was a fair education in politics.[19]

Mitchel McLaughlin, from Derry, was twenty years old in 1966. He described his background and the Easter 1966 commemorations:

My own parents weren't involved at all in republicanism. But my maternal grandmother was a member of Cumann na mBan and had very – right through her life, and she died when she was eighty-six years of age – she had very staunch republican principles and I think it was clearly some kind of seminal influence. And then the Easter 1966 celebrations of the original rising in 1916, the fiftieth anniversary, there was a small demonstration and I think that was my first action.[20]

The Tyrone republican and McLaughlin joined the Movement in 1966. That spring foreshadowed the future. Independent republicans blew up Nelson's Pillar in central Dublin. Loyalists, threatened by the heightened nationalism, organized a new Ulster Volunteer Force (UVF) and announced they would execute known IRA men.

A group of UVF activists, based in Belfast, set out to kill Leo Martin but could not find him. Instead, they killed two West Belfast Catholics, John Scullion and Peter Ward. Scullion is considered the first victim of the 'Troubles'. In a botched attempt at torching a Catholic bar, the group also firebombed the home of a 77-year-old Protestant widow who died from her injuries. The Stormont Prime Minister, Terence O'Neill, banned the UVF and described it as 'this evil thing in our midst'. Gusty Spence and two others were convicted of the murder and, in time, Spence would become an iconic figure among loyalists.[21]

Easter commemorations were often held at the graves of the martyred republican dead, and the ceremony often included a decade of the Rosary. In a letter published in the May 1966 issue of *The United Irishman*, Roy Johnston argued that the commemorations were sectarian. The accusation offended many people and added to the tension in the Movement. Seán Mac Stiofáin believed that 'the real target of this Marxist criticism was not sectarianism, but religion as such'. Mac Stiofáin stopped distribution of the paper in Cork and Kerry, and encouraged others to do the same. In reply, the Army Council ordered him to sell the paper and suspended him for six months. Mac Stiofáin did not go easily and that autumn he was re-elected to the Council. The leadership had more success getting rid of other traditionalists. The entire North Kerry Sinn Féin Comhairle Ceantair (Regional Council) was expelled for refusing to circulate a leaflet – 13 cumainn and 250 members were eliminated.[22]

The elimination of dissent coincided with success on the political front. In August 1966, the Wolfe Tone Societies of Dublin, Belfast and Cork sponsored a conference on civil rights in Maghera, County Derry. And, at a meeting in Belfast in January 1967, the Northern Ireland Civil Rights Association (NICRA) was born. NICRA had five objectives:

> To defend the basic freedoms of all citizens;
> To protect the rights of the individual;
> To highlight all possible abuses of power;
> To demand guarantees for freedom of speech, assembly and association;
> To inform the public of their lawful rights.[23]

The IRA was involved, but NICRA was much more than the conspiracy that some unionists believed. It was a fragile coalition of trade unionists, communists, liberal unionists, middle-class nationalists and Irish republicans. Its first 'chairman' was Betty Sinclair, a communist and Secretary of the Belfast and District Trades Union Council.

To maintain unity, NICRA left the 'national issue' out of civil rights demands. The organization adopted the slogan 'British Rights for British Subjects' and focused on three issues: job discrimination, housing discrimination and political discrimination. There was clear evidence that nationalist/Catholics were intentionally under-employed. Harland and Wolff shipbuilders was one of the largest employers in Northern Ireland; of 10,000 employees, only about 500 of them were Catholic/nationalist. Politically, nationalists were underrepresented on several councils. In Dungannon, for example, there was a small nationalist majority, but unionists controlled the town. No Catholic family had been allocated a permanent home in Dungannon for more than thirty years. Segregation, gerrymandering and housing policy made it more likely that nationalists lived in substandard homes, had a lower quality of life and were more likely to emigrate. Emigration was important because Catholics had a higher birth rate than Protestants. Owners of businesses were allocated multiple votes and, because Protestants were more likely to own businesses, that benefitted the unionist/Protestant community. 'One Man One Vote' signs were a prominent feature of NICRA marches.[24]

The unionist reaction to NICRA and the Republican Clubs was predictable and polarizing. Accusations of discrimination were denied and denounced. The Minister for Home Affairs at Stormont, William Craig, banned the Republican Clubs.

As the civil rights campaign was starting, the Republican Movement was fragmenting. Richard Behal, a 1950s veteran, was part of a group that attacked the British warship *Brave Borderer* in Waterford Harbour and then launched a mini-campaign in Kilkenny. He was court-martialled and, in essence, exiled.[25] A group of socialist republicans in Cork circulated an anonymous news-sheet, *An Phoblacht* (The Republic), that was critical of the leadership and a group of leftists in Dublin split and formed The Saor Éire (Free Ireland) Action Group. They are best known for a series of bank robberies – 'fundraising operations' – and killing Garda Richard Fallon in April 1970.[26]

At Bodenstown in 1968, the Cumann na mBan women objected to including the Connolly Association's banner in the march to Tone's grave. It was agreed that the banner would not be displayed but, at the last minute, the Connolly Association went ahead and raised it. Cumann na mBan marched from Sallins to the cemetery but refused to march back. Peig King described the event:

They didn't march because of the red flag ... It was the way we were brought up, because there was so much communism then. Personally, I found that the people I knew who called themselves socialists didn't seem to agree with our socialism. You know, they were more militant in their own aspect of things and I found them to be more or less dictators. That was my impression of them. But it wasn't my decision not to walk, it was the Executive of Cumann na mBan [that] made that decision and as a member you didn't walk ... up to that time, it was people that you believed in and that you could align with were invited to march, but when people come along and force themselves on you, come down to Bodenstown, put up their banner and march, that was a problem. They weren't invited, they were told they couldn't march but they insisted on marching.[27]

Goulding considered Cumann na mBan a 'traditional apolitical group' and a source of 'right-wing intrigue'. The next issue of *The United Irishman* carried the news that Cumann na mBan units had been disbanded. In reply, a statement from the Cumman na mBan Executive pointed out that it was an 'autonomous body of the Republican Movement' and only its members could disband it. Those signing the statement included Susie Mulcahy and Annie Long, in Limerick, and Nellie McCarthy, in Cork. They were, respectively, the wives of Paddy Mulcahy and Des Long and the sister of Gearóid Mac Cárthaigh, three critics of the Goulding leadership.[28]

Goulding and company pressed on and the Movement became involved in social agitation. The Dublin Housing Action Campaign grew out of the Sinn Féin Citizens' Advice Bureau and advocated for the homeless in Dublin. Members chained themselves to condemned houses and interrupted meetings of the Dublin City Council.[29] Some of the 'traditionalists' were wary but supported the agitation. Ruairí Ó Brádaigh talked about this:

All these things, this development during the sixties was all welcomed and everybody took part in it. And anyone who just didn't seem to be part of it just faded out of it or went to the tide thing or something [drifted away]. But we were all there banging away – MacStiofáin against the big German farmers in Meath. And I was against the American fishing boats that had ultrasound and were scooping [fish] off the [ocean floor] off the west of Ireland. And the land agitations here in the midlands as well. And, we were all in this, petitions and all.[30]

Ó Brádaigh and his wife, Patsy, helped develop a credit union in Roscommon. J.B. O'Hagan and his wife, Bernadette, were members of the Civil Rights Association Committee in Lurgan.[31] The Dublin government organized a commemoration of the fiftieth anniversary of the opening of Dáil Éireann and Joe Clarke, a Dáil official in 1919, was invited. Outside the event, the Dublin Housing Action Committee protested Dublin's housing shortage and inside, when Éamon de Valera began his address, Clarke stood up and denounced his 1916 commanding officer with: 'The declaration of Independence and the Democratic Programme of the First Dáil were never implemented. The homeless are being put in jail. Ireland is still occupied by British troops ...'[32] Eighty-six-year-old Clarke was removed from the room, crutches and all. Under the leadership of Cathal Goulding and Tomás Mac Giolla, the IRA and Sinn Féin openly declared for a thirty-two-county democratic *socialist* republic.[33] Joe Clarke, Seán Mac Stiofáin, Ruairí Ó Brádaigh, J.B. O'Hagan et al. did not resign.

In the summer of 1968, NICRA became involved in direct action. In Caledon, County Tyrone, an open house was allocated to a 19-year-old unmarried Protestant woman while Catholic families were left on a waiting list. There were protests and Austin Currie, the Nationalist Party representative at Stormont, and two others squatted in the house. They were evicted and fined And, when Currie tried to raise the issue at Stormont, he was ordered out of the room. When he shouted, 'All hell will break loose, and by God I will lead it', no one anticipated what was about to be unleashed.[34]

The NICRA executive organized their first civil rights march and, on 24 August 1968, 2,500 to 3,000 people walked the four miles from Coalisland to Dungannon. They reflected the diversity of NICRA: Betty Sinclair, communist and trade union activist; Gerry Fitt, of the Republican Labour political party and the MP for West Belfast; Eddie McAteer, leader of the Nationalist Party; Bernadette Devlin, a student at Queens University; and Tomás Mac Giolla, President of Sinn Féin. On the outskirts of Dungannon, they were stopped by a police barricade and learned that they had been banned from the centre of town, the Market Square. Behind the barricade were 'Paisleyites' and loyalists, armed with clubs and chatting with police officers. There were some scuffles with the police and a few people were struck with batons. The organizers calmed things and the march became a civil rights rally with Betty Sinclair, Gerry Fitt and Austin Currie addressing the crowd and the rally ending with the singing of 'We Shall Overcome'.[35]

A second march was scheduled for Derry, which was a model of housing and political discrimination. The city's wards were drawn so that the Protestant/unionist minority controlled the city.[36] Even the city's name was controversial. For nationalists, it is 'Derry', from the Irish

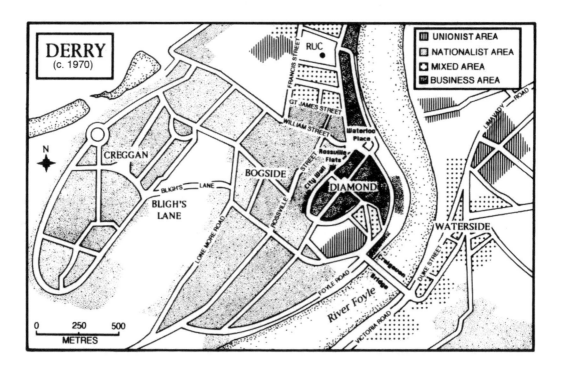

word for oak grove, *doire*. Unionists refer to the city as 'Londonderry', which dates from the Plantation of Ulster. On 5 October 1968, five to six hundred people met outside the city's walls and set off for the Diamond, the city's centre and a symbol of Protestant supremacy. They were stopped at Duke Street, outside the city gates, and then attacked by the RUC. A future republican arrived on the scene and, in his words:

As I said, not being one of the immediate 600 that were on the street, I arrived late. And we were talking about the fact that most – a great number of the people who were there, if they had foreseen the violence that was going to be meted out to them by the RUC, probably would not have been there. It probably would have been called and turned into a meeting somewhere else where they could discuss it. And things might not then have assimilated, the Movement itself would never have gotten off the ground – most unlikely. But the Stormont reaction through the RUC was so vicious and so naked in its sectarianism and its determination to hold on to the power, and its complete and utter – not reluctance, reluctance implies that perhaps you would give something – utter denial of rights to a huge proportion of the community ...

Q: What does it do to you when you see the establishment react that way?

A: It scares you shitless. It just frightens you so much that because it's – controlled violence is something that builds up but, it builds up in such a way that the operation of the state inculcates into people an acceptance for a certain standard of state violence, of state manipulation, of state control. Sectarian hatred, which decides policy in the North, is so naked when it lets go that it is naturally excessive because it is sectarian in nature and uncontrolled. It is excessive and there's no way of controlling it. So, when the RUC drew their batons, it wasn't a case that they pulled their batons to hit people. They pulled their batons and attacked the crowd to destroy the people on that street ... The very beginning of the attack on the crowd, the first person to be hit is a man who is shouting at the police, 'For God's sake can we not settle this peaceably?' or something to that effect. But he's got his hands outspread and he gets what looks like a baton in the balls. It may have been a thrust to the stomach – the same effect it would be – but he screams and he just goes down and then he's batoned as he goes down. They really got into him. ... No one of any sort of rational mind can cope with that sort of attack. It's instant panic – just distilled fear to get out of the way, to get anywhere. They used a water cannon then. If you didn't get out of the fucking way of the water cannon, they ran you down.[37]

The assault was recorded on film and televized in Ireland, Britain and the United States. Eighty to ninety people were treated for injuries, including Gerry Fitt, MP, who was hospitalized. Marchers stoned the police and a riot developed with the police pushing the crowd into the Catholic Bogside ghetto where there was rioting through the night. The march was a watershed and it is considered the start of the 'Troubles'.

The rioting and battles with the police in Derry continued into the next week. Barricades were erected to protect neighbourhoods. The Derry Citizens Action Committee, with Ivan Cooper as Chairman and John Hume as Vice Chairman, was created. Cooper was a member of the Labour Party and a Protestant. The Nationalist Party withdrew from Stormont. Students in Belfast marched on William Craig's home and formed their own civil rights group, People's Democracy (PD). The attack mobilized nationalists and, in November, 15,000 people turned up for another march in Derry. The mobilization brought concessions with Derry Corporation agreeing to a points system for the allocation of houses and Terence O'Neill announcing there would be additional reforms, including the end of company votes. Civil rights protests were working for the nationalist community.[38]

Cathal Goulding, Seamus Costello, Tomás Mac Giolla and others in the leadership wanted to take advantage of the situation, but they were stymied by people like Seán Mac Stiofáin and Ruairí Ó Brádaigh. At the convention in the Autumn of 1968, Goulding found a way around them by increasing the Army Council from seven to twenty members. Seán Mac Stiofáin commented:

> [Goulding] proposed that the Army Council be enlarged to twenty. Now I opposed it because I knew that he was looking for a majority on the Army Council which he couldn't get up to then. When it was a seven-man Army Council it was four-three and, by increasing the Army Council to twenty and making sure that some of his own nominees, a lot of his own nominees got in, he had a built-in majority then of about thirteen to seven ... something like that. And yes, there were Northerners on that Army Council. But it was a stupid move. It is hard enough at times to find a safe place for seven men to meet. Then it is [more difficult] to find a place for twenty to meet.[39]

Goulding also undermined Cumann na mBan by arguing that, because of 'the development of feminist equality all round', there was no need for a special women's organization. It was at this point that the IRA agreed to admit women volunteers.[40]

In December, Prime Minister Terence O'Neill stated that 'Ulster stands at the crossroads' and called for restraint. He asked that 'men of goodwill to come together' and accept reform. NICRA was willing to work with O'Neill and called for a truce period without marches or rallies. People's Democracy, in stark contrast, wanted to keep the pressure on.[41] On 1 January 1969, students set out on a four-day trek from Belfast City Hall to Derry, in a march that paralleled the famous Selma to Montgomery march by US civil rights activists in 1965. The marchers included several young people who would become very prominent: Michael Farrell, Bernadette Devlin, Eamon McCann and Dolours and Marian Price. The march was provocative and the organizers got the trouble they expected. They were harassed along the route by the police, the B Specials, loyalist extremists and Paisleyites. On 4 January 1969, the RUC stood by as a mob attacked marchers at Burntollet Bridge, about five miles from Derry City. They staggered into Derry, were stopped by the RUC and then counter-demonstrators showered them with bricks, stones and bottles.

There was another riot in Derry and that evening the police went into the Bogside, beat people up and threw stones through windows. The Derry republican who commented earlier described the situation:

> you weren't safe anywhere, especially if you lived in the ghettos, because they were just charging in with their armoured cars at that stage, and jeeps, and really going into the houses and dragging people out and

beating them up. And nobody was safe – nobody – kids, youngsters of five – There was an old lady who lived in St Columb's Wells, eighty-six years old. Eleven cops went in one night; they were drunk. They had been drinking wine from a bar just inside the walls up above where Rossville Flats are in Derry. And they went down; they were making up songs about ... 'Hey, hey, we're the Monkees, we're gonna monkey around.' Remember the group in the States, the Monkees? Well that was on television at the time so they'd made up their own sectarian version of it. They went into a lot of the houses in St Columb's Wells and they beat people up. And one old lady was hospitalized. She was eighty-six and she got batoned up. The people realized that it was coming to the stage, it was unspoken, but that the violence that was going to ensue from then on was going to be guns.[42]

Barricades again went up and 'You are now entering Free Derry' was painted on one of the gable walls in the Bogside. When the situation had calmed, the Citizens Action Committee convinced people to take down the barricades but, at the next Army Council meeting, Seán Mac Stiofáin urged Goulding to allow attacks on the RUC. Goulding refused.

The Belfast to Derry march and the violence raised the political consciousness of Irish nationalists and brought them onto the streets of Northern Ireland. A respondent from Dungannon described the mobilization:

Initially you didn't get the big crowds that you expected. And then it started to mushroom. The more violence there was, the more people wanted to stand up. And be counted. And that's what you will find. The more violence there is against another of their own, the more people will come out. If one man's knocked down, there's ten more to replace him ...[43]

Civil rights marches, counterdemonstrations and rioting became common.

Terence O'Neill was caught between Unionist hard-liners in his own party who wanted nothing changed and civil rights supporters demanding change. And Prime Minister Harold Wilson in London was putting pressure on O'Neill to resolve the situation. In an attempt to shore up his political position, O'Neill made the mistake of suspending his own government and calling a snap election. He was returned as Prime Minister, but his critics in the Unionist Party, especially William Craig and Brian Faulkner, were also re-elected. On the nationalist side, civil rights candidates effectively wiped out the Nationalist Party. Eddie McAteer, the party leader, lost his seat to John Hume, who ran as an Independent. In the spring of 1969, Terence O'Neill resigned as Prime Minister at Stormont and was replaced by Major James Chichester-Clark.

The change at Stormont did not bring relief, however. A by-election for the Mid-Ulster seat at Westminser, scheduled for April 1969, presented an opportunity for nationalists and republicans. The republican leadership considered putting forward a candidate but passed because it was clear that nationalists wanted someone who would represent them in London. A compromise candidate, Bernadette Devlin of People's Democracy, won the seat. Devlin was twenty-one years old, an outstanding speaker and a strident spokesperson for change. There was also a series of bomb attacks, attributed to the IRA but actually the work of the UVF. And, in Derry, RUC officers chasing after teenagers broke down a door and attacked Sammy Devenny, who was seriously injured.[44]

It was obvious there would be more trouble and, at an IRA meeting in May, Ruairí Ó Brádaigh raised the issue of defence:

> *So at this meeting, I said that it was obvious that from the way things were going, that each time it was going on to a higher and higher level and it was quite obvious that there would be shooting soon. And what was being done about [it]? ... [Paddy] McLogan had told me about that type of thing in Belfast in the twenties. You got people together who aren't necessarily volunteers but who are prepared to act in a defensive capacity in their street. And that they gathered all the weapons they could – sporting weapons, any type of weapon, and they had them available at a certain point, and the people took turns in staying up at night, and with patrolling or staying on the alert in one particular house at a strategic position. And, I said, 'What was being done about that? Were there any weapons and would they be ready?'*

Goulding believed that if they organized an armed defence of the nationalist communities it would alienate unionists and Protestants who supported civil rights and encourage more loyalist counter-violence. It would also provide the hardliners at Stormont with the excuse they needed to engage in widespread repression. According to Ó Brádaigh:

> *So Goulding got up and [made] a statement – famous statement. He said, 'It is not our job to be Catholic defenders. When the time comes, we'll put it up to the official forces, the British Army and the RUC, to defend the people.' So I was disgusted of course, saying that was for the birds. 'Put it up to them, yes, and if they don't do it. And then what happens? And then what happens to us?' So there it all was – the thinking. So I said, 'I'd like to ask a further question.' I said, 'What arms are available in Belfast?' So Goulding looked down at [Billy] McMillen, who was O/C Belfast, and McMillen got up and he said, 'Enough for one job or one operation.' So I said, 'Whatever that means.' [Laughs] And, in fact, it turned out that they had what we had in the South. They had one of everything for training purposes. They had one knife and they had one sub-machine gun, they maybe had a couple of revolvers.[45]*

The election of Bernadette Devlin showed Goulding and company that their strategy was working. Without abstentionism one of their own might be a high-profile MP instead of Devlin. They had missed out on that opportunity but believed their hard work was paying off. In a crisis, the British might force the unionist establishment to confront extremists in their own community. That would open the door to more political change, threaten unionist domination and potentially destabilize the province. Goulding was not about to militarize the situation.

In the middle of July 1969, 67-year-old Francis McCloskey was found beaten to death after the RUC had baton-charged a crowd in Dungiven, County Derry. Two days later, Sammy Devenny died from his wounds.[46]

The leadership's critics saw Goulding choosing reform over revolution. They were convinced that Northern Ireland was beyond reform and began recruiting like-minded people. Gerry McKerr, who lived in Lurgan, commented:

Well, it came about actually during the Civil Rights Movement, I became involved as I was approached by persons and asked to give an account of what my ideas were about the situation. And I had attended a number of civil rights meetings and protests which were met, of course, by the RUC rather violently. And I decided that I would have settled for civil rights, one man one vote, I would've settled for equality and a better way of life. But I realized that this was not the way things were going to turn out because of the brutality that was meted out by the RUC against the protesters. And I decided that revolution was the only answer, total revolution of the entire system. And it wasn't going to come about by marching and protesting because we were beaten from the streets. So, I decided there was no other option but there has to be a reaction against the violence by actually using violence. It's the only way to get the ideas across and to achieve an equality state. But, in the process of that, I had decided that one unified Ireland was the only solution and that – and that process of thought. And I willingly went along with old republicans who had asked me my opinion and I decided that revolution was the only answer to what was happening in the North.[47]

McKerr was twenty-five years old and not a wild-eyed student radical.

In July 1969, ironically, the British government gave the traditionalists a platform from which to attack Goulding and company. A campaign seeking the repatriation of the bodies of Peter Barnes and James McCormick, hanged in Birmingham in 1940, was a magnet for the opposition. The Belfast contingent included Joe Cahill, Jimmy Drumm, Billy McKee and Jimmy Steele. Ruairí Ó Brádaigh was also involved. The British released the bodies of Barnes and McCormick and they were reinterred in Ballyglass Cemetery in County Westmeath. In his remarks at the ceremony, Steele challenged the leadership:

> Our two martyred comrades … went forth to carry the fight to the enemy, into enemy territory, using the only methods that will ever succeed, not the method of the politicians, nor the constitutionalists, but the method of soldiers, the method of armed force. The ultimate aim of the Irish nation will never emerge from the political or constitutional platform. Indeed one is now expected to be more conversant with the teaching of Chairman Mao than those of our dead patriots.

Jimmy Steele had spent more than twenty years in prison for the cause and was a legend in Belfast. Dublin GHQ dismissed him from the IRA.[48]

5

THE SPLIT (AUGUST 1969–JANUARY 1970)

There was one hundred and nine pound in funds and a collection of rusty guns.

– Seán Mac Stiofáin[1]

In Northern Ireland, there are two major marches on the Protestant/unionist calendar. The first celebrates the victory of Protestant William of Orange over Catholic James II at the Battle of the Boyne, in 1690. The height of the marching season occurs on 12 July and in 1969 there was widespread rioting. The second commemorates the relief of Derry in 1689 from a siege by James II's army. The 'Apprentice Boys of Derry' march on the second Saturday in August. In 1969, civil rights marches had been banned and some nationalists hoped the Apprentice Boys' march would be banned, too. As it turned out, that was naively optimistic.

Following the Apprentice Boys march, on 12 August 1969, there was another major riot in Derry. The RUC again pushed nationalists into the Bogside and this time people pushed back and put up barricades. The police fired CS (tear) gas and tried to remove the barricades but were kept back by showers of petrol bombs and stones launched from the top of Rossville Flats. In the thick of the fighting was the MP for Mid-Ulster, Bernadette Devlin.

News of the 'Battle of the Bogside' spread and, in support of Derry, nationalists attacked RUC stations in Coalisland, Newry and Strabane. The next day there was more rioting in Derry; there were fires in Dungannon and Dungiven, roads were blocked in Newry, RUC stations were attacked in Belfast and there were clashes in Lurgan. In Dublin, 4,000 people marched in protest to the British Embassy and Sinn Féiners addressed a rally at the GPO.

Jack Lynch, who had succeeded Seán Lemass as leader of Fianna Fáil and as Taoiseach, called an emergency cabinet meeting. Fianna Fáil had a history of confronting the IRA and Sinn Féin, but the party's roots were still very green. Several ministers, including Charlie Haughey, Neil Blaney and Kevin Boland, urged Lynch to take a strong stand. That evening, he spoke to nationalist Ireland, stating that 'The Stormont government evidently is no longer in control of the situation' and that 'The government of Ireland can no longer stand by and see innocent people injured and perhaps worse.' Lynch announced that the Irish government had asked the British government to apply for a United Nations peacekeeping force and that field hospitals were set up in Donegal to assist people fleeing across the border. Terence O'Neill replied with, 'We must and we will treat the government which seeks to wound us in our darkest hour as an unfriendly and implacable government, dedicated to the overthrow by any means of the statutes which enjoy the support of the majority of our electorate.'[2] Neither Lynch's speech nor O'Neill's reply calmed the situation.

In Derry, the RUC was outnumbered and every attempt to enter 'Free Derry' was countered with petrol bombs and stones. On 14 August, the British government sent in troops to replace the RUC and B Specials, and the nationalists saw it as a victory. The Derry republican who described the civil rights protests also described the arrival of the British Army:

> *I can't say that I was antagonistic towards them as soon as they appeared because a lot of people felt a great sense of relief. It took someone who was brought up in the republican tradition to know that it was just another stage of oppression. People accepted superficially; it was a relief to people. They had beat the RUC into the ground and the guns were the next thing. And the RUC had used their guns on two occasions in Derry and they had used them more frighteningly in Belfast where they actually killed in August. So, when the Brits arrived it was getting to the stage when it culminated in what is now known as the Battle of the Bogside, and the support – all the rest of the rioting in the North was support for Derry at that time. It was to take pressure off Derry because Derry has always been the focal point for that sort of agitation. People knew that when they started firing in gas in so much quantity and people were really ending up in hospital in bad shape ... petrol bombs weren't really sufficient any more. And where do you go from here?[3]*

Derry settled down but conflict continued in other places. On the night of 14 August, the B Specials fired on a crowd in Armagh as a civil rights rally was breaking up, killing John Gallagher.[4] An Armagh republican described the event:

> *It started on 12th August in Derry, in '69, when the riots started in Derry. And then Armagh erupted on the fourteenth night. There was a civil rights meeting in Armagh – an indoor meeting, actually, because the [B] Specials were mobilized. The town, the whole centre of Armagh was like an armed camp and it was – I don't know if you've seen the old footage of the National Guards in the States, during the riots, the civil rights riots in the States with the rifles stacked in the street – it was virtually an armed camp. I remember – I wasn't at the meeting, but my brothers and my sisters were at it. And they come out of the meeting and there was a crowd of Specials and one word, one word following another and the next thing there was a baton charge and the Specials opened fire.*

He also described what happened next:

> *And then the bubble burst. Then you saw the full apparatus of the state going into action. The next morning you had raids, people were arrested. And people with republican backgrounds were arrested and detained for a short period of time. But then that's when the realization came that the only answer – the only answer for political change was through the bomb, you know?*

The respondent was from a 'very strong' republican background. He joined Na Fianna Éireann.[5]

Irish republicans use words like pogrom to describe what happened in Belfast. Tom Fleming lived in North Belfast:

It was about 13th or 14th August of 1969. I was coming home from work. I had been to a bar down the Crumlin Road and then the barman said he would have to close the shop, or the pub, because there was rioting further up the street. And they came into the street. I saw petrol bombs being thrown by both sides and the RUC all massed on the Protestant side along with the loyalists. I came back home, had my supper and then there was a lot of talk but it was more and more aggro going on and fighting out on Crumlin Road. As the night grew on, I saw the fires in the sky ... [6]

The RUC killed two nationalists in Ardoyne and, on the night of 14 August, loyalists and the RUC attacked the Lower Falls in West Belfast. Fra McCann witnessed the attack:

I don't think anybody expected anything on the scale of what had happened. Again, I was fairly young and fairly naïve at the time. And I wasn't really aware. All that I seen was loyalists coming down with RUC and the B Specials attacking ... at the front of Divis Flats. Most of that part of them was burned to the ground. And if you go up to the school around the corner from Divis Flats, St Comgall's School, and you look at the front of it, the walls are still riddled with bullet holes from the early ... from '69–'70 – which was attacks by loyalists and by the RUC. I stood on the stoop and watched women trying to carry their children with loyalist mobs coming after them – couldn't even get their belongings out of the houses and the whole houses were burnt down around them. And RUC men and B Specials actively took a part in that. [7]

Among the dead was nine-year-old Patrick Rooney who was shot by a 'tracer' bullet fired from a Browning machine gun mounted on an RUC armoured car. Rooney was in his bedroom in Divis Flats. [8]

The Clonard lies between the nationalist/Catholic Falls Road and the Protestant/loyalist Shankill Road in West Belfast. On the afternoon of 15 August, a loyalist mob from the Shankill Road set fire to Catholic homes in Clonard and burned out Bombay Street. One of the victims was 15-year-old Gerard McAuley. *Belfast Graves*, a tribute to republicans who have 'given their lives for their country', states that he was 'shot dead in Waterville Street on August 15th 1969 while defending Clonard from attack by rampaging Orange mobs'. McAuley was a member of Na Fianna Éireann and the first republican activist killed in the 'Troubles'. [9]

Belfast republicans saw the IRA as a defence force that would protect them from loyalists and the RUC. Goulding's IRA was missing in action, however. The defenders in West Belfast were 1940s IRA veterans like Liam Burke, Albert Price and Seamus Twomey. Joe Cahill commented: *'The actual defence of what they called Divis Street on the 15th of August, the weapons that were produced then weren't IRA weapons. They belonged to an auxiliary group, and I remember it was something like eight weapons altogether. They would have been ex-prisoners who had banded together.'* [10] One of the defenders was Billy McKee. He was asked about his return to the Movement:

Well, actually, the way I want to put it was I didn't return to the Movement, I returned to the people that were being attacked at the church just around the corner here. I don't know whether you know it – burned a whole flat of houses, old age pensioners. And I got out of work to come up and it was already

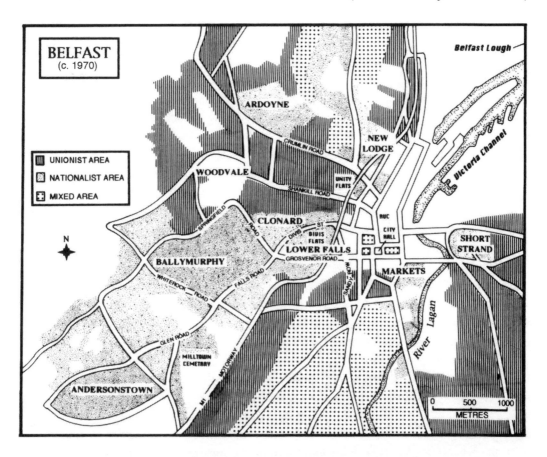

over. Well, I come up that night and I came around the corner down at the bottom of the street here.
And they came down from the Shankill Road. There could have been thousands of them. It was dark,
darkness. And they came down and they yelled [unclear] they intended to burn the rest. Their intention
was Clonard Chapel. They had a belief that the Chapel and Clonard [Monastery] were mainly for to
convert Protestants into the Catholic faith. Whatever it was, they had this in their mind, that they were
trying to convert Protestants into it – which I'd never heard tell of. But they had this belief and they were
going down, drunk and everything. And there was a – when they got down there to the bottom of the hill
a team of men were waiting on them to defend the area here. And there was a lot of shooting. And that
night there was people that never would have touched the IRA with a forty-foot pole, even in its heyday,
but they came out for to defend our area. And I was with them.[11]

Joe Cahill described his return:

we had been meeting and talking about what was possibly going to happen. We didn't expect it to happen
as quickly as it did. It happened very, very quick. So, once it came, any dissension there was, any fallout
there was, was thrown to one side and everybody reported … the pogrom started on the 14th, 15th of
August. On the 15th, the day of the 15th or 16th of August, it was known that IRA headquarters

had been set up in the Andersonstown area in Belfast. There was a particular base there which is very well known to everybody and it was an automatic thing. Just go and say what can I do to help, I'm here. I'm reporting back as it were.[12]

Seamus Twomey also reported back.

Jim Sullivan, who was second in command to O/C Billy McMillen, became Chairman of the Citizens Defence Committee in West Belfast.[13] Sullivan and McMillen supported the Goulding leadership but their situation was not made easier by the return of disgruntled and militant veterans who distrusted Goulding. Joe Cahill explained:

after the 15th of August, defence groups were set up. They wouldn't have been under the control of the IRA, whereas the IRA people would have been there, certainly ... there was tremendous distrust of the IRA ... because the IRA, they had been let down. In fact, it was nothing unusual to see written up on the walls, IRA – I Ran Away ... I was one of the prominent republicans in Belfast. People actually spat at me and said. 'You have deserted the people.' The immediate thing was the defence groups were set up in different areas. And that was the start, if you like, of the regrouping. People realized that whilst they were setting up the defence group, that the people who had been on it were either IRA men or ex-IRA men. So there was a natural thing that they were thrown up as the leaders. And that was the rebuilding of the IRA in Belfast.[14]

Included in the rebuilding were teenagers who had joined the defence groups. One respondent was a teenager in Clonard who joined Na Fianna Éireann:

The Clonard area in '69, Bombay Street is in the area. The Clonard is completely – it's smaller. It has thirteen streets, right? At the bottom of the street [it is a] fringe off the Shankill Road area. In '69 the area was attacked from the Shankill Road along Lawnbrooke Avenue by B Men, which were sort of paramilitary reservish policemen. The Loyalists attacked the area. At that time, there was only a couple of hunting guns in the area – like shotguns. Nobody was able to defend the area. So, I decided the best way to defend the area is to get involved in the Republican Movement.

British Troops arrived on the Falls Road on 15 August and in North Belfast the next day. Like Derry, many Belfast nationalists welcomed the troops but, in contrast to Derry, Belfast has a deeper republican tradition. The young man from Clonard was from a republican family:

I was very suspecting because both – well my Mom, telling me stories about them. When they came into the Clonard area, people were frightened because they had no means of defence against the RUC and the loyalists. They [the British Army] were looked upon as protectors or someone who would stop these people from murdering all around them. But, I remember talking to my Mom at that time and she says, 'Watch where they point their guns.' They were protecting us but the guns were in our direction.

Over a three-day period, 7 people were killed, another 150 were injured by gunfire and 150 had their homes burned out.[15]

The Belfast IRA expected more trouble and asked the Dublin leadership for weapons. The Dublin leadership was worried that more guns would cause more bloodshed and turned down the request. Joe Cahill, Jimmy Drumm and Leo Martin went south looking for weapons from kindred spirits who also did not trust the leadership. On 17 August, Cahill picked up weapons from John Joe McGirl in Leitrim. That same day, Seán Mac Stiofáin took direct action and led an IRA attack on the RUC station at Crossmaglen, South Armagh. A week later, Mac Stiofáin and Dáithí O'Connell met with disenchanted Belfast republicans Joe Cahill, Jimmy Drumm, the brothers John and Billy Kelly, Leo Martin, Jimmy Steele and Seamus Twomey.[16]

British soldiers patrolling the streets were a temporary solution to deep problems in Northern Ireland. The Home Secretary in London, James Callaghan, established the 'Hunt Commission' and gave it responsibility for reviewing the RUC and B Specials and recommending changes in policing. At the end of August, Callaghan toured the North and met with political leaders, like James Chichester-Clark, and with nationalists still behind barricades in Derry.[17] The Dublin government established a cabinet committee on Northern Ireland that included Ministers Charlie Haughey and Neil Blaney, and placed funds at their disposal. Haughey, the son-in-law of Seán Lemass, was an incredibly ambitious politician but he also had a complicated relationship with the IRA. As the Minister for Justice, he took a hard line against the IRA campaign in the early 1960s though he was also the son of a 1920s IRA veteran from County Derry.

Like everyone else in Fianna Fáil, Haughey saw himself as a republican.[18] Michael Moran, the Minister for Justice, received a report that an unidentified cabinet minister had met with Cathal Goulding and promised that the government would not interfere with the IRA if they ended their activities in the Republic of Ireland. When he was asked about this, Haughey confirmed that he had met with Goulding but said, 'There was nothing to it. It was entirely casual.' It was more than a casual meeting and several links would develop between Fianna Fáil and the IRA. Sources report that Charlie Haughey's brother Padraig met with Cathal Goulding in London and gave him money. Another report has Padraig Haughey meeting John Kelly in London and Kelly meeting in Belfast with Captain James Kelly of the Military Intelligence Division of the Irish Army. Charlie Haughey directed funds to publish a news-sheet, *Voice of the North*. The paper's directors included two Goulding critics, Seán Keenan and John Kelly. Fianna Fáil supporters also met with Belfast dissidents John Kelly, Joe Cahill, Jimmy Drumm, Billy McKee and Jimmy Steele. In the middle of all of this, the Irish Army offered to set up a weapons training camp in Donegal if the IRA would stop independent training.[19]

Conflict in the North brought a variety of people into contact with Movement activists. Ruairí Ó Brádaigh commented:

> *The whole thing was very loose. You had a Sinn Féin meeting in Dublin, you'd have some of these Stormont MPs speaking on the platform. You'd have a civil rights meeting in Athlone and we had Paddy Devlin [a 1940s IRA veteran and MP at Stormont for the Northern Ireland Labour Party] and Paddy O'Hanlon [a civil rights activist and independent Nationalist MP at Stormont] speaking at it. I was at one in Mullingar and Austin Currie arrived down for it. You had a whole – from August to December '69 – you had a whole mad situation of blocs and all this type of thing.*[20]

The situation was so loose that, on 22 September 1969, the Belfast dissidents attempted a coup. A group that included Joe Cahill, John Kelly, Leo Martin, Billy McKee, Jimmy Steele and Seamus Twomey interrupted a Belfast Brigade meeting, produced weapons and told Billy McMillen they were taking over. McMillen and Jim Sullivan negotiated a compromise. McMillen continued as O/C but added some of the dissidents to the Brigade Staff. They also agreed to break with Dublin and set up a Northern Command, to remove Cathal Goulding and three others from the Army Council and not to attend the next IRA convention.[21]

Billy McMillen was not in a position to follow through on all of these changes. He remained in touch with Goulding and no one left the Council. That gave the disenchanted reason enough to start setting up their own organization. In effect there was a mini-split in Belfast. Joe Cahill highlighted the issues:

> In spite of the fact that everybody was sort of reporting back to the IRA, there was still the belief that, within the coffers of the IRA, there was sufficient arms to defend. And it was discovered there was no arms at all – that the IRA wasn't an armed body. The then leadership had failed the people of the North, had let them down. So there was complete opposition then or virtually complete opposition to the leadership of the IRA at that particular time. People felt that they couldn't trust them any longer. And they asked for the removal of a number of key personnel. This is in Dublin, as far as Belfast was concerned. They asked for the removal of a number of key personnel and didn't get that, so the natural outcome was the formation of the Provisionals.[22]

Seán Mac Stiofáin, who was in touch with Leo Martin, became a go-between between Goulding and McMillen and the Belfast dissidents.[23]

Dissatisfaction with Goulding and company, and a desire for weapons, was not confined to Belfast. J.B. O'Hagan was the key republican in Lurgan:

> I was at a couple of meetings and one of them – particularly the last one was in Dundalk … Roy Johnston was the principal man who came up from the Republican Movement in Dublin. He spoke about social issues which, I said, that was all right. But then in the question and answer afterwards, I queried, 'What about the military end?' So I didn't get the answers that satisfied me. During the riots in Lurgan, during the civil rights riots, we were involved heavily. There was a lot of fighting, rioting, attacks by the unionist population, the RUC, the B Specials into our areas. And there was a lot of rioting, fighting. And at one stage, I said to one of the boys – who was sort of in charge of weapons – I said, 'I think we should get some stuff into town because this is getting very tough,' you know what I mean? That we'll have to defend our areas. So, when he went out of town and came back and he said, 'There's no weapons.' I said, 'Where are they?' He says, 'Some of the members of the Republican Movement have come from Dublin. They [were] ordered from Dublin – took the weapons away.[24]

Senior IRA veterans were looking for weapons while the British tried to reform Northern Ireland.

In mid-October, the Hunt Commission released its report which recommended disarming the RUC, replacing the B Specials with a locally recruited regiment of the British Army that would actively recruit Catholics and placing the British Army General Officer Commanding, Lieutenant General Sir Ian Freeland, in charge of security. The unionist community was outraged and Belfast erupted in riots. The Revd Ian Paisley described it as 'an absolute sell-out to the republicans and the so-called civil rights movement which is only a smokescreen for the republican movement' and called on Harold Wilson to resign as Prime Minister. In rioting along the Shankill Road the British Army shot dead two Protestants and the loyalist UVF shot dead RUC Constable Victor Arbuckle. Constable Arbuckle's death completed an interesting trifecta of the conflict. Loyalists killed the first victim (John Scullion, 1966), set off the first bombs (April 1969) and killed the first member of the security forces.[25]

By this time the IRA and Sinn Féin had settled into pro- and anti-Goulding camps. Roy Johnston describes himself and Tomás Mac Giolla as 'politicizers' at Sinn Féin Coiste Seasta (Leadership Committee) meetings: '*the CS meetings during this period were basically being carried by RJ and TMaG on behalf of the leading politicizers. The role of Joe Clarke was to put a glowering negative presence on the process, backed by Tony Ruane, and fortified by SMacS [Seán Mac Stiofáin] from time to time*' [emphasis in original].[26] The Goulding leadership publicly complained through *The United Irishman* that Charlie Haughey, Neil Blaney and Kevin Boland were trying to take over the 'Civil Rights and anti-Unionist forces'. Because of his involvement with *Voice of the North*, Seán Keenan was dismissed from Sinn Féin.[27] Dáithí O'Connell, who was the O/C in Donegal and a member of the expanded Army Council, walked out of a meeting to protest a GHQ decision and he was promptly suspended from the IRA.[28]

J.B. O'Hagan (second from right), Annual Wolfe Tone Commemoration, *c.* 1970. Courtesy of Seamus Murphy

In mid-December, the dispute over the future of the Movement was decided at the IRA Convention. General Headquarters staff and the Chief of Staff arrange IRA conventions and this one was held in North Roscommon. As agreed in September, Belfast was not represented, but also missing were delegates from the west who were opposed to the leadership, including Paddy Mulcahy and Denis McInerney who were not picked up at pre-arranged locations. From the start, the opposition considered it a rigged Convention.

Two important motions were on the agenda. The first called for the IRA to enter into a 'National Liberation Front' with other 'radical left' organizations. Cathal Goulding argued that successive IRA campaigns had failed 'because the people were not committed to, or involved in, the struggles'. Abstract ideals were not enough, what mattered were, 'Wages, working conditions, standards of living, housing, personal freedom, voting rights, equality with other sections of the community in the exercising of all these basic rights.'[29] The traditionalists were not opposed to social activism but they disagreed on why they were engaged in the activism. Ruairí Ó Brádaigh discussed this:

> *I remember Mac Stiofáin putting it very clearly. He says that this type of activity, agitational activity, will be followed up by political action which would crystalize the thing much more clearly and would end up in military action – against the British Army in the North ... You would go into political action, as well as the agitation and then you would go into military actions as well as the political and the agitational. But instead of that, they wanted to stop short at the political and divert the political into constitutional. Well, then you're reaching into – that was going on from '65 until '69, when they made a final bid. And just at the time, in the middle of their final bid, the North blew up.*[30]

The traditionalists refused to discuss or vote on the National Liberation Front motion and it was passed. The second motion called for, 'all embargoes on political participation in parliament be removed from the Constitution and Rules of both bodies [the IRA and Sinn Féin]'.[31] If passed, the motion would allow participation in the Dublin, Belfast and London parliaments. It would change a principle to a tactic and the dissidents were actively opposed.

In *Revolutionary in Ireland* and in interviews, Seán Mac Stiofáin made it clear that he wanted to avoid a split. Goulding and the others went too far according to Mac Stiofáin:

> *I didn't want to split the Movement. I would far rather have had some way we could settle the thing without the split. In fact, I believe that the biggest crime that Goulding, and MacGiolla and Seán Garland and others committed in the late sixties was that they didn't resign from the Republican Movement and form the Worker's Party there and then. And they could have shaken hands with us and said we no longer agree with the policies of the Movement, and therefore we're leaving to set up our own organization; you're welcome to come with us if you want. And if they had done that, there would have been no bitterness, no recrimination, no armed clashes and there would have been a basis for a certain amount of cooperation. But, instead, they wanted to have their cake and eat it. They wanted this image of being republican yet they were departing from the republican policies.*[32]

Ruairí Ó Brádaigh's perspective was much the same. The motion violated basic principles and would turn the Movement into something 'contrary to its nature':

> *I'm always inclined to say look, if you're tired, Jesus, just opt out. And if you want to start something else, start it. Even a constitutional party. Start it and at least there won't be any bitterness and there'll be a certain amount of good will until you get to power. But don't start trying to convert the Republican Movement into what it's not. Something which is contrary to its nature because you will – you'll end up with an upheaval. And a dirty one.*[33]

The final vote was twenty-eight to twelve in favour of ending abstentionism And, because they believed the vote was rigged, the traditionalists considered it illegitimate. They did not walk out, but from that point they refused to participate in deliberations or go forward for membership on the IRA Executive and Army Council.[34]

Immediately after the Convention, the opposition began organizing a second convention. Mac Stiofáin left for Belfast where he joined an in-progress meeting of people planning to set up an independent Northern Command. Those present included 1940s veterans Joe Cahill, Jack McCabe and Harry White. They agreed to set aside their plan and send four representatives to a second convention. Ruairí Ó Brádaigh contacted Dáithí O'Connell, who asked, 'What's going to happen?' Ó Brádaigh replied, 'The minority is going to expel the majority.'[35]

Twenty-six people – thirteen delegates and thirteen visitors – attended a second IRA Convention held two weeks after the first. The visitors included the missing delegates from the first convention, representatives from Belfast and a few interested others like O'Connell. One of the first things they did was appoint Seán Mac Stiofáin to chair the proceedings. If the first convention was illegitimate, this one started the process of fixing that by overturning the motions from the earlier convention. They also elected a new Executive Council which then elected a new Army Council – Joe Cahill, Leo Martin, Paddy Mulcahy, Seán MacStiofáin, Ruairí Ó Brádaigh, Dáithí O'Connell and Seán Treacy – and they gave themselves a name. The 1916 Proclamation had declared a 'Provisional' government. Dáithí O'Connell suggested they would be the 'Provisional' IRA until a proper convention could be organized. The other group became known as the 'Official' IRA.[36]

The Army Council elected Seán Mac Stiofáin as Chief of Staff. He had been in the organization for twenty years, had served time in prison and had a reputation for hard work and efficiency. Most important, Mac Stiofáin had fought Goulding and the new direction every step of the way. He spoke about his appointment:

> *I was considered by the Army Council to be the best person available … and they felt that I had leadership qualities. I had worked my way up from the bottom to the top inside of, what, ten years? Was it ten or twenty years? But I'd been active over a long period of time. Any job I had in the IRA I'd been successful in. I was Director of Intelligence for three years before that. I had been O/C down in Cork and Kerry and… I got new units organized when I came up to County Meath so I was well known for being energetic, and disciplined and steady-headed … The person who proposed me as Chief of Staff was*

a Belfast man. And he said that, in the opinion of the Belfast Staff, the one person who understood the North better than anybody down here was myself.

Mac Stiofáin was also willing to put his life on hold:

And, literally, when I was appointed Chief of Staff, I had to put my career – I had a good job at the time, a job I was very interested in – I was working as a financial organizer for Conradh na Gaelige, the Irish language movement – literally, I just had to do away with my career, my family and everything and just leave it like that. I actually put everything into the Movement because there was very little resources. There was one hundred and nine pound in funds and a collection of rusty guns.[37]

Mac Stiofáin's peers recognized his commitment and his talents. Ruairí Ó Brádaigh described him as 'perfect' for the job: '*I had a lot of respect for MacStiofáin. I thought he was a very good man in a particular situation ... idealistic and all that kind of thing. He was very much for the Irish language and so on.*'[38] J.B. O'Hagan described Mac Stiofáin as the 'proper man' for the position, as someone 'genuine' and 'very sincere'.[39] The Provisionals wanted a Chief of Staff who was committed to the Army, efficient and sincere. They got that in Mac Stiofáin.

They sought out like-minded republicans. Mac Stiofáin described approaching Cumann na mBan: '*I met them shortly after the split and they immediately agreed that they'd pledge their allegiance to the new republican leadership.*'[40] The Cumann na mBan leadership released a public statement supporting the Provisionals. Ruairí Ó Brádaigh met with Tom Maguire, the surviving member of the group that delegated the powers of government from the Second Dáil Éireann to the Army Council. On the last day of December, Maguire released his own public statement:

An IRA Convention, held in December, 1969, by a majority of the delegates attending, passed a resolution removing all embargoes on political participation in parliament from the Constitution and Rules of the IRA.

...

I, as the sole surviving member of the Executive of Dáil Éireann, and the sole surviving signatory of the 1938 Proclamation, hereby declare that the resolution is illegal and the alleged [IRA] Executive and Army Council are illegal, and have no right to claim the allegiance of either soldiers or citizens of the Irish Republic.

...

I hereby further declare that the Provisional Executive and Provisional Army Council are the lawful Executive and Army Council respectively of the IRA and that the governmental authority delegated in the Proclamation of 1938 now resides in the Provisional Army Council and its lawful successors.[41]

The Provisionals could claim that they were the rightful heirs and defenders of the All-Ireland Republic of 1919–22 – whether or not anyone else agreed with them.

The army had split and the two sides prepared for the Sinn Féin Ard Fheis, which was held at Dublin's Intercontinental Hotel on the second weekend of January 1970. On the agenda was a motion allowing Sinn Féin representatives to take their seats in the Dublin, Belfast and London parliaments. Supporters of the Provisionals pointed out that, according to the Sinn Féin Constitution, recognizing Leinster House, Stormont or Westminster was 'an act of treachery' and the motion was unconstitutional. The Officials organized the Ard Fheis and ignored the objection. When it all came down to a vote, however, the motion passed (153 in favour and 104 opposed) but not with the required two-thirds majority needed to change the Constitution. A delegate quickly proposed a vote of allegiance to the Official Army Council, which only required a simple majority. The motion was seconded and the walkout began with Seán Mac Stiofáin making his way to the microphone and saying, 'Now lads, it's time for us to leave.'[42] Ruairí Ó Brádaigh, Joe Clarke, Des Long, John Joe McGirl, Tony Ruane and about half of the room started for the door. In the commotion, someone slugged Mac Stiofáin in the chest.[43]

They reconvened in a pre-arranged location, Kevin Barry Hall in Parnell Square. Their actions paralleled the Provisional IRA of a few weeks earlier, in part because some of them attended both meetings. They elected a twenty-person 'Caretaker Executive' that would maintain Sinn Féin until a proper Ard Fheis was organized. Ruairí Ó Brádaigh was elected Chairman. The other officers were his brother, Seán Ó Brádaigh, Director of Publicity; Walter Lynch, Secretary; and Tony Ruane, Treasurer. Following standard procedure, several members of the Provisional IRA leadership were elected to the Caretaker Executive, including Seán Mac Stiofáin and Paddy Mulcahy along with Ruairí Ó Brádaigh (see Figure 2).[44] A rumor would later develop that a seat on the Army Council was reserved for the President of Sinn Féin, but Ó Brádaigh was already on the Council.

Other than their commitment and experience, they had few resources. They had walked away from the party's headquarters, given up a newspaper and cut their membership by about half. Frank Glynn asked John Joe McGirl what they would do for funds:

> 'Well', he [McGirl] says, 'a very good question'. 'Well', I said, 'here's a ten pound note'. And I put the first ten pound note on the plate. And I said to him, 'Do a collection before we leave here.' And he got ninety pound or something before we left. And a lot of fellows could hardly afford a ten-shilling note or a pound note or whatever it was at the time. But I know we got ninety pound that night.[45]

Seán Ó Brádaigh arranged a loan for a newspaper – *An Phoblacht* – and the first issue appeared at the end of the month with the headline, 'On This Rock We Stand'. They were standing on the 'Rock of the Republic' and from that position they declared, 'we refuse to budge'.[46]

Understanding the Split

There is a tendency to view the split as the response of militants to the debacle of August 1969 – the more militant Provisionals separating themselves from the more political Officials. But this view ignores the fact that, in their words and deeds, the Officials were quite militant. The January issue of *The United Irishman* claimed, 'The war against Britain has never been halted and will never

Northern Six Counties	Southern 26 Counties
Charlie McGlade, Belfast (1930s), living in Dublin	Ruairí Ó Brádaigh, Chairman, Longford/Roscommon (1950s)
	Seán Ó Brádaigh, Director of Publicity, Editor, *An Phoblacht*, Longford/Dublin (1950s)
Liam Slevin, Fermanagh (1950s)	Uaitéar Ó Loinsigh (Walter Lynch), Secretary, Dublin (1950s)
	Tony Ruane, Treasurer, Mayo (1910s)
	Eamon Mac Thomáis, Dublin (1950s)
	Seán Mac Stiofáin, Meath (1940s)
	Seosamh Ó Clerigh (Joe Clarke), Dublin (1910s)
	Pádraigh Maolchatha (Paddy Mulcahy), Limerick (1920s)
	Larry Grogan, Louth (1920s)
	John Joe McGirl, Leitrim (1930s)
	Peter Duffy, Louth (1930s)
	Cáit Bean Mhuinhneacháin (Kathleen Moynihan), Longford (1940s)
	Caoimhín Mac Cathmhaoil (Kevin Campbell), Mayo (1940s)
	Frank Glynn, Galway (1950s)
	Deasún Ó Longáin (Des Long), Limerick (1950s)
	Denis McInerney, Clare (1950s)
	Seán Ó Gormaile (Seán Gormley), Galway (1950s)
	Thomas O'Neill, Dublin (1950s)

FIGURE 2

Sinn Féin Caretaker Executive: January 1970 (approximate year of recruitment in parentheses)

be halted as long as Britain claims a right to legislate for Ireland.' This was not just rhetoric since, from the split through to May 1972, the Official IRA killed people because 'Only an armed, determined people will be listened to with respect.'[47]

Another simplistic view is that the split was caused by the IRA's failure to defend Belfast in August 1969 and that the Provisionals arose like the Phoenix, 'Out of the Ashes'. Certainly young people flocked to the IRA after August 1969, and many of them ended up in the Provisionals. But teenagers in Belfast defending their neighbourhoods did not create the Provisional IRA or the Sinn Féin Caretaker Executive. In *Tyrone's Struggle*, Gerard Magee quotes a pre-1969 IRA volunteer who commented, 'I didn't need to be struck over the head by an RUC baton to become an active republican.'[48] Middle-aged Irish republican veterans, like Paddy Mulcahy, a 53-year-old insurance agent, created the Provisionals. The vast majority of the people on the first Army Council and the Caretaker Executive did not live in Belfast or even Northern Ireland.

'Defending the people of the north' and the Provisionals' rising 'Out of the Ashes' became phrases that summarized five interrelated issues that led to the split, as described in the first issue of *An Phoblacht*:

- Recognition of Westminster, Stormont and Leinster House
- Extreme Socialism leading to totalitarian dictatorship
- Failure to protect our people in the North in August 1969
- Abolition of Stormont and direct rule from Westminster
- Internal methods in operation in movement for some time.[49]

The Provisionals believed that the leadership had moved so far to the left that they were Stalinists ('totalitarian dictatorship') and used 'internal methods' to stifle dissent.[50] Seán Mac Stíofáin described the internal issues:

> There was also the question of the internal discipline in the Movement, of which there were double standards. If you favoured the new policies, you could get away with anything. If you didn't, you were severely disciplined for the slightest infringement of rules or regulations … there was this hard Marxist rhetoric, which was unacceptable to a lot of us, and unacceptable to the vast majority of the people of Ireland – the people we depended upon for support.[51]

The importance of abstentionism is seen in John Joe McGirl's response to the split. He was close friends with Cathal Goulding and was probably the most politically engaged of anyone in the Movement in 1969/70. He had represented Sinn Féin on the Leitrim County Council since 1960. At the Ard Fheis, he explained his opposition to abstentionism with the comment, 'men have died opposing Leinster House, men have been killed for refusing to enter that assembly'. For a year and a half after the split, McGirl tried to reconcile the differences between the Provisionals and the Officials, but he insisted the 'Officials' would have to accept abstentionism.[52]

Ending abstentionism was a key issue because the Officials could not reform Stormont without first taking seats in that assembly. They thought they could pursue revolution *and* constitutional politics – at least that is what they told their supporters. In contrast, the Provisionals believed that in order to get someone elected armed struggle would have to be limited or ended altogether. They also believed that Stormont was beyond reform. The Provisionals wanted a direct confrontation with the British, without unionists and Stormont in the middle. Abstaining from constitutional politics made it easier to confront the British directly through armed struggle.

Ruairí Ó Brádaigh was and would remain the most articulate spokesperson for the abstentionist position. For him, taking seats in Stormont, Leinster House and Westminster violated Irish republican principles *and* was a strategic mistake. *Constitutional* politics lead to reform, not revolution. According to Ó Brádaigh, when revolutionaries take seats in a parliament:

> You get like those you work with. You become part of the machine … You become part of the status quo. You become like it, you become part of it and then you defend it. Because you have to defend, because there's a crowd of madmen like us loose. You're caught in no-man's land. That's what happens to you. And then you use secrets because you're under a blitz from the crowd you have left, and you seek refuge with the others. And it's what happened to John Redmond [in the 1910s] and everything else [Collins, de Valera etc.]. That's what parliaments are for. Parliament is a replacement for civil war. You talk it

out, instead of in the streets. But if you think you can keep one leg in the streets and the other leg in parliament, you've a bloody awful mistake.

From this perspective, sincere republicans are corrupted by constitutional politics. When Éamon de Valera became Taoiseach of the Irish Free State in 1932, no one imagined that, within a decade, a Fianna Fáil government would intern and execute former comrades or let them die on hunger strike. Ó Brádaigh was also concerned about the future:

> *I remember saying to them, 'That's all very fine, you want to do this now' – in discussions at the Army Conventions, the Sinn Féin Ard Fheis's – 'You want to do this now. Well I'll tell you, as far as I'm concerned, and plenty of people like me, we're not going along with you. No matter what support you've got, we're not going along with you. [We're] going to where we are going. Now, what I want to know, from you now – now, not in ten years' time – what are you going to do with us?' A challenge, an answer. 'What are you going to do with us, how are you going to cope with us?' There'd never come an answer. And I know well what you'd do to us – put us against the bloody wall and behind the barbed wire and six feet under. That's what you'll do with us ... Of course they were too smart to say that but this is the logical outcome of the whole damn thing.[53]*

There was no reason to believe that Goulding et al. were special and immune from the political processes that led de Valera to turn on his comrades.

Over the course of the 1960s, the Irish Republican Movement divided into two camps. Within each camp people became like-minded, in part because they were more likely to speak with each other than they were to speak with people in the other camp. Geography influenced this in-group interaction. Cathal Goulding, Tomás Mac Giolla, Seán Garland and Mick Ryan all lived in Dublin and the progressives were Dublin-centred. Seamus Costello lived in nearby Bray, County Wicklow and Roy Johnston was in Dublin. Rural traditionalists led the opposition and no one on the first Provisional Army Council was in Dublin: Mac Stiofáin was from England and lived in County Meath; Ó Brádaigh was from Longford and lived in Roscommon; Paddy Mulcahy lived in Limerick; Sean Tracey lived in Laois; Dáithí O'Connell was from Cork but had moved to Donegal. Joe Cahill and Leo Martin were from Belfast, not Dublin. Most of the people on the 'Caretaker Executive' were from the south and west; only two of them were from Northern Ireland.

At the time of the split, the Republican Movement was a small conspiracy. The leaders had been involved for decades and everyone pretty much knew everyone else. Within two groups or blocs of activists, people became even closer. The Dublin leadership met with each other, shared their thoughts and came to similar conclusions about the Movement's future. The rural traditionalists/abstentionists met with each other, shared their thoughts and came to a different conclusion. Defence of the North may have split Belfast, but abstentionism split the Movement.

A Fianna Fáil Plot

There remain allegations that Fianna Fáil created the Provisionals.[54] At the extreme, some argue that Fianna Fáil supported the Provisionals because they feared the development of radical Irish republican politics as led by Cathal Goulding, Tomás Mac Giolla and so forth. The allegation is more than a little far-fetched. Sinn Féin, at that time, was not even registered as a political party, North or South. John Kelly, the Belfast republican, offered a summary of the Fianna Fáil–Provisional relationship, 'At the time we, to be quite honest, didn't much care if there were strings attached to the guns or not.'[55]

After August 1969, politicians from several political parties were sympathetic with the republican position. Cathal Goulding did not trust Fianna Fáil but neither did those who went with the Provisionals. In 1957, even though he had been elected to the Dublin parliament, a Fianna Fáil government interned Ruairí Ó Brádaigh. He did not forget it and, on Fianna Fáil's involvement in creating the Provisionals, Ó Brádaigh commented:

> *I had no contact or no part in any of the meetings with Fianna Fáil people or any of the meetings with Free State Army officers ... and to think that I would touch with the barge pole anything organized by Fianna Fáil – ... they were up to no good. They were trying to short circuit and defuse the whole Northern situation, whereas we were trying to convert it into a revolutionary situation.*

He also commented on the claim that Fianna Fáil financed the Provisionals:

> *These defence committees included all kinds of people in the North, including republicans ... it's like saying that the Provisional IRA was started with Fianna Fáil money, which is a downright lie, as we all know to our cost. We all did it out of our own pockets ... And if some of our members were members of defence committees, so were the Officials members of defence committees. If money came from Dublin to pay members of the defence committees in Belfast who were out all night on the streets patrolling and weren't able to go to their work in the morning – if our members were at that, yes, they did get money the same as the Officials got the money. But that was for the families ... But this then is converted into the other thing like that [Fianna Fáil financing the Provisionals]. You know? It's a smear.*[56]

For the Belfast dissidents, Fianna Fáil support probably made the September coup more attractive, and the possibility that Fianna Fáil would help import weapons may have made the split a little easier for those in the know. But the Provisionals were going to be created with or without Fianna Fáil.

Any links between the Provisionals and Fianna Fáil were broken in the spring of 1970 when Taoiseach Jack Lynch found out about an arms shipment and sacked Charlie Haughey and Neil Blaney. Kevin Boland then resigned from the cabinet and Captain James Kelly, republican John Kelly, Belgian businessman Albert Luykx, and Haughey and Blaney were arrested and charged with conspiracy to import arms. The charges against Blaney were dropped and, over the course of two 'Arms Trials', the others were acquitted. Charlie Haughey would forever be linked with the allegation that he ran guns for the Provisionals. It was a badge of honour for some and a cause of shame for others.

6

WAR (JANUARY 1970–DECEMBER 1971)

*At one end, at Bombay Street, no, at the corner of Cupar Street, you had IRA snipers, right?
On the top of Mackies Machinery you had British Army snipers and they were firing away at one
another.*

– Armagh republican[1]

Immediately after the split, the two IRAs and the two Sinn Féins competed for the allegiance
of their members. What no one knew was that, within two years, Northern Ireland would be a
war zone. Ironically, the increase in violence had more to do with British mismanagement of the
situation than it did the Provisionals or the Officials.

Choosing between the two groups was easy for some activists. Seán Lynch, for example, was
an ardent abstentionist and had a relationship with Ruairí Ó Brádaigh that went back decades. Ó
Brádaigh's father was shot in an arms raid in 1919 and Lynch's father helped save his life. Lynch
went with the Provisionals, as he explained:

> *At that particular time I had no bother at all deciding myself because ... the Catholics had been harassed
> and everything was happening to them down in the North. The Officials didn't seem to be doing anything
> about it – nothing for the defence. And that was one of the reasons why I had no – I nearly even hadn't
> to think about what side I'd be on ...*

Asked if he was an abstentionist, Lynch replied: 'Ahh, yes, yes I am – against Leinster House.'[2]

Phil O'Donoghue returned from South Africa in 1969 because 'the country was going to
hell at that stage'. He approached the split carefully:

> *For a long time I didn't want to get involved with the factions. I just couldn't see any forward movement
> with the various elements, you know? I just couldn't see it. And when you know some of these people you
> say to yourself, 'Jesus, who'd be following them?' But, anyway, at the end of the day most of them were
> genuine enough but got carried away ... both sides.*

With time, O'Donoghue went with the Provisionals:

A few fellows asked me, would I help. And I said I would but I wasn't going to take any definite decisions on that. So I just helped out for a while ... The Jewish resistance were like that. They would go off to sea and wouldn't be seen for years. And the next thing would be, the fellows would be going to a meeting and there's all these old friends. The Republican Movement is like a siren at night calling you back.[3]

In *Man of War, Man of Peace*, David Sharrock and Mark Devenport report that Gerry Adams was a 'semi-independent' for about six weeks before joining the Provisionals.[4] Richard Behal, who had returned to Ireland, would remain an independent until after Bloody Sunday.[5] Some people chose the Officials and then switched, as described by Mitchel McLaughlin:

I didn't actually go immediately with Provisional Sinn Féin. At the time of the split, I actually stayed with the Official Republican Movement, mainly because of their politics which undoubtedly were more progressive than the more kind of nationalistic rhetoric that I was hearing from the likes of Ruairí Ó Brádaigh and people like that. What decided me, and I mean it was a fairly rapid process – I mean I'm talking about within two or three months of the split, I concluded that those accusations that were being made about the Officials abandoning the national question, and ... [becoming involved in] constitutional politics, were actually true.[6]

In *Martin McGuinness: From Guns to Government*, Liam Clarke and Kathryn Johnston report that McGuinness joined the Officials in 1970 and then switched to the Provisionals.[7]

The Movement had pretty much split down the middle.[8] As people chose sides, the Provisionals rebuilt. In *Revolutionary in Ireland*, Seán Mac Stiofáin writes that they began with an organization 'that was only a nucleus. Outside Belfast the battalions were very much paper battalions.'[9] Their most valuable asset was experience. Ruairí Ó Brádaigh commented: *'The [1950s] campaign kept faith with the past and it handed on a tradition to the future. And in practical terms it provided an officer corps for the 1970s. And all that accumulated experience – it wasn't a case of going back to the forties men.'* It had been seven years since the end of the previous campaign, but twenty-five since the 1940s. Ruairí Ó Brádaigh again: *'the 1940s people, while I'm sure they would have been all right for help and advice, and all that type of thing, by '69 they wouldn't be able to contribute the way we were able to do it.'* Ó Brádaigh acknowledged that activists from the forties, like Joe Cahill and John Joe McGirl, were involved:

Yes, there were. And Twomey ... but that would be quite thin on the ground ... There were a lot more fifties people. It's like when we were in the Curragh in the fifties and looking around us, the number of twenties people were – you had McLogan, you had Larry Grogan and then you had local men like Danny Gleeson and so on. But at top level, you just had a very few. The forties people were fine, especially the younger forties people but there wouldn't have been so many of them. No, it was very important that the fifties people were there and available and fit into place – very important, and especially as the situation developed very quickly. Experience is a very difficult thing to replace.[10]

Top-level positions were filled right away. Dáithí O'Connell became IRA Director of Publicity. Jack McCabe became the Quartermaster. Gearóid Mac Cárthaigh (Gerry McCarthy) was appointed the O/C of Cork and was heavily involved in training, as were Seán Tracey and Paddy Ryan. Ryan has been described as one of Mac Stiofáin's right-hand men.[11]

Belfast was especially important but Billy McMillen and Jim Sullivan supported the Officials. The Belfast Brigade was divided into three battalions and Mac Stiofáin appointed Billy McKee as the O/C. McKee's staff officers were: Seamus Twomey, Adjutant; Leo Martin, Intelligence Officer; Tom O'Donnell, Finance Officer; Seán McNally, Quartermaster; and Jimmy Steele, Publicity Officer. Albert Price was in charge of the part-time/reserve Auxiliary IRA. In Derry City, the leading Provisionals were Seán Keenan and Tommy McCool. In Tyrone, where the IRA did not split, the O/C was John Paddy Mullen, another veteran from the 1950s. In Tyrone, there would be a 'steady transition' to the Provisionals over time.[12]

Compared to the new recruits, their officers seemed middle-aged and out of touch. Billy McKee, in particular, was socially conservative and a devout Catholic. At the same time, the younger people deeply respected McKee and the other leaders.[13] Brendan Hughes, nicknamed 'Darkie' because of his complexion, joined the West Belfast IRA after August 1969. He commented on the early leadership: *People like Ruairí Ó Brádaigh, Seán Mac Stiofáin, Dáithí O'Connell and that sort of calibre person – we would have been in awe of them ... Billy McKee, yeah, that sort of calibre – they were the heroes for people like me.*[14] The senior people had kept the Movement together during the lean years. They attracted others who saw their political analysis as the correct one – the Officials were going constitutional, Northern Ireland was beyond reform and the British only responded to physical force.

The first item on the agenda was weapons, especially for new units. Experience helped with that, too. Seán Mac Stiofáin spoke about acquiring arms:

> *Immediately after the split formed there were units springing up like mushrooms. And then every time a unit formed, the first thing was, 'What stuff can you issue us?' Right? And it was a semi-nightmare getting something for them. And what I did, I knew – and I'd been around for a long time previous, and in spite of all this stuff that was sent, collected in the Autumn of '69, and went mostly into Belfast and other areas – that there was still stuff around. And I just appointed a couple of organizers and told them to go ahead and get around the country and screw what stuff was there in the twenty-six counties out. From that, they came up with – it was amazing the amount of weapons that were collected, say in January and February, and March of 1970. You had sub-machine guns, rifles, short arms, automatic shot guns – all useful gear for the kind of thing we were preparing for, which was defensive action.*[15]

Some of the weapons had been around for a very long time. Thompson machine guns were smuggled into Ireland in the 1920s. The Thompson resurfaced in the 1940s and again in the 1950s. There were still 'scores' of them in 1970, as Ruairí Ó Brádaigh explained:

> *There were roughly – there were 200 plus Thompson guns [in '56] ... There were about 50 Sten guns, which had been captured. There were 250 Lee Enfield rifles, from World War Two. They were in use by the British at that stage and, in fact, while the Free State Army still had the World War One, Mark III Lee Enfield, we had already got the – captured from the Brits [in arms raids] – the World War Two*

ones. In the early fifties we were in advance of them. So that would be 500 plus between shoulder weapons and sub-machine guns. And then about ten or twelve Bren guns, light machine guns.

Q: In 1970, in addition to the 'scores' of Thompsons, would some of that other material still be around?

A: Oh yeah, oh yes. Standard. As to the numbers, I suppose the rifles would be in scores, too – be in the region of 100, I'd say.[16]

Overseas supply lines were organized. By April of 1970, material was arriving in Ireland, including more sophisticated ArmaLite AR15 and AR-18 assault rifles.

Dáithí O'Connell visited New York, where three veterans from the 1920s, Michael Flannery, Jack Magowan and Jack McCarthy had created the Irish Action Committee. O'Connell also met with Mayo-born George Harrison who, along with Liam Cotter, had supplied the IRA weapons in the 1950s. Seán Keenan then visited New York and helped Flannery, Magowan and McCarthy organize the Irish Northern Aid Committee (NORAID). Its mission was to support the families of the inevitable prisoners that would result from the developing IRA campaign. Later, there would be allegations that NORAID was involved in gun-running.[17]

While the Provisionals organized themselves, demonstrations, counter-demonstrations and riots continued. Stormont passed the Public Order (Amendment Act), which required seventy-two hours' notice for a march; trade union marches were exempt. People's Democracy immediately staged a sit-in at Queen's and NICRA organized demonstrations throughout Northern Ireland and in the UK. In the background, there was paramilitary violence. By the end of February 1970, loyalists and republicans had set off twelve bombs.[18]

In the spring, both the Officials and the Provisionals celebrated the Easter Rising. There were disturbances in Armagh, Derry and Lurgan. Catholic–Protestant clashes went on for three days in Belfast and, for the first time, British troops fought with Catholic/nationalist crowds. Nationalists attacked with petrol bombs and the British responded with CS gas. Ed Moloney, in *A Secret History of the IRA*, reports that Billy McKee was the Belfast O/C and that Gerry Adams, who maintains that he never joined the IRA, was the O/C for Ballymurphy. According to Moloney, they disagreed on strategy. McKee wanted a direct confrontation with the British and sent in a unit to start a gun-battle. Adams stopped them in order to let the rioting further radicalize people. It was the right political move, but McKee was furious.[19]

Young people reassessed the situation. Fra McCann describes the Lower Falls/Divis Flats area of West Belfast:

A lot of people were under the false impression, and the Church played a big part in it, saying that the British were in to protect the nationalists. But if anybody looks back on it now, the British were here to uphold the state that they had imposed on the nationalist population. The RUC were stretched to the full limit. They were almost near breaking point. And if it went on any longer, the whole thing would have collapsed. So the British came over to prop up that state.

Q: Would you have realized that at the time?

> A: *Not really, no. It wasn't really until later, 'til I started reading and looking at the situation – go back, go back in my mind especially, you know, [about] the situation at the time. But one thing that has always stuck in my mind is when the British Army came onto the streets. It was just at the top of Albert Street. I remember one morning standing with a tricolour and this fellow yelled at me and he was shouting, 'Youse will rue the day the British ever set foot on them.' And he was talking about our streets. And that was the day the British Army came onto the streets. Because most people have – most elderly people have had a lot of experience with the British troops back in the '20s and things like that ... That one statement has always stuck in my mind, even though I was fairly young at the time.*[20]

Young people in Derry had a similar experience:

> *The British came in. And there was a certain relief. People did give them tea and sandwiches. It wasn't all loyalists ... people were going up and talking to them, and asking them where they were from and all the rest of it. And I talked to quite a few. It was an interesting situation because we had been at war with the police. That's what it came down to. And then these guys arrived and suddenly the cops are pulled right out of it and not allowed to do anything unless they're accompanied by the Brits and whoever else in charge. We had seemed to win a victory, and the Brits saying we're in this. They were in the vacuum actually – it was a vacuum situation I suppose. And the Brits hadn't, at that stage, been pushed to do anything. They were just there. And they could act to you, and they'd talk to you and they were ordinary characters ... I would have accepted them as being there and I wouldn't have been naturally antagonistic to them. But it didn't take long for my antagonism to build up because the first day that I saw barbed wire had been put across a street to stop a march or a protest and it was in the same areas where we were never allowed to march before, like in the city centre, in the Diamond and whatnot. Nothing had really changed. And then, of course, one day I saw a bit of a hassle going on with Brits and some people were trying to march and the batons were pulled. And I recognized one of the Brits that was doing the batoning was one of the guys I had been speaking to. And he saw me and he said, 'Look, go on, get the fuck out of here.' And I said, 'No, you can't tell me to do that. I know you're all right, I know you're a sound enough character because I've spoken to you but this is my town and I'm allowed to be here.' And he says, 'I'm just fucking telling you for your own good because we're going to start using gas.' 'Well', I said, 'that's too bad because I'm going to be over there. So it looks like we're on opposite sides after all.' And that's really then when it started. But that didn't prompt me to run looking for a gun or for the IRA.*[21]

What was happening in Belfast and Derry was happening on nationalist streets throughout the North. In the summer of 1970, the political landscape for much of the next twenty-five years was being put in place.

In a Westminster election, Edward Heath and the Conservatives replaced Harold Wilson and Labour. In Northern Ireland, republicans did not contest the election and moderate nationalists benefitted. Prominent civil rights supporters Gerry Fitt, of the Republican Labour Party, and Bernadette Devlin, a nationalist-republican 'Unity' candidate, were re-elected in West Belfast and Mid-Ulster. Frank McManus, another 'Unity' candidate, won in Fermanagh-South Tyrone; he was the brother of IRA volunteer Pat McManus, killed during the 1950s campaign.

Unionists had lost West Belfast, Mid-Ulster and Fermanagh/South Tyrone in previous elections. Those losses were tolerable. More important, cracks were appearing in the Unionist Party. In January 1970, Terence O'Neill had resigned from Stormont and Revd Ian Paisley, running as a Protestant Unionist, won the by-election. The Protestant Unionist Party, which foreshadowed the Democratic Unionist Party (DUP) that Paisley would co-found, was more loyal and more Protestant than the unionist establishment. On the other side, moderates had defected from the Unionist Party and formed the Alliance Party, which was avowedly non-sectarian and supported reform. In the Westminster election, Paisley was elected MP for North Antrim, the Unionist Party lost two seats and the party's vote was down significantly.[22]

At the end of June, the honeymoon between nationalists and British troops took another hit in Belfast. Protestants celebrated the 'Little Twelfth', an Orange festival that serves as a precursor to 12 July marches. There were Protestant–Catholic riots and, in North Belfast, Provisional IRA defenders shot dead three Protestants. In East Belfast, a mob attacked the Short Strand, a Catholic enclave, and tried to petrol bomb St Matthew's Catholic Church. The British Army turned down an appeal for help because they were so busy elsewhere and could not spare the personnel. Billy McKee and the Provisional IRA stepped in and shot dead two Protestants and mortally wounded two others. A Catholic defender, Henry McIlhone, was shot dead and McKee was seriously wounded. McKee became a legend and the Provisionals secured their reputation as defenders. The next day, Sir Ian Freeland, the General Officer Commanding (GOC) of British forces in Northern Ireland, announced that anyone carrying a firearm was liable to be shot without warning. The Ulster Defence Regiment (UDR), which had replaced the B Specials, was mobilized along the border.

The Provisionals were already moving from defence to offence but it was a deadly transition. That weekend they lost their first volunteers through a premature explosion. Tommy McCool, Joe Coyle and Tommy Carlin, three middle-aged men, were building bombs in McCool's kitchen in Derry when something ignited the mix, killing McCool and his two daughters, 9-year-old Bernadette and 4-year-old Carol. Joe Coyle died the next day and Tommy Carlin died in hospital almost two weeks later.[23]

On 3 July 1970, the British Army made worse an already difficult situation in Belfast. Troops raided the Lower Falls looking for weapons and nationalists saw it as the confiscation of their defences. There was plenty of violence in the Protestant/unionist community, but only the Lower Falls was raided. There was a riot, barricades went up and petrol bombs were thrown at the soldiers. It was an Official IRA stronghold and they had a gun-battle with the British. More troops arrived and the area was drenched with CS gas and placed under a curfew. Over a thirty-six hour period, the troops shot dead two nationalists and a freelance photographer, and killed another nationalist by running him down with an armoured car. Adding insult to injury, British Army press officers drove two triumphant Unionist Ministers from Stormont through the area – 'Their army driving them around the ruins', in the words of historian J. Bowyer Bell. The curfew was finally breached when a a group of women pushing prams and carrying milk, bread and other supplies broke through the British lines. They were led by Máire Drumm, Jimmy's wife and a leading member of Cumann na mBan. During the curfew, the British Army confiscated guns, homemade bombs and thousands of rounds of ammunition. They left behind wrecked homes and a ruined relationship with Belfast working-class nationalists.[24]

In August, there were major riots in Belfast and Derry and a booby-trap bomb in a stolen car killed two RUC constables in Crossmaglen – they were the first police officers killed by the Provisionals. The situation was still 'loose', in that Gerry Fitt condemned the 'dastardly crime' and then, on the same day and with Paddy Devlin, attended the funeral of Jimmy Steele, who had died suddenly at the age of sixty-three. Steele's most recent contribution to the Provisionals had been founding *Republican News*, the northern complement to *An Phoblacht*. Thousands of people turned out to hear Seán Mac Stiofáin praise an uncompromising republican legend. At Steele's funeral, Ruairí Ó Brádaigh approached Máire Drumm and asked if she would be interested in joining the Caretaker Executive – she was. Proinsias Mac Airt took over as editor of *Republican News*.[25]

Shortly after the Steele funeral, Ivan Cooper, Austin Currie, Paddy Devlin, Gerry Fitt, John Hume, Paddy O'Hanlon and Paddy Wilson, MPs at Stormont and civil rights activists, formed the Social Democratic and Labour Party (SDLP). They described the Party as left of centre and in favour of civil rights, and called for the reunification of Ireland through the consent of the majority. Almost immediately the SDLP replaced the Nationalist Party as the voice of constitutional nationalism in Northern Ireland.

Although the Provisionals' young recruits saw their leadership as middle-aged and socially conservative, they saw the SDLP leadership as middle-aged, middle-class, hypocrites. In the summer of 1968, Gerry Fitt had warned, 'If constitutional methods do not bring social justice; if they do not bring democracy to the North, then I am quite prepared to go outside constitutional methods.'[26] Two years later, the Provisionals were 'outside' constitutional methods but not the SDLP. The republican from Armagh offered these comments:

> *The people who raised the Catholic people's expectations was the so-called politicians of the time – the Austin Curries, the Gerry Fitts, the John Humes who was later to come – because I remember very vividly in my mind, about '67, there was an election meeting and, I don't know if youse have it in the States, but there was a street corner meeting. And I remember Fitt and Austin Currie, and I think Paddy Devlin was there. And they were up and they were ranting and raving about a united Ireland and all the rest of it. And it's very ironic. They raised the people's expectations. They took the people onto the streets, right? They said, 'This is the way to do it.' They took 'em on the streets. And then when the balloon burst they left them on the streets. And they stood back, they said, 'Oh no, no, no, this isn't for me.*[27]

The SDLP opened an office near Queen's University, in middle-class south Belfast.[28]

In September 1970, the republican counter to constitutional nationalism ended its 'Provisional' period. An IRA convention with delegates from all thirty-two counties confirmed that *they* were the heirs of 1916 and the true defenders of the republic. This included an address from Tom Maguire who told them that 'the authority of the last sovereign parliament for all Ireland now rested with them'. The delegates also confirmed the decision taken in 1968 to allow full membership to women; Cumann na mBan was not represented, and objected after the fact.[29] At the end of the convention, the delegates elected an Army Executive which then elected a slightly younger and more Northern Army Council. Denis McInerney from Clare and Billy McKee, who had recovered from his injuries, replaced Paddy Mulcahy and Seán Tracey. Otherwise, Seán Mac Stiofáin, Ruairí Ó Brádaigh, Dáithí O'Connell, Joe Cahill and Leo Martin were all re-elected, and Mac Stiofáin remained as C/S. At the Sinn Féin Ard Fheis the next month, the Caretaker Executive was dissolved and a proper Officer Board and Ard Chomhairle were elected. Several people made the seamless transition from one group to the other. Ruairí Ó Brádaigh became President of Sinn Féin, his brother Seán continued as Director of Publicity and so on.[30]

The 'Provisional' period was over, but to the press and public 'Provos' was a great label and it stuck. The Officials who, instead of wearing a pin, would stick glue-backed Easter Lilies to their lapels, became the 'Sticks' or 'Stickies'.[31] As Brian Hanley and Scott Millar describe in their definitive work, *The Lost Revolution: The Story of the Official IRA and the Worker's Party*, the two groups would move further and further apart.

Home Secretary Reginald Maudling wanted to keep violence at an 'acceptable' level.[32] In theory, the British Army patrolled the streets as peacekeepers. In practice, they tried to impose order like an army. That approach drove young nationalists into the arms of veteran guerrillas organizing an insurgency, especially in Belfast. Nationalists may have been in the minority in Belfast, but there were still 200,000 of them.[33] In 1971, this respondent was a young teenager living in West Belfast:

> *Going to school, getting your school bag took off you and searched. Sometimes you would have got your books torn out of your school bag and kicked over the road. Things like that there. After school they'll attack your bus and you get that there stopped. And about five of them search you again. There's sometimes four or five – you'd probably get searched three or four times before you got to school.*

He joined Na Fianna Éireann.[34]

On 6 February 1971, there was rioting through the night in North Belfast and the British Army shot dead James Saunders and Bernard Watt. Watt was another civilian victim. Saunders was the first Provisional IRA volunteer killed by the British Army. That night, the Provisionals claimed their first British soldier, Gunner Robert Curtis of the Royal Artillery; Curtis was the first British soldier killed by the IRA since the 1920s. The next day, James Chichester-Clark announced that, 'Northern Ireland is at war with the Irish Republican Army Provisionals.'

Competition between the Provisionals and the Officials contributed to the deteriorating security situation. There were confrontations in Belfast and Charlie Hughes, a well-known Provisional and a defender of St Comgall's School in 1969, was shot dead by the Officials. A truce was quickly arranged but, before everyone got the news, Tom Cahill, Joe Cahill's brother, was shot and wounded.[35] Charlie Hughes's death is notable for two reasons. It was early in the conflict and British soldiers were photographed saluting the cortege as it made its way to Milltown Cemetery; such signs of respect for a fellow soldier were ended quickly. And while the truce held, the Provisionals were bitter, especially Billy McKee. According to Brendan Hughes, Charlie's cousin, *'Billy took that very, very bad – Billy McKee did – and I don't think he ever forgave the Officials, the Stickies for the killing of Charlie Hughes.*[36] Billy McKee commented on the suggestion that he never forgave the Officials:

How could I? In case you don't know, it was me they thought they shot. They thought they shot me that night. Outside – I arrived shortly after they shot Charlie. They had no reason to do that. We already had a meeting with McMillen and them … there had been an agreement – to stop it … And there was a dozen of them at this house. Proinsias Mac Airt and myself walked out of the house and there was three boys standing on the far side … And [Mac Airt] went down to the house on Cyprus Street and Charlie and a couple of our lads were in it. So they came out of the house to go somewhere. And they [the Officials] were under the opinion because I had left the meeting house with Mac Airt that it was me – and as soon as the lads came outside the door, they opened fire on them – shot him. And that was the main – that brought about the real feud. That was the start of it. There was no – it never should have happened – after a meeting. And everything was just – you go your way and we go our way. You do what you think is right and we'll do what we think is right and let it go at that. But no. They came out – and it was me they thought they shot that night.[37]

There would be more conflict with the Officials.

The Provisionals were becoming harder and creative. The day after Charlie Hughes died, the Belfast IRA used a 'honey-trap' to lure three off-duty Scottish soldiers from a bar. Brothers John and Joseph McCaig, aged 17 and 18, and Dougald McCaughey, 23 years old, were each found shot in the back of the head on a mountain road; they were probably shot while relieving themselves. The *Belfast Telegraph* accurately described the killings as 'cold-blooded executions for purely political purposes'. James Chichester-Clark flew to London seeking help. More British troops were sent over, but it was not enough for Chichester-Clark and he resigned. Brian Faulkner, another member of the unionist establishment, became Prime Minister at Stormont.[38]

The British Army took a harder line. Senior officers trying to control rioting in Ballymurphy had been meeting with Billy McKee, Proinsias Mac Airt, Leo Martin and Liam Hannaway, describing them as 'community leaders'.[39] McKee and Mac Airt were arrested on a trumped-up charge of possessing weapons and ammunition.[40] After an interview with the BBC, Leo Martin was arrested and charged with membership and promoting the IRA. The Provisionals were deep enough that McKee, Mac Airt and Martin were quickly replaced. It was probably at this point that J.B. O'Hagan joined the Army Council, as McKee's replacement. It appears that Joe Cahill, the O/C of Belfast's Second Battalion, also took over as the O/C of Belfast, and that Cahill appointed Gerry Adams as O/C of the Second Battalion. Adams's reported adjutant was Ivor Bell and his Operations Officer was Brendan Hughes. Paddy Ryan probably replaced Leo Martin on the Council; as it turned out, the journalist refused to identify Martin and he was acquitted.[41]

Spring became summer and there were more riots and explosions. In July, after four straight nights of rioting, the British Army shot dead Seámus Cusack in Derry. They claimed he had raised a rifle against them though witnesses contradicted the claim. There were demonstrations the next day and the British shot dead Desmond Beattie. The police claimed he was getting ready to throw a nail bomb though, once again, witnesses contradicted the claim. The unionist establishment defended the shootings. The SDLP called for an independent inquiry and when that did not happen, they withdrew from Stormont. The Provisionals used the events for their own ends. At a Sinn Féin rally, Máire Drumm offered the remark for which she is best known –

'It is a waste of time shouting, "Up the IRA!" The important thing is to join.' She was jailed for six months for sedition. On the morning of 12 July 1971, there were ten explosions in Belfast along the route of an Orange Order march and a soldier was shot dead later that day.[42]

Brian Faulkner was the Stormont Minister for Home Affairs when internment was introduced in 1956. It was a standard response to unrest and Faulkner believed it would work again. There was a 'dry run' in late July and, on the morning of 9 August 1971, the British Army implemented 'Operation Demetrius' and raided homes throughout Northern Ireland.[43] In Lurgan, they went looking for J.B O'Hagan. As he described it: *I knew that they'd done a dry run for internment about two weeks before the actual date of internment. And I said to myself, "Well, internment's coming." So while I was working, I stayed out of the house at night.* O'Hagan was one of several leading Provisionals who slipped the net though they did pick up his 16-year-old son, Felim. Bernadette O'Hagan described the incident:

> *On that Monday morning of internment, they came and actually I stood beside one of the soldiers and saw the paper in his hand. And he had photographs. And he had Joe and the three oldest sons' photographs. And they were coming for the four of them. He insisted that Felim was Fintan. He kept saying, 'You're Fintan.' He didn't answer them. The young girl, Dara, at the time was only seven or eight years old. And she kept shouting and insisting, 'That's not Fintan, that's our Felim. That's not Fintan.' But they insisted that this was Fintan. And they dragged him out of the house that morning – at about half six, in his pyjamas, and brought him to the local Army base. And we learned later that they sussed around the priests in the parochial house, through the local RUC, 'Was this Fintan O'Hagan?' and gave his description, his age and all that. And then they found out that it wasn't – that it was Felim O'Hagan. So they let him out to walk home at eight o'clock on that summer morning in his pyjamas.[44]*

The British had identified Gerry McKerr, who lived just outside Lurgan, as a 'player' and McKerr's home was raided:

> *At about half past five in the morning the door was kicked in and the window at the side of it, the glass window was smashed, and they came up the stairs. I was still in bed – my wife and I were still in bed. And I was arrested, told to get dressed quickly and taken out by the scruff of the neck out through the door and put in an army tender. There were no RUC that I can remember at the scene, only British soldiers. And I was taken to a barracks in Lurgan where we were processed, along with others.*

Because of dated information, several of those arrested were long retired from the IRA; an attempt was made to arrest a man dead for four years. Of the 342 people arrested that day, 116 were released within 48 hours. Many of them reported that they had been mistreated while in custody.

In most instances, families learned that their loved ones were being held in huts at an old RAF base named Long Kesh, near Lisburn. There was no information, however, about Gerry McKerr and eleven others: Jim Auld, Joe Clarke, Mickey Donnelly, Kevin Hannaway (a cousin of Gerry Adams), Paddy Joe McClean, Francis McGuigan, Seán McKenna, Patrick McNally, Michael Montgomery, Patrick Shivers and Brian Turley. They, along with Liam Rogers and Liam Shannon who were arrested in October, became known as the 'Hooded Men'. Gerry McKerr described what happened:

[I was] taken to Ballykinlar Camp, which is an army camp on the coast of County Down. I was held there for two and a half days, being processed, interrogated, given different 'stress positions' as they're called, such as lying flat on your back and your feet in the air. And you were given various exercises to do which I was quite capable of doing at the time ... after all the men were processed and released or taken away ... the last four left in the room were myself, Patrick McNally, Seán McKenna, now deceased, and Brian Turley ... About an hour or so into the sleep, we were rudely awakened by soldiers who had come in, ordered us up and ordered us to run around the room. And this went on for a further three or four hours. And I asked to go to the toilet – I had to go to the toilet while running on the spot, which I found rather difficult to do at the time. Seems funny now but I thought, well at least it's coming to an end. But later that morning, we were hooded and told we were going to another place. [We were] placed into a helicopter and, after an hour's journey, we were thrown out of the helicopter. I didn't know how far we were from the ground but we were still in the air, but apparently we were only hovering about a foot or two from the ground. But we were kicked out with the hoods over our heads, bundled into a room – we still had the hoods. And I remember seagulls calling and the smell of salt air ...

We were looked at by a medic, stripped naked. And I remember saying to the medic, 'You realize what's happening and you're party to this.' He didn't speak. [He] declared me fit ... [I] was given a pair of overalls, greenish-type overalls, stripped naked, barefooted. [I was] put in the overalls with a bag over my head and placed against the wall in the stress position, which means hands against the wall, feet wide apart, and left there for hours on end. There was a very loud noise – I had no idea where I was – like steam hissing out of a boiler at a very high rate and extremely loud. I could hear voices screaming as well. People, I imagine, were coming to my ear behind my back and screaming in my ear, as well, until I couldn't – I was unable to stand. I just fell. And as I fell, I was placed against the wall again. And this went on ad infinitum it seemed to me. Finally I did collapse ... I was up and down, up and down – continually beaten, in the ribs particularly – a knee up the arse, head banged against the wall. And finally, I remember being taken into a room and there were two plain-clothes people in the room, and the bag was whipped off my head and I was immediately accosted with questions that I couldn't understand and I hadn't any idea what they wanted but my mind was sort of in a daydream – 'Was this really happening? What is going on here? Am I in a dream? Should I wake up?' I had no idea what they were asking because I was in such a state. I hadn't eaten, I hadn't any water and I thought I would eventually awaken from this nightmare – eventually. But I began to come around and I realized they were asking me about my involvement, particularly with the IRA. I just says, 'No. No.' He said, 'He's not cooperating, get him out of here' and it was back to – back to the wall and the noise. At some stage thereafter, I was taken out and put on a helicopter and I said, 'Well that's it. I've cracked that.' But I was taken, after about an hour's journey, to another place where I met police who gave me a severe beating. And the bag was whipped off my head and before me was a desk with three police behind the desk and one said to me, 'You are Gerard McKerr?' of a particular address. I thought I was in Crumlin Road. I thought I was home. And he leaned over and stuffed a document in my pocket and says, 'Take him off.' The police escorted me rather painfully to the helicopter again. And it was back to square one ...[45]

After about a week of rumours, and after a writ of Habeas Corpus was filed, the mis-treatment ended. McKerr was sent to Crumlin Road Jail for a few months and then on to Long Kesh. A British investigation, the Compton Report (1971), later concluded that McKerr and the others had been ill-treated but not brutalized or tortured.[46]

The SDLP, the Nationalist Party, Republican Labour and the Civil Rights Executive met and released a statement pledging non-cooperation with Stormont or Westminster until internment was ended. They also called on the public to withhold rents and rates.[47]

Civil rights groups organized anti-internment rallies. The Provisionals went to war.[48] The republican from Armagh was in Belfast on the morning of 9 August. He described the day:

The way I can describe it is, it was like Beirut. It was just total warfare on the streets – total warfare ... My brother lived on a street in Belfast called the Kashmir Road, in the Clonard. And the fellows from the Clonard were taken to – there was an old Army barracks in Cupar Street. It was an old tailor's cum men's shop and it was converted into a temporary Army billet. And that's where we were taken. Now the Protestants, when we were being taken down into it, there was about forty Protestant women – it always stuck in my mind – on the far side of the road, laughing and joking and sneering. They knew what was happening. They were aware of the fact that they were moving our men and they knew what was happening ... at Bombay Street, sorry no, at the corner of Cupar Street, you had IRA snipers, right? On the top of Mackies Machinery, you had British Army snipers and they were firing away at one another.[49]

Fourteen people were killed in political violence that day. In Belfast, members of the Parachute Regiment killed six civilians in the 'Ballymurphy Massacre', including Father Hugh Mullan. Father Mullan left the shelter of a home to offer last rites to a shooting victim. Waving a white cloth and making his way back to the house, he was shot dead.[50]

On Friday 13 August, the British Army held a press conference on the Falls Road and a spokesman explained that their troops had killed more than twenty gunmen, the leadership of the IRA had been lifted and the organization was decimated. Just up the road and at almost the same time, Paddy Kennedy, a Stormont MP, introduced Joe Cahill at another press conference. Cahill explained that only two Provisionals had been killed and only thirty were interned. One of the deceased volunteers was Paddy McAdorey, rumoured to have been involved in the killing of the three Scottish soldiers in March; Martin Meehan was an alleged accomplice. Things were going well, said Cahill, although they needed more ammunition. The British Army was humiliated and Cahill became a public figure.[51]

Because it would be a propaganda coup if the British caught Cahill, Mac Stiofáin ordered him to Dublin. Mac Stiofáin also tried to take advantage of Cahill's notoriety and sent him on a tour of the United States. However, Cahill was stopped in New York, held for a week and then returned to Dublin. In the meantime, reports have Cahill's subordinates moving up the ranks in Belfast, with Seamus Twomey taking over as the O/C Belfast and Gerry Adams becoming his adjutant. Ivor Bell became the Brigade Staff Operations Officer and Brendan Hughes became O/C of the Second Battalion.[52] In August 1971, there were 100 explosions in Northern Ireland and 35 people were killed. The dramatic escalation of violence after internment is shown in Figure 3.[53]

Joe Cahill, Annual Wolfe Tone Commemoration, c. 1970. Courtesy of Seamus Murphy.

For many young nationalists, internment confirmed that Northern Ireland was beyond reform. A Fermanagh republican commented:

> *Internment, if you like, was a watershed in the Six Counties. On 9 August 1971, hundreds of people were taken from their homes and interned on the orders of Brian Faulkner. The British troops were used to do the operation. And obviously, as a young person at that time in youth – it was an experience that obviously would leave an impression. And then that would be the reason why I would have got involved – once you see your next door neighbour being taken and dragged and frog-marched and put into the British Army lorry and when he's not back in four weeks ...*[54]

Recruits flocked to the Provisionals. Fra McCann described the Lower Falls and Divis Flats: *'there was about a hundred people arrested in this area ... friends of mine [their] fathers were taken away and their*

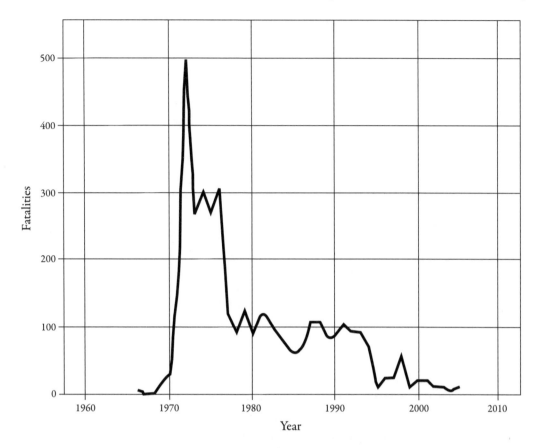

FIGURE 3
Deaths from Political Violence, Irish Conflict, 1966–2005

brothers were taken away and next thing you know they were tortured, they were taken and beaten up ... I would say that it had a big effect on the Movement. I mean, it was counterproductive.' The Fermanagh Republican, Fra McCann and many others joined the Provisionals following internment. In February 1972, McCann was interned on the Maidstone, a prison ship in Belfast Harbour.[55]

Internment forced senior Northerners like J.B. O'Hagan and Joe Cahill to go on the run but it also allowed them to devote themselves full time to a rapidly expanding movement. J.B. O'Hagan became the lead organizer for Armagh, Monaghan and Tyrone. He described his activities:

I stayed in the North for, I suppose, about three or four weeks. Word came from Chief of Staff Seán Mac Stiofáin that he wanted me down to Dublin. So I went down and I had a bit of a talk with him. He told me would I have a look around Armagh City and would I take a trip into Tyrone and see how things were there. Because there was no organization as such at that time. So I done that and came back to Lurgan, met some of the other boys who weren't interned, see how they were. Got word again from Seán Mac to go out. I was to take part in an operation – got the weapons and all over the border. Just then,

85

whoever was gathering intelligence then, the intelligence failed. So I told him we couldn't do this operation. I was actually getting into a car to come over to the North again when word came through would I stay in Monaghan and start organizing camps, organizing people, and, more or less, would I link in with Tyrone and parts of Armagh and get an organization going.[56]

Another key veteran from the 1940s was John Joe McGirl, who owned a small pub in Ballinamore. McGirl, who still represented Sinn Féin on the Leitrim County Council, was the key person to the west of O'Hagan, organizing Fermanagh, Leitrim and Cavan.

The Provisionals were growing quickly and the leadership was constantly busy. When he became Chief of Staff, Mac Stiofáin put his career on hold and became a full-time activist. Asked how the Provisionals got from 1969 to 1972, he replied, *'Sheer hard work. I personally put in between fourteen to eighteen hours a day, seven days a week.'*[57] Around this time Ruairí Ó Brádaigh took a leave of absence from his position as a secondary school teacher in Roscommon and Dáithí Ó Connell gave up his teaching job in Donegal and moved to Dublin. These were not arm-chair revolutionaries. In December 1971, Jack McCabe, the Quartermaster, was killed while mixing explosives at his Dublin home. In one interpretation, McCabe's death was evidence of a lack of expertise and a sign that the Provisionals were desperate. In reality, McCabe was experimenting with explosives and without enough regard for his personal safety because he was trying to keep up with demand.[58]

One critic has minimized the rights that were denied Northern nationalists and suggests that Terence O'Neill's reforms were 'continually outpaced' by insatiable demands from the Civil Rights Movement that were really rooted in a desire for a united Ireland. Provocative actions by groups like People's Democracy produced unrest that was manipulated by the Provisionals and internment was simply an 'own goal' by the British that further alienated nationalists. Another critic acknowledged that Northern nationalists 'suffered from social, political and economic discrimination' but then clinically described internment as a 'counterproductive policy' in contrast to the Provisional IRA's 'campaign against liberal democracy'.[59]

In addition to blaming the victim, these critics miss or intentionally ignore the politics of Northern Ireland in 1971. Governments can implement reform while simultaneously engaging in repression. British soldiers arrived on the scene as supposedly neutral peacekeepers but Seán Mac Stiofáin, Joe Cahill, Seán Keenan, Jack McCabe, Billy McKee, Ruairí Ó Brádaigh, Dáithí O'Connell, J.B. O'Hagan, Paddy Ryan and a host of other senior figures in the Movement saw their arrival as an opportunity for war. Mac Stiofáin et al. argued that Northern Ireland could not be reformed and that a united Ireland was the only logical way forward. Their goal was to convince others that their interpretation was the correct one. No matter how many reforms had been introduced, liberal democracies do not arrest people without charge and hold them indefinitely without trial. Internment was a violation of basic civil rights. The 'Hooded Men' were tortured in the 'liberal democracy' of Northern Ireland. If the Civil Rights Movement had achieved 'British Rights for British Subjects', then internment would never have been implemented.[60] By implementing internment, the Northern Ireland and British governments confirmed the Provisionals' interpretation of British rule in Ireland.

7

The Year of Victory (1972)

When you look down over a scope you know what you're shooting and you can see if a man's armed or not, especially when the people were out in open spaces when they were shot.

– Derry republican on 'Bloody Sunday'[1]

An Phoblacht's headline for the first issue of the new year declared, '1972: Year of Decision'. The accompanying article began with 'England is on her knees; Stormont is finished ...'[2] It was optimistic and shows how well things were going. Anti-internment sentiment was high and the Provisional IRA was riding a wave of success.

The *Maidstone* was considered 'escape-proof'. However, internees on the overcrowded ship saw a seal swimming nearby. If the seal could get in through the security fencing then they could get out. Seven internees covered in boot polish slid down the anchor rope, made their way through the fencing and swam to shore. They hijacked a bus and were spotted driving into the Markets area. The British surrounded the area and claimed everything was under control. The 'Magnificent Seven' surfaced at another embarrassing press conference.[3]

Dundalk was flooded with 'on the runs' from Belfast and things were wild enough that it was nicknamed 'El Paso'. One of the 'on the runs' was Martin Meehan, a senior figure from Ardoyne who had a knack for being at the centre of the action. A few days after the *Maidstone* escape, there was a four-hour gun battle between the IRA and the British Army across the Louth–South Armagh border. The event was widely reported by the press. Meehan's comment, 'We pasted them', was the headline in Dublin papers. The war was going very well, even if the Irish police arrested Meehan and seven others the next day.[4]

On 30 January 1972, the British Army gave the Provisionals reason to claim that 1972 might, in fact, be the 'Year of Victory'.[5] More than 20,000 people showed up in Derry for an anti-internment march that was banned. Towards the end of the march, youths began stoning British troops, which was fairly typical, and the British Army responded with rubber bullets and CS gas, which was also typical. Members of the Parachute Regiment moved in to make arrests and then opened fire, shooting twenty-six unarmed people and killing thirteen of them. A fourteenth victim died later.[6] The British Army claimed that they were returning fire from gunmen. In an interview with the BBC, future terrorism expert Colonel Maurice Tugwell said that only gunmen and bombers were fired on and claimed that four of the dead were on the Army's wanted list– the allegation was repeated by the British Information Services. Independent sources at the scene disputed the British account and the claim about the wanted list was retracted.[7]

The effect of Bloody Sunday cannot be underestimated. Standing on Derry's walls the next day, John Hume told an Irish radio interviewer that, 'Many people down there feel that now it's a united Ireland or nothing. Alienation is pretty total.' Suddenly, throughout Ireland and internationally, the Provisional IRA was a people's army. After Bloody Sunday, the IRA in Derry was literally signing up volunteers on clipboards. A teenager from Derry, who was not from a republican family, joined the Provisionals just after Bloody Sunday:

> There was no event before [Bloody Sunday] … it more or less brought to the fore the attitude amongst the majority of the people in the six counties – it showed you the bad, the blatant aspects of British rule in Ireland. That's been there for centuries. And it just brought it to the fore. And people seen then that Sinn Féin was the only alternative … it showed me the state wasn't going to be reformed. Any state that goes out and shoots down people in peaceful protest, it's quite obvious.[8]

The British response to Bloody Sunday added to the damage. Lord Widgery's inquiry into the event was released in April 1972 and the summary blamed the victims: 'There would have been no deaths in Londonderry on 30 January if those who organized the illegal march had not thereby created a highly dangerous situation in which a clash between demonstrators and the security forces was almost inevitable.'[9] Colonel Derek Wilford, officer commanding of the First Parachute Regiment, was awarded an OBE.

Recruitment into the Provisionals was a *social* process. The young man from Derry who, at one time, was friendly with British soldiers, commented: *'[Bloody Sunday] didn't change my attitude and, in particular, it wasn't an emotional response that, "I hate the Brits and it's about time I did something". It was just that I'd always been concerned, I'd always been motivated towards things Irish and it was just another – it was just another act of political vandalism on Irish people.'* For him, Bloody Sunday completed a process that began with the Civil Rights Movement.

> As soon as civil rights started things started to fall together for me. All the little bits of information and facts and evidence that I had picked up from whatever source – be it just casual comments from people around me, just watching peoples' attitudes – and then going to school through the working class, the Bogside ghetto area, from my friends not having things, just observation. When civil rights began it all began to gel for me and build up towards some main picture. And the picture was that, my gut feeling and the way I had been brought up to respect other people's rights wasn't being done by the state. And, therefore, all the stories and mythologies and all the rest of it had to have some foundation. And so I started talking to more people and reading more about it.

This political transformation was experienced collectively, shared with peers:

> The Republican Movement, it may have historical background, yes, but essentially it got off the ground because it came out of the community and it was a community that accepted it because it was its own

people. And, therefore, I suppose you could say that it was my contemporaries that, if anybody influenced, would have influenced me to join …. I didn't join because my friends were in the Movement. That's not the reason I joined. I was motivated to join the Republican Movement because I knew that the people who were in it were sincere. I mean, a 19-year-old kid or an 18-year-old kid who makes a conscious decision to go out and fight a vastly superior army on the streets, to take on a government and all its forms and to change society – he may not think in terms of vast political thought about how society's going to be changed by him, but if he makes that conscious decision instead of happily waiting until he gets his welfare cheque, and then goes off and plays pool or drinks beer and goes to dances – they're denounced as being mindless thugs but that is just not true. It could never for me be a description of them.

The Civil Rights march in October 1968, the 'Battle of the Bogside' in August 1969, internment and Bloody Sunday showed that the RUC, the Northern Ireland government, and the British government were not legitimate. He continued:

It wasn't natural that I thought, 'The gun was the only answer.' But when you went out to riot and saw the RUC coming into the area – they used to invade the areas and they'd break down doors and they'd go into people's houses and they'd beat them up. Once I saw that, then there was no problem with rioting … The British were killing our people, they were locking them up and they were nothing more than Stormont.

The respondent was not in Derry to witness Bloody Sunday, but the attack on his community and the community's response brought him home:

I wanted to know more closely what was happening at home and, therefore, it was logical to come home. And come home I did. And I think probably from the first week I was home that the decision was there and made because things had changed so much … The intense presence of the British soldiers in the streets, the antagonistic attitudes of the RUC, the whole heavy aura of military oppression … it was very much like a real miasma of military oppression in the state. The lack of privacy, the intervention in every form of your life, social or otherwise. It was impossible to avoid … I became then permanently active [laughs] in … August–September of '73 … I joined the IRA.

For some recruits, such as those from republican families, the process of recruitment was completed quickly. They were 'ready-made', the state violence confirmed the politics of their elders. For others, state violence started a political reassessment that eventually led them to conclude that political violence was the answer to the problems affecting Northern Ireland. And for some recruits, it was entirely a social decision based on personal connections. The Derry respondent recalled:

That was very common in the early years … if I knocked about with Seamus and Seamus joined the IRA and I usually went drinking on a Saturday night with Seamus but now we were going bombing Brits. It's logical that Seamus is my mate and I know him and I trust him and I, therefore, can get on with him. And we go and do it. What the fuck, we go and bomb Brits.[10]

Recruits like 'Seamus' and his friend would become more political with time. All of them ended up in the Provisionals.[11]

Bloody Sunday's influence was massive. The Dublin government withdrew its ambassador from London and called for a national day of mourning to coincide with the funerals, which were held the following Wednesday. After three days of protests, a crowd of 20,000 people gathered outside the British Embassy in Dublin. A bomb blew in the front door, petrol bombs were thrown and the building went up in flames. The political climate had changed so much that the charges against Martin Meehan and those arrested with him were dropped.[12]

Among the people in the crowd outside the Embassy was Val Lynch. Unlike many of the new recruits, he was married, employed and raising a family. Lynch's father had been a member of the IRA's Dublin Brigade in the 1919–22 era. He followed Michael Collins into the Free State Army as an officer, but over time he became disenchanted and gave up his commission. No longer interested in those who accepted the Treaty, and not welcomed by the Fianna Fáil crowd who had rejected the Treaty and then compromised, he was underemployed the rest of his life. Val Lynch grew up in a household very interested in the republican cause but not actively involved in the Movement. In his words, 'It was always there.' The Civil Rights Movement heightened his interest and Bloody Sunday brought him into the Provisionals:

> *And then in '68, that was when civil rights came up in the North of Ireland and that led on up 'til Bloody Sunday. And it was after Bloody Sunday that I myself became really interested or involved, and from there to this day [1984] I'm still involved, more or less ... And then there was the loyalist pogroms, of Belfast, where they started systematically burning out Catholics – thousands of them [refugees] arrived down here in the South – burned down their homes and run them out generally. And then the culminating point was Bloody Sunday, in Derry ... And I was outside the British Embassy here in Dublin when it was burned down. So after that I got actively involved in Sinn Féin.*[13]

Bloody Sunday affected Irish people of all ages. A 12-year-old in Dublin watched his family's reaction to the event.

> *I remember my father was off work for three days. There were strikes everywhere. I remember – the thing that really stands out in my mind is seeing the funeral in the church – just the solemnity of the occasion, just the thirteen coffins laid out ... and my mother saying – telling me to be quiet and have a little respect for it.*

A year later, Na Fianna Éireann was recruiting in his neighbourhood: *'They had kind of a leafleting campaign. And all these leaflets come around to the door and I got hold of one.'* He became a republican scout.[14]

The personal characteristics of IRA volunteers who died in the early years of the conflict show the influence of internment and Bloody Sunday (see Appendix 2). The first volunteers killed on active service were often middle-aged men with families, like Tommy McCool (43) and Joe Coyle (45). After internment, the volunteers killed on active service were of mixed ages and life situations. In December 1971, Jack McCabe was killed in Dublin and John Bateson,

James Sheridan, and Martin Lee were killed in a premature explosion in South County Derry. McCabe was 55 years old, a veteran of the 1940s campaign. Bateson and Sheridan were 20-years old, Lee was 17. *Tírghrá: Ireland's Patriot Dead* does not mention a republican background for any of them. Provisional IRA volunteers killed on active service following Bloody Sunday were younger, exclusively male and typically from Belfast. As an example, between 4 March 1972, when 18-year-old Albert Kavanaugh was killed in an explosion, and the end of May 1972, when Joseph Fitzsimmons, Jackie McIlhone, Martin Engelen and Edward McDonnell were killed in an explosion, eighteen Provisional IRA volunteers died on active service. Only 29-year-old Edward McDonnell was more than twenty years of age.[15]

Because of the rapid growth of the IRA from 1970, the leadership did not properly organize and train the new recruits. In the early years of the campaign, a large number of volunteers were killed in explosions and training accidents. Joe Cahill discussed this:

> *The young lads who came in who were seventeen, eighteen, would depend on the likes of myself to pass on my knowledge to them. And again, we didn't have the same opportunities then, because the thing whole was thrown onto us. There was an influx of volunteers into the IRA. There wasn't time to train them. There wasn't time to educate them. And I remember actually in '69 and '70, a lot of volunteers, their first training with weapons was when they went out to fire them.[16]*

As described in *Lost Lives: The Stories of the Men, Women and Children Who Died As A Result of the Northern Ireland Troubles*, three days after Bloody Sunday, 17-year-old John McErlean joined the Provisionals. Only two months later, McErlean and two other teenagers, Samuel Hughes and Charles McChrystal, were killed in a premature explosion.[17]

After Bloody Sunday, there was so much support that volunteers could operate openly in 'no-go' areas that were established in parts of Belfast, Derry and some of the smaller cities. A veteran of the Belfast Brigade described the situation:

> *you could have straightly, even if you were in trouble, have gone into any house and expected that people would give you some sort of assistance.*
>
> Q: *How many people in the local population would have known that you were in the IRA?*
>
> A: *Probably, well, all the active republicans. The republican support that's in the area, all would have known. And then, I suppose, just anybody that was in any way perceptive, you, know? Because if you were seen, for example, with someone who was just out of internment or ... if you went in and out of a call house in a street, anybody on the street who'd seen you going into that house would know you were in the IRA.[18]*

The British were not in a position to confront the Provisionals with a massive show of force. Instead, the British Army and the RUC supported by the Army patrolled areas as best they could and, over time, better intelligence brought better results. In the spring of 1972, Gerry Adams was picked up in a dawn raid in West Belfast and ended up interned on the *Maidstone*. A couple of months later, the *Maidstone* internees, including Adams, were transferred and joined about 500 others in Long Kesh.[19]

By this point, the IRA's economic war was in full swing. The goal was to wreck the Northern economy but the cost in lives was appalling. On the first Saturday in March 1972, central Belfast was crowded with shoppers. It was early in the conflict, so when two ladies left a package at the Abercorn restaurant it was not suspicious. The package exploded, killing two women and injuring another seventy people. The coroner described the result as 'pathological murder of the most depraved kind'. The bomb seemed to confirm what the media was saying – the Provisionals were a bunch of mindless bombers.[20]

The leadership met the next day and decided to prove that they were in control and that the violence was political. A seventy-two-hour ceasefire would show that they could turn the violence off if they wanted. Proving the violence was political would be more difficult and they agreed to approach Frank McManus and ask him to read their demands into the record of the House of Commons. Seán Mac Stiofáin and Ruairí Ó Brádaigh met with him at the Sinn Féin Head Office. Mac Stiofáin could be brash whereas Ó Brádaigh tended to take a long-term view. The meeting did not go well, as described by Ó Brádaigh:

> *Mac Stiofáin and myself met McManus in Kevin Street and Mac Stiofáin asked him to stay out of Westminster – during this period, he was to stay out of Westminster. And McManus refused. So Mac Stiofáin did something, which is typically Mac Stiofáin – he jumped up and left. So I stayed talking to him because I knew what was going to happen, and which did happen, [which] was that later on the Movement wanted something done about prisoners and they wanted someone to approach McManus and put him in the picture. So I went along and did it because Mac Stiofáin didn't feel he could because of the way they had parted company.[21]*

Following the meeting with McManus, the Provisionals approached John O'Connell, a Labour Party TD in Dublin with connections to Harold Wilson, Leader of the Labour Party opposition in London. John O'Connell passed on to Wilson three Provisional IRA demands:

1. An immediate withdrawal of British armed forces from the streets of Northern Ireland coupled with a statement of intent as to the eventual evacuation of HM forces and an acknowledgement of the right of the Irish people to determine their own future without interference from the British government.
2. The abolition of the Stormont parliament.
3. A total amnesty for all political prisoners in Ireland and England both tried and untried and for those on the wanted list.

As a sign of good faith, they announced that a seventy-two-hour ceasefire would start at midnight, Friday 10 March 1972.[22]

Harold Wilson passed the proposals on to Prime Minister Edward Heath and then asked to meet with the Provisionals. Because Wilson was only Leader of the Opposition, Mac Stiofáin was opposed but, according to Dáithí O'Connell, the 'collective leadership decided otherwise'. At a secret meeting in Dublin, Dáithí O'Connell, Joe Cahill and John Kelly, explained their demands and Wilson expressed his concern that if Stormont were abolished there would be a sectarian backlash. The Provisionals disagreed, and Dáithí O'Connell would later write that he noticed Wilson was clearly interested in the future of Stormont. When Wilson notified the Provisionals that he was going to refer to the meeting in the House of Commons, they took it as an indication that something had changed. On 20 March 1972, Wilson made public the first of many secret British–IRA meetings. That same day, a Provisional IRA car bomb in the middle of Belfast killed two RUC men, an off-duty UDR soldier and four civilians.

At the end of March, the British confirmed a change in their approach. Edward Heath informed Brian Faulkner that security powers would be transferred to Westminster and Faulkner and his Stormont cabinet resigned. Westminster then suspended the Stormont government and parliament, and William Whitelaw, Leader of the House of Commons, was appointed Secretary of State for Northern Ireland. The Provisionals saw the fall of Stormont as a major victory, as did the Unionists. Brian Faulkner commented, 'And when it was made clear to me that the United Kingdom Government could not give an assurance of any further positive measures against terrorism, I felt bound to ask whether the end of violence was being sought not, as we have always asserted, by defeating the terrorists, but by surrendering to them.'[23]

Two weeks later, the sectarian backlash that Harold Wilson had feared was underway. Loyalists bombed Kelly's bar in Belfast and fired on people helping clean up the area. The attack escalated into a series of three-way gun battles between loyalists, the British Army and the Provisionals. A few days after this, the Provisionals bombed the Blue Bell bar in South Belfast, and Na Fianna Éireann scouts fired shots at Protestant workers as they walked home from work in West Belfast.[24] The escalation of conflict extended to prisoners. In mid-May, fifty-year old Billy McKee led forty Provisionals in Crumlin Road Jail onto a hunger strike for political status.

The Provisionals wanted a direct confrontation with the British and they saw the fall of Stormont as a major step in that direction. Their claim that they were leading the way to the Republic received another boost when the Official IRA announced a unilateral ceasefire at the end of May. The Officials had tried to wed constitutional politics and guerrilla war and failed, as predicted by the Provisionals. The Officials were responsible for sectarian attacks on unionist politicians like Jack Barnhill, who was the first victim of political assassination in Ireland since the 1920s, and their military campaign had stumbled. Three weeks after Bloody Sunday, an Official IRA car bomb went off at the headquarters of the Parachute Regiment at Aldershot, England. They claimed it was in retaliation for Bloody Sunday; in fact, the operation had been planned for some time but, either way, Aldershot was a disaster. Seven people were killed – a Catholic chaplain, five cleaning women and a gardener. In the statement announcing their ceasefire, the Officials condemned the Provisionals for waging a sectarian bombing campaign. The Provisionals' reply noted the attacks on Protestant politicians and the Aldershot bomb.[25]

Late in the spring of 1972, the outcry over Bloody Sunday had diminished enough that the Dublin government began confronting the Provisionals. Under the Offences Against the State Act (1939), non-jury courts were established. Then, the Sinn Féin headquarters was raided and

Joe Cahill was arrested. Ruairí Ó Brádaigh was on the phone with the *Irish Times*, complaining about the Dublin raid, when his own home was raided and he was arrested. Seán Ó Brádaigh was arrested the next day.[26] The leadership knew that, at some point, the Dublin government would go after them. Therefore, they had agreed that if they were arrested on trumped-up charges they would immediately go on hunger strike. Ruairí Ó Brádaigh recalled:

> they took two documents which – they wouldn't tell me what these incriminating documents were – and based on them, then, I was a member of the IRA ... So eventually, when – I couldn't imagine what they were – when they finally produced them, the first was a draft statement from my brother Seán, who was Publicity Director, who suggested – but this was commonplace – a statement on the following lines making these points, and the other one was a copy of a statement from the Republican Publicity Bureau that had been circulated the previous March or something like that, which any journalist or any public figure was likely to have a copy [of]. I remember asking, 'Would it be surprising for Mister John Hume to have a copy of this document?' ... They grasp at anything ... they released Seán after a week. There was absolutely – they hadn't anything, documents, nothing. In his case, they just took him in and said, 'You're a member of the IRA.' And this was totally ridiculous so he went on hunger strike. All three of us went on hunger strike. So, after a week, he was out. After a fortnight, I was out. And after three weeks, Joe Cahill was out.[27]

Most people can go without food for about thirty days and not suffer lasting damage to their health. The cases against the Ó Brádaighs and Cahill collapsed and they recovered quickly. The hunger strike in Crumlin Road, however, was approaching thirty days and becoming serious and, when a rumour spread that Billy McKee had died, there were riots in Belfast.

The day of the Belfast rioting, Seán Mac Stiofáin, Dáithí O'Connell, Séamus Twomey and 22-year-old IRA Commander Martin McGuinness held a press conference in Derry. They offered a seven-day truce in exchange for a meeting with William Whitelaw at which they could discuss the Provisionals' demands. Whitelaw immediately rejected the offer, saying he could not respond to an 'ultimatum from terrorists'. John Hume and Paddy Devlin, of the SDLP, then intervened and approached Whitelaw. Because the SDLP had not met with the British since the introduction of internment, Whitelaw saw their approach as an opportunity to build a relationship with the SDLP and also slow the violence. He accepted two IRA preconditions for a secret meeting. First, paramilitary prisoners in Northern Ireland would be provided 'special category status', political status in all but name. That ended the hunger strike in Crumlin Road. Second, Gerry Adams would be released from Long Kesh so he could participate in the meeting.[28] The request to include Adams showed the British how much the leadership respected his strategic thinking.

Adams was called to the Long Kesh gate and told he was being released. He suspected the other internees were playing a trick, but waiting for him were Dolours and Marian Price.[29] They were the daughters of Albert Price and the nieces of Bridie Dolan, and were from a staunch republican background. Bridie Dolan was a Cumann na mBan volunteer who had been seriously injured in an accidental explosion during the IRA's 1940s campaign; she remained devoted to the

Provisional IRA Press Conference, 13 June 1972. From left: Martin McGuinness, Dáithí O'Connell, Seán Mac Stiofáin, and Seamus Twomey. Copyright Larry Doherty.

cause until her death in 1975 and is listed on the Provisionals' Roll of Honour. The Price sisters drove Adams to Belfast where he was briefed on developments. A few days later, Adams and Dáithí O'Connell met with Philip Woodfield, of the Northern Ireland Office, and Frank Steele, of British intelligence, to make arrangements for the meeting with Whitelaw. The Provisionals announced that a truce would begin at midnight on Monday 26 June 1972, 'provided that a public reciprocal response was forthcoming from the armed forces of the British Crown'. Whitelaw responded publicly and positively.[30]

Two days later at a press conference in Dublin, Dáithí O'Connell and Ruairí Ó Brádaigh revealed the Provisionals' political solution to the conflict – *Eire Nua* (New Ireland).[31] O'Connell was the lead author, but it was a collaborative effort which took the progressive social and economic programme that Sinn Féin developed in the 1960s and added a federal scheme based on the historic Irish provinces of Ulster, Leinster, Munster and Connaught. Ruairí Ó Brádaigh explained their approach:

> *And he [Dáithí O'Connell] said, 'Look, why don't we start by reuniting Ulster? The nine counties.' And then we would have a two and a half to five per cent unionist majority, but with all this idea of maximum devolution at the lowest possible level. Regions and the districts would go out into the local majority ... [with] the policing at local level and so on.[32]*

One of their models was the Swiss Canton system. The goal was a secular, decentralized government for all of Ireland that would safeguard the rights and traditions of both the unionist and nationalist communities. The key feature was Dáil Uladh, which would be a nine-county parliament comprised of the six counties of Northern Ireland plus Cavan, Donegal and Monaghan. Unionists would still have a modest majority, but the nationalist vote would be large enough to influence outcomes and there would be a chance for cross-community cooperation on some issues. As an alternative to Stormont, the Provisionals established a regional parliament, Dáil Uladh (Dáil Ulster), with an office in Monaghan.

Éire Nua was original to the Provisionals. It was endorsed by the Army Council and federalism was voted into Sinn Féin's Constitution. Sinn Féin also tried to establish regional parliaments in each of the four Irish provinces, but failed. Unfortunately for the Provisionals, the scheme was pretty much ignored by everyone else. Agreeing to meet with terrorists was risky for the British and there was no way they were going to endorse the Provisionals' political solution to the conflict. Unionist politicians were worried about the truce, did not trust the British and hated the Provisionals. They wanted Stormont back, not a Provisional scheme that cut into their majority. Loyalists feared the truce signalled a British–IRA deal. Over the first weekend of July 1972, five Belfast Catholics were abducted, hooded and beaten, and shot dead. Unidentified republicans assaulted and shot dead two Protestants in North Belfast that same weekend.[33]

Even some of the Provisionals were not interested in Éire Nua and federalism, or Sinn Féin. It seemed the IRA was winning the war and activists wanted to be part of it. In an interview, Marian Price commented: *We looked at Sinn Féin as the lesser group in the Republican Movement. If somebody wasn't up to snuff for the Army, we sent them to Sinn Féin. It was for people who were not good enough for the Army.*[34] Sinn Féin's junior status is also seen in the delegation that met with Whitelaw. According to Seán Mac Stiofáin, 'The delegation was an Irish Republican Army one. I chose the members.'[35] Ruairí Ó Brádaigh confirmed this: *'It was purely an Army delegation. They were there representing the IRA. They weren't representing the Movement, in the larger sense. It was specifically, and they were there as, an IRA delegation.*[36] Mac Stiofáin's view was that the British were most interested in 'the military situation'. He turned down a suggestion to include a senior Sinn Féiner. If something developed, then Sinn Féin could become involved.

Mac Stiofáin put together a delegation that was a mix of senior and junior people.[37] The senior people were himself, Dáithí O'Connell and Seamus Twomey. The junior people were Ivor Bell, one of the younger veterans from the 1950s, Gerry Adams and Martin McGuinness. Mac Stiofáin and O'Connell were from the South while Twomey, Bell and Adams were from Belfast. McGuinness represented Derry and Dublin solicitor Myles Shevlin, a Sinn Féiner, was included as a note taker. On Friday 7 July, and accompanied by Frank Steele, they were flown from the RAF airfield at Aldergrove, Belfast, to an RAF base in Oxfordshire. From there, they travelled to the Cheyne Walk home of Paul Channon, the Minister of State at the Northern Ireland Office. The British group included William Whitelaw, Philip Woodfield, Frank Steele and Channon.

According to Mac Stiofáin's account, Whitelaw opened the meeting by 'telling us what he wanted to do for "the people of Northern Ireland"'.[38] Mac Stiofáin then read the three demands from a prepared statement. The British account of the meeting summarizes these as:

i.   the British government should recognize publicly that it is the right of the whole of the people of Ireland acting as a unit to decide the future of Ireland;

ii.   the British government should undertake to withdraw the British Army from Ireland by 1975;

iii. the expected conditions on internment and amnesties.[39]

Dáithí O'Connell gave Whitelaw a copy of Éire Nua and explained the political programme. In the discussion that followed there were two 'clashes'. Whitelaw denied that British troops would fire on innocent civilians. Martin McGuinness, after a look at Mac Stiofáin who gave the go-ahead, brought up Bloody Sunday and the shooting of Cusack and Beattie. And when Whitelaw told them that the Ireland Act of 1949 provided 'constitutional guarantees to the majority in Northern Ireland', Mac Stiofáin countered that another parliamentary act could set that aside. In his autobiography, *Before the Dawn*, Gerry Adams writes that some of the best 'interventions' came from Myles Shevlin.[40]

As they spoke about the timing and arrangements for the next meeting, Adams asked that they adjourn. In private, according to Adams, Mac Stiofáin exclaimed, 'Jesus, we have it!' That was the opposite of how Adams saw things. After further discussion, the two sides agreed that the British could take a week to respond to the proposals and that there would be twenty-four hours' notice before conflict would be renewed. Whitelaw asked for an assurance that the meeting be kept confidential and Mac Stiofáin agreed, 'as long as it was not contrary to the interests of the Republican Movement to do so'. Whitelaw said that if news of the meeting became public, 'All bets are off.' Adams replied, 'That means all bets are off, then.'

Going into the meeting, the British saw Dáithí O'Connell as the Provisionals' chief strategist and he did not disappoint them. After the meeting, they understood why the Provisionals also wanted Adams there. Their assessment of Adams was that he recognized there were political dimensions to the conflict that could not be solved only through military action. The British Cabinet account states, 'Mr. Mac Stiofain was very much in charge.' They were not impressed, and Frank Steele would later comment that Mac Stiofáin behaved like Montgomery, 'telling the German generals what they should and shouldn't do if they wanted peace'. Seamus Twomey and Ivor Bell came off as militarists naïve enough to believe that 'one more heave' by the IRA would drive the British out. Steele described Myles Shevlin as 'a creep', which may say more about Steele than it does Shevlin.[41] The British correctly concluded that the Provisionals were not going to accept anything less than a declaration of intent to withdraw and that they would either restart their campaign 'or disengage and wait for a better opportunity'. Whitelaw later described the meeting as a 'non-event': 'The IRA leaders simply made impossible demands which I told them the British government would never concede. They were, in fact, still in a mood of defiance and determination until their absurd ultimatums were met.'[42] On the plane back to Belfast, Frank Steele commented that their demands were unrealistic and told Dáithí O'Connell that the British Army lost more soldiers in road accidents in Germany than they did in Northern Ireland. It was callous, but true.

The Provisionals knew that the British had the resources for an unlimited number of four hour-long gun-battles. Mac Stiofáin and O'Connell and others in the leadership who did not attend the meeting – Joe Cahill, Denis McInerney, Ruairí Ó Brádaigh, J.B. O'Hagan and Paddy Ryan, for example – had been in the IRA for years. They had joined a small conspiratorial clan and thanks to them the Movement was bigger and stronger than it had been since the glory days of the 1920s. They had literally bombed their way to the bargaining table. The question was whether or not they could get something out of continuing the truce. Seán Mac Stiofáin and Dáithí O'Connell wanted it to continue and see where it might lead. Others were convinced that the longer the truce lasted the more it hurt the Provisional IRA. The Belfast IRA was especially concerned. In *Before the Dawn*, Gerry Adams would write that he suspected the British were simply exploring the political landscape and were not going to concede anything. Martin McGuinness would later comment, 'I had learned in two hours what Irish politicians still haven't learned: that the British don't give easily.'[43]

On the Sunday following the British–IRA meeting, there was a confrontation in West Belfast. The Ulster Defence Association (UDA), an umbrella organization for loyalist vigilantes, had stopped the Housing Executive from re-housing nationalists in what had been Protestant homes in Lenadoon. Loyalists, British soldiers and the Provisional IRA were on the scene in a tense standoff. Late in the afternoon, the nationalists tried to unload furniture from a truck and a British Army vehicle rammed it. A crowd of about 3,000 people started throwing stones at the soldiers. The British fired rubber bullets and CS gas; Seamus Twomey told the British commander that they had violated the truce. According to Brendan Hughes, it was a manufactured incident. Twomey wanted to end the truce and arranged for Hughes and two others to start shooting on his signal. When the crowd stepped back, the Provisionals began shooting and the British returned fire. At 9 pm the Provisionals in Dublin put out an official announcement that the ceasefire was over. That was an understatement.

There were six explosions in Derry and, in Belfast, ten people were killed in violence that day. In Ballymurphy, British soldiers shot dead 13-year-old Margaret Gargan; Father Noel Fitzpatrick, a Catholic priest giving her last rites; 30-year-old Patrick Butler, who was killed by the same bullet that killed Father Fitzpatrick; and 14-year-old David McCafferty, who was trying to help Father Fitzpatrick. Whitelaw blamed the IRA for breaking the truce. The Provisionals replied by making it public that they had met with him. In the House of Commons, Whitelaw explained that he met with the Provisionals 'in order to save lives' but the Provisionals' demands were 'unacceptable to any British government'. He added, 'I want to make it perfectly clear that terrorism and extremism in the community cannot be tolerated, that the rule of law and justice must be restored.' Violence raged in Northern Ireland while Brian Faulkner and the Ulster Unionists complained about 'appeasement'. And, ten days later, an IRA delegation led by Joe Cahill met with Harold Wilson and Merlyn Rees at a cottage in Buckinghamshire.[44]

The Cahill–Wilson meeting did not lead anywhere, evidently because the British had already made a decision to focus on the IRA. The day after the truce broke down, William Nield, Permanent-Secretary at the Northern Ireland Office, wrote a letter to Sir Robert Armstrong, Secretary to Prime Minister Heath, summarizing what happened next. Nield contrasted the 'few hundreds [*sic*] of effective members' of the IRA with the 'confederation' of vigilante and loyalist groups, 'now 25,000 strong and supplied with arms', and expressed Whitelaw's anxiety in facing two subversive forces:

> the Army can neither ally with one or the other because both are challenging the authority of the government; nor can they take on both at once with anything like their present strength, quite apart from the considerable sympathy for the UDA which the 2 1/2 years of bombing has aroused in the Army's auxiliary security forces, i.e., the Ulster Defence Force and the Royal Ulster Constabulary.[45]

The implications are clear. It would be easier for the British Army to take on the IRA than the loyalists and the British knew that members of the RUC and UDR were open to collusion with loyalists.

The Provisionals wanted to show the British that they were 'speaking from strength' and organized a 'bomb blitz' to show the cost of ignoring them. Early on Friday 21 July, a bomb derailed a freight train between Portadown and Lurgan and put the Dublin–Belfast line out of commission. Thirty-four more bombs went off in Northern Ireland that day. Three car-bombs caused extensive damage in Derry but no casualties. The day is remembered for the twenty-two bombs that went off in Belfast, nineteen of which exploded in a span of seventy-five minutes early in the afternoon. *The Guardian* reported, 'It was impossible for anyone to feel perfectly safe. As each bomb exploded there were cries of terror from people who thought that they had found sanctuary, but were in fact just as exposed as before.'[46] Two bombs claimed nine victims – a member of the RUC, two British soldiers and six civilians, including three teenagers. 'Bloody Friday' was the Provisional IRA's complement to Bloody Sunday.

Seán Mac Stiofáin claimed the targets were 'industrial, commercial, or economic ones' and that the British deliberately disregarded warnings 'for strategic policy reasons' – to weaken support for the Provisionals. In reality, the Belfast Brigade grossly miscalculated the mass confusion that would result from so many bombs. There were warnings but some of them were unclear. Even if the warnings had been clear, there was no way for the police, soldiers and firefighters to clear that many areas at the same time. Brendan Hughes later admitted that he was the 'operational commander' and responsible for organizing the bombs. He also claimed that the entire Belfast Brigade staff planned the operation, including Seamus Twomey, Ivor Bell and Gerry Adams. According to Hughes, they did not intentionally target civilians, but 'the risks were far too high, and even if there wasn't any collusion or deceit on the part of the British, I don't believe they were capable of handling so many bombs at one time'.[47]

After Bloody Friday, William Whitelaw was willing to speak to just about anyone but the Provisionals, and there was no reason to hold back the British Army. More troops were sent over and, on 31 July 1972, 21,000 British soldiers, 9,000 members of the UDR and 6,000 RUC officers cleared the 'no-go' areas. The Provisionals anticipated 'Operation Motorman' and offered no resistance. The day is also remembered for three car bombs that killed nine people in the village of Claudy, County Derry. The Provisionals denied responsibility but no one believed them.[48]

Operation Motorman was effective and the level of violence was immediately reduced. For example, in July 1972, ninety-five people were killed in political violence in Northern Ireland. There were were fifty-six fatalities in August and forty-one fatalities in September.[49] It was not an acceptable level, but it was much improved. Operation Motorman also gave the British a platform from which they could introduce a series of political initiatives. Whitelaw invited the leaders of the constitutional parties to a conference in Darlington, England. Brian Faulkner and the Ulster Unionists, the Alliance Party and the Northern Ireland Labour Party accepted. The SDLP turned down the invitation because internment continued. However, after the conference, the Northern Ireland Office issued a discussion paper that gave the SDLP a chance to provide input and join the dialogue. Heath also welcomed a 'Green Paper' from the Irish government and agreed to a meeting in the autumn with Jack Lynch in London. For its part, the Irish government took steps to appear friendlier to Protestants, for example by deleting the section of the Irish Constitution that gave a special position to the Catholic Church.[50]

The Dublin government also stepped up its efforts against the Provisionals. The Sinn Féin head office was raided, literature was confiscated and the party secretary, Walter Lynch, was arrested. A three-month closure notice was put on the front door. The cases against Joe Cahill and the Ó Brádaigh's had collapsed in the spring because the law required evidence. The Minister for Justice introduced legislation amending the Offences Against the State Act (1939) so the *opinion* of a senior police officer would be enough to convict someone of membership of an illegal organization. Máire Drumm was arrested after a speaking engagement in County Westmeath.

The most irritating Provisional was Seán Mac Stiofáin. It was public knowledge that he was Chief of Staff and he did not back away from the attention, making public appearances, giving press interviews and so on. In the spring, Mac Stiofáin had slipped into Derry and offered the oration at the funeral of Colm Keenan, Seán Keenan's son who, with Eugene McGillen, was killed by the British Army. A parcel bomb sent by loyalists went off at Mac Stiofáin's home, injuring his eye; he put on a temporary patch and kept going. In spite of calls for his arrest and a heavy police presence, in the autumn he slipped into the Sinn Féin Ard Fheis, offered the leadership's annual message to cheering delegates and then slipped out. On 19 November 1972, just after a taped interview with Kevin O'Kelly, of Radió Teilifís Éireann (RTÉ), the Dublin police finally caught up with Seán Mac Stiofáin.[51]

Mac Stiofáin was a 'perfect' Chief of Staff in 1969. He was dedicated and sincere, a take-charge kind of person who could lead an organization as it got off the ground. Since then, his ego had grown with the IRA's success and he had clashed with others, especially Dáithí O'Connell. One complaint was that Mac Stiofáin did not bring together GHQ staff for meetings but instead worked directly with individuals. It was efficient for the C/S but it also kept others out of the decision-making process. Whether or not he was difficult, the Movement had prospered and that limited his internal critics.[52] But when he was arrested, his ego got the better of him. The plan had been for members of the leadership to go on hunger strike if they were arrested on trumped-up charges. In that situation, a hunger striker slowly wasting away would put enormous pressure on the authorities. The police had evidence against Mac Stiofáin, however, including the taped interview with O'Kelly. Still, he one-upped Cahill and the Ó Brádaighs and immediately went on a hunger *and* thirst strike. At most, he might last twenty days. The hunger and thirst strike also put enormous pressure on the Movement to rally in his support. They came through and very quickly Sinn Féin had a continuous picket outside Mountjoy Jail. Mac Stiofáin had also put enormous pressure on himself.

It was a dramatic situation. Mac Stiofáin was arrested on a Sunday and, on the following Friday, Jack Lynch met with Edward Heath in London and Mac Stiofáin appeared before the Special Criminal Court. The case was delayed until Saturday and RTÉ went ahead and broadcast the controversial interview. RTÉ is Ireland's 'national public service broadcaster'; the Dublin government sacked the RTÉ Authority. Kevin O'Kelly refused to identify the voice on the tape, but a police officer testified that, in his opinion, it was Mac Stiofáin's voice. That was enough and Mac Stiofáin was sentenced to six months in prison for membership of an illegal organization. At that he said, 'It may as well have been six years. I will be dead in six days.' A judge replied, 'Unfortunately, that is something over which we have no control.' Kevin O'Kelly received a three-month sentence for contempt, journalists walked off the job in support and Irish radio and television went off the air for two days. A bomb exploded in Dublin and the next day, 5,000 people marched to the Mater Hospital where Mac Stiofáin was wasting away. Inside the hospital, the Special Branch exchanged shots with an IRA unit trying to rescue him. The rescue failed, the unit was arrested and Mac Stiofáin was whisked away by helicopter to the more secure military hospital in the Curragh.

The Mac Stiofáin drama would end quietly. After two days in the Curragh, Father Seán McManus, Frank's brother, convinced Mac Stiofáin that if he died there would be bloodshed in the South and it would rebound against the Movement. Mac Stiofáin began to drink liquid but stayed on hunger strike. That ended the immediate threat to his life, but it was an anti-climactic outcome for people who had rallied in support of an uncompromising hard-man on the quick path to martyrdom. The hunger strike continued and there were reports – fair or not – that Mac Stiofáin was drinking orange juice. Instead of being a rallying point, Mac Stiofáin and his hunger strike became a distraction. Eventually, after fifty-nine days without food, an irritated Army Council ordered him to end the fast.[53]

The Dublin government did not stop with Mac Stiofáin and sent the amendment to the Offences Against the State Act to Dáil Éireann. Fine Gael TDs were initially opposed to the amendment because it threatened civil liberties. Then, in the middle of the debate, loyalists set off bombs in central Dublin. Two people were killed and scores were injured. Because of the convenient timing, and the technology involved, there remain suspicions that British intelligence was also involved. In spite of their concerns for civil liberties, the Fine Gael TDs abstained and the amendment was passed.[54]

Armed with new powers, the police tried to arrest Dáithí O'Connell but they missed and he went on the run. Ruairí Ó Brádaigh, in contrast, was president of a legal political party and he refused to go on the run. He was arrested again and charged with membership of an illegal organization.[55] And on the last day of the year, Martin McGuinness and Joe McCallion were arrested in Donegal and charged with possession of explosives, ammunition and membership.

In January 1973, based on the opinion of a senior police officer that he was a member of the Provisional IRA and his own refusal to confirm or deny membership, Ó Brádaigh was convicted and sentenced to six months in prison. McGuinness and McCallion beat the possession charges but were also convicted of membership.[56] Ó Brádaigh, McGuinness, McCallion and Seán Mac Stiofáin all ended up in the Curragh.

So ended 1972 – with the Provisionals on the defensive and with several of their leaders on the run or in prison. Yet, they were still a larger and more capable revolutionary organization than anything seen in Ireland since the 1920s. And they still believed they could win. In court, Martin McGuinness stated, 'I am a member of the Derry Brigade of the IRA and I am very, very proud of it.' If McGuinness had thought the war might last another twenty-five years, it is very unlikely that he would have been so naïve as to admit membership.

8

THE PROVISIONALS ADAPT (1973–1974)

I suppose it probably just slowly disintegrated as the British intelligence improved ... You were more careful about the call houses you were using and there would have been a slow input until you got to the position where you weren't using that procedure at all ...

– Belfast republican 4[1]

After Operation Motorman, the London and Dublin governments continued to repress dissent while they searched for a political middle in Northern Ireland. Ironically, it would all lead to another conversation between the British and the Provisionals.

Internment was extended to women with the first victim being 19-year-old Liz McKee. She was arrested, interrogated for a week and, on 1 January 1973, became the first of more than sixty women internees in Armagh. Interning women was a controversial decision and led to several protests.[2] Although most of them were young and single, Geraldine Taylor was married with children:

I went in for six weeks but they had massive protests and things outside because my husband was interned at the same time. They got me released for the sake of my three children. There was big write-ups in the papers and all about it as well and photographs of my mother and my three children. And then my sister put a stop to it because she thought it was too much for me, my family, which she was right because a lot of news media were only using them and it was too stressful. So she stopped it.[3]

Because witnesses and jurors were threatened with intimidation, the British introduced non-jury courts (Diplock Courts) in terrorist cases. A telephone number was advertised so the public could provide confidential information. British troops and the RUC patrolled city streets and the countryside supported by helicopters. Tens of thousands of homes were raided and, between 1 April 1973 and 1 April 1974, four million cars were searched.[4]

British soldiers killed nationalist civilians and got away with it. A Newry republican described the night that 12-year-old Kevin Heatley was shot dead in February 1973:

There was rioting and then one night ... the Brits come into the housing estate so everybody came out and one night there was a crowd came out ... and they came in and they were drunk and they just blew the head off this young fellow. A twelve year old. Twelve years old, just blew his head off. And tried to say that he was armed. But they got off like. I mean, the soldier that murdered that young boy, he was sentenced to three years in spite of the fact that there was forty witnesses from the estate that went to his trial and told exactly what happened. That the young fellow was just sitting on the wall and just – the next thing he was just shot dead. And he was sentenced to three years' imprisonment. And then he went back to England. He appealed and got it quashed on appeal. He never done a day's jail.[5]

Corporal Francis Foxford was the first serving member of the British Army charged with 'unlawful killing'. And he did serve more than a day in jail. Foxford was found guilty, sentenced to three years in prison, transferred to England and then granted bail *after a week*. Three months, later the Northern Ireland Court of Criminal Appeal overturned his conviction 'on the grounds of irregular conduct by prosecuting personnel'.[6]

The Provisionals adapted to changing conditions. Joe Cahill replaced Seán Mac Stiofáin as C/S. Máire Drumm became Acting President of Sinn Féin. When they completed their sentences, Ruairí Ó Brádaigh, Martin McGuinness and Joe McCallion pretty much picked up where they left off. Mac Stiofáin's situation was more complicated because he had destroyed his own credibility. Some key people were very upset with him, especially in Belfast, and he did not return to the IRA leadership. He was still a committed republican and joined the staff of *An Phoblacht*.

Operation Motorman made it more difficult for the Provisionals to operate and easier for the British to collect intelligence. The no-go areas were gone and the Provisionals moved away from call houses. A veteran of the Belfast Brigade commented:

I suppose it probably just slowly disintegrated as the British intelligence improved, you know? How they've changed. You were more careful about the call houses you were using and there would have been a slow input until you got to the position where you weren't using that procedure at all … You'd have seen the O/C in the morning for an hour and then the call house as such wouldn't have been used the whole day. So you wouldn't have people running in and out all day. You'd have done the meeting, decided and then maybe done a meeting at three o'clock in the afternoon or the following morning. So it was – the security problems would have been cut down in that way. So it was just a – probably a progression. I mean things just didn't – you didn't drop one way of doing things and switch to another. Things change slowly.[7]

Security was also an issue. Tom McNulty in East Tyrone was arrested in the spring of 1971. The unit suspected that a Monaghan-based veteran from the 1950s, presumably George Poyntz, had set them up. When internment was introduced the investigation was lost in the shuffle.[8] It was a deadly mistake because the informant remained in place. Adding to that mistake, along with the flood of recruits brought in by internment and Bloody Sunday came more informers.

Over the course of the conflict, few people from Tyrone were executed as alleged informers.[9] In contrast, the Belfast IRA was ruthless. Their first victim was Edward Bonner, on 2 October 1972, in West Belfast. Bonner's execution has largely been overlooked because of other events that day. Brendan Hughes had unearthed two informers, Seamus Wright and Kevin McKee, who revealed that the British were using local businesses as fronts to collect information. One was a massage parlour in North Belfast and another was the Four Square Laundry. The laundry service drove into and out of neighbourhoods, picking up clothes that were then tested for weapons and explosives. The day Edward Bonner was killed, the IRA attacked the massage parlour and shot up the Four Square Laundry's van, killing at least one British soldier. They also abducted Seamus Wright and Kevin McKee.

Wright and McKee were a serious issue because they were from prominent families. In order to limit public embarrassment and to send a cruel message to others, they were 'disappeared'; their bodies were finally found in a bog in County Meath, in 2015. Jean McConville would be the most prominent of the disappeared. She was a widow and the mother of ten children and the Provisionals believed she was spying for the British in Divis Flats. Four women dragged her out of the bathroom at gunpoint and left her terrified children to fend for themselves. It was not until 2003 that her body was recovered from a beach in County Louth. Brendan Hughes, in Ed Moloney's *Voices From the Grave: Two Men's War in Ireland*, would later implicate Gerry Adams and Ivor Bell in disappearing Jean McConville.[10]

The Provisionals also adapted by developing more sophisticated weapons. Petrol bombs made from milk bottles were replaced by incendiary devices powered by 1.5 volt batteries that produced an intense fireball. An early mechanism used to delay bombs was to wrap soldering wire around a clothes peg. When the wire loosened, tacks placed at the end of the peg came together and completed an electric circuit. But if the wire loosened too soon, the consequences were deadly. Safety fuses were developed and timers were added. In the summer of 1973, a homemade mortar exploded in a launching tube and killed Dan McAnallen and Patrick Quinn, two volunteers in East Tyrone. Quinn was only 16 years old. In his memoir, *The Informer: The Real Story of One Man's War Against Terrorism*, Seán O'Callaghan reports that Kevin McKenna, the leader of the Tyrone unit, and Jim Monaghan, an engineer credited with inventing the IRA's mortar, improved the firing system at a bomb factory in Kerry.[11]

The Provisionals also drew on an underutilized resource – women. Some were in the IRA while others were in Cumann na mBan. A respondent commented:

> *The girls were very, very – became very experienced. They burned the six counties down with incendiary devices. They were brilliant – brilliant, and without them, the Army would never have survived. At the height of internment, when men were very low on the ground, women took up their positions. Women of Cumann na mBan took up their positions and kept it all going until the men were released ...*
>
> *Q: Why didn't they maintain their positions when the men were released? ...*
>
> *A: Well, they were filling positions within the Army, within the Irish Republican Army. Naturally when the men came out they would take back their own position because they weren't in the Irish Republican Army, they were in Cumann na mBan. Do you understand? And then they took their own positions in Cumann na mBan again.*

In 1973, three Cumann na mBan volunteers, Vivienne Fitzsimmons (Downpatrick), Pauline Kane (Newcastle) and Anne Marie Petticrew (Belfast) were killed in premature explosions. In December 1974, Ethel Lynch, an IRA volunteer in Derry, was also killed in a premature explosion.[12]

Mass mobilization had ended, but the Movement still attracted Southern Irish recruits. Josephine Hayden, originally from Waterford, joined Cumann na mBan in Dublin. She described her recruitment:

At the time I joined in around 1973, things were really very bad at that time in Belfast and places. And I was away. I was working in Jersey at the time, but there came a point where I just said, 'I have to go home and do something about this.' I would have come from a very republican, nationalist house. And my mother was a teacher and I remember her teaching Irish history. I remember once she wrote up on the wall, 'IRA', right? On the blackboard. And I remember her saying, 'If the cigire comes in', that's the inspector, 'that means Ireland reunited again.' Then she proceeded to tell all of us about the Irish Republican Army and the true history, not what the state history would have been but the true history of the Irish struggle for freedom. She would have been very nationalist and republican and her mother was as well. Her mother now would have been a very strong Sinn Féin supporter.[13]

In May 1973, several prisoners in Portlaoise resigned from Saor Éire; some of them switched to the Provisionals.[14]

In contrast to the 1950s, the active service volunteers were mostly Northerners. Southerners were mostly involved in support roles, like hiding weapons and running training camps, though there were exceptions. Pat Ward, originally from Donegal, joined the IRA in England. He ended up on active service in Derry and also operated along the Fermanagh/Cavan border.[15] Other Southerners who operated in the North in these years include John Noonan from Dublin, Seán O'Callaghan from Kerry and Tony Ahern and Dermot Crowley from Cork. Noonan was active in Newry and ended up in Long Kesh.[16] In *The Informer*, O'Callaghan writes that he was sent to the Donegal border for special training. There he met Pat Doherty, the 'quartermaster for the Donegal IRA' who was responsible for training camps and bomb factories. O'Callaghan would go on to organize bomb-factories in Kerry and Leitrim and was on active service with the East Tyrone Brigade. In the spring of 1974, for example, he was one of forty volunteers involved in a mortar, rocket and machine gun attack on a UDR base in Clogher, County Tyrone, that killed UDR 'Greenfinch' Eva Martin. She was the first female member of the security forces killed in the conflict. A couple of months later, O'Callaghan walked into a pub in Omagh and shot dead RUC inspector Peter Flanagan. Tony Ahern and Dermot Crowley grew up in the same housing estate in Cork and are among the few Southerners killed on active service. Ahern was 17 years old when he was killed in a premature explosion in Fermanagh, in May of 1973. Six weeks later, 18-year-old Dermot Crowley was killed transporting a bomb in Tyrone.[17]

The Provisionals internationalized the conflict. There was always an Irish-American connection, even if the US authorities excluded Joe Cahill, Ruairí Ó Brádaigh, Dáithí O'Connell and company. Cahill, travelling in disguise, became the primary liaison with Northern Irish Aid. Denis McInerney travelled the world for the Provisionals. His most important work was arranging a meeting between Colonel Muammar Gaddafi and Joe Cahill; Gaddafi was dressed in perfectly creased fatigue pants and wore a battle jacket for the occasion. The Libyan connection became public in March of 1973 when Cahill, McInerney and a couple of others were arrested off the

Cumann na mBan dinner in Limerick, early 1970s. Front row, from left: Máire Drumm, Patsy Ó Brádaigh, Susie Mulcahy, Annie Cahill, Marie Quinlivan and Líta Ní Chathmhaoil. Back row: Paddy Mulcahy, Ruairí Ó Brádaigh, Jimmy Drumm and Joe Cahill. Ó Brádaigh family collection.

coast of Wexford on board the *Claudia* with five tons of weapons. When a judge described Cahill as the 'ringleader', he replied, 'You do me an honour.'[18]

On the political front, while on the Continent and in the United States, Richard Behal had realized how important it was to 'to get the Irish case out of Ireland' and explain to the world that it was a colonial problem. He described the development of Sinn Féin's International Department:

> *I was preaching all the time the value of an international front. ... Wolfe Tone went to Paris in 1798. We had – in Emmet's time, in the Young Irelanders' time – Thomas Francis Meagher and all. You had Australia. You had America. You had a global dimension – in the First War, in the Black and Tan War, we had representatives in Paris, and we even sent a delegation to the Versailles peace negotiation. So I said, 'It's nothing new. It's that we somehow or other lost our international perspective in the twenties, after the twenties.' And it was time for us to regain it and get back out there. So I was given a small amount of money and told, 'Go and see what you can do.'*[19]

Behal set up a base in Brussels and with Ruairí Ó Brádaigh and Seán Keenan established political connections with a variety of movements, including ties to Basque, Breton, Catalan, Kurdish, Palestinian, Scottish and Welsh cultural minorities.

As Chief of Staff, Seán Mac Stíofáin had had reservations about bombing England. The benefits were the international news that a bomb in London would generate and letting the English people know what life was like in Northern Ireland. Having spent six years in English prisons, he also knew first-hand how difficult it was to operate there. As the O/C of Belfast, Joe Cahill had developed a reputation for approving operations and, after taking over as C/S, and just before leaving for Libya, Cahill approved bombing London.

The Belfast Brigade put out a call for volunteers for a high-risk operation and built four car bombs that were driven to London via the Dublin–Liverpool ferry. After parking them near high-profile targets, the operators headed for the airport. At two in the afternoon, warnings were telephoned to the *Times*, giving the police an hour to clear areas. It was not enough time and, when bombs exploded at the Old Bailey and Whitehall, 180 people were injured and one person died of a heart attack. The two other bombs were defused and, as expected, the bombs were a major news event. Expanding the campaign to England, along with the arrest of seven men and three women at Heathrow, including Dolours and Marian Price, Gerry Kelly, Hugh Feeney and Roy Walsh would have long-lasting consequences.[20]

The two bombs that were defused had been spotted prior to the telephone warnings, which suggested there was an informer. The capture of the team at Heathrow was a sign of poor planning. Shutting down Heathrow and checking every passenger was a predictable response to the attack. GHQ stepped in and shifted control over operations in England from Belfast to Dublin. Brian Keenan, the Belfast Quartermaster, was placed in charge. Keenan, who grew up in Belfast, had lived in England for six years. He was known for his leftist politics, being very organized and clever. Years later, in an interview for *An Phoblacht*, he described the beginning of the English campaign:

> The IRA leadership was constantly reviewing its war strategy, looking for ways of extending and expanding its campaign. Out of this outlook emerged the IRA's campaign in England. England was a very important theatre of war for both the IRA and the British. All modern states rely on transport, communications and power. These were the targets of the England campaign.

Keenan avoided 'in and out' jobs and looked for unknown operators who could quietly slip into and out of the Irish community in England. One of them was Harry Duggan; his family – and the police – thought he had been killed in a premature explosion in the North. Duggan was, in fact, alive and well and on active service in England under an assumed name.[21]

The threat of arrest was constant and the Provisionals organized themselves so there would be smooth transitions. When someone in a leadership position was arrested, the adjutant took over on a temporary basis and then the Army Council, or the brigade or battalion leadership, met and appointed a successor. After Cahill was arrested on the *Claudia*, for example, Seamus Twomey became C/S and J.B. O'Hagan became his Adjutant. Also, as more and more senior people were arrested, younger people moved into leadership positions. It is reported that, when Twomey became C/S, Gerry Adams became the O/C of Belfast, Ivor Bell became his Adjutant and Brendan Hughes became the Brigade's Operations Officer.[22]

Because the Provisionals tried to minimize direct confrontation with the Irish police, Fianna Fáil never implemented internment.[23] In the South, the level of repression would never reach the levels experienced in the North. Following an Irish general election in the spring of 1973, however, the threat of harassment and arrest did significantly increase. A Fine Gael–Labour coalition government was formed in Dublin and they took a much harder line than did Fianna Fáil. It appears that the new ministers were trying to justify the choices of a previous generation.

The Taoiseach was Liam Cosgrave, the son of William Cosgrave who had supported the Treaty and succeeded Arthur Griffith as President of the Irish Free State in 1922. The Minister for External Affairs was Garret FitzGerald. His father, Desmond FitzGerald, was a pro-Treaty1916 veteran who served in William Cosgrave's cabinet. The Minister for Justice was Paddy Cooney, the nephew of Seán Mac Eoin, a highly regarded IRA commander who sided with Michael Collins. Conor Cruise O'Brien, of the Irish Labour Party, was Minister for Posts and Telegraphs. Cruise O'Brien had previously served in the Ministry for External Affairs and with Ireland's delegation to the United Nations. A self-described liberal, he saw the Provisionals as the 'the greatest and most abiding threat' to the security of the Republic of Ireland. One of his first decisions was to informally ban Sinn Féin from Irish radio and television, even if they were a legal political party.[24]

With the pressure on the Provisionals in Northern Ireland and the Republic of Ireland, the London government set out to resurrect the Northern Ireland Assembly. They began by interning loyalists, in February 1973. The move sparked outrage in the unionist community. A mob attacked an RUC station, a firefighter was shot dead by a sniper and shots were fired at the British Army. The 'United Loyalist Council' called for a one-day general strike and there was a total blackout of electricity in parts of Northern Ireland.[25] Interning loyalists was part of a political strategy that had more to do with courting the moderate SDLP and Dublin than it did confronting loyalists.

In March, William Whitelaw published a White Paper – 'Northern Ireland Constitutional Proposals' – which proposed a seventy-eight-seat 'power-sharing' Assembly for Northern Ireland. At the top of the Assembly was an Executive that, by design, would force the two communities to share power. Whitelaw's target audience was the middle ground of Northern Irish politics – unionist moderates in Brian Faulkner's Ulster Unionist Party (UUP) and nationalist moderates in the SDLP. Instead of ending internment, they would also intern loyalists and, therefore, appear more even-handed. A proposed Council of Ireland brought the Dublin government into the mix as a potential ally of the SDLP, and also offered a hint of a united Ireland in the future. At first, the SDLP kept their pledge of no involvement in government unless internment was ended. Then, according to Paddy Devlin, Whitelaw 'promised that he would deliver on internment'. For more than half a century the nationalist community had been on the political and social margin of Northern Ireland. In a new Northern Ireland Assembly, they would have a share of power. Whitelaw's promise was enough. The SDLP agreed to contest an election scheduled for June 1973 and to take seats in a new Northern Ireland Assembly.[26]

In contrast, and even if they had not been banned in the North, Sinn Féin was not interested in participating in the Assembly. The more politically-minded, however, did want to challenge the SDLP. Ruairí Ó Brádaigh commented: *I was still in prison in the Curragh but our people outside wanted to contest these [elections] to prevent the SDLP from – who had been formed in 1970 – to prevent them from getting a strong grip. But, there was opposition, principally from Belfast, and it wasn't carried through.*[27] Because there was no republican alternative, the election became a contest between moderate unionists and the SDLP versus unionist extremists who did not want power-sharing or a Council of Ireland. The result was mixed and complicated. Faulkner's supporters in the Ulster Unionist Party won twenty-four seats. In combination with others, including nineteen seats won by the SDLP and eight seats won by the Alliance Party, moderates won forty-eight of the seventy-eight seats. At the same time, anti-Assembly unionists, including seven seats won by people in Faulkner's own party, eight seats won by the DUP (led by Revd Ian Paisley) and seven seats won by Vanguard (led by William Craig), won more seats than Faulkner's moderates.[28] Moderates were in the overall majority, but moderate unionists were outnumbered by anti-Assembly unionists. On the nationalist side, the SDLP cemented its position as the voice of the nationalist community in Northern Ireland.

For the Provisionals, the war remained their top priority but, soon after the election, the war effort took a serious hit in Belfast. A raid netted Gerry Adams, Brendan Hughes and Tom Cahill, and Adams took a severe beating that ended with the comment, 'Well, Gerry, what was it you told Mr. Whitelaw? All bets are off?' Another raid in North Belfast netted almost the entire Third Battalion staff. Ivor Bell became O/C Belfast, the Third Battalion was reorganized and the war continued. Adams, Hughes and Tom Cahill ended up in Long Kesh.[29]

In Long Kesh, the focus was on returning to the war, not politics. Brendan Hughes was asked to comment on Éire Nua, Sinn Féin's political programme:

> *I'm talking about the '73 period. I wasn't even interested in Éire Nua. All I wanted was out, I just wanted out of prison to get back to war ... I escaped out of internment. But it was set up for me to escape, to get back and restart the war ... you escaped out of prison to go back to war. And Gerry was the main mover in getting me out of prison.*[30]

Gerry Adams was twice caught trying to escape.[31] Hughes was successful. He was sewn into an old mattress and dumped into a garbage lorry. He got lucky – soldiers checking the rubbish just missed him with a spear. After the truck went through the camp's gate he waited for a bit and then jumped off and hitched a ride to Newry. From there he took a taxi across the border. Brian Keenan met up with him in Dundalk and took him on to Dublin, where he stayed at the home of Harry White, the 1940s veteran and the uncle of another Long Kesh internee, Danny Morrison. Within a couple of weeks, Hughes was back in Belfast as Ivor Bell's Operations Officer, albeit with dyed hair.[32]

An escape in the autumn of 1973 was one of the most creative prison breaks ever. Seamus Twomey had been arrested near the border in Monaghan and joined Joe Cahill, J.B. O'Hagan and Kevin Mallon in Mountjoy Prison, in the heart of Dublin. On 31 October, a hijacked helicopter landed in the exercise yard. Twomey, O'Hagan and Mallon went out 'over the wall', as described by O'Hagan:

> *The helicopter was supposed to come in at half two and it didn't come in until half three. So we were sort of worried but then we learned afterwards that the helicopter pilot, when he heard that he was being hijacked to bring three people out of Mountjoy, he said, 'If I go in now with the weight of the fuel I have*

we'll not be able to lift off.' So your man made him circle for an hour and use up some fuel and then it came in about half three. Kevin Mallon got in first. I got in second. Twomey got in and he started lifting off. I hadn't even the door shut. I said, I had my hand by the door, 'I can't get this shut.' So I was up in the air before we got it shut. I was afraid of Twomey falling out. [Laughs] So, I got it shut. Looking down on Dublin was tremendous. You see the cars just like toys and then went on to Baldoyle, an old racecourse. And [we] got out, thanked the pilot and the pilot said the best of luck ...[33]

When Twomey had been arrested, Eamonn O'Doherty, a former British Army paratrooper and another veteran from the 1950s, took over as Chief of Staff.[34] After their escape, Twomey joined Doherty's GHQ staff in Dublin and O'Hagan headed north to the border. Mallon was re-arrested.

Eamonn O'Doherty was the last Provisional IRA Chief of Staff from the South. When he was arrested in the summer of 1974, Twomey again became C/S with Brian Keenan as his Adjutant.[35] J. Bowyer Bell, in *The Irish Troubles: A Generation of Conflict*, describes Keenan as 'Twomey's most important aid'. Because of the helicopter escape, IRA prisoners were moved south to the more secure Portlaoise Prison, in County Laois. That same summer, Kevin Mallon and eighteen others used smuggled gelignite to blow a hole in the gates. He went out 'through the wall' and rejoined the leadership.[36]

The senior Provisionals – Joe Cahill, Jimmy Drumm, Kevin Mallon, Billy McKee, Ruairí Ó Brádaigh, Dáithí O'Connell, J.B. O'Hagan, Paddy Ryan and Seamus Twomey – had known each other for decades. They were long-term members of a revolutionary movement who trusted each other and knew how to keep a secret. But after three plus years of guerrilla war, some of the younger people were moving into leadership positions. And as the younger people moved into the leadership, the lustre of senior people faded. After the 1972 truce fell apart, the leadership stayed in touch with the British but they kept it to themselves. When others found out, it contributed to a developing lack of trust which Brendan Hughes spoke about:

There was a period in 1973 before I was arrested, when I got information that Jimmy Drumm was meeting with the British. I was the O/C of the Belfast Brigade at that time and I arrested him – Jimmy Drumm, at the Army house on the Ormeau Road – and asked him what the hell was going on. I didn't know what was going on. He admitted to me that he was meeting, that he met some doctor at the Royal Victoria Hospital. That was all he admitted to me. But there was some sort of secret negotiations going on that I didn't know about. This was in '73. This is after I escaped and before my second arrest ... after the whole Belfast Brigade almost was wiped out. So, there was a mistrust there of people of that – people like Ruairí and Dáithí and the rest of them – the leadership of that period.[37]

Some of the internal difficulties would have been smoothed over if there had been an IRA convention, but security issues prevented that. Brendan Hughes was arrested for the second time in the spring of 1974 and joined Gerry Adams, Ivor Bell et al. in Long Kesh.[38]

The O/C of the Long Kesh Camp Council was Liam Hannaway, a Belfast IRA veteran of from the 1930s and Gerry Adams's uncle. After Gerry McKerr was transferred into Long Kesh, he was brought onto the Camp Council, which he described:

it was run democratically, but we discovered a group within Long Kesh who were affiliated only to Belfast and only took their orders from Belfast and done interrogations which we didn't know about for quite a while until it was discovered. We intercepted a 'comm', which is called a communication, which said – it was for the O/C ... it wasn't meant for the O/C of the camp and the Camp Council, it was meant for the O/C of this group that was in contact with Belfast. And in it, it said, I remember reading the wording, it said, 'Whatever you do, do not let this fall into the hands of the Rosary Bead Brigade', which meant the older IRA type, the Liam Hannaway type and John O'Rawe type and Seán Keenan type of solid traditional IRA. And we found out who it was addressed to and who it came from, which I won't mention at the time but you can use your imagination. And we uncovered this group and challenged them. And they said they were entitled, quite entitled, to interrogate people who came in and that included beatings and other sorts of torturous activity. And I asked, simply asked them, 'But who interrogated you? Do you want to go through this procedure?' I said, 'Certainly no one interrogated me. Do you want to do this procedure on me?' To which he answered nothing, just stonewalled. The various machinations that were going on at that time for some reason – and I had been a young man in my mid-twenties, I only thought in straight lines. I couldn't see that – no one could do this. It must be something that the Brits have introduced for some reason to cause dissention. Could it be? ... I couldn't see anybody being devious. You've declared yourself as a republican. You've taken an oath ... Most of us didn't believe in religion. And it was changed from the oath to an affirmation, that you agreed to obey your superior officers, et cetera, et cetera. And I thought that if any man would take that and still be devious, I couldn't see it. I say, I thought in straight lines, that to be a republican you must be as I saw the older men – the solid men like the Seán Keenans and the Liam Hannaways.[39]

The younger, Belfast-based inmates in Long Kesh would eventually dominate the Provisional IRA and Sinn Féin.

While the Provisionals fought on, the British brought together the moderates in Northern Ireland and the Fine Gael–Labour government to discuss Whitelaw's proposals. In the autumn of 1973, at a conference in Sunningdale, England, the British and Irish governments, the SDLP and Brian Faulkner and the Ulster Unionists charted a way forward. In a major change from Fianna Fáil's approach, the Dublin government agreed to the principle of consent for Northern Ireland – Northern Ireland's status would be unchanged unless a majority of the people living there agreed to a united Ireland. Dublin also agreed to make it easier to prosecute persons in the Republic who were accused of crimes in Northern Ireland. The British government agreed to phase out internment 'as soon as the security situation permits' and 'affirmed' the possibility of a united Ireland – if a majority of the people in Northern Ireland desired unification, the British would support it. The two governments agreed to enhance cross-border collaboration through the proposed 'Council of Ireland'.

The Provisionals rejected the Council of Ireland and condemned the Irish government for collaborating with the British. William Craig, Ian Paisley and the loyalists condemned Brian Faulkner for collaborating with Dublin.[40]

On 1 January 1974, the British government transferred the powers of government to the Northern Ireland Executive. Brian Faulkner became 'Chief Executive' and Gerry Fitt became 'Deputy Chief Executive'. The cabinet was comprised of UUP and SDLP representatives plus

Oliver Napier of the Alliance Party. The SDLP group included: John Hume, the Minister of Commerce; Paddy Devlin, the Minister of Health and Social Services; and Austin Currie, the Minister for Housing, Local Government and Planning. Napier was the Legal Minister and head of the Office of Law Reform. Unfortunately for those involved, British politics, unionist and loyalist extremists and SLDP hypocrisy undermined the Executive. Against the recommendation of John Hume, Prime Minister Heath called a Westminster election. As the SDLP feared, it became a referendum on power sharing and the already fragile Executive. Anti-Sunningdale unionists came together and formed the United Ulster Unionist Council (UUUC).

In the nationalist community, the backdrop to the election was a high-profile hunger strike by the Price sisters, Hugh Feeney and Gerry Kelly who had received life sentences. In Northern Ireland, they would have been political prisoners but in England they were criminals. They demanded repatriation to Ireland and the British countered with force-feeding. In a letter to her family on her twentieth birthday, Marian Price described her day:

> this is how our force-feeding went on Friday 1st Feb. I was pulled off my bed and carried bodily by the arms and legs from my cell to the room where it takes place. I was put in a chair, my legs were held and my arms put up my back and held tightly. My head was then bent and my nostrils choked in an attempt to make me open my mouth. I opened my lips to breathe but clenched my teeth. Pressure was put on my chin a number of times to make me open my mouth but I managed to keep it closed. I was then blindfolded and a metal clamp was used to force my teeth apart. This was screwed in place; the wooden gag was inserted and the blue tube pushed into my stomach. After the liquid had been poured in, the clamp and the gag were removed, and then the blindfold and I was then practically carried back to my cell. I needn't tell you I was nearly in hysterics and was given a whiff of smelling salts, and the result of the whole thing was I was force-fed as I had been on the previous 58 days ...[41]

The hunger strike and the force-feeding generated enormous publicity. It helped their cause that the Price sisters looked a lot more like two attractive college students – which is what they would have been without the conflict – than they did mindless bomber terrorists.

The election, scheduled for 28 February 1974, gave Sinn Féin another opportunity. The British were claiming that the IRA was undemocratic and without a mandate. Putting forward hunger strikers as 'Republican' candidates would highlight the hypocrisy of the ban on Sinn Féin and bring more attention to the prisoners. The Provisional IRA rejected the idea. Ruairí Ó Brádaigh commented:

> we did attempt again to have the Price sisters and Hugh Feeney and Gerry Kelly as candidates. They were on hunger strike at the time. But the Army was against it and they insisted because of the conflict taking place in the North they would have a dominant say in what was happening. They wouldn't interfere in local elections in the twenty-six counties. And that was because of the thing in the six counties. Their judgement was it would damage the ongoing struggle.

Q: If it was a poor vote?

A: Yes. We didn't think that there would be and Albert Price – who was Dolours and Marian's father – he went forward as an Independent in West Belfast against Fitt. And he did quite well, although all our people were boycotting it.[42]

Gerry Fitt was re-elected MP for West Belfast, but Albert Price received 5,662 votes (11.9 per cent) and finished third out of five candidates. The Provisionals and the Price sisters had more support than some people realized.[43]

In Britain, the election brought back Harold Wilson of Labour as Prime Minister and he appointed Merlyn Rees as Secretary of State for Northern Ireland. One of Rees's first acts was to de-proscribe Sinn Féin, the UDA and the UVF, which suggested a political approach would be forthcoming. However, hard-line anti-Sunningdale candidates in the UUUC won 51 per cent of the Northern Irish vote and took eleven of the twelve seats at Westminster. Paisley and Craig were among those elected and the Northern Ireland Executive was severely wounded.

Actions taken by SDLP ministers hurt the Executive's credibility among nationalists. In 1971, Austin Currie had condemned internment and urged people to withhold their rates and rent in protest. More than 10,000 tenants were still on the rent and rates strike and, as Minister for Housing, Local Government and Planning, it was Currie's job to resolve the situation. In April 1974, he announced that payments had to be made and that a penalty would be levied against the very people who had followed his earlier advice. In his memoir, *All Hell Will Break Loose*, Currie describes his dilemma:

> I was coming to terms with the harsh realities of political life. It was necessary, inevitable, and unavoidable. Nonetheless, I knew that the contrast would be highlighted – to my disadvantage – between what I had just announced and my declaration on a public platform in Coalisland, just two-and-a-half years earlier, that rent should not be paid and should never be paid. Yet that statement too, in the context and time it was made, while not inevitable, was, to me, equally necessary and unavoidable.[44]

Political compromise for some; SLDP hypocrisy for others. A respondent from Tyrone commented on the decision:

> *Well, you have the Austin Curries, and from the civil rights emerged the SDLP. And for a while they seemed to be the only nationalist sort of a political group. Sinn Féin wasn't really heard of at that stage. And to a certain extent, until things happened, the people withheld the rent because of internment. And Mister Currie, Mister Austin Currie of the SDLP, he encouraged them. And he says now we can win something by withholding rent and rates and so on ... he told them to go ahead and spend it, not save it to pay it back. And people were gullible enough to go and spend their money, not pay any rent. And that went on for over a year, maybe longer. And there's that much has happened that I just can't recall exactly what year and what date, but then you had people being threatened with eviction and Mister Currie wasn't*

to be seen. After telling them to go and spend the rent, then he told them to start paying it back … And that's the type of politicians we had at that stage. So something had to be done to change that.[45]

The SDLP was sharing power with the Ulster Unionists, Austin Currie was a Minister, internment continued, and 'something had to be done to change that'. A large segment of the nationalist community would never embrace the SDLP. The Assembly and the Council of Ireland crashed a month after Currie's announcement.

On Tuesday 14 May, and in response to calls that it be re-negotiated, unionist and nationalist moderates in Stormont endorsed the Sunningdale Agreement. The next day, the Ulster Workers Council, a coalition that included Craig and Paisley, trade unionists and loyalist paramilitaries, called a general strike in Northern Ireland. Workers cut power to utilities, paramilitaries set up roadblocks and factories closed. On the afternoon of Friday 17 May, three car bombs exploded without warning in central Dublin and a fourth bomb exploded in Monaghan. It was the loyalist response to Dublin's interference in Northern Ireland. Thirty-three people were killed – the highest total for any single day in the conflict.[46] The following Monday, barricades cut Belfast off from the rest of Northern Ireland. Journalist Robert Fisk, in *The Point of No Return: The Strike Which Broke the British in Ulster*, described the scene:

> From ten miles away it was possible to see long columns of brown and jet-black smoke twisting wearily into the dawn sky over Belfast as UDA men set fire to stolen lorries, cars and even bicycles on makeshift barricades ... Masked UDA men told the driver of a grain lorry in Great Victoria Street to leave his cab, then they swung the vehicle and its trailer across the road – normally one of the busiest in Belfast – between a motor showroom and the regional office of the AA. Beside York Road railway station in north Belfast, where trains normally left for Coleraine, Derry and the towns of western Ulster, Protestants set fire to overturned cars and effectively cut off the Shore Road and part of the docks. Every one of these incidents was watched, sometimes from only a few yards away, by policemen and soldiers ... When confrontation seemed almost inevitable, it was the Army who withdrew.[47]

A state of emergency was declared and Harold Wilson denounced the strikers as 'thugs and bullies' who were assaulting democratic methods while 'sponging on Westminster and British democracy ... Who do these people think they are?'[48] In spite of the denunciation, Heath was unwilling to directly confront the strikers. After fourteen days of mayhem, Brian Faulkner submitted his resignation and the Executive collapsed. With it went the Council of Ireland and control of Northern Ireland reverted to London. [49] The war continued.

The Provisionals set off bombs in Birmingham, London, Manchester and Yorkshire.[50] Two more prisoners, Michael Gaughan and Frank Stagg, joined the Price sisters, Gerry Kelly and Hugh Feeney on the hunger strike. On the sixty-fifth day of his fast, 3 June 1974, Michael Gaughan died of pneumonia. His family claimed that a feeding tube had punctured his lung and killed him. It was reported that Gerry Kelly was blind and the others were in bad shape.[51] Faced with more deaths, widespread concerns about the Price sisters and a medical staff under increasing pressure not to participate, the British stopped the force-feeding and began negotiating. As described by Marian Price:

> *the Home Secretary at that time was a guy called Roy Jenkins who was actually going to leave the Labour Party and he went on to form a different party in England, a more middle of the road party, not as left wing. But one of the Home Office psychiatrists who used to come to visit us in Brixton, he was firstly sent in order to certify us to say that we were mentally unstable and that was to give them a reason, a legal reason to force-feed us. But he was a very nice man and he said no, he couldn't do that because our problem was we were probably too sane, as he put it but he was actually a personal friend of Roy Jenkins and, of course, when he came to visit us we always talked politics with him and things like that. And then he went on to tell us that he was a friend of Roy Jenkins and he assured us that Roy Jenkins was a very noble man and honorable man and things like this. And when the British offered us the deal that we would be returned to Ireland before the end of 1974, he also said if Roy Jenkins gives it – because I wanted it in writing and they refused to give it in writing – and Peter Scott, who was the Home Office psychiatrist, he assured us that Roy Jenkins was a very honorable man and that if he gave his word he would do it – he would do it.*[52]

The prisoners accepted the offer and ended their fasts. And Michael Gaughan was given a martyr's funeral. An IRA colour guard escorted him from Parkhurst Prison on the Isle of Wight to Kilburn, London, and a funeral mass at Sacred Heart Church. Then Gaughan was flown to Dublin and escorted across Ireland to Ballina, County Mayo, where Dáithí O'Connell delivered a fiery funeral oration. The British were appalled and the funeral contributed to anti-Irish sentiment in England.[53]

In spite of the Dublin–Monaghan bombs, the informal media ban and the harassment of activists, Sinn Féin was slowly building a political organization in the South. Seán Lynch was a candidate for the Longford County Council in the Southern local elections, held after the Gaughan funeral. Lynch described a raid on his family's farm the morning of the election:

> *In 1974, on a Tuesday morning – it's dole day … the day where the people sign on at the local barracks for the unemployment assistance … and my house would be in full view of the road and a whole lot of people were going to sign that morning but my yard was filled with police cars and Army trucks and the house was surrounded with Irish soldiers. They were around the whole house and some of them were in view of the road and were talking to all those people going to sign. It's the image – they'd say, 'Oh hey, what's going on up here?' As a matter of fact, one neighbour of mine … came running down to see what had happened. And they held him up. What is he running for and all this sort of thing … they were intimidating the people. They were saying not to vote for me.*[54]

Seán Lynch topped the poll in North Longford.

Sinn Féin did well in the west, where Frank Glynn and Paddy Ruane were re-elected to the Galway County Council. Another councillor was elected in Clare and, along the border, Fra

Browne and James McElwain were elected in Louth and Monaghan, and John Joe McGirl was re-elected in Leitrim. It was the second time that McGirl had been elected while a prisoner. At Easter, he was mistaken for Seamus Twomey and arrested in Belfast. There were no charges against him but instead of letting him go he was interned in Long Kesh. The total number of Sinn Féin councillors was trivial when compared to the larger parties, and yet they had representatives on six of the twenty-six county councils. It was a reasonable result given the conditions.[55] That autumn, the Gardaí raided *An Phoblacht's* office in Dublin and seized equipment. Eamon Mac Thomais, the editor, and Líta Ní Chathmhaoil were arrested and charged with 'printing and publishing an incriminating document'.[56]

Whatever the level of repression, there was no let-up in the war. Prisoners in Long Kesh, McGirl among them, were tired of poor facilities, poor food and heavy-handed guards. On 15 October, they set the place on fire. As the camp burned, the British Army saturated them with CS gas and then let those without huts spend the night outside in the cold October air. The next day, soldiers entered the burned-out area, fired away with rubber bullets and re-asserted control.[57] A month later, there was an attempted escape through a tunnel in which Fra McCann was involved:

> *a number of us escaped from the prison through a tunnel that we had dug and were caught just approaching the motorway. And there was a guy with us who was shot dead by the British Army ... Hugh Coney was shot dead. I was actually laying beside him when he was shot dead. We were re-arrested. We got bad beatings after the escape.*[58]

Up to that point, Hugh Coney, McCann and the others had not had been charged with a crime. Coney was dead. McCann and several others were found guilty of attempting to escape from 'lawful custody' and their status was changed from internee to sentenced prisoner.[59]

In the autumn of 1974, the bombing campaign in England targeted pubs frequented by military personnel. Four soldiers and a civilian were killed in Guildford and a bomb thrown into a pub in Woolwich killed another soldier and a civilian. James McDade, of North Belfast, was killed planting a bomb in Coventry. It was in this context that Irish journalist Mary Holland interviewed Dáithí O'Connell. The IRA's Director of Publicity looked into the camera and threatened, 'I bring it home to the British Government that the consequences of war are not going to be kept solely in Ireland; they are going to be felt on the mainland of Britain.' On 21 November 1974, bombs in two Birmingham pubs killed twenty-one people.[60]

The Birmingham bombs were not what the leadership had planned. Ruairí Ó Brádaigh described his personal reaction to Birmingham:

> *Well, of course, this wasn't on the agenda at all. It was inconceivable, if you like. If you ask me what do I think of the atom bombing of Hiroshima or Nagasaki, I would have the same answer, or, indeed, some of the other things that happened like Dresden and Hamburg and Berlin and also some of the bombings by the Axis Powers and some of the other outrageous things they did. So there it was. These were just ordinary people. I think there was an Irish person among the twenty-one killed, but that is neither here nor there. And incidentally, just in moving among people, people were much more likely to have a relative*

> *in a pub in Birmingham than in a pub in Belfast or Derry – the people from the twenty-six counties. So, I would say that it would not have been acceptable to the Movement.*[61]

The Provisionals denied responsibility.

The British response was immediate. In forty-eight hours, the House of Commons passed the Prevention of Terrorism (Temporary Provisionas) Act (PTA). The PTA allowed arrest without warrant, detention without trial for up to seven days and the exclusion of citizens of Northern Ireland from Great Britain. Roy Jenkins described the powers as 'draconian' but justified. The Birmingham bombs affected Irish people in England in a variety of ways as Marian Price explained:

> *In November '74, there were the Birmingham bombs and Roy Jenkins stood up in the House of Commons and said that he was no longer going to return us home because of the Birmingham bombs. Peter Scott then let us know that Roy Jenkins did that to save his political career because if he had sent us home in light of the Birmingham bombs his political career would have been finished.*[62]

The transfer of the Price sisters, Gerry Kelly and Hugh Feeney was put on hold, and anti-Irish sentiment led to more victims.

Any young Irish person living in England was suspect. The first person arrested under the Prevention of Terrorism Act was Paul Hill. He was one of several Belfast natives living on the margin in London. Hill was not involved in the Guildford bomb. In custody, he did mention that he had travelled over from Belfast with Gerry Conlon, but Conlon wasn't in the IRA either. In his sad memoir, *My Father's Watch*, Gerry Conlon's teenage cousin Patrick Maguire described what happened:

> In the opinion of the police, they were murdering bastards, and once they were in custody they were treated as the police believed murdering Irish bastards deserved to be treated: they beat them, they deprived them of sleep and food, and they threatened to hurt or kill their families or loved ones. The only way Hill and Conlon could see of making the police stop doing this was to tell them what they realized the police wanted to hear. They agreed that they were part of the IRA unit that had been planting bombs throughout the autumn, and they said the IRA's bombmaker was Mum ... they believed the idea that Mum was an IRA bombmaker was so preposterous that it wouldn't stand up in court. Big mistake.[63]

The 'Guildford Four' – Paul Hill, Gerry Conlon, Paddy Armstrong and Carole Richardson – and the 'Maguire Seven' – the Maguire family plus Guiseppe Conlon, Gerry's father and Anne Maguire's brother-in law – were convicted in spite of alibis and evidence of coerced confessions. The 'Birmingham Six' – Hugh Callaghan, Patrick Hill, Gerard Hunter, Richard McIlkenny, William Power and John Walker – another group of innocent Irish people, were convicted for the Birmingham bombs.[64] It was in this climate that several people involved with Sinn Féin in Britain left for Ireland, including Mick Timothy, who left Manchester for Dublin, and Eddie Fullerton, who went home to Donegal.[65]

Ironically, the Birmingham bombs contributed to peace. As Brendan Hughes had discovered, the Provisionals were in contact with the British. They were also meeting with members of the Protestant clergy, including Revd William Arlow. Arlow was the Deputy Secretary of the Irish Council of Churches and was in contact with Frank Cooper of the Northern Ireland Office. Before Birmingham, arrangements had been made for a high level meeting in December at Smyth's Village Hotel, in Feakle, County Clare. The Provisionals who attended described themselves as the 'political and military leadership of the Republican Movement': Máire Drumm, Seamus Loughran, Kevin Mallon, Billy McKee, Ruairí Ó Brádaigh, Dáithí O'Connell, J.B. O'Hagan and Seamus Twomey. The clergymen involved were also top-level: Revd Arlow; Revd A.J. Weir, Clerk of the Assembly of the Presbyterian Church in Ireland; Bishop Arthur Butler of the Church of Ireland; Dr Harry Morton, President of the British Council of Churches; and Stanley Worrall, former headmaster of Methodist College, Belfast, and Chairman of the New Ulster Movement.[66]

The clergymen were searching for a path to peace. Their view was that the more bombs there were the less likely Protestants would agree to a united Ireland and the less likely the British would withdraw. They had drafted a document that they hoped would lead to a ceasefire and they wanted input from the Provisionals. The Provisionals expressed their own desire for peace. The catch was that peace had to be coupled with a British declaration of intent to withdraw. After much discussion, the two groups separated so each could consider what the other had said. Then the republicans learned that the Special Branch was on the way, as described by Ruairí Ó Brádaigh:

> So then, after much discussion, they withdrew and they were formulating their ideas as to how this bridge could be constructed when the police struck. They had gone upstairs ... When we told them that we had got an intelligence report to the effect that the place was going to be raided and that a number of people would have to go, they were very dubious. They thought that this was some excuse, that we didn't want to participate any longer.[67]

Because of the Mountjoy escape plus Kevin Mallon's escape from Portlaoise, J.B. O'Hagan, Seamus Twomey and Mallon were the most wanted people in Ireland. The police had been after Dáithí O'Connell for two years, even if he did not face a specific charge. They left, as described by J.B. O'Hagan:

> Somebody came in and said, 'Look, the cops know about us.' So Twomey looked at me and said, 'We'd better hit the road.' So it was just a sort of a general talk. Some said no, they wouldn't – they can't do it because the clergy are here and they wouldn't raid the place. So, while they were talking like that, I went up to the room that Seamus Twomey and I had and I packed our bags and I came down and said, 'Seamus we've got to go.' [Laughs] ... So he said, 'I think we better.' Some of the boys started to say, 'Ah well, they wouldn't raid, it'd be a terrible thing to raid the Protestant clergy, et cetera.' So Twomey give the orders, 'Out.' I think Billy McKee was told to stay. He wasn't on the run and Rory Brady wasn't on the run ... [O'Connell] left in a different car. We left then and we were actually back in Dublin before we heard the place was raided.[68]

Ó Brádaigh, Billy McKee, Seamus Loughran and Máire Drumm were warming themselves by the fire when the police came in carrying machine guns. When asked where the others were, McKee replied, 'Upstairs'. The clergymen were up against the wall before the Gardaí realized who they were.[69]

The meeting became public and generated speculation that a ceasefire was in the works. It also generated positive publicity for the Movement. In an interview with the *Irish Times*, Dr Arthur Butler commented, 'We were all most impressed by their attitude, with their fair-mindedness, and we were so pleased to find that they were talking seriously and deeply and with great conviction and had listened very carefully to what we had to say.'[70] During this period, Revd Harold Good was Director of Corrymeela Community Centre for Reconciliation. Revd Good knew Dr Harry Morton, one of the clergymen at Feakle. Morton was struck by a connection that he established with Dáithí O'Connell, as described by Revd Good:

> *I mean, here are two men from totally different backgrounds. One who was a Methodist minister, had been president of the Methodist Conference in Britain, was the General Secretary of the British Council of Churches. English. Protestant. Ordained. David O'Connell was a leader in the Republican Movement and had come from a totally different Irish Catholic republican background. Harry Morton said, when somebody asked him, 'Was it not very scary to be with these people?' He said, 'The scariest thing was how much I had in common with him and how much we enjoyed each other's conversation.' And he said, 'We could've gladly gone off for a couple of weeks together to discuss the books we had read and what we thought about them.' Now by all of that, I don't think he was saying that they agreed on everything. In fact, I think knowing Harry Morton, the little bit that I did know of him, what he would have enjoyed was perhaps their disagreement. You know, the engaging with people who had different views and different perspectives but who respected each other. Respected each other's intellectual integrity. ... Harry would've totally disagreed with – the reason he was there was to try and persuade the Provisionals to move away from violence ... the purpose for the meeting was to try and get some kind of message across that this was counter-productive ... what he was saying was, we were two people who had many of the same interests but a different approach.*[71]

Knowing the raid was coming probably made the leadership look more credible to the clergymen. The Provisionals also welcomed the positive publicity as a counter to the negative publicity of the Birmingham bombs. After two and a half years of war, the Provisionals were about to return to the bargaining table. During that time, 848 people had died in the 'Irish Troubles'.[72]

9

A DEADLY TRUCE (1975)

We had to make an attempt for the sake of the people that were suffering all over the North.

– Billy McKee[1]

Working for peace would lead the Provisionals into an open-ended and controversial bi-lateral truce or unilateral ceasefire, depending upon one's perspective. Terrorism experts have suggested that by negotiating with the Provisionals the British let them off the hook. Paul Wilkinson, in *Terrorism and the Liberal State*, writes:

> With the benefit of hindsight it is now possible to see that the army had practically beaten the Provisional I.R.A. by December 1974. Hence the Provos' Christmas truce, and their so-called 'cease-fire', proffered in January 1975, were declared from a position of desperate weakness: they had been decimated as a military force and they urgently needed time to lick their wounds, recruit and train new members, await the release of their key men from internment, and regroup.[2]

However, some Provisionals argue that the British tricked the leadership into believing they were going to withdraw from Ireland and that the truce was a disaster. While the leadership negotiated in good faith, the British reorganized their counterinsurgency and then almost destroyed them.[3] What happened in 1975 is very important for understanding the course of Provisional Irish Republicanism.

After the Feakle meeting, the leadership laid out four demands: a 'constituent assembly' would draft an all-Ireland constitution; the new constitution would include a provincial parliament for the nine counties of Ulster (Dáil Uladh); the British would publicly commit to withdrawing within twelve months of the adoption of the all-Ireland constitution; and there would be an amnesty for political prisoners. The clergymen were asked to pass the demands to Merlyn Rees. As a sign of their good faith, they also made Rees an offer: if the security forces limited their activities, then the Provisional IRA would enter into a ceasefire over the Christmas and New Year holidays.[4]

Rees was very interested because he was working on another plan to bring back the Northern Ireland Assembly. A Northern Ireland Office (NIO) White Paper had proposed an election to a Constitutional Convention that would consider which kind of government would 'command the most widespread acceptance' throughout Northern Ireland. The seventy-eight elected representatives would not have legislative or administrative power. Instead, they would meet for six months in inter-party talks and submit a report that, if approved by Westminster, would lay out a plan to devolve government back to Northern Ireland. Power sharing and an 'Irish Dimension' were open issues for discussion. How they would figure into the final plan would be left to the Convention. According to his memoir, *Northern Ireland: A Political Perspective*, Rees believed that the 'political wing' of the Provisional IRA's leadership realized that 'there was no possibility of a military victory' and wanted to participate in the Convention. He told the clergymen that a ceasefire would 'create a new situation' and stressed that it had to include England.[5]

The IRA Army Council does not publicize its members. Deliberations are conducted in secret and there is always a certain amount of speculation when it comes to accounts of who voted which way and why. Observers suggest that the Council at this time included Seamus Twomey (C/S), Kevin Mallon, Billy McKee, Ruairí Ó Brádaigh, Dáithí O'Connell, J.B. O'Hagan and perhaps Seamus Loughran. Some accounts have Ruairí Ó Brádaigh and Dáithí O'Connell pushing for a Christmas ceasefire and record the vote as five to two in favour. There are also claims that the negative votes were from the only two Northerners on the Council. No matter how they voted, there were five Northerners on the Council, not two.[6] J.B. O'Hagan was probably one of them, and he did not support the ceasefire:

Q: *The ceasefire in '75 ... would you have supported that?*

A: *No ... we met at Feakle.*

Q: *Right.*

A: *So we did. And then through that – there was the longer truce at Christmas, you know what I mean? Usually [we] had three days' truce at Christmas but the decision was to have two weeks, to involve the New Year. And not just Christmas, and through the New Year. I objected to that, too ... I was against all truces actually, at Christmas. I thought that we should – all right, the volunteers should have said, 'Look, hold off boys.' But I don't see why we should have said that publicly – said there was a truce and allow the Brits to have their free time after what they have done all year, raiding houses and things. My attitude was why should they think they're gonna have peace around Christmas?*[7]

The Provisional IRA announced they would suspend operations from 22 December 1974 to 2 January 1975.

On Christmas Day, Ruairí Ó Brádaigh looked out of the front window of his home and saw Brendan Duddy, a businessman from Derry, walking up to the house. Duddy describes himself as a 'pacifist, anti-war and anti-violence all my life'. He was one of a handful of people serving as links between the Provisionals' leadership and British officials like Frank Cooper and Michael

Oatley, of the British Secret Intelligence Service (SIS). Duddy delivered a letter requesting a meeting to establish structures for a British withdrawal from Ireland. As described in *Behind the Mask: The IRA and Sinn Féin,* by journalist Peter Taylor, Ó Brádaigh was 'astonished' and arranged for Duddy to meet with the leadership. At the meeting, Billy McKee asked, 'Well, what's on the agenda?' Duddy, not aware that McKee asked the question, answered, 'Withdrawal' and explained that the British wanted Michael Oatley to meet with Billy McKee.[8] McKee was surprised, *I've often wondered why they were so anxious to talk to me because I hadn't met any of them before. I was only out of prison. I wasn't long out of prison after they were putting me in jail. [Laughs]*[9] Seamus Twomey asked McKee if he would meet Oatley. McKee was willing, but only with a witness. It was the first of several decisions that would have serious implications for the Provisionals.

The Army Council extended the ceasefire and on 7 January 1975, Billy McKee and Joe McCallion met with Michael Oatley at Brendan Duddy's home in Derry.[10] At this meeting McKee again asked about the agenda. Oatley's reply was, 'Withdrawal', and he added, 'We need your help.' The British wanted to withdraw without a bloodbath and they wanted the Provisionals to meet with loyalists as part of the process. It was an exploratory meeting and nothing was arranged. However, Merlyn Rees released more internees and, in the House of Commons, announced that representatives of the Northern Ireland Office had met with Sinn Féin, the UDA and the UVF. He also stated that with a 'genuine and sustained cessation of violence' the British Army's presence might be reduced and the RUC might take over the 'major law and order role'.[11]

The Provisionals wanted a lot more than the release of internees and suggestions of what might happen. They also had to worry about the Dublin government. Ruairí Ó Brádaigh explained: *'[Kevin] Mallon was arrested during this in January, during that unilateral ceasefire. And, of course, it didn't help matters because he was one of the principals in the ongoing situation.'*[12] Mallon went back to Portlaoise Prison where the Dublin government was taking a hard line. Ten prisoners, including Kevin McKenna, Gearóid Mac Cárthaigh, Colm Dalton and Pat Ward went on hunger strike on New Year's Day, 1975.[13]

The ceasefire ended at midnight on 16 January 1975 and the Provisionals went back to war. However, at 2 am Ruairí Ó Brádaigh received a phone call telling him to get in touch with Brendan Duddy. This led to more meetings that were broadened to include Proinsias Mac Airt and Jimmy Drumm, who met with Michael Oatley and James Allan. With the meetings behind the scene, the war continued. Over the next couple of weeks, the Provisionals killed British soldiers in Belfast and Fermanagh, a police officer in Tyrone, a Protestant teenager in North Belfast and a 7-year-old Catholic in Armagh. In Fermanagh, British soldiers killed IRA volunteer Kevin Coen. In Belfast, a premature explosion killed IRA volunteers, John Stone and John Kelly.[14]

J.B. O'Hagan was also arrested that January, in Dublin. As O'Hagan describes it, his arrest may have made it easier for the Provisional–British negotiations since he was opposed to a truce. After Feakle but before his arrest, O'Hagan had discussed the situation with Seamus Twomey:

> *Seamus Twomey and I were together after that [Feakle] and we talked it over. And we said we should ignore the Brits and go hell for leather all summer. You know, as best we can. ... And we had more or less made up our mind – because Seamus and I were together all the time actually, because we were on*

the run at that time. And I got the surprise of my life when the truce was announced in February … I was very, very, very, very surprised.[15]

According to Billy McKee, O'Hagan was not so much opposed to a truce as he was opposed to the involvement of Seán Mac Bride in the process. McKee recalled:

it wasn't that he wasn't in favour of the truce, no. I don't know – I thought he was, now. He only said he was against – I wanted [a third party] and it was decided about it – I said, 'We should have a man, an outsider, that could sit in with it and stand over it in case they came and said we were out telling lies or making false promises or so forth …' And I proposed Seán Mac Bride. And Seán Mac Bride would have done it. But Joe B. O'Hagan was totally against it because he says he was one of the men who caused a split in the IRA starting Clann na Poblachtach [in 1946]. And me and him had a few disagreements, not fights – the next day we were talking and all. But eventually I said, 'Okay.' I agreed. O'Connell talked me out of it. Well, Dave had a good influence on me. And I had a good bit of influence with Dave, too.[16]

Memories are always tricky and subsequent events can lead to re-interpretations. J.B. O'Hagan ended up in Portlaoise and would not be implicated in decisions made by the leadership. The leadership had to make those decisions. They also had to deal with an important political development.

The Gardiner Commission's review of terrorism and human rights in Northern Ireland was released at the end of January 1975. The report brought into focus the Northern Ireland Office's White Paper, a statement from Merlyn Rees the previous April about a 'return to normality' and his more recent comment about the RUC taking the major law and order role. The Gardiner Report found that special category status for prisoners and internment might have made sense in the short term but the longer the conflict continued the more they were a problem. Both policies reinforced the view that the conflict was political. Rees was going to 'normalize' the 'Troubles' by phasing out internment and ending special category status. Politically inspired special category prisoners would be transformed into criminal terrorists.

In addition, moving the RUC onto the front line would 'Ulsterize' the security situation and help isolate the conflict to Northern Ireland. Fewer soldiers would be killed, the British public would be insulated and less likely to question the government's decisions and so on. Whether or not this was part of Rees's initial calculation is unclear, but another benefit was that the RUC was about 90 per cent Protestant and the UDR was almost exclusively Protestant. Having the almost exclusively Catholic Provisionals attacking the almost exclusively Protestant RUC and UDR would make the Troubles that much more sectarian and Irish with the neutral British caught in the middle. Normalization, Ulsterization and criminalization were a stroke of genius.[17]

The Provisionals' 'political and military leadership' could not have understood the full implications of the British plan, but Billy McKee had led the hunger strike that won special category status. There was no way they would go along with criminalizing IRA prisoners. Ruairí Ó Brádaigh commented:

I think it was the 31st of January, this came out and they brought us a copy of the Gardiner Report. And they had a typewritten memo along with it saying that this was simply a report, that it wasn't a decision to do anything. Whereupon we went into them and we said, did they realize that they were playing with fire? Did they not know about people wearing blankets in Portlaoise Prison, south of the border? For seven years in the forties – ended in a hunger strike and a climb down by the government ... [Did they not know] that this was touching a very raw nerve, as far as republicans were concerned? And, were they out of their minds? Did they not realize the responses that they could trigger and that this would go so deeply into the Irish psyche – that what they would be doing would be attempting to criminalize prisoners of war and freedom fighters and that all hell would break loose?[18]

The replacements for O'Hagan and Kevin Mallon in the leadership are unknown, but they also would have been aware of the implications of the Gardiner Report.

One person who may have rejoined the Army Council at this time is Joe Cahill, who was released from Portlaoise for health reasons late in January 1975. Cahill did not return home but settled into Dublin where he would be one of several Belfast Provisionals found in the Sinn Féin Head Offices. Even though Cahill was constantly followed, he was able to meet with Dáithí O'Connell and Seamus Twomey and, at their request, served as an intermediary with the Minister for Justice's office to resolve the hunger strike in Portlaoise. Unfortunately, the strike did not end before Pat Ward's health was permanently damaged.[19] By this point, the British–Provisionals negotiations had become very detailed, with each side developing terms for what the Provisionals called a 'bi-lateral truce' and the British called a 'position paper' on a unilateral Provisional IRA ceasefire.

Both sides wanted to avoid a repeat of what happened at Lenadoon in 1972. Therefore, the NIO agreed to set up 'Truce Incident Centres' in North and West Belfast, Armagh, Derry, Dungannon, Enniskillen and Newry. They were staffed by civil servants and connected to the NIO by telephone.[20] If a dispute could not be resolved locally then Proinsias Mac Airt and Jimmy Drumm would intervene. Ruairí Ó Brádaigh again:

There were two aspects to it. First of all there was a truce monitoring arrangement in incident centres – set up in each of the six counties. That meant that there was a phone number available on both sides and complaints could be channeled through and an attempt made to iron out the difficulty that arose at a local level. If that failed ... there was an arrangement that officials from the Northern Ireland Office could get in touch with people in Belfast if a resolution wasn't made at local level. And Jimmy Drumm, among others, would be in contact with them. And if it were impossible to settle it on the telephone, there were arrangements that they could meet face to face to deal with this.[21]

There was enough agreement between the two sets of terms that the Army Council agreed to go forward with the truce even if nothing was signed.

Seamus Twomey was Chief of Staff and his input would have been very important for the final decision. Dáithí O'Connell was Chairman of the Army Council and, although he never met with the British, O'Connell was one of the 'architects' of the situation and was considered a strategic thinker. Whatever reservations Seamus Twomey may have had earlier, there was

INSTRUCTIONS 20. 1. '75.

TERMS FOR BI-LATERAL TRUCE

1. Freedom of movement for all members of the Republican
    Movement.

2. A Cessation of all harassment of the civilian population.

3. A Cessation of all raids on lands, homes and other buildings.

4. A Cessation of arrests of members of the Republican Movement.

5. An end to screening, photographing and identity checks.

6. Members of the Republican Movement reserve the right to
    carry concealed short arms solely for the purpose of self-defence.

7. No provocative displays of force by either side.

8. No reintroduction of R.U.C. and U.D.R. into designated areas.

9. Agreement of effective liaison system between British and
    Republican Forces.

10. A progressive withdrawal of troops to barracks to begin with
    the implementation of the bi-lateral truce.

11. Confirmation that discussions between representatives of the
    Republican movement and H.M.G. will continue towards
    securing a permanent ceasefire.

12. In the event of any of these terms being violated, the
    Republican Movement reserve the right of freedom of action.

ENDS

Provisional IRA terms for a Truce, January 21, 1975.

Provisional Irish Republican terms for a truce agreement, 20 January 1975. Ruairí Ó Brádaigh 'Truce Notes'. Personal copy.

unanimous agreement on the truce, as confirmed by Ruairí Ó Brádaigh: *'In fact, all decisions taken in that period with regard to the truce were unanimous decisions … All of those decisions could not have been decisions unless there was consensus. And there was consensus.*[22] Billy McKee's account is similar to that of Ó Brádaigh. McKee was asked if Twomey had opposed the truce:

> *Not against it. He spoke – he gave his opinion about the truce and everything. We all – he didn't say any more against it than we all said at the time. But they all talked together and they agreed … Everybody*

agreed. Yes. We all agreed … The only difference was when they asked about – I said, 'Bring Seán Mac Bride in.' Joe B. O'Hagan was totally against it.[23]

The Provisionals agreed to send three representatives to 'Formal Meetings' in Derry: Ruairí Ó Brádaigh, Billy McKee and, based on information in the the UK National Archives, Joe McCallion. Ruairí Ó Brádaigh's 'Notes' on the meetings show that the representatives, or at least Ó Brádaigh, consulted with the Army Council on a regular basis. The input of Twomey and O'Connell was especially important.[24]

On Sunday, 9 February 1975, the Provisionals announced they would suspend operations the next day. Merlyn Rees then announced that meetings with Sinn Féin had produced a ceasefire and that the Northern Ireland Office would open truce incident centres to facilitate communication if problems arose. It was not part of the agreement but, in an important move, Sinn Féin also opened incident centres. Mitchel McLaughlin and Martin McGuinness worked the centre in Derry. Seamus McCusker, the IRA's Northern Director of Intelligence, worked in the North Belfast centre. Proinsias Mac Airt, Marie Moore, Danny Morrison and Tom Hartley worked in the West Belfast centre.[25] Danny Morrison described the West Belfast centre:

Billy [McKee] called me one day … when the ceasefire was called. We were asked would we monitor what were called 'the truce incident centres.' And there was a single republican in those centres in contact with the Northern Ireland Office in case there was any military breach of the ceasefires … we monitored the ceasefire and we slept in the office. It was the Sinn Féin press offices, but it was called the 'Truce Incident Centre.' Then it became the 'Incident Centre.' It was colloquially known as a 170 A. That was its address [on the Falls Road].[26]

Most of the complaints involved some kind of harassment from the security forces and almost a thousand of them would be lodged over the following eight months. The incident centres also gave Sinn Féin a public presence in the North. Journalists could find activists for interviews and, for the younger people, it was their first opportunity to engage in community politics. The downside was that the security forces kept tabs on who visited the centres.[27]

The leadership agreed to the truce for two reasons. Ricky O'Rawe, in his memoir, *Blanketmen: An Untold Story of the H-Block Hunger Strike*, writes that Billy McKee believed the truce would give the Provisionals time 'to recuperate'. McKee confirmed this, and commented: *We were going through a bad period and when we got this word about wanting to meet us … I remember talking to Twomey, and Twomey agreed. Dave O'Connell was there and he was fully behind and he says, "It would be a Godsend" … But we said this will give us a breather anyway.'* In addition, they were morally obligated to explore the opportunity. McKee was asked if he trusted the British:

Well – I couldn't say I could – couldn't say that I trusted them. But we had to make an attempt for the sake of the people that were suffering all over the North. We had to make an attempt to do something … They were practically telling us they were going to withdraw, you know? They were. And we said, 'Give us a date when you'll get out. Should be five or ten years, fifteen years.' [We] said, 'Give us a date, make it public, when youse are gonna get out. Then or before it,' I said, 'we'll call the campaign off.[28]

Ruairí Ó Brádaigh also believed the leadership had a responsibility to explore the situation:

> *You were asking me a question as to how we felt when going into these meetings. Well, I suppose it was a moment in history, in its own way. And it was a feeling of responsibility that people had to make the very most of this if there was a way out of this centuries-old conflict. There was a way of getting British withdrawal in whatever manner.*[29]

The leadership was very aware that the British had used similar situations to undermine other insurgencies. In Kenya in the 1950s, the British pursued the 'China Peace Initiative' and collected information on suspects at the same time. When the peace initiative failed, they implemented Operation Anvil and interned thousands of suspects. Mau Mau never recovered. The Provisionals were taking a calculated risk and they knew it.[30]

The British representatives included Michael Oatley, James Allan and Donald Middleton.[31] Officially, they represented the Northern Ireland Office under the direction of Merlyn Rees and Frank Cooper; the Provisionals assumed they were also working for British intelligence. It is unclear if the British representatives were out in front of Rees and the NIO when they suggested a British withdrawal or if they were following Rees's lead. The 'Constitutional Convention' provided a cover for the meetings and fit with Rees's statements that they were meeting with Sinn Féin. The truce/ceasefire also fit with his plans to normalize Northern Ireland. If the Provisionals could be persuaded to participate in the Convention, the chance of success was that much greater. If the truce fell apart and/or the Convention failed, the British would limit conflict to Northern Ireland and pursue a war of attrition.[32] As recommended by the Gardiner Report, they began working on a new prison next to Long Kesh.

A fundamental problem with the truce was that other actors were not bound by either party's terms.[33] Point 4 of the Provisionals' terms, for example, included 'A Cessation of arrests of members of the Republican Movement.' There was no guarantee that the RUC, the Gardaí or the police in England would observe that. Additionally, there were no obligations for other paramilitary groups. Seamus Costello had split from the Officials and created the People's Liberation Army (later, the Irish National Liberation Army (INLA) and the Irish Republican Socialist Party (IRSP).[34] A week into the truce, the Officials shot dead Hugh Ferguson and sparked an INLA–Official IRA feud that also claimed the life of Billy McMillen, the Officials' O/C in Belfast. There were also unplanned events. At the end of February, the British were outraged when an unarmed police officer, Stephen Tibble, was shot dead in London by an IRA volunteer fleeing arrest. A bomb factory was discovered in the area.[35]

The Dublin government, Unionist politicians and the SDLP had not been consulted. Ian Paisley accused Rees of cutting a secret deal with the Provisionals and called for an independent state of Ulster. The loyalist plan – to the degree that there was one – was to kill so many Catholics that the nationalist community would demand the IRA quit its campaign. For the loyalists, the incident centres looked like bases that the Provisionals would use to police their own neighbourhoods, a possible first step in a withdrawal process. They stepped up their efforts and, on the first day of the truce, two Catholics were killed in Tyrone and another was killed in Belfast.

Insight into the Formal Meetings is found in the notes kept by Ruairí Ó Brádaigh.[36] They show that the leadership was largely focused on two issues: obtaining a declaration of intent to withdraw and better conditions for prisoners. On the other side, the British used the possibility of a withdrawal to try and entice the Provisionals into the Constitutional Convention. The Convention was, they said, 'a sign that H.M.G. no longer wants to dictate terms in Ireland'. The Convention election was scheduled for the end of May 1975 and they wanted Sinn Féin to participate. According to Ó Brádaigh's notes:

> The point was made that R.M. [Republican Movement] wants a 32-county convention. The Brits replied that such was not possible because they rule 6 counties only. R.M. said the Brits should advocate R.M.'s solution publicly to the Dublin government who would find it impossible to decline. The Brits then said that Sinn Fein should attend the convention (6-county) and there advocate an all-Ireland convention. Perhaps an all-Ireland convention could follow after the 6-county convention. At any rate the 6-county convention may produce ideas which would lead to agreement, the Brits said.[37]

The Notes also show that the truce was troubled from the start. 'INSTRUCTIONS' from the Army Council dated 19 February raise the issue of the republican representatives 'wasting time with a big number of meetings' and quote from an article in the *Economist* that suggested the Movement had been 'conned and taken for a ride'.[38]

In order to keep the Provisionals engaged, internee releases and troop reductions were presented as concessions. By the middle of March, 160 of 570 internees had been released and the British representatives claimed it was a sign of 'British goodwill'.[39] The Price sisters were transferred from Durham to Armagh Prison and that, too, was viewed as a concession. It was not clear, however, that the internee releases and the Price sisters' transfer were direct results of the truce. Marian Price spoke about the transfer: *'We ended our hunger strike on June 7 1974, and we were transferred on 18 March 1975.'* She was asked if the transfer was a result of the truce: *'It probably was a contributing factor … he [Roy Jenkins] was going to leave the Labour Party anyway. Peter Scott informed us that Roy will take care of old business before he goes. So maybe I'm being too generous to the man but I do think that sending us home was him cleaning house before he left office.*[40]

By the end of March, the British had been speaking privately about a withdrawal for three months and had not delivered. At the Easter commemoration in Belfast, Seamus Twomey challenged them to go public with a declaration of intent to withdraw.[41]

The next Formal Meeting was scheduled for 2 April. To emphasize Twomey's challenge, the Provisionals bombed a travel agency in Belfast and released a statement indicating it was their first violation of the truce. At the meeting, the British asked for patience and refused to make a public declaration of intent. Their excuse was a desire to avoid the slaughter that happened in Congo after Belgium's sudden withdrawal. Ó Brádaigh underlined their response in his notes:

> With reference to S.T. speech in Belfast at Easter, a firm (public) undertaking is totally and absolutely out of the question. This would lead to a Congo-type situation which both Brits and R.M. wish to avoid. Grave statements lead to the opposite happening.

If on the other hand R.M. helps H.M.G. to create circumstances out of which the structures of disengagement can naturally grow, the pace quicken immensely once the ground work is laid. The only way to develop is to get the ground work right. H.M.G. cannot say they are leaving Ireland because the reaction will prevent that happening. They cannot make a stark definite statement.[42]

The British also claimed that the nationalization of Harland and Wolff shipyards in Belfast was another sign they would disengage. The Provisionals 'rejected' this. Within a week, Hugh Feeney and Gerry Kelly were secretly transferred to Long Kesh but that did not stop the drift.[43]

The next Formal Meeting was scheduled for 10 April. The day before the meeting, the Belfast IRA blew up the recently restocked House of Fraser department store in central Belfast. Billy McKee described the incident:

the day before [the explosion] there was about a million pounds of stuff put in their basement. Perfumes and different stuff was brought in. And the bomb went off and it blew the whole lot to hell ... And we had a meeting the day after it, in Derry. And I was on it ... I'm not sure who he was – but he was, you knew he was an ex-officer. [He] came in real dictating and kept on about us blowing the place ... tore into me for a while and the other one. And I asked him, I said, 'You trying to tell me now the truce is over?' And he said, 'I'm not trying to tell you that.' And I said, 'So what are you trying to tell me?' So he turned his head and he walked out ... he said, 'That belonged to the House of Fraser.' And I said, 'I don't give a damn whose it is' ... I didn't know who the House of Fraser was. I didn't care.

From McKee's perspective, the truce was seriously damaged and subsequent meetings 'amounted to nothing'.[44]

The Provisionals were upset with British politicians who were dragging their feet. The British Army was upset with British politicians because they were bargaining with the Provisionals. Frank King, General Officer Commanding of the British Army in Northern Ireland, publicly complained that Merlyn Rees was releasing known terrorists. He also claimed that his forces would have beaten the Provisionals in a matter of months if not for political interference. An article on the 'Bloody Truce' in *Time* quoted an unidentified officer: 'We have always been cynical about it. The Provos will maintain the cease-fire to get as many of their men released as possible and then start again after the elections. By now they are all well rested, well fed and well trained.'[45] Politicians in Dublin were also upset. Ruairí Ó Brádaigh described the situation:

[Dáithí] O'Connell was one of the architects of that situation and the Dublin government were very uneasy about this bi-lateral truce and the on-going talks. In fact, the British used to say to us that the Dublin government is getting increasingly twitchy. It's not an expression we would use – increasingly twitchy about these talks. And the SDLP were, of course, openly hostile, and so on. But, we learned that, in fact, the Dublin government set up a special unit of the Special Branch and with no other mission except to hunt O'Connell down.[46]

```
            FORMAL MEETING                           2.4.75.

                                            (b)

The acceptability of R.M. as a respectable movement has greatly increased
they said. It is now viewed as a serious political movement which should
be listened to. This is an enormous gain. It will be lost if R.M. goes
back to war.

There is no magic way forward. The only way is slow, too slow for the
members of R.M. and the Leadership is unable to tell them. There is a
communication problem here. A way out of the difficulty would be: show
the members R.M.s role and its advantages. The Brits wish to discuss be-
forehand with R.M. the method of doing this.
The pressures on R.M. may force them to give away more than they realise.
This is an extremely historic moment. It may never happen again for a long
time. The responsibility on P.M. is enormous. History and the future of
the Republican ideal are at stake. The alternative to going back to war
is to accept a rate of progress which is slow but will increase as it
goes along.
Finally

With reference to S.T. speech in Belfast at Easter, a firm (public) under-
taking is totally and absolutely out of the question. This would lead to a
Congo-type situation which both Brits and R.M. wish to avoid. Grave state-
ments lead to the opposite happening.

If on the other hand R.M. helps H.M.G. to create circumstances out of
which the structures of disengagement can naturally grow, the pace quicken
immensely once the ground work is laid. The only way to develop is to get
the ground work right. H.M.G. cannot say they are leaving Ireland because
the reaction will prevent that happening. They cannot make a stark defin-
ite statement.
If one looks at events: Harland & Wolfe have been nationalised but are
retained separately from the other British Nationalised Industries. The
tendency is towards eventual British disengagement. The hints are there
but will stop if R.M. goes back to war.
The whole British Army in Ireland is programmed to fight R.M. The diff-
iculty is to re-programme it quickly. The important thing is to believe
in each others sincerity.

Truce Agreement
With regard to the Balkan Street incident, the B.A. received information
that weapons were held. In the event the information proved false and the
B.A. tried to put the disruption right. Here the Brits alleged that the
Republican T.I.C. "agreed at first but later disagreed". This was re-
jected by R.M.
```

Notes from the 2 April 1974 'Formal Meeting' with a summary of the response to Seamus Twomey's challenge that Easter. Personal copy.

If the British withdrew, Dublin would have a mess on their hands. Garret FitzGerald was the Minister for Foreign Affairs. In a memoir, *Just Garret: Tales From the Political Front Line*, he writes, 'From mid-1974 until the latter part of 1975 we suspected that Wilson was contemplating such a withdrawal from Northern Ireland.' FitzGerald discussed the situation with other politicians. John Hume was concerned about what would happen if the British withdrew. FitzGerald met with Margaret Thatcher, Leader of the Opposition in the House of Commons, and Airey Neave, her Shadow Secretary of State for Northern Ireland. They were pro-Union Conservatives. FitzGerald expressed his opinion that it was a mistake for the British to speak with the IRA. Neave, who was outspoken in his opposition to power sharing and the Price sisters' transfer, wondered if the Conservatives should call for the abolition of the incident centres. Merlyn Rees told FitzGerald that he was 'not very optimistic about the Convention, and feared that if it failed, pressure in Britain for a withdrawal from Ireland might mount'.[47] The Provisionals were not the only people who suspected the British might withdraw.

The British Army, the Conservative opposition, unionists, the SDLP and the loyalists were confused and concerned. So were some republicans. Danny Morrison commented:

> *Let me explain the situation on the ground in Belfast. First of all there's a ceasefire called. Right? So, the IRA volunteers on the ground are told to go home. It's okay, they can rest and not be arrested ... The ceasefire broke down, the IRA volunteers were told to go out, to go back out on active service. In Belfast, here a man called John Kelly and John Stone, who I was in jail with – John Stone – went out on an operation and the bomb blew up and killed both of them. Then, a few days later, right after that funeral, the ceasefire's back on again. Now, that's okay, you know, if the ceasefire's going somewhere or if there's gains coming from it and tangible gains and you know what the strategy is. None of us knew what the strategy was – if it was a tactic. We were misinformed.*[48]

In *Blanketmen*, Ricky O'Rawe writes: 'I also felt the frustration of that period, of going to Battalion "call-houses"… and of asking where we were going with this ceasefire, only to be told that the leadership knew what they were doing and that we needed to be patient.'[49] Some Provisionals were impatient. Loyalists bombed two Belfast bars in March and another in April, and continued their attacks on Catholics civilians. In reply, the IRA bombed the Mountainview Tavern on the Shankill Road, killing four Protestant civilians and a loyalist. They also shot dead a Protestant civilian and a loyalist.[50]

If Merlyn Rees truly believed that the political wing of the Provisionals wanted to participate in the Constitutional Convention, he was sorely mistaken. During a formal meeting the republicans were asked if they would ever participate in elections. Their reply was intentionally vague – 'such a decision would be taken in the light of the circumstances at the time'.[51] The leadership consisted of pretty much the same people who had founded the Provisionals in 1969 – Joe Cahill, John Joe McGirl, Billy McKee, Ruairí Ó Brádaigh, Dáithí O'Connell, Paddy Ryan, Seamus Twomey and company. They rejected constitutional politics then and they rejected them in 1975. Ruairí Ó Brádaigh and Dáithí O'Connell may have been more political than the others, but all of them were militant republicans committed to a united Ireland. The leadership wanted a declaration to withdraw. They were not interested in bringing back a Northern Ireland Assembly, with or without power sharing. Sinn Féin boycotted the election.

As it turned out, the Convention election showed that Northern Ireland was more polarized than ever. The winners were the anti-Sunningdale unionists led by William Craig and Ian Paisley. The UUUC won forty-seven of the seventy-eight seats. One of the elected candidates of Craig's Vanguard Unionist Progressive Party was David Trimble, a Lecturer of Law at Queen's University who would become very prominent. Moderates in the Ulster Unionist Party, still led by Brian Faulkner, won only five seats. Compared to the 1973 Assembly election, the UUP was down nineteen seats. The SDLP actually increased its vote and still lost two seats relative to 1973 (nineteen versus seventeen). When the inter-party talks opened on 8 May 1975, the UUUC was in control.[52]

The Army Council 'Instructions' for the first Formal Meeting after the election reflected the results. The representatives were told, 'R.M. should press H.M.G. to make the Declaration of Intent so that the convention can be given the task of drafting a constitution in the contest [sic] of a British withdrawal. This would give a purpose to the convention and would rescue something from the shambles.' The Army Council also wanted something done about the 'intolerable' sectarian killings. Things were so bad in mid-Ulster that an area bounded by Portadown, Pomeroy and Aughnacloy became known as the 'murder triangle'. Finally, they wanted more prisoners transferred home. At the top of the list was Frank Stagg, who was considering another hunger strike.[53] Just before the meeting, the RUC and the Provisional IRA made things even more difficult.

Shane O'Doherty was a bomb-maker from Derry, and he was special. He had masterminded a letter-bombing campaign that wreaked havoc in Britain, including sending two ounces of gelignite to 10 Downing Street. The British wanted O'Doherty arrested and, at the beginning of the truce, he was one of a few volunteers who were told that it was not safe to surface. Six weeks into the truce, he was told he could go home. For more than a year, the RUC had been watching the house and he was arrested the day the Convention opened. It was a clear violation of Point 4 of the Provisionals' terms. They invoked Point 12, which gave them 'right of freedom of action'. RUC Constable Paul Gray was patrolling Derry's walls when he was shot twice in the back with a high-powered rifle and killed.[54] The British were, again, outraged at the loss of life, as described by Ó Brádaigh:

> The shooting of the R.U.C. man in Derry was a totally disproportionate action to the arrest of Shane Doherty [sic]. They regard it as an act of political folly because no government can afford to appear to accept that type of incident if it hopes to survive. The effect of the Derry Brigade Staff action is to put a stop to progress.[55]

The British announced that troop levels would not be reduced and the negotiations deteriorated. There were more truce violations and more reprisals and the British announced they were postponing the release of internees. The Provisionals accused them of using prisoners as hostages and, in mid-June, cancelled further meetings.[56]

Like the Provisional–British talks, there was no progress with the Convention. The delegates spent their time discussing procedures and potential structures, but they could not reach consensus on anything of substance. The British suggested to the Provisionals that it was a sideshow but something necessary before they could disengage. A 'REPORT' in Ruairí Ó Brádaigh's papers contains the following:

Wednesday 25. 6. 75

A. did all the talking. The Brits were uninterested in the outcome of the Convention. They had not the slightest intention of getting drawn back into the Northern Ireland situation. 'R.M. should not be watching day to day press comment on the Convention because it did not matter. In fact the N.I. office were freezing out the Convention members. This is part of a deliberate policy of disengagement and R.M. should appreciate that it was at the very heart of decision making.'[57]

When the Convention took a six-week recess, the British pressed for another Formal Meeting. Another note from the British echoed what Michael Oatley had said six months earlier – withdrawal was the goal but it would take time and they needed help:

We feel that the efforts by our representatives over the past seven Months to achieve a permanent peace in Northern Ireland should be regarded as evidence of our complete sincerity. We look in return for a rejection of the politics of violence. There is however no quick solution to the problems which have been with us for many years. We are concerned, as we believe are the representatives of the Provisional Sinn Fein, to avoid the emergence of a Congo-type situation in Northern Ireland. We should like to include this matter and the question of sectarian forces as points for discussion with your representatives. We propose a meeting on Tuesday 22nd July at 10.30 pm.[58]

The Provisionals considered the invitation and prepared to re-start the campaign.

At an operational meeting in South Armagh, IRA commanders were told the truce was going nowhere and that they should get ready to ease back into the campaign.[59] The meeting was secret but the Provisionals' intentions were not. Martin McGuinness claims that he left the Provisional IRA in 1974. Whatever his status, at a commemoration in Derry he called for a public declaration from the British, or else: 'Let me make it clear here to-day that if no such declaration is made, be sure then that the I.R.A. will once again go on the offensive until the declaration is made, and the principles for which our dead comrades made the supreme sacrifice are realized.'[60] Martin McGuinness was an uncompromising hard-liner.

Another younger person who was developing a larger if different kind of profile was Danny Morrison. He had a flair for words and occasionally wrote for *Republican News*. Morrison described being asked to edit the paper:

I became editor because there was an argument. The former editor had had a major fallout with Billy McKee ... So Billy called me in and says, 'Would you be – do you think you could do this even for a

week or two?' I don't know what the exact row was with Sean McCaughey, who was the previous editor.
It may have been over something that he wrote in the paper — I think it was. So, I came in and took
over the paper.[61]

One of the more important decisions Morrison made was to arrange for Gerry Adams to write
a column. Adams, because he was caught trying to escape, was one of the sentenced prisoners
in Long Kesh. His first column was smuggled out and written under the pseudonym 'Brownie'.
It was titled, 'Inside Story' and appeared on 16 August 1975. Even though 'everybody knows
terrorists can't type', Brownie managed to describe life in the camp.[62]

Another important change in the Movement that July came when the Special Branch finally
caught up with Dáithí O'Connell, who had been on the run for two and a half years. Seized
with O'Connell were documents that brought the Dublin authorities up to speed on the truce
negotiations, at least from the perspective of the Provisionals. O'Connell was found guilty of
membership and ended up in Portlaoise. His replacement on the Army Council is unknown.
Likely candidates include Joe Cahill, if he was not already on the Council, Brian Keenan, who
had recently been released after twelve months in Portlaoise, and Martin McGuinness. Kieran
Conway, in *Southside Provisional: From Freedom Fighter to the Four Courts*, reports that Cahill became
Adjutant General upon O'Connell's arrest. With O'Connell's arrest, the number of Southerners
on the Army Council was reduced to one person — presumably, Ruairí Ó Brádaigh.[63]

Following O'Connell's arrest, the Derry Brigade set off three bombs at 'Crown buildings'.
Another bomb in South Armagh killed three British soldiers.[64] In spite of the violence, the
Formal Meetings were re-started on 22 July[65] and Northern Ireland sank deeper into sectarian
conflict.

At the end of July, the Miami Showband, a popular music group based in Dublin, was
returning from a show in Banbridge. They were outside Newry when their minibus was stopped
at what looked like a UDR checkpoint. In fact, a loyalist gang supported by active duty UDR
soldiers had stopped them. The band members were being searched when a bomb exploded
prematurely at the back of the minibus. If the bomb had gone off while the group was driving
on to Dublin, it would have looked like they were transporting explosives for the IRA. That
would have supported the claim that there was not enough security along the border and would
have contributed to a general mistrust of Southern Ireland — musicians transporting bombs. The
explosion killed some of the band members and some of the loyalists. In an attempt to kill the
witnesses, loyalists shot the surviving band members, two of whom survived.[66] Two weeks later,
the Belfast IRA bombed and shot up the Bayardo Bar, an alleged UVF hangout. Five Protestants
were killed and scores were injured.

These attacks are often cited as evidence of a Protestant/loyalist-Catholic/Provisional IRA
sectarian war in Northern Ireland. The Miami Showband attack also provides clear evidence of
loyalist–security force collusion. Indeed, at one of the Formal Meetings, the British admitted 'in
confidence' that one of the men charged in the attack was 'a serving member of the U.D.R.'.[67]
The British also complained that 'an internee released from L.K. on June 17th' had been charged
with participating in the Bayardo Bar attack. As Billy McKee and Dáithí O'Connell had hoped,

and as General King had feared, released internees were returning to the IRA. The Bayardo Bar attack is also remembered because of the involvement of a former seminary student, Brendan 'Bik' McFarlane.[68]

The Northern Ireland Constitutional Convention reconvened in August and the SDLP and UUUC representatives tried to find a formula for a 'voluntary coalition' that would share power. They were at an impasse as Northern Ireland went back to war. British soldiers killed 10-year-old Stephen Geddis with a plastic bullet. They claimed they had fired into a crowd of people throwing stones at them; the claim was disputed. The IRA bombed the London Hilton and a booby trap claimed the life of a bomb disposal expert. Then the 'Republican Action Force' – a cover name for local Provisionals – sprayed the Tullyvallan Orange Hall in South Armagh with machine gun fire. Five Protestants died and with them went any chance that the UUUC would compromise on majority rule and share power with the SDLP. In mid-September, Brendan Duddy wrote in his diary, 'My efforts at mediation seem useless' and Merlyn Rees publicly denied that there was or ever had been a bilateral truce.[69]

The Provisionals, or at least Ruairí Ó Brádaigh, took a business-like approach to the truce. The struggle for a democratic socialist republic did not end with the truce, it was only being pursued on a different 'front'. Ó Brádaigh was asked about the ending of the truce:

Q: *So then the end of it in September, I mean, are you depressed or is that business, too?*

A: *No, that's business too. It didn't work out. So this is what happens. There you are. And so what?*

Q: *So you go on?*

A: *That's right. Yes, yes, yes. But satisfied that we had done everything that we could possibly do in this situation to bring matters to a successful conclusion, from our viewpoint ... we weren't fooled by the Brits in any way. And we knew the Brits to be what they are and that is clever scheming politicians who will go to any length to secure their own position ... and snare people. But they did not ensnare us. We felt, at the time, duty bound to respond to the offer that was made and to explore it for what it was worth. And when it became blatantly obvious that this situation wasn't going anywhere, it was a case of back to war. And the so-called peace lasted seven and a half months. It wasn't a real peace in the sense that there can be no real peace under the British hegemony. But, as well as that, you had a simmering conflict all the time. And the British were violating the truce terms and reprisals were being taken by the republicans and you had the loyalists, assassination – a campaign stronger than ever and then they – the republicans – were seeking out some of these leading loyalist death squad people to punish them.*[70]

On 22 September 1975, the Provisionals set off eighteen bombs in Northern Ireland. Without question the truce was over. Unlike on Bloody Friday, the only fatality that day was Margaret Hale, a Catholic civilian killed in a UVF gun and bomb attack on a bar in County Armagh. There was no formal statement ending the truce; however, three days later at a Sinn Féin press conference, flanked by John Joe McGirl, Marie Moore, Joe O'Neill and Seán Keenan, among others, Ó Brádaigh countered Merlyn Rees and said there had been a truce. Because the meetings had been held in confidence, and because the British were *still* communicating with them, he refused to offer details.[71]

Through a 'sub-intermediary', the British complained that the 'deliberate display of violence' and the 'public slanging match' were leading to renewed conflict. A personal note attached to the message asked, 'Should you not think carefully?' The British pressed for another meeting but the Provisionals refused unless two conditions were met – 'Full implementation of all 11 points agreed upon' *and* 'The purpose of the meetings to be the devising of structures of British disengagement from Ireland.'[72] Instead of accepting the conditions, Merlyn Rees announced that, as of 1 March 1976, paramilitary prisoners would no longer receive Special Category Status. Rees also banned the UVF but not Sinn Féin. On 14 December 1975, Frank Stagg went back on hunger strike for repatriation to Ireland.

Whether it was intentional or a quirk of scheduling, the British Cabinet sub-committee on Northern Ireland did not formally address the issue of withdrawal until 11 November 1975, after the truce had ended. Harold Wilson, it appears, was relatively open-minded on the issue. After the Ulster Workers' Strike, and at Wilson's insistence, civil servants had drawn up a plan whereby troops would be pulled out over a four-month period and Northern Ireland would be given dominion status, like Canada and Australia. Merlyn Rees, the Dublin government and the SDLP helped kill the idea. In a letter to *The Guardian*, Merlyn Rees would later write:

> The option of withdrawal was seriously considered in Cabinet sub-committee between 1974–76. As Secretary of State I was firmly against such a policy and was supported by the elected Irish government in Dublin, the SDLP, the NILP, the Northern Trade Unions and the British Labour Movement ... Withdrawal would lead to an independent, smaller Northern Ireland, loyalist dominated.

The likelihood that the British would withdraw from Ireland was always low. Yet, it was a possibility. The risk taken by the Provisionals' leadership was reasonable given the circumstances. In December 1975, the last of the internees was released and the final piece of 'normalization' was in place. Merlyn Rees closed the Northern Ireland Office's incident centres and the British settled in for a war of attrition.[73]

On 11 February 1976, there was one final Formal Meeting. Ó Brádaigh's summary says, 'No concrete result.'[74] The next day, Frank Stagg died in Wakefield Prison after sixty-two days without food.[75] The truce was long over and the Provisionals had entered a very difficult period.

10

Reorganizing for a Long War (1976–1978)

They had been through the legal system and there's where the legal system got them to: forced confessions, beaten up and thrown into jail.

– Tyrone Sinn Féiner, 1977 recruit[1]

By the end of 1975, more than 1,500 people had been killed and thousands more injured by political violence in Northern Ireland. The Provisionals were responsible for about half of the fatalities and had suffered significant losses. The 'Roll of Honour' lists more than one hundred Provisional IRA and nine Cumann na mBan volunteers who died on 'active service' between August 1969 and 31 December 1975. One of the oldest of the volunteers killed was 46-year-old Peter McNulty. He was killed in a premature explosion during an attack on an RUC station in Castlewellen, County Down. Sixteen members of Na Fianna Éireann were killed between 1969 and the end of 1975, many of them in accidental shootings and training accidents. One of the youngest of the Provisionals killed was 13-year-old Seán O'Riordan, who was shot by the British Army during a gun battle in West Belfast.[2]

The truce had failed and the war would go on, but before they could do anything about it, the Provisionals faced a series of problems. The Official IRA still had guns and they still engaged in punishment shootings and robberies. There were inevitable confrontations and, on 29 October 1975, the Belfast Provisionals went after them with a vengeance and shot nineteen people, one fatally. The Officials refer to the attacks as a pogrom and they responded in kind. In two weeks, ten more people were dead, including Seamus McCusker, killed by the Officials, and 7-year-old Eileen Kelly, killed by Provisionals looking for her father. Two Belfast priests, Fathers Des Wilson and Alec Reid, were able to mediate a truce but the feud sorely damaged the Provisionals. They may have outgunned the Officials but they also gave the media good reason to portray them more like gangsters than a national liberation army.[3]

A rogue unit in Limerick contributed to the gangster image. Eddie Gallagher and his comrades kidnapped Dutch businessman Dr Tiede Herrema and demanded the release of Rose Dugdale, Gallagher's girlfriend. She was an English heiress and one of the more interesting of the people associating with the Provisionals. After an embarrassing siege, Herrema was freed and Gallagher's group was arrested; Dugdale stayed in Limerick Jail.[4] An IRA unit in London didn't help the image, either. Tired of IRA bombs in London, Ross McWhirter, of *Guinness Book of*

Records fame, called for the death penalty for the bombers and announced a £50,000 reward for information that led to arrests and convictions. He was shot dead at his home. After another attack, the unit was spotted and chased across London and they ended up in a flat on Balcombe Street, with hostages. After a six-day siege, on 12 December 1975, the hostages were released and the London police arrested Eddie Butler, Hugh Doherty, Joe O'Connell and Harry Duggan. Duggan was supposedly buried in County Mayo; Doherty was the brother of Donegal republican Pat Doherty. Unfortunately, their arrest did not end the 'Balcombe Street Gang' saga.

The group accepted responsibility for an extensive list of operations, including the Guildford and Woolwich bombs for which the Guildford Four and Maguire Seven had been convicted. The authorities thought it was another Provisional IRA trick. In his statement from the dock, Joe O'Connell pointed out the miscarriage of justice, 'We have recognized this court to the extent that we have instructed our lawyers to draw the attention of the court to the fact that four totally innocent people – Carole Richardson, Gerard Conlon, Paul Hill and Patrick Armstrong – are serving massive sentences for three bombings, two in Guildford and one in Woolwich.' Their convictions were based on false evidence and 'police lies', O'Connell said. Sadly, it was easier for the authorities to keep innocent Irish people in prison than it was to admit that their criminal justice system was flawed. O'Connell, Eddie Butler, Hugh Doherty and Harry Dugan received multiple life sentences plus additional years. The Maguire Seven and Guildford Four had their appeals denied.[5]

The New Year brought more trouble when loyalists attacked two families in South Armagh and killed six Catholics. In retaliation, the 'Republican Action Force', a cover name for local Provisionals, stopped a mini-bus loaded with workers at Kingsmill. The lone Catholic was told to 'run up the road' and the eleven Protestants were shot; only one victim, shot eighteen times, survived. The Kingsmill Massacre was a blatant sectarian attack and yet some Provisionals justified it. In *The IRA*, journalist Tim Pat Coogan describes asking an unidentified spokesperson, 'Why?' The reply was, 'It stopped the sectarian killings in the area, didn't it?'[6] That may have worked in South Armagh, where Protestants were in the minority and the IRA had strong support. In Belfast, it seemed like nothing could stop the sectarian tit-for-tat killing. In the autumn of 1976, loyalists would claim their most prominent victim, Máire Drumm, who was killed while awaiting surgery at the Mater Hospital. By that point the 'Shankill Butchers' – a group of loyalists that included Lenny Murphy and Robert 'Basher' Bates – had taken their own brand of violence to another level. They began with Francis Crossan, a 34-year-old married man and father of two children. Crossan was walking home after a few drinks in a social club. He was hit on the head with a wheel brace, dragged into a taxi and had his skull fractured and his throat slit. Between the autumn of 1975 and the spring of 1977, the 'Shankill Butchers' would torture and kill nineteen people. Most of them were innocent, randomly chosen, Catholics.[7]

The way the truce ended, the feud with the Officials and the sectarian attacks all contributed to a feeling that the Provisionals had lost direction, especially among the younger people. Danny Morrison talked about this period:

> I remember talking to a young lad called Seán McDermott, and he and I were saying to each other – I remember it being in a house in Andersonstown – we were saying, 'Where is this going? Is this ceasefire

on or is it off?' Because it had never been called off and yet IRA units were back operating again. Friends of mine were killed on active service and we didn't – well, the leadership had been intimating and actually using the pages of An Phoblacht *and* Republican News *to broadcast claims that it was over. When Rolls Royce pulled out of East Belfast, we were told that it was the beginning of an economic withdrawal and that the British were preparing to go. We were actually told it could well be a civil war situation and that we should prepare for it. Other problems were that, while the Brits were telling the leadership or these civil servants that were meeting leadership representatives ... the prison administration was also telling, for example, Davy Morley [O/C of prisoners in Long Kesh] ... not to worry – that the jail that was being built on the other side of the wall, that is the H-Blocks were for ordinary prisoners. And this led to a lot of resentment that, while they were preparing for their next strategy which was criminalization, Ulsterization and normalization, we were being fed a rather naïve interpretation of what the British were at ... and then again in October 1975, in Belfast here, the feud starts ...it was a very despairing period – despairing and lost.*[8]

A group of prisoners in Long Kesh was convinced the truce was a disaster. They watched it unfold from a distance, but they were on-site as a state-of-the-art prison was built next door – HMP Maze. Logic dictated that they ask the question, 'If the British are withdrawing, why are they building a new high security prison?' Brendan Hughes was critical of the ceasefire:

one, because I thought there was no strategic advantage for us at the time of going into a ceasefire. Two, because I think the ceasefire was manipulated by the British and then the Movement was drawn into a sectarian war where we were no longer fighting the British. We were fighting each other. And sectarianism and the sectarian war that the IRA allowed themselves – allowed itself to be brought into. That's why I was so critical of it. And I seen, in 1972, I believed the British tried to involve us in a long drawn out ceasefire. In 1975, I seen a long, drawn-out ceasefire developing. So, I was critical of the Movement, of the leadership at that time because it allowed itself to be drawn into that trap.

Hughes commented on ceasefires in general: '*Soldiers, or volunteers, soldiers have to be doing something. And when you're not shooting at the British other things develop – feuds. And I think that that's a dangerous period when you get into the situation when soldiers stop shooting. You lose the enemy and another enemy develops and it develops into feuds.*'[9] Hughes was in Cage Eleven of Long Kesh and discussed these issues with his fellow prisoners. The Belfast Provisionals who at one time or another were in Cage Eleven included Gerry Adams, Ivor Bell, Tom Cahill, Jim Gibney, Gerry Kelly, 'Bik' McFarlane and Bobby Sands.[10]

Questions about the truce and the sense that the IRA had lost direction contributed to operational problems. While some internees returned, others drifted away. Joe Cahill commented:

once it's an extended truce, then it's detrimental to the Republican Movement. From the point of view that a certain amount of normalization set in. And it's hard to get away from that again. You'd have various degrees of commitment as far as the volunteers are concerned. You'd have 100 per cent commitment and it would be down the hill, maybe to zero per cent commitment, or maybe 60 per cent commitment. They would be on the run. They would establish a sort of normal routine. But during a ceasefire, or a truce, when they could go back and live with their families – getting a job, getting a wage and enjoying normal life – it's very hard to get them to give that up.[11]

Not everyone agreed with the critics, however.

Ricky O'Rawe was on active service in West Belfast until his arrest in 1977. In his memoir, he describes sharing a prison cell with Brendan Hughes:

> I disagreed with The Dark's view that the IRA was almost defeated, though. I could speak only from a local perspective, but in Ballymurphy, with a glut of good men and women at our disposal, we never felt that we were staring into the face of defeat. Equally at the daily Battalion call-house meetings, I met the OCs from the other companies in west Belfast, and never once did I leave with the impression that they thought they were on the verge of being defeated.[12]

According to Billy McKee, he and Seamus Twomey had conversations 'day in and day out'. McKee recalled a conversation in January 1976:

Q: Were you thinking of calling off the campaign?

A: Oh no. I said if we ever needed to call it off we could always say, 'At least we got rid of Stormont.' … I wasn't planning to call it off. It was never called off at that time …

Q: Was the truce a mistake?

A: See, no, it wasn't a mistake. We didn't lose anything by it. When it was called off and we went back to war again we were as strong as we ever were, maybe stronger. It wasn't a mistake. No, no … In the '75 truce we gave nothing away. We came out of it stronger than we was when it started.[13]

Not only did the IRA get back released internees, they probably also benefitted from a more committed army.

When the truce broke down, volunteers who returned to active service chose to give up a 'normal life' for the second time. They were experienced and committed, and, unlike naïve teenagers, they knew what they were getting back into. Seán Mac Stiofáin compared the volunteers of the early 1970s with the volunteers of the late 1970s:

A lot of people came into the Movement in '71–'72 as a reaction to certain events – you had the pogroms in '69, you had the attacks on East Belfast and North Belfast in, say, June 1970, you had various acts of British repression, like the killing of civilians in that area [unclear], and then you had Bloody Sunday. You had internment, torture, Bloody Sunday, right? And always, every time these things happened, there would be a wave of recruits into the IRA. And I suppose a lot of those people, again, they didn't last the pace like. The people who did stay on, and the younger volunteers that came in and those who lasted the pace, well they had – I won't say they were more committed, but they were certainly – well, those who had been there since '71 were those that had become battle-hardened and were experienced. Those who were soldiering on after the '75 Truce, they would be, obviously they were very committed, very dedicated and possibly more politically – a high degree of political consciousness.[14]

Whether or not the truce was a disaster, it did help Sinn Féin. The British closed their incident centres but Sinn Féin kept theirs open. That gave the Provisionals a public presence in the working-class Northern communities.[15]

The volunteers who returned to active service after the truce include iconic figures like Mairéad Farrell and Bobby Sands. Farrell was arrested in the spring of 1976, after bombing the Conway Hotel. Also on the operation were Seán McDermott, who was killed by an RUC reserve officer as they withdrew, and future hunger striker Kieran Doherty.[16] Sands was released from Long Kesh in the spring of 1976 and rearrested only a few months later after a furniture factory was fire-bombed. Also arrested in the incident were Joe McDonnell, a future hunger striker, and Seamus Finucane, from a prominent republican family.[17]

A brief look at the activist careers of three volunteers, Paul Marlowe, Frank Fitzsimons and Joey Surgenor, offers a sense of the IRA after the truce.[18] Marlowe was an ex-British paratrooper who had served with the Special Air Service (SAS) in Malaysia and Aden. In late 1969/early 1970, he joined the Provisional IRA in Ardoyne, North Belfast. Because of his background, he quickly became a Brigade level Training Officer. He was interned, released and joined the Engineering Department in Belfast. Marlowe is credited with developing their version of a Claymore mine. In the autumn of 1976, Paul Marlowe was thirty-one years old, married, the father of three children and a very experienced operator. Frank Fitzsimons was from the Short Strand in East Belfast and he was on the barricades in 1969, but did not join the Provisional IRA until 1973. After only a few months on active service, he was arrested at a British Army checkpoint for possession of ammunition. Fitzsimons was released from Long Kesh in 1975. That autumn, he was twenty-nine years old, married and the father of two children. Joey Surgenor was also from the Short Strand and also helped with the barricades in 1969. Unlike Fitzsimons, Surgenor went directly into the Provisional IRA, at the age of seventeen. He helped defend St Matthew's Church in June 1970 and was arrested in October 1971 for causing an explosion. He was a 24-year-old bachelor when he was released from Long Kesh in June 1976.

Collectively, Paul Marlowe, Frank Fitzsimons and Joey Surgenor had more than fifteen years of experience in the Provisional IRA. Only Fitzsimons was from a republican family but all three had been imprisoned or interned. In the autumn of 1976, they set out to bomb a British Army post located next to the Belfast gasworks. Their bombs exploded prematurely, the gasometer caught fire and they were killed in a huge fireball. The Provisional IRA lost three experienced activists. Every loss was important, but it was also the seventh year of the campaign. There were hundreds, if not more than a thousand, experienced and dedicated volunteers who were willing and able to go on active service.

Whatever the difficulties they faced, the Provisionals were also recruiting new members. State violence was still an important source of recruits, including violence from years earlier. A teenager from Derry:

I was brought up in a nationalist area. There was a Protestant area on the edge of it and, in 1969, 1968–69 when the troubles first started, it was my first experience of loyalist brutality. When I seen B Specials coming on my street – I was only eight or nine years of age at the time – coming onto my street and smashing homes up, coming into my house and assaulting my father and wrecking my house, that was my first involvement. It wasn't my involvement but it was my experience.

He was 14 when he formally became involved:

Fourteen ... '75–'76. There was nothing really happening then. Political status had been taken away from our prisoners and I had grown up through the Troubles, through Bloody Sunday, through all that, the different incidents. Seeing the Brits walking the streets and things like that, I just didn't like it. And it played on my mind from 1968–69, until then. And then, when I was old enough, when I thought I was old enough to get involved, I got involved ...

Q: Did your older brothers or sisters get involved ... Would they have influenced you to get involved?

A: No, no way. No one has had an influence on me. I'll tell you the only thing that had an influence on me being involved was when I seen a B Special coming into my home and hitting my father, assaulting my father and wrecking my home ....[19]

Because of the violence, many Southerners avoided the North.[20] And because of censorship, the Provisionals' message often went unheard. New Southern recruits were often brought in through a process that made the conflict in the North personal for them. Seán Crowe, for example, joined Sinn Féin around this time. He was from Dublin and there was a family history of involvement, but an important part of his recruitment was a visit to Derry, which he described:

I suppose if you go back to the grandparents, they were republicans. Grandfather fought in the Tan War. But that wouldn't necessarily have an influence on me, although my father would be republican ... I sort of got interested by reading and then around the seventies, there was a lot happening at that time. I used to watch it on television. I was reluctant to get involved initially in that I felt it was going to take over my life. And I went up to Derry. I think it was in 1975 – about three years after Bloody Sunday ... just talking to people, basically. There was no real sort of one [reason] you could say that made me want to join but I suppose that had a big influence on me at the time. There was a lot of things happening prior to that as well but I suppose that was the significant thing, you know? Shortly after that – I was sort of on the fringe of things prior to that, in that we were involved in the Irish Civil Rights Association which was active at the time ... You had a hunger strike, I was involved in some of the marches, you had the hunger strike in Portlaoise and that. But I hadn't actually made the decision to join. And then when I did come back from Derry then I got involved locally in a branch of Sinn Féin.[21]

In the North, the Provisionals were an attractive option for many young, working-class nationalists. In the South, they were fewer in number, but there were still recruits.

The fact that their opponents were constantly improving their counterinsurgency may have contributed to the belief that the IRA was weaker. Security continued to become tighter and harder. The Emergency Powers Bill (1976), an Irish complement to the Prevention of Terrorism Act in Britain, gave the Gardaí the right to hold suspects for seven days before charging them. The penalty for membership of an illegal organization was increased to seven years. As a complement to the legislation, the 'Heavy Gang' was established to interrogate suspects.[22] Conor Cruise O'Brien, the Minister for Posts and Telegraphs, described Sinn Féin as a 'public relations agency for a murder gang' and formally banned them from radio and television.[23]

It was standard procedure to try and intimidate new recruits and younger activists. Seán Crowe was first arrested in 1976:

> I was arrested with the Heavy Gang, in Dublin … We were putting up posters – 'Join the Republican Movement', anti-EEC type posters. And because they were of a political nature the detectives arrested us … Frightening experience. Yeah, I was sort of young and naïve and you didn't really know the score. They just held us for twenty-four hours and released us … It wasn't illegal or anything. We were just putting up posters.[24]

Crowe remained active in Sinn Féin, though others were scared off.

In the North, special category status ended on 1 March 1976. The British saw the Maze Prison as a state-of-the-art facility that complemented one of the most progressive approaches to crime in Europe. Prisoners who accepted criminal status and conformed would receive 50 per cent remission – for each day served the sentence was reduced by one day. The republican prisoners rejected everything about the place. They continued to call it Long Kesh or the 'H-Blocks' – each building had a central corridor connected by four wings so it looked like an 'H' from the air – and they refused to conform. Ciaran Nugent was the first Provisional sent to the H-Blocks. When asked his sizes for a uniform, he replied, 'You have got to be joking.' He wore the uniform once, for a visit with his mother. He told her that she would not see him for three years, adding, 'If they want me to wear a uniform they will have to nail it on my back.' Naked and wrapped in a blanket, he was the first 'blanketman'.[25] Gerry Hodgins was arrested in May 1976 and he explained why he went on the blanket:

> Because I believed I was a political prisoner at the time, that the offenses which I was held for were all politically motivated ones. And I didn't see the logic in the British government – saw again that had them offenses been committed before the first of March 1976, I would be a political prisoner. It turned out I was arrested on the fourth of May 1976, which is only two months after the date. Yet, they were saying that you weren't a political prisoner, you were a criminal. So, I wasn't prepared to – and it's a personal thing where you didn't want to criminalize yourself. And then the whole struggle would be criminalized, by wearing a prison uniform, a prison uniform and accepting that you were a criminal.[26]

The blanketmen lost all privileges – no radio, no television, no newspapers, no visitors and no remission. Mairéad Farrell was the first woman convicted after the withdrawal of political status. Women in Armagh Prison were not required to wear a uniform but they were required to perform prison work. She refused and was locked up for twenty-one hours a day, lost her remission and was denied visits and parcels. Because prisoners who refused to wear a uniform were denied visits, people on the outside were not fully aware of their conditions. [27]

In the autumn of 1976, Roy Mason succeeded Merlyn Rees as Secretary of State for Northern Ireland. He was a former miner from South Yorkshire and his focus was on security, not White Papers and political initiatives. In his autobiography, *Paying the Price*, he described his approach:

> Almost my first public statement in the Province stressed that I wanted criminals caught by the RUC and punished as criminals – not 'politicals'. I warned, 'Peace, democracy and personal well-being are being destroyed by these men. They are torturing their own people. The criminals have violence in their souls, so ingrained that they turn on their own kith and kin.'[28]

Under Roy Mason, Sir Kenneth Newman was appointed Chief Constable and the RUC was reorganized. Intelligence information was centralized via computers. Castlereagh Holding Centre, in Belfast, was transformed into a specialized interrogation centre. During the truce the RUC had collected information on republicans and their associates. In 1976, more than 700 people were charged with Provisional IRA-related offenses. That was more than twice as many as the year before. Section 10 of the Prevention of Terrorism Act (1974) allowed the police to detain someone without charge for up to forty-eight hours. Under Section 12, the Secretary of State could extend the detention for five more days. The RUC used seven-day detention orders to try and break suspects. Complaints of assault in custody also doubled.[29]

Castlereagh became notorious. In a hand-written account that was smuggled to the Association for Legal Justice and subsequently published in Denis O'Hearn's, *Nothing But an Unfinished Song: Bobby Sands, The Irish Hunger Striker Who Ignited a Generation*, Bobby Sands described his mistreatment:

> I was punched very heavily across the head, ears, face and eyes. I was kicked on the legs, my head was smashed against a wooden wall; I was punched on the body as well. After this beating which lasted 4–5 minutes I was calmly told to sit down. A few things were said when they were beating me. I did not hear what they were. I was given a cigarette as if nothing had happened. I was completely taken unaware. I was very shocked. I was then told that what I got was only a taste of what I would get unless I gave the right answers to their questions.[30]

Sands, Seamus Finucane and Joe McDonnell received fourteen years each for possession of ammunition and a firearm, and they joined the blanket protest. Tommy McKearney was an IRA commander in Tyrone when he was charged with killing a part-time member of the UDR. Journalist Peter Taylor, author of *Beating the Terrorists: Interrogation in Omagh, Gough and Castlereagh*, presents McKearney's account of his interrogation in Castlereagh:

the most traumatic piece of torture came towards the end of the seven days. I think, looking back on it now, that the interrogators believed that they would make one last attempt to have me break. They brought in maybe four to six hefty policemen in civilian clothing. They pressed me to the floor and brought in a bin liner and put it over my head and started to tighten it around me so that I couldn't breathe. It was through that that I sustained several injuries, notably a black eye which was the most obvious sign.

Dr Albert Irwin, an RUC surgeon, examined McKearney after the interrogation. Taylor also presents Dr Irwin's description of McKearney: 'he was pale, nervous, and exhausted. He had a black eye that looked fairly recent and bruises whose colour suggested they were five to six days old. His forehead was swollen and many of the muscles at the back of his neck, forearm and abdomen were swollen and tender. His fingers were trembling.'[31] Dr Irwin reported the mistreatment to the Police Authority but nothing happened. McKearney was sentenced to twenty years and went on the blanket.

Mistreatment of suspects was not confined to Castlereagh, as shown by Gerry McGeough's description of his arrest in 1977:

> In the classic dawn raid type of thing, where they come into the house and they were all over the place and corralled all the members of the family into one room and arrested me and took me away. So that would have been spring of '77. And it was quite a horrendous experience because it was basically a beating session. There was no subtlety about it whatsoever and one didn't expect subtlety either, I might add. But having said that, it's still a dreaded experience. Everybody feels they're gonna get it at some stage. And it was almost to be expected given where we were living and the times in which we were living. And looking back on it, who did these people think they were? They were pulling in basically children. You know, we were just like sixteen, seventeen, eighteen.

McGeough, from Tyrone, described his interrogation:

> I think I got off quite lightly, all things considered, but the particular barracks that I had been taken to, which was Cookstown, was notorious. People had been beaten unconscious in it, in the course of the previous twelve months. So it was probably a psychological operation on their part bringing us there in the first place. It was absolutely filthy. I mean appallingly dirty. The cell that I was being held in was – I don't know if there was a light in it but if there was there certainly wasn't much. But it was absolutely filthy. And it offered absolutely nothing other than a slab and people had urinated all over; there was probably vomit here and there. It was a disgusting place. But anyhow, the actual interrogations themselves revolved around – [I was] asked my name. Once I gave my name, I was beaten. It was, 'We asked you your effing name, you little effing Fenian.' And so you could see you weren't going to make much progress there.

The police were less interested in his name than they were in beating him:

They just gave me a whack – a good thump on the back, knocked me down and said, 'You were asked your effing name.' And then – from then on it was a series of slapping and pushing and kneeing to the sides of the leg and occasional punch into another. And, on one occasion, I wrote a request to see a doctor and this guy came in – and probably I would've been slapped around a little, my hair would've been all ruffled and a few bruises or marks anyhow – and he said, 'Oh, there's nothing more than you'd get in a good rugby match'. That was his attitude. So there wasn't making much progress there. And it was just a matter of knuckling down and taking what was coming.

McGeough was released without charge. The arrest and interrogation were a 'standard experience' for people of his age who were active in republican circles.[32]

The beatings were effective in that many suspects broke or signed false confessions. In the late 1970s, more than three quarters of the convictions in paramilitary cases in Northern Ireland resulted from confessions.[33] In an interview with the *Daily Express*, Roy Mason described the new approach, 'We are squeezing the terrorists like rolling up a toothpaste tube. We are squeezing them out of their safe havens. We are squeezing them away from their money supplies. We are squeezing them out of society and into prison.'[34] The beatings were also counterproductive in that those who did not break were hardened. And whether or not suspects provided information, they had friends and relatives who were upset.

The mistreatment also showed that the SDLP was largely powerless and had been powerless for years. A young woman from County Tyrone, explained her decision to join the Movement in 1977:

I recognized that the nationalist people were oppressed, and I felt that it was my duty to do something about that …

Q: What was happening here in '77?

A: It was the H-Blocks, the controversy at that time. Political status had been taken away in 1976 …

Q: Instead of joining Sinn Féin, why didn't you join the SDLP?

A: In 1977, I witnessed a lot of my friends being arrested, taken to Castlereagh and beaten up, forced to sign confessions. Remanded for a number of months and convicted on trumped up charges. And some of them who are released today, some of them got life. And there was no other movement [that] took an interest. There was no other movement prepared to do anything about it. There was no other movement prepared to stand up against British rule. So, therefore, I chose this path.

Q: Okay, seeing that happen to your friends, that would make you angry, to say the least, wouldn't it?

A: The fact – okay, that it happened to my friends, yes, but the fact that it was so unfair and so unjust made me realize just how unjust the Brits are, and [how] unjust the society that I come from.

Q: Yeah. There wouldn't have been any legal way to help your friends … I mean, through the court, through the legal system?

A: It's been the legal – the Diplock Court, a nonjury court. And there's no way – they had been through the legal system and there's where the legal system got them to: forced confessions, beaten up and thrown into jail.

Q: Would you say that a series of events led you to get involved or, like, one event?

A: It was a series of events, but, in 1977, probably because I'd become older and more aware, but it was a series of events that led up to it. And Bloody Sunday was the one thing that really sticks out in my mind and I was a twelve year old – just about that age. And, again, I wasn't present at the march but I saw it on TV and that really stuck in my mind – the way that people were shot down and slaughtered down on the streets. I couldn't believe – at that age – that these people were allowed to do that – there was a peaceful march. People were unarmed and defenceless.[35]

In March 1977, the SDLP issued a detailed statement expressing concern about the mistreatment of suspects, and in June 1977, Austin Currie, Paddy Devlin, Gerry Fitt and Michael Canavan, the SDLP spokesman on law and order, met with the Chief Constable.[36] It was not until March 1978, and only after an Amnesty International investigation was made public, however, that Roy Mason appointed Judge Harry Bennett, QC, to lead an inquiry into the RUC interrogation procedures.

Even with the Bennett inquiry underway, the abuse continued. In January 1979, Dr Irwin examined Dan McCann after six days in Castlereagh. McCann had two black eyes, bruises from his nose to his cheekbones and bruises on his thighs, knee and back. In an interview with Mary Holland that was broadcast on the London television show 'Weekend World', Dr Irwin made public his concerns. By his account, he had seen more than 150 suspects who had been abused in custody. Although Roy Mason and the RUC disputed the allegation, the Bennett Report, released in March 1979, confirmed that suspects had injuries that 'were not self-inflicted and were sustained in police custody'. The publicity forced Mason to implement changes to interrogation procedures, including regular visits by medical officers and closed-circuit TV in interview rooms. Allegations of abuse declined; so did the conviction rate in paramilitary cases.[37]

Beating confessions out of suspects was only one of many approaches available. The RUC would adapt, too. In the meantime, the beatings, Provisional IRA violence, the Shankill Butchers, Paisley's denunciation of unionist sellouts, Dublin's hard line and the SDLP's powerlessness all contributed to a general hardening of attitudes. Tom Fleming's path to the Provisionals, for example, was different from that of most recruits. He was born in Belfast in the 1920s. Unlike the Billy McKees and Joe Cahills of that world, he served in the Royal Navy during the Second World War. In August 1969, teenagers like Joey Surgenor defended their areas and joined the Provisionals. Fleming, in contrast, was in his early forties. He helped displaced families find homes and then became a staffer in the office of the Ardoyne Relief Committee. A few years later, he was a candidate for the Republican Labour Party. Fleming described his later move to Sinn Féin:

From the start of the '69 Troubles, I became actively aware of the place – provocation and oppression of the people in Ardoyne. And, too, I became involved in welfare work as such and [with] families who were displaced from their homes through the Troubles. And from that it has just gradually stemmed from hardening attitudes 'til I became a member of the Republican Movement somewhere in 1978 ...

Q: What was happening in 1978?

A: The civil rights marches, they were earlier. In '78 – '78 was just – gradually that I had become, what I'd say positive in the thinking of the whole general situation and I thought I may as well join the Republican Movement as this was the closest thing to my ideals, and play an active part in it.

Fleming joined the staff of the Sinn Féin advice centre in Ardoyne.[38]

The new recruits joined organizations that were changing. After Operation Motorman, the Provisionals adapted. After the truce, they reorganized. In Long Kesh, Gerry Adams, Ivor Bell, Brendan Hughes and Gerry Kelly were involved in discussions that would have a huge effect on the IRA and Sinn Féin. Brendan Hughes described the discussions:

We actually pushed the education program in the prison on other liberation struggles. '76–'77, myself and Ivor Bell, Gerry Adams ... actually produced a program ... There was a great debate going on within the prison at that period, after the ceasefire period, '76–'77. And we had a massive politicization program going on, especially within Cage Eleven, which is where myself and Gerry Adams were placed. And there was a great debate going on within the prison. It was before that – during the ceasefire period, on the outside and on the inside – there was a debate going on. And I was thinking we were opposed to the ceasefire on the inside. And Gerry was constantly writing articles under the name Brownie, but which were censored, actually [by Republican News] ... They censored his articles at the time ... because he was critical of the ceasefire. This whole debate was going on within the prison. I mean, at one period – and this isn't widely known – I was leaving the Movement and packed my bags to leave Cage Eleven and was going up to Cage Thirteen, which was the INLA cage at the time. And I was talked out of it by Gerry. Gerry convinced me to stay.[39]

The prisoners and the leadership on the outside realized that the British were not leaving and that they were in for a long war. The leadership viewed Gerry Adams as the most strategic thinker of the younger activists. In late 1975 or early 1976, he was asked to develop a reorganization plan.[40]

A 'Staff Report', presumably developed by Adams, with the assistance of Ivor Bell plus input from others, argued that the Provisional IRA had to 'gear ourselves toward a long-term armed struggle'. The report addressed two key issues – RUC interrogation procedures and an outdated organizational structure. The report explained that:

> The three-day and seven-day detention orders are breaking volunteers, and it is the Republican Army's fault for not indoctrinating volunteers with the psychological strength to resist interrogation.
>
> Coupled with this factor, which is contributing to our defeat, we are burdened with an inefficient infrastructure of commands, brigades, battalions and companies. This old system with which Brits and [Special] Branch are familiar has to be changed ... Army men must be in total control of all sections of the movement.[41]

The 'Green Book', a manual for IRA recruits, was developed. The Green Book provided information on Irish republican history, the IRA Constitution and standing orders, the nature of guerrilla war and so on. Arrest, interrogation and torture were addressed in detail. The most important point was to say nothing – 'the best defence is to remain COOL, COLLECTED, CALM, and SAY NOTHING.'[42]

The report proposed moving to four-person cells (active service units), especially in urban areas 'where the biggest proportion of our support lies anyway'. The current battalions and companies would be dissolved and their volunteers placed in either 'operational cells' or the 'civil administration'. The cells would be specialized – 'sniping cells, execution, bombings, robberies, etc'. Finance would be funnelled through the cell leader. A brigade or command area quartermaster would control weapons and explosives.[43] In theory, the cell system would minimize the threat from lower-level agents and people who broke under interrogation; agents at a higher level were still a threat, however.[44] Because the RUC was not acceptable, the 'civil administration' would serve as the local police force and provide punishment-beatings and kneecappings for drug dealers, sex offenders, thieves and thugs. The civil administration would also serve as an employment agency for newly released prisoners, finding them jobs in bars and social clubs, on building sites and as taxi drivers. It also gave the IRA a presence in communities that was independent of the active service units/operational cells.[45]

Another important feature of the reorganization was the creation of Northern and Southern commands between the Army Council and brigade commanders. Northern Command included the six counties of Northern Ireland and the border counties – Louth, Monaghan, Cavan, Leitrim and Donegal. Southern Command covered the rest of the country. The Northern Commanders were almost exclusively Northerners, where the war was fought. Southerners became almost exclusively involved in support activities – importing and hiding weapons, training camps, bomb making, finance/robberies and providing safe houses. With the Northern Command came a change in the leadership's approach. Even when Seán Mac Stiofáin was in charge, the Chief of Staff and GHQ did not micro-manage. Commanders had a great deal of authority and units had a large amount of discretion in choosing operations, especially in the countryside. The Northern Command centralized authority. As Tommy McKearney describes it, 'Northern Command penetrated every crevice of the IRA.' Because some of the Southern leadership positions were filled by Northerners on the run, the Provisional IRA became that much more Northern focused.[46] Northern Command also put the people fighting the war in full control of the Army. It is reported that the Northern Command met for the first time in November 1976 and that Martin McGuinness was the first O/C. The first O/C for the Southern Command is not publicly known.[47]

Histories of this period present young Northerners like Gerry Adams, Martin McGuinness and Ivor Bell as the architects of the reorganization of the Provisional IRA, but that is too simple. Certainly Adams, Bell and McGuinness, along with Brian Keenan, had an important influence on the Movement in the late 1970s. The situation was more complex than the young Northerners simply taking over after the truce, however. Adams and Bell, even if they wrote the 'Staff Report', were in Long Kesh when it was implemented. Seamus Twomey was C/S and

Joe Cahill, Billy McKee and Ruairí Ó Brádaigh were probably on the Army Council. In *A Secret History of the IRA*, journalist Ed Moloney reports that two others on the Council were Martin McGuinness and Brian Keenan, with Keenan serving as Twomey's Adjutant and Director of the England campaign. If this is correct, the old leadership still had a majority. Also, for the senior people, the reorganization would not have been a radical departure. Twomey, Cahill and McKee knew first-hand that the IRA had a Northern Command in the 1940s. Ó Brádaigh was Chief of Staff during the 1950s campaign which started with 'flying columns' and quickly shifted to more efficient 'battle teams' that were, in essence, cells or active service units.

If reports of the Army Council's membership are correct, then Cahill, McKee, Ó Brádaigh and Twomey would have been involved in key decisions like asking Gerry Adams to work on the reorganization plan, the appointment of Martin McGuinness as O/C of Northern Command and asking Pat Ward to work on the Green Book. Gerry Adams was released from Long Kesh in early 1977 and was evidently co-opted onto the Army Council. Twomey, Cahill, McKee and Ó Brádaigh would have been involved in that decision. In an administrative sleight of hand, Twomey could have stepped off the Council and made room for Adams because, as C/S, he would still have been able to attend meetings.[48] Two prominent activists who probably were not directly involved in the reorganization were Dáithí O'Connell and Kevin Mallon. While the Provisionals were reorganizing, they were in Portlaoise leading Martin Ferris, Bobby McNamara and several others on a mass hunger strike. That strike ended after forty-seven days, with no direct concessions from the Fine Gael–Labour coalition government.[49]

Change is difficult for all kinds of organizations, and Ed Moloney also presents the Army Council's reaction to the reorganization. Joe Cahill and Billy McKee were opposed but Seamus Twomey, Brian Keenan and Martin McGuinness supported it. Gerry Adams, presumably, supported the reorganization.[50] If disagreement over the best way forward slowed implementation, changes in the Council probably made it easier to finish the job. In the summer of 1977, there was another Provisional–Official feud in Belfast.[51] Observers report that Gerry Adams was instrumental in calming the situation and then went after Billy McKee, who had not consulted the Army Council before giving the go ahead to attack the Officials. McKee's influence was fading when he developed health problems and stepped off the Council.[52] Then, in December 1977, the Gardaí arrested Seamus Twomey in Dun Laoghaire.[53] It is widely assumed that Gerry Adams succeeded him as Chief of Staff.[54] Who replaced Billy McKee and Seamus Twomey on the Council is unknown, but one possibility is Ivor Bell who was released from Long Kesh in 1977. Bell, presumably, also supported the reorganization.[55]

Not all of the Staff Report's recommendations were implemented. In a move that echoed Cathal Goulding a decade earlier, the report recommended that Cumann na mBan be dissolved with the best women 'incorporated in IRA cells structure and the rest going into Civil and Military administration'.[56] It was an attempt to control women activists and the idea met with resistance. Líta Ní Chathmhaoil described joining Sinn Féin and then Cumann na mBan:

> *I joined Sinn Féin in 1970, and very soon I realized I wanted to become more involved, and I joined Cumann na mBan at that time.*

Q: Why is it important that there's a separate women's organization?

A: I think it's important from the point of view that women tend to become subsumed — well at that particular time women's role was more subservient than it would be now [2009]. Women were only just kind of standing up and being counted. And I think it was always important for the Republican Movement that women had a separate voice and could stand up for themselves because, even now, I think that women in the male military organization are very much at the mercy of their male counterparts. And I would rather, as a woman, have my own voice and be able to make it known.

Q: Why — this may be an obvious question — but why would women be at the mercy of their male counterparts?

A: Well, I suppose it is an obvious question but, at the same time, it's thousands of years of conditioning, isn't it? That women are … not up to that kind of thing and they're only suited for doing certain jobs. Also, my experience has been that some people use them as a sort of a cover rather than as a partner, you know? Like women are used to go somewhere with a man or something like that, that they wouldn't be given equal status … It's not really intentional in many cases, and with many men in the Republican Movement, it wouldn't happen at all, but there was an element there, especially in the seventies, that tended to treat women as a cover really rather than in a partnership.[57]

Between 1969 and 1978, six Cumann na mBan volunteers died in premature explosions. Every one of them was killed alongside a male Provisional IRA volunteer. According to another activist, the male-dominated Provisionals benefitted from a women's organization:

where they [women] can go when they have complaints and get them dealt with if these Army men were abusive to them in any way, shape or form or thought they [were special] and the girls [were] put down or made to feel small. They also — [Cumann na mBan] would take up their complaints and would deal with it and get it resolved … if the girls felt that at some stage that [something was] risky … [and] they had voiced their opinion within the cell, [but] the cell wouldn't listen. Cumann na mBan could go to the Army and they could go and listen to the girl about the operation.

The Cumann na mBan Executive turned down the Staff Report recommendation and they remained a separate organization. But, because it was seen as the more elite organization, some women left for the Provisional IRA. The final Cumann na mBan volunteer killed on active service was Rosemary Bleakley who, along with IRA volunteer Martin McDonagh, was killed in a premature explosion on 13 January 1976. The two Provisional IRA women killed on active service after 1976 were Mairéad Farrell, who was killed with Dan McCann and Seán Savage in Gibraltar (1988), and Patricia Black, who was killed with Frankie Ryan in England (1991).[58]

Tables 2 and 3 show how the reorganization influenced the Provisional IRA.[59] In 1972, the Provisional IRA killed 130 members of the security forces, including 95 British soldiers. Then, the number of security forces killed declined for three straight years, especially with the truce in

TABLE 2

Political Violence Northern Ireland, 1969–80

	Persons Killed	Persons Killed by Provisional IRA	Security Forces Killed by PIRA	British Soldiers killed by PIRA	Shootings	Explosions
1969	14	0	0	0	73	9
1970	25	15	2	0	213	153
1971	174	89	56	40	1,756	1,022
1972	470	243	130	95	10,631	1,382
1973	252	128	75	55	5,019	978
1974	220	140	63	43	3,208	685
1975	247	103	31	14	1,803	399
1976	297	150	50	13	1,908	766
1977	112	70	31	15	1,081	366
1978	81	56	30	14	755	455
1979	113	93	59	38	728	422
1980	76	45	27	9	642	280

1975. In 1976, the number of security forces killed increased, but it fell again in 1977 and was steady in 1978. The large increase in 1979 is attributed to one incident, eighteen British soldiers killed at Warrenpoint. In 1980, the number of security forces killed by the Provisional IRA was its lowest level in a decade. The influence of Ulsterization is also seen in Table 2. Of the sixty-three members of the security forces that the Provisional IRA killed in 1974, forty-three of them were soldiers. Of the fifty members of the security forces killed in 1976, only thirteen of them were soldiers. Ulsterization helped isolate the conflict to Northern Ireland and made it appear sectarian.

Information that is specific only to Provisional IRA shootings and bombings is not available. However, the Provisionals were the most active paramilitary organization in these years and changes in the level of their violence are reflected in the annual counts. Shootings and explosions peaked in 1972, fell steadily through 1975 and then increased in 1976. In 1977, the number of shootings and explosions decreased and continued to decline to 1980. The tables show that the reorganization led to a significant decrease in IRA activity. A benefit of less activity was that the Provisional IRA needed fewer volunteers and new recruits.

The introduction of Northern Command, the cell structure and the Green Book's stress on saying nothing made the Provisional IRA more secure and more efficient. Table 3 shows that, in the early years, one member of the security forces was killed for every seventy-four incidents (shootings and explosions). In 1975 and 1976, one member of the security forces was killed for every fifty-nine incidents. Between 1977 and 1980, the Provisional IRA killed one member of the

TABLE 3

Northern Ireland Incidents (Shootings and Explosions) and Security Force Deaths, 1969–88

Year	Number of Incidents	Security Force Deaths	Ratio Security Deaths: Incidents
1969	82	1	1:82
1970	366	2	1:183
1971	2,778	59	1:47
1972	12,013	148	1:81
1973	5,997	79	1:76
1974	3,893	52	1:75
Subtotal	**25,129**	**341**	**1:74**
1975	2,202	31	1:71
1976	2,674	52	1:51
Subtotal	**4,876**	**83**	**1:59**
1977	1,447	43	1:34
1978	1,210	31	1:39
1979	1,150	62	1:19
1980	922	26	1:35
Subtotal	**4,729**	**162**	**1:29**
1981	1,540	44	1:35
1982	766	40	1:19
1983	690	33	1:21
1984	527	28	1:19
1985	386	29	1:13
1986	564	24	1:23
1987	910	27	1:34
1988	791	39	1:20
Subtotal	**6,174**	**264**	**1:23**
1969–1988	**40,908**	**850**	**1:48**

security forces for every twenty-nine incidents. There were fewer incidents, but they were more deadly for the security forces.

The cell structure and scaling back the bombing campaign also made the Provisional IRA safer. In 1976, fifteen volunteers died in explosions or were shot dead by the security forces – one volunteer was killed on active service for every 178 incidents (2,674/15). In contrast, between 1977 and 1980, one volunteer was killed on active service for every 295 incidents (4,729/16).[60]

The tables show that the truce was not a disaster for the Provisional IRA. The years 1974 and 1976 represent the twelve months before the truce (but include the ceasefire from 22 December to 31 December 1974) and the first full year after the truce. In 1974, the Provisional IRA killed fewer people (140) than they did in 1976 (150). And in 1976, they killed fewer members of the security forces (fifty) than they did in 1974 (sixty-three). But the figures for the two years are not dramatically different. In 1977, after the reorganization, shootings, explosions, and persons killed declined dramatically. It was not the truce but the reorganization that caused the decrease in Provisional IRA operations. For activists who had experienced the highs of 1972, especially for the young Northerners who had been active in the war zone, the dramatic decrease in operations probably did contribute to a perception that the truce hurt the Provisional IRA.

The British immediately recognized the importance of the reorganization. A British Army intelligence document, dated 2 November 1978, was intercepted and leaked to the press. According to, 'NORTHERN IRELAND: FUTURE TERRORIST TRENDS':

> The Provisionals cannot attract the large numbers of active terrorists they had in 1972/73. But they no longer need them. PIRA's organization is now such that a small number of activists can maintain a disproportionate level of violence. There is a substantial pool of young Fianna aspirants, nurtured in a climate of violence, eagerly seeking promotion to full gun-carrying terrorist status and there is a steady release from the prisons of embittered and dedicated terrorists ...
>
> *Popular Support.* Republican terrorists can no longer bring crowds of active sympathizers onto the streets at will as a screen for gunmen. Indeed there is seldom much support even for traditional protest marches. But by reorganising on cellular lines PIRA has become less dependent on public support than in the past and is less vulnerable to penetration by informers ...

The document's conclusion begins with, 'The Provisionals' campaign of violence is likely to continue while the British remain in Northern Ireland ...'[61]

The good news for the Provisionals was that the reorganization was a success and they could probably continue the 'Long War' forever. The bad news was that the war might last forever.

11

STALEMATE (1978–1980)

You'd just be waking up there in the morning to – nothing really. And all you had was a cell. There'd probably be two in the cell. The cell was filthy. You would have a lump of sponge as your mattress and three blankets.

– Gerry Hodgins[1]

When Seamus Twomey was arrested in December 1977, the Provisional IRA's reorganization was well underway if not complete. The arrest was one of a series of changes that put the young Northerners in charge of a reorganized Provisional IRA that could pursue a 'long war'.

Continuing forever was very different from winning. The 'Staff Report' also suggested developing a new front – politics:

> Sinn Féin should be radicalized (under Army direction) and should agitate about social and economic issues which attack the welfare of the people. SF should be directed to infiltrate other organizations to win support for, and sympathy to, the movement. SF should be re-educated and have a big role to play in publicity and propaganda depts., complaints and problems (making no room for RUC opportunism). It gains the respect of the people which in turn leads to increased support for the cell.[2]

The 'Brownie' articles that Gerry Adams wrote for *Republican News* would become synonymous with the call for Sinn Féin to become more political.

An article entitled, 'The Ard Fheis', for example, describes a Sinn Féin convention in Long Kesh. 'Brownie' writes of a motion from Brendan Hughes that 'Sinn Féin organize a massive agitation campaign in the Free State and that they affiliate themselves with all anti-state groups.' Kevin 'Dee' Delaney seconded the motion and put forward an 'impassioned attack on the social, economic, and political policies being implemented by the constitutional parties in Leinster House'.[3] Brownie urged the development of class politics and he defended armed struggle.

Danny Lennon was released from Cage Eleven in the spring of 1976. That summer he was shot dead by the British Army while transporting a rifle. The car he was driving continued on and hit Anne Maguire and her children. She was severely injured and three of the children were killed. The press, in a standard response to tragedy, condemned the 'men of violence', but there

Funeral of Bobby Sands, MP, 7 May 1981. Members of the Sands family, including his young son, are pictured. Courtesy of Val Lynch.

Danny Devenny's iconic mural of Bobby Sands, a tourist attraction on the gable wall of Sinn Féin's Falls Road offices, with two famous quotations: 'Everyone, Republican or otherwise has their own particular role to play' and '… Our revenge will be the laughter of our children'. © Robert White.

Gerry Adams in front of a Falls Road mural, 1980s. Bobbie Hanvey photographic archives, John J. Burns Library, Boston College.

Mitchel McLaughlin addressing a 'Peace Talks Now' rally, Navan, County Meath, 22 July 1995. Seated is Joe Reilly. © Robert White (from video of the event).

Gerry Adams and Richard McAuley, Easter Commemoration, Dublin, 2006. In 2004, authorship of the famous 'Brownie' article admitting membership in the IRA was attributed to McAuley; most observers assume the author was Gerry Adams. © Robert White.

Revd Ian Paisley and Martin McGuinness, the 'Chuckle Brothers', February 2008. Dara Mac Dónaill, *Irish Times*.

Fourteen Sinn Féin Teachtá Dála (TDs) at Dáil Éireann/Leinster House, February 2011. Centre: Gerry Adams. Front row from left: Seán Crowe, Caoimhghín Ó Caoláin, Mary Lou McDonald, Sandra McLellan, Brian Stanley, Peadar Tóibín. Second row from left: Aengus Ó Snodaigh, Pádraig Mac Lochlainn, Michael Colreavy, Dessie Ellis, Pearse Doherty, Jonathan O'Brien, Martin Ferris. Cyril Byrne, *Irish Times*.

From 'Provisional' Sinn Féin to 'New' Sinn Féin: Dublin Councillor Cathleen Carney Boud (in 1916 period dress and hat), Sinn Féin Vice President Mary Lou McDonald, and Sinn Féin President Gerry Adams sing 'Amhrán na bhFiann' ('The Soldiers' Song') at the conclusion of ceremonies at Arbour Hill, Sinn Féin 'Lost Leaders March', 25 March 2016. © Robert White.

Seán Crowe, TD. Sinn Féin 'Lost Leaders March', from Kilmainham Gaol to Arbour Hill, Dublin, part of the 100th anniversary of the Easter Rising commemorations, 25 March 2016. © Robert White.

Part of a Sinn Féin poster at their 'Cumann na mBan 100th Anniversary Celebration'. Wynn's Hotel (where Cumann na mBan was founded), Dublin, 2 April 2014. The poster repeats Sinn Féin's claim that Cumann na mBan ceased to exist in the 1980s. © Robert White.

Ruairí Ó Brádaigh funeral, 8 June 2013. St Coman's Cemetery, Roscommon Town. Peig King (back to the camera) and Cecilia Conway (facing forward) of Cumann na mBan fold the Irish national flag (tricolour) to present it to the Ó Brádaigh family. © Robert White.

Josephine Hayden, in Cumann na mBan uniform and flanked by a colour party of the republican movement, Republican Sinn Féin Annual Wolfe Tone Commemoration, Bodenstown, June 2015. © Robert White.

was also an unexpected groundswell of outrage coupled with a widespread desire for peace. Betty Williams, a housewife in Andersonstown, Mairead Corrigan, Anne Maguire's sister, and Ciaran McKeown, a journalist and experienced community worker, organized the 'Peace People'. Rallies for peace drew thousands of people and crossed the Catholic/Protestant divide.

'Brownie' wrote an eloquent response to the events, 'In Defence of Danny Lennon'. He expressed sympathy for the Maguire and Lennon families, and described Danny Lennon:

> Like us all he made mistakes but he was a good young man, a socialist by instinct and an IRA operator by choice. He wanted an Ireland free of the profit-motive, free of fighting, free from sectarianism and free from violence. He did not fight for some outdated ideal, some abstract thing: he fought for a society in which the Irish people could be truly a sovereign people.[4]

The Peace People was a short-lived phenomenon.[5] Only days after the Maguire children were killed, 12-year-old Majella O'Hare was shot in the back and killed by a British soldier in South Armagh. The Peace People did not organize protests and the soldier was subsequently acquitted of manslaughter. The reluctance to condemn state violence left some nationalists wary. Ironically, when Betty Williams and Mairead Corrigan were awarded the Nobel Peace Prize in 1977, they lost more support. Instead of putting the award back into their organization, they kept the funds. As for Brownie, in one of his more interesting columns he wrote, 'Rightly or wrongly, I am an IRA Volunteer and, rightly or wrongly, I take a course of action as a means to bringing about a situation in which I believe the people of my country will prosper.' That would come back to haunt and, years later, Adams's long-term aide Richard McAuley would take credit for that column.[6]

The call for more politics was made public at the 1977 Wolfe Tone Commemoration. The keynote speaker was Jimmy Drumm, Máire's widower. His speech is viewed as a watershed for two reasons: he acknowledged that the British were not going to withdraw and he argued that the Provisionals had to combine armed struggle with revolutionary politics. Only later was it revealed that Gerry Adams and Danny Morrison wrote the speech, which included the following:

> We find that a successful war of national liberation cannot be fought exclusively on the backs of the oppressed in the 6 counties, nor around the physical presence of the British army. Hatred and resentment of this army cannot sustain the war, and the isolation of socialist Republicans around the armed struggle is dangerous and has produced at least in some circles the reformist notion that 'Ulster' is the issue, which can somehow be resolved without the mobilisation of the working class in the 26 counties ... The British Government is NOT withdrawing from the 6 counties ...

Drumm's speech is often portrayed as a bridge between two distinct periods in the history of Provisional Irish republicanism – the apolitical early years when Sinn Féin was a support group and the post-truce era when people like Gerry Adams, Danny Morrison, Tom Hartley and

Mitchel McLaughlin brought politics to the Provisionals and began the transformation of Sinn Féin into a political party.[7]

It was an important speech, but other than acknowledging the British were not leaving, much of the content was not new. The Provisionals were declared socialists from their beginning. As early as 1972, Ruairí Ó Brádaigh and Dáithí O'Connell had warned that armed struggle alone would not force a British withdrawal. They had tried to build Sinn Féin into a political force and, in spite of censorship and harassment, there were twenty-six Sinn Féin councillors in the South. That number paled when compared to Fianna Fáil and Fine Gael; but if Sinn Féin was not engaged in politics, then what were people like Frank Glynn, Seán Lynch and John Joe McGirl doing as county councillors and why were voters re-electing them? O'Connell and Ó Brádaigh had developed and promoted a political programme, Éire Nua, that offered an Irish solution to the conflict.

In response to Drumm's speech, an editorial in the *Belfast Telegraph* asked a fundamental question, 'If the British are not going and if the Provisionals need mass working-class support, what is the point of the campaign of violence? How can they engage loyalists in dialogue when they are shooting them down?'[8] The answer was the social and economic programme and federalism of Éire Nua – often lost in the discussion of Drumm's speech is his praise for the programme: 'We are continually accused of having been devoid of political thinking, dependent entirely upon the bullet and bomb – so once again – We were the very first to issue a comprehensive policy that embraces all 32 counties, a policy that we are certain, if enforced, would lead to a just and lasting peace.'

It seemed that no one noticed Éire Nua.

In *Republican Voices*, by Kevin Bean and Mark Hayes, Tommy McKearney comments on the political debate in the 1970s:

> I remember Ruairí Ó Brádaigh or Dáithí O'Connell asking me (and probably others) whether it was feasible to run Kevin Mallon as a local councillor in Tyrone. To be honest we didn't think much of it; in fact we didn't even think it was possible!
>
> Yet politics existed without having parliamentary politics. Parliamentary politics was not on our agenda in those early years. The anti-H-Block pro-blanket men protests were the type of politics we would have paid attention to. Lobbying, leafleting, action campaigns being set up and so on, even street dramas were part of the campaign. How can this be described as non-political?[9]

Sinn Féin was a political organization, even if some Provisionals didn't notice, or care.

In the early years, because they believed victory was just around the corner, politics and Sinn Féin were unimportant for many Provisionals. In *Ardoyne: The Untold Truth*, a comrade described Paul Marlowe, who was killed in the attack at the Belfast gas works: 'Paul was very politically aware but he had no time for politicians. His idea was to get the war finished first and keep as many volunteers alive as possible. There would be time for politics after that.'[10] The 'Year of Victory' came and went and the teenage recruits of the 1969–74 era became seasoned veterans. Some of them wondered why they had not won the war. Gerry Adams, Danny Morrison, Tom

Hartley, Mitchel McLaughlin et al. gave them an answer – they were not political enough. The answer was not new but what was new was the messenger.

In spite of a decade's worth of violence, public opinion polls showed that the call for more political engagement might actually resonate with voters North and South. A 1978 political opinion survey found that 72 per cent of the respondents in the Republic of Ireland were 'anti-partition' and that almost 68 per cent of them saw a united Ireland as the 'most Workable and Acceptable' solution to the Northern Ireland problem. In the Northern Ireland Attitude Survey (NIAS), collected at the same time, 39 per cent of nationalists identified some form of a united Ireland as the 'Most Workable and Acceptable Solution' to the problem.[11] Transforming sympathy for a united Ireland into votes for Sinn Féin would not be easy, however.

In the South, most people avoided Northern Ireland.[12] And for those Southern voters who were interested in Northern Ireland, Fianna Fáil had been courting them for decades, especially when they were out of power. In the debate on the Emergency Powers Bill (1976), Jack Lynch described it as 'unnecessary and dangerous'. In the same speech, however, he denounced the Provisionals as, 'enemies of cooperation between the people of Northern Ireland within the North and between the North and South, and the enemies of the genuinely held national aspirations of the great majority of the Irish people towards the unity of our people'. Fianna Fáil's status as the 'Republican Party' continued to play well with the electorate and, in an election just after Jimmy Drumm's speech, they were returned to power with Lynch as Taoiseach. In power, of course, Lynch did not seek the repeal of the Emergency Powers Bill and his government retained the media ban on Sinn Féin that had been instituted by Conor Cruise O'Brien. The election is also noteworthy because the new cabinet included Charlie Haughey as Minister for Health and Social Welfare. It was an amazing comeback for a politician who had been accused of running guns to terrorists. According to Jack Lynch, Haughey had 'purged whatever indiscretion he was involved in'.[13]

In the North, Sinn Féin faced enormous obstacles. It was an all-Ireland party, but Southern leaders like Ruairí Ó Brádaigh, Dáithí O'Connell and John Joe McGirl were excluded and could not openly cross the border to help organize things.[14] There was also a price to be paid for Provisional IRA blunders. In February 1978, a firebomb at the La Mon House restaurant in County Down claimed twelve lives and injured dozens more. The Provisional IRA admitted that their warnings were 'inadequate'. One of the warning calls was received *after* the bomb went off. Gerry Fitt referred to the bombers as 'depraved animals'[15] and the RUC went after Sinn Féin.

Gerry Adams and nineteen others were arrested. In Adams's case, he was shown photos of the La Mon victims but not physically mistreated in Castlereagh. After seven days, he was charged with membership, denied bail and sent to Long Kesh to await trial. It was common for republicans neither to confirm nor deny membership of the IRA. That way, the suspect did not recognize the court and gave the authorities no information. The approach often ended in a conviction. Adams denied the membership charge and threatened to sue Belfast newspapers describing him as a senior figure in the Provisional IRA. With justification, Sinn Féin claimed he was the victim of a 'Show Trial'. The evidence against him included quotations from the 'Brownie' articles, the fact he had been in Cage 11 and a speech he gave to the 1977 Ard Fheis. It took six months, but the charges were dismissed.[16]

The RUC tried to shut down *Republican News*. The office was raided and staff members went on the run. Delivery drivers and the printer were arrested. At one point, the Belfast Officer Board of Sinn Féin and the editorial staff of *Republican News* was in jail and yet they still published the paper.[17] The RUC caught up with Danny Morrison in the autumn of 1978. He described what happened:

> *I was on the run in '78 when the British government tried to close down* Republican News. *It kept raiding the office, seizing copies of the paper, raiding the printers in Lurgan owned by ... a member of the SDLP. They actually arrested that man and charged him with IRA membership and conspiracy – which, you know, he was completely innocent. He was just a businessman. But this is the extent they went to intimidate people from publishing us. And I was eventually arrested. I got arrested the day that Adams got out. Adams had been charged with IRA membership from the night of La Mon, in February '78 and I had been on the run until the 29th of September '78. That was the day he got out. And I was coming from his press conference when [I was caught by] undercover people who had been following a friend of mine ... So, I got charged with IRA membership, conspiracy.*[18]

The evidence against Morrison included IRA statements in his handwriting. His defence was that they were part of his work as editor of *Republican News*.

At Morrison's bail hearing, he noticed that the police had also picked up a statement from loyalists that was in his handwriting. The statement was for an article he was writing for *The Irish People*, the Irish American paper. Considering the evidence, Morrison asked why he had not also been charged with membership of the Ulster Volunteer Force. The judge put the question to the prosecutor who replied, 'Don't be ridiculous.' Morrison had a point and the judge granted him bail. The attempt to suppress *Republican News* actually backfired. Danny Morrison again:

> *Up until 1978, I never used my name. If you were coming to me as a journalist, you wouldn't know who I was. I'd always give you a false name. But once we were charged and came out of court, I then started to say, 'My name's Danny Morrison. I'm the editor of* Republican News.' *Tom Hartley would say, 'I'm the manager of* Republican News.' *Other members would turn to them and say, 'I'm in charge of publicity.' 'I'm spokesperson on housing', right? And suddenly, as a result of the Brits trying to close us down, it forced us into a public stance. And now we started to put a public face on the Movement in the North which had been missing for several years, because Máire Drumm had been assassinated in 1976, Seamus McCusker had been assassinated in 1975.*

The charges against Morrison were withdrawn.

In the background, the prisoners in Long Kesh and Armagh suffered. Almost two years into the blanket protest, the outside world knew relatively little about the culture of resistance they were creating. Confined behind a cell door, they communicated with each other by shouting back and forth from their cells.[19] In order to limit eavesdropping, they taught themselves Irish. And yet, Bobby Sands was already beginning a publicity campaign that would put Long Kesh at the centre of the Movement. On his own initiative, Sands decided to parallel the Brownie articles and write about the blanket protest. Using a ballpoint pen refill and writing on toilet paper, his first article was entitled, 'On the Blanket'. It was dated 23 October 1977, smuggled out of Long Kesh through a visit with his mother and then published in *Republican News*. Sands wrote, 'We are all Republican Prisoners-Of-War here, and there is nothing that the Prison Authorities, the Northern Ireland Office, or the British government can say or do to change this.'[20]

In the spring of 1978, an important change came when Brendan Hughes was convicted of rioting and assault. Hughes lost his special category status and was transferred from the 'Cages' of Long Kesh to the cells of the H-Blocks. He went from being 'Mister Hughes' to '704 Hughes'. He was twenty-nine years old, and five to ten years older than most of the blanketmen who saw him as a kind of elder statesman. With an endorsement from the outside leadership and the support of the prisoners, Hughes became their O/C. His first suggestion was that they end the blanket protest, cooperate with the administration and then wreck the prison system from within. They respected Hughes, but after two years of principled protest, they turned him down. Most of the prisoners refused to take visits. Hughes's second suggestion was that they start taking them.[21]

The trade-off for having to put on the prison uniform for a visit was more contact with the outside world, which was largely limited to visits from priests and the occasional court appearance. By meeting with people they trusted, the prisoners were able to exchange 'comms' with GHQ – messages written on cigarette or toilet paper and wrapped tightly in tin foil. Depending upon the prisoner and the visitor, a quick kiss or a brief embrace would also send in a pen, tobacco and cigarette papers that were quickly tucked away in prisoners' rectums. They even managed to smuggle in the parts for a small crystal radio.

The authorities caught on and introduced the 'mirror search'. Prisoners were forced to bend over and have their anuses searched. The prisoners resisted, the guards became more aggressive and the conflict escalated. When prisoners left their cells to go to the toilet or take a shower, the warders tried to force them to put on pants. Prisoners refused and were beaten. Finally, Brendan Hughes ordered them to stay in their cells and they began a 'no wash' protest. The prisoners broke the cell windows and tossed out their excrement. They poured their urine under the door. The authorities replaced the broken windows with Perspex and pushed the urine back into the cells with rubber brooms. The prisoners then smeared their excrement on the cell walls. Prison warders poured undiluted disinfectant into the cells.[22]

In the spring of 1978, Bobby Sands was placed in a cell adjacent to Brendan Hughes. One of the most important decisions Hughes would make was to ask Sands to serve as his Public Relations Officer. Sands began editing statements that Hughes sent out on behalf of the prisoners and they developed a close relationship. Sands would also make his own important contribution to prison literature. On cigarette papers and toilet paper, he wrote poems, including the ninety-six verse 'The Crime of Castlereagh'. His book *One Day in My Life* was folded like an accordion and hidden up his backside. Under the pen name 'Marcella' – his sister's name – Sands's articles for *Republican News* gave the public a direct line into Long Kesh. Sands also wrote letters to social and political leaders who might aid the cause.[23]

One of Sands's letters, in Irish, went to Tomás Ó Fiaich, the Archbishop of Armagh. As a member of the clergy, Ó Fiaich was entitled to visit his parishioners and, in the summer of 1978, he visited the prisoners, condemning their conditions the next day:

Having spent the whole of Sunday in the prison, I was shocked at the inhuman conditions prevailing in H-Blocks 3, 4, and 5, where over 300 prisoners were incarcerated. One would hardly allow an animal to remain in such conditions, let alone a human being. The nearest approach to it that I have seen was the spectacle of hundreds of homeless people living in sewer pipes in the slums of Calcutta. The stench and filth in some cells, with the remains of rotten food and human excreta scattered around the walls, was almost unbelievable. In two of them I was unable to speak for fear of vomiting.[24]

The statement boosted morale but did not change the conditions. In an interview reprinted in *The Pensive Quill*, Thomas 'Dixie' Elliott commented:

I was in the cell with Tom McElwee during the winter of '78, where we nearly froze to death. It was when they started forced washing. The thing that stands out for me was when it was coming up to Christmas '78. Tom was a hard man and he said 'look if these screws start hitting us, I'm going to hit back'. I said no problem I'll hit back too. They took us to a clean wing where one of the screws started poking me and Tom with scissors. We both looked at each other and just started hitting. They battered us, nearly killed us and threw us in the back of a wagon, naked and sent us to the boards where we were put on a no.1 diet of bread and water, which was a starvation punishment.[25]

On the outside, the Provisional IRA attacked prison warders. The victims included Albert Miles, deputy governor of the Maze, and prison officer Agnes Wallace, shot outside Armagh Gaol.[26]

The war was in the North, the prison crisis was in the North and the IRA's leadership was firmly rooted in the North. Observers report that when Gerry Adams was arrested, Martin McGuinness took over as C/S and Ivor Bell became Northern Commander. When Brian Keenan was arrested in March 1979, Kevin Mallon became Director of Operations.[27] The young Northerners set their sights on Sinn Féin. They began with a merger of *Republican News* and *An Phoblacht*. Danny Morrison described *Republican News* at the time:

unfortunately for An Phoblacht, *because of its geographical location, our war news was up to date and intimate because we had access to the IRA on the ground. We could go to the IRA in Belfast and they would tell us, 'Well, that bomb was 900 pounds. This is how the device was armed. This was how many volunteers were involved in planting it. There were so many shots fired. These were the weapons that were used.' Right? So, we were getting all this very sexy type information – very sharp news approach – whereas* An Phoblacht *was getting it like two weeks later because they weren't Northern based ... from '76–'77 onwards, we were covering the H-Blocks, the blanket protest, the beatings in Castlereagh. I mean we really, really went past the law. We were libeling people all over the place ... But we didn't care because our resources couldn't be traced. What were they going to do? When they did raid the office, when the British Army or the RUC did raid our office on the Falls Road, they took our telex machine, which was like a huge machine about the size of that chest of drawers and they fucked it out the window into the back of a lorry. It didn't belong to us. We were renting it ... none of our machinery was owned. And what were they going to do? I didn't own a house. Was an RUC man going to sue us?*

Early in 1979, Deasún Breatnach indicated he wanted to step down as editor of *An Phoblacht*. Morrison explained what happened next:

> *I had argued at leadership level that the papers should merge and that was agreed. There had been people who had opposed the merger – people in the North, sound people, like Marie Moore for example. Marie thought that* Republican News *was a better paper than* An Phoblacht *and that in merging with* An Phoblacht *it would lose its identity. Other people didn't like the idea of losing the name* Republican News. *There was no name decided upon. All that was left for the future. And what actually happened was that I was called down to Dublin ... My sense of the meeting was that Ruairí [Ó Brádaigh] and Dave [O'Connell] thought or felt that they could have put Dave in as editor, right? ... Because that was the way the meeting was going and Deasún wasn't prepared to stay on. So, I spoke to Mick Timothy ... the business manager of* An Phoblacht *– a very efficient manager. And he was sort of an ally of mine – fed me what the politics were, what was going on ... Dave thought and Ruairí thought that* Republican News *and* An Phoblacht *wouldn't be merging for maybe another six months to a year. And I got the sense that they were – as I said, Dave would be in charge of it, he would look after it. And I just cut the ground from under him. And I said, 'That's okay. The papers are merging next week.' And I did it.*

Because of the dynamics in the Movement at that time, Morrison had the authority to make the decision. The balance of power had shifted. Morrison again:

> *I could see that they were taken aback and that it was another, in a sense, loss for them. And the papers merged. And then the talk became that the* Republican News *had taken over* An Phoblacht *because what I did was I brought my entire editorial staff in Belfast on board, including the designer people, and* An Phoblacht, *at that stage, didn't really have a full-time staff.*[28]

The first issue, on 27 January 1979, had the headline, 'Out of the Ashes'. The merger was part of a general challenge led by the younger people.

Gerry Adams, Danny Morrison, Tom Hartley and others pushed Sinn Féin to the left. One proposal called for the elimination of all private property in Ireland. Several of the younger people were opposed to federalism, a key element of Éire Nua. Danny Morrison commented:

> *We were quite aggressive. You know, in retrospect I can understand the sense of hurt that people like Ruairí and Dave had because they were doing their best and then you had these newcomers – not newcomers because we were around for ten years before that – but, we thought we had all the answers. We had pails of energy, full of ideas, prepared to borrow; we were quite eclectic in the political ideas that we had. We wouldn't have been tied totally into the traditional republican orthodoxy. We were interested in the left-wing politics in England and Europe, movements in America.*[29]

In 1979, the Army Council withdrew its support for federalism and created a situation in which Sinn Féin policy was not in sync with IRA policy. At the Sinn Féin Ard Fheis (held in January 1980), the younger people challenged federalism, which they believed was unrealistic. Morrison discussed this:

As far as I could see there was no demand for a parliament in Leinster, Munster and Connaught ... Why complicate your basic political demand? It was unnecessary baggage. Now there could be an argument for regionalization, of course, and there is but this cumbersome structure of four provincial parliaments feeding into a national parliament – we had enough trouble on our hands maintaining an armed struggle, a political struggle. We had the H-Block/blanket protest, the women in Armagh Jail. We were trying to raise resources to fight the struggle. We were constantly losing people. People were getting killed. People were going to jail. And then to talk about something that the bulk of the membership in the North were saying, 'Huh? What's this?'... from a very early stage I just – I didn't warm to the Éire Nua policy. And I wasn't in a minority at that.[30]

Ruairí Ó Brádaigh, Dáithí O'Connell and Richard Behal led the defence of federalism, but the fact that Sinn Féin's political programme was under attack from within was another sign that things were changing.

It didn't help Ó Brádaigh and company that stalwart supporters like Joe Clarke (1976) and Larry Grogan (1979) passed away from natural causes. Christine Ní Elias, a strong advocate for Éire Nua, was smeared as a British agent and left. A byproduct of the Elias situation was that Walter Lynch, party secretary since the 1970 Caretaker Executive, quit.[31]

The senior people suspected that the young Northerners were intentionally being extreme in order to force them out. At the same time, the move to the left made the party more attractive for others not interested in the traditional approach. A veteran of People's Democracy who was involved in left-wing groups through much of the 1970s became more interested in Sinn Féin. He commented:

I came to republicanism in a somewhat circuitous fashion in so far as – like many people of my generation, I was essentially sort of left. Initially my politics were much more left-leaning than reflected in the Republican Movement at the time. So I would have been involved in more left organizations within Belfast and then, as Sinn Féin became more to reflect politics on the ground and to adopt more a libertarian, left wing stance, then I became interested in Sinn Féin ...

Q: Okay. Would you be from a republican family?

A: Emphatically not ...

Q: When you got involved, what was your goal for the Movement?

A: I think when I became involved I was anxious that the left-leaning and progressive elements within republicanism should be supported. And in becoming involved in Sinn Féin I was very much – I saw myself very much as being part of that left-leaning progressive element within republicanism. My goal was to ensure that that situation continued – that the Republican Movement would not become an elitist military organization or not slip back into being an elitist military organization – that republicanism should reflect the politics of people on the ground, politics of the communities – of the communities from which they came, and that they evolved a political strategy which had meaning for those groups ... it was a case of having gone through other political organizations and sort of worked my way steadily towards it. When I became involved in republican politics, it was still not a left-wing organization. There were still elements of the organization which I had difficulty with. The backward-looking, green nationalist, parochial, Catholic aspect of republicanism was still very much around. And I had difficulties with that. So no particular individual influenced me, but the evolution of individuals, both members of the IRA and members of the Republican Movement who were clearly not from that perspective in life, would have influenced me ... it was the beginning of that period of republicanism where you no longer felt it necessary to hark back to the sort of pioneer pin-wearing, Gael-Irish speaking group who, I presume, had kept the Republican Movement going when it wasn't very fashionable. And certainly it was that aspect of republicanism that I found most difficult to deal with. I wanted a progressive, active and politicized Republican Movement.[32]

In contrast to the typical teenage recruit who suffered from RUC and British Army harassment, this respondent was older and much more politically aware.

Of course, state violence was still an important source of younger and less politically-minded recruits. This respondent, from Derry, was seventeen when he joined in the late 1970s:

The reason why I got involved was because the brother, my brother, was arrested in the late 1970s and he was sentenced, he got a life sentence, you know? And it was just, I knew a few people that was already in Sinn Féin and it was just, more or less, talking to them and getting to know them better and all that ....

His brother's arrest and conviction, whether or not they were justified, were part of a general pattern of repression that affected him and his fellow working-class nationalists:

the Brits raided the house, you see, about twelve times in two weeks. Like, they usually hit the house every week, one or two times. But I remember one time we were all sitting on the house and the brother – he was sitting on our hedges. It was a good day and he was sitting out on the copper fence in the garden and the Brits came along. There was a wee black Brit that just pushed him over the hedge then, you know? Then they lifted him and they lifted my Mom. Half the street was out then. There was murder in the street. But they did harass us a lot ... there's people in these towns that have never been p-checked by a Brit. They have never been stopped by a Brit. [A p-check is] when the Brits stop you and ask you for all your personal – like what's your name, your date of birth, all that there. I'd say there's people in this town that doesn't even know what it's like ... the people that I'd be talking about there is the people that come from, say, middle class to upper class families.[33]

Nowhere was the repression more evident than in the H-Blocks.

In January 1979, the prison authorities tried to break the blanketmen by isolating their leaders. They seriously underestimated the solidarity that would be generated by bringing together a group of committed activists who shared hardship. For nine months, a group of prisoners which included Brendan Hughes, Bobby Sands, Bik McFarlane, Paddy Quinn, Laurence McKeown, Gerry Hodgins, Pat McGeown, 'Dixie' Elliott, Jake Jackson, Larry Marley, Ricky O'Rawe and Seanna Walsh were together in H-Block 6. Instead of being isolated, they were able to communicate more easily and their camaraderie and commitment was increased. The move also enhanced their status. When the group members were finally redistributed to other blocks, they were welcomed as leaders, elites. In Laurence McKeown's *Out of Time: Irish Republican Prisoners, Long Kesh 1972–2000*, Anthony McIntyre comments, 'I had a sense of relief when the men in H6 were reintegrated into the rest of the camp. I felt the Blocks were being strengthened. H6 had become an intellectual nucleus within the jail. Men had learnt from their debates and the standard of Gaelige [Irish] was high.'[34] The blanketmen were better organized and their leaders were more committed. They were also considering a hunger strike. Their final decision on that would be influenced by changes in Britain and the inability of outside groups to help them.

In the spring of 1979, Margaret Thatcher put forward a vote of no confidence in James Callaghan's Labour government. Ironically, two Irish MPs, Gerry Fitt in West Belfast and Frank Maguire in Fermanagh/South Tyrone, sealed Callaghan's fate. Fitt was upset with Roy Mason and the mistreatment of suspects by the RUC. He also opposed the Labour government's plan to increase the number of parliamentary seats in Northern Ireland, which he believed would strengthen the unionist position. He abstained. Maguire had been interned in the 1950s and was very concerned about conditions in the H-Blocks and Armagh. He rarely attended parliament and still had not made his maiden speech. Maguire travelled to Westminster and abstained in person and Callaghan's government fell.[35] The conflict in Ireland influenced the forthcoming election in another way.

Airey Neave, who had escaped from Colditz in 1941, was a war hero with close ties to British intelligence and was very pro-Union. He was also the architect of Margaret Thatcher's rise to the leadership of the Conservative party and was slated to become Secretary of State for Northern Ireland. A few days after the vote of no-confidence, an INLA car bomb killed Neave as he drove out of the House of Commons' parking garage. The INLA's 'spectacular' had a deep effect on Thatcher. In her memoir *The Path to Power*, she wrote: 'I felt only stunned. The full grief would come later: With it also came the anger that this man – my friend – who had shrugged off so much danger in his life should be murdered by someone worse than a common criminal.'[36] The Conservatives won the first of four straight victories. Thatcher became Prime Minister and appointed Humphrey Atkins Secretary of State for Northern Ireland. Gerry Fitt was re-elected in West Belfast and Frank Maguire was re-elected in Fermanagh/South Tyrone.[37]

Two events added to Thatcher's distaste for Irish republicans. Lord Mountbatten was a cousin of the Queen and uncle to Prince Philip. For years he had ignored the security risk and vacationed in Sligo, in the west of Ireland. And for years the Provisionals knew he was there and did nothing about it. On the morning of 27 August 1979, an IRA bomb ripped through his boat as it left Mullaghmore harbour for the sea, killing Mountbatten, members of his family and a local boy piloting the boat, Paul Maxwell. That afternoon, at Warrenpoint in County Down on the other side of Ireland, an IRA bomb exploded as a British Army convoy passed an empty lorry. Six soldiers were killed and several others injured. The IRA unit anticipated the British response and, as a helicopter with reinforcements was landing, another bomb, hidden beneath the field base, exploded, killing twelve more soldiers. Eighteen soldiers and Mountbatten on the same day – a double 'spectacular'.[38]

The Mountbatten assassination and Warrenpoint bombs had several consequences. They boosted morale and showed that the new leadership was clever, creative. The rest of the world was shocked that the IRA would target an 80-year-old man and his family, whether or not they were royal. At the invitation of Cardinal Ó Fiaich, Pope John Paul II was scheduled to visit Catholic and Protestant parishes in Armagh. The visit was relocated south to Drogheda. In a homily for a mass that drew an estimated 250,000 people, the Pope asked his fellow Catholics to turn away from violence 'On my knees I beg of you to turn away from the paths of violence and to return to the ways of peace … Violence destroys the work of justice.'[39] The leadership believed they were fighting a just war; the Pope did not mention British violence. They could not condemn him and they could not ignore his remarks. An IRA statement noted the 'widespread support' that they had and blamed the Stormont and British governments for the situation, 'In all conscience we believe that force is by far the only means of removing the evil of the British presence in Ireland.' A Sinn Féin statement stressed the Pope's message that 'each human community – ethnic, historical, cultural or religious has rights that must be respected'. At a press conference in Dublin, Sinn Féin's Director of Publicity, Seán Ó Brádaigh, faced an aggressive British press corps who wanted to know if the IRA was going to call a ceasefire.[40]

The Mountbatten attack also had a 'profound' effect on Seán O'Callaghan, the Kerry republican. In his memoir, O'Callaghan writes that he had resigned from the IRA in 1975 after concluding it was a sectarian, Catholic defence organization. The Mountbatten attack was a 'final straw'. He contacted a Garda Special Branch officer and became an unpaid informer 'from the inside'.[41] In an interview, O'Callaghan offered the following: *'My view is this. I joined the IRA. I turned against the IRA because I despise it for many reasons, desperate reasons, particularly its Northern Ireland context, its Northern Ireland stuff, its sectarian stuff … I found it disgusting – still do to this day.'*[42] Back in the IRA, O'Callaghan became actively involved with the Southern Command. The O/C was Dáithí O'Connell who, according to O'Callaghan, was replaced by Pat Doherty in the summer of 1980.

Following standard procedure, Sinn Féin did not contest the Westminster election that brought Margaret Thatcher to power. The first election for the European Parliament was scheduled for June 1979, however. Ruairí Ó Brádaigh, who saw the European Economic Community (EEC) as the 'new colonialism, the super-power of Europe', wanted to contest it. In a 1972 referendum, 17 per cent of voters in the Republic of Ireland opposed joining the EEC. In 1975, 47 per cent of the Northern Ireland electorate voted that the United Kingdom should leave the EEC. Sinn Féin could tap into that opposition and Ruairí Ó Brádaigh saw a political opportunity:

> *we wanted to contest the EEC elections and there was a bit of a fuss. I was the principal person encouraging it … and Adams was the principal person against it … our view was that the line had been clearly drawn in the North between anti-imperialists and colonialism. And we wanted the same thing to happen in the South. And we had our eye on the people, the 17 per cent that had voted against the EEC membership and so on. And we weren't advocating going over to Brussels and taking part in all of these committees. What we were saying was, do we galvanize all this support and go over to Brussels and read a statement setting out the Irish national position and then becoming some kind of ambassador, in the event of success, which we*

didn't really believe it would be? But you had to provide for it – that we would then have an Ambassador at large around the world ... we had a committee to deal with all of this and it was lost by one vote.[43]

The British claimed that the IRA and Sinn Féin were a criminal conspiracy. The IRA claimed they had widespread support. For some Provisionals, it was too risky to participate in the European election and find out how much support they really had.

The election, held on 17 June 1979, was a major triumph for Revd Ian Paisley, who seemed to be against everything. Paisley, the leader of the DUP, tapped into unionist opposition to change. He topped the poll with 170,000 votes and took the first of three seats. The election was also a triumph for John Hume, who took the second seat with 140,000 votes.[44] Hume was in the process of becoming the leader of a less socialist and more nationalist version of the SDLP. By this point, Paddy Devlin had been expelled after complaining that the party was 'populated with straightforward nationalists' who were Catholic and conservative. Following the European election, Humphrey Atkins invited the SDLP to inter-party talks. Gerry Fitt, the party leader, accepted the invitation. John Hume, however, insisted that Irish unity be on the agenda. Fitt disagreed and the SDLP Executive backed Hume which resulted in Fitt's resignation and complaint that the party was no longer socialist; Hume was elected party leader.[45]

Whether Gerry Fitt or John Hume led the SDLP, a large section of the working-class nationalist community remained uninterested. The Sinn Féiner from Derry was asked why he joined Sinn Féin instead of the SDLP:

> *I just never looked at the SDLP as a party, you know? ... The SDLP was the last thing in my mind ... They're too middle class, too snooty – don't have anything at all [unclear]. See, even their politics ... I can't give you a reason for it, at the minute. Just that – it never even crossed my mind. I looked upon the SDLP as another part of the British establishment. The only radical party at that time was Sinn Féin, that's about it.*[46]

Radical or not, Sinn Féin boycotted the EEC election. Bernadette (Devlin) McAliskey, the former MP for Mid-Ulster, showed that was a mistake. McAliskey was actively involved in anti-H-Block protests as a member of the 'Relatives Action Committee'. She ran as an Independent Republican, advocating for the prisoners and received 33,000 votes. Even with that result, opposition to elections was so strong that a motion preventing Sinn Féin from contesting local elections in the North was passed at the 1980 Sinn Féin Ard Fheis.

The election and the Relatives Action Committee did help move the H-Block/Armagh issue higher on the Provisionals' agenda. Kieran Nugent, the first blanketman, completed his sentence and Sinn Féin sent him on a tour of Ireland and the United States – he was arrested in New York just before he was scheduled to appear at a press conference organized by Irish Northern Aid. In the autumn, a 'Smash H-Block' conference was organized in West Belfast. The conference was open to anyone who supported the prisoners, whether or not they supported armed struggle, and attracted more than 600 people. Separating the prisoners from armed struggle, it was hoped, would make it easier to attract humanitarian support.

The Relatives Action Committee sponsored the conference, but it was organized by the Provisionals. The discussion ended with a resolution, proposed by Gerry Adams and seconded by Tom Hartley, endorsing a seventeen-person 'Smash H Block Committee' (to become the National H-Block/Armagh Committee) that was supposed to spearhead a publicity campaign and mobilize support to force the British to concede political status. The committee was dominated by Provisionals but its Chairman was an independent, Father Piaras Ó Duill, who had a long-term interest in prisoner issues. Others on the committee included Gerry Adams, Miriam Daly of the IRSP, Fergus O'Hare of Peoples' Democracy, Joe Stagg (Frank's Stagg's older brother) and solicitor Pat Finucane. Bernadette McAliskey would become a prominent spokesperson for the committee.[47] As described by Gerry Hodgins, the prisoners supported the Committee:

> So we knew there was a hunger strike tradition but it was always something, if you raised it, then it would be up for discussion but it was never sort of grasped at with anybody saying, 'That's the way forward. That's the way we're going to do it.' It was always something that you didn't want to talk about, you didn't want to consider, until you were absolutely sure that there was no other avenue left open. The first time we discussed the hunger strike was 1979. Now, the whole reaction then was to put it on ice and not do it, to give a chance to the recently formed H-Block, the new H-Block/Armagh Committee on the outside, which was formulating the five demands and trying to create as broad a movement as possible, within Ireland and internationally, to put pressure on the British government.[48]

The five demands were: no prison uniform; no prison work; free association; full remission of sentence; and visits, parcels and recreational/educational facilities. Political status in all but name.

The National H-Block/Armagh Committee organized a conference in Dublin, more protests and more tours. Fra McCann was released from Long Kesh soon after the Committee was formed. He talked about his release:

> I was the first prisoner who got out who wasn't force-washed. Kieran Nugent and all, they'd had their beards cut, they had been washed and their hair cut. So I got out and I was what they said looked like what a blanketman was supposed to look like – long hair, a big beard ... the family and the people in the car park had run over and they were hugging you and you were in just total shock because you came out of probably one of the worst nightmares that you ever went through ... and the minibus turns to go out of Long Kesh and Kieran Nugent bent over and says to me, 'Are you reporting back?' And I said, 'For God's sake Kieran, let me get into the house and get something into me.' And that was just the nature of the thing. And I says, 'Well, you know I am' ... And I'd never publicly spoken in my life. And the other guy turns around and says to me, 'Don't touch your hair, don't touch your beard.' And the next thing was, you were being sent off in the communities and then the length and breadth of this country.

After touring Ireland, McCann was also sent to the United States. And like Kieran Nugent, he was arrested in New York.[49] In January 1980, the IRA shot dead Graham Cox, a 35-year-old warden at Magilligan prison. In June 1980, loyalists killed Miriam Daly, a member of the H-Block/Armagh Committee.[50]

The H-Block/Armagh protests brought in recruits. Brian McDonald, who grew up in Clones on the Monaghan/Fermanagh border, explained his involvement:

> *The event that decided me to get involved in republican politics, or to examine republican politics, was the emergence of the Peace People and the way they were hyped up by the media in 1976. And, early in 1977, I went up to Belfast for myself to see what it was like. And [I] found that the whole Peace People thing was a myth – that they weren't supported by ordinary working class Catholics or working class nationalists … it was a big shock … I began to reexamine my own position as a virulent anti-republican, which I was. And it was like a road to Damascus conversion over a period of time.*

McDonald became interested in the H-Block/Armagh protests and met activists:

> *I got interested, went to meetings on the H-Block issue … that was the issue that really brought me into actual involvement – active involvement, going to marches … rather than just passive support. Similarly, because of my friendship with a few people who were politically involved as republicans I began to get visits from Special Branch policemen here and I was involved in nothing. I was a member of nothing. And they came around, they laid allegations at my door that I was a member of the IRA or the INLA and this kind of thing, without a shred of evidence and it was totally false because I wasn't even in Sinn Féin. I was in nothing at that point. It was simply because I had friendships … And that was a very big factor. I said. 'Well to hell. If they're going to hassle me, you know, I might as well be, too – actually doing something, actually getting involved' … By 1978, I had come to the position where I did want to actually get involved. I didn't know to what extent. I was scared out of my wits, definitely – and coming from a very comfortable background. I have a middle class background and boarding school education, which isn't that ordinary in the Republican Movement. It was just a totally different lifestyle and that took a couple of years … In 1979, I began working with a fellow who was on the run himself. He got involved [unclear] as a young fellow, sixteen, who had to go on the run near eighteen. And his whole life was sitting down here in the South. And living in the same flat as him, not only working with him but living in the same flat, it began to make me think. He wasn't a particularly committed republican but, at the same time, his whole life had been destroyed because of what's happening up there. And then I began to meet other people who I knew had been in jail … definitely friendships are a big thing in it. If you know a republican it's much more likely, I suppose, that you're going to become actively involved.*[51]

The Anti-H-Block/Armagh campaign helped counter state censorship and brought activists into contact with potential recruits.

In Armagh Prison, about twenty-five women refused to conform to regulations. In February 1980, prison warders kept them from going to the toilet and their chamber pots overflowed. When the cells doors were finally opened, they dumped the pots onto the landing. That was the start of their 'no-wash' protest.[52]

In Long Kesh, there were around three hundred blanketmen. They decided that their only option was a hunger strike. Gerry Hodgins spoke about the decision:

Poem written by an unidentified prisoner in Armagh Women's Prison, signed 'M. Farrell' but not in Mairéad Farrell's handwriting (probably 1980). Courtesy of Richard Behal.

while they tried very hard, they [The National H-Block/Armagh Committee] failed to move the British Government, just because the British Government wasn't going to be moved – not through any fault of their own or any failing of their own. So, whenever that sort of last avenue that we had failed, we didn't have any other option but the hunger strikes.[53]

In a final attempt to resolve the situation, the prisoners appealed to Cardinal Ó Fiaich for help. Ó Fiaich persuaded the Provisional IRA to stop shooting prison warders and, over a period of months and with Father Alec Reid as an intermediary, he negotiated with Humphrey Atkins and the Northern Ireland Office.

Brendan Hughes and Bobby Sands had already begun planning a hunger strike. They sent out a 'comm' only to discover that the leadership was opposed. In reply, Gerry Adams argued that Margaret Thatcher would simply let hunger strikers die.[54] A failed hunger strike, everyone knew, could destroy prisoner morale and demoralize support on the outside. However, in *Republican Voices*, Tommy McKearney explains that the prisoners had to do something or the protest might fall apart: 'Many solid Republican volunteers were physically unable to sustain the protest and began to conform to prison regulations. By mid-1980 the protest was approaching a crossroads. We were fast approaching a situation where 50 per cent of the Republican prisoners were conforming and if that happened our case was lost.'[55] Gerry Hodgins described their conditions:

> *Desperate. Every day was just the same. About the only things that broke up the day was dinner time and tea time. I mean, you'd just be waking up there in the morning to – nothing really. And all you had was a cell. There'd probably be two in the cell. The cell was filthy. You would have a lump of sponge as your mattress and three blankets. Across the window ... the bars were concrete but on the outside there was an iron drop put over it – and then on the outside a Perspex box [was] built around it ... Very dull – you can't see through it. It would let a certain amount of light through. So that was your whole world for whatever amount of time you were there – two, three, four, five years or whatever.[56]*

Late in the summer of 1980, Cardinal Ó Fiaich announced a 'breakthrough'. The apparent concessions were then denied. Danny Morrison, who had succeeded Seán Ó Brádaigh as Sinn Féin's Director of Publicity, was an intermediary between Brendan Hughes and Cardinal Ó Fiaich. In a letter published in *Then The Walls Came Down: A Prison Journal*, he described what happened:

> in September 1980, Atkins told him that the British government would let the prisoners wear their own clothes. Ó Fiaich was delighted, sent word to the H-Blocks, headed off to Rome for a conference and while his plane was in the air the British government announced that it wasn't their own clothes the prisoners were getting but government-issue civilian-type clothes. Ó Fiaich was shattered by the duplicity. The prisoners then announced they were going on hunger strike.[57]

Morrison visited Brendan Hughes in Long Kesh and told him that the Ó Fiaich initiative had failed. Hughes told Morrison they were going on hunger strike.[58]

By the time the hunger strike began in October 1980, Brian McDonald had joined Sinn Féin. He commented: *'When the first hunger strike began in 1980, I'd already joined Sinn Féin. I'd joined them early that year. Because I just decided I had been hanging in the wings for too long.'[59]* The hunger strike would bring in more people 'hanging in the wings'.

12

FOR BOBBY (1980–1981)

And in the hunger strike you just seen that they didn't really care about us at all. And they would use
any means to put us down.

– 1981 Sinn Féin recruit[1]

One hundred and forty-eight blanketmen volunteered for the hunger strike. At a 'staff meeting' during mass, the prison leadership, including Brendan Hughes, Bobby Sands, Bik McFarlane and Jake Jackson agreed they wanted six hunger strikers who would represent a broad geographic area. Hughes and Sands both wanted to represent Belfast and County Antrim, but Hughes had the final word and took the spot. Four others were chosen relatively quickly – Leo Green (Armagh), Raymond McCartney (Derry), Tom McFeeley (South Derry) and Tommy McKearney (Tyrone).

Seán McKenna (Down/Monaghan) was desperate to be chosen but Hughes had reservations. McKenna was in poor health but he also had impeccable credentials. McKenna was seventeen in August 1971 when he and his father were interned. His father was one of the Hooded Men and never recovered from the experience; he was forty-five years old when he died of a heart attack in 1975, and he is listed on the 'Roll of Honour'. Seán McKenna was the O/C of H5 and refused to take no for an answer and Hughes relented. The seven hunger strikers 'echoed' the seven signers of the 1916 proclamation and the seven members of the Army Council.[2]

Hughes also had to worry about the women in Armagh and the INLA. The men were concerned that women hunger strikers would be a distraction, especially if the women became critically ill before the men.[3] Through couriers and comms, Hughes, Mairéad Farrell and the leadership worked out a deal. After thirty or so days without food the body starts to feed on itself. After about fifty days it starts to shut down. Around the sixtieth day without food, hunger strikers go blind, become deaf and then lapse into a coma. They usually die between the sixtieth and seventieth day of their fast. Gerry Adams suggested, and Hughes and Bobby Sands agreed, that women prisoners would join the fast at about the mid-point of the men's fast.[4] The INLA had thirty-four prisoners on the protest and John Nixon, their O/C, wanted two prisoners on the strike. Hughes offered them one and Nixon, who was from Armagh, took the spot.[5]

The Provisionals agreed that when Hughes went on hunger strike, Bobby Sands would become the O/C and Bik McFarlane would take over as Public Relations Officer (PRO).

McFarlane was not eligible for the strike because his involvement in the sectarian attack on the Bayardo Bar made him a liability with the media.[6] Danny Morrison and Tom Hartley would be the key contacts between the prisoners and the Provisionals on the outside. And if there were negotiations with the authorities, the prisoners wanted Morrison and Gerry Adams to represent them.[7] Hughes, Green, McCartney, McFeeley, McKearney, McKenna and Nixon refused food on 27 October 1980. In solidarity, 200 conforming prisoners in Long Kesh joined the blanket protest.[8]

Irish prisoners on hunger strike in British jails pricked the consciousness of nationalist Ireland and crowds attending H-Block/Armagh protests started growing. Caoimhghín Ó Caoláin is a cousin of Feargal O'Hanlon who was killed on the famous Brookeborough raid in 1957. When the hunger strike started, Ó Caoláin was in his late twenties and comfortably employed in banking. He explained his involvement in the H-Block protests:

> I recall very clearly that the prison protest in Long Kesh specifically but also in Armagh ... was very prominent within the political climate of the day here in Ireland. I became aware of it and interested in it through the work of the Relatives Action Committee and the other campaigning groups, but it actually took the hunger strike period of 1980 before my conscience was sufficiently disturbed by my spectator role of all that was unfolding in my own country. And that was, for me, a catalyst in my life. I was working in comfortable employment and I had to make the conscious decision to get actively involved myself, which I did.[9]

People who were already involved worked harder. Brian McDonald commented: 'when the first hunger strike began, I gave up my job and went to work for Sinn Féin full-time because I had a degree from university at that stage ... and I thought that I might be useful to the Movement.[10] There were black flag protests and mock funerals in Belfast, Derry, Cork, Dundalk, Limerick and Tralee, and a march in Dublin attracted 11,000 people.[11] On 1 December 1980, thirty-six days into the strike, Mairéad Farrell, Mairéad Nugent and Mary Doyle refused food.[12] The next day, the seven men were moved to the prison hospital.[13]

If the hunger strike continued, Christmas would be their fifty-ninth day without food and the situation would be desperate. Third parties tried to intervene, John Hume meeting with Humphrey Atkins to try and broker a deal on humanitarian grounds, and Charlie Haughey, who had succeeded Jack Lynch as Taoiseach, meeting with Margaret Thatcher in Luxembourg. Then, on 8 December 1980, Thatcher visited Dublin for a summit. She was the first British Prime Minister to visit Dublin since 1921. Haughey urged Thatcher to find a way to save face and allow the prisoners to end the strike but Thatcher's view was that there would be no concessions while the hunger strike continued. Yet, after the Dublin summit, a joint communiqué suggested something would come from the visit. At a press conference, however, Haughey overstepped and described an 'historic breakthrough' that might ultimately lead to a change in the constitutional status of Northern Ireland. The unionists were infuriated and Thatcher then embarrassed Haughey by announcing they had not discussed the constitutional status of Northern Ireland.[14] None of this helped the prisoners.

Behind the scenes, the British reactivated the Michael Oatley–Brendan Duddy link to the Provisionals[15] and on 10 December, the Northern Ireland Office offered the prisoners a deal. John Blelloch, an Undersecretary of State at the NIO, visited each prisoner and read out a document outlining reforms *if* the strike were ended, including a concession on clothing. Blelloch left a copy in each cell but refused to negotiate with Brendan Hughes. After Blelloch left, Bobby Sands was allowed in, Hughes showed Sands the document and Sands told Hughes of the secret link with the British. They suspected the British were testing the prisoners and would offer a better deal if the prisoners held firm. The British were never going to formally concede 'political status' but the prisoners had not fully considered what might be an acceptable alternative. Sands issued a statement describing the NIO proposal as 'irrelevant to the extreme' and brought another twenty-three prisoners onto the hunger strike.[16]

On 18 December, the fifty-third day of the strike, Seán McKenna was very weak and Tommy McKearney was going in and out of consciousness. The prison doctor told McKearney's mother that he had about twelve hours to live.[17] The prison governor, the Chief Prison Officer and a civil servant met with the hunger strikers – Bobby Sands was excluded. According to Brendan Hughes, 'They told us that they were prepared to concede, not political status, not the five demands, but something similar.' The hunger strikers asked to see the details in writing. It was in this context that Seán McKenna asked Hughes, 'Promise me that you won't let me die.' Hughes told him, 'I won't let you die', but while they waited for a written document McKenna slipped into a coma. The doctor told Hughes that McKenna would only last a few more hours.

Brendan Hughes was in a very difficult situation. If he took McKenna off the strike, the British would see it as sign of weakness and it might hurt support on the outside. He also wanted to keep a solid front, but if he let McKenna die, everything would change. The British might take a harder line and the prisoners could lose whatever concessions they had gained; it might all have been for nothing. As McKenna was being wheeled away for transfer to a military hospital, Hughes shouted, 'Feed him!' That ended the hunger strike in Long Kesh.[18]

Around the time Brendan Hughes ended the Long Kesh strike, Michael Oatley met Father Brendan Meagher at Aldergrove Airport and gave him the written offer. Meagher delivered the document to Clonard Monastery where Gerry Adams, among others, reviewed it and saw that it was less than they had hoped for. Father Meagher then delivered the document to Brendan Hughes in Long Kesh. Hughes, who could not see well enough to read, gave it to Bobby Sands who was visiting him. Sands's reaction was the same as that of Adams and company – the British had given them nothing concrete. Back in the H-Blocks, Sands delivered the news to the other prisoners with, 'Ní fhuaireamar faic' ('We didn't get anything'). In a comm to Adams he wrote, 'Dorcha [the Dark] panicked when they rushed Seán to the hospital.'[19] In Armagh, the women heard on the radio that the strike was over but Danny Morrison was not allowed in to confirm the news. The next day, and only after consulting with Síle Darragh their O/C, Farrell, Nugent and Doyle ended their fast.[20]

The Provisionals pretended it was a victory and a National H-Block/Armagh Committee statement claimed that the 'strength of a roused people' had made it possible. Prisoners who took visits acted like they had a lasting deal. In reality, Bobby Sands was already considering another hunger strike[21] and the National H-Block/Armagh Committee almost lost one of its most prominent supporters. In mid-January 1981, an undercover patrol of British soldiers watched loyalists bash in the front door of the County Tyrone home of Bernadette McAliskey. She and her husband Michael were shot and severely wounded. The loyalists were arrested *leaving* the house. It was the sixth attack on H-Block activists and the Provisionals retaliated. Sir Norman Stronge was 86 years old, a veteran of the Battle of the Somme and a former Speaker of the Stormont parliament. The family was part of the unionist elite and had lived for generations at Tynan Abbey, in County Armagh. Sir Norman and his son James were shot and killed and their home burned to the ground.[22]

In Long Kesh, Bobby Sands tried to work out a compromise. The prisoners, for example, were told there would be a concession on clothing. Two wings of prisoners who went off the dirty protest were moved to a clean wing with furniture and issued prison clothes. However, when their families sent in their own clothes, they were put in storage and the prisoners were told that they would receive them only after the protest ended and they accepted the prison regime, unchanged. The prisoners then wrecked their cells and destroyed the furniture. In retaliation, the prison administration moved them back to dirty wings with no clothes, no mattresses, no blankets, no water and left them there for fourteen hours. Sands began planning a second hunger strike.[23]

Observers suggest that the Army Council at this time was Martin McGuinness (C/S), Gerry Adams, Ivor Bell, Joe Cahill, Ruairí Ó Brádaigh and two others, perhaps Kevin Mallon and Kevin McKenna. They were very concerned because another failed hunger strike could wreck everything. Adams, the presumed Chairman of the Army Council, would have run meetings and represented them with outsiders.[24] A message from Adams to Sands made it clear the leadership opposed a second strike: 'We are tactically, strategically, physically and morally opposed to the hunger strike.'[25] Ruairí Ó Brádaigh also had reservations:

> *Who wants a hunger strike? Who in their sane mind wants a hunger strike. Nobody wants a hunger strike. This whole situation had gone on since 1976 ... It moved from a strip strike to a no wash protest. And then in, I think, October of 1980, the first hunger strike started. And it ended ... fifty-three days [later] when the famous thirty-two page document was made available. And there was a settlement on that basis. And Bobby Sands was the O/C of the prisoners there. So when this was reneged on, he felt totally let down ... he felt that this situation had to be repaired and he felt, apparently, a certain degree of responsibility for the settlement that had taken place. And he said, 'Right, I'm standing down as O/C and I'm going on hunger strike on the first of March'... Nobody wants a hunger strike and nobody was – I mean it's so ridiculous – nobody was ordering anybody to go on hunger strike. You can't order people to go on hunger strike ... but if a hunger strike started, you have to back it up.[26]*

The British would not take a second strike seriously until the fifty-third day. It was almost certain that prisoners would die, possibly for nothing.[27]

Sands knew he would probably die and organized the strike accordingly, including bequeathing his writings to the Provisionals.[28] The leadership wanted Seanna Walsh to take over as O/C.

Instead, Sands insisted on Bik McFarlane becoming O/C. Sands had a personal relationship with Walsh that pre-dated the H-Blocks; he suspected that Walsh would not let him die while McFarlane would.[29] It was agreed that if there were meetings with the Northern Ireland Office, then McFarlane had to be present. The INLA were planning their own second hunger strike but Sands stopped it. According to Tony O'Hara, Sands told his brother Patsy, 'If you go on this alone, you will be forever on your own in this Prison.' The INLA agreed to a joint second strike.[30] A hunger-strike committee on the outside was formed which included Gerry Adams, Danny Morrison, Jim Gibney, Tom Hartley and Martin McGuinness. If the authorities asked for talks then McFarlane was supposed to insist that Danny Morrison and Gerry Adams be present. They had still not considered what might be an acceptable offer.

Sands would be the first of four men on a staggered hunger strike. That way each person would only be responsible for himself – the Hughes–McKenna situation would not be repeated. Francis Hughes, from South Derry, would join the fast a week after Sands. Hughes was an IRA legend, the most wanted man in Ireland when he was arrested following a gun-battle that left an SAS man dead, another wounded and Hughes severely wounded. He got around the H-Blocks on a crutch because surgery left one leg shorter than the other. Patsy O'Hara, from Derry and the INLA, and Raymond McCreesh, an IRA volunteer from South Armagh, would follow Hughes. If hunger strikers started dying, the spectre of death would be constant.[31]

Bobby Sands began his fast on 1 March 1981, the fifth anniversary of the introduction of criminal status. Bik McFarlane became O/C and Ricky O'Rawe became the PRO. A statement put out by O'Rawe and Danny Morrison ended with:

> We have asserted that we are political prisoners and everything about our country, our arrests, interrogations, trials and prison conditions, show that we are politically motivated and not motivated by selfish reasons or for selfish ends. As further demonstration of our selflessness and the justness of our cause a number of our comrades, beginning today with Bobby Sands, will hunger-strike to the death unless the British government abandons its criminalization policy and meets our demand for political status.[32]

On 2 March, the prisoners ended the dirty protest in order to focus attention on the hunger strike.[33] On the fifth day of March, fate intervened and Frank Maguire, the MP for Fermanagh/South Tyrone, died of a heart attack.

In his autobiography, *Before the Dawn*, Gerry Adams claims that Jim Gibney suggested putting Bobby Sands forward as a candidate in the by-election for Maguire's seat. Adams writes, 'We had been developing an electoral strategy, but almost by definition we had no experience of electoral contests. While we thought and talked about having a prisoner go forward, it was only following the intervention of Bernadette Devlin McAliskey in the constituency that Jim Gibney raised the possibility that Bobby Sands should stand in the election.'[34] Cathleen Knowles, then a joint-General Secretary of Sinn Féin, says it was Dáithí O'Connell's idea and that the Belfast crowd was opposed:

Dáithí O'Connell, who was the political and military strategist of the Movement at the time, Sinn Féin and the Republican Movement, was a great thinker and he thought that the only way perhaps to save his [Bobby Sands's] life on hunger strike was to put him forward as a candidate. And this met with opposition. And he brought it to the smaller committee ... that meets weekly. It's called the Coiste Seasta. It's a standing committee and there's usually about eight people on that committee. And I was General Secretary at the time so I was taking the minutes. And he did speak to me beforehand that this was his intention, to bring it up. Now, he met with a little opposition. There was not opposition so much as reluctance to accept that that could happen ... That he could actually stand as a candidate or that it would do any good or that it would prevent him dying on hunger strike. So he did bring it up. I think it was Tony Ruane, who's long dead, who seconded the motion. And they said, 'Well, we can't really make a decision because we're just this small body. It has to go to the Ard Chomhairle' – to the Executive, the National Executive. And it went to the National Executive. And on the National Executive you had a lot of Belfast people, including Tom Hartley, Gerry Adams and Pat Doherty [in Donegal] and a few people like that ... [Joe Cahill and I] were joint-General Secretaries. And so they would all be there and they were more than reluctant. They were opposing it because, they said, 'If this fails it would be a terrible blow to the Movement.' So Dave had to convince them that – he went back to Terence Mac Swiney's death and what had happened after his hunger strike [in 1920]. The whole world had awakened to what was going on – British occupation of Ireland – and that it had ended up in this man's death, approaching death on hunger and thirst strike because he had been a mayor, Mayor of Cork, that his predecessor had been shot dead [Tomás Mac Curtain] and that this could happen again – that we could get the whole world behind us and opposed to British imperialism and that was his main theme, you know? ... But after all sorts of debates and trying to convince those – it was mainly Belfast who were opposed to this – he did convince them in the end to go ahead and we would stand Bobby Sands ... Jim Gibney is a nice guy. No way did he have anything to do with it ... I was there.[35]

Ruairí Ó Brádaigh was there, too. He confirms Knowles's account and says of Gibney, 'Success has many fathers.'[36]

Putting Bobby Sands forward as a candidate was not a simple matter. Sinn Féin had not contested Fermanagh/South Tyrone since 1966 when Ó Brádaigh was the candidate. Nominations were due by 30 March and the election was 9 April. Sands was from Belfast and, in Long Kesh, there was no way to build a personal connection with voters. Noel Maguire, Frank's brother, Bernadette McAliskey and Austin Currie were also interested in going forward as candidates. A split nationalist vote would produce the disastrous result of electing a unionist. There was also a very strong anti-election sentiment among Irish republicans.

While these issues were being considered, the prisoners stuck to their plan. Francis Hughes refused food on 15 March. A week later, and to the surprise of the INLA, Raymond McCreesh and Patsy O'Hara joined the strike on the same day. Tony O'Hara would later comment, 'To our astonishment Raymond was put on the same day to minimize the impact of the 1st INLA joining the protest.'[37] On 23 March, Sands was moved to the prison hospital.[38]

Because much of the Sinn Féin leadership was excluded from the North, the election convention to discuss Sands's candidacy was held in the Swan Hotel, in Monaghan Town.[39] A majority of the Fermanagh/South Tyrone activists were against running Sands as explained by Owen Carron:

> Yes, I was there. And the meeting actually voted not to nominate him … the people who were there from leadership level at the meeting … weren't able to convince the ordinary grass roots people on the ground in Fermanagh/South Tyrone because, you have to remember, that Sinn Féin hadn't entered electoral politics ever before or republicans hadn't – they didn't see themselves in that light. There was a tradition in that area of an independent republican MP. And everybody thought that the brother of the man who died would have automatically sort of fitted into that role. And so there would have been a certain bit of internal disorder and confusion. And, I suppose, it went back to the fact that really ordinary rank and file Sinn Féin people were not politicized. They were just sort of, if you like, IRA supporters – republican supporters.[40]

The failure of the first hunger strike and the recent events also influenced the decision. Gerry McGeough also attended the meeting:

> I remember Dáithí O'Connell was there and a number of others and people just voiced their opinions. I think the fear was probably we'd been beaten down so much and we'd had such a sense of euphoria with the gains from the previous winter, from the previous fall – the hunger strike we were referring to, once it was called off, the deflation. There was such a sense of people just – the morale collapsed … particularly when it emerged that they had achieved nothing. And it was kind of like, 'Oh, here we go again.' And getting the next campaign going, the next hunger strike going, was like whipping a dead horse. It really was just – people were saying, 'What is the point?' – until Frank Maguire died and then suddenly all the possibilities opened up. And, of course, bear in mind Bernadette McAliskey, who had been very active … had been shot and seriously wounded … The Stronges were shot dead and this was all in our general neighbourhood I should point out … via the loyalists, or whatever way you want to look at it, but the British side were starting to punch back a little … I got the feeling that perhaps people just didn't want another defeat, you know? And deep in their psyche the Northern Catholics had been just, our history has been a long, long, legacy of defeat.[41]

The opportunity was too important to pass up and the leadership was persistent. A second meeting the same night overturned the decision, as Owen Carron explained:

> myself and a few people … had words afterwards with Gerry Adams and a few of the people that were there. And we were convinced that it was a good idea. So we decided – so then there was a whole second meeting later on. I think it was in Cootehill [County Cavan], which is also not far from Clones [in County Monaghan]. And time was running out, you see, because you had to have this nomination in. So then it was decided to nominate Sands. And I was nominated as his election agent at that meeting – that second meeting. And then we had the problem of trying to get him to be delivered, to be the sole nationalist candidate … if there was three nationalist candidates, the one unionist – because of the voting system – would win.[42]

Owen Carron was a teacher and member of the Fermanagh H-Block committee. As Sands's election agent, he was, in effect, the candidate.

One of the first things Carron did was to visit Long Kesh and have Sands sign his nomination papers.[43] Sands appeared on the ballot as an 'Anti H-Block, Armagh Political Prisoner'. Various sources have Gerry Adams and/or Jim Gibney meeting with Bernadette McAliskey and Noel McGuire. Cathleen Knowles reports that Ruairí Ó Brádaigh and Dáithí O'Connell visited potential candidates. In support of the prisoners, McAliskey and Maguire decided they would not go forward as candidates.[44] That put pressure on Austin Currie and the SDLP to do the same or risk alienating nationalists who did not necessarily support the Provisionals but did not want Sands to die. To the dismay of Austin Currie, the SDLP withdrew his nomination and called on voters to boycott the election. Currie commented, 'I am unhappy and that is the only comment I am prepared to make.'[45] Humphrey Atkins refused to allow journalists into the H-Blocks so Owen Carron, Gerry Adams and Danny Morrison became the public face of the Provisionals.

The election came down to Bobby Sands and Harry West of the Official Unionist Party – Provisional IRA gunman vs unionist farmer. For the British and the unionists, a vote for Sands was a vote for murder. The Provisionals in Derry contributed to that image. The Provisionals were boycotting the census, claiming it was being used to gather intelligence. Two days before the election, they shot dead Joanne Mathers, a young mother who was working part-time as a census enumerator.[46] Whether or not the nationalists of Fermanagh and South Tyrone saw the attack on Joanne Mathers as murder, they supported Bobby Sands. He was elected with 30,493 votes versus 29,046 for West. It was a massive indictment of criminalization. There were victory parades throughout the country; in Belfast, they ended in riots. The British and unionists were stunned and Harry West commented, 'I never thought the decent Catholics of Fermanagh would vote for a gunman.'[47]

It was hoped that Sands's victory would lead to a breakthrough but, instead, Margaret Thatcher issued a blunt statement, 'Crime is crime is crime. It is not political, it is crime. And there can be no question of granting political status.'[48] In spite of appeals from the Vatican, the European Commission on Human Rights, the Irish Commission for Peace and Justice and Taoiseach Charlie Haughey, neither Sands nor Thatcher backed down.

On 5 May 1981, after sixty-six days without food, an emaciated Bobby Sands – his fillings having fallen out, his organs shut down, the whites of his eyes turned orange from toxins released – died. Belfast erupted in riots and black flags were flown throughout nationalist Ireland. Irish republicans stopped traffic in Dublin and international interest soared. A crowd estimated at 100,000 people listened to an oration from Owen Carron and watched an IRA colour guard fire a volley of shots over the casket. It was all caught on camera and the world saw that Bobby Sands was much more than a gunman.[49]

Francis Hughes, Raymond McCreesh and Patsy O'Hara were growing weaker and there was no question that Thatcher would let them die, too. Joe McDonnell, who was married and the father of two young children, was scheduled to replace Sands. McDonnell did not put his name forward for the first strike because, in his words, 'I have too much to live for.' He refused food

The firing party prepares to offer a final salute to Bobby Sands, 7 May 1981. Several activists from Dublin are pictured, including Val Lynch (with camera). Pacemaker Press.

on 8 May 1981.[50] Francis Hughes died four days later and there were more protests and riots. A Derry republican commented:

There is always emotionalism involved in everything. It's impossible not to have it. You're not human if you're not emotional in certain circumstances. I worked my ass off during the hunger strike, right? ... in publicity and whatever. It doesn't matter a damn what I was asked to do, I just did it because that was what we required. But when Sands died – and I mean I expected him to die, from the word go I expected him to die – I didn't have any illusions about it. I was shocked and I was stunned when Hughes died. And right up the line, I felt every time – I was in tears when Hughes died. I just – I was on O'Connell Bridge [in central Dublin]. I couldn't believe that it had happened. I saw that I had the same emotional reaction right through to the end. And to this day it's something that – I'm sure everybody's experienced in their life at some stage something that always triggers an emotional response and can literally bring tears on right there and then on the spot, you know? And you can't rationalize over it. And what you do is you generally choke them back. But that's precisely how I feel about the hunger strike ... it didn't make me any less rational in what I was doing because my reaction that day was not – I did, I freaked a bit on the bridge because there was a couple that wanted to kneel down and say the Rosary and I lost my head and started shouting at them, 'Get out and block the fucking traffic', because we were down at a black flag protest anyway. So we then – like, there was about seventy or eighty got out and in the way and just sat there and blocked all the traffic at rush hour because it was around five o'clock. And I left – I mean I didn't even stay with it. I went out and bought black markers in a stationery shop and sheet of card and came back and wrote up posters. It doesn't make you any less rational as long as you understand what you're doing and why you're doing it. It can affect you emotionally and it really upset me but it doesn't – it shouldn't have made me less rational.[51]

Brendan McLaughlin, an IRA volunteer from County Derry, replaced Francis Hughes.

Rioting was constant. The day Bobby Sands died rioters stoned a milk lorry in North Belfast driven by two uninvolved Protestants. The lorry crashed, killing the driver and his son, Desmond and Eric Guiney. The day Francis Hughes died, a soldier in West Belfast shot 14-year-old Julie Livingstone in the head with a plastic bullet; she died the next day. A few days later, an IRA landmine killed five soldiers in South Armagh. That afternoon in Belfast, a soldier shot 12-year-old Carol Ann Kelly in the head with a plastic bullet; she died three days later. In Derry, an RUC land rover, driving away from a crowd of stone throwers, ran over 33-year-old Joseph Lynch.[52]

A Protestant from East Belfast described how the blatant repression raised the consciousness of many different people:

For a long time I thought I was British. I didn't really know what I was, actually. When I was younger, I went to England to work due to the high unemployment at home and then I was made very aware of my identity, and it was Irish. I was left in no doubt that I was a Paddy. And – you know the old stories about people going to try to find flats, somewhere to live in London, where the signs are in the window, 'No Irish', 'No Coloureds' – it was a good thing to experience because it did give me a perception, it did give me an education which I might not necessarily have gotten if I had stayed in the North. But certainly that made me very aware of my identity. Then moving from my loyalist area, through other locations, finally to end up in a republican area was a great experience … To experience the continual daily harassment, the constant harassment – it's a great education as well – to see the poverty as well … the lack of any hope … the lack of facilities. Just seeing young kids, young intelligent kids with an amazing amount of potential, and an amazing amount of intelligence, of ability … They would never get a job except perhaps the most menial, if they were lucky.

With the hunger strike mobilization, he joined Sinn Féin in 1981:

During the hunger strike period the number of plastic bullets fired in Belfast was incredible. I think the figures for the North actually break down to one plastic bullet fired every three minutes during the month of May during 1981. And where I lived, there were plastic bullets being fired every day. It got to the stage where you would hear the bullets being fired and you wouldn't necessarily look out the window to see what was happening. It was just taken as a regular run of the mill thing. And I witnessed that personally myself, them firing plastic bullets at wee kids who were trying to throw stones which they could hardly lift.

Youngsters of five and six trying to throw stones at British Army saracens, armoured saracens – and they would fire plastic bullets at them. Their whole attempt to terrorize us, to keep us down, to prevent us from making ourselves heard. And then the hunger strike, of course. The hunger strike was, I suppose, the culmination of a series of events. And in the hunger strike you just seen that they didn't really care about us at all. And they would use any means to put us down.[53]

Between March and October 1981, more than 29,000 plastic bullets fired in Northern Ireland killed seven nationalist/Catholic civilians.[54]

In the midst of this massive mobilization, local elections were held in Northern Ireland on 20 May 1981. The year before, the Sinn Féin Ard Fheis had passed a motion stating they would not contest this election. The hunger strike mobilization showed how that decision was a colossal mistake and there was not enough time to fix it. With Sinn Féin on the sidelines, the SDLP lost nine seats and the Irish Independence Party, which supported the prisoners, picked up twenty-one. Gerry Fitt, of the SDLP, was replaced on Belfast City Council by Fergus O'Hare, of People's Democracy and the H-Block/Armagh Committee.[55] The day after the election, Raymond McCreesh and Patsy O'Hara died. When O'Hara's family received his body, his nose was broken and there were cigarette burns on him.[56]

There were unexpected consequences of the funerals, protests and riots. Charlie Haughey was a canny politician who, along with Fianna Fáil, supported Irish unity. Aware that there were IRA and INLA prisoners in Southern jails, when Liz Hughes, Francis Hughes's sister, asked if he supported the five demands, Haughey refused to answer the question. He also put off calling a general election until the first wave of the strike had passed. Then, with at least a month before Joe McDonnell would be critical, he dissolved Dáil Éireann.[57] Haughey played politics and the prisoners stayed the course: Kieran Doherty, a Provisional from Belfast, refused food on 22 May; Kevin Lynch, an INLA volunteer from Dungiven, refused food the next day; and Martin Hurson, an IRA volunteer from Tyrone, refused food on 28 May. The only deviation came when it was discovered that Brendan McLaughlin was bleeding internally. The plan was for him to die on hunger strike, not from a perforated ulcer. McLaughlin was ordered to end his fast.[58]

On Friday 29 May 1981, there was a meeting in the Sinn Féin Head Office in Dublin to consider the upcoming Leinster House election. Even with Bobby Sands's win and the local election results in the North, some Provisionals were still very cautious. Ruairí Ó Brádaigh commented:

I know that in '81 even, that down here, that Gerry Adams was very nervous about this electoral involvement … people who were ringing up and wavering about contesting or not and he was inclined to discourage them … People from places like Clare or Wexford that wanted to contest, or would they contest, and all that type of thing, et cetera and so on. And he was inclined to discourage them.[59]

At the meeting, a report that Wexford was 'not very hopeful' prompted Adams to suggest 'we withdraw from Wexford and Clare – go ahead with Cork'.[60] Richard Behal, however, reported that people in Clare were enthusiastic. Under Articles 2 and 3 of the Irish Constitution, persons born in Northern Ireland were citizens of the Republic of Ireland. Those present agreed to put forward six Provisionals and three INLA/IRSP 'Anti-H-Block/Armagh' prisoner candidates:

Constituency	Candidate
Cork North Central	Mairéad Farrell/IRA-Sinn Féin
Sligo/Leitrim	Joe McDonnell/IRA-Sinn Féin
Cavan/Monaghan	Kieran Doherty/IRA-Sinn Féin
Longford/Westmeath	Martin Hurson/IRA-Sinn Féin
Louth	Paddy Agnew/IRA-Sinn Féin
North Kerry	Seán McKenna/IRA-Sinn Féin
Dublin West	Tony O Hara/INLA-IRSP
Waterford	Kevin Lynch/INLA-IRSP
Clare	Tom McAllister/INLA-IRSP

Except for Paddy Agnew, who was from Dundalk, all of the candidates were from Northern Ireland. Four of them – Joe McDonnell, Kieran Doherty, Martin Hurson and Kevin Lynch – were on hunger strike. The minutes also show that, 'G. Adams wanted it noted that he proposed dropping all areas with the exception of S/L L/WM C/M Louth' [Sligo/Leitrim, Longford/Westmeath, Cavan/Monaghan, and Louth]. That would have eliminated the three INLA/IRSP candidates and the lone woman, Mairéad Farrell.

Although Sinn Féin had not contested a Leinster House election since 1961, capable and experienced people were available. The Director of Elections was Dáithí O'Connell. Caoimhghín Ó Caoláin, in Monaghan, directed Kieran Doherty's candidacy; County councillors John Joe McGirl and Seán Lynch were the election agents for hunger strikers Joe McDonnell and Martin Hurson; and Richard Behal was Director of Elections in Clare. The prisoners did their part with Tom McElwee, a cousin of Francis Hughes, joining the strike three days before the election. Anti-H-Block/Armagh candidates received 42,803 first-preference votes and shook up politics in the Republic of Ireland. Kieran Doherty was elected in Cavan/Monaghan and Paddy Agnew was elected in Louth. In Waterford and Sligo/Leitrim, Kevin Lynch and Joe McDonnell were 300 and 315 votes short of election, respectively. In Longford/Westmeath, Martin Hurson received more than 4,500 first preference votes. If Gerry Adams's recommendation had been implemented, it would have cost the campaign more than 15,000 votes.[61]

The prisoners' success came at the cost of Fianna Fáil. Doherty and Agnew, for example, took the seats of Fianna Fáil incumbents and Fine Gael and Labour formed a coalition government with Garret FitzGerald as Taoiseach. The election is also noteworthy because, after eleven years, the Officials, now organized as Official Sinn Féin/The Workers' Party, elected their first TD, Joe Sherlock in Cork. The party was still led by Tomás Mac Giolla and actively opposed the prisoners' demands, even if four hunger strikers – Francis Hughes, Patsy O'Hara, Kevin Lynch and Mickey Devine – were, at one time, members of the Official IRA.[62] Following the election, Paddy Quinn, a South Armagh Provisional, refused food.

In the early 1970s, events like internment and Bloody Sunday had broken down the barriers that made it difficult for people to support political violence. A Kerry republican explained how the same thing happened in 1981:

> *And I made new friends from the H-Block ... An awful lot of people whom I didn't know got to know me ... the main fact is I actually became a member, we'll say, of the Movement is – was the H-Block situation. I always supported it. Deep down I was always kind of glad that there was an odd British soldier shot, that the struggle kept going in Northern Ireland, to get Ireland free ... There was thousands of people marching in this town ... We took over the GPO here in town – flew a black flag out the window for about an hour. We stopped the train, buses ...*

The H-Block/Armagh protests brought thousands of potential recruits into contact with active republicans. The hunger strike also exposed, for some at least, the hypocrisy of Fianna Fáil. The Kerry republican described his family's background: *'Well, my grandfather was in the Old IRA, as it was termed. And he was interned in the [unclear] like that and he was on hunger strike himself ... My father and mother have changed ... before the H-Block situation I think they would be Fianna Fáilers.*[63] A young woman from County Sligo had a similar experience:

> *Even people who have no interest in, or were totally against Sinn Féin and all that, it took over everybody's mind here, the hunger strike did. It was a normal topic of conversation to be going on. So it was just in listening to discussions ... there'd be pickets, black flag pickets or postering or whatever. I mean, young people my age when they could be going out, having a few drinks or having the craic [good time] or going to pictures or just having the fun, would be going out postering in the evenings or selling the paper or going to meetings. And that kind of thing really affects you ... Fianna Fáil calls itself the Republican Party. It's a joke and it's been proved the last few years*
>
> *Q: What proved it?*
>
> *A: The H-Block situation proved it ... my mother and father and all these other people, in the last generation, my father's generation, would always say with half the smile, 'Charlie's one of the lads.' But they found out different during the H-Block. And a lot of people are very upset about that – that generation. And it's very difficult for someone like my father or mother to change. All through the years they've been bleating out telling people that Fianna Fáil are the Republican Party and when they found out that they weren't, it was very difficult for them to change.*[64]

Fianna Fáil talked about a united Ireland; hunger strikers were dying for a united Ireland.

The hunger strike also showed that the British and Margaret Thatcher were unreasonable. An activist from Dublin:

> *The hunger strike really highlighted it to me.*
>
> *Q: What did it highlight?*

> A: *The British intransigence, the British government's intransigence at the time. They wouldn't, they refused to talk to the strikers even. It was ten men – they were prepared to give up their lives, to give everything for what they believed in … That was the end.*

> Q: *The end of?*

> A: *The end of me sitting on the sidelines just looking in, buying the odd paper. I decided then that I'd be actively involved. If these men can give life itself surely I can give up a couple of nights a week and a few hours.*[65]

The activist from Sligo:

> *it was due to her fucking intransigence on the thing. And it wasn't as if they were asking for the world. … – the general mood would be – even if they had done something wrong or they're in there, 'This isn't right.' That kind of attitude. But I think if the Brits had given in, even a bit, it would have defused it, but they were fueling it, really.*[66]

A respondent from Fermanagh joined in 1981:

> *It was in June, after everything, at the time of the hunger strike. That was – would have [been] the time. I think it influenced a lot of people during the hunger strike. … I think that the British government were unprepared to do anything to stop them from dying … she could have done something to stop those deaths.*[67]

Mickey Devine, an INLA volunteer from Derry, joined the fast on 22 June 1981.

With four hunger strikers dead, the Irish Commission for Justice and Peace (ICJP) tried to arrange a deal between the prisoners and the Northern Ireland Office. Three representatives from the Commission – Hugh Logue of the SDLP, Dermot O'Mahoney, the Auxiliary Bishop of Dublin, and Father Oliver Crilly, a cousin of Tom McElwee – met with Michael Allison, the NIO minister in charge of prisons, members of the H-Block/Armagh Committee and the hunger strikers. At the end of June, Humphrey Atkins issued a six-page statement that rejected any concessions but also acknowledged efforts by Charlie Haughey and the ICJP to resolve the impasse.[68] The British also strengthened their hand.

On 2 July, the Representation of the People Act 1981 was given Royal Assent. Under the Act, persons imprisoned for more than a year in the United Kingdom or the Republic of Ireland were 'disqualified' from membership in the House of Commons.[69] In the by-election to replace Bobby Sands, there would not be another prisoner candidate. Mitchel McLaughlin described how attitudes were changing:

> *I suppose really the story goes back to the hunger-strike intervention by Bobby Sands. And, I mean, they came to Derry and I was a member of the National H-Block Committee at that stage. I was a fairly prominent republican activist then. And they had asked people to go up and work for Bobby Sands and I refused. I was a committed abstentionist and I was actually anti-electoralism. So, I didn't work for Bobby Sands. Once the Bobby Sands thing happened, I realized how short-sighted in my beliefs I had been.*[70]

The Provisionals nominated Owen Carron as an 'Anti-H-Block Proxy Political Prisoner' candidate for Sands's seat.

The ICJP renewed their efforts and this time there was progress. Michael Allison told them that if the hunger strike was ended, then the prisoners could have their own clothes. When this was reported to the prisoners, they were interested. At the same time, Bik McFarlane was concerned that the ICJP was undermining the prisoners.[71] Ricky O'Rawe and McFarlane decided to introduce some 'realism' into the situation. On 4 July, they issued a statement that backed off from the demand for 'political status'. Instead, and for the first time, they broke down the five demands and focused on their substance. The statement outlined 'the basis of a solution, without loss of principle to either side in the conflict', and it had a much bigger impact than they expected.[72] With the support of Margaret Thatcher, the Brendan Duddy backchannel was again reactivated.[73]

Duddy, codenamed 'Mountainclimber', delivered a message to the Provisionals. The British were willing to make concessions that went beyond what the ICJP was proposing, *if the hunger strike ended immediately*. While the media focused on the ICJP, Danny Morrison quietly slipped into Long Kesh and met with Bik McFarlane.[74] A British condition was that the communications remain secret, so only a few prisoners – including Bik McFarlane, Ricky O'Rawe, Jake Jackson, Pat McGeown, Seanna Walsh and Joe McDonnell – were told of the contact.[75] In order to keep the ICJP from interfering with the British–Provisional negotiations, Gerry Adams met with Father Crilly and Hugh Logue and revealed that the Provisionals were in contact with the British and Adams asked the ICJP to withdraw. The ICJP commissioners were upset and surprised but, instead of withdrawing, they met with Michael Allison and gave him a document that they believed would end the hunger strike.[76]

Gerry Adams waited for more information from 'Mountainclimber'. In *Before the Dawn*, he writes:

> The representatives of the British government with whom we on the hunger strike committee were in contact used to leave it until someone was at a very weak point on hunger strike before entering into negotiations … Very early one morning I and another member of our committee were in telephone discussion with the British from a living-room in a house in Andersonstown when, all of a sudden, they cut the conversation, which we thought was quite strange. Then, later, when we turned on the first news broadcast of the morning, we heard that Joe McDonnell was dead.[77]

Joe McDonnell died on 8 July 1981, the sixty-first day of his fast. Adams writes that the British misjudged the timing of their negotiations and McDonnell died sooner than expected.

Joe McDonnell's death marks a turning point when the authorities became harder, more callous. The morning McDonnell died, Nora McCabe, a 33-year-old housewife and mother of three, went out to buy cigarettes. She was standing on a street corner in West Belfast when an RUC officer killed her with a plastic bullet. Na Fianna Éireann tried to burn buses at the Falls Road bus depot and 16-year-old John Dempsey was shot dead by the British Army. Dempsey was only 4 years old when the Provisionals were created. The day after McDonnell died, a soldier in Ardoyne shot dead 15-year-old Danny Barrett as he was sitting innocently on a garden wall. At McDonnell's funeral, the British Army and the RUC went after the republican colour guard and attacked mourners; Gerry Adams's brother Paddy was shot and arrested in the confrontation.[78] On 13 July 1981, less than a week after Joe McDonnell, Martin Hurson died after only forty-six days on his fast. Matt Devlin, a Provisional from Tyrone, replaced Hurson.

The hard line scared people and the unending deaths demoralized them. Some family members and some members of the clergy, especially Father Denis Faul, started calling for the strike to end.[79] The Kerry republican commented:

> You had thousands upon thousands of people and business people, clerical people, the whole lot and it was a really big thing. But then when the second one died, people began to fall off. Do you know? The longer the campaign went on, the less emotion was involved and people were getting used to the idea that the hunger strikers were dying and here's your job. The people and the ordinary worker on the street were the only ones left to support now. The clerical people and all the rest of them or the business people wouldn't come out. They were closing their shops and it was costing them money to close their shops. And, I think the parties, the political parties, called their people at the line and said, 'Look, these guys are using ye for their own gains', and all the rest of it.[80]

A Dublin republican described the feeling at the time:

> It was all in a wave of emotion, kind of. It was a very emotional period at that time – just thousands of people in the streets. I really thought that it was getting together then. But after, say, the first seven died, six or seven hunger strikers died, then it started to slacken off. People realized that the British weren't going to give in.[81]

Garret FitzGerald's government took a harder line. In Dublin, an Anti-H-Block/Armagh rally brought out 10,000 people for a march from the GPO to the British Embassy. They ran into the Gardaí, massed twelve deep and a baton charge left more than 200 people injured.[82]

The state violence was frightening. People were frustrated. Kieran Doherty was approaching his sixtieth day without food and Brendan Duddy wrote in his diary:

> The position has gone dead. Neither side can nor will move. everyone is tired Time is running out It is 1-33 am July 20th I am almost defeated I cannot move forward. THE British are asking for their plan to be accepted, A won't move Noel is saying He is finished for all time I am so tired I can't save K Doherty's life It is so tragic
>
> It is regrettable that a solution does not seem possible
>
> 2.25am July[83]

The prisoners wondered if the strike should continue.[84]

Father Faul arranged for Gerry Adams to meet with the hunger strikers' families. They, in turn, asked Adams to go into Long Kesh and tell the prisoners to end the fast. The Army Council had ordered Seán Mac Stiofáin off his fast and *someone* had intervened and gotten Brendan McLaughlin to end his hunger strike. Adams replied that the hunger strike was the prisoners' decision, that the Army Council had opposed the hunger strike and that the IRA could not order the prisoners to end their fast.

Adams, Owen Carron and Seamus Ruddy did receive permission to visit Long Kesh. Carron was the political heir of Bobby Sands – *if* he was elected – and Ruddy represented the IRSP. On 29 July, they met with hunger strikers Mickey Devine, Matt Devlin, Tom McElwee, Pat McGeown, Laurence McKeown and Paddy Quinn, plus Bik McFarlane. Kieran Doherty and Kevin Lynch were not healthy enough to attend the meeting. In *Nor Meekly Serve My Time*, Laurence McKeown describes Adams's presentation:

> It was a grim picture. There were no ifs or buts. Really he was spelling out for us what we in a sense knew but didn't like to think through. The Brits had already allowed six men to die and they would likely allow more to die. Certainly there was no movement to indicate that they desired a speedy resolution to the protest.

Adams told them they could come off the strike and no one would object; it was their decision. They chose to stay on hunger strike. Adams, Carron, and Ruddy also visited Kieran Doherty and, when Adams told him that if he stayed on the fast he would be dead in a week, Doherty replied, 'Thatcher can't break us, I'm not a criminal.'[85] On the last day of the month and after forty-seven days without food, Paddy Quinn went into a coma. His mother intervened and saved his life.[86]

There was another wave of deaths. Kevin Lynch died on 1 August after seventy-one days; he was replaced by Liam McCloskey, also of the INLA. Kieran Doherty died on 2 August after seventy-three days; Doherty's fast was the longest. He was replaced by Pat Sheehan, a Provisional from Belfast. Tom McElwee died on 8 August after sixty-two days; Jackie McMullan, another Belfast Provisional, replaced McElwee. The tenth and final hunger striker to die was Mickey Devine, on 20 August 1981. It was election day in Fermanagh/South Tyrone and Owen Carron received more votes than Bobby Sands to win the seat.[87]

It appeared that nothing had changed. Garret FitzGerald and Margaret Thatcher refused to meet with Carron and he was denied a visa to visit the United States. Worse, the strike was falling apart. Mickey Devine was not replaced because the INLA had run out of volunteers.[88] Five more Provisionals would join the fast, but as hunger strikers slipped into a coma, their families intervened. Finally, on 3 October 1981, the hunger strike was formally ended and, within days, the prisoners were given their own clothes.[89] Thatcher had won but, with time, the prisoners would wreck the prison from within, as Brendan Hughes had suggested years earlier.

Gerry Hodgins was one of six prisoners on the hunger when it ended. Hodgins, who went twenty days without food, recalled:

you have to be over twenty-one, and you have to be absolutely sure of the decision you're making. You wouldn't be asked to go on it. You have to volunteer for to go on it and, volunteering to go on it, you would be contacted by senior people, outside, and they would just write and tell you that you've volunteered for a hunger strike – tell you exactly what you've volunteered for, in very clinical terms – that if you go on that strike that you're going to be dead and that's it. You've no more family or nothing, so think about it. And then you can think about it again and write back and apply and say you do want to go ahead or you don't want to go ahead. And then, eventually, when you're accepted, you'd just be kept on a short list to be called until you're told what date you go on hunger strike. So, a lot of men, I would say, would not want to take that step, saying okay, look for the first time in your life maybe death seems like it's just around the corner. A lot of men, a lot of people don't want to die; I think it's a natural human instinct to live instead of die. So, that is the big – that to me was the big thing of overcoming. I mean, you have to stand and sort of analyse your situation and place yourself in the context of your family and your friends. And you try to imagine what it would be leaving them. If I die, are they going to survive, are they going to be okay? And you have to work on that yourself. And then you have to sort of – whenever you make your final decision – get a visit with your family and explain to them exactly what you're doing and why you're doing it.[90]

One interpretation of the strike is that it was a mass suicide caused by desperate conditions and no relief in sight, but of the twenty-three hunger strikers in 1981, only four of them were serving life sentences. If he had conformed to prison regulations, Mickey Devine would have been released a few months after the hunger strike ended.[91] Gerry Hodgins described the connections among the prisoners.

The only hunger striker that I never knew was Kevin Lynch. He was only a matter of a couple of hundred yards away from me but I never met him because he was in a different Block. But, just through the years of imprisonment and moving from – being moved from different wings or blocks, I'd got to know all the rest of them. There was three of them [unclear] the wing I was in. That was Raymond McCreesh, Francie Hughes and Martin Hurson. And, as for the rest, for a while I was – I spent time in a cell with Bobby Sands, in H6 in 1979. Tom McElwee was in the one we were in. So I knew them all very well. Some I was very close to...

Q: *The fact that you knew them well, would that have influenced your decision to go on the strike?*

A: *It would. I think you had a unique situation in the H-Blocks, where people had lived through that sort of regime. We had all come through it together and there was that bond between all the men there. It was sort of – I think it was just a unique situation. I don't think that you'd ever see it repeated – that the friendship and the comradeship that built up amongst men there, it had everybody clinging together and everybody sort of thought and acted as a group – that if one was going to be beaten or anything everybody took it just as bad.*[92]

The hunger strikers were inspired by camaraderie.

There were deep personal connections between the hunger strikers and their contacts on the outside. Bobby Sands was in Cage Eleven with Brendan Hughes, Bik McFarlane and Gerry

Adams. Sands wrote articles for *Republican News*, edited by Danny Morrison. Sands was arrested with Joe McDonnell; McDonnell replaced Sands on the strike and one of Sands's cellmates in the H-Blocks was Tony O'Hara, Patsy's brother. Patsy O'Hara and Mickey Devine were on the same operation that led to Devine's arrest and conviction; O'Hara was arrested and released. Francis Hughes and Tom McElwee were first cousins and operated in the same IRA unit, and Francis Hughes and Raymond McCreesh shared a cell for fourteen months. Raymond McCreesh was arrested with Paddy Quinn. Kieran Doherty was on the operation that led to Mairéad Farrell's arrest and he was also on active service with Joe McDonnell. Doherty was arrested with John Pickering who was on the strike when it ended. Kevin Lynch and Liam McCloskey were childhood friends; they were arrested on the same day and shared a prison cell; McCloskey replaced Lynch on the strike. These personal relationships generated camaraderie, trust and a willingness to sacrifice.[93]

Social connections like these were not confined to Long Kesh. In Armagh, three women prisoners on the protest gave birth. Instead of leaving the protest and connecting fully with their children, they stayed with their comrades. Because they were only allowed a half hour visit every four weeks, they and their children suffered.[94] The personal connections between the hunger strikers reflect, in microcosm, the social connections, camaraderie and solidarity that sustained the Provisionals in general.

In the beginning, the hunger strikers thought they might win. As hunger strikers died, the expectation of success faded and their commitment to their comrades increased. In a way, 'success' changed from winning political status to refusing to quit. Consider the following from Gerry Hodgins:

Q: *You said initially you thought you would get the demands. When did you come to question that … ?*

A: *I think when Bobby Sands died. It was definite then that they weren't going to give any one of them.*

Q: *But you still went on the hunger strike then?*

A: *Yeah. Because it was a chance, it was the struggle that we were in. The loss of Bobby was a very big loss; it was really something that everybody felt real badly about. But I believed we had to fight on at the time and that to just give up then would have been a total waste of life – for Bobby. It would have been a waste of all the years that we had been engaged in the blanket protest and it also would have been a major setback for the Republican Movement for us to stand down at that time.[95]*

The hunger strike was filled with camaraderie, commitment, sacrifice and emotion. It was also a political act that led to more than 1,200 demonstrations involving more than 350,000 people. The 1981 hunger strike started a process that would transform the Provisionals.[96]

CODA

In *Blanketmen* and *Afterlives*, Ricky O'Rawe presents a compelling argument that, on 5 July 1981, Danny Morrison delivered a formal offer from the British to Brendan McFarlane. According to

O'Rawe, he and Bik McFarlane discussed the offer, agreed that it was enough and sent out a comm accepting it. They received a comm back from Gerry Adams indicating that the offer was not enough. They assumed the Army Council had rejected the offer and were 'shattered'. According to O'Rawe, McFarlane sent comms expressing reservations about rejecting the offer but then Joe McDonnell died. Eventually they received a comm blaming the British for brinkmanship in a 'battle of nerves'. O'Rawe also states that there was a second offer after Martin Hurson died.

Gerry Adams is portrayed as a deceitful manipulator who misled the Army Council, misled the hunger strikers and deceived their families in order to get Owen Carron elected. In this light, the meeting on 29 July 1981 between Adams, Owen Carron, Seamus Ruddy and the hunger strikers is much more interesting. O'Rawe's position is that Adams did not tell them that the prison leadership accepted the 5 July offer only to have it rejected from the outside, and he argues that, by leaving the decision with the prisoners, Adams effectively guaranteed that they would stay on the strike. Considering the sacrifices that had already been made, none of them would want to be the first to end the strike. Was Owen Carron there to remind the hunger strikers that if he lost in Fermanagh/South Tyrone then it would all have been for nothing?[97]

O'Rawe's allegations were immediately disputed. Danny Morrison, for example, wrote in *Daily Ireland* that he was 'astonished'.[98] Bik McFarlane complicated the dispute by denying there was an offer – 'I couldn't have accepted something that didn't exist.' In fact, several sources provide details on the 5 July offer.[99] The key question is whether or not the prison leadership accepted an offer that the outside leadership then rejected. David Beresford in *Ten Men Dead* presents a comm dated 7 July 1981, from 'Bik' to 'Brownie', that reads, 'I don't know if you've thought on this line, but I have been thinking that if we don't pull this off and Joe dies then the RA [IRA] are going to come under some bad stick from all quarters.'[100] *Something* prompted that message. A plausible explanation is that the outside committee turned down the offer hoping to get more from the British. When McDonnell died, they were under incredible pressure to make sure Owen Carron was elected and to hide the fact they had turned down a deal.

As Thomas Hennessey notes in *Hunger Strike: Margaret Thatcher's Battle with the IRA 1980–1981*, it is impossible to prove or disprove Ricky O'Rawe's account. O'Rawe has his supporters and Bik McFarlane has his.[101] One of the more telling pieces of the controversy is a visit O'Rawe describes in *Blanketmen*. His visitor wanted to know if he was writing a book about the hunger strike and would he be willing to speak to Gerry Adams. O'Rawe asked the visitor if he knew about the Brendan Duddy/Mountclimber offer. The reply was, 'Bad things happen in war, Ricky.'[102]

13

THE ARMALITE AND THE BALLOT BOX
(1981–1983)

'[A police officer] stopped at the office door and he knew that I could hear him and he said, "They shoot children", and he was reciting what he had just read on the book cover but he was pointing the gun into the office. And I remember that was a pretty explicit threat.'

– Tyrone republican[1]

The hunger strike changed everything. Bobby Sands's image would become iconic and his writings would become synonymous with the Provisionals. Sands's poignant comment, 'Our revenge will be the laughter of our children', looked to the future from a desperate time. His argument that, 'Everyone, republican or otherwise has their own particular part to play' would be the guide to transforming Sinn Féin into a political party. The hunger strikes had brought in a massive number of new recruits; some Anti-H-Block/Armagh committees went directly into Sinn Féin as cumann (clubs).[2] Sands, the icon, and the new recruits were part of something new replacing something old.

Following the hunger strike, the tension between the old leadership and the young Northerners resurfaced. At the Ard Fheis in the autumn of 1981, the delegates passed a motion that Sinn Féin contest *every* election. It was an incredible flip-flop from the year before. During the debate, Danny Morrison offered his famous quip, 'Who here really believes we can win the war through the ballot box? But will anyone here object if, with a ballot paper in one hand and an Armalite in this hand, we take power in Ireland?'[3] The armalite and ballot box strategy nicely summarized the goal of combining revolutionary politics with armed struggle. Another motion, put forward by Gerry Adams and seconded by Morrison, called for the deletion of federalism from the Sinn Féin Constitution. Morrison referred to federalism as a 'sop to Loyalists' and argued that 'you will have as much trouble getting the loyalists to accept a nine-county parliament as you will in getting them to accept a united Ireland, so why stop short?' A majority supported Adams and Morrison, but not the two-thirds' majority required to change the Constitution. The federalism fight was not resolved and, in the process, hard feelings were created.[4] Seán Mac Stiofáin, for example, was upset by insulting comments directed at Ruairí Ó Brádaigh and Dáithí O'Connell. He walked out and resigned from Sinn Féin.[5] When the Ard Fheis ended, the new

Danny Morrison, Sinn Féin parade and march in Downpatrick, County Down, 1980s. Bobbie Hanvey photographic archives, John J. Burns Library, Boston College.

Ard Chomhairle was split into two camps, Ó Brádaigh–O'Connell versus Adams–Morrison, with the latter on the rise.

In January 1982, Danny Morrison and Owen Carron flew to Canada from where they hoped to quietly slip into New York and promote the armalite and ballot box strategy at an Irish Northern Aid testimonial dinner. They were stopped at the border but the arrest had a silver lining since a judge in Buffalo granted them bail and they travelled extensively while awaiting a deportation hearing. They met more people and generated more publicity than if they had quietly slipped into and out of New York City.[6] A month later, however, the armalite and ballot box strategy failed its first test.

The Fine Gael–Labour coalition fell apart over budget issues and an election was called for February 1982.[7] On the Ard Chomhairle, everyone but Ruairí Ó Brádaigh and Charlie McGlade, a Belfast veteran from the 1930s who lived in Dublin, wanted Sinn Féin to fight the election. Ó Brádaigh contrasted June 1981 with February 1982:

> *[In 1981] the elections have already been postponed twice because hunger strikers were dying. We need to introduce a new factor. Sands has died, Hughes has died, O'Hara and McCreesh have died. We want to do something about it or these men are just going to die like flies. We need to galvanize support. This is an opportunity. We have the ear of the people. Bernadette Devlin was the spokesperson for the*

H-Block Committee. She could get on radio and television and so on, we couldn't. So, this was the push and eventually it was agreed and it was done and you know the results. But then, the following February or March when there was another general election, I was totally opposed to it. I said, 'We are going to do badly. This election isn't about H-Block, it is about the price of butter and children's shoes.' And, 'What have we to say to that? How can we affect this type of thing? We are getting into the rather ordinary constitutional politics and we are a revolutionary movement and we won't do anything like the H-block [vote]. We are not centre stage, we are not going to get radio and television, we won't have the paper [newspaper media] here …we had quite some standing as a result of the H-block situation and we will come down and we will suffer and it will be bad for our morale and it will be bad for the morale of the public and the view of the public in general.' And here I was left with one person, Charlie McGlade from Belfast, on the Ard Chomhairle supporting me … everyone else was mad for a contest … Defending the seats that had been won in the H-Block campaign… And, of course, Gerry Adams never turned up.

Q: For the Ard Chomhairle meeting?

A: Yes.[8]

In June 1981, Anti-H-Block/Armagh candidates received more than 42,000 first preference votes and won two seats in Leinster House/Dáil Éireann. Eight months later, Sinn Féin received 16,894 first preference votes, elected no one and learned the hard way that it was not relevant in the typical general election in the Republic of Ireland.[9]

The election was also a learning experience in another way. Neither Fianna Fáil by itself, nor Fine Gael and Labour in combination, had a majority in the Dáil. The Officials – Sinn Féin/The Workers' Party – elected three TDs and their support was essential if Charlie Haughey wanted to return as Taoiseach. In 1970, the Officials accused Haughey and Fianna Fáil of creating the Provisionals. In 1982, the revolutionary socialists in Sinn Féin/The Workers' Party cut a deal with him. In exchange for a promise to protect workers in a poor economy and to publish a progressive social and economic program, their TDs voted for Haughey. Tony Gregory got an even better deal. He had been elected as an Independent to represent Dublin's impoverished inner city and, in exchange for Gregory's support, Haughey agreed to a massive investment in new housing and jobs in the area.[10]

The deal making showed the political power that a small political party and even a single politician might have under the right conditions. That caught the attention of the Provisionals, as Ruairí Ó Brádaigh recalled:

I remember a function in Longford after the '82 result and the Officials were calling themselves Sinn Féin/The Workers' Party at that stage and they won three seats … and fringe people at this function, which was raising money to pay expenses, were saying, 'Well, look here, why don't we go in there and take part and look at the way the Worker's Party can do it. And besides that, we want the guards [police] off our back' and all that type of thing. So that is the ordinary people saying we want to convert to a constitutional political party, want to cease being a revolutionary movement. And this had the very effect that I feared at the time. Adams said he couldn't see that at all, but he didn't turn up to that Ard Chomhairle meeting which meant that he could distance himself from the decision.[11]

One of the notable features of Haughey's second term as Taoiseach was his strong stance against the British invasion of the Falklands/Malvinas, which infuriated Thatcher. In her memoir she writes of the 'terribly unhelpful stance taken by the Irish government during the Falklands War ...'[12]

Anglo-Irish relations were at a low point and Haughey's government was unstable because of the way it was put together. The discovery of a murder suspect in the Attorney General's apartment, which Haughey described as 'grotesque, unprecedented, bizarre, and unbelievable', added to the instability of the the 'GUBU' government. When Fianna Fáil published its budget proposal, Sinn Féin/The Workers' Party withdrew their support because it included cuts in government spending. Ireland had its third election in eighteen months and Fine Gael, who put forward Garret FitzGerald as a more trustworthy choice than Charlie Haughey, had their best vote since 1927. FitzGerald formed a government with Dick Spring, the new leader of the Labour Party, as Tanaiste. Sinn Féin/The Workers' Party lost a seat and was out of government; it was seen as the price they had paid for working with Fianna Fáil. Tony Gregory, in contrast, was re-elected and the 'Gregory Deal' and renovations in central Dublin are part of his legacy.[13] Sinn Féin did not contest this election.

In the North, and in stark contrast to the South, Sinn Féin thrived, with the former truce incident centres becoming neighbourhood advice centres. A Tyrone republican described the party's approach:

part of that, pursuing that electoral strategy, was starting up advice centres, Sinn Féin advice centres. And so we needed a Sinn Féin Advice Centre ... and the only office available was ... opposite the RUC barracks. Some people said to me maybe it's not a good idea, people will not go into the office, it's right opposite the barracks. And I said, 'No, people don't care about them. We'll have our Sinn Féin office opposite the barracks.' And I went every morning right about 9:30 and opened that door and went into the office.

The Advice Centres helped build a connection with the community and, according to the Tyrone republican, they also made it easier for the RUC and the British Army to monitor and harass Sinn Féin:

It was a steady flow of people and we put our little booklets in the window and all the paraphernalia and all the literature and whatnot. And I remember we had this little book in the window and the front cover was, 'They Shoot Children', and it was referring to the plastic bullets. And I remember one day the RUC walked [by on patrol] ... there was a number of them walking on one side of the street and a number keeping a certain distance from each other in army style. And I remember one of them standing with his gun, and it looked like the gun that discharges plastic bullets, and he stopped at the office door and he knew that I could hear him. And he said, 'They shoot children', and he was reciting what he had just read on the book cover but he was pointing the gun into the office. And I remember that was a pretty explicit threat.[14]

RUC harassment was not new or unexpected. In response to the hunger strike mobilization, the British added more sinister tactics to their counterinsurgency, beginning with supergrasses – informers willing to testify against groups of people.

Christopher Black was an IRA volunteer from Ardoyne who had already completed one spell in prison. When he was rearrested in the autumn of 1981 he was not interested in another jail term. In exchange for immunity and a guarantee of safety for his family, he implicated more than forty people in terrorist offenses. In a non-jury courtroom in Northern Ireland, the uncorroborated testimony of an informer was often enough for a conviction. Black's testimony led to the conviction of twenty-two people and caused a major disruption in the IRA. Gerry Bradley and Brian Feeney, in *Insider: Gerry Bradley's Life in the IRA*, write that:

> Black wiped out Ardoyne and the Bone. The Crum [Crumlin Road Jail] was bunged: three in a cell for a while. He had a terrible domino effect, too. People stopped leaving their doors open. They were scared to help. They had seen people charged for stupid little things. They couldn't trust the IRA any more. Black had an effect on morale and confidence for years.[15]

Between 1982 and 1985, supergrasses led to the arrest of more than 400 alleged terrorists – Provisionals, INLA/IRSP supporters and loyalists. Allegations from thirteen Provisional IRA supergrasses accounted for charges against more than two hundred people. By definition, informers are deceitful and they are often lousy witnesses and with time the supergrass initiative collapsed. For example, eighteen of Christopher Black's victims successfully appealed their convictions. In the meantime, serious damage was inflicted on the Provisionals. One of the more prominent victims was Jim Gibney, an important Sinn Féin strategist and alleged 'person of authority and importance in the IRA'.[16]

The British also tried to counter the mass mobilization with a new political initiative. James Prior, who had replaced Humphrey Atkins as Secretary of State for Northern Ireland, published a White Paper, 'Northern Ireland – a Framework for Devolution', that proposed an election to a seventy-eight-member Assembly that would serve as a consultative body. If 70 per cent of the representatives agreed, then direct rule would devolve from London to Belfast one department at a time. 'Rolling devolution' would be the third attempt to resurrect the Northern Ireland Assembly in less than a decade. The Provisionals saw it as another attempt to bring back Stormont and called for a boycott and, unlike in 1973 and 1975, they nominated candidates for the election. The SDLP were committed to power sharing, which was not included in the White Paper, and suspected a new Assembly would be unworkable. They also feared they were being outflanked by Sinn Féin and, after much deliberation, the SDLP followed Sinn Féin's lead and nominated candidates who, if elected, would boycott the Assembly.[17]

Several of Sinn Féin's candidates were connected to the hunger strike, beginning with Owen Carron, MP, and including Gerry Adams, Danny Morrison and Benedict McElwee, the brother of Tom McElwee. J.B. O'Hagan, who was from Lurgan but lived across the border in Monaghan, and Martin McGuinness, seen as an IRA commander and not a Sinn Féin politician, were also candidates. One interpretation of O'Hagan's and McGuinness's candidacy was that they represented an endorsement from the senior Army leadership of Sinn Féin's involvement in elections. Indeed, there are reports that the election was important enough that Martin McGuinness and Gerry Adams stepped down as Chief of Staff and Adjutant General so they could focus on the campaign. Apparently they remained on the Army Council, with Ivor Bell as C/S and Pat Doherty as Adjutant General.[18]

Most of the younger people had never voted let alone organized a political campaign. Candidates had to be identified, proposed and seconded and each candidate required an assenter who would publicly sign on as a supporter. Mitchel McLaughlin, who was seen as the political complement to the military-minded Martin McGuinness, commented:

> In October of '82, we had decided that we would contest the Assembly elections. And Martin McGuinness, who was also equally abstentionist, he agreed to stand as the candidate. We had [debated] as to who should be the candidate and it was agreed that he would be and I would be his Director of Elections. Up until that point in time, neither of us had ever been in a polling station. So he was a candidate and I was his Director of Elections and neither of us ever voted. … He won that election in Derry. It was a major breakthrough for us and a significant set-back for the SDLP.[19]

The election stunned the Irish and British political establishments. Owen Carron topped the poll in Fermanagh/South Tyrone and Gerry Adams topped the poll in West Belfast. In Derry, Martin McGuinness finished second behind John Hume but still had enough votes to be elected. Danny Morrison was elected in Mid-Ulster and Jim McAllister was elected in Armagh.[20]

Sinn Féin received 64,191 (10.1 per cent) first preference votes. Even if the SDLP received almost twice as many votes (118,891; 18.8 per cent) and won more than twice as many seats (14 vs 5), the election was a shock. Anyone paying attention knew that, with more experience and better organization, Sinn Féin might have taken three more seats at the SDLP's expense.[21]

To some degree, people voted for Sinn Féin because they were new faces and it was the first Northern election after the hunger strike. McLaughlin explained:

> I think in those circumstances – I mean, it's emotional, it was hype, it was novelty. And we were running somewhat ahead of our actual vote. You know, there was people just by the novelty and the excitement of it, and maybe a wee bit of a kick-back against the system, who were voting for us as an alternative as opposed to a close examination of what we stood for or for our politics as such – the fact that we were an alternative to the tired, kind of middle-class, middle of the road, middle-aged SDLP.[22]

Alienated nationalists had been uninterested in the SDLP for more than a decade. A young republican from Derry City, for example, wanted nothing to do with John Hume:

> He's right done well sitting with his own private house up there – two cars and ordering another one [sarcastically]. He's really heavy working class like. He's got all these big fancy cars. If I was … working class, as Hume claims to be, and I had cars like that there, I don't know, I'd want to stay unemployed

all my life ... the only people that accept Hume in this town now is that sort of older generation ... Sinn Féin's a radical party and the young fellows ... see Sinn Féin and Sinn Féin members getting harassed. It's a fact of life ... you never see any SDLP man or their car getting stopped ... they can see that we're part of ... that we're working class with them. They can see we're going through the same kind of business as they are. And that's why they tend to identify more with us than they do with the SDLP.[23]

Sinn Féin gave a new and radical voice to young nationalists. With Sinn Féin and the SDLP boycotting, the Assembly was effectively scuttled. The success came at a price, though. Just after the election, Peter Corrigan, an ex-prisoner who had moved into Sinn Féin and served as Jim McAllister's election agent, was out for a walk with his brother and son. Loyalists drove by and strafed them with a submachine gun, killing Corrigan.[24]

A couple of weeks later, the British added another dimension to their counter-insurgency – targeted state violence. Gervaise McKerr was in his early thirties and had been operating in the IRA's North Armagh Brigade for a couple of years. Seán Burns and Eugene Toman were childhood friends and ten years younger than McKerr. They were arrested for rioting during the second hunger strike and held on remand until March 1982. Toman and Burns joined the North Armagh Brigade the day they were released and, along with McKerr, the police believe they planted a landmine in October 1982 that killed three RUC officers. In mid-November, the three of them drove up to a roadblock that was staffed by a special unit of the RUC. More than 100 bullets were fired into the car and they died at the scene. The RUC claimed they drove through the roadblock though forensic evidence suggested something different. Gervaise McKerr, for example, was shot in the chest while either getting out of the car or just after getting out of the stationary car. Contrary to British denials, the evidence suggests that Gervaise McKerr, Seán Burns and Eugene Toman were the first of a series of 'shoot to kill' victims.[25] In seven incidents between 1982 and 1992, twenty-six Tyrone IRA volunteers were shot dead in ambushes when they might have been arrested.[26]

The election increased Sinn Féin's profile and credibility and Danny Morrison was busy enough that he stepped down as editor of *AP/RN*. His successor was Mick Timothy, the author of a popular column entitled 'Burke's at the Back'.[27] The Troops Out Movement invited Gerry Adams to London and Ken Livingstone, leader of the Greater London Council, agreed to meet with him. Thatcher's government quickly took care of that and William Whitelaw, the Home Secretary and former Secretary of State for Northern Ireland, excluded Gerry Adams, Martin McGuinness and Danny Morrison from entering Great Britain. Livingstone, nicknamed 'Red Ken' because of his progressive politics, and two Labour councillors travelled to Belfast and met with Adams, Danny Morrison et al.[28]

In the South, the hunger strike cast a long shadow and continued to bring people into the movement. Caoimhghín Ó Caoláin, for example, left banking and became the General Manager of AP/RN:

it was the selflessness and the great courage of the ten young men who died on hunger strike and their comrades ... that motivated me sufficiently to take the conscious decision to become politically active and that culminated, in the following year of 1982, with my making the decision to leave my then employment of some twelve years and to go full-time with Sinn Féin.[29]

During the hunger strike, Seán Crowe had worked full-time for the Movement. At first, he returned to his job: *'I was in full paid employment and I was up on a charge of rioting at the British embassy and I decided then that I was going to pack in the job.'*[30] The young woman from Sligo who was involved in the H-Block/Armagh protests was gradually brought into Sinn Féin:

> *Well, I didn't really kind of decide. What happened was that Seán, my boyfriend, was working for Sinn Féin and he had to drop out for a couple of months. He was doing exams, so they needed somebody. So I said I would step in, fill the space while he was gone and then finish and drop out when he came back. But by the time he came back, I was so interested that I decided to stay on and they decided that they would keep me on. That's the way it happened. I didn't make any decision or I didn't always want to work in here. I had no interest in politics or anything like that beforehand.*[31]

Inevitably, the rapid growth of Sinn Féin in the North was compared with the party's slower growth in the South. There was another troubling comparison. The Southern leadership – people like Ruairí Ó Brádaigh and Dáithí O'Connell – looked, dressed and talked like the middle-aged family men that they were. They seemed out of touch, from a different generation, compared to Adams, Carron, McLaughlin, McGuinness, Morrison et al.[32]

Given the result from the year before, there was going to be a re-match on federalism at the 1982 Ard Fheis. Just before the Ard Fheis, Gerry Adams went too far in trying to advance the new direction, as described by Ruairí Ó Brádaigh:

> *I was confronted by Adams who demanded that I condemn Éire Nua.*
>
> *Q: Condemn it?*
>
> *A: Yes, at the Ard Fheis. That I was a source of scandal. That the prisoners, who to my mind have been orchestrated, the prisoners in Long Kesh were opposed to this. That, now, the Army had dropped this policy – that was known well, that this was the situation. And there was I as President of Sinn Féin and I was still pursuing this policy. So that I was a source of scandal to the young volunteers and so on. And that I should get up there at the coming Ard Fheis in '82 and denounce it. [Laughs] Please.*

It says something about his position in the Provisionals that Gerry Adams felt sure enough to demand that Ruairí Ó Brádaigh denounce a policy that Ó Brádaigh had publicly and proudly endorsed for more than a decade.

The young Northerners saw Éire Nua and federalism as a 'sop' to unionists. Ó Brádaigh saw it as a non-sectarian bridge to unionists who would have to live in a united Ireland; that was important to him, if not Adams and company. Ó Brádaigh was also sure of his own position. He had been President of Sinn Féin since 1970 and had been in the IRA leadership since the 1950s.

Sinn Féin was the junior partner to the IRA, and they had some overlapping members, but they were separate organizations. The IRA could not simply dictate orders to Sinn Féin. Ó Brádaigh commented:

> So I said that this idea hadn't come from Sinn Féin. It had come from the Army Council of the IRA who made a public statement a week or so, maybe less, after internment. It was their policy and that Sinn Féin agreed with it ... And it was an original idea, that it came from within the Movement itself, it wasn't imported from anywhere ... And that this was a way of resolving the situation and I thought that getting rid of it would make the struggle much more difficult for young people out there fighting and sacrificing themselves ... No way would I do that ... I had carried out my duty, as instructed by Sinn Féin and by Ard Fheis's, and the Army agreed with it. It was their idea from the start and if the Army leadership had changed and the Army policy had changed – I thought that was regrettable but that I wasn't going to change with it ... I said, 'No way, if you want a new song, you get a new singer.'[33]

Ó Brádaigh threatened to resign as President.

At an Ard Fheis, the delegates typically re-elect members of the Officer Board and the Ard Chomhairle. Candidates are often unopposed and the leadership tends to evolve over time, as people resign, become ill or, on occasion, are arrested. Ó Brádaigh had a lot of friends and supporters and there was no succession plan in place. If he quit just before the Ard Fheis, it would be a 'scandal' but Ó Brádaigh refused to continue as President of Sinn Féin unless the 'ultimatum' was withdrawn. It was withdrawn but, at the Ard Fheis and after more than four years of trying, Adams and his supporters got the two-thirds vote required to remove federalism from the Sinn Féin Constitution. Several senior people, including Richard Behal, Joe O'Neill and Tom Sullivan left the Ard Chomhairle. They were replaced by younger people who embraced the new direction. Ó Brádaigh continued as President and Dáithí O'Connell and Cathleen Knowles stayed on as officers, but they were in the minority.[34] And Gerry Adams's stock continued to rise.

In the spring of 1983, Seamus Kerr won a by-election for the Omagh District Council. When he took his seat, it was the first time since the 1920s that a Sinn Féiner had served on a Northern council. On 9 June 1983, Sinn Féin rocked the political world by contesting 14 of the 17 Northern Irish constituencies and receiving 102,701 votes (13.4 per cent overall and 43 per cent of the nationalist vote). Gerry Adams took the West Belfast seat from Gerry Fitt and Danny Morrison lost Mid-Ulster by only seventy-eight votes. In Fermanagh/South Tyrone, Owen Carron lost his seat because the SDLP fielded a candidate and split the nationalist vote, but he received almost 21,000 votes versus the 10,000 for the SDLP candidate.[35] It was another watershed, showing that the Sands and Carron results of two years before were not a fluke. One of the benefits from the election was that the British were forced to lift the exclusion order on Adams. With Joe Austin, he visited London at the personal invitation of Ken Livingstone. They met with journalists, were escorted into the House of Commons by Labour MP Jeremy Corbyn and, in general, were a media sensation.[36] In everything but title, Adams was the leader of Sinn Féin.

Sinn Féin's success upset a variety of people. At the end of June, Alex Maskey won a by-election for a seat on the Belfast City Council. When he entered the Belfast City Hall chambers for his first council meeting, he was met with boos and jeers. Maskey began his maiden speech in Irish and the unionist councillors started screaming and stamping their feet.[37] Garret FitzGerald was also alarmed by what was happening in Belfast. In *All in a Life*, FitzGerald describes a memorandum he wrote with Peter Barry, his Minister for Foreign Affairs:

> At a recent by-election in the Lower Falls area of Belfast the Sinn Féin vote had exceeded that of the SDLP by a margin of over three to one. If Sinn Féin's electoral support in Northern Ireland were to exceed that of the SDLP, the situation there could get out of control and threaten the whole island, for in those circumstances the IRA might seek a violent confrontation with the unionists and try to follow this by an attempt to destabilise the Republic.[38]

FitzGerald tried to stem the Sinn Féin tide with its own political initiative.

When he had returned as Taoiseach, FitzGerald set out to find a way to counter the nationalist alienation that was fuelling Sinn Féin. He began with the New Ireland Forum, which was designed to support the SDLP and start repairing the damage that Charlie Haughey had inflicted on Anglo-Irish relations. As FitzGerald describes it, the Forum was:

> open in principle to Unionist Party participation and in practice to hearing the unionist case put to it at least semi-officially, but that would be designed in such a way that it would help to restore the SDLP's self-confidence; and second, to have through this forum a more secure base from which to move towards my objective of a new arrangement with Britain that would reduce the alienation of the Northern nationalist minority and thus strengthen constitutional nationalist politics against inroads by the IRA's political party, Sinn Féin.[39]

Paisley and the DUP and the UUP, led by James Molyneaux, refused to attend. The Alliance Party and the Workers' Party (which had dropped the Sinn Féin label) also passed. Sinn Féin was not invited and thus, the New Ireland Forum was a series of meetings and public presentations involving representatives of constitutional Irish nationalism, as led by FitzGerald of Fine Gael, Dick Spring of the Irish Labour Party, John Hume of the SDLP and Charlie Haughey of Fianna Fáil. They met for the first time at Dublin Castle in May of 1983.

With the Forum underway, FitzGerald reached out to Margaret Thatcher and James Prior, and to show he was serious, he let Thatcher know that he was willing to discuss amending Articles 2 and 3 of the Irish Constitution, which claimed the entire island for the Dublin government. In return, FitzGerald wanted a 'substantial package' of reforms and he wanted to discuss the possibility of London–Dublin 'joint authority' over Northern Ireland.[40] His biggest problem was convincing the British that there were good reasons that nationalists were alienated from the political process in Northern Ireland.

Nationalists had experienced internment without trial, Bloody Sunday, non-jury courts, the mistreatment of suspects in custody, supergrasses and, most recently, shoot to kill. The following is from the Derry republican who described his journey from civil rights protester to

Provisional IRA volunteer in the aftermath of Bloody Sunday. Nothing in the intervening decade had persuaded him that he had made the wrong decision. On 9 August 1983, Private Ian Thain killed Thomas 'Kidso' Reilly in West Belfast. Thain said that he thought Reilly was reaching for a hidden pistol but Reilly was shirtless, unarmed and shot in the back. The respondent offered his interpretation of the event, *'he deliberately shot Kidso Reilly, who was the roadie for the Bananarama group. He ran up to him and shot him at point blank range. He knew the man wasn't involved in anything, he knew the man wasn't armed but he did it.'* Reilly was the 140th civilian shot dead by the British Army. In December 1984, Thain became the first British soldier sentenced to life in prison for murder while on duty in Northern Ireland.[41] On the surface, it appeared that justice was served and the 'rule of law' was enforced. The Derry respondent was not convinced:

> *Now all sorts of pleas could be made and have been made for similar circumstances in the past, where he was under pressure, it was the war zone on his nerves and the terrible pressures they were under and all. And so people have been let off in similar circumstances. ... The British Government sacrificed Private Thain in those circumstances because it suited them to put somebody away for it. Also, because it impinged on the consciousness of an awful lot of people, not only in Ireland but especially England, because the group is based there. And then, internationally, because the pop scene is a different thing altogether. And a lot of kids who might know sweet FA [fuck all], well, who know an awful lot about politics, current present day politics but aren't interested in them and who couldn't name the Prime Minister, for example, will tell you every individual member of every band and their nicknames as well. So that would impinge on the conscience of a lot of people. So there's a political decision behind putting Thain away ... he is just merely a sacrifice and it hasn't changed policy one whit. Similarly, they put a couple of RUC men on trial. A great majority are acquitted, maybe one or two get small sentences and invariably then these are suspended sentences and put to one side. Any UDR man that commits a crime is an ex-UDR man by the time he comes to court. It doesn't change the situation, and I am intelligent enough – now that doesn't make me any different from the great majority of ordinary people, I'm just the exact same – I'm street-wise enough to know what's right and what's wrong. And that's not going to change my opinion by locking up one or ten or twenty Brits.*[42]

After serving less than three years of a life sentence, Private Thain was released on parole and allowed to return to the British Army.[43]

Sinn Féin was a legal political party and it was also a threat to the establishment. Advice centre workers were arrested and threatened:

> *six o'clock in the morning ... there was a big, big knock on the door and the house was surrounded by RUC and they'd [come for me]. So they arrested me and took me to the barracks ... I went to wash my face and couldn't find a towel in the bathroom so I had to bop into the living room to get the towel and my father was sitting there and it was like, I felt terrible for him. I didn't feel terrible for myself. I felt terrible for him ... 'Oh, gosh, they have come to this house and this is not fair on him' ... So they released me after two days. But during that time all they done was threaten me and told me to leave the office and go back to work [at a previous job] and that, if I didn't do that, that I would get to know every corridor of the*

barracks, that I would be able to walk around blindfolded. They promised me they would persecute me if I didn't. They could tell me that there was going to be dead meat in a couple of weeks' time ... and Brian Campbell and Colm McGirr were shot dead about three weeks later. And I didn't really listen. I didn't see the significance of that because people were dying every day. And this is typical of what they would say anyway and they just were more or less telling me what they knew about me and it was an intimidatory exercise. I remember being released that evening and my mother saying, 'Maybe you should take the day off tomorrow.' And I said, 'No way. I am not taking no day off. I'm going back. I'm going back.' I remember feeling the sense of absolute defiance. You think you're going to intimidate me? You think you are going to take me and say all them things to me and threaten that I will know the barracks blindfolded? That's fine. I'm prepared to take this chance and I opened the door and walked in. So they knew that didn't work.[44]

The respondent was in Sinn Féin. Colm McGirr, twenty-three, and Brian Campbell, nineteen, were members of the Tyrone Brigade and they were attractive victims for a shoot-to-kill policy, especially Campbell.

In Long Kesh, the prisoners had taken advantage of relaxed conditions and, while engaging in prison work, had organized an escape. On 25 September 1983, they took over sections of the prison and nineteen of them got away. The escapees included some of the most high-profile prisoners: Dermot Finucane (Pat and Seamus's brother), Gerry Kelly, Bik McFarlane, Pádraig McKearney (Tommy's brother) and Seamus Campbell – Brian's brother.

Brian Campbell and Colm McGirr were fairly typical of IRA volunteers at the time. They were from republican families and both of them had been arrested and threatened by the security forces. In December 1983, they were climbing through a hedge on their way to check an arms dump when an undercover SAS unit opened fire and killed them at the scene; a third volunteer escaped. They were the first active service volunteers killed after the 'Great Escape'. At their funerals, the Provisionals highlighted the wedding of armed struggle with Sinn Féin's election success. The mourners included Gerry Adams, Martin McGuinness, Danny Morrison and Owen Carron. Owen Carron gave the oration at McGirr's funeral and Danny Morrison gave the oration at Campbell's funeral. Seamus Campbell was never recaptured.[45]

The rise of Sinn Féin worried the authorities in Northern Ireland, the Republic of Ireland and Britain but it also worried some of the Provisionals. Several sources report that Ivor Bell was upset that, during the Westminster election, the Belfast IRA supported Gerry Adams as a candidate by limiting their operations.[46] A blunder like La Mon or the shooting of Joanne Mathers could have cost Adams the election. Ruairí Ó Brádaigh, Dáithí O'Connell and their supporters were worried that the Provisionals were following the Officials into constitutional politics. They were not opposed to politics but they were opposed participation in *parliamentary politics*. Ó Brádaigh was still upset by the transformation of the Officials:

Jesus, they were calling us terrorists and gunmen and so on. These guys came and slept in this house. They – I had them at table, had my kids on their knees. And they were bringing stuff around and training. And now they're all calling us bloody militarists and gunmen. The cheek of them! Do you know what I mean? It's a bit thick.[47]

Ó Brádaigh and Ivor Bell wanted to slow things down and were in the minority. Events would strengthen the hand of those who wanted more politics.

Ivor Bell was one of almost thirty Provisionals arrested on the word of Robert 'Beano' Lean, another supergrass. Even though Lean retracted his statement and Bell was released, the damage was done and he was out as Chief of Staff. Observers identify Kevin McKenna of Tyrone as his successor.[48] Another person who left the leadership around this time was Kevin Mallon, who once described Gerry Adams as the kind of person who, if the roof were falling in, would 'act as if he had planned it to fall in exactly that way'.[49] Mallon was another veteran from the 1950s and had a close personal relationship with Ó Brádaigh and O'Connell. In *A Secret History of the IRA*, Ed Moloney reports that the kidnapping of the racehorse Shergar (in February 1983) and of businessman Don Tidey (in November 1983) led to Mallon's departure as IRA Director of Operations. No one knows for sure what happened to Shergar; an Irish soldier and reserve police officer were killed in the hunt for Tidey, who was rescued. Neither kidnapping brought in any money and both were publicity disasters.[50]

In Sinn Féin, Gerry Adams, Danny Morrison, Tom Hartley et al. outnumbered Ó Brádaigh, O'Connell and Cathleen Knowles. Tired of losing votes and aware that the situation was not going to change, just before the 1983 Ard Fheis, all three of them announced that they would not continue as officers. Ó Brádaigh's decision was expected but O'Connell's and Knowles's decisions were a surprise. After a bit of scrambling, and subject to ratification by the delegates, John Joe McGirl agreed to succeed O'Connell as one joint vice-President. Phil Flynn of Louth agreed to replace Adams as the other and Denise Creggan agreed to replace Knowles as one of the General Secretaries.

In his outgoing presidential address, Ó Brádaigh was not bitter, although he did get in a dig while praising the new leadership:

> We hand over the great Sinn Féin organisation to a new generation, more vigorous and more successful at the polls than at any time since 1918. We are gratified that in the 1980s they have at last accepted what many of us on the ard chomhairle were saying right through the 1970s, that we should be involved electorally in the six counties first of all and in the twenty-six counties when opportune.

The press was speculating that a split was looming but he denied it, adding that there would be no splits as long as there was 'no departure from the basic principles'. His theme was that constitutional democrats are not trustworthy. He was an elected member of the Dublin parliament when the constitutional politicians of Fianna Fáil sent him to an internment camp in 1957, 'The rules of democracy, then as now, for those who sought and gained democratic support for policies that might upset the Leinster House apple-cart, was the same as that which the Thatcher "democrats" employed after they had murdered Bobby Sands, MP for Fermanagh/South Tyrone. When the rules no longer suit, they simply change the rules.'[51] He finished by welcoming the new leadership and wishing them well and the delegates then endorsed a new President and Officer Board. The new Ard Chomhairle was sympathetic to the new leadership and included Owen

Carron, Pat Doherty (Donegal), Tom Hartley, Martin Ferris (Kerry), Martin McGuinness and Rita O'Hare (Belfast).[52] Only two years after the hunger strike, Gerry Adams was President of Sinn Féin.

There is every reason to believe that he had spent several years pursuing the position and yet, in his first presidential address, he praised Ó Brádaigh's leadership and denied any personal desire for the office – 'I was extremely reluctant to let my name go forward.' Adams claimed that 'The emphasis needs to be upon the 26 counties' and that his preference was for 'a leader who was based in this area'. It's an interesting comment considering he is still President of Sinn Féin. Adams also noted that Sinn Féin was an abstentionist party and 'it is not my intention to advocate a change in this situation'.[53] Ruairí Ó Brádaigh saw Sinn Féin as one of two wings of the Irish Republican Movement. Gerry Adams was going to turn Sinn Féin into a political party.

Much of Adams's address paralleled what any President of Sinn Féin would have said: in the North they faced a shoot-to-kill policy, unemployment and poverty; in the South they faced a 'neo-colonial state' that entered the EEC on the coattails of the British. There was also the traditional appeal to Protestants by asking for their help in building a new Ireland – 'Republicans do not seek a sectarian state,' he said. Of course, the year before Sinn Féin had dumped a policy that reached out to those same Protestants.

14

ADAMS TAKES COMMAND (1983–1985)

*I don't think any tears should be cried over people who have been great heroes of the past and suddenly
are not any more today because that's the way it is.*

– Derry republican[1]

Following the 1983 Ard Fheis, Gerry Adams led Sinn Féin and a majority on the Army
Council supported his vision. There was still opposition to the new direction, however.
Since it can call an Army convention at which policies will be debated and a new leadership
might be elected, the IRA Executive serves as a check on the Army Council. Ruairí Ó Brádaigh
was no longer President of Sinn Féin, and if Ó Brádaigh had been on the Army Council, he
was off it after New Year's Day 1984 when he was seriously injured in a tragic car accident.
However, six of the twelve people on the Executive agreed with Ó Brádaigh and one of them
was Paddy Ryan, a comrade from the 1950s who was still upset with Goulding et al. Two other
likely critics were Dáithí O'Connell, who was co-opted onto the Executive in 1980, and Ivor
Bell, who it is reported was co-opted onto the Executive after the supergrass evidence against
him was withdrawn.[2] Adams's efforts to change Sinn Féin were also slowed by an attempt on
his life.[3]

During the 1983 Westminster campaign, Gerry Adams and four other activists got into a
confrontation with RUC officers who had had pulled down an Irish tricolour. The group was
charged with obstruction and the case went to trial in the spring of 1984. Adams was in a
car driving away from court in central Belfast when another car pulled alongside and loyalists
opened fire, hitting four of the five occupants. Adams was hit in his neck, shoulder and arm.
The driver, Bob Murray, was not injured and drove on to the Royal Victoria Hospital in West
Belfast; all of them survived. The loyalists were immediately arrested by undercover police
officers, which prompted speculation that they could have stopped the assassination attempt
but chose not to.

While Gerry Adams recovered from his injuries, Garret FitzGerald plotted a course for
constitutional nationalism, even if it disenfranchized voters. Coalition ministers refused to meet
with delegations that included elected Sinn Féin representatives.[4] FitzGerald also continued with
his attempt to unite constitutional nationalism. The New Ireland Forum released its report in
May 1984 and the report offered three scenarios for a 'new Ireland':

a. a 'unitary state';
b. a 'federal/confederal' state that combined the twenty-six counties of the Republic of Ireland and the six counties of Northern Ireland; and,
c. 'joint authority' where the Dublin and London governments shared responsibility for Northern Ireland.[5]

FitzGerald wanted to use the report as a framework for bringing the unionist political parties and the British government into a conversation on the future of Ireland. He was unsuccessful as the unionists dismissed the report out of hand.[6] At a press conference, Charlie Haughey undermined FitzGerald and the report with the statement, 'the only solution is as stated in the report: a unitary state with a new constitution'. Haughey also insulted the unionists by saying that no one was entitled to deny the 'natural unity' of Ireland.[7] Haughey was out of power and could be ignored but FitzGerald needed Thatcher's help if Dublin and London were going to work together to counter nationalist alienation.

By May of 1984, there was enough evidence of a shoot-to-kill policy that John Stalker, the Deputy Chief Constable of the Greater Manchester Police Force, was asked to lead an inquiry into the conduct of the RUC. His efforts were troubled from the start. At Stalker's first meeting with the RUC Chief Constable, Sir John Herman, he was given terms of reference that were drawn up by the Chief Constable, a clear conflict of interest. In his memoir, *The Stalker Affair*, he writes, 'It became obvious that we could not trust anyone ...' In one of the incidents Stalker investigated, British intelligence (MI5) had placed a recording unit in a hayshed that was used as an IRA arms dump. The RUC, unaware of the device, shot Michael Tighe and his friend, two innocent teenagers who were checking out the shed. Tighe was killed, his friend was severely wounded and the incident was recorded. Stalker discovered that the tape was destroyed but there was a transcript. The Chief Constable refused to show him the transcript unless Stalker signed a 'declaration of secrecy' which Stalker refused.[8]

The degree to which the criminal justice system in Northern Ireland was troubled was made abundantly clear only a few days after Stalker began his investigation. Three RUC officers had been charged with murdering Eugene Toman, who was shot dead with Seán Burns and Gervaise McKerr in the first shoot-to-kill incident. The presiding judge, Lord Justice Maurice Gibson, acquitted the officers and then offered remarks that made international news:

> I wish to make it clear that, having heard the entire Crown case, I regard each of the accused as absolutely blameless in this matter. That finding should be put on their record along with my own commendation as to their courage and determination for bringing the three deceased men to justice, in this case, to the final court of justice.

Although he later denied that it was his intention, in effect Lord Justice Gibson had endorsed killing unarmed suspects. Garret FitzGerald used Gibson's comments and the criticism they generated in Ireland, Britain and the US to show Thatcher that the nationalist community in general was losing faith in the system. (In 1987, a Provisional IRA landmine killed Justice Gibson and his wife, Cecily, as they drove home from a holiday.)[9]

Not that it was needed, but the 1984 European election further showed that the two governments needed to do something. Revd Ian Paisley again topped the poll, with 230,000 votes (33.6 per cent) and whilst the result was expected, it was still distressing for anyone seeking middle ground in Northern Ireland. The high-level of support for uncompromising unionism contributed to the alienation and sense of minority status among nationalists. The good news for Dublin and London was that Danny Morrison directly challenged John Hume and lost. Hume took the second seat with 151,000 votes (22.1 per cent) and John Taylor of the Ulster Unionists took the third and final seat with 147,000 votes (21.5 Per cent). Even though Morrison finished fourth (91,000 votes; 13.3 per cent), Gerry Adams claimed the result as a victory: 'I consider it a victory that our vote held, that it is a republican vote, clearly anti-imperialist and anti-EEC, a republican vote as opposed to a nationalist or a Catholic vote, that it is ideologically sound, that it is not going to fluctuate, that it can be built upon.'[10] Adams had a good point. Whatever their reasons for voting Sinn Féin, the bottom line was that three years removed from the emotion of the hunger strikes the political wing of an armed insurgency had received 91,000 votes.

Dublin and London were also frustrated because the conflict was expanding in unpredictable ways. In 1981, five people associated with Irish Northern Aid – Michael Flannery, George Harrison, Tom Falvey, Daniel Gormley and Joseph McLaughlin – were arrested and charged with gun running. The next year, Gabe Megahey and four others were arrested trying to purchase missiles for the IRA from an FBI agent. The arrests ended an important source of weapons; Harrison had been running guns to the IRA for decades. The case against Flannery and his colleagues, however, took an unexpected twist when the defendants admitted they were trying to send guns to the IRA but claimed that they believed their supplier, George DeMeo, was a CIA agent and that they had the blessing of the United States government. After all, the United States had secretly provided weapons to insurgents in places like Cuba, Guatemala and Haiti. Why not Ireland? To the amazement of the prosecution, the group was acquitted. Five months later, Michael Flannery was the Grand Marshall of New York's 1983 St Patrick's Day parade.[11]

The Provisionals were not allowed into the US, so Tom Hartley suggested a 'fact-finding' tour for Irish-Americans. In the summer of 1983, more than eighty of them met with Joe Cahill in Dublin, travelled about Ireland with Fra McCann and met with Gerry Adams, Danny Morrison and Martin McGuinness, among others. In the 'bandit country' of South Armagh, they met with Jim McAllister and were treated to an IRA checkpoint. With a Canadian television crew filming and a British helicopter overhead, the Irish-Americans cheered as balaclava-clad volunteers, armed with Armalites and a machine gun, waved them on. The tour ended with Irish Northern Aid leading the annual anti-internment march up the Falls Road. One of the speakers that day was Martin Galvin, Irish Northern Aid's spokesperson and editor of *The Irish People*.[12] The tour was irritating but, when another was organized for the following summer, the Dublin government was not about to ban a bunch of Irish-American tourists. The British, less concerned about Irish-America, banned Martin Galvin from Northern Ireland so, when the tour buses crossed the border, they were stopped and searched but Galvin was not with them. As the Irish Americans made their way across Northern Ireland, the media wondered if he would turn up for the annual anti-internment march and rally in Belfast.

On 12 August 1984, there was a heavy RUC presence as the marchers walked up the Falls Road and into the heart of West Belfast. Twice plastic bullets were fired at kids throwing stones. When the march arrived outside Connolly House, Sinn Féin headquarters in Andersonstown, more plastic bullets were fired in response to more rocks thrown. Perhaps 3,000 people sat down in the street or stood around the edge of the crowd and listened to speakers, including an address from a representative of the Troops Out Movement in England. Gerry Adams was then called to the podium and he gave the Irish-Americans a glimpse of his charisma. The RUC were out to get Galvin and the media were primed to record it. Adams mocked the authorities with: 'We have a perfectly peaceful, passive demonstration of people sitting down and we have the press here. Now if we act in a disciplined fashion, the RUC and British soldiers will be forced before the cameras of the world's press to expose themselves.' The crowd laughed and Adams ended the introduction with:

> Wouldn't it be a terrible disappointment if Martin Galvin didn't turn up? Now to the RUC and to the British soldiers and those in charge, if you want to kill men, women and children, this is your opportunity, because we are not moving. I would like to welcome Martin Galvin of Irish Northern Aid.[13]

It was a set up and the RUC played into his hands. Galvin bounced up onto the platform and plastic bullets started flying. Galvin described the event:

> *It's just tragic what happened. I get called to the platform and I was supposed to then, just at some point, give a speech, melt into the crowd, change clothes, do other things and then be guided or escorted by republicans who were on the side. And it turned out there was a fellow there that I knew very well ... as soon as I got up, the British opened fire with plastic bullets into the crowd – started to charge in, land rovers, everything. I saw that. And this guy [that I knew] started shouting, saying, 'run, run.' So I thought he was picked to lead the way for me and I jumped down right next to him. And I realized – he kept shouting, 'run, run' – that he had nothing to do with the people trying to get me away. I had now lost track of them and there was havoc and I couldn't find them. What I did was, I stood on the side on – there was a fence right on the side of Connolly House. I just figured they are going to be looking for some people running, they're going to charge into the house. And they did ... I was against that fence for a long time and then just after everything went by me, I was able to get away from there. Just by acting like nothing had happened or blending into the crowd in that way, just acting like I was not trying to run away.*[14]

The RUC booted their way into Connolly House and fired more plastic bullets, hitting Mick Reilly of Sinn Féin in the face and shattering his jaw. Behind them was John Downes, who had been shot in the chest at almost point-blank range and killed. He was the fifteenth fatality caused by plastic or rubber bullets and all of the victims were nationalists.[15]

The RUC claimed they were policing a riot but that was news to the people seated on the street when the 'riot' started. Because the media filmed the event it was a public relations disaster for the RUC and, in Irish-America, there were still people willing to send guns to the IRA.

In the autumn of 1984, an arms shipment from Boston was scheduled to arrive off the coast of Kerry aboard the *Valhalla*. On the American side, James 'Whitey' Bulger's criminal gang organized the shipment. In Ireland, Ivor Bell was in charge of the operation and was supported by Martin Ferris, O/C of Southern Command, and Seán O'Callaghan, the Southern Command Director of Operations and still an informer. Ferris led a group that sailed on the *Marita Ann* and met the *Valhalla* about 200 miles off the coast. O'Callaghan arranged safe houses for personnel and arms dumps for the weapons. He spoke about it:

> For about three or four weeks before the Marita Ann set sail, or the Valhalla set sail, I was asked to provide a number of houses in different areas. That's what I was asked to do. Yeah. And because I'm a clever kind of cunt at the end, I said, look let's place them in a newspaper called the Irish Post [a newspaper for the Irish community in Britain]. If you're placed in the Irish Post, it's like you're asking can a couple of English people come and live in your house in Kerry or whatever the case might be. So Ferris looks at me and says, 'Seán, you were always a clever cunt. Do all that stuff.' And the day before the Marita Ann went off to meet the Valhalla, Martin put his hand up to me like that and said, 'What do you think? We'll do it together mate?' I said, 'No, not on this occasion, I'm sorry.'[16]

O'Callaghan was also tasked with keeping tabs on the Irish police. That was easy. After saying goodbye to Ferris, he phoned his police contact with the news that the operation was going ahead as planned. The Irish navy intercepted the *Marita Ann*, the crew was arrested and seven tons of weapons were captured. It was the largest seizure of weapons since the *Claudia* had been stopped and Joe Cahill arrested.

It was clear that an informant had compromised the operation but Seán O'Callaghan had impeccable credentials and was not a suspect. He was from a republican family and was personally responsible for shooting dead RUC Inspector Peter Flanaghan. For good measure, the Gardaí arrested O'Callaghan along with several other Kerry republicans; he was released after forty-eight hours. O'Callaghan took over from Martin Ferris as the O/C of Southern Command and a rumour was circulated that the informer was on the American side.[17]

As events would later show, Seán O'Callaghan was only one of several informers in the Provisionals. Nevertheless, the organization was big enough and compartmentalized enough that informers could not stop everything. Only a few months after the *Marita Ann* was captured, the Provisionals almost pulled off what would have been their most spectacular operation. The Conservative Party had scheduled its annual conference for Brighton, on the south east coast of England, for mid-October 1984. It was public knowledge that Margaret Thatcher, her cabinet and other party officials would stay in the Grand Hotel. At some point during the summer, Patrick Magee checked into the hotel as 'Roy Walsh' and carefully hid a bomb in his room; Roy Walsh was in prison in England, having been arrested with the Price sisters, Gerry Kelly, Hugh Feeney et al. for the London bombs of 1973.

Provisional IRA bombs had come a long way since then. In *The IRA: The Bullets and the Bombs*, A.J. Oppenheimer describes the bomb that targeted Margaret Thatcher as 'both very simple and very complex – a terrorist "masterpiece"'.[18] A timer from a home video recorder primed the bomb for detonation and it was wrapped in film to avoid tracker dogs. The recorder was set for 3 am on the morning of 12 October 1984, the last day of the conference. When the bomb went off, the centre of the Grand Hotel collapsed and took with it much of the front of the building. Thatcher was not injured but five people were killed, including Anthony Berry, MP, and Roberta Wakeham, wife of the Chief Tory Whip.[19]

It was 'terrorism' at its best, showing their faithful followers that the Provisionals' new leaders were both creative and bold. The bomb was seen as payback for the hunger strikers. An IRA statement claiming responsibility for the attack contained a warning, 'Mrs. Thatcher will now realise that Britain cannot occupy our country, torture our prisoners and shoot our people in their own streets and get away with it. Today we were unlucky, but remember we only have to be lucky once – you will have to be lucky always. Give Ireland peace and there will be no more war.'[20] There was also a strategic element to the attack. In 1988, and as Sinn Féin's Director of Publicity, Danny Morrison placed the bomb into the context of the 'long war' strategy:

> It isn't a question of driving the British Army into the sea. It's a question of breaking the political will of the British government to remain. And that's why ten years ago the IRA stated the theory of the long war. And it was – that was to prepare, mentally prepare volunteers for a long war and secondly, to show to the British government it doesn't matter if we don't beat you this year, or next year or the following year, we are still gonna be here and you're still going to be in trouble. And the Thatcher government knows, and any British government that succeeds Thatcher knows, Thatcher had a very lucky escape in Brighton. And if the IRA bomb in Brighton had come off properly you were talking about a massive blow against the British establishment, and which could have been the straw that broke the camel's back.[21]

It was important for the Provisionals that they could strike directly at Thatcher, even if they missed.

It is unknown what might have happened had the Brighton bomb killed Thatcher and several members of her cabinet, but it certainly would have had a major influence on events. As it was, Thatcher was not killed and she was not intimidated. The afternoon of the attack, in her address as leader of the Conservative Party, she described the bomb as

> an attempt not only to disrupt and terminate our conference. It was an attempt to cripple Her Majesty's democratically elected government. That is the scale of the outrage in which we have all shared. And the fact that we are gathered here now, shocked but composed and determined, is a sign not only that this attack has failed, but that all attempts to destroy democracy by terrorism will fail.[22]

Thatcher was steadfast in her opposition to terrorism, which she would define in *The Downing Street Years* as 'The calculated use of violence – and the threat of it – to achieve political ends.'[23] The fact that Northern Irish nationalists might consider themselves victims of state terrorism through internment, Bloody Sunday, shoot to kill and so forth evidently did not register with her.

Garret FitzGerald was convinced that the only way to counter terrorism in Ireland was if the Dublin and London governments worked together while Thatcher, it appears, was willing to go it alone. At a summit meeting in Chequers about a month after the Brighton bomb, FitzGerald suggested that Articles 2 and 3 of the Irish Constitution could be amended in exchange for a package of reform in Northern Ireland. Douglas Hurd, the new Secretary of State for Northern Ireland, replied that the Irish Constitution did not limit the ability of Thatcher's government to make changes in Northern Ireland. It caught the Irish delegation off-guard because, for years, they had been told that Articles 2 and 3 were a major stumbling block. The Forum Report, in spite of Charlie Haughey's comments at his press conference, still represented a potential basis for a conversation on the future of Ireland. At a press conference following the Chequers summit, Thatcher was asked to comment on the Forum Report. She dismissed more than a year's worth of work by Garret FitzGerald:

> I have made it quite clear – and so did Mr. Prior when he was Secretary of State for Northern Ireland – that a unified Ireland was one solution that is out. A second solution was confederation of two states. That is out. A third solution was joint authority. That is out. That is a derogation from sovereignty. We made that quite clear when the Report was published. Northern Ireland is part of the United Kingdom. She is part of the United Kingdom because that is the wish of the majority of her citizens.[24]

Thatcher's 'Out! Out! Out!' humiliated Garret FitzGerald. And yet, in his own way, he was just as determined as Thatcher. At a meeting of the European Council, he met with her privately and pleaded for 'extra sensitivity' after 800 years of misunderstanding. She was receptive and the two governments continued their dialogue.

For reasons very different from those of Garret FitzGerald and Margaret Thatcher, Ivor Bell also tried to slow Sinn Féin. Bell led a group of activists in Belfast who were upset that resources were being redirected to the party. Bell stopped the transfer of funds from the IRA to Sinn Féin that would have supported contesting local elections in the North, scheduled for May 1985, and he called for an IRA convention at which the disenchanted could challenge the Army Council's support for Sinn Féin.[25] Gerry Adams is a calculating and clever person and, if reports are accurate, he was not about to allow anyone to organize an IRA convention unless he was sure of its outcome.

Also, supporters of the armalite and ballot box strategy had a response to the argument that the IRA was being held back. The loss of the *Marita Ann* hurt but the Libyan connection had been reactivated. More weapons were on the way and they were proof that politics would complement armed struggle, not replace it. Depending upon who tells the story, Ivor Bell was outmanoeuvred by Gerry Adams or Martin McGuinness. Most likely, as they had for several years, the two of them worked together to protect their positions and push their agenda. In *The Informer*, Seán O'Callaghan writes that Ivor Bell was charged with insubordination, expelled from the IRA and threatened with execution if he tried to set up a rival organization. Whatever happened, Bell and the others were out of the way.[26]

In May 1985, Gerry Adams's approach was vindicated when Sinn Féin put forward ninety-one candidates in the Northern Ireland local elections. As usual, they faced harassment and three candidates were arrested during the campaign: Francie Molloy, in Dungannon, and Cathal Quinn and Seamus Donnelly, in Omagh. In Armagh, Tommy Carroll – the brother of shoot-to-kill victim Roddy Carroll – received death threats. His mother was arrested and kept from voting. In spite of the harassment, Sinn Féin held its vote at 12 per cent and elected fifty-nine councillors. The result in Belfast was especially impressive where Sinn Féin elected seven councillors versus six for the SDLP. Overall, the impact of the election was far greater than Sinn Féin electing 59 out of 566 total councillors (compared to 101 for the SDLP). Unionists refused to participate in councils that had Sinn Féin representatives and seventeen of Northern Ireland's twenty-six councils had to be adjourned. The armalite and ballot box strategy was threatening the stability of Northern Ireland.[27]

In the South, censorship, harassment and the fear of violence kept most voters away from Sinn Féin. Broadly, the party courted the same kind of voter who supported Sinn Féin in the North – people in working-class and underserved areas who were alienated from mainstream parties. Although there were fewer such voters in the South, Dublin presented an opportunity. Sinn Féin argued that the major political parties had abandoned the inner city and the impoverished areas on the outskirts, Ballymun in North Dublin and Tallaght in South Dublin. By working with groups like Concerned Parents Against Drugs, Sinn Féin engaged in direct action to help local communities. For example, John Noonan, Sinn Féin's organizer in Dublin, met with drug dealers and told them to 'change their way or face the consequences'. The drug dealers were no doubt aware that Noonan had been on active service in the North and was an ex-prisoner.[28]

In the anti-drug campaign, crowds would gather outside the home of an alleged drug dealer and chant 'Pushers out!' Inevitably kids in the crowd would bang on the front door and harass those inside. The police claimed it was vigilantism but activists countered that they were helping people help themselves while their government and the police did nothing. The Sligo republican, who lived in Dublin, commented on Dublin Sinn Féin:

> I think they're doing well, for all the obstacles that they come up against. I mean, they won't meet them. They're getting great support. It must be admitted they're doing well in the drugs thing. I don't believe this crack that they're all, the media blown up and Michael Noonan [the Minister for Justice] talking about how Sinn Féin has taken over the whole thing. The way it is is, Sinn Féin are involved because there are concerned parents in any community – that these committees are set up and this crack about vigilantes – if the police – if the guards [Gardaí] were doing their jobs there wouldn't be any need for this.[29]

The grass-roots activism helped Sinn Féin build a base in working-class areas of Dublin and smaller towns. However, there was no one in Leinster House/Dáil Éireann to counter charges of vigilantism or defend the party at the national level. The grass-roots campaign was based in local communities and pretty much stayed there.

A month after the Northern election, 122 Sinn Féin candidates contested seats on local authorities throughout the Republic of Ireland. The candidates included Eddie Fullerton and Joe

O'Neill in Donegal, Des Long in Limerick, John Noonan in Tallaght, Richard Behal in Killarney and Seán O'Callaghan in Tralee. Only thirty-nine Sinn Féiners were elected, which was more than the eleven seats won in 1979, but a far cry from the dramatic results in the North. One of the unsuccessful candidates was Seán O'Callaghan, who would leave the Provisionals for the second time at the end of 1985. He was exhausted and stressed out, and resigned from the Ard Chomhairle and stepped down as O/C of Southern Command.[30]

There was a breakthrough in Dublin where Christy Burke was elected to one of five seats that would represent the North Inner City. Burke was from the area and, while he was only in his mid-thirties, he had been in the Movement a long time. He had joined Na Fianna Éireann as a kid and in the 1970s served time in Portlaoise; he was an ideal candidate. In his words:

> You see, Sinn Féin in Dublin here didn't have any political strategy in relation to community issues up 'til about 1981. So they then had a series of meetings and decided we would need to go full-time in order to serve the public ... so I chose to go for full-time political activist ... And they [voters] knew I came from a working class, very deprived background and they could identify with me. And during that three year [period] I was involved in many issues. I was one of the founder members of the Concerned Parents Against Drugs where local communities used to meet and march to the homes of drug pushers and, in a peaceful way, intimidate them from living in the flat complexes and they would leave. And in 1985, I got elected.[31]

Tony Gregory, who represented the area in Dáil Éireann, was re-elected to represent the area on Dublin City Council. Just after the election, Burke and Gregory were arrested in a sit-down protest in the city centre in support of Moore Street traders. Their view was that the police spent too much time harassing people trying to make a modest living selling small items to tourists and passersby and not enough time going after heroin dealers. They were sincere politicians and committed to their constituents but Burke and Gregory were also only two of fifty-two Dublin City councillors.[32]

The response of the mainstream parties to even limited success by Sinn Féin was predictable. Frank Glynn was re-elected in Galway but Galway County Councillors who were members of Fine Gael were told not to work with him. Sinn Féin did best in Monaghan where Caoimhín Ó Caoláin topped the poll and was elected to the County Council. Sinn Féiners were elected to local councils in Castleblaney, Clones and Monaghan Town[33] but steps were taken to minimize the party's influence. Peter McAleer was elected to the Urban District Council in Clones:

> when I was first elected, myself and another colleague in 1985, Sinn Fein councillors were a new thing ... and two of them were in this town and we found whenever we were elected we were marginalized by the major parties. Obviously it's only a small town council with nine councillors sitting on it and, as I say, there were two of us but we were kept off everything – housing committees and stuff like that that should have been open to any of the councillors ...[34]

A Fianna Fáil–Fine Gael pact kept Sinn Féiners off the important committees in Clones.

By keeping Sinn Féin at bay and patiently working with the British, Garret FitzGerald's government finally realized its most significant diplomatic achievement. After two years of dialogue with Margaret Thatcher and successive secretaries of state for Northern Ireland – James Prior, Douglas Hurd and Tom King – the Anglo-Irish Agreement (AIA; or, Hillsborough Agreement) was signed at Hillsborough Castle in County Down. The British and Irish governments agreed to work together to isolate Sinn Féin and counter the Provisional IRA. The formal status of Northern Ireland was unchanged and, under the AIA, the two governments:

(a)   affirm that any change in the status of Northern Ireland would only come about with the consent of a majority of the people of Northern Ireland;

(b)   recognize that the present wish of a majority of the people of Northern Ireland is for no change in the status of Northern Ireland; and,

(c)   declare that, if in the future a majority of the people of Northern Ireland clearly wish for and formally consent to the establishment of a united Ireland, they will introduce and support in the respective Parliaments legislation to give effect to that wish.[35]

The cornerstone of the Anglo-Irish Agreement was an 'Inter-Governmental Conference' that gave the Dublin government a consultative role in security, legal matters and the administration of justice in Northern Ireland. With better coordination between the Garda Siochána and the RUC, cross-border security would be enhanced.

Fine Gael, Labour and the Workers' Party supported the AIA. Charlie Haughey and Fianna Fáil were opposed. They were upset that they had not been included in the negotiations and, being out of power, they also looked to the next general election. Haughey claimed the high ground on the national question and argued that the AIA recognized the authority of Britain in Northern Ireland and, therefore, was in contradiction to Articles 2 and 3 of the Irish Constitution. The AIA was approved in Dáil Éireann with a vote of eighty-eight in favour and seventy-five opposed.

In negotiating the AIA, Margaret Thatcher had not consulted unionist politicians, however, and they were outraged. An anti-Agreement rally at Belfast City Hall attracted an estimated 200,000 people. Revd Ian Paisley roared, 'Where do the terrorists operate from? From the Irish Republic! That's where they come from! Where do the terrorists return to for sanctuary? To the Irish Republic! And yet Mrs. Thatcher tells us that that Republic must have some say in our Province. We say never, never, never, never!' A huge 'Belfast Says No!' banner went up at Belfast City Hall. Unionist councillors and MPs refused to meet with British ministers and, in the House of Commons, Harold McCusker, the UUP MP for Upper Bann, described how the British government had failed its loyal subjects in Ulster:

I stood outside Hillsborough, not waiving a Union flag – I doubt whether I will ever wave one again – not singing hymns, saying prayers or protesting, but like a dog and asked the Government to put in my hand the document that sold my birthright. They told me that they would give it to me as soon as possible. Having never consulted me, never sought my opinion or asked my advice, they told the rest of the world what was in store for me ... Does the Prime Minister realize that, when she carries the agreement through the house, she will have ensured that I shall carry to my grave with ignominy the sense of the injustice that I have done to my constituents down the years – when in their darkest hours, I exhorted them to put their trust in the British House of Commons, which one day would honour its fundamental obligation to them to treat them as equal British citizens? Is it not the reality of this agreement that they will now be Irish–British hybrids and that every aspect – not just some aspects – of their lives will be open to the influence of those who have coveted their land?

The vote in the House of Commons was 473 in favour and 47 opposed.[36] Unionist opposition did not end there.

Paisley and the DUP formed an anti-Agreement 'Unionist Pact' with James Molyneaux and the Ulster Unionists. Unionist MPs at Westminster resigned their seats and the resulting by-elections became a referendum on the AIA in Northern Ireland. The results were mixed but anti-Agreement Unionists received more than 418,000 (71.5 per cent) votes and won 14 of the 15 seats available. At the same time, the overall anti-AIA vote was less than the 500,000 they had hoped for and, in Newry and Mourne, Seamus Mallon of the SDLP took the seat from the UUP.[37] Still, unionist protests against the AIA carried into the spring of 1986. In the six months following the signing of the Agreement, on-duty RUC officers were attacked hundreds of times and several officers had their homes attacked. And whether or not it was a result of the AIA, there was also evidence of a more even-handed approach by the RUC. In March 1986, the RUC defended Catholic homes in Lisburn from attacks by loyalists. The next month, at a march in Portadown, an RUC plastic bullet killed Keith White. He was the first and only Protestant victim of the bullets.

The Provisionals also rejected the Anglo-Irish Agreement. From their perspective, the Agreement was designed to prop up the SDLP and the only reason Dublin and London were collaborating was because they were threatened by the Provisional IRA's armed struggle in combination with Sinn Féin's politics. The AIA was more evidence that the armalite and ballot box strategy was working. The Sligo republican was re-interviewed just as the Anglo-Irish talks were coming to a conclusion:

> The moves that are on at the moment, I don't know what's going to happen. I think it's a lot of talk or whatever. But if it ever, ever happened that the Brits said, 'Right, we are pulling out and this is the set-up we're going to leave behind and' – you know, it will all be nicely talked out and everything. They would claim that it was because it was all talked out and everything, but the only reason there are any talks on at the moment is because of the war in the North and because they know they can't beat them. They've said it themselves anyway. They can't beat the IRA.[38]

The former Provisional IRA volunteer from Derry was also re-interviewed that autumn. His comments on constitutional politics and the Anglo-Irish Agreement capture the alienation and distrust of Northern nationalists:

it's British constitutional politics that have produced the situation in the North of extreme sectarian hatred on one side of the community who have allowed themselves to be bred into it, and they make the laws which maintain an extremism. And, therefore, the mere thought of constitutional politics in the North makes me blench. And I cannot see any honesty emanating from anyone who would take part in what they term constitutional politics ...

Q: Do you think constitutional politics can ever succeed in the sense of ending partition?

A: Well, again, it comes back to the point that – it depends what constitutional politics you're talking about. If it's constitutional politics based on SDLP subservience to Westminster and the Home Office and British governmental policy of the day, no. It's just an impossibility because it goes against, it immediately goes against anything Irish. As far as the twenty-six counties engaging in constitutional politics ... the Anglo-Irish talks, I think, are a very good pointer as to what exactly is involved. You have the incredible situation where Charlie Haughey, up until today, which is months after the talks were instituted, it's presumed did not know, although he is the opposition, the main opposition in government ... and, therefore, will possibly in the next time around form the next government. He should definitely be part [of the talks] because it's the future of the twenty-six counties that's being decided vis-a-vis their compliance or acceptance or working hand in hand with Britain. That's incredible in the first place, that they wouldn't apprise him in one way or another ... Secondly, the unionists are not being consulted in the North and that's just point of fact. They're not being consulted ... it's amazing that they're talking to the SDLP and the Free State Government and ignoring the loyalists. So, on both sides, if that's constitutional politics, no thanks – pure and simple.[39]

The Provisionals were disenchanted with constitutional politics and did not trust constitutional politicians. Ironically, their leaders wanted to take Sinn Féin in that direction.

In the North, the armalite and ballot box strategy was working and, because of the Anglo-Irish Agreement, unionist extremists were engaging in outrageous behaviour. At one point, Peter Robinson, Ian Paisley's lieutenant, led a group across the border and into Clontibret, County Monaghan, and took over the local Garda station. They were quickly arrested and the incident was condemned in Dublin and London, but it also contributed to the sense that the unionist community was desperate.[40] In the South, Sinn Féin was growing much more slowly and remained marginalized. The leadership concluded that the problem was Sinn Féin's policy of not taking seats in the Dublin parliament. Martin McGuinness commented:

I think that many of us who came into the Movement in the '68, '69, seventies – I joined the Movement in late 1970 – that many of us came into a Movement which had many of its policies and attitudes already firmly established by previous generations. And many of these policies were established by people who were, in our opinion, great republicans ... But, I think that all of us, including many of those people themselves, recognized and understood that our politics had to evolve, that our politics, our attitudes, had, at times – certainly not our principles but our attitudes – had to change to meet the circumstances which we were faced with. And also had to take on board the view that there is a massive opposition out there against the Republican Movement … And we felt that it was incumbent upon us to, if the IRA on one hand was using guerrilla tactics and methods to tackle the British forces of occupation militarily, that political activists and freedom seekers within Sinn Féin also had to look at the obstacles which our opponents were putting up in order to defeat the rise of Sinn Féin, which had been very successful in the six counties and not successful in the twenty-six counties.[41]

Mitchel McLaughlin also spoke about the changes:

I think that my attitude was actually formed by that kind of clearly very principled and very rigid republican orthodoxy which was rooted in the Civil War. And, you know, the people who were influencing me – I mean was a major influence on my life – was Seán Keenan … Up until that point I just had accepted it as republican dogma and I only really began to examine it after the Bobby Sands election. And then once I started to examine it I think that the conclusion that we should contest in the twenty-six counties, in the Leinster House elections, was a logical conclusion.[42]

Danny Morrison's perspective was similar to that of McGuinness and McLaughlin:

I think the importance of Leinster House is that we break out of political isolation in the twenty-six counties and, as it is, our voice is suppressed by state censorship on radio and television and it makes it very difficult. And the people who sell our newspaper are harassed. And it makes it very, very difficult to get the republican message across. But I do think that there is a receptive republican audience there just waiting to be tapped, so that, if there was another way of breaking out of isolation which did not involve going near Leinster House, I would support it. But from a practical point of view it is the only way of breaking out of isolation. And, therefore, I support that … I think that what we are recognizing is the fact that the vast majority of the people in the twenty-six counties consider it as their institution, while all republicans consider it as an illegitimate institution. I am recognizing that fact. I am not recognizing it as being legitimate because it cannot claim to be the government of Ireland – as it does in Articles 2 and 3 of the Constitution – and yet do nothing about it. So, therefore, it can't be – it's not fully legitimate. It's not living up to its own claims about its own identity.[43]

Taking seats and participating in the Dublin parliament would be a pragmatic move to help Sinn Féin grow in the South. At the 1985 Sinn Féin Ard Fheis, there was a motion on the agenda that 'abstentionism be viewed as a tactic and not as a principle'. Gerry Adams did not speak on the motion. Tom Hartley's contribution included the statement that there was a principle 'riding above all principles and that is the principle of success'. Seán Crowe argued that those who had sold out over the years 'were not republicans'. The motion was defeated by a vote of 181 opposed and 161 in favour.[44]

Figure 4 presents the Sinn Féin Officer Board and the Ard Chomhairle elected by the delegates in 1985.[45] Compared to 1970, the party had changed dramatically. The only person left from the Caretaker Executive of 1970 was John Joe McGirl. The only other founding figure in the Sinn Féin leadership was Joe Cahill, who had been on the first Army Council. The importance of

Officers	Ard Chomhairle Members
Gerry Adams, President	Martin McGuinness
John Joe McGirl, Vice-President	Danny Morrison
Joe Cahill, Treasurer	Jim McAllister
Seamus McGarrigle, Treasurer	Mitchel McLaughlin
Denise Creggan, Secretary	Francie Molloy
Tom Hartley, Secretary	Seamus Kerr
Rita O'Hare, Editor *AP/RN*	Aine Nic Mhurchadha
Brian McDonald, Director of Publicity	Seán Crowe
Seán McManus, Chairperson	Mary McGing
Pat Doherty, National Organizer	Caoimhghín Ó Caoláin

Source: Information found in AP/RN and other Sinn Féin documents.

FIGURE 4

1985–86 Provisional Sinn Féin Ard Chomhairle

Belfast is seen by the presence of Adams, Cahill, Tom Hartley, Danny Morrison and Rita O'Hare in the leadership. If accounts can be trusted, Adams, Cahill, Morrison and Pat Doherty also represented the IRA leadership. The one person missing was Owen Carron as the RUC claimed that they could link him to an assault rifle discovered on a farm and Carron, believing he would not receive a fair trial, had jumped bail and crossed the border.[46]

Many of those in the 'new' leadership had been involved in leadership positions for more than a decade. It had been ten years since Morrison became editor of *Republican News* and Adams had been a Sinn Féin officer since 1977. It all seemed part of a natural political evolution, replacing the old with the new. The Derry republican commented:

> *Sinn Féin, after many years of maturation, it's become a much more realistic political force now than it was. I mean, partially that lovely expression, 'Weeding out process', where people give what they can to the Movement and if they're left behind or if their politics aren't suited then that's a natural process of elimination. I think that also is revolutionary progress and it has to be accepted as such and I don't think any tears should be cried over people who have been great heroes of the past and suddenly are not any more today because that's the way it is.*

The rank and file had watched the new leadership move up the ranks, often leading from the front, taking risks, suffering hardship and staying true to the Movement. Adams, McGuinness, Morrison and Rita O'Hare, for example, had been interned and/or jailed. Pat Doherty's brother, Hugh, was serving multiple life sentences for his role in the Balcombe Street gang. The membership respected the leadership. The Derry republican again:

Everybody's affected by the mythology. And, therefore, the more eminent members of the Republican Movement, who are naturally picked up on by the press and the media and vilified, but the image has to be built up first so that they can vilify them. I mean they naturally become someone to be admired if you're pro or in favour of a war of liberation ... Martin McGuinness once had the name as the IRA leader – I mean in the Daily Mail *or the* Mirror *or somebody ran a front-page photograph of him – 'The Butcher Boy'... In fact there was a press conference held. And they ran this photograph up as 'The Butcher Boy', because he had worked for a butcher's in Derry. But they, of course, were saying that he was a mass murderer. That did no end of benefit to Martin's standing in the community because everybody says, 'Well fuck the Brits. Martin's one of our people.'*[47]

The Sinn Féin rank and file distrusted constitutional politics and constitutional politicians but they trusted their leaders because they were 'our people'.

In hindsight, the motion to view abstentionism as a tactic and not as a principle was a test. The leadership needed to know how far they were from having a majority of delegates agree to change Sinn Féin's Constitution and allow elected representatives to take seats in Leinster House. Three hundred and forty-two delegates voted. For a two-thirds majority, they would have needed 221 votes meaning they were 60 short. The leadership spent the next year finding those votes.

15

A SECOND SPLIT (1986)

It's what you're about yourself. It's what you believe in and it's what you're struggling for. And if you're afraid of every change you make, that it's going to corrupt you, then there's something wrong with your own fundamental beliefs.

– Pat Doherty[1]

The new leadership wanted elected Sinn Féiners – if and when that might happen – to take their seats in Leinster House and challenge the Dublin government but realizing that vision was complicated because it required changing the constitutions of two separate organizations. Sinn Féin's Constitution could be changed at an Ard Fheis. Because of the war, however, the Provisional IRA had not met in convention since 1970; a convention would have to be organized and held in secret. There was also the delicate situation of activists with dual membership. Under the IRA Constitution, Leinster House was a proscribed organization and members who advocated taking seats could be dismissed or charged with treason. The IRA's Constitution would have to be changed before dual members could advocate changing Sinn Féin's Constitution. Most important, it would be a disaster if the leadership tried to change either constitution and failed.

The IRA Convention was held in September 1986. It can safely be assumed that the leadership would not have gone forward with the Convention if they were not sure they would win the vote. Indeed, steps were taken to guarantee success. Paddy Ryan, an outspoken critic of the Adams and McGuinness leadership, was dismissed from the Army Executive.[2] Each county was entitled to send delegates and in some of them there was strong opposition to taking seats in Leinster House. Therefore, six counties were reorganized into two regional areas – Sligo-Roscommon-Longford and Wicklow-Wexford-Waterford.[3] Because the Convention was held in secret, few details of what transpired are available. What is known is that three key veterans from the 1940s, Joe Cahill, John Joe McGirl and J.B. O'Hagan, supported the leadership.

The main argument of those who opposed taking seats in Leinster House was that it would put the Provisionals on a slippery slope that would eventually lead them into constitutional politics and away from armed struggle, as the Officials and Fianna Fáil and Cumann na Gaedheal/Fine Gael had discovered before them. It was an argument that Ruairí Ó Brádaigh had made in 1969 and would have made again in 1986. In his words: *Parliament is a replacement for civil war. You talk it out instead of in the streets. But if you think you can keep one leg in the streets and the other leg in Parliament, you've a bloody awful mistake.'*[4] The argument was that parliaments corrupt even the best of Irish republicans. Taking seats in a parliament starts a process that ends in failure. The counter-argument was that the Officials and their predecessors were corrupt before they became involved in constitutional politics, that they had planned on ending armed struggle all along. To show that they were different from the Officials, the army leadership unveiled their plan to move into constitutional politics and, at the same time, take the armed campaign to another level. Weapons had arrived from Libya that more than made up for the loss of the *Marita Ann*. More were on the way, including Semtex explosives, AK-47 assault rifles, RPG-7 rockets and Soviet made heavy machine guns, DshKs (*Dushkas*).[5]

The leadership also had a plan. In January 1968, the North Vietnamese had launched the 'Tet Offensive' and, in a series of surprise attacks, captured the city of Hue and briefly occupied the US embassy in Saigon. The US Army rallied but at a cost of 2,000 soldiers killed and heightened anti-war sentiment that influenced US politics, including President Johnson's decision not to seek re-election. The Libyan weapons would be used to escalate the campaign, an Irish Tet Offensive. Accounts have Martin McGuinness and Tom 'Slab' Murphy being moved into key roles in the Provisional IRA – with Murphy, from South Armagh, appointed Director of Operations and charged with developing the plans for an Irish Tet and McGuinness, a soldier with a sterling record as a leader, returning as Northern Commander and implementing the plan.[6]

The promise of taking the campaign to another level, in combination with Sinn Féin taking revolutionary politics into the Dublin parliament, was an effective counter to any arguments that may have been made by people like Ruairí Ó Brádaigh, Dáithí O'Connell, and Joe O'Neill or others like them. Three-quarters of the delegates voted in favour of ending the ban on Leinster House and the IRA's Constitution was changed. As in 1969, the opposition did not walk out, and some of those opposed to the change were unwilling to split the Army in a time of war. Seamus Twomey voted no and was then elected to the Army Executive. He joined the Executive, effectively endorsing the leadership and the decision to enter Leinster House.[7] The Convention and its result were not made public until 16 October 1986, when *AP/RN* announced on its front page an 'Historic IRA Convention'.[8] The Sinn Féin Ard Fheis was scheduled to open two weeks later.

Gerry Adams tried to limit any damage from the Convention by meeting with members of the opposition. For meetings with Ruairí Ó Brádaigh and Joe O'Neill, Adams took with him a special guest – Brendan Hughes who was just out of Long Kesh and had been appointed to GHQ staff. Hughes described the meetings:

> *I was only out a week or so, a couple of weeks or so and I was brought to a meeting, yeah. In Athlone with myself, Paddy Doc [Pat Doherty] and Gerry to meet Ruairí …*
>
> *And I didn't – I was naïve again. We met Ruairí in Athlone, in a restaurant in Athlone. I know now why I was there. I was there to give Ruairí some sort – or to give credence to what was going on. And that I was seen as the military person, I was seen as the soldier and that's what I was actually because I knew that weapons were coming in. I knew that. And I think I was used by the leadership – by Gerry and the leadership at that period, to try and influence Ruairí. We left that meeting and Ruairí was not*

impressed at all … He welcomed me and shook hands with me and then gave me whatever welcome he could but he was not convinced. We left there and went to Donegal after meeting Ruairí – to meet Joe O'Neill and Joe was quite forthright to him. He was quite forthright about it. He says, 'That fucking man will not influence me.' Me – talking to me.

Q: Talking about you?

A: Yeah. Yeah. He says, 'He's not going to change my mind.' Again there was no hostility towards me but he knew more than I did, what was going on.

Hughes says that he, Adams and Doherty were 'quite tame' and that he was surprised at how upset Ó Brádaigh was.[9] Ó Brádaigh had heard it all before, and more weapons and Brendan Hughes did not change the fact that what was a bad idea sixteen years earlier was still a bad idea. History was repeating itself. Ruairí Ó Brádaigh later commented: *'It was said that it wasn't the same and so on, but if it quacks like a duck, waddles like a duck, et cetera, et cetera, it's got to be a duck, which it was and has been seen.'*[10] Ó Brádaigh was involved in his own set of meetings, including one with Tom Maguire.

Maguire was ninety-four years old and the only one left from the small group of people who, in 1938, had devolved the powers of government from the Second Dáil Éireann to the IRA Army Council. It may have been convoluted and ancient history to the younger people, but the implications of taking seats in Leinster House were very real for Maguire. He was being asked to ignore the fact that he had spent a lifetime refusing to acknowledge the legitimacy of the Dublin parliament – in essence, the same Free State parliament responsible for the execution of his 17-year-old brother in 1923. In 1969, Seán Mac Stíofáin, Ruairí Ó Brádaigh, Dáithí O'Connell, Joe O'Neill, Joe Cahill and the others refused to follow Cathal Goulding into Leinster House, and Maguire endorsed them. In 1986, Ó Brádaigh, O'Connell, O'Neill and their supporters refused to follow Gerry Adams, Joe Cahill and company into Leinster House, and Maguire endorsed them. A public statement from Maguire paralleled the one he issued in 1969:

> There is no difference between entering the partition parliament of Leinster House and entering a partition parliament of Stormont.
>
> I speak as the sole surviving Teachta Dála of the Second Dáil Éireann and as the sole surviving member of the Executive of the Second Dáil Éireann.
>
> In December, 1969, as the sole surviving member of the Executive of the Second Dáil Éireann, I recognized the Provisional Army Council … The majority of delegates to a recent IRA Convention purported to accept the Leinster House partition parliament, and in so doing broke faith and betrayed the trust placed in their predecessors in 1969 …[11]

For those so inclined, Maguire's statement was more evidence that 1986 was a repeat of 1969/70.

What happened in private was next played out in public at the Ard Fheis, which was held in the Mansion House in Dublin. The Sinn Féin leadership followed standard practices for packing a political convention by splitting some cumainn in two and making sure that the majority in the new and the old cumainn were 'sound', that is, they supported the change. One-person cumainn were created. People who refused to keep quiet or get out of the way were dismissed. Des Long was on the Caretaker Executive in 1970 and had remained an ardent abstentionist. Munster Sinn Féin elected him as their regional representative to the Ard Chomhairle and, when he was asked to resign, he refused. Long was dismissed from the Ard Chomhairle. Seán Keenan was Honorary Life President of Derry Sinn Féin and Tony Ruane was Vice President for Life of Sinn Féin. They were also ardent abstentionists and neither was allowed into the Mansion House.[12]

In order to allow more time for debate, the Ard Fheis opened on Friday evening, 30 October. The debate on abstentionism was scheduled for Sunday and, in his presidential address on Saturday evening, Gerry Adams played his trump card – the Provisional IRA supported taking seats in Leinster House:[13]

> I would remind you that the Army Authority of Óglaigh na hÉireann, the rank and file volunteers, assembled in the General Army Convention, has democratically made a judgement on this issue and that Óglaigh na hÉireann has remained united in its determination to pursue the armed struggle and is united in its confidence in us and in our ability to pursue the political struggle.
>
> There was no walk-out from the IRA by IRA Volunteers.

It was up to the delegates if they wanted to follow the Army's lead, but 'To leave Sinn Féin is to leave the struggle', he told them. He also argued that history was not repeating itself: 'To compare us to the Stickies is an obscenity ... For anyone who has eyes to see, it is clear that the Sticky leadership had abandoned armed struggle as a form of resistance to British rule as part of their historic new departure into British and Free State constitutionality.' Left unmentioned was the fact that, for more than two years, the Officials had tried to combine armed struggle and constitutional politics and then concluded that it would not work. Instead, Adams focused on the need to develop politics:

> We must develop a 32-County wide political struggle. This is the most important task facing us at present. While consolidating our base in the 6 Counties, we must develop a popular struggle here in the 26 Counties to complement the struggle in the 6-County area. Of necessity this means, in order to advance at the level of people's consciousness, the removal of abstentionism in regard to Leinster House.

The 'central issue' was not abstentionism but the 'the failure of successive generations of republicans to grasp the centrality, the primacy and the fundamental need for republican politics'.

Pat Doherty, on behalf of the Ard Chomhairle, began the formal debate the next day by putting forward Resolution 162, 'That this Ard-Fheis drops its abstentionist attitude to Leinster House ...' Without naming anyone, Doherty praised the new leadership and attacked the old leadership:

our leadership, your leadership, who are these people who are spearheading change; where did they come from? Well let me tell you. They were the people who, along with others, were doing all the things that were required to be done on the ground at local level during the years 1969 to 1975. They were the people who after the disastrous 1975 truce moved into middle leadership and national leadership and started to pick up the pieces and push the Movement forward once again. They are the people who moved into the Sinn Féin leadership from 1980 to the present, and have led Sinn Féin to various propaganda successes.

Doherty laid the foundation for what would become the accepted interpretation of the rise of Gerry Adams and Martin McGuinness into the Provisionals' leadership. They had saved the Provisionals from the disaster of 1975 and, by combining armed struggle with revolutionary politics, they had made Sinn Féin radical and relevant. Doherty also challenged the argument that entering Leinster House would compromise armed struggle.

From as far back as the '50s, military action in the 26 Counties has been ruled out. Is there anyone in this hall today seriously saying that we should confront the Free State on a military front? Of course there is not. Therefore the only way we can confront the Free State is by political means, as part of an overall national struggle.

Doherty had a point: How could armed struggle be compromised where it did not exist?

John Joe McGirl was one of the very few people who, in 1969, attended the first IRA convention that caused the split, the second IRA convention in which the Provisionals were created *and* the 1970 Sinn Fein Ard Fheis, and he followed Pat Doherty. In 1985, McGirl voted that abstentionism was a principle. Now, however, he seconded Pat Doherty's motion and then spoke from personal experience to argue that history was not repeating itself. In 1969/70, the Goulding leadership had 'abandoned Irish freedom and the Irish struggle'. Now, the 'situation is reversed. We have an army fighting 16 years which will continue to fight until British rule is defeated.' Adding to the weight of his remarks, he explained that other founding Provisionals agreed with him:

When this policy was mentioned to me I didn't hastily make up my mind. I went to people like J.B. O'Hagan, Joe Cahill, Seamus Twomey and others who were close to me at that period in 1969 and we agreed that it was necessary to make change if we were not going to hand down this struggle to another generation.

McGirl denied that he was abandoning comrades who had been executed by the Free State, men who had 'walked round the prison yard with me'. Instead, he was pragmatically fighting the damage caused by abstentionism:

If you take a county council, we go and we mobilise support and with limited success. The next parliamentary election comes and we don't contest it, the people we have built up are gone into Fianna Fáil and Fine Gael. We talk to the young people today, we tell them of our effort for freedom, we tell them that we are interested in their livelihood. And we are interested in people because that's what this struggle is about. And when young people come in looking for work, I'll say that it's the politicians in Leinster House who are to blame for their plight and the British occupation of their country. And the answer I get, no matter how I convince them, is, why will you not represent us there?

McGirl probably had more close ties with the young Northerners than any other senior Southern republican. He was the centre of a clandestine network along the Leitrim, Cavan and Fermanagh border. He had been arrested in Belfast and was interned in Long Kesh when the prisoners burned the place. It was a sign of respect that, in 1981, he was asked to speak at the funeral of hunger striker Joe McDonnell in Belfast.

Joe Cahill followed John Joe McGirl. Like McGirl, he was in the Sinn Féin leadership through the transition from old to new and as Sinn Féin's Treasurer he was based in the Dublin headquarters in Parnell Square and built relationships with the younger people there. In his remarks, Cahill focused on armed struggle,

> Like John Joe, in many ways I haven't changed. The dedication and commitment which brought me to the foot of the scaffold in 1942 is the same in my heart today as it was then, and will be until the day I draw my last breath. The only thing that has changed as far as I'm concerned is that age is against me and I can't be in the field with the freedom fighters today because of that. I thought I had to make those remarks.

In 1969, the leadership was 'corrupt' and 'had sold out the military spirit' whereas he and McGirl had been soldiers:

> When the holocaust of August '69 came, there was nothing there to defend the people. And I make it public now, that on the 17th of August when, along with other people, a few of us had to leave Belfast and come down here in search of arms, John Joe McGirl was the man who gave me arms in Leitrim.

The delegates went wild with applause. It was well known that Cahill resigned from the IRA in 1965 and he drew on his own experience, asking those thinking about a walkout to reconsider.'That was a mistake,' he said, 'I should have stayed on and fought.'

The delegates who spoke against the motion included Richard Behal, Liam Cotter, Brendan Magill, formerly Sinn Féin's national organizer in Britain, and Caoimhín Mac Cathmhaoil and Frank Glynn, who had been on the Caretaker Exective in 1970. Glynn commented on his remarks:

> *What I said to the floor was that the whole thing hinged on John Joe McGirl ... And I appealed to John Joe McGirl – and he left the stage when I was speaking – to stay with the genuine Republican Movement and that if he did stay that he would have carried the day ... I think if John Joe McGirl*

hadn't gone – I'm certain in fact that if John Joe McGirl hadn't gone and sided with Adams there is no way that they would have carried the day. There is no way of that happening.[14]

Ruairí Ó Brádaigh spoke towards the end of the debate.

Ó Brádaigh, like McGirl, was one of a select few as he had attended both IRA conventions in 1969, the Sinn Féin Ard Fheis in 1970 and he was still involved. He began by questioning the debate itself. Holding a copy in his hand, he pointed out that according to the Constitution of Sinn Féin 'no person who approves or supports candidates going into Leinster House, Stormont or Westminster shall be admitted to membership or allowed to retain membership'. Technically, the entire debate was out of order and those advocating taking seats in Leinster House should have been dismissed. If the motion passed, he warned, Sinn Féin would eventually take seats at Stormont and Westminster and end up collaborating with the British.

He asked a question that has perplexed Irish republicans since the Anglo-Irish Treaty: 'where are our revolutionary socialists, how do they expect to build a democratic socialist republic out of Leinster House? How can serious social change come out of Leinster House? How can the fundamental change in property relations come out of Leinster House?' His answer was, 'No way can it do that.' The argument was rooted in principles that had been in place for decades. His conclusion was that 'we have not been wrong for 65 years'. His critics were aware that after sixty-five years of principles they were no closer to the republic than they had been in 1921.

One of the last to speak was Martin McGuinness and he did not hold back. McGuinness rejected any notion that the leadership would enter a Northern Ireland Assembly or Westminster, and he rejected the claim that entering Leinster House would compromise the IRA campaign:

> First of all, I would like to give a commitment on behalf of the leadership that we have absolutely no intention of going into Westminster or Stormont ... I reject the notion that entering Leinster House would mean an end to Sinn Féin's unapologetic support for the right of Irish people to oppose in arms the British forces of occupation. That, my friends, is a principle which a minority in this hall might doubt, but which I believe all our opponents clearly understand.

McGuinness, the hard man, said what the delegates wanted to hear:

> Our position is clear and it will never, never, never change. The war against British rule must continue until freedom is achieved ... If you allow yourselves to be led out of this hall today, the only place you will be going is home. You will be walking away from the struggle. Don't go my friends. We will lead you to the Republic.

As he finished, McGuinness built on Pat Doherty's opening remarks and attacked the old leadership: 'what you are witnessing here is not a debate over one issue, but two: abstentionism and the leadership of the republican struggle ... The reality is that the former leadership of this Movement has never been able to come to terms with this leadership's criticism of the disgraceful attitude adopted by them during the disastrous 18-month cease-fire in the mid-1970s.' The attack was audacious given that, at most, the 'ceasefire' in 1975 lasted eight months. The crowd gave him a roaring standing ovation.

Seán McManus, the party Chairperson, announced the final result: 429 in favour of taking seats in Leinster House, 161 opposed and 38 abstentions. With 419 votes required for a two-thirds majority, Adams, McGuinness and company carried the day and Sinn Féin's Constitution was changed. The presence of 250 more delegates versus the year before was not lost on the opposition. Frank Glynn commented:

> I said to Ruairí when he rushed out at that time, 'Stand and call for a recount', because I don't believe that the count was a hundred per cent genuine. There was a very, very narrow margin in the count and it was just a show of hands. But I do believe that if it was properly checked through at the time that Adams wouldn't have carried a majority because it was well known at the time that he gave out cards, admission cards to a lot of people that they knew were favorable because they held regional meetings and local meetings.[15]

Instead of seeking a recount, Ruairí Ó Brádaigh, Frank Glynn, Dáithí O'Connell, Joe O'Neill, Geraldine Taylor and around a hundred other delegates walked out of the Mansion house.[16] They reassembled in the West County Hotel, in the Dublin suburbs, and formed Republican Sinn Féin (RSF). The counterfoils of the delegate cards, which are raised in the air to signify a vote, were destroyed the next morning, making a recount impossible.[17]

Understanding the Split

On the surface, the 1986 split was caused by a conflict between the old leadership and the new leadership, Ó Brádaigh and O'Connell versus Adams and McGuinness, but the split was more complex than that.

There is a tendency to view the Provisionals from the perspective of the people fighting the war, especially the young Northerners who dominated from the late 1970s. In fact, there were four broad sub-groups of Provisionals. The sub-groups, or what Karl Mannheim refers to as 'generational units', were loosely organized around the geography and the timing of recruitment into the Irish Republican Movement: pre-1969 Northerners; pre-1969 Southerners; post-1969 Northerners; and post-1969 Southerners.[18]

Pre-1969 Irish republicans were part of a conspiratorial clan. Post-1969 Irish republicans, especially those recruited in the early 1970s and during the hunger strikes, were part of a mass mobilization. Northerners lived in a police state that marginalized the Irish way of life. Southerners, even if they rejected the Dublin government and experienced state repression, lived in a country that claimed the entire island of Ireland for the 'republic' and embraced an Irish way of life. Southern Ireland was a safe-haven for Northerners. All four sub-groups are important for understanding the course of Provisional Irish republicanism. Everyone agreed on the same

	Pre-1969 Provisionals	Post-1969 Provisionals
N O R T H E R N	Gerry Adams, President **(1964)** Joe Cahill, Treasurer (1930s) Jim McAllister **(1962)** Mitchel McLaughlin **(1966)** Francie Molloy **(mid-1960s)**	Rita O'Hare, Editor, *AP/RN* (1970s) Tom Hartley, Secretary (1970s) Martin McGuinness (1970s) Danny Morrison (1970s) Seamus McGarrigle, Treasurer (1970s) Seamus Kerr (1970s)
S O U T H E R N	John Joe McGirl, Vice President (1930s)	Denise Creggan, Secretary (1970s) Pat Doherty, National Organizer (1970s) Sean McManus, Party Chairperson (1970s) Brian McDonald, Director of Publicity (1979/80) Aine Nic Mhurchadha (1970s) Seán Crowe (1970s) Mary McGing (1980s) Caoimhghín Ó Caoláin (1980s)

FIGURE 5

1985 Sinn Féin Ard Chomhairle as Generational Units
(year of recruitment in parentheses)

goal – a united, democratic and socialist Ireland. Within each group, activists interacted with each other, shared experiences and developed a common view on the best way to achieve the goal. Across groups, however, there were important differences.

Figure 5 presents the 1985 Ard Chomhairle as generational units.[19] Only two members of the Ard Chomhairle, John Joe McGirl and Joe Cahill, joined the Movement before the 1960s. Gerry Adams, Jim McAllister, Mitchel McLaughlin and Francie Molloy joined the Movement as young men in the early to mid-1960s. Their experiences as activists would have been strongly influenced by the events of the late 1960s and early 1970s. The influence of post-1969 events is seen in the fact that the majority of Ard Chomhairle members were recruited between the early 1970s and the early 1980s. Without state violence and the hunger strikes, many of them would have never gotten involved. Abstentionism was probably never all that important for some of them. Their biographers write that Gerry Adams did not immediately go with the Provisionals and that Martin McGuinness first joined the Officials.[20] Mitchel McLaughlin acknowledges that he first went with the Officials and then switched to the Provisionals.

When they were recruited, the young Northerners accepted abstentionism as a political philosophy that they inherited and did not question. The war continued, they became more interested in politics, experienced the election results that followed the hunger strikes and they came to see the refusal to take seats in Leinster House as an obstacle that had to be overcome. The young Northerners were also convinced that what had happened to the Officials would not happen to them; that the situation was different. Mitchel McLaughlin was asked if the split in 1986 was different from the split in 1969:

> Oh it was, definitely, it was clearly different. I'm not a neutral and I don't claim to be a neutral but I think for even the most neutral and objective of people it clearly was different in so far as those people, unfortunately, you know – I would have a lot of social contact with them. Some of them I would remember with deep affection. In political terms they never actually went anywhere. They almost went back to a 1970 decision. Their analysis of what was happening in 1970, I think, was justified, although their politics, as I say, was always a social concern. But their analysis of what was happening in 1986 was, I think, flawed by virtue of the fact that their politics hadn't developed in the intervening period. And they were recognizing in 1970 that the Officials were, in fact, looking to abandon the national question ... that was simply another group of republicans choosing to join the constitutional family and abandon the struggle to resolve the national question. Now, when they try to then apply that argument, that analysis to 1986, where it totally fell down was that there was this actual, unique combination of armed struggle to confront the presence of the British Army on the streets with an attempt to broaden the base of the struggle and bring more people into the political dimension of it. So, I mean they were hanging a label that was appropriate in 1970 onto the Movement in 1986.[21]

Danny Morrison offered similar comments:

> I was for abstentionism, and still am for abstentionism with respect to Stormont and Westminster, but not Leinster House. I think the difference is that all of the people who, in the past, had a policy of abstentionism towards Leinster House and who [then] advocated taking seats in Leinster House were actually being deceptive in so far as they had it in their minds from the outset that they were going to be co-opted by the system. And it wasn't a question then of it being done – that is, that no matter what you put in the sausage machine it comes out as sausage. I think they intended coming out as sausages. Our position is not that. Our position is not that secretly we aspire to become what is termed constitutional politicians and that we have to be disingenuous about the way we do it and we have to fool our supporters and slowly take them down that road.[22]

In terms of generational units, the young Northerners knew each other well. Adams, Hartley, Morrison and Rita O'Hare were all from Belfast. Refusing to take seats in Leinster House was probably never as important as the war in the North. The young Northerners had to convince others to go along with them.

The easiest group to convince was probably the young Southerners – technically, persons born outside Northern Ireland who joined the Movement after August 1969. Pat Doherty, for example, was born and raised in Glasgow. The young Southerners were typically recruited in response to events in the North, like internment and Bloody Sunday or the hunger strikes. Solidarity with what their contemporaries in the North were experiencing brought them into the Provisionals. They also trusted the leadership of people like Gerry Adams, Danny Morrison and Martin McGuinness, who had taken Sinn Féin to a new level. Pat Doherty recalled:

> it was said by one of the people who were opposed to the change that if you lie down with dogs you'll get up with fleas. And [a delegate supporting the motion] said something like, 'It's not our intention to lie down with dogs, it's our intention to kick the dogs out of the woods.' Well, you see, it's what you're about yourself. It's what you believe in and it's what you're struggling for. And if you're afraid of every change you make, that it's going to corrupt you, then there's something wrong with your own fundamental beliefs. And I don't think there's anything wrong with our fundamental beliefs. I think they're sincerely held and I think the people who hold them know why they hold them and they're not into being corrupted by power and prestige.[23]

For some of the younger Southerners, abstentionism was never important. Brian McDonald was the Director of Publicity and a member of the Ard Chomhairle. He was asked if he had supported the dropping of abstentionism:

> Oh, yeah. Yes. I don't see why republicans should put up obstacles to themselves or maintain obstacles. There was certainly no principle for me.

> Q: Would you have always thought that? …

> A: Yeah. Well, as you're obviously aware, I didn't come from a traditional republican background. So I don't have – the only holy grail that I have, if I have a holy grail, is the removal of the British presence and the unity of Ireland. After that, everything for me is negotiable. I hope it's a socialist republic, you know? But I hope at least it's a socially conscious republic. I hope that it's all those things. And I think that's obviously what Sinn Féin's program is. But things like abstentionism I just felt – I'm a historian and while I can admire the faithful few, I don't see the rationality of holding onto their position in entirely different circumstances … if this generation did this, then we must do that … And it was no way to run a political or revolutionary movement. You've got to be adaptive. And I think that's the credit of Adams and them is that they have adapted.[24]

Taking seats in Leinster House was part of the political development of the Provisionals. A respondent from Tipperary commented:

> I was in favour of it because I thought it would open up political avenues. I never believed we would get seats … I didn't believe that we were going to get seats at any stage. That we were so far behind politically – the political organization was [behind] – that if we were to make inroads we would have to be seen as a political party and we weren't … When I joined the organization [in the early 1970s], at first, to

be honest about it, I was abstentionist through and through. But the more involved I became with people locally and then on the ground I felt that, yeah, that if we were to make any inroads – and they always told us, you only represent 1 per cent. You only represent a half per cent.[25]

A Dubliner recruited during the hunger strike mobilization commented: *'Actually I would have agreed at the start that Sinn Féin shouldn't take seats in Leinster House but through more involvement and more reading and developing politics I would have discarded that view.*[26] Several of the young Southerners were not raised in republican families. They had little or no connection with the Treaty debates and the Irish Civil War that had confirmed abstentionism as a principle. The ongoing war in the North was immediate.

Convincing the pre-1969 Northerners to support taking seats in Leinster House was essential. The support of J.B. O'Hagan and Seamus Twomey, seen as two key IRA veterans, and the support of Joe Cahill, who was in the IRA and Sinn Féin leadership, was important because they could deny the argument that history was repeating itself. Just as important was their close relationship with John Joe McGirl, who was highly regarded by everyone. It was not so much that people like J.B. O'Hagan wanted Sinn Féin to participate in the Dublin parliament but that they saw the cost of refusing to participate. O'Hagan was asked if he supported the dropping of abstentionism:

I supported it, yes. I had doubts about it but I supported it … the way I looked at it was 99 per cent – maybe 100 per cent of the people in the twenty-six counties considered it to be their legitimate government. So, taking a pragmatic view of things, I said, 'Well, we're isolating ourselves. We need to get a voice if possible in the Dáil and get into politics 100 per cent in the twenty-six counties.[27]

According to Joe Cahill, he was an exception since, as he described it, abstentionism was never that important to him. Cahill was asked to compare 1986 with 1969:

1969, 1970 – I must say at the very start that I have a very open mind on the question of abstentionism – as far as the twenty-six counties is concerned. I have a very closed mind as far as abstentionism is concerned in the North of Ireland or in England. I don't think we should take seats there. In the twenty-six counties I have a very open mind and always have. Now, I don't believe that the split that took place in '69/'70, was over abstentionism. I believe that the split that took place then was over the failure of the IRA to defend the people of the North. That was the main reason that there was a split. Albeit, abstentionism was used as a vehicle for the split, if you like … I believe that, in order to make progress in the twenty-six counties, attendance in Leinster House is very, very necessary. The people down here – we're not fighting a war down here. We're not at war with the authorities down here. So, in order to gain support, we have got to be seen to help the people in social and economic issues and the only way you can do that is to take part in the political process down here. And, as abstentionists, you're not taking part in the political process and you're merely asking people to support the IRA. People want to – if you're looking for support, they want something from you. So down here, they want support on social and economic issues.[28]

Cahill has a reputation as someone who tended to accommodate himself to whatever way the majority was going; critics describe him as 'a yes man'.[29] For more than a decade he had been ensconced in Dublin, keeping an eye on things as a new leadership rose up in Belfast. In 1969/70, he was fine with supporting the more militant Provisionals *and* abstentionism. In 1986, the new leadership wanted to pursue armed struggle and take seats in Leinster House and he was fine with it. Each decision was the pragmatic one for him.

There are two more issues to consider. First, Joe Cahill, J.B. O'Hagan, Seamus Twomey and their contemporaries were raised Irish and Catholic in a state that was British and with a Prime Minister who boasted, 'we have a Protestant parliament and a Protestant state'. They were victims of Stormont and so were the young Northerners, who promised they would never take seats in a Northern Ireland Assembly. Second, Cahill and the others had been in the IRA for half of a century. Their days on the front lines had passed and they knew it. Hence, Cahill's comment, 'age is against me and I can't be in the field with the freedom fighters today'. John Joe McGirl was ill and passed away in 1988 and Seamus Twomey passed away after a long illness in 1989. They had willingly paid a price for their activism – Cahill, O'Hagan and McGirl were jailed in the 1940s, the 1950s and the 1970s; Twomey was jailed in the 1940s and the 1970s. But they also felt a responsibility toward those who followed them and, as McGirl described it at the Ard Fheis, 'we agreed that it was necessary to make change if we were not going to hand down this struggle to another generation'. Their status in life and in the Provisionals, in combination with camaraderie amongst themselves and close ties to the young Northerners, prompted them to go along with taking seats in Leinster House.

Broadly, the pre-1969 Southerners were the one group that refused to go along with taking seats in Leinster House. Like members of the other groups, they had their own shared experiences and close interaction. Several of them were raised in republican families and they tended to live outside Dublin – Ruairí Ó Brádaigh in Roscommon, Joe O'Neill in Donegal, Seán Lynch in North Longford, Des Long in Limerick, and so on. In many ways, the pre-1969 Southerners were the children of the people who lost the Irish Civil War and refused to accept the result. Abstentionism was important to them in 1969/70; it was still important in 1986.

For them, what happened at the West County Hotel was a repeat of what happened in 1970. Figure 6 presents the Republican Sinn Féin Executive that was established on 2 November 1986.[30] Of the twenty-one people listed, only two of them were from Northern Ireland. Five of the six officers of the new party were Southern republicans from the 1950s. Ruairí Ó Brádaigh, Dáithí O'Connell and Des Long had been members of either the first Provisional IRA Army Council or the Sinn Féin Caretaker Executive or both. Twenty people were on the Caretaker Executive. Only ten of them, all of them from the South, were still involved in November 1986. Nine of them opposed taking seats in Leinster House – the exception was John Joe McGirl, which again shows how important his support was for Adams and company.

For the pre-1969 Southern republicans, the principles that maintained the Movement over the years were still important. Frank Glynn had personal experience with the temptations of constitutional politics:

Officers	
Dáithí O'Connell, Cork/Dublin	Cathaoirleach (Chairman)
Ruairí Ó Brádaigh, Longford/Roscommon	Urlabhraí (Spokesperson)
Cathleen Knowles, Dublin	Secretary
Des Long, Limerick	
Joe O'Neill, Donegal	
Frank Graham, Dublin	

Organizing Committee	
Pat Ward, Donegal	Jim Neary, Galway
Emer O'Connor, Limerick	Liam Cotter, Kerry
Bernadette Cullen, Donegal	Declan Curneen, Leitrim
Anne Magee, Fermanagh	Cathleen Sheils, Dublin
Emmet Walsh, Offaly	Gerard Mooney, Sligo
Diog Ní Chonaill,* Dublin	Michael Noonan, Tipperary
Seosamh O Maoileoin, Westmeath	Conor Corr, Tyrone
Martin Morris, Tipperary	

*Dáithí O'Connell's daughter.

FIGURE 6

Republican Sinn Féin Executive, November 1986

I could see that the other lads were, and I knew from my own background, too, that when you get a taste of politics after a while a lot of people want to go for the political scenario. And the political scenario, once you accept it, you're bound by it. So then where does the Republican Movement go for it to keep a legitimate Republican Movement? The heart and soul has gone out of it ... I used to have to pinch myself when I was elected to Galway County Council now and again because you're rubbing shoulders with all these politicians saying to you, 'You're a bloody fool. You're an idiot. If you joined our party ... we'd put you up as a TD and you'd have a good salary and you'd be a Minister and'– you know? They keep saying this to you – number one. Number two, you see the trappings of power, you're rubbing shoulders with – there's Ministers coming down, there's a dinner out here, there's an official opening out there ... unless you're staunch that will wear you down.[31]

At the 1970 Ard Fheis, John Joe McGirl had said, 'men have died opposing Leinster House, men have been killed for refusing to enter that assembly'.[32] McGirl was willing to set that aside but others were not. Seán Lynch was asked if Leinster House was the legitimate government of Ireland:

No, no, no, it was – they are the result of the British government of Ireland Act. In no way, morally or any other ways, it's not. And that's one of the reasons why I would oppose it. In no shape or form there.

> *The best of men could be alive today, Cathal Brugha and all those others, if they wanted to accept it then. And that was – the pressure that was put on them – Liam Mellowes for instance. They postponed his execution, to see would he accept it [the Treaty].*[33]

The pre-1969 Southerners were in the minority and lost the vote. They knew that, in walking out, they would give up all of the material resources associated with the Provisionals, including Sinn Féin offices scattered throughout Ireland and a newspaper but they still walked out.

The Aftermath of the Split

From the perspective of Adams and company, the split was regrettable but of limited consequence. Sinn Féin's account has only thirty delegates walking out of the Ard Fheis.[34] Sinn Féin has also tried to make sure that the split is seen through their eyes.

Martin McGuinness and Pat Doherty had argued that the disagreement was less about abstentionism and more about the old leadership refusing to accept responsibility for the 1975 truce/ceasefire. That interpretation was reinforced in interviews with journalists and academics. In 1990, in reply to being asked if he agreed with McGuinness's assertion that the 1975 ceasefire was a disaster, Joe Cahill said: *'Well, I would agree with him on that … I've always maintained that it was a disaster, you know? It got nowhere. As has been proven since, it got nowhere. I think that the then leadership fell for a British ploy.'*[35] In 1990, Mitchel McLaughlin commented:

> *We're talking about honourable people here. But [they made] a very significant and serious mistake. The republican struggle was almost destroyed as a result of that truce. They were negotiating with the British on a totally false premise and, in the meantime, the British were building the H-Blocks. The British were pulling together their Ulsterization and their normalization programme and all of that was being put in place while these sincere and genuine republican leaders thought they were negotiating with a British government that was prepared to consider withdrawal from Ireland. And what happened was they didn't read it as early as those people who lived in the war zone. So here in Derry and in Belfast there was reaction against that.*[36]

The interpretation that the old Southern-based leadership fell for a British ploy became the accepted history of the Provisionals.[37] Jonathan Powell, the former advisor to Prime Minister Tony Blair, writes in *Great Hatred, Little Room: Making Peace in Northern Ireland*, 'the IRA leadership agreed to a ceasefire in 1974–75. This is seen now by IRA members as an unmitigated disaster in which Volunteers' morale plummeted and the movement was penetrated. The southern leadership of the movement had been duped by false promises.'[38] Whether or not the truce was a disaster is debatable. And the truce cannot be laid at the feet of Southern republicans who did not live in the 'war zone'. In 1975, five of the seven members of the Army Council were Northerners, Seamus Twomey of Belfast was C/S, and two of the representatives who met with the British were Northerners.

Stubborn facts like these were conveniently ignored by the Provisionals and often missed by commentators. Gerry Adams and Martin McGuinness saving the Provisionals and developing revolutionary politics via the hunger strikes is a simpler story when compared to the complexity of what actually happened. Because Adams and McGuinness won the debate, and because the war was in the North, journalists and academics often looked to them and Danny Morrison, Tom Hartley and so forth for interviews. As a result, the voices of Southern republicans are often missing from books and articles on the conflict in Ireland. As an example, for *Feminist Identity Development and Activism in Revolutionary Movements*, Theresa O'Keefe only presents 'field work in the North of Ireland', thereby missing the story of Southern republican women, including Southern women in Cumann na mBan after 1986.[39]

Adams and company also benefitted from having watched Official Sinn Féin very carefully control their image as they morphed into the The Workers' Party, diverting attention from their own background and attacking the Provisionals as sectarian terrorists.[40] With the Officials as a model, the post-1986 Provisionals have promoted their own version of history and helped others ignore alternative versions. Not mentioning Dáithí O'Connell's role in suggesting that Bobby Sands contest Fermanagh/South Tyrone is an example. Activists who did not go along with the leadership were 'former' republicans and that view made its way into accounts. In his biography of Bobby Sands, *Nothing But An Unfinished Song*, Denis O'Hearn describes Tommy McKearney as someone who 'left the Republican Movement in 1986'. McKearney only left the Provisionals. He was still in Long Kesh and formed the League of Communist Republicans. As a result, he and other prisoners faced 'an environment in which the leadership within the prison encouraged hostility and isolation in order to stamp out opposition' to the decision to take seats in Dublin. When the Sands biography was published, McKearney was involved in the 'Republican Writers' Group', was editor of *Fourthwrite: For a Democratic Socialist Republic*, and still a republican.[41]

Cumann na mBan opposed taking seats in Leinster House. The Provisionals claim they 'ceased to exist' in the 1980s when in fact they still exist and are still opposed to taking seats in Leinster House.[42] The denial of the existence of Cumann na mBan is an interesting approach considering the Provisionals pride themselves on being progressive on women's issues. A majority of Na Fianna Éireann scouts were opposed to taking seats in Leinster House but because they were children and teenagers, the Provisionals could more easily manipulate them. The organization's constitution was changed to allow members to support taking seats in Leinster House and it caused a split. Some of the membership did leave for the Provisionals. Those who remained undid the change and then carried on as Na Fianna Éireann.[43] Today, Na Fianna Éireann is an independent organization that is closely aligned with Republican Sinn Féin. As far as the Provisionals are concerned, after the 1994 ceasefire Na Fianna Éireann morphed into Ógra (Young) Shinn Féin.[44]

Personal Consequences

Lost in many accounts of the split are its deep personal consequences. Even those who supported taking seats in Leinster House were taken aback by the negativity and personal attacks at the Ard Fheis. The republican from Tipperary stated:

the first time I ever saw it was the '86 Ard Fheis. I mean where people openly, openly criticized the leadership. It was something I didn't like and the reason why I didn't like it was because I thought, right, [people] have made mistakes but who genuinely believed at the time that they were doing the right thing. And let those who are first to cast a stone … It's sad. I find it – one of the people that I was very friendly with [name] … If there is someone I'd idolize … it would have been [him]. It would have really, really hurt. What he used to do was he would stop my wife and ask her how I was.

Q: He wouldn't talk to you?

A: No. That's the way it got, right? I remember going to his funeral.[45]

The leadership was based in Belfast and the vast majority of the members there stayed with the Provisionals. The few Belfast Provisionals who did not go along with the change included Bob Murray and Geraldine Taylor. Taylor was asked if she had any regrets in having walked out of the Ard Fheis and gone with Republican Sinn Féin:

No. It's been – from '86 after the walkout to now [2009], it was a very lonely time. Make no mistake about it, especially here in Belfast where I was part of a big, big movement and all of a sudden you find yourself on your own. Friends stop speaking to you. It was a very lonely time. It broke my heart. Make no mistake about it. I cried so at nights. Why was I there? Why did I stay there? The only thing that kept me going was the thought of the men and women, boys and girls, who were buried in Milltown Cemetery. They died for what I believed in and they died for what they believed in – the freedom of their country – and I couldn't give it up. I had to keep going for their sakes, for their beliefs and for what they died for. But it was a very lonely time.[46]

There were personal losses on both sides of the Atlantic. Martin Galvin commented:

Michael Flannery was my mentor when I joined Irish Northern Aid. We used to travel around the country. He would tell me stories, give me instruction. I learned a great deal from him. I was very close to him. In 1986, when there was a division, it was heartbreaking for me. It was not something that I wanted. To go against Michael Flannery, that was just very, very difficult.[47]

Flannery, along with George Harrison and Joe Stynes, would organize an alternative Irish-American support group, Cumann na Saoirse Náisiúnta (National Irish Freedom Committee).[48]

In Ireland, Frank Glynn, Dáithí O'Connell, Geraldine Taylor and the others did not go 'home', as Martin McGuinness had hoped. In a short period of time they would bring back Éire Nua and federalism, have their own newspaper, *Saoirse*, and a head office in Dublin. In effect, they were a social movement in waiting, waiting for the Provisionals' leaders to prove them right. As far as the Provisionals were concerned, they were irrelevant: RSF – 'Retired Sinn Féin'.

Coda

The Provisional IRA also split in 1986, but very few people knew that. During the Sinn Féin Ard Fheis, there was a private meeting between Ruairí Ó Brádaigh, Des Long, Joe O'Neill and Pat Ward on one side and Gerry Adams, Martin McGuinness, John Joe McGirl, Kevin McKenna and Mickey McKevitt, among those on the other side. Adams and company wanted to know if the abstentionists were planning a split if the vote went against them. The discussion was heated at times and Ó Brádaigh refused to answer the question. Des Long and Joe O'Neill finally confirmed that, if the motion passed, there would be a walkout. As the meeting came to a close, the abstentionists were warned not to form another IRA. John Morrison, in *The Origins and Rise of Dissident Irish Republicanism*, reports that Tom Murphy warned Ruairí Ó Brádaigh, 'Now Ruairí don't be starting anything.'

When the abstentionists reassembled at the West County Hotel, a journalist asked Dáithí O'Connell if they had their own army. He replied, 'We have no military organisation at this stage.' Within a couple of weeks, the Continuity Army Council was established with O'Connell as its Chief of Staff. No one had any interest in a Continuity IRA-Provisional-PIRA feud. As long as the Provisional IRA (PIRA) remained active, the CIRA would wait quietly on the sidelines.[49]

16

THE PLAN FAILS (1987–1990)

What would render invalid the prospect of success was a weariness, was a disillusionment, was a lack of regeneration within the Republican Movement. And that hasn't occurred. And that's what's most important.

– Danny Morrison[1]

With the benefit of hindsight, the 1986 Sinn Féin Ard Fheis was the final phase in the implementation of the Staff Report of the late 1970s. Cumann na mBan was gone, Na Fianna Éireann was on the way out, and Sinn Féin was unfettered by tradition. The Provisionals were on the cutting edge of revolutionary politics, finally in a position to fully embrace the armalite and ballot box strategy.

The Provisional IRA had travelled a long way since the mid-1970s. As the IRA implemented the Staff Report following the Truce, the 'civil administration' grew and the Provisionals became more and more deeply involved in the lives of people living in republican areas. The civil administration also empowered activists in a way that was different from directly prosecuting the war.[2] To a degree, Sinn Féin in the North was built on the back of the civil administration. They found jobs for ex-prisoners in local bars, on construction sites, driving taxis and so on. They also provided a criminal justice system for people who did not trust the RUC. Drug dealers, joyriders, sex offenders, thieves and thugs were beaten or knee-capped.

The IRA in general became more bureaucratic and the number of active service operators was reduced to perhaps one to two hundred volunteers. They were a mix of seasoned veterans and the best of the new recruits. Departments became more specialized and compartmentalized, more focused on specific tasks. Internal security examined failed operations, debriefed released prisoners and searched for informers. Quartermasters monitored arms dumps scattered throughout Ireland. Supply lines brought material into the South that engineers turned into increasingly sophisticated bombs, mortars, and rockets and then sent North.[3]

With the bureaucracy came 'middle managers', which had pluses and minuses. Many of them had been operators, which gave them credibility, and, because they no longer went on operations, they were likely to stay in place and that provided stability. On the downside, and like any other bureaucracy, some of the middle managers stayed in their positions for too long. Keeping someone in a position of influence helped make that person beholden to the leadership.

It also created a situation in which a middle manager could become more interested in staying a middle manager than in taking risks prosecuting the war. There was also a security issue. An agent in a management position, like Seán O'Callaghan, had access to a large amount of information and enough influence to cover his or her tracks. It appears that the Provisionals made a colossal blunder with the security department. John Joe Magee and Freddie Scappaticci were in the department's leadership and there are credible allegations that both were agents. If so, the persons in charge of executing informers were informers themselves. There are credible allegations that the security forces let them get away with murder.[4]

The reorganization and the rise of Sinn Féin also changed the nature of involvement. For example, in 1983, Ricky O'Rawe was released from Long Kesh and Tom Hartley asked him to take over the republican press centre in Belfast. O'Rawe accepted the position and was pleased to discover, courtesy of Danny Morrison, that he was now attached to GHQ and, therefore, his operating days were over.[5] Martin Meehan, who had been O/C of Ardoyne, was released from Long Kesh for the second time in 1985. Meehan was forty years old and had every intention of returning to active service; he assumed everyone felt the same. To Meehan's dismay, he discovered that members of the civil administration were not expected to go on operations and that new recruits were even allowed to choose between different departments: civil administration, intelligence, active service and so on.[6]

The Provisionals' plan in the winter of 1986–7 was to have Sinn Féin challenge the status quo in the twenty-six counties by taking seats in Dáil Éireann and to have the Provisional IRA make the six counties ungovernable by stepping up the armed campaign. The plan would fail because of British agents, Provisional IRA blunders and Margaret Thatcher's willingness to use everything she could against them.

Only a few months after the Ard Fheis, Labour withdrew from the coalition government in Dublin and Sinn Féin was presented an opportunity to contest a Leinster House election without abstentionism. Expectations were high, even though Gerry Adams had warned that removing abstentionism would not be a 'magic wand' and that 'the election after the next one will be the first serious test of our ability to win major support'.[7] On 17 February 1987, after its most aggressive political campaign since the 1920s, 27 Sinn Féin candidates for Dáil Éireann received only 32,933 votes. That was almost double the vote of February 1982, but less than 2 per cent of the total vote. It was also 10,000 fewer votes than the H-Block/Armagh candidates of 1981. Sinn Féin was a long way from being able to 'kick the dogs out of the woods'. The best result was in Cavan-Monaghan where Caoimhghín Ó Caoláin received 4,129 votes (7.3 per cent) and finished seventh out of ten candidates.[8] Charlie Haughey, the master politician, put together another coalition government and, for the third time, he was Taoiseach.

Soon after the election, Sinn Féin published what they said was a major policy document, *A Scenario for Peace*.[9] In terms of substance, there was not much that was new in the document. For example, 'It is for the Irish people as a whole to determine the future status of Ireland.' The document offered unionists 'a settlement based on their throwing in their lot with the rest of the Irish people and ending sectarianism'. Brian Feeney writes that '*A Scenario for Peace* cut no ice with unionists – very few read it. It was dismissed with derision by the SDLP and ignored by the British.'[10] As it would turn out, the most interesting part of the document was the opening statement: 'This document is presented by Sinn Féin for discussion and as an answer to those who claim that there is no alternative to the continuation of British rule.' *A Scenario for Peace* was a call for a dialogue with the major constitutional parties in Ireland. Such a dialogue would probably have been impossible if Sinn Féin still had an embargo on Leinster House and all those abstentionists had not walked out.

On the military side of the Provisionals' plan, there was disagreement on the best way to take the campaign to another level. The leadership was following a 'political guerrilla' model in which activists remained in their communities. That allowed people to have dual roles in Sinn Féin and the IRA and helped connect the IRA with the community. The approach also left activists vulnerable. The RUC could arrest them and their friends and, for seven days, interrogate, cajole, bribe and intimidate them. If the wrong person broke, it was a disaster for an active service unit (cell). The security forces also passed information to loyalists and known activists were assassination targets. A group of IRA volunteers in East Tyrone, led by Jim Lynagh and Padraig McKearney, wanted a change in tactics.[11]

Lynagh and McKearney argued that the choice was 'total war or no war at all', and they wanted total war. They suggested creating an independent active service unit that was not tied to a specific geographic location, similar to the flying columns of the 1920s. With the unit constantly on the move, the RUC would not be able to monitor activists when they left home, met with friends and so on. Informers would be more exposed because they would have to separate from the column in order to pass on information. Also, operators in a mobile unit that was constantly on the go would be out of the reach of loyalist assassins. Lynagh and McKearney were respected operators and could not simply be ignored. Between Portlaoise, Long Kesh and Magilligan, the two of them had spent more than a decade in prison. Lynagh has been described as a 'ruthless gunman' but he was also a political guerrilla in the sense that, in 1979, he was elected to the Monaghan Urban District Council, although he had to go on the run in the early 1980s. McKearney had been on the run since escaping from Long Kesh in 1983 and the family was highly regarded. His brother Tommy was on the 1980 hunger strike, in the mid-1970s the press had described his sister Margaret as 'Britain's most wanted woman' and, in 1974, his brother Seán was killed in a premature explosion along with another volunteer, Eugene Martin.[12]

Mid-Ulster is filled with rolling hills and valleys, and its small towns and villages had pockets of hard-core IRA sympathizers. An independent flying column might have wreaked havoc in East Tyrone and become a model for similar columns in other areas. Kevin McKenna, the Chief of Staff, was from Tyrone and lived in nearby Monaghan. The base of power was in urban Belfast, however, and evidently neither McKenna nor the Belfast leadership was interested in having an independent column operating in the Tyrone countryside. In 1988, Danny Morrison, as Sinn Féin's Director of Publicity, was asked to comment on the IRA campaign. In response, he said:

> *The IRA relies on public support and has to carry out operations within a perception by our supporters of what is acceptable and what is unacceptable. And the IRA has never poisoned the water supply in a British Army base ... What the IRA is trying to do is walk a tightrope, and it's trying to maintain*

a very dignified and civilized and limited form of guerrilla warfare. It could be that if the IRA hadn't been doing that for this last twenty years and had said, 'We are going to bomb, we are going to close down the London underground, we are going to make the streets of London unsafe for the public, we are going to sicken them with being in Ireland,' maybe that would have worked, maybe the Brits would have been pulling out of here five years ago, but that is not something about which you could be proud, about which you could justify. It might be efficacious. It'd bring about the desired end. And that's also debatable. It may have brought, actually, down more repression on your head than you could handle. ... the reason why the IRA would not have done it is because the IRA is fighting a popular war which requires popular support, and which requires some ground rules.

At the time Lynagh and McKearney offered their proposal, the Provisional IRA had killed more than 1,400 people and was responsible for several atrocities, including Bloody Friday, the Birmingham pub bombs, the Kingsmills massacre and the La Mon House firebomb. If they wanted, the Provisional IRA could have delivered an atrocity every day. Danny Morrison also commented:

The fact remains that the IRA has never set out a policy to car bomb civilians in England whereas it's an everyday event in the Middle East. They just put 150 pounds of TNT in the middle of the street, blow the street away and then they come back and do the same thing the next day.[13]

If the Provisionals were going to follow 'ground rules', they needed a central command structure that could control active service units. The East Tyrone Brigade already had a reputation for independent action. Turning them loose in the countryside would have been too risky, and the leadership turned down the idea of an independent flying column. Tommy McKearney, in *The Provisional IRA: From Insurrection to Parliament*, argues that keeping activists in their own areas was a strategic blunder that 'allowed British intelligence to inflict more damage on the IRA than might otherwise have been the case'.[14] The damage was especially heavy in East Tyrone.

Over an eighteen-month period in the mid-1980s, the East Tyrone Brigade had successfully attacked RUC barracks in Ballygawley, Coalisland and Dungannon, hotels in Cookstown and Dungannon, and restaurants in Ballyronan and Kildress. On the evening of Friday 8 May 1987, an active service unit set out for the RUC barracks in Loughall, a nearby village in County Armagh. A mechanical digger was commandeered and the bucket was filled with explosives. With a scout car in front of him, Declan Arthurs drove the digger to Loughall where they met up with a hijacked Toyota van driven by Eugene Kelly. Paddy Kelly, the O/C, was in the van's front passenger seat. In the back were Jim Lynagh, Padraig McKearney, Seamus Donnelly, Tony Gormley and Gerard O'Callaghan. Gormley and O'Callaghan climbed onto the digger and off they went. Because of an informer, high-quality surveillance, or a combination of the two, waiting for them was a special unit of SAS.[15]

Arthurs drove past the barracks and then made a sudden turn and drove through a perimeter fence and Paddy Kelly got out of the van to provide back up. Arthurs lit the fuse to the explosives and the SAS opened fire. The eight volunteers died in a hail of bullets – some of them were shot running from the scene. Declan Arthurs was shot thirty-six times; Seamus Donnelly was shot twenty times. Two civilians, brothers Anthony and Oliver Hughes, drove onto the scene and the SAS assumed it was another scout car. Anthony Hughes was killed and Oliver Hughes was shot fourteen times but survived. There was almost five minutes of continuous shooting during which the explosives went off and destroyed a section of the police barracks, injuring two RUC men inside.[16] With the Loughall ambush, the possibility of 'total war' in Tyrone was lost.

The 'Loughall Martyrs' represent the largest number of Provisional IRA volunteers killed in one event. They offer a profile of active service operators in the mid-1980s. As shown in Table 4, the senior members of the unit were Padraig McKearney, Jim Lynagh, Patrick Kelly and Gerard O'Callaghan, ages thirty-two, thirty-one, thirty and twenty-eight, respectively. Each of them had been arrested and spent a year or longer in custody and then returned to the IRA. They would have known each other well: in the 1970s, Padraig McKearney and Jim Lynagh probably overlapped for a time as sentenced prisoners in Long Kesh; in 1980, McKearney was arrested with Gerard O'Callaghan.[17] One of their contemporaries described the prison experience:

> It's just you go through everything with everyone. You live with someone twenty-four hours a day. Now, you're all in separate cells but it is an unbelievable experience. I didn't know what to expect. Regarding jail, it is totally different because everyone I was in there with was in there for a belief – a political belief as opposed to being in there for crime, armed robbery, for self-gain. And the characters and the people were excellent. And I would say this over and over: people who would make politicians, solicitors, lawyers at any other time were in jail for political arrest. People with great influence. And everyone worked for one another. But it was a family atmosphere. Everyone was there for everyone else. We slagged. We joked. We got on with it. But lads were in there for sixteen, seventeen years. And they had been in that same place for sixteen, seventeen years, not been out for a day for that time, and they still totally believed. And it gave a bond. I think what the state actually wanted was the people in jail to break – to break you. It has the opposite effect. It definitely has the opposite effect when it comes to republicans ... Just the friendships that I built up – that experience, that whole experience of a community spirit was in the jails certainly. I can't really explain but – I don't want to do it again, I didn't want to do it the first time – but I'm glad I've had that experience.[18]

Between the beginning of 1986 and the end of 1989, twenty-six Provisional IRA volunteers were shot dead by the security forces or died in premature explosions. All but one of them was male; the exception was Mairéad Farrell. Eleven of them were thirty or more years of age and eight of them were married with children. Fourteen of them joined the Provisionals in 1975 or earlier. Paddy Kelly, Jim Lynagh, Padraig McKearney and Gerard O'Callaghan were experienced and committed comrades, like many of their peers in the IRA.[19]

The younger members of the unit were Eugene Kelly (no relation to Paddy Kelly), Tony Gormley, Declan Arthurs and Seamus Donnelly, aged twenty-five, twenty-four, twenty-one and nineteen years, respectively. They are described as 'close friends as well as comrades'. Kelly, Gormley and Arthurs were from Galbally and joined the Provisionals during or just after the

TABLE 4

Provisional IRA Volunteers killed at Loughall, May 1987

	Age	Place of Birth/ Where Lived	Married	Children	Year Joined the IRA (approximate)
Padraig McKearney	32	Moy, Co. Tyrone	No	0	Early 1970s
Jim Lynagh	31	County Monaghan	No	0	Early 1970s
Paddy Kelly	30	Dungannon, Co. Tyrone	Yes	3	1975/76
Gerard O'Callaghan	28	Benburb, Co. Tyrone	No	0	1976
Eugene Kelly	25	Galbally, Co. Tyrone	No	0	1982
Tony Gormley	24	Galbally, Co. Tyrone	No	0	1981
Declan Arthurs	21	Galbally, Co. Tyrone	No	0	1982
Seamus Donnelly	19	Cappagh, Co. Tyrone	No	0	1984

hunger strikes. Donnelly was from Cappagh, which is near Galbally, and was a neighbour of Martin Hurson's family. At one point or another, each of them had been arrested for suspected paramilitary activity. Declan Arthurs spent most of January 1987 in and out of Gough Barracks. He was arrested, held for seven days, released, rearrested and so on.

John Joe McGirl and J.B. O'Hagan led the guard of honour as it carried Jim Lynagh's coffin across the Tyrone/Monaghan border.[20] Gerry Adams offered the funeral oration during which he used the event to attack the hypocrisy of Fianna Fáil and Charlie Haughey:

> A few short months ago, the people of this state elected a Fianna Fáil government of sorts. Their leader made many brave noises about a British withdrawal being a prerequisite for peace in this island. He described the Six-County state as a non-viable social and economic unit. He chose Bodenstown to denounce British policy, Fitzgerald's collusion in that policy and the actions of the British crown forces. That was when he was looking for votes ... You owe him no allegiance, he has broken every promise he made.[21]

What Adams did not say, and it is not clear how many people were aware, is that he was in the process of reaching out to Haughey and Fianna Fáil, and the SDLP.

Father Alec Reid was born in Tipperary and joined the Redemptorist community at Clonard Monastery. The Redemptorists are known for their engagement with the community and a vow of poverty. Reid had developed a relationship with Gerry Adams[22] and a few weeks after Lynagh's funeral, through Father Reid, Gerry Adams contacted Charlie Haughey and John Hume and asked them to participate in a dialogue on creating an alternative to armed struggle. Haughey and Hume were interested but wary. Haughey had to worry about the legacy of the 'Arms Trial' and was not willing to meet with Adams in person. He did authorize 'party-to-party' meetings but Hume suspected Adams was trying to use him. If it became public that Hume met with Adams it would add to Sinn Féin's credibility just before a Westminster election. The unionists and some of his own people would also condemn him for meeting with terrorists. Hume met several times with Father Reid but wisely held off on meeting Adams.[23]

In the June 1987 Westminster election, Sinn Féin directly challenged the SDLP in several constituencies and lost. Adams was re-elected in West Belfast but, in Derry, Martin McGuinness lost to John Hume by 15,000 votes. In Newry and Armagh, Jim McAllister finished 19,000 votes behind Seamus Mallon. Overall, Sinn Féin's vote was down and the SDLP's was up. The SDLP also picked up a seat when Eddie McGrady won in South Down.[24] The ballot box half of Sinn Féin's plan was not doing well, and there was more trouble with the IRA's campaign.

On 1 November 1987, French customs officers seized the *Eksund* in the Bay of Biscay and captured 150 tons of weapons. It was the final shipment from Libya and, with its capture, the authorities realized that other shipments had gotten through. Follow-up operations uncovered arms dumps in Counties Cavan, Donegal, Dublin, Limerick and Meath and the plans for an Irish 'Tet' suffered a major blow.[25] Ten days later, 11 November – Remembrance Day ('Poppy Day') – there was another atrocity. The unionist community in Enniskillen turned out to watch a parade and commemorate the War dead of the Commonwealth of Nations. As the parade ended, a bomb exploded and a building collapsed onto the crowd. Eleven people were killed, all of them Protestant. There were already allegations that the Provisionals were engaged in ethnic cleansing, targeting the sons of Protestant families along the Fermanagh border to clear the area.[26] The IRA claimed that electronic 'countermeasures' had triggered the bomb. No one believed it. At best, bombing a Remembrance Day ceremony was grossly incompetent. The alternative explanation was that it was a sectarian attack on the Protestants of Fermanagh. In Dublin, 50,000 people signed a book of condolence.

One of the Enniskillen victims was twenty-year-old Marie Wilson, a nurse. She was standing next to her father when the bomb exploded. In an interview with the BBC, Gordon Wilson described the event:

> We were both thrown forward, rubble and stones and whatever in and around and over us and under us. I was aware of a pain in my right shoulder. I shouted to Marie was she all right and she said yes, she found my hand and said, 'Is that your hand, dad?' Now remember we were under six foot of rubble. I said 'Are you all right?' and she said yes, but she was shouting in between. Three or four times I asked her and she always said yes, she was all right. When I asked her the fifth time, 'Are you all right, Marie?' she said, 'Daddy, I love you very much.' Those were the last words she spoke to me … I miss my daughter and we shall miss her but I bear no ill will, I bear no grudge. She was a great wee lassie; she loved her profession. She was a pet and she's dead. She's in heaven and we'll meet again.

Gordon Wilson was a devout Methodist and he forgave his daughter's killers, saying, 'I shall pray for those people tonight and every night.'[27] The grace he exhibited in the interview and throughout the rest of his life had a larger impact on the Provisionals than most people could imagine. Another person who was committed to peace and would have a tremendous influence on the Provisionals is John Hume. Hume referred to Enniskillen as 'an act of sheer savagery' and then went ahead and met with Gerry Adams in January 1988.[28] When the meeting was made public, the reaction from some quarters was predictable. Ian Paisley accused Hume of seeking allies with 'the political wing of the PIRA murderers'.[29] No one knew that Northern Ireland was about to suffer more carnage.

In March 1988, Mairéad Farrell, Dan McCann and Seán Savage were in Gibraltar to bomb the British military stationed there. Like the Loughall Martyrs, they were experienced operators and the leadership gave them the assignment because they were 'sound' and trustworthy. They were also, in the words of J. Bowyer Bell, 'innocents abroad'. Farrell was probably the most identifiable woman 'terrorist' in Western Europe. One of the more widely distributed photos of the dirty protest shows her in Armagh Gaol surrounded by faeces and menstrual blood. Her face appeared on posters for the 1981 Leinster House election and, when she was released in 1986, the press sought her out for interviews. McCann's mistreatment was part of the investigation into Castlereagh and he was a blanketman. Savage was the nephew of Billy McKee and, in the early 1980s, McCann and Savage were arrested based on supergrass evidence; the man retracted and they were released. Whether Farrell, McCann and Savage were done in by informers or their own high profiles, the SAS were waiting. The initial reports claimed that they were killed in a shootout and that a bomb was found. In the House of Commons, Sir Geoffrey Howe, the Foreign Secretary, was forced to offer a clarification:

> When challenged, they made movements which made the military personnel operating in support of Gibraltar police to conclude that their own lives and the lives of others were under threat. In the light of this response, they were shot. Those found were subsequently found not to have been carrying arms.[30]

A Thames Television production, *Death on the Rock*, included eyewitness testimony that they were shot while surrendering and then finished off with bullets to the head as they lay on the ground.[31]

Being murdered on the streets of Gibraltar by the elite of the British Army turned the 'Gibraltar Three' into icons. McCann's status, in particular, was transformed. He had been caught up in Ivor Bell's challenge of the leadership and dismissed. With little alternative he had returned to the fold, as described by Brendan Hughes:

> *Dan was very, very critical at the time but found himself on the outside. And Ivor would have been the most critical one at the time – Ivor Bell. And Dan was seen as being part of Ivor Bell's group. And Ivor was court-martialled. And Dan and the rest of the whole squad ... all got court-martialled. And they lost ... and, so, people like Dan found themselves outside ... once they'd lost there was nowhere else for them to go except drift away or to come back in. And Dan came back in. And if Dan had been killed at that period it would have been terrible. And when Dan come back and died in Gibraltar, he was a hero. But a few weeks before, a few months before, he was seen as a dissenter.*[32]

The funeral for Mairéad Farrell, Dan McCann and Seán Savage was the largest since the hunger strike. Tucked into the crowd in Milltown Cemetery was Michael Stone, a loyalist armed with grenades and a pistol. Stone started tossing grenades and shooting at mourners as the coffins were being lowered into the republican plot. Television crews filmed him make a deadly retreat down the hill to the M1 motorway, pursued by young men who would stop and wait for a grenade to explode before renewing their chase. They caught up with Stone on the motorway and began beating him. Stone was unconscious when the RUC arrived and arrested him. In his wake, he left a stunned crowd and a trail of victims, including three fatalities.

Three days later, another huge crowd gathered for the funeral of IRA volunteer Caoimhín Mac Brádaigh, one of Michael Stone's victims. Incredibly, two corporals in the British Army, Derek Wood and David Howes, out of uniform and in an unmarked car, suddenly drove into the cortege. Black taxis blocked their escape and mourners assumed it was another loyalist attack. When Corporal Wood pulled out a pistol and fired a shot, the crowd stepped back, for a moment. Wood and Howes were pulled from the car, beaten to the ground and stripped to their underpants. After they were identified as British soldiers, the IRA shot them and left them to die on waste ground. In her account for the *Irish Times*, journalist Mary Holland described one of the soldiers being dragged away: 'He didn't cry out, just looked at us with terrified eyes as though we were all enemies in a foreign country who wouldn't have understood what language he was speaking if he called out for help.'[33] Father Reid was in the crowd and pleaded with the IRA not to shoot them, as described in *Lost Lives*: 'One of the most enduring pictures of the troubles

Father Alec Reid gives the last rites to a British soldier killed by the Provisional IRA, 19 March 1988. News Syndication.

shows him kneeling beside the almost naked bodies of the soldiers, his face distraught as he administered the last rites.'[34] Like Michael Stone's attack, the incident was captured on video and, via television, the rest of the world saw what an awful place Northern Ireland could be.

The RUC used the video to arrest several people for their involvement in the murder of Corporals Wood and Howes, including Pat McGeown who was on the 1981 hunger strike; when he had lapsed into a coma, his wife had taken him off the fast. The RUC also wanted to question Father Reid but, through a contact in the Northern Ireland Office, Reid asked Chief Constable John Herman for help. If Reid were forced to cooperate with the RUC, it would end his role as an intermediary for Gerry Adams just as his service was starting to bring results. Reid was not questioned.[35]

In April 1988, John Hume, Seamus Mallon, Austin Currie and Seán Farren met with Gerry Adams, Danny Morrison, Tom Hartley and Mitchel McLaughlin. When the meeting was made public, Margaret Thatcher expressed her distaste, telling the House of Commons that, 'members of this government have had no contact whatever with Sinn Féin and will have no contact with them'. Tom Campbell, of the Alliance Party, criticized Hume with: 'for one who is seriously suggesting he wishes to engage in dialogue between all sections of the community, this is an astonishing move. The fact that Mr. Hume has chosen to meet with Sinn Féin in the aftermath of the Enniskillen murders is a sad commentary on this so-called desire for dialogue.'[36] A month later, a Fianna Fáil delegation that included Dermot Ahern, a TD for County Louth, and Martin Mansergh, met in Dundalk with Gerry Adams, Mitchel McLaughlin and Pat Doherty. Mansergh described the meeting:

> Adams went out of his way to be fairly polite, courteous and gentle – not to be too intimidating. Adams did a majority of the talking. Adams is, as we all know, both intelligent and articulate. The meeting was essentially a 'getting to know you' exercise.[37]

From the perspective of Fianna Fáil, it was not clear how serious the Sinn Féiners were in making the approach. It seemed that Sinn Féin was only interested in an open-ended dialogue, without commitments.

Broadly, Sinn Féin, the SDLP and Fianna Fáil agreed on two things. They wanted a united Ireland and they wanted the future of Ireland to be determined by the people of Ireland. Sinn Féin saw the meetings as a chance to explore a possible 'pan-nationalist' front that the British would have to take seriously. At the April SDLP–Sinn Féin meeting, for example, the Sinn Féiners suggested jointly approaching the Haughey government and asking it to lead an international effort for national self-determination. Where the three groups disagreed was on the importance of armed struggle.

Fianna Fáil and the SDLP saw political violence as counter-productive. In the spring of 1988, Danny Morrison offered his thoughts on constitutional nationalism and the British government:

> Even if there was no SDLP and Sinn Féin held all nationalist seats and said to the British government, 'Now will you leave our country?' the British would not go. Even if Sinn Féin were the government in

the South of Ireland and Sinn Féin held all the seats in the North, and said, 'Now will you leave our country?' Britain would still refuse to go. Now, isn't that clear? If Fianna Fáil said that to the British government tomorrow, 'Leave Ireland', they won't go. If the SDLP tomorrow said, 'Leave Ireland', they will not go. So it's not a question that all that's wrong is that the SDLP and the Dublin government aren't calling upon the Brits to leave Ireland, or that all that's wrong is that Sinn Féin doesn't occupy the SDLP and Dublin government positions to meet the simple demand to leave Ireland. The fact is the Brits will not leave Ireland. And they will not leave Ireland because they are here for their own strategic interests. They are maintaining their grip here because they do not want to see Ireland become a neutral, independent democracy. They want to dictate the political complexion of this island and, although it is, at times, obnoxious to them and it causes them problems internationally, because of the methods they have to used to remain here, still and all, they are more prepared to use those methods in order to keep their grip here than to surrender control to the sovereign Irish people.[38]

Although the three groups were far apart, the meetings did show the Provisionals that *if* they ended the military campaign it might open the door to a discussion about a pan-nationalist front.

The Provisionals were a long way from ending the campaign. Although the security forces had seized a huge amount of weapons and there would not be an Irish 'Tet', the IRA had enough pistols, assault rifles, semtex, mortars and rockets to continue for a very long time. There had been losses, like Loughall and Gibraltar, but there were also successes. British Army headquarters in Northern Ireland was located in Thiepval Barracks, in Lisburn. Every June, British soldiers participated in a fun run that supported the local YMCA. It was a community event and no one expected the Provisionals would bomb it but, for 1988, they put a bomb under an unmarked military van and killed six soldiers. A couple of months after the Lisburn attack, soldiers returning from leave drove over a bomb on the Ballygawley–Omagh Road in Tyrone and eight soldiers were killed. Ten days after Ballygawley, the SAS hit back and three members of the mid-Tyrone IRA, Gerard Harte, the O/C, his brother Michael and Michael Harte's brother-in-law Brian Mullen, were shot dead.[39]

There was another stalemate in Northern Ireland. After twenty years, the Provisionals still had not won but they had not lost, either. Danny Morrison was asked if the failure to win after twenty years was evidence the Provisionals could not win:

Well, I can counter that. The Catholics have [been able to sit in the British parliament] since 1829 and social democracy hasn't been able, or the methods of social democracy haven't [been able], to drive the British out. In 1978, you probably had people in what was then Rhodesia lecturing the Patriotic Front and saying, 'You've been fighting for six years and you haven't won, why not just give up?' when, in fact, they won in the seventh year. Or in Vietnam, you fought the French and you fought the British, you know? And you fought the Americans, and the Americans haven't left. They're still sending them. In fact, they're sending in another twenty-five to thirty thousand soldiers. Why not just give up? It's not a question of that. If you give up what you actually do, you're sowing the seeds for another generation. And there has been almost 3,000 people killed in the North of Ireland this last twenty years. Now, if you had, and this isn't being cynical or inhumane, but if those three thousand casualties had been suffered at the time of partition in the cause of sticking it out ... it's quite possible that we would now be living in an independent Ireland ... And also, because something hasn't been achieved after twenty years, it does not render invalid the prospect of success.

What would render invalid the prospect of success was a weariness, was a disillusionment, was a lack of regeneration within the Republican Movement. And that hasn't occurred. And that's what's most important. The fact that, despite all those losses, despite the fact that thousands have gone to jail, hundreds of IRA Volunteers have been killed, despite the losses, the material losses and propaganda defeats down the years, the British government knows that it faces a very professional, well-disciplined, well-organized, guerrilla army, which it, let's face it, after twenty years hasn't been able to defeat. And you're talking about – let's just look at the British point of view – you're talking about a small organization, a criminal organization, masterminded by godfathers, who are lining their own pockets, and they can't wipe them out? A superpower can't wipe them out? So that is the question. Their argument is invalid. And what they are facing is a patriotic organization which has popular support.[40]

What might come from the contacts with constitutional nationalism was unclear. What the Provisionals did know was that they had a base level of support that could even withstand a disaster like Enniskillen. Although the SDLP withdrew from the meetings after the Ballygawley bomb, John Hume and Gerry Adams stayed in touch with each other. The Provisionals also maintained the connection with Fianna Fáil.[41]

Also, while the Republican Movement as a whole may not have been weary and disillusioned, some former Provisionals were. In the autumn of 1988, Seán O'Callaghan walked into Tunbridge Wells police station in England and told an officer that he wanted to admit to murdering an RUC Special Branch detective inspector in 1974.[42] It was the beginning of a strange saga for O'Callaghan.

The British had their own 'ground rules' – they were not going to bulldoze the homes of Sinn Féin supporters, for example. While the security forces contained the IRA, Margaret Thatcher's government worked to isolate and 'demonize' Sinn Féin. A ban was introduced that prohibited broadcasting statements from eleven Irish political and paramilitary organizations with Sinn Féin as the primary target. Broadcasters had difficulty interpreting the ban and it led to a strange situation where viewers would see someone like Gerry Adams speaking but hear the voice of an actor, like Stephen Rea. It was awkward and confusing but also effective since, in response to the ban, there was a noticeable decrease in requests for interviews with Sinn Féin. The effects of demonizing Sinn Féin extended beyond television interviews.[43]

The Finucanes, like the McKearneys, were one of several families that were deeply connected to the Provisionals. John Finucane, who was killed in a car accident, is listed on the IRA Roll of Honour. Seamus Finucane was arrested with Bobby Sands and he was in a relationship with Mairéad Farrell when she was killed. Dermot Finucane was one of the nineteen successful escapees from Long Kesh. Their brother, Pat Finucane, was a solicitor and his firm, Madden and Finucane, represented republicans. Loyalists assumed that he was in the IRA and, even if he was not a member, Pat Finucane was irritating because he was a good attorney. With Finucane as his solicitor, Pat McGeown was acquitted of charges related to the attack on Corporals Wood and Howes. Finucane was also the lead attorney in a case in which the European Court of Human Rights ruled that seven-day detention without legal representation violated the European Convention.

Early in 1989, the Prevention of Terrorism Act was up for renewal and the Thatcher government faced serious opposition from civil libertarians. The RUC Special Branch passed to Douglas Hogg, a Conservative MP, a dossier indicating that Pat Finucane was 'associating closely with IRA/SF personnel'. In the House of Commons, Hogg told the Select Committee examining the PTA that, 'I have to state as a fact, but with great regret, that there are in Northern Ireland a number of solicitors who are unduly sympathetic to the cause of the IRA.'[44] Seamus Mallon, the SDLP's MP for Newry and Armagh, immediately objected to the 'appalling' accusation. Hogg had violated protocol and identified an attorney with a client's cause. The Law Society also filed an objection and it was in this context that British intelligence received information that Pat Finucane's life was at risk. They did not pass that information on to him.

On the evening of 12 February 1989, the Finucane family was eating dinner in North Belfast when loyalists burst through the front door. Pat Finucane was shot fourteen times and killed, his wife was wounded and their children were traumatized. An investigation would later reveal that Brian Nelson, a loyalist working for British intelligence, had given the assassins a photo of Pat Finucane with Pat McGeown. The attack was not an isolated event and two days after Pat Finucane was killed, loyalists shot dead Sinn Féin Councillor John Davey outside his home in South Derry.[45] A month after this, the IRA ambushed an unmarked car and killed two RUC superintendents, Harry Breen and Bob Buchanan. They were returning from a meeting with Gardaí in Dundalk and there is speculation that the IRA had an agent in the Irish police force.[46]

The British used administrative tactics to isolate Sinn Féin. Prior to local elections in Northern Ireland, scheduled for May 1989, the Elected Authorities (Northern Ireland) Act was passed. Candidates were required to sign a pledge that they would not express support for a proscribed organization or 'acts of terrorism', defined as violence for political ends. Sinn Féin took a pragmatic approach and their candidates signed the declaration.[47] Republican Sinn Féin, which was formed because its supporters saw taking seats in Leinster House as a violation of republican principles, argued that signing the pledge amounted to a 'public disowning' of the right of Irish people to engage in armed struggle.[48] They stuck to their principles and paid a price for it. Their candidates refused to sign the pledge and their nomination papers were rejected meaning that three sitting Councillors – Eamon Larkin in Newry and Mourne, Frank McCarry in Moyle and Mickey McGonigle in Limavady – lost their chance for re-election.

The results of the 1989 Northern Ireland local elections suggest that the anti-Sinn Féin policies were having a cumulative effect. The results may also reflect a developing weariness among Sinn Féin voters. In 1985, Sinn Féin won 59 seats, received 75,600 votes and shook the establishment. Four years later, Sinn Féin won 43 seats and received 69,000 votes. It was the second straight election in Northern Ireland in which the SDLP gained while Sinn Féin lost.[49]

The restrictions of the Elected Authorities Act effectively wiped out Republican Sinn Féin as a political force in Northern Ireland. In the South, there were only a few RSF councillors still in place, including Joe O'Neill in Donegal and Frank Glynn in Galway, and yet, the party's principled stand still attracted recruits. Des Dalton grew up in a Fianna Fáil home in County Kildare and joined Ógra Fianna Fáil as a teenager. He described his personal political journey:

> *Fianna Fáil came into government in 1987, and I began to see that the rhetoric that Fianna Fáil had played of being republican and so on wasn't living up to the reality of what they were actually doing in power. And I was railing against this within Fianna Fáil as a sixteen year old, somehow feeling that this was a betrayal of what I viewed Fianna Fáil and grew up believing them to be ... The reality was Fianna Fáil had long departed from any kind of a republican position and I looked at what they had done from the 1930s on and the internment and the executions in the forties and so on. So, by the age of seventeen, I just came to the realization that I'm basically railing against the machine here ... At that point I resigned from Fianna Fáil and looking at the alternatives, I suppose you would naturally say the alternative would have been to join Provisional Sinn Féin ... and I felt looking at them that fine, yes, at this present moment in time I would be probably 95 per cent in agreement with where they were – that would have been 1989. But looking at that and where they had at that stage, they had decided to drop their policy of abstention and so on, and recognize the twenty-six county state. I felt that yes, fine, I could join them now but I could see myself fourteen, fifteen, even twenty years down the road, I said to myself, I could see a departure coming because I could see the same basis was there as with The Workers' Party as with Fianna Fáil and so on. So, after much consideration, looking at Republican Sinn Féin, and I had read a copy of Saoirse [RSF's paper], as I said, I was well aware of who people like Ruairí Ó Brádaigh were, and so on. I decided at that point in time to join Republican Sinn Féin ... I felt that the most consistent revolutionary ... Irish republican revolutionary organization that was there was Republican Sinn Féin ...*

Republican Sinn Féin was attracting more interest than observers realized. In part, it was through the influence of republican families:

> *There were a number of young people that, again there was a stereotype of Republican Sinn Féin at the time. There was a joke at the time in the Provisionals that in 1986 they got Gerry Adams and we got the geriatrics [laughs]. But when I joined, there was quite a number of young people there actually within it despite the stereotype. Now, I suppose a number of them would have been coming from republican families.*[50]

Whether or not the Provisionals considered them irrelevant, RSF, Cumann na mBan, and Na Fianna Éireann refused to go away.

The Provisionals had reached out to the SDLP and Fianna Fáil in order to broaden their political options. They also looked to the United States, where they wanted a more sophisticated and political approach from their supporters. To do that, they toned down their anti-capitalist/pro-socialist rhetoric and became more directly involved. Joe Cahill, who had been sneaking into the US since the 1970s, was the key liaison with Irish-America. That responsibility was shifted to the Foreign Affairs Department, based in Belfast. Brian McDonald and his wife moved to New York and began working with Irish Northern Aid. McDonald spoke about his role:

it was a very difficult job to do in managing a transition – from a pseudo kind of a, well I shouldn't say pseudo but a militaristic type organization or one that would have seen itself in those terms. Some of the leadership at least in Irish Northern Aid at that time – and to try and steer Irish-America towards political activism as opposed to that purely 'RA, 'RA, 'RA-ing and seeing themselves simply as a support group for the IRA – that was the objective and that was the high point … We met a lot of great people though and we were blown away in the States with the amount of really, really solid people – people who were a thousand miles away and had absolutely no gain out of it whatsoever and yet did enormous, enormous work. It was incredible.

Internal conflict among Irish-Americans made the work stressful. There was also the occasional odd person that all political organizations manage to attract, as McDonald described:

those who pulled away, the Friends of Irish Freedom [in 1989] and that kind of a group, were extremely bitter, extremely bitter. And I was at the receiving end, I suppose, of a lot of that and some people I would have thought better of before, you know? You learned maybe that people were a wee bit unbalanced [laughing]. And that's the problem, I suppose. That was the thing you discovered in the States, too – that revolutionary movements attract some very, very peculiar people, mad people who insinuate themselves into the movement because they'll do anything, they'll do all the jobs … I remember a friend of mine [said] … that how the Americans, the Feds, if you like, had broken up the left in the west coast of America was to encourage the ultra-leftist thing. They were so left wing they were right wing and insinuated themselves into the organizations and broke them up from inside. And I felt that way about some of the people maybe that were involved over there.[51]

After a year, McDonald and his wife returned to Ireland. His replacement was Denis Donaldson. Donaldson had impeccable credentials. He had helped defend St Matthew's Church in 1970 and was among a group of prisoners profiled in *AP/RN* in the autumn of 1972: '22, born in Belfast, he is a married man'. Donaldson was 'the studious type, always exploring every possibility to further his education' and 'A small likeable lad …'[52] In Long Kesh, he was friends with the most famous Provisional of them all, Bobby Sands. One of the more famous photos of IRA prisoners shows Donaldson's arm draped over the shoulder of the much taller Sands. Contrary to expectations, when Donaldson arrived he behaved strangely. Brian McDonald talked about the handover:

I had to brief him for three weeks. He was never off the phone, never off the phone. He was the all-American boy after one day – reverse baseball cap, the sneakers with the tongue out and he wanted to be the all-American boy and I just thought he had a swagger. And his attitude was absolutely atrocious, I thought, from the word go. And he told us, quite openly, that his objective – that he would see Galvin gone … They wanted to send over somebody who could get along with people, who would try to bring things together as much as possible … Obviously the Friends of Irish Freedom, they were the problem. But instead, he was coming over to target those who hadn't gone away, those who hadn't left the Movement, and to create what was a trauma and I really do think he sewed the seeds of a movement against Galvin within Northern Aid ... it would have been in the interest of the British military intelligence and the British government to see Galvin destroyed because Galvin was their thorn in the side.

Martin Galvin also commented on Donaldson's behaviour:

And then the first night when he came out, I took him out along with a guy named Gabriel Megahey who was with Irish Northern Aid at that time ... we met him just to try to tell him a little bit about what was going on, and just brought him out that night for a couple of drinks ... After I left Gabe Megahey called me the next day and said, 'Denis said that you're finished in terms of Irish Northern Aid', which just made no sense to me. I mean, I had just come back from meetings in Ireland and was considered the top of the list or something. I called the guy in Ireland who had sent Denis. He said, 'This is ridiculous, we don't know what he's talking about.' I asked Denis; he totally denied it, said that Gabe must have drank too much or something which made no sense to me. It was just totally ridiculous but I noticed Denis seemed to be, there were a number of things that bothered me. Number one: a number of the stronger people in Irish Northern Aid, some people who had been very good members, he was all of a sudden downgrading them and bringing in people who didn't have much of a background with the organization. Number two: it just seemed to bother me he was able to give his own name. He was someone who had been in jail in Ireland who normally wouldn't have been allowed out and he just would go into the Northern Aid office, give his own name, brag about being in the IRA, do that over the phone. There were a number of things like that that struck me as very strange ... I made a number of complaints about him and was very happy when he went back to Ireland.[53]

Donaldson's replacement was Hugh Feeney, who was famous for being on hunger strike with Gerry Kelly and the Price sisters. Feeney was arrested and deported and Denis Donaldson was allowed back into the US and replaced Feeney.

In the summer of 1989, Peter Brooke succeeded Tom King as Secretary of State for Northern Ireland. Brooke, and the British in general, were painfully aware of the cost of the ongoing stalemate. That autumn a time bomb at the British base in Deal, Kent killed ten members of the Royal Marines' regimental band.[54] There was also a sense in the air that the British establishment might be coming to terms with some of their own blunders. After years of unfailing efforts by civil libertarians like Sister Sarah Clarke and investigative journalists like Chris Mullin, the convictions against the Guildford Four – Paddy Armstrong, Gerry Conlon, Paul Hill and Carole Richardson – were quashed. They were released on 19 October 1989 and their release brought that much more attention to the plight of the Maguire Seven and the Birmingham Six, whose convictions were quashed in 1991. Sadly, it was too late for Guiseppe Conlon, Gerry's father and an in-law of the Maguire's. An innocent man, he died a prisoner in Hammersmith Hospital in January 1980.[55]

On his 100th day in office, journalists were invited to an interview with Peter Brooke. Derek Henderson of the Press Association brought up the 'Mexican stand-off position' and asked if the British might 'sit down one day and talk to Sinn Féin?' To the surprise of everyone, Brooke replied:

I'll need to give you a slightly elaborate answer to that because there are obviously a number of factors which weigh with it. The first factor is that I would recognise that in terms of the late 20th century terrorist, organised as well as the Provisional IRA have become, that it is difficult to envision a military defeat of such a force because of the circumstances under which they operate, though the security forces can exercise a policy of containment to enable, broadly speaking, normal life to go on within the province. So in that sense it would require a decision on the part of the terrorists that the game had ceased to be worth the candle, that considering the lifestyle they have to adopt, that the return which they were securing from their activities did not justify the costs that it was imposing in personal terms on those who were engaged in their activities … if in fact the terrorists were to decide that the moment had come when they wished to withdraw from their activities, then I think that government would need to be imaginative in those circumstances as to how that process should be managed.

The follow-up was even more interesting. Henderson commented that it was a remarkable statement and quite an admission that the government might consider 'speaking to the Gerry Adams and Danny Morrisons of this world'. Brooke replied: 'Let me remind you of the move towards independence in Cyprus and a British minister stood up in the House of Commons and used the word "never" in a way which within two years there had been a retreat from that word.'[56] Brooke's comments were major news and they contributed to the sense that times were changing. That November, the Berlin Wall was breached.

17

CEASEFIRE (1990–1994)

I would certainly be much more open minded than I was, say, in 1980.

— Mitchel McLaughlin, 1990[1]

In early January 1990, in a speech at Bangor, County Down, Peter Brooke showed he was serious about ending the stalemate in Northern Ireland. Brooke called for inter-party talks among the 'constitutional parties' that would provide a basis for the devolution of power from London. The speech was ambitious since, because of the Anglo-Irish Agreement, Unionists politicians still refused to meet with British officials. In response to Brooke, James Molyneaux and Revd Ian Paisley demanded the suspension of the Anglo-Irish Intergovernmental Conference (AIIC) as a precondition for talks. Sinn Féin called for an all-Ireland, all-party conference without any pre-conditions.[2]

Accounts suggest that the Army Council at the start of 1990 was comprised of Kevin McKenna as C/S plus Gerry Adams, Joe Cahill, Pat Doherty, Martin McGuinness, Danny Morrison and Tom Murphy.[3] If Morrison was a member of the Army Council, that changed at about the time of Brooke's speech. Alexander 'Sandy' Lynch was arrested by IRA internal security and interrogated by John Joe Magee and Freddie Scappaticci. Lynch admitted he was an informer and also told a story that appeared to confirm a shoot-to-kill policy. Lynch's situation was brought to the attention of Danny Morrison:

> *I was at home on a Sunday, 7th [January 1990], when 'Anto' Murray [John Anthony Murray], who was an ex-internee and who I knew, arrived at my door and had a message for me from a man called Patrick, which is not his real name. Patrick was in the IRA. I knew I could trust him, and the story was that the IRA had suspected a member, Alexander 'Sandy' Lynch, of being an informer. Some things had gone wrong; he was the common denominator. They had picked him up. They had interrogated him. He had admitted to being an informer but he told a story which was intriguing. Some time earlier ... two separate active IRA service units were involved in planning an attack ... The police and the Army made a cock up and apparently two separate units, perhaps involving both the police and Army and undercover, hit the house at the same time and opened fire on each other. And a policeman was killed. [An] RUC man was killed.[4] Sandy Lynch told the IRA that his handlers were going ballistic about this and they*

257

were putting him under pressure to set up, presumably for assassination, two members of the Republican Movement ... And they [the IRA] did a deal with him. They said to him, 'Would you appear at a press conference and name your handlers and tell the story?' And he said he would. So that was the information I was given.

Morrison wanted to assess Sandy Lynch's credibility. He went on:

I wasn't gonna put him in a press conference if he turned out to be Walter Mitty because my credibility and the credibility of the party would've been – say, I walk into the house and I discover this guy's a balloon, he's made all of this up, this doesn't stand up to scrutiny. This isn't gonna be good – me putting him up in a press conference ... If he turned out to be good propaganda, he was going on a press conference on Monday morning or as soon as I organized it.[5]

Martin Ingram and Greg Harkin, in *Stakeknife: Britain's Secret Agents in Ireland*, tell a different story.[6] In this version, because the IRA was concerned that innocent people had been executed, they put in place a policy that required a review by an Army Council representative before final decisions were made on informers. Thus, Freddie Scappaticci set up Danny Morrison and Sandy Lynch was the bait. Danny Morrison described what happened:

So as we went through the door I could hear jeeps, the heavy sound of jeeps sweeping into the area. And I said, 'Anto, there's the Brits. The fucking Brits, there's the fuckin' cops' ... So I bolted out the door – right through the back door. Tried to climb over a fence and a soldier shouted, 'Halt or I'll shoot.' And he was in another garden, but instead of going over that fence I went over another fence. Walked into the house next door.

In the first house, the soldiers found Sandy Lynch, 'Anto' Murray, and former hunger striker Gerry Hodgins, among others, watching a football match. Danny Morrison was next door:

they kicked in the door and came in through the house that I was in. And I was sitting on the sofa. They asked me what I was doing. I said I was visiting. They brought me into the kitchen. They brought in the soldier and the soldier says – he was asked, 'Is that him?' And he says 'Yes, that's the guy who climbed over the fence.' So I was arrested. So we went to Castlereagh. Obviously, I never took part in the interrogations. They asked questions; I never opened my mouth.

The group faced a variety of charges; Morrison was charged with membership of a proscribed organization, false imprisonment and conspiracy to murder.

Morrison was sent from Castlereagh to Crumlin Road Jail where he met up with Seanna Walsh, the O/C. Also in Crumlin Road was Seán O'Callaghan, who had been transferred from England to await trial. The Provisionals suspected he was an informer and were concerned that he would turn into a supergrass so they were keeping an eye on him. Morrison described meeting with O'Callaghan:

Seanna had been arrested some months earlier and charged with possession of a mortar bomb. And I go over and sit beside Seanna and we're yarning away and Seanna says to me, 'Your old mate's over there'. I says, 'Who?' He says, 'O'Callaghan, Seán O'Callaghan'. And he was sitting at the table on his own. And, he says, 'Nobody talks to him. But I talk to him; I walk around the yard with him and I reassure him that everything's okay.' So I says, 'I suppose I might go over and say hello to him.' So I went over and I said, 'Seán what about you?' And he got up. And the first thing he says to me is, 'Danny, I'm not an informer, do you think I'm an informer?' and I says, 'Absolutely not Seán', and Seanna is sitting behind his back going – rolling his eyes at me. So I says to him, 'So tell me what happened.' He says he was unhappy and hitting the drink. He ran away from Tralee, met a girl ... moved in with her in England. Couldn't cope. Gave himself up. Made a statement.

O'Callaghan claims that they had a two-hour discussion on the Provisionals' 'peace strategy' during which Morrison told him the 'republican struggle was being slowly strangled' and it was 'time to form a nationalist consensus involving the Irish government, the SDLP and Irish America'.[7] O'Callaghan passed this on to the RUC. Morrison remembers it differently. He commented:

Why would I tell him anything? I already know that he's an informer, right? ... The IRA, when I came into jail, was beginning to release the Libyan weapons to the units. It had introduced semtex about a year before. It was now letting the 12.7, the DShK heavy machine guns out. [They] had flamethrowers. The IRA was beginning to release the equipment. So in actual fact, the expectation was the exact opposite. The expectation was that the war was going to be intensified. This business about peace actually didn't come about until I'm in the jail.[8]

Seán O'Callaghan pleaded guilty to several charges and received life sentences for the murders of Peter Flanagan and Eva Martin, plus 539 years for other offenses. 'Anto' Murray and Danny Morrison were sentenced to eight years in prison. Gerry Hodgins received twelve years because of his previous conviction.[9]

Considering Seán O'Callaghan's behaviour and the fact that Danny Morrison had just been set up, it's hard to believe Morrison would have been willing to discuss anything sensitive with him. Even if he had, O'Callaghan could not have passed on anything the British and RUC didn't already know through other informers, including Denis Donaldson and Freddie Scappaticci. The key was that the Provisionals were changing, becoming more open-minded, and the British knew it. Mitchel McLaughlin was deeply involved in building Sinn Féin through the 1980s and helped develop *A Scenario for Peace*. He was interviewed in the spring of 1990:

My frame of mind is now that I wouldn't say never, even in respect to Westminster. There is a principle there – I have examined it – and my position now, having examined it, is that abstentionism [from Westminster] is the correct approach. But I'd be making my own kind of decision on that, there'd be nobody really handing it down to me. I'll review that and if somebody could [make] arguments to us for attending to Westminster, or attending the Assembly, I think I would have a much more open mind about examining those issues. Although I'd be guided by the fact that there are republican principles as to whether or not we go along with it. At the moment I wouldn't. I would be very hard to convince. But I would certainly be much more open minded than I was, say, in 1980.[10]

Peter Brooke had been briefed on the British–Provisional contacts in 1975. Because any contact between the British and the IRA would be highly controversial, the details of what followed that briefing may never be fully known. However, at Easter 1990, Michael Oatley, the MI5 agent involved in those talks, visited Brendan Duddy, an intermediary in 1975. Oatley's story was that he was upset at being turned down for a promotion and was about to retire. He was in Derry to discuss the possibility of becoming an 'independent, highly-paid consultant'.[11]

Mitchel McLaughlin, early 1990s. Bobbie Hanvey photographic archives, John J. Burns Library, Boston College.

What exactly happened next and why is unclear, but on 28 June 1990 *AP/RN*, ran an interview with a spokesperson for the 'General Headquarters Staff of Óglaigh na hÉireann' who denied media speculation about a possible ceasefire. The spokesperson said, 'If the British declare publicly their intention to withdraw from our country within a specified period of time, then and only then would the idea of a cease-fire be contemplated.' That was standard information but what followed was interesting, 'The IRA have always made it clear that they are willing to talk to the British at any time they show a genuine desire to bring about peace and democracy in Ireland.'[12] That was a response to Michael Oatley's visit.

Gerry Adams, in *A Farther Shore: Ireland's Long Road to Peace*, writes that Peter Brooke had concluded that 'reactivating the "line" might be useful' and that the British contacted the 'Derry link'. Brooke has confirmed authorizing the contact and, because it was through a third party, felt he could publicly deny any dialogue with the Provisionals. In October 1990, Oatley visited Brendan Duddy again and 'intimated' that 'if he had to be in a room with MG [Martin McGuinness], he wouldn't run away'. Arrangements were made for Martin McGuinness to meet Michael Oatley at Duddy's home.

In describing the invitation to meet with Michael Oatley, Gerry Adams writes of himself and Martin McGuinness, 'Even though we had reservations, if the British government wanted to engage with us, we had a duty to facilitate this, even in a cautious exploratory way ... The only possible reason London wanted any dialogue with republicans was to achieve an IRA cease-fire.' McGuinness has stated, 'we felt a moral imperative to explore any overtures from the British'. Ironically, their comments parallel those of Ruairí Ó Brádaigh and Billy McKee on the 1975 talks.[13] Adams also refers to the hard line taken by IRA spokespersons and suggests there was a divide, that the 'Sinn Féin leadership had to persuade the Army leadership of the merits of the strategy we were developing.' He does not mention any overlap between the leaders of the two organizations.

The reality was that, twenty years into the campaign, the Provisionals were in an increasingly difficult situation. Dropping abstentionism from Leinster House had not changed Sinn Féin's fortunes in any significant way. In addition to the informer problem, the security forces were everywhere.[14] There were fifty-five British military installations in Belfast. In Derry, there were eleven barracks, three permanent vehicle checkpoints and twenty roads that led to the border were closed. The Provisionals took great pride in the 'Bandit Country' of South Armagh, but it was not a liberated zone. There were thirteen spy posts and nine RUC–British Army barracks supplied by heliports. Surveillance was constant and made even simple things like owning a car difficult. A Belfast republican spoke about this in an interview:

> *I had one [a car] a lot of years ago. It was sort of like a banger – just got tortured in it. I thought the Peelers [RUC] used to hide on the corner and wait for me to come out and get in it ... because you had the car and they'd be able to see everywhere you went. They knew if the car was about you were about ... Plus, they probably had it bugged as well, like – because they arrested me one time and took the car off me ... And then after that they were able to tell me, 'What were you doing in such and such a place?'... if you've got a car, it's going to be bugged. It's just routine. Like your phone's bugged, right? And there's a good*

possibility that your house would be bugged. If it was raided, anytime the house is raided we always have to search the house afterwards. Take the floor boards up ... Just to check for bugs and what have you.[15]

The constant presence of the security forces affected the entire community. In most cities, teenagers out for a joyride worry about the police. In West Belfast, they had to deal with British soldiers in a war zone. One evening in September 1990, soldiers fired on a stolen car and killed the driver, 17-year-old Martin Peake, and a passenger in the back seat, 18-year-old Karen Reilly. The soldiers claimed Peake had run a checkpoint but Reilly had been shot in the back and an RUC officer on the scene told his superiors that the checkpoint story was a cover up. The officer's stance was a major change from the early 1970s and helped convict Private Lee Clegg of murdering of Karen Reilly. Clegg received a life sentence and was sent to prison.[16]

The police and Army were everywhere and the campaign was reaching its limit. At some point that autumn the IRA leadership endorsed 'proxy bombs'. Patsy Gillespie was married, the father of three children and a cook at the Fort George British Army base in Derry. Because of his job, Gillespie was considered a collaborator and legitimate target. On 24 October 1990, he was one of three men who were kidnapped, strapped into cars loaded with explosives and sent on their way. One of the car bombs killed a soldier at a checkpoint outside Newry; the driver was injured but survived. The second bomb failed to explode at an RUC station in Omagh. The human bomb that was Patsy Gillespie was exploded via remote control at a checkpoint on the Donegal–Derry border, killing him and five soldiers and bringing widespread condemnation down on the Provisionals. At Gillespie's funeral, Bishop (later Cardinal) Cahal Daly condemned the IRA with: 'They may say they are followers of Christ. Some of them may even still engage in the hypocrisy of coming to church, but their lives and their works proclaim clearly that they follow Satan.' More proxy bombs brought more condemnation and the practice was abandoned. The outrage over the proxy bombs showed the cost of violating the 'ground rules'.[17]

Martin McGuinness met with Michael Oatley just before or just after Patsy Gillespie was killed. He attended the meeting 'on a listening brief' and, according to his account, 'I said very little and was non committal on all aspects of republican policy.' Evidently, McGuinness did not have a republican witness, which was an important change from 1975.[18] During the meeting, Oatley acknowledged that the Provisional IRA could continue indefinitely, but also pointed out that they were contained. There was no military victory in sight and there never would be. McGuinness was the youngest member of the IRA delegation that met with the British in 1972. Oatley pointed out that, at some point, a new generation would take over, just as his generation had taken over for Twomey, O'Connell, Ó Brádaigh, McKee, etc. Oatley told McGuinness that he was retiring but if the Provisionals were interested he could reopen the British–Provisionals link and turn it over to his successor. Brendan Duddy's papers show McGuinness telling Oatley, 'the Brits would need to have a clear agenda of what their position would be in the event of a cessation'.[19]

The most interesting part of the meeting came in the last half hour. As described in Duddy's papers, Michael Oatley and Martin McGuinness discussed fishing: 'M.G. fantasized about what it must be like to be free to travel around Scottish trout and salmon areas, stay in B&Bs etc. and not have to worry about security forces constantly on your back. M.O. was fascinated by this.' Like every Irish republican since Wolfe Tone, Martin McGuinness could travel and fish all he wanted if any of three things happened: the Provisionals could win, he could walk away from the struggle or the British and the Provisionals could cut a deal. The Provisionals were not going to win any time soon and, having promised that he would lead them to 'the republic', quitting was not really an option. Giving up a leading position in a revolutionary movement and going to work as a 44-year-old butcher's apprentice was probably not attractive either. Martin McGuinness describes himself as a pragmatist.[20] He told Michael Oatley that the Provisionals were interested in a dialogue.

An immediate benefit of the meeting was that Michael Oatley passed on to Denis Bradley, a former priest who also served as a go-between, the text of a speech Peter Brooke was scheduled to deliver in London on 9 November 1990. Brooke consulted with John Hume, among others, and stated in public that Britain was a neutral party: 'The British government has no selfish strategic or economic interest in Northern Ireland: our role is to help, enable and encourage. Britain's purpose, as I have sought to describe it, is not to occupy, oppress or exploit, but to ensure democratic debate and free democratic choice.' In a sense, it was the British response to *A Scenario for Peace*, Sinn Féin's position in their talks with the SDLP and Fianna Fáil, and Martin McGuinness's comment on the British 'agenda' in the event of a cessation.

Of course, the Provisionals needed convincing. Gerry Adams writes in *A Farther Shore* that Brooke 'wasn't telling the truth as we understood and experienced it'. The Provisionals had a valid question: If the British wanted to ensure democratic debate, then why did they support a sectarian state? In the spring of 1991, for example, the RUC refused to allow an International Women's Day march into Belfast city centre because a banner written in Irish would cause 'insult' to people there. The banner read '*La Idirnaisiunta na mBan*' (International Women's Day).[21] It was one of countless examples of Irish people being denied the basic right to express themselves in Northern Ireland.

Michael Oatley retired and was replaced by Colin Ferguson. With Brendan Duddy and Denis Bradley as go-betweens, the Provisionals and the British began exchanging messages. Events would later show that these messages were part of several secret conversations underway. Adams was meeting with John Hume, Hume was in touch with Brendan Duddy and with the loyalists, and there were also meetings at Clonard Monastery between Protestant ministers Revd Ken Newell and Revd Sam Burch, Catholic priests Father Reid and Father Gerry Reynolds and Gerry Adams, Aidan McAteer and Tish Holland.[22] Only a select few in the Provisionals were fully aware of what was going on. And what was going on was important enough that it continued in spite of a change in government and another attempt to assassinate the British Prime Minister.

Margaret Thatcher had been in power since 1979. She faced a troubled economy and a decline in support from her Cabinet leading to her resignation. Her successor, John Major, supported continued contact with the Provisionals. The Provisionals welcomed him to his new position with mixed messages. Gerry Adams, following the example of Ho Chi Minh, sent Major a personal letter in an attempt to engage 'with the person who now had responsibility for British policy in Ireland'.[23] And in December 1990, the IRA called their first Christmas ceasefire in fifteen years.

But in the new year, they stepped up the bombing campaign, essentially adopting a twin-track approach – talking about peace and bombing England as much as possible. There were fifteen IRA bombs in England in 1990. In 1991, there were thirty-six and in 1992 there were fifty-seven. Major received a personal message from the IRA in February 1991 – a jerry-rigged van was parked 200 yards from No. 10 Downing Street and mortars were fired by remote control. One of them exploded in the back garden, shaking the building and shattering glass – another near-miss. Inside No. 10, the British Cabinet was discussing the Gulf War. They reconvened in another room.[24]

Although the Provisionals could take the war to England, they knew they had stalled. In December 1991, a prominent Sinn Féiner was asked if the party was growing. The reply was 'No', and he offered the following:

> There's many, many reasons. I never believed, from the beginning, that the removal of abstentionism was a panacea that would suddenly solve our problems. I just saw it as removing a major barrier. The reason that we're not growing is that the whole establishment consensus, allied with censorship – very, very, very strong censorship – which is portraying the republican struggle for what it is not and giving us no opportunity to present our own analysis, our own arguments or even to answer their arguments – that we are being squeezed all the time. And the climate out there is such that we haven't grown. It's fairly frosty. I think what we have to do is survive the frost, because we will grow when it thaws.[25]

At Christmas 1991, the Provisional IRA called another three-day ceasefire.[26]

It was part of their mythology that, like the Phoenix, the Provisionals had risen from the ashes of 1969 to defend the nationalists of the North. In the early 1990s, the Provisionals could not even defend their own people. Although innocent Catholics were always an option, the loyalists took greater pleasure in killing Provisionals. Sinn Féin Councillors, Eddie Fullerton on the Donegal County Council and Bernard O'Hagan on the Magherafelt Council, were assassinated. The first victim of political violence in 1992 was Kevin McKearney, youngest of the prominent McKearney family. Loyalists walked into the family's butcher shop in Moy, shot him dead and fatally wounded his uncle, Jack McKearney.[27] When the IRA campaign had a success, there was a sectarian reply. In mid-January 1992, a van filled with workers who had spent the day repairing Lisanelly British Army base in Omagh drove over a Provisional IRA bomb at Teebane Crossing in County Tyrone. Eight workers were killed and six more were injured; all of them were Protestant. Teebane set off a series of events. Loyalists killed Catholics in East Belfast, Antrim and North Belfast. In early February, an RUC officer posing as a journalist attacked the Sinn Féin press office in West Belfast, killing Pat McBride and Paddy Loughran of Sinn Féin and a visitor, Michael O'Dwyer; the officer committed suicide. The next day, loyalists killed five Catholics at a betting shop in South Belfast. The Catholic/nationalist community was paying a heavy price for the Provisionals' liberation struggle.[28]

In contrast, the British–Provisional conversation in combination with a secret conversation between the British and the loyalists began to influence events. For example, the Irish government agreed to a temporary break in meetings of the Anglo-Irish Intergovernmental Conference (AIIC) so that Peter Brooke could bring together the UUP and DUP for a meeting with the SLDP and Alliance parties at Stormont. As part of this, the British passed on to the Provisionals that the 'Combined Loyalist Military Command (CLMC)' would go on ceasefire while the inter-talks were underway.[29] The Brooke talks only lasted a month and they had to be suspended to avoid a unionist walkout as the date for the next AIIC meeting approached. The talks were important, however, because, for the first time in more than a decade, the major constitutional parties met in a formal setting. They would continue to meet off and on, and with Sinn Féin on the sidelines. It was also important that the British, the Provisionals and the loyalists were communicating, if only indirectly.

At the 1992 Ard Fheis, Sinn Féin unveiled *Towards a lasting peace in Ireland*. The document was more sophisticated than *A Scenario for Peace* and began with the caution that, 'an end to conflict does not, of itself, lead necessarily to a lasting peace'. *Towards a lasting peace in Ireland* actually drew on the Anglo-Irish Agreement and argued that London and Dublin (the 'two "sovereign" powers') had a joint responsibility to pursue peace: 'They have the power to effect the necessary change.' The document invited third-party involvement, noting that 'in today's "global village" it is also an international responsibility'. There was also a reply to Peter Brooke's claim that the British did not have interests in Northern Ireland:

> Today the British government maintains partition in response, it claims, to the wishes of the unionist people. They back up this stance with misleading propaganda about a blood bath should they leave. They have now added to this scare claim the spurious argument that while they prefer the union they have 'no selfish strategic or economic reason' for maintaining partition. The British government cannot have it both ways. It cannot on the one hand claim a 'preference' for maintaining the union while on the other hand claiming no strategic or economic interests in being in Ireland.

If the British truly did not have a strategic interest in Ireland, then they should stop supporting unionist excesses. The document issued a challenge: 'there is an onus on those who proclaim that the armed struggle is counter-productive to advance a credible alternative'.[30] The Provisionals wanted London and Dublin to give them a good reason for ending armed struggle. They were about to get help from Dublin.

In February 1992, it was revealed that Charlie Haughey had authorized the tapping of journalists' phones in the 1980s. Haughey resigned and, in the rough and tumble world of Fianna Fáil politics, his successor as leader of Fianna Fáil and Taoiseach was Albert Reynolds. Only a few months earlier, Reynolds had been sacked as Minister for Finance because he had challenged Haughey. Haughey and John Hume briefed Reynolds on the 'private discussions' with the Provisionals, which went against the government's public stance. Reynolds writes in his autobiography:

I was very clear in my mind as to what might work and I was prepared to go the distance with it. I knew we could only make progress if we developed a relationship with all the elements – the Republican and Nationalist parties of Sinn Féin, IRA and the SDLP, the Unionist parties (UUP and DUP), and the Loyalist paramilitary groups, the UDA, the UVF and their army council, the Combined Loyalist Military Command: everyone had to be brought to the table and into dialogue. It was the only way.[31]

Albert Reynolds did not have the arms trial baggage of Charlie Haughey and was in a better position to move the dialogue along.

Sinn Féin was demanding that they be included in the Brooke talks without pre-conditions. That spring, Northern nationalists were given a chance to show their support for that demand. In a Westminster election, on 9 April 1992, Sinn Féin's vote fell again (78,291 votes; 10 per cent) and the SDLP had its best election ever (184,445 votes; 23.5 per cent). In West Belfast, Joe Hendron challenged Gerry Adams and won – 17,415 vs 16,826 votes. In Foyle (Derry), John Hume again embarrassed Martin McGuinness – 26,710 vs 9,149 votes.[32] Adams was no longer an MP and Sinn Féin had no mandate for inclusion in anything. In Britain, it was widely assumed that, in the midst of a recession and after thirteen years in power, the Conservatives could not win again. Instead, they squeaked out another win and John Major remained as Prime Minister, but with a reduced majority.

The day after the election, an IRA bomb at the Baltic Exchange in London killed three people and caused an estimated £800 million in damages.[33] That single bomb caused more damage than the total damages thus far for the conflict in Northern Ireland.

It was in John Major's interest to continue the secret dialogue. In a Cabinet shuffle, Patrick Mayhew replaced Peter Brooke as Secretary of State for Northern Ireland and Mayhew picked up where Brooke left off supporting inter-party talks, with Sinn Féin excluded. He also supported the secret contact with the Provisionals.

Four years earlier, Danny Morrison had said, 'what would render invalid the prospect of success was a weariness'. The election result suggested weariness had set in. In an article that he submitted to *An Phoblacht/Republican News*, entitled 'A Bitter Pill', Morrison offered his interpretation of the Westminster election:

I am not one for doom and gloom, for defeatism or surrender, but the election results were very bad for Sinn Féin, for the IRA, and for the struggle, in whatever order you prefer. The trend is going in the direction of our vote in the twenty-six counties – downwards – and I hope that no one will have the temerity to claim the opposite or accuse me of overreacting … It is a situation out of which it [the IRA] cannot simply bomb its way … When the Sandinistas lost the election in Nicaragua two years ago they were under big pressure to go back into the mountains and melt back into the barrios and resume armed struggle. But they stood their ground, swallowed the bitter pill and went into opposition because they realized that with their still considerable support they could fight a popular rearguard action … Some day we shall be faced with the same choice. We should never allow the situation to decline to the extent that we face such a decision from the depths of an unpopular, unseemly, impossible-to-end armed struggle or from the point of brave exhaustion – another one of the 'glorious defeats' with which our past is littered …

The article was rejected. The editor, Míceál Mac Donncha, explained that he agreed '99 per cent' with Morrison but 'it would have been seized upon by our opponents'. Morrison decided to stop writing for *AP/RN* and focus on an Open University course and writing a novel.[34]

That spring, those in favour of dialogue received a boost from the United States. At the Irish American Presidential Forum in New York, candidate Bill Clinton indicated that, if elected, he would appoint a special peace envoy for Northern Ireland. In response to a question from Martin Galvin, Clinton also said he would provide a visa for Gerry Adams. Galvin, editor of *The Irish People*, asked a prepared question:

> *It used to be the Irish papers' editors would ask the questions, they'd put it on. That was the format … it was something like, 'Would you if you were president end the policy of the censorship by visa denial, and grant the visa to Gerry Adams?' I don't recall the exact wording, but I was the one selected to present that question. And Clinton answered 'Yes'. And that was a major development. He then took off in New York afterwards which was probably just coincidence. He won the New York primary and started to think that the Irish issue was not a bad one. The British criticized him unjustly, for some reason. They seemed to be more sympathetic to George Bush, Sr.*[35]

Bill Clinton was very aware that John Major and the Conservatives favoured President George H.W. Bush. In his memoir, *My Life*, Clinton writes, 'Two Tory campaign strategists came to Washington to advise the Bush campaign on how they might destroy me the way the Conservative Party had undone Labour Party leader Neil Kinnock six months earlier.'[36]

The Westminster election confirmed that Sinn Féin had peaked and, even if the IRA could blow up central London, the truth was the British could ride out the 'long war' forever. As an example, the main cross-border checkpoint outside Newry was along a rail line. In May 1992, the IRA stole a van, modified it to run on rails and loaded it with 2,000 pounds of explosives. In the dark of night, a stolen mechanical digger lifted it onto the rails. The van was put in gear and when it reached the checkpoint the explosives were triggered by remote control. The checkpoint was destroyed, a soldier was killed and twenty-three more were wounded. No matter how clever the IRA was, the British had virtually unlimited resources – they rebuilt a more secure checkpoint.[37]

The IRA campaign had its limits, but in the summer of 1992, the secret discussions bore fruit. Hume and Adams, with input from Fianna Fáil through Father Alec Reid, forwarded a document to London that *might* serve as the basis of a joint Irish–British declaration that could trigger a peace process. The 'Hume–Adams Document', which is presented in Eamonn Mallie and David McKittrick's *The Fight for Peace: The Secret Story Behind the Irish Peace Process*, was a plan for peace that involved London and Dublin. Traditionally, the Provisionals wanted a united Ireland

and they rejected the idea that unionists had any kind of a veto over what the majority of the Irish people wanted – the principle of 'unionist consent'. In 'Hume–Adams', the Provisionals sought 'self-determination' and it was implied that this was subject to unionist consent:

> The British Government accepts the principle that the Irish people have the right collectively to self-determination, and that the exercise of this right could take the form of agreed independent structures for the island as a whole … The British Government will use all its influence and energy to win the consent of a majority in Northern Ireland for these measures.

The plan called on the Taoiseach to establish a 'permanent Irish Convention' that would address divisions among Irish people that stand in the way of 'self-determination'. Embedded in the final paragraph was an offer of a ceasefire: 'The convention will be open to all democratically mandated political parties in Ireland which abide exclusively by the democratic process and wish to share in dialogue about Ireland's political future and the welfare of all its people.' As Eamonn Mallie and David McKittrick describe it, the document contained 'constructive ambiguity'.[38] At Bodenstown in June, the Provisionals followed up with a speech by Jim Gibney who has been described as a 'kite-flyer' for Gerry Adams.[39] Up until 1980, Sinn Féin policy called for a 'phased withdrawal' by the British. At the Ard Fheis that year, Gibney put forward a motion calling for 'the immediate and total withdrawal of British troops from Ireland'. The motion passed and was a sign that younger and more radical Northerners were taking over the Provisionals. Twelve years later, Gibney bluntly stated what the Provisionals had been hinting, namely that there had been 'evolutionary changes' in republican thinking over the decade:

> These cover many issues, the most pressing one being the need for peace in our country. *We know and accept that the British government's departure must be preceded by a sustained period of peace and will arise out of negotiations* [emphasis added]. We know and accept that such negotiations will involve the different shades of Irish nationalism and Irish unionism engaging the British government either together or separately to secure an all-embracing and durable peace process.[40]

The Provisionals were suggesting they might trade a ceasefire for a seat at a negotiating table. Other things were changing, too. That summer, the Ulster Defence Regiment was joined with the Royal Irish Rangers to create the Royal Irish Regiment; the controversial UDR was now a part of history.[41]

Late in the summer, Albert Reynolds reopened contact with Sinn Féin, though it was contrary to government policy and only a few people in Fianna Fáil were told of the decision. Des O'Malley, the leader of his coalition partner, the Progressive Democrats, was kept in the dark.[42] In October 1992, there was another Sinn Féin–Fianna Fáil meeting. Martin Mansergh, who represented Taoiseach Albert Reynolds, described how the tone of the conversation had changed:

When we re-engaged directly from 1992 on it was actually a concrete project ... It was not explicitly stated and we did not press for it but, yes, this was different from '88. With post-'92, this was something capable of being brought to a conclusion. The odds were against success, based on the outcome of previous attempts. But the situation had changed.

Nobody doubted the material capacity of the Provisional IRA to continue but there comes a point in a prolonged stalemate with no prospect of a breakthrough when the psychological will to continue weakens. So there is a danger of implosion ... I think the Republican Movement was wise to move when they did.[43]

At the end of the month, Colin Ferguson (Michael Oatley's successor) had his first face-to-face meeting with Martin McGuinness. With McGuinness was Gerry Kelly, the former London bomber, hunger striker and the leader of the 1983 escape from Long Kesh. Kelly had been arrested in Amsterdam (with Bik McFarlane), extradited and served out his sentence; Gerry Adams describes him as a 'Sinn Féin colleague'.[44]

In an election in the Republic of Ireland in the autumn of 1992, no party won an overall majority. Albert Reynolds put together another coalition government, this time with the Irish Labour Party led by Dick Spring, who became Tanaiste. Reynolds did brief Spring on the contact with the Provisionals and the possibility of a joint Anglo-Irish declaration. Spring was interested and suggested the Irish government might reach out to unionists by softening its stance on Articles 2 and 3 of the Constitution. In time, and through his press officer, Fergus Finlay and Irish peace activist Chris Hudson, Spring would develop his own relationship with the loyalists.[45] With respect to Sinn Féin, the election was that much more evidence that they had stalled. The party received only 27,809 votes (1.6 per cent). Six years after deciding to take seats if elected to Leinster House, they still could not match the Anti-H-Block/Armagh vote of 1981.[46]

What was working for the Provisionals was happening in secret. In a speech at Coleraine, Patrick Mayhew responded to the Hume–Adams document:

Unity cannot be brought nearer, let alone achieved, by dealing out death and destruction. It is not sensible to suppose that any British government will yield to an agenda for Ireland prosecuted by violent means ... provided it is advocated constitutionally, there can be no proper reason for excluding any political objective from discussion. Certainly not the objective of a united Ireland ... In the event of a genuine and established cessation of violence, the whole range of responses that we have had to make to that violence could, and would, inevitably be looked at afresh.[47]

If the Provisional IRA declared a ceasefire, Sinn Féin would be invited to talks.

In February 1993, the British received this message:

The conflict is over but we need your advice on how to bring it to an end. We wish to have an unannounced ceasefire in order to hold a dialogue leading to peace. We cannot announce such a move as it will lead to confusion for the Volunteers because the press will interpret it as surrender. We cannot meet the Secretary of State's public renunciation of violence, but it would be given privately as long as we were sure that we were not being tricked.[48]

They assumed the message was from Martin McGuinness. John Major convened a special Cabinet meeting and then sent the reply that their response to an IRA cessation would be 'bold and imaginative'. The next day, there was another atrocity when bombs at a crowded shopping centre in Warrington, England, killed a 3-year-old child, John Ball, and critically injured a 12-year-old, Timothy Parry, who died a few days later. The Warrington bomb almost destroyed what would become the peace process.[49]

Gordon Wilson, who had spoken so eloquently after his daughter was killed in the Enniskillen tragedy, had become a prominent advocate for peace and reconciliation. His message resonated with many people and Albert Reynolds appointed him to the Irish Senate. After the Warrington bomb, Wilson asked for a meeting with the Provisional IRA. They agreed and for two hours he tried to persuade them to stop the violence. The IRA representatives, aware of Wilson's loss and sincerity, apologized for Enniskillen and said they also wanted peace, but they also stuck to the old argument that the cause of the conflict was the 'the ongoing violent denial of Irish national rights'. When it was all over, Wilson believed it had been a waste of time, that the Provisionals had not heard him and, when the meeting was reported in the media, Wilson's critics said he was naïve. Peter Robinson of the DUP complained that Wilson had 'boosted' the IRA campaign. David Trimble of the Ulster Unionists complained that Wilson had been manipulated to divert attention from the Warrington bomb.[50]

The Provisionals *had* listened to Gordon Wilson. Unfortunately, their representatives were not in a position to reveal how close they were to a cessation and how impressed they were with his appeal. Revd Harold Good, who knew Gordon Wilson, described Wilson's influence on the Provisionals:

> *When Gordon Wilson died [1995], one of my fellow Methodist ministers was doing the thought for the day on radio that morning. We have a thought for the day each morning on our local radio. And he was asked to speak because Gordon Wilson had died the day before. And my friend, Eric Gallagher [who was at Feakle in 1974], went on air. He spoke about the importance of Gordon Wilson's contribution and he said, 'For him it was a sadness, that when he went to the IRA' – he got the opportunity to go and talk to the leadership of the IRA – 'and his great sadness was that he felt they didn't hear him. That it made no difference.' Well, I went to the funeral a couple of days later and I saw a leading light in Sinn Féin after the sermon. He was very brave to be there, very brave to be there. And after the service, in the church hall, the Methodist church hall in Enniskillen, there was an opportunity for people who were invited for a cup of tea, as they do after funerals in Ireland. And there was this man, a very significant leader in the Movement, sitting on his own because nobody was talking to him. And I went over to sit with him, brought my cup of tea over and I did sit with him, and I said to him, 'You know about the thought for the day that morning?' And I said, 'Eric was saying the great sadness for Gordon was that he felt that the Republican Movement did not hear him, did not listen when he went to see them. It was*

a brave thing for him to do, to go to see them.' And he said, 'I would like to tell you, they did hear him. They did listen.' And he said that made a huge impact upon them and was one of the key factors in helping them to move more effort towards an alternative.[51]

The British and the Provisionals continued to exchange messages and, in March 1993, there was another face-to-face meeting. And when the Provisionals brought up what had happened in 1975, the British said they had not been serious then 'but they were now'.[52]

On the surface, it appeared that nothing could end the stalemate. Whether it was by accident or design, the first of two revelations by a journalist helped move things along. Eamon McCann broke the story that Gerry Adams was seen entering John Hume's home and it was front-page news. Hume was condemned for meeting with terrorists and responded with, 'it's a highly sensitive process. I am working for a lasting peace.' Hume and Adams issued a joint statement that included the following: 'Everyone has a solemn duty to change the political climate away from conflict and towards a process of national reconciliation which sees the peaceful accommodation of differences between the people of Britain and Ireland and the people of Ireland themselves.'[53] The day of the Hume–Adams statement, a bomb in the City of London killed a *News of the World* photographer and devastated the financial district, causing an estimated £1 billion in damage. The revelation that Hume and Adams were meeting put pressure on Dublin and London to help them, and the Warrington and City of London bombs showed the cost of the stalemate. At the same time, the bombs made it impossible for Dublin and London to acknowledge they were meeting with the Provisionals.

The British and the Provisionals continued to exchange messages and there was another face-to-face meeting.[54] In the autumn, Irish-America became more involved. Sinn Féin had backed off enough on its socialist rhetoric that business and political leaders, led by former Congressman Bruce Morrison, visited Northern Ireland and met with several people, including Gerry Adams. Bruce Morrison had been a law school classmate of President Clinton and had organized Irish-Americans for Clinton. A peace process involving London, Dublin and the United States was coming together[55] but then there was another atrocity.

The loyalist campaign had continued with recent victims including Martin Lavery, in December 1992, and Seán Lavery, in August 1993. They were the brother and son of Bobby Lavery, a Sinn Féin councillor in North Belfast. When the IRA received information that senior loyalists were meeting above Frizzell's fish shop on the Shankill Road, they organized an attack. On 23 October 1993, two volunteers entered the shop with a short-fused bomb, so short that it went off as they delivered it. The bomb exploded and the building collapsed, killing 22 year old Tom Begley of the Provisional IRA and nine Protestant civilians. None of the Protestants were connected with loyalism and two of the dead were children. The Shankill bomb was seen as another in a series of sectarian attacks on the Protestant community.

Gerry Adams then contributed to the perception that he was talking out of both sides of his mouth. He said there was no excuse for the attack but then, as a sign of respect for the deceased and in order to maintain his own credibility as a republican, he helped carry Begley's coffin in his republican funeral. Albert Reynolds was 'appalled' by the bomb. John Major was 'furious and seething' on seeing photos of Adams carrying Begley's coffin and, in the House of Commons, said that the thought of sitting down and talking with 'Mr. Adams' and the Provisionals would turn his stomach. 'We will not do it,' he said. The loyalist response to the Shankill Road bomb was to kill two Catholics in separate attacks and six more plus a Protestant in an attack on the Rising Sun Bar in Greysteel, County Derry.[56]

Northern Ireland, London and Dublin were then rocked when journalist Eamonn Mallie broke the story of the secret British–Provisional dialogue. John Major denied it, Martin McGuinness confirmed it and Secretary of State for Northern Ireland Patrick Mayhew denied it again. Mallie then produced a 'speaking note' with instructions from Mayhew to the British representative and Mayhew was forced to confirm that there had been a dialogue. But he was again deceptive, claiming the contact began in February 1993, with the 'conflict is over' note. The British released copies and summaries of the dialogue/communications that fit his story. Sinn Féin then released a more detailed and credible set of documents showing the contact dated from mid-1990 and denying they were the source of the February communication. Mayhew backtracked again and issued a corrected set of documents. It was a shocking turn of events given John Major's comments after the Begley funeral and, in the House of Commons, Ian Paisley called Patrick Mayhew a liar.[57]

The revelations fuelled speculation that a peace process was indeed underway and, in mid-December 1993, Albert Reynolds and John Major came through with the 'Downing Street Declaration', a twelve-point document that built on 'Hume–Adams'. The Prime Minister, on behalf of the British government, agreed to let the people of Ireland 'exercise their right of self-determination', but he also affirmed unionist consent. A united Ireland depended on 'the democratic wish of the greater number of the people of Northern Ireland on the issue of whether they prefer to support the Union or a sovereign united Ireland'. The Taoiseach, on behalf of the Irish government, also affirmed the consent principle and acknowledged that Articles 2 and 3 of the Irish Constitution 'are deeply resented by Northern Unionists'. Both governments accepted that Irish unity could only be achieved 'peacefully and without coercion' and only if 'a majority of the people of Northern Ireland are so persuaded …' Both governments also confirmed that 'democratically mandated parties' that were committed 'to exclusively peaceful methods' would be invited to participate in a dialogue on the way forward. On their own, and at an appropriate time, the Irish government would establish a 'Forum for Peace and Reconciliation' that would make recommendations on building trust and agreement between the nationalist and unionist traditions.[58]

Northern Ireland was on the brink of peace and, in the House of Commons, John Hume expressed 'deep appreciation' for John Major and Albert Reynolds. James Molyneaux raised questions but did not reject the declaration. The most negative comments came from Revd Ian Paisley – 'Doctor No' – who denounced John Major:

> It is a tripartite agreement between Reynolds, the IRA and you. You have sold Ulster to buy off the fiendish Republican scum and you are prepared to do this notorious deed with such speed that time is not given for the Christian burial of their latest victim, a member

of the RUC. You will learn in a bitter school that all appeasement of these monsters is self-destructive.[59]

The Provisionals stalled. Both governments had endorsed the consent principle and there was no timetable for the 'dialogue', let alone a date for a British withdrawal. They would be invited to talks *if* they gave up the weapon that made them important and they knew, to quote Joe Cahill, 'once it's an extended truce, then it's detrimental to the Republican Movement'. If they flatly rejected the declaration, however, they would lose John Hume and Albert Reynolds, almost a decade's worth of work and the leadership would be discredited. Mitchel McLaughlin said that Sinn Féin would be studying the Declaration 'in depth'. Gerry Adams commented that the 'deliberations will take some time' and required clarification from Dublin.[60]

Having promised they would never stop short of a victory, the Provisionals' leadership had to be careful. It did not help that the more there was speculation about peace the more relevant Republican Sinn Féin became. Their Ard Chomhairle released a statement: 'Eighteen percent of the people living in Ireland cannot have the monopoly of decision over the future of this country thus maintaining a veto over the other 82%. The nationally-minded people according to the Major–Reynolds Declaration have no rights whatsoever.'[61] Many Sinn Féiners agreed with that analysis. Republican Sinn Féin also delivered the message that there might be another IRA lurking. Tom Maguire, patron of Republican Sinn Féin, had passed away in July 1993, at the age of 101 and, in February 1994, *Saoirse* reported: 'On the 75th Anniversary of the First (All-Ireland) Dáil hÉireann [21 January 1994] a firing party of Volunteers of Óglaigh na hÉireann – the Irish Republican Army – loyal to the principles of the late Comdt-General Tom Maguire rendered military honours at his grave in Cross, Co Mayo.' The report and accompanying photograph fuelled speculation that the IRA had split, which Martin McGuinness denied.[62]

The Provisionals asked the British for 'clarification' of the Downing Street Declaration. John Major had a slim majority in the House of Commons and relied on the support of James Molyneaux and the Ulster Unionists. The British reply was that the Declaration spoke for itself and they refused to meet with or respond to direct communications from Sinn Féin without an IRA ceasefire. Albert Reynolds and Bill Clinton were more friendly. The Dublin government allowed the media ban to lapse and, for the first time in years, Sinn Féiners appeared on Irish radio and television. President Clinton approved a visa for Gerry Adams and in a forty-eight-hour visit he appeared on 'Good Morning America', 'Larry King Live' and the front page of the *New York Times*.[63]

The Provisionals were realizing the benefits of a peace process and it was obvious that a ceasefire would bring more. They also knew that a ceasefire might drive more of a wedge between the moderate Ulster Unionists and the more extreme Democratic Unionists led by Paisley, weakening both parties in the process. Additionally, if the British truly did not have a 'selfish strategic or economic interest' in Ireland and were committed to 'democratic debate and free democratic choice', a ceasefire should force them to make changes in Northern Ireland that guaranteed equal treatment of nationalists. In time, the sectarian, undemocratic state of Northern Ireland might collapse under its own contradictions. Help from the Clinton White

House could hasten that collapse and then anything was possible. And there was another issue to consider – loyalists were killing more and more Catholics/nationalists in what they said was the defense of Ulster while also sending the message, 'You stop, we stop.'[64]

The leadership was also aware that what they had suffered had been passed to another generation, as John Joe McGirl had warned. A young woman from Belfast who was born in the early 1970s was asked why she became involved. She replied:

> Long story. I suppose during the hunger strike, I'd seen so many arrests, within the family, you know? Because my family is sort of – I was born into a republican family. And when – my father being shot with plastic bullets and my brother's being shoved out of houses and stuff like that there ... being trailed out of the house by the RUC, arrested and interrogated when he was sixteen, and just sort of everyday just seeing the beatings in the street, stuff like that. And the uncles, they would be in the prison ... I suppose I just took it from the family really. It's just I have never really known anything different.

She joined the Provisionals as a teenager and was still a teenager when her first child, a daughter, was born. She was arrested in the early 1990s, after the birth of her second child. She continued:

> It was hard, it was hard for the first child I had [Katie], she was a year and a half, because I had that bond with her, you know? With Fiona [the second child] I didn't have that bond ... plus I knew the RUC was looking for me. So it was – once I came out of the hospital, I went into a sort of hiding. So the kids were getting messed up a lot, so I said, 'I will just go back to my own flat'. And I had been getting raided every week and that morning they just came for me.

In custody, she learned that the father of her second child was an informer. The abuse from the RUC was so bad that she actually looked forward to being transferred to prison. In her own words:

> Seven days of interrogations, sometimes three or four hours of constant interrogation – and you get a break for an hour and back in for another four hours. And they're beating you and kicking you, calling you all these dirty names. And they have this, like a file, you know, of your whole movements that they have – so many years. So they can tell me company I had kept, where I walked and who I've been with and all that information because I was in under an informer. So, all that there, and they knew my movements and had been watching me all these years ... The interrogation was – sometimes it's hurtful because you find out a lot that you never knew about your life. They can tell you things that you don't even know about ... The person who I was in over was my ex-boyfriend, who I had the child to, the child that was eight weeks old. So he had told them everything about me.

Her arrest and conviction affected her relationship with her children:

> But I found that I missed Katie a lot when I went in. I found it hard. But you get your head then, you have to concentrate and you just say you can't sit around moping all day, 'My kids this' and 'My kids

that' and 'I miss my kids.' Okay, you miss your kids, you can't do anything about it; like it or not, you're in prison here. Nobody is going to feel sorry for you here... The way I done it was I got myself settled in jail, got to know the whole place and the so-called rules and then, bang, it just hits you. You're in prison here and you start missing your kids. The first visit with your children would probably be the worst. Your first Christmas visit away from them, 'cause you always remember Katie squealing after me, clinging on, 'Mommy! Mommy!'... it breaks your heart, times like that there.[65]

There were more than 700 Irish republican prisoners scattered throughout Ireland, England, Western Europe and the United States. More than one hundred of them were serving life terms.[66] If the leadership called a ceasefire, there would be no more arrests and, in time, relief for the prisoners. Unless something changed, the prisoners would waste away.

At the 1986 Ard Fheis, Martin McGuinness had said, 'Our position is clear, and it will never, never, never change. The war against British rule must continue until freedom is achieved.' Eight years later, they had the Downing Street Declaration and the leadership had to choose between continuing an unwinnable war that brought hardship to their community or take a chance and call a ceasefire. Reports show that there was serious opposition to a ceasefire in both the Provisional IRA and Sinn Féin.[67] A three-day IRA ceasefire over the Easter period gave the leadership some breathing room as they developed a way to take a chance and keep their options open. In the summer of 1994, the TUAS document was circulated internally and those who might be reluctant to support a ceasefire, like the rank-and-file IRA, were told TUAS stood for 'Tactical Use of Armed Struggle'. If a ceasefire did not work, they would go back to war. Others, who wanted a ceasefire, were told that TUAS stood for 'Totally Unarmed Strategy'.

The document, later leaked to the press, acknowledged that they did 'not have the strength to achieve the end goal' and that 'The D.S.D. [Downing Street Declaration] does not hold a solution.' However, after prolonged discussion and assessment the Leadership decided that if it could get agreement from the Dublin government, the SDLP, and the Irish-American lobby on basic republican principles which would be enough to create a dynamic that would considerably advance the struggle, then it would be prepared to use the TUAS option ...'[68] The Provisionals approached Albert Reynolds for help. In exchange for a ceasefire and an end to IRA recruiting and training, Reynolds agreed to support including Sinn Féin in a Forum on Peace and Reconciliation.

It was in this context that the Army Council met and agreed to a temporary ceasefire. Ed Moloney, in *A Secret History of the IRA*, records that those in favour of the ceasefire were Gerry Adams, Martin McGuinness, Joe Cahill, Pat Doherty and one other person from South Armagh. Kevin McKenna was opposed and Tom Murphy expected Cahill to vote against the ceasefire and planned on doing the same. When Cahill voted for the ceasefire, Murphy abstained. Moloney also reports that Mickey McKevitt, the Quartermaster, and Gerry Kelly, the Adjutant General, attended the meeting but did not vote. Kelly supported the ceasefire but McKevitt was opposed.[69] The Sinn Féin leadership supported the decision but then Gerry Adams, Pat Doherty and Joe Cahill were the President, Vice President and Treasurer of the organization. Martin McGuinness was a member of the Ard Chomhairle. Before following through on the ceasefire, the Provisionals settled a score. Earlier in the year, loyalists had attacked a Sinn Féin function in Dublin and killed Martin Doherty of the Dublin IRA. The Provisionals believed that Martin Cahill, a Dublin gangster who worked with loyalists, was involved. He was shot dead.[70]

In late August 1994, Joe Cahill was granted a visa to enter the United States. Speculation by the press that Cahill was allowed in to brief Irish-American supporters on a forthcoming ceasefire was confirmed with a formal announcement: 'Recognising the potential of the current situation and in order to enhance the democratic peace process and underline our definitive commitment to its success the leadership of Óglaigh na hÉireann have decided that as of midnight, Wednesday, 31 August, there will be a complete cessation of military operations. All our units have been instructed accordingly.' Over the four years it had taken Gerry Adams and Martin McGuinness to 'persuade' the Army leadership to pursue a peace strategy, the Provisionals had killed more than 120 people. Twenty-eight Provisional IRA volunteers and twelve Sinn Féiners had been added to the 'Roll of Honour'.[71]

18

PEACE, WAR, PEACE (AUGUST 1994–JULY 1997)

The war is over and the good guys lost.

– Bernadette McAliskey[1]

There was hope that the ceasefire would lead to a lasting peace. Unfortunately, the peace was unstable from the start though, for the Sinn Féin leadership, it was a time for celebration. Gerry Adams and Martin McGuinness appeared at a rally at Connolly House. Joyriders waving Irish flags and a parade in West Belfast were caught on film and the video was distributed to supporters as evidence of a significant breakthrough.[2] However, the more people were removed from the Provisionals leadership, the more they wondered if the war was really over.

Albert Reynolds expressed relief with the comment, 'As far as we are concerned, the long national nightmare is over.' John Major welcomed the ceasefire but added that it should be 'clear and unambiguous' that the violence had ended. Revd Ian Paisley commented, 'The only way you could prove that there would be a permanent cessation is by the surrender of their killing machine, their Semtex stores, their guns, their mortars and their equipment.' James Molyneaux was more conciliatory but, in effect, said the same thing: 'I'm very glad that there has been a halt to the killing in Northern Ireland and throughout the United Kingdom and I hope that those who have influence with the IRA will now be able to make the halt permanent.'[3] Loyalists on the Shankill Road organized a march with banners that read, '25 Years and Still British.'[4] The Provisionals were not willing to make the ceasefire 'permanent' because they did not want to confirm that they had lost.

There was dissent in the ranks as described by Tony Catney, of the Belfast IRA, who spoke about his experience to Peter Trumbore, a political scientist in the United States:

So the fork in the road for me was the 31st of August 1994 when as an IRA volunteer I was summoned to be given the briefing as to why there would be a ceasefire at 12:00 that night. And the guy doing it gave me the reasons why, and then foolishly enough asked for people's opinions ... and I said, 'My opinion is this is all bollocks ... You sat in February of this year and sent IRA volunteers out on operations that have resulted in them lying in the H-blocks of Long Kesh at this moment in time on the basis that all of the talk about ceasefires was mischievous and that it was being put out by the Brits ... and this hasn't been done from a position of strength by the IRA it has been done as an admission of weakness and that's my honest opinion on it.' And he says, 'If you ever repeat that outside of this room', that I'd be charged with treason.[5]

The prisoners had not been consulted and were confused. The young mother from Belfast commented:

> I didn't know how to take it, you know? Because it came all the sudden, nobody knew it was coming. So it was a shock. And we were just sitting there and people were smiling for a couple days. I says, 'What are we smiling about?' Here's me, 'We are sitting in prison and they call a ceasefire, what the hell happens to us here?' And I couldn't accept it. I just felt at that stage that the way forward was to fight because that is the only time that Britain listens to you, you know? … Somebody actually sat me down and says, 'Look, this is the reason for it.' Sat and explained to me, 'We'll have to try this'… And some of the girls were jumping for joy and everything else and I was going, 'What are you doing this for? What are you celebrating for?'[6]

The Belfast republican, Tony Catney and most Provisionals were willing to wait and see if Sinn Féin could move the struggle forward.

For RSF, the *unilateral* ceasefire was proof that their analysis was correct, that constitutional politics leads to compromise. Their interpretation attracted some dissenters, including Joe 'Tiny' Lynch in Limerick:

> at the Ard Fheis in 1986 I asked Des Long, 'Des, this war is going to be hopefully brought to a successful conclusion'… And Des said, 'Well, we're not going into Leinster House.' Well, I wasn't too worried about Leinster House, I was worried about the war going on. As to me, politics would come second … And why split the organization and that? So I stayed with them in '86 and they guaranteed us the war would go on until there was a declaration of intent to withdraw.

Joe Lynch learned about the ceasefire from television. As far as he was concerned, it 'was breaking the contract'. Des Long, who also lived in Limerick, visited Lynch: *'I asked him, were they [Republican Sinn Féin] going to carry on? And he said, "Of course we're carrying on." So I said, "Right oh, you have my support and whatever I can do."'*[7] In spite of the sceptics and a few defections, the peace process moved forward.

Gerry Adams, Rita O'Hare, Jim Gibney and a few others met with John Hume and Albert Reynolds to discuss the Forum for Peace and Reconciliation.[8] Mairéad Keane started setting up an office in Washington for a new support group, Friends of Sinn Féin.[9] Gerry Adams and Richard McAuley visited the US and met with members of the State Department. In New York, Adams debated Ken Maginnis, of the Ulster Unionists, on *Larry King Live*. Adams came across as moderate and thoughtful while Maginnis refused to shake hands with him, saying, 'I'm not going to get involved in a gimmick for the American public; Gerry Adams controls an organization which controls 100 tons of guns.' While Adams was in the US, the peace process received another boost when the Combined Loyalist Military Command announced their ceasefire.[10] By the end of October 1994, John Major had lifted the order that excluded Adams and Martin McGuinness from England, road-blocks on several unapproved North–South roads had been removed and Albert Reynolds had opened the Forum for Peace and Reconciliation in Dublin.

Sinn Féin was also gaining new recruits that more than compensated for defections. The ceasefire made Sinn Féin more attractive to people who wanted a united Ireland but were wary of being associated with violence. In contrast to young people who joined to defend their neighbourhoods or to hit back at the establishment, they wanted to be part of Sinn Féin's political development. A student at Queen's University, from a middle-class nationalist background, explained why he joined Sinn Féin in the autumn of 1994:

> *Because I'd already been involved really in republican politics and, at that point, that juncture, it was my opinion that people being involved in Sinn Féin explicitly, and importantly, was an important means of popularizing republican politics – developing republican politics – and enhancing the prospects for a just and democratic lasting peace settlement.*

> *Q: ... you've been involved in republican politics? ...*

> *A: Yes, in community groups particularly. So it's from that background that I would have come to it as a particular emphasis on social and economic rights, and human rights issues ... One of the [community] groups was a campaign against discrimination which also promoted the Mac Bride principles [an Irish-American fair employment campaign] and ultimately that led to community boycott action in the North of Ireland and abroad. So it was republican politics in so far as it was personal.*[11]

New recruits more interested in politics and less interested in armed struggle, 'Ceasefire Sinn Féiners', were a part of the transformation into mainstream politics.

In November, the peace process received two different kinds of jolt. The IRA robbed a post office in Newry and killed a postal worker, Frank Kerr[12] and the Dublin government immediately suspended the release of nine prisoners. An IRA statement claimed that the 'cessation' was complete but then a vigilante group calling itself Direct Actions Against Drugs (DAAD) began killing alleged drug dealers in Belfast. The 'civil administration' was keeping volunteers busy and policing neighbourhoods. The inability of the Provisionals to completely distance themselves from violence would cause issues throughout the peace process.

The second jolt involved Albert Reynolds and allegations that someone in his government had interfered with the extradition of a priest accused of child molesting.[13] Dick Spring withdrew Labour from the Fianna Fáil coalition and took them into another coalition with Fine Gael and Democratic Left, a new party that had emerged from a split in the Workers' Party. John Bruton of Fine Gael became Taoiseach and Dick Spring continued as Tanaiste. Even though Bruton would never develop the kind of relationship that Albert Reynolds had with Sinn Féin, the peace process withstood the jolts. The Dublin and London governments released some prisoners and President Clinton appointed George Mitchell, the former Senate Majority Leader, as his special advisor on Northern Ireland.[14]

In February 1995, the British and Irish governments published the 'Framework Documents', which were influenced by the inter-party talks of the early 1990s and the Downing Street Declaration.[15] The documents called for a ninety-member assembly for Northern Ireland with checks and balances that 'would command the confidence' of both communities plus North–South institutions that would 'promote agreement among the people of the island of Ireland ...' That framework had been an option since Sunningdale. The unionists were adamantly opposed to the North–South institutions. Paisley referred to the Framework Documents as a 'one-way street to Dublin'. The documents were important because they provided a starting point for discussion.

For Sinn Féin, the people who would participate in that discussion were very much the same people who had led the party since 1983. Figure 7 presents the Sinn Féin Ard Chomhairle that was elected at the 1995 Ard Fheis, and shows how stable the leadership was.[16]

The Provisionals believed that all-party negotiations on the future of Ireland would begin fairly soon after the Provisional IRA went on ceasefire. John Major's government depended upon Unionist support, however, and the British and the Unionists wanted proof that the ceasefire was permanent. In a speech in Washington, in March 1995, Patrick Mayhew announced that before Sinn Féin would be invited to talks, the IRA had to meet three conditions:

1. A willingness to disarm progressively;
2. A common understanding of what decommissioning would actually entail; and

Officers:		
Gerry Adams	Belfast	President
Pat Doherty	Donegal	Vice-President
Lucilita Bhreatnach	Dublin	General Secretary
Mitchel McLaughlin	Derry	Chairperson
Rita O'Hare	Belfast/Dublin	Press Officer
Joe Cahill	Belfast/Louth	Joint-Treasurer
Dessie Mackin	Belfast/Louth	Joint-Treasurer
Members:		
Owen Carron	Fermanagh/Leitrim	
Bairbre de Brún	Dublin/Belfast	
Jim Gibney	Belfast	
Pat McGeown	Belfast	
Dodie McGuinness	Derry	
Martin McGuinness	Derry	
Francie Molloy	Tyrone	
Caoimghghín Ó Caoláin	Monaghan	
Pat Trainor	Monaghan	

FIGURE 7
Sinn Féin Ard Chomhairle, elected March 1995

3.   As a sign of good faith and demonstration of the practical arrangements, the actual decommissioning of some weapons.[17]

Sinn Féin immediately complained that there had been no pre-conditions and flatly rejected the 'Washington Three'. They also courted Irish-American support and, at Easter, Gerry Adams was invited to the White House where John Hume introduced him to President Clinton.[18]

The pre-conditions sent the peace process into a stall at the same time that there was more evidence of another IRA. Six people were arrested in Dublin and charged with possession of weapons. One of them was Josephine Hayden, the Joint-General Secretary of Republican Sinn Féin and a member of Cumann na mBan. Republican Sinn Féin was not so much opposed to peace as they mistrusted the British. Seán Lynch, who represented RSF on the Longford County Council, was interviewed in the summer of 1995 and, when asked if armed struggle still had a role in bringing about a united Ireland, he replied:

> *We all want peace. You know that we all want peace. But I can't see peace coming after what's happened now. The British government have never stated that they were going to disengage from Ireland. All the talk. They never apologized to the Irish people for anything ... it has happened in every generation, the armed struggle. I would imagine that, in the future, it would happen again.*
>
> *Q: ... if there had been no armed struggle over these twenty-five or so years, do you think that the British would be even engaging in talks?*
>
> *A: Oh, no, I wouldn't think they would. The British government are very, very deceptive and cunning people – even with all this talk – bringing in different meanings into words and all this, and that's what always happened here. And as [Terence] McSwiney said, 'They can lie like hell.*[19]

Republican Sinn Féiners were convinced the Provisionals' ceasefire was a mistake. Some Provisionals suspected the same thing. The longer the ceasefire lasted, the more the Provisionals' leaders needed something from the British to show their followers that they were on the right track. They never got it. The first official Sinn Féin–British meeting was in April 1995, when Michael Ancram, Patrick Mayhew's deputy, met with a Sinn Féin delegation led by Martin McGuinness. In May, Gerry Adams and Patrick Mayhew met privately in Washington, but there was no formal meeting.[20] The ceasefire had been in place for nine months.

Irish republicans had, for years, argued that the justice system treated their prisoners differently. There were hundreds of republican prisoners and many of them had served more than twenty years in prison. Their fate contrasted starkly with the treatment of Lee Clegg, the soldier sentenced to life for the murder of Karen Reilly.[21] Clegg was released on license after only four years in custody and allowed to return to the British Army. When Clegg's release became public in the summer of 1995, there were riots. Belfast Sinn Féin organized a peaceful demonstration to protest Clegg's release and it was attacked by the RUC. Then there was a major confrontation in Portadown, in County Armagh. There was a strong loyalist presence in the area and the town sits in the southwest corner of what was known as the 'Murder Triangle'.

Protestants in Portadown take great pride in their heritage. The Orange Order there dates from 1796. Since 1807, Protestants in the area have celebrated the victory of King William over Catholic King James II (in July 1690) by marching along a route that goes from the centre of town to a small church at Drumcree, holding a service there and then circling back to Portadown. Over time, the Drumcree march became a large part of the area's Protestant culture. It also became more controversial as more and more Catholics moved into the area. They were not interested in being insulted by marchers and bands passing by their homes and, in the 1980s, complaints led to a change in the outbound route. In the spring of 1995, the Garvaghy Road Residents Group asked for a change to the return route. The Orange Order refused to meet with them. The group appealed to Patrick Mayhew and the response from the Northern Ireland Office was that the police were in charge of parades. A meeting with the RUC was no help so the residents' group took direct action.

On the morning of Sunday 9 July 1995, about 500 nationalists sat down on the Garvaghy Road. In order to avoid a confrontation, the RUC stopped the Orangemen at Drumcree. Crowds grew on both sides of a blockade; loyalists tried to push through and the police responded with plastic bullets. Conflict spread and there were riots in loyalist areas, more roads were blocked and the port of Larne was sealed off. A similar stand-off developed along the Ormeau Road in Belfast.

After two tense days, it appeared that mediators had worked out a settlement. On 11 July, the Garvaghy Road residents agreed to allow members of the Portadown Orange Lodge to march in silence in exchange for a promise that future marches were dependent upon their consent. However, once past the disputed area, the marchers joined up with a huge crowd and claimed a victory over the Garvaghy Road group. David Trimble, the Ulster Unionist MP for the area, and Revd Ian Paisley, were photographed raising their arms in triumph. Paisley declared that it was 'one of the greatest victories during the past twenty-five years for Protestantism in Northern Ireland'. Adding insult to injury, the Orange Order denied there had been any agreement about future marches. The next day in Belfast there was a major riot at the Ormeau Road flashpoint.[22]

Drumcree affected both communities. Among republicans it showed how little things had changed and among unionists it raised the profile of David Trimble. Compared to James Molyneaux, Trimble was twenty-five years younger and a much stauncher defender of Ulster. About a month after Drumcree, Molyneaux resigned as leader of the Ulster Unionists and Trimble was elected his successor.

By the summer of 1995, Sinn Féin had very little to show for the Provisional IRA's ceasefire. Fra McCann, Sinn Féin's representative for the Lower Falls on the Belfast City Council, was interviewed that summer. He commented:

> *I believe that the RUC will never change ... They still take the numbers of registrations of cars. They still stop people in the street. They still harass the youth. And they're trying to put this clean image across. And the people that you see on the road, I believe, are doing no more than gathering intelligence ... the areas are still heavily patrolled by armoured vehicles, RUC vehicles.*[23]

Sinn Féin organized *Saoirse* (Freedom) demonstrations in support of the peace process. At one of them, about 200 demonstrators tried to stage a sit-down picket in Donegal Square, in Belfast City Centre. The RUC attacked with batons and demonstrators were arrested.[24] McCann contrasted the treatment of Orangemen and loyalists with that of nationalists:

> *To give you an example of where they're thinking is if you look at what happened over the twelfth of July. To break what they called nationalist authority down, they sat down on roads. They blocked roads right across the six counties. They blocked the main port in Larne refusing to let lorries get on and off for twenty-four hours. And the RUC never did anything. And last Friday – and a couple of Fridays before it – Sinn Féin called a protest in the centre of the city here. And we sat in the middle of the road. And it was met by violence by the RUC. And I – so the nationalist – nothing has changed in that field. They still see the RUC as purely a sectarian force.*

Like Republican Sinn Féiners, the Provisionals did not trust the British. Fra McCann again:

> *I think that the British have a history and a record of being the most devious bastards – and I am not going to change my opinion. I think the way that they've handled the past year has been atrocious … What you actually have is the Brits using that period first of all to try and split the Movement. And then to drag this thing out as long as possible. And anything that has been given – which have been slight changes – anything that has been given has had to – they've had to be dragged to the table screaming to get it out of them.*[25]

Seán Crowe was Secretary of the Sinn Féin delegation to the Forum for Peace and Reconciliation. He also was interviewed in the summer of 1995:

> *Q: If the IRA decided tomorrow that they'd hand in all their guns, like the British have been asking, do you think the British would then be forthcoming and do all-party talks?*
>
> *A: No. I think they'd come up with some other hurdle. I don't think the IRA are going to hand over the arms tomorrow anyway. I think it's semantics. The IRA have said on numerous occasions that there was going to be no – they weren't going to be handing over arms. This whole thing of preconditions and so on.*

And yet, publicly at least, the Provisionals remained optimistic and patient. Seán Crowe explained: *'It was the IRA initiative – the cease-fire, the cessation – that brought about this whole process. The potential is still there for a peaceful resolution to the conflict.'*[26] The Provisionals were trying to make the ceasefire work.

In the middle of July, Gerry Adams and Martin McGuinness met secretly and for the second time with Patrick Mayhew and Michael Ancram.[27] The British were still committed to the Washington Three and the Provisionals were still not interested in decommissioning. Unlike in 1975, however, the conversation involved more than leading Provisionals meeting with British representatives. Dick Spring suggested an international commission for 'peace and disarmament' with an American as the Chair. The British were opposed to US involvement, but they also knew that doing nothing would eventually lead to a disaster. They were also no longer in a position where they could just ignore the Irish government. The two governments put forward a proposal in which an international commission of experts would address the decommissioning issue while London and Dublin organized multi-party talks.[28]

The secret meetings were made public and at a press conference on the Falls Road, Gerry Adams was guarded when asked about the international commission, saying:

> Well, I have to say that I don't know. I'm very, very loath to get involved and to get engaged in what at this time is a lot of speculation. And I'm very mindful that, you know, like the other parties in this, the British government could be using that speculation to put a good spin on a conversation. They could be creating or attempting to create an illusion of movement without any real movement. I note – and I think it's very important to note and to underline the fact that Patrick Mayhew yesterday reiterated the British government's position – that there could be no movement to all-party talks unless the IRA decommission some of its weapons. So I have to ask them, is this commission a notion or a device or an idea to bring about a decommissioning of IRA weapons in order to fulfill a British precondition?

Adams did not flatly reject an international commission on decommissioning. He did express frustration with the delays:

> We are eleven months into an IRA cessation. We are three years into the initial dialogue and contact between Sinn Féin and the British government … We've had nearly a decade of bilaterals and trilaterals and ups and downs but we need to move. We need to move with some urgency. We need to bring all of the people together around one table under the basis of equality to resolve all of the issues which are perplexing all of us.[29]

Although Adams and Mayhew officially met at the end of July, by mid-August Adams began dropping hints of a return to war. At a rally at Belfast City Hall, someone yelled, 'Bring back the IRA.' Scripted or not, Adams replied, 'They haven't gone away, you know?'[30]

All of the parties involved wanted peace, even if they did not necessarily agree on what that meant or how to achieve it. That autumn, there was a series of meetings that would have been unimaginable in 1975.[31] Prime Minister John Major met with Taoiseach John Bruton; Revd Ian Paisley and Peter Robinson of the DUP met with vice President Al Gore and Tony Lake, the United States' National Security Advisor; David Trimble of the Ulster Unionists met with Bill Clinton; Mary Robinson, the President of Ireland, met with Queen Elizabeth; and Gerry Adams met with Nancy Soderberg of the US National Security Council. There were also private meetings involving Protestant clergymen, like Revd Harold Good and Revd Ken Newell, and Catholic priests like Fr Alec Reid. Out of these conversations came an agreed upon two-track approach to end the impasse. A three-person international arms commission, under the chairmanship of George Mitchell, would work with the paramilitaries on decommissioning. The second track consisted of all-party negotiations. Sinn Féin could participate in preparatory talks while the arms commission consulted with the different parties. The Mitchell Commission would file a report in January 1996 that would then serve as the basis for negotiations.

In support of George Mitchell, and as a sign of his personal interest in the peace process, President Clinton toured Britain and Ireland late in the autumn.[32] He addressed the Houses of Parliament and Dáil Éireann, and became the first sitting United States president to visit Northern Ireland. At a reception in Belfast, Ian Paisley lectured him on the 'error of his ways'. And on a tour of West Belfast, his car pulled up at a bakery shop and he met briefly with Gerry Adams, who had come a long way in a short period of time.

The Mitchell Commission was underway when the 'Continuity Army Council' finally revealed itself. A public statement on 6 January 1996, confirmed its existence: 'We wish to clarify our position to the people of Ireland. We are neither Official nor Provisional and rejecting reformism we remain revolutionary as the true Óglaigh na hÉireann, Irish Republican Army.' The statement was signed 'B Ó Ruairc'. Brian Óg Ó Ruairc, from the Irish midlands, was the last hold-out of the seventeenth-century Irish chieftains opposed to the English invasion; he died without yielding. A second statement included portions of a letter written in 1987 by 'Comdt General' Tom Maguire that validated the Continuity IRA: 'I hereby declare that the Continuity Executive and the Continuity Army Council are the lawful Executive and Army Council respectively of the Irish Republican Army, and that the governmental authority, delegated in the Proclamation of 1938, now resides in the Continuity Army Council, and its lawful successors.' In the eyes of its supporters, the 'Continuity' IRA was the legitimate Army of the Republic, holding in 'trust' the powers of government of Dáil Éireann.[33] Other than firing shots over Tom Maguire's grave, however, they were inactive.

The Mitchell Commission delivered its report a few weeks later.[34] In order to 'take the gun out of Irish politics', the Commission recommended that participants in all-party negotiations commit to:

1. Democratic and exclusively peaceful means of resolving political issues;
2. The total disarmament of all paramilitary organizations;
3. Agree that disarmament must be verifiable to the satisfaction of an independent commission;
4. Renounce for themselves, and to oppose efforts by others, to use force, or threaten to use force, to influence the course or the outcome of all-party negotiations;
5. Agree to abide by the terms of any agreement reached in all-party negotiations and to resort to democratic and exclusively peaceful methods in trying to alter any aspect of that outcome with which they may disagree; and
6. Urge that 'punishment' killings and beatings stop and to take effective steps to prevent such actions.[35]

The Commission recommended 'parallel decommissioning'. Instead of disarming prior to all-party talks, decommissioning would occur *during* the talks. It was a creative way to get Sinn Féin into the negotiations (*if* they accepted the Mitchell Principles), keep the Provisional IRA on the sidelines and potentially make the 'Continuity' IRA irrelevant. Then John Major intervened.

In consulting with the Mitchell Commission, unionists had suggested an election precede the all-party negotiations. David Trimble, for example, argued that the people of Northern Ireland should be involved in the selection of representatives who would discuss their future. The Provisionals and the SDLP saw an election as another attempt to delay progress and were opposed. The report only noted the idea but John Major used it to propose an election to a forum that would precede all-party negotiations.[36] Major's proposal delighted the unionists and upset the nationalists.

John Hume called for a fixed date for the start of all-party talks. Gerry Adams accused John Major of 'unilaterally dumping' the Mitchell Commission report. It was another example of British deceit. The Belfast Provisional who was surprised by the ceasefire, now an ex-prisoner, commented:

> the cessation was called, it showed the people what Britain is really like because every time Sinn Féin or the nationalist people went forward they moved the goalpost. It just seemed we weren't getting anywhere because every time we were doing something positive or thinking positive or talking positive, Britain was coming up with something else. … When we worked our way around the first condition they've come up with other conditions – this is the only way you can get around the talking table, and all this hand in arms … they have to understand that it is a war here and they have to accept that they caused this conflict.[37]

The Provisionals were not the only ones frustrated with the lack of progress. Revd Harold Good recalled:

> this small group of people from the Methodist Council on Social Responsibility got into a relationship with some of the people like Tom Hartley, Alex Maskey, Jim Gibney and some of the folk who were the more visible face of Sinn Féin, but who also were very much involved in the total Republican Movement – Jim Gibney and people like these who had served their time in prison. As we got into that conversation we sensed that there was a desire to find another way. So in those conversations, we began to build up trust … And we did some important, some very important representation after the ceasefire of the mid-nineties when there was no response – nothing coming back from the British government. We tried to represent the republican frustration and the huge concern and anxiety of the people that we were talking with – that is, there was no practical, positive response from Westminster, that there was a limit as to how long people could hold back the very radical wing from doing something else. And I can remember going to officials in Northern Ireland and representing this and they were saying, 'We don't give in to threats.' We were saying, 'This isn't threats. This is people telling us that if there isn't a good response there will be a reaction from some. And this is a fact of life.' We were actively seeking to represent republican leadership frustration at the highest levels. Then we had Canary Wharf.[38]

The IRA Executive Council met and voted eleven to one to have an Army Convention. That would take time to organize and, in the meantime, the Army Council also met and voted unanimously to go back to war. After seventeen months on ceasefire and with nothing to show for it, on 9 February 1996, the Provisional IRA announced the ceasefire would end at 6 pm. At 7 pm, a truck bomb exploded at Canary Wharf, killing two people and causing an estimated £100 million in damage to London's business district.[39] The return to war did not go smoothly, however. Within a fortnight, Edward O'Brien, a 21-year-old Provisional from Wexford, was killed and three civilians were injured in a premature explosion on a London bus.[40]

As for the peace process, it went forward without the Provisionals. The Northern Ireland Forum for Political Dialogue, in Belfast, replaced the Forum for Peace and Reconciliation and an election was scheduled for May 1996.[41] The new Forum would be a talking-shop with representation determined by a complex election scheme that allowed up to ten political parties to send delegates. The election would also determine the delegates who would be invited to attend all-party negotiations on the future of Northern Ireland. If its representatives were elected, Sinn Féin was welcome to participate in the Forum. Without an IRA ceasefire, they would be excluded from the negotiations. Sinn Féin argued that the Forum was a return to Stormont, a new Northern Ireland Assembly with the old in-built unionist majority. They said they would not participate.[42] They did contest the election and the pre-conditions, Lee Clegg's release, moving the 'goalpost' and so on helped Sinn Féin to its best election since 1955. The party received 116,000 votes (15.5 per cent) and finished fourth with seventeen representatives elected to the negotiations.[43] Sinn Féin was still behind the Ulster Unionists (thirty seats), the DUP (twenty-four seats) and the SDLP (twenty-one seats) but they were significantly ahead of the Alliance Party (seven seats) and the two loyalist parties (Progressive Unionist Party, two seats; and Ulster Democratic Party, two seats).

The Provisional IRA then tried to rob a postal truck carrying pension and social security funds in Limerick. Garda Jerry McCabe was killed and his partner seriously wounded and any claim that Sinn Féin had on a mandate for inclusion in the negotiations was worthless.[44]

When John Major and John Bruton jointly opened the all-party talks at Stormont, Sinn Féin was excluded.[45] Representatives of the loyalist parties, still on ceasefire, were admitted. As it worked out, the Sinn Féin delegation missed a lot of bluster and conflict that, for the next year, produced nothing. For example, George Mitchell waited in an office for two days while the delegates argued about his role. Mitchell finally took his seat with Ian Paisley yelling, 'No! No! No! No!' When he stopped yelling, Paisley denounced the imposition of Mitchell on the negotiations and walked out. Their first order of business was that all of the political parties involved accept the Mitchell Principles which they did, including Paisley and the DUP who walked back in. Three days later, an IRA bomb destroyed the centre of Manchester.

Unionists and loyalists were tired of what they considered meddling by the Dublin government and the willingness of the British to admit Sinn Féin to the negotiations if the IRA went back on ceasefire. That summer, they took a stand against concessions. When Hugh Annesley, the Chief Constable, announced that Orangemen would not be allowed to march down the Garvaghy Road, it was seen as a challenge. Another standoff at Drumcree led to riots in Protestant areas of Ballymena and Carrickfergus.[46] Mid-Ulster loyalists, led by Billy Wright, added to the tension by killing Michael McGoldrick, a Catholic taxi driver from Armagh. Loyalists blocked motorways and Belfast airport was shut down. The DUP withdrew from the negotiations and Paisley addressed the Drumcree crowd with: 'I do not promise an easy victory this time. It was easy last year. Now we've all the power of the British government against us aided and abetted by the skunks from Dublin. We are fighting for the promise of the life to come and that's worth fighting for and that's worth dying for.'[47] With an estimated 60,000 loyalists converging on Portadown, the Chief Constable reversed his decision, the RUC cleared nationalist protesters and Orangemen were allowed to march down the Garvaghy Road. Northern Ireland erupted in riots – unionists in triumph and nationalists in anger. In Derry, Dermot McShane was run over and killed by a British Army vehicle.[48] The SDLP announced it was withdrawing from the Forum[49] and a bomb wrecked the Killyhevlin Hotel, near Enniskillen.

It was the first bomb in Northern Ireland since the August 1994 ceasefire. It was assumed the Provisionals were responsible, but they denied it. This time, they were telling the truth. After weeks of speculation and rumour, the Continuity Army Council released a statement through the Irish Republican Publicity Bureau:

> The action near Enniskillen on July 14 was carried out by Volunteers of the Irish Republican Army under the direction of the Continuity Army Council.
>
> This military operation against an economic target was an immediate reprisal for the killing of an Irish citizen by British troops the previous night and the general campaign of terror by British Forces against the Nationalist population at that time … military action will continue to be taken against British occupation in Ireland until such time as the British Government withdraws finally from our country.[50]

It was the first military operation by the 'dissidents'. Ruairí Ó Brádaigh, the President of Republican Sinn Féin, was interviewed in the autumn of 1996 and provided a context for the attack:

> *A lot of people say, 'Oh, it's good that you're there in case all this goes wrong' and all that type of thing. I say, 'It's going wrong by the day and been going wrong since '86, and it's time they saw it' … the Provisionals only speak for themselves. They call this unilateral, unconditional and indefinite ceasefire. They called it, so it is binding on them. They speak only on themselves, not binding on other people. So there it is. And if we were all dead and gone tomorrow … the whole lot, there would be people to carry on. That is one thing I am so sure of.*[51]

The Enniskillen bomb was the start of the Continuity IRA's campaign. The Provisionals were trying to end their campaign but, because they had returned to war, they were excluded from the peace process.

In essence, the Provisionals had gone back to the 'armalite and ballot box' strategy. The Canary Wharf and Manchester bombs showed what the IRA could do and the Sinn Féin vote showed that they had grass-roots support. Joe Cahill, who was a member of the Army Council and the Treasurer of Sinn Féin, was interviewed in September of 1996. When asked if there was still a role for armed struggle, he replied:

Joe Cahill (1990s). Bobbie Hanvey photographic archives, John J. Burns Library, Boston College.

Well, I believe there is. I've always had the firm conviction that the political and the Army go together, that one can't go ahead without the other. And I think that has been proven over the ceasefire period. That was probably the best opportunity there's been, since 1920–21, to do something about the situation in Ireland. And it was ignored – ignored because there was a ceasefire. Maybe if there had of been more military action during that period of time or if the ceasefire hadn't lasted so long there may have been a lot more done. But I think once the British particularly had got a ceasefire they were prepared to live with that and happy to live with it. Drag it out.

Q: The British demand for an IRA ceasefire before continued negotiations, what would be your opinion?

A. Well, again, that's ludicrous because of the election results in the North – the mandate that Sinn Féin has. They're entitled to be there, irrespective of what the IRA are doing. And entitled to speak for the people that voted for them. So it's absolutely ridiculous that they're not in there at the present time because of the mandate that they have.[52]

The leadership knew that the armalite and ballot box strategy had already failed once and they also knew that the IRA had been weakened. That autumn, J.B. O'Hagan was asked to compare the current situation with 1975:

Well, I thought we were – a truce this time was from a position of strength. The Movement was strong. Now, whether it would be just as strong now is doubtful. Like after the truce. But it was from a position of strength. I supported it. Looking back, maybe we were naïve in the sense that a unilateral truce wasn't the thing. We should have maybe got more promises from the Brits and got concessions from them. I don't know. Hindsight's very, very nice … it's like you could have had ten alternatives but you've only one decision when it comes to the point.[53]

The twin track of pursuing war while demanding participation in peace talks had a high price. On 23 September 1996, Diarmuid O'Neill was killed in a raid in London – he was unarmed and could have been arrested.[54]

It was in this context that Gerry Adams released his autobiography, *Before the Dawn*. Adams had already authored an edited collection of his Brownie articles, *Cage Eleven*, and a memoir, *Falls Memories: A Belfast Life*. He cultivated the image of a 'revolutionary-intellectual' and the peace process had turned him into an international 'terrorist-celebrity'. Journalist Suzanne Breen, in an insightful article for the *Belfast Telegraph* entitled 'Down through history the working class has always been cannon-fodder in wars', commented on Adams and the Provisionals' strategy:

As Eoghan and Teresa O'Neill travelled to England to identify their son's body, Sinn Féin president Gerry Adams launched his autobiography. He claimed to have considered cancelling it following the death but 'reluctantly' went ahead … Diarmuid O'Neill's life wouldn't have made an international bestseller. He grew up in London of Irish-born stock who later moved back home … The Sinn Féin President visits the White House and parties with Donald Trump, Bianca Jagger and Oliver Stone. He enjoys Hollywood treatment in the US. There is even talk of a film of his life … There won't be a film about the short life of Ed O'Brien … There is less talk now of a 32-county socialist republic and more of a negotiated settlement and parity of esteem for Catholics and Protestants within Northern Ireland. But a public announcement of this policy change would threaten the leadership's power base … bombing England is no longer aimed at Irish unity. It's a negotiating tactic to ease Sinn Féin's way into all party talks … If the republican leadership possesses a shred of humanity, it should inform its grassroots of its new position and the compromises entailed …'[55]

Whether or not Gerry Adams's internal critics read Breen's column, she had nicely summarized their concerns. In the first week of October, the Provisionals carried out their first attack in

Northern Ireland since the ceasefire. Two IRA bombs exploded at Thiepval Barracks, British Army Headquarters in Northern Ireland, killing one soldier and wounding several others.[56]

In October, the Provisional IRA finally met in convention. Journalist Ed Moloney reports that Mickey McKevitt and Frank McGuinness led the disenchanted. They were members of the Army Executive and the directors of the quartermaster and engineering departments, respectively.[57] McKevitt's criticism was helped by the fact that his partner was Bernadette Sands, the younger sister of Bobby Sands. The leadership, however, still had the trust of most activists. The ex-prisoner was asked if she believed that the leadership had been fooled: *'No, they haven't been fooled. They tried. You know, I feel they have been trying, I mean they really want – they really want peace here in Ireland.'*[58] The leadership, in good faith, had taken a chance. It had not worked out and they had properly moved on.

Accounts of the convention suggest that Martin McGuinness, Chairman of the outgoing Army Council, offered a report to the delegates and promised that they would not enter talks and that there would not be another ceasefire. That was enough to keep the support of most of the delegates. Frank McGuinness and Mickey McKevitt were re-elected to the Executive, but so were supporters of the leadership. The accounts have several members of the outgoing Army Council being re-elected, including Gerry Adams, Martin McGuinness, Pat Doherty, Kevin McKenna (C/S) and Tom Murphy. It is reported that they were joined by Brian Keenan, who was released from prison in England in 1993, and Martin Ferris. Keenan was a critic of the ceasefire but also a long-time supporter of Adams.

In an interview for *An Phoblacht/Republican News*, Keenan would later comment: 'the IRA was morally obliged to look at alternative options to continuing the war, especially if there was a viable alternative. I was skeptical and supportive in equal measure.' Martin Ferris, Seán O'Callaghan's victim in 1984, was another supporter of the peace process. He was released from Portlaoise Prison in September 1994 and immediately appointed to the Sinn Féin Ard Chomhairle. Ferris was also a delegate to the Forum on Peace and Reconciliation. The biggest change involved 77-year-old Joe Cahill, who was off the Council for the first time in twenty years though he continued as Treasurer of Sinn Féin.

As Northern Ireland moved into the spring of 1997, the Provisionals were at war, Sinn Féin was on the sidelines and the negotiations were going nowhere. The talks were adjourned in the run-up to a Westminster election that would change everything.[59] Sinn Féin's vote went up again (126,921 votes, 16.1 per cent) and they moved past Paisley and the DUP to become the third largest political party in Northern Ireland, behind only the Ulster Unionists of David Trimble and John Hume and the SDLP. Gerry Adams won back the seat in West Belfast and Martin McGuinness, who was never going to top John Hume in Derry, was elected in Mid-Ulster. Sinn Féin again claimed they had a mandate for inclusion in the negotiations and this time the IRA did nothing to compromise it. Perhaps most important, after eighteen years of Conservative governments in London, the Labour Party won a landslide victory. Tony Blair replaced John Major as Prime Minister and the peace process was rejuvenated.

Tony Blair had a family connection to County Donegal and, with a huge majority in the House of Commons, he was in a position to make history as the Prime Minister who brought peace to Northern Ireland. He chose Belfast for the site of his first major speech as Prime Minister and he offered something to both communities. He calmed unionist fears:

> Northern Ireland is part of the United Kingdom alongside England, Scotland and Wales. The Union binds the four parts of the United Kingdom together … Northern Ireland is part of the United Kingdom because that is the wish of a majority of the people who live here. It will remain part of the United Kingdom for as long as that remains the case.

He supported nationalist aspirations: 'We are also determined to build trust and confidence in public institutions. Incorporation of the European Convention on Human Rights into United Kingdom law will help protect basic human rights. We want to increase public confidence in policing through measured reform …' Blair also challenged the Provisionals: 'My message to Sinn Féin is clear. The settlement train is leaving. I want you on that train. But it is leaving anyway, and I will not allow it to wait for you. You cannot hold the process to ransom any longer. So end the violence. Now.'[60] Blair did not depend on the support of unionist MPs and could deliver on his promises. Sinn Féin wanted a timeline for the negotiations and Blair made it clear that May 1998 was the deadline for a settlement, with or without Sinn Féin.

At the beginning of June 1997, the all party-negotiations reconvened without Sinn Féin. Political change in the Republic of Ireland then reinforced the view that there was a developing opportunity for peace that would include Sinn Féin.[61] In an election held on 6 June 1997, Fianna Fáil was returned to power in coalition with the Progressive Democrats. Bertie Ahern, who had been a minister in Albert Reynolds's government, became Taoiseach. Ahern supported the peace process and he would develop a very positive relationship with Tony Blair. Meanwhile, ten years after dropping abstentionism from Leinster House, Caoimhghín Ó Caoláin topped the poll in Cavan–Monaghan and was elected to Dáil Éireann.

Caoimhghín Ó Caoláin was not a reformed-militant, ex-prisoner. Instead, he dressed and carried himself like a bank offcial, which was his professional background. He also was not a 'Ceasefire Sinn Féiner'. He was the cousin of Fergal O'Hanlon, killed on the famous Brookeborough raid and immortalized in the song 'The Patriot Game'. Ó Caoláin had served on the Monaghan County Council for more than a decade and his politics were much more sophisticated than 'Brits out'. Interviewed in the autumn of 1996, his comments show why he was the right person at the right time for a movement making a transition from armed struggle to constitutional politics:

> *Republicanism is a political ethos that is – that has I think maybe been misrepresented in terms of the Irish experience. And I guess that republicans themselves are not just a little at fault in this. For many people, it conjures up only the idea of Brits out and opposing the imposition of partition or the British presence or whatever it is. But I've often thought that for me it is much, much more than that. And I certainly would like to think whether the British were involved in Ireland or had remained involved in Ireland as they do, I would have hoped that the republican ideal, the republican ethos and what it stands for in terms of its political tenets would have attracted me in any event … liberty, equality, fraternity.*

And the liberty in terms of – it does not mean just the liberty of the country. It's the liberty of the people in it. It has to also have respect for all minority opinion. If we're talking about democracy in terms of freedom and liberty, well then you could only evaluate the quality of that democracy by the way it treats its minorities. And those are minorities in terms of social groups, in terms of women, in terms of sexuality, in terms of – we'll say ethnic groups. There are so many manifestations here in Ireland that you could point to. I mean, how do you claim that the travelling community have the same liberty as those of the settled community here in the Irish experience? So for me it's just not about Brits out and about Irish independence but it's also about the liberty and independence and rights and justice that must apply right across the board.[62]

Caoimhghín Ó Caoláin was the first Sinn Féin TD to take a seat in the Dublin parliament since 1922. Even if he was only one of 144 TDs, his election was seen as a major breakthrough.

Things were coming together for Sinn Féin. They were excluded from the negotiations but, to the dismay of the unionists, Tony Blair agreed to parallel meetings with Sinn Féin. The Mitchell Commission then offered a way around the decommissioning impasse.[63] If the Provisional IRA declared a second ceasefire, Sinn Féin could join the substantive negotiations while the Independent International Commission on Decommissioning organized a parallel discussion of the weapons issue. In late June or early July, the seven members of the Army Council met and assessed the new situation. They voted unanimously to call another ceasefire.

According to Ed Moloney's account in *A Secret History of the IRA*, when the Army Council met with the Army Executive, Martin McGuinness explained the logic behind a second ceasefire.[64] There was a new British government, Sinn Féin's vote was on the rise North and South and the decommissioning pre-condition had been sidestepped. The new Fianna Fáil government and the Clinton White House would keep the British committed to the formal start and end dates for the negotiations – 15 September 1997 and 1 May 1998. There would be no new preconditions and the length of the ceasefire would be fixed. If the negotiations failed the unionists and the British would be blamed, and if the Provisional IRA had to go back to war, it would be with a stronger Sinn Féin with a representative in Dáil Éireann.

At least three of the twelve people on the Army Executive were very upset – the Chairman, Seamus McGrane, Frank McGuinness and Mickey McKevvitt. They had not been consulted before the Army Council had voted and they had been promised the previous autumn that there would not be another ceasefire. Other than complain, however, there was not much they could do. Journalists John Mooney and Michael O'Toole report in *Black Operations: The Secret War Against the Real IRA*, that when the discussion became heated Martin McGuinness told them, 'If you don't like it, elect a fucking new Army Council.'[65] On 19 July 1997, the leadership of 'Óglaigh na hÉireann' announced that the 'unequivocal restoration of the ceasefire of August 1994' would begin at noon the next day.[66]

Gerry Adams had been pursuing peace for at least a decade. It had been almost seven years since Martin McGuinness had met with Michael Oatley. The Army Council knew that a second ceasefire might provoke another split and, no matter what happened, the Army would be weakened even more. They also knew that the war was not winnable and it was time to cut a deal. The campaign had wrecked lives for a generation. Marriages fell apart because a spouse was unwilling or unable to put life on hold and wait out a partner's prison sentence; children grew up in single parent households because their father or mother was in prison or had died on active service or was killed by loyalists. With the benefit of hindsight, other issues may also have influenced their decision.

Every large organization suffers from personality clashes and misbehaviour by its members. Chief of Staff Seán Mac Stiofáin grated on some people. Maria McGuire left the Provisionals after Bloody Friday, writing a tell-all memoir, *To Take Arms: My Year With the IRA Provisionals*, in which she claimed that she had an affair with Dáithí O'Connell; O'Connell denied the affair.[67] It is reported that Brian Keenan and Martin McGuinness did not get along.[68] Some transgressions are of a different kind and threat.

In the late 1980s, Gerry Adams's niece and her mother (his ex-sister-in-law) approached the RUC. They claimed that his brother, Liam Adams, would beat his wife and, after she fled the house, he would molest his daughter. They were disappointed to discover the RUC was more interested in collecting information on Gerry Adams than pursuing a paedophile. The allegation was withdrawn and they turned to Gerry Adams for help. He believed them and arranged for a meeting with Liam Adams, who denied everything. The allegation remained private and Liam Adams remained involved with the Provisionals. By 1997, the RUC and presumably British intelligence had known for a decade that there was credible evidence that the brother of the President of Sinn Féin was a paedophile. At any time that information might be used against Liam or Gerry Adams and the RUC did not have a reputation for treading softly.[69]

The Liam Adams case reflected a more general problem – that the 'civil administration' could not properly police neighbourhoods and, because of this, people suffered. Máiría Cahill, for example, is the grandniece of Joe Cahill. She alleges that as a 16 year old, in August 1997, she was raped by a volunteer in the Belfast IRA. Two years later, she reported her allegation to the 'civil administration' and was then forced to participate in a humiliating investigation with a kangaroo court that included a confrontation with the man who raped her.[70] Máiría Cahill's accusations are disputed and the alleged rape would have occurred after the ceasefire. Her specific situation would not have influenced the Sinn Féin or Provisional IRA leadership's decision to enter the second ceasefire. However, Máiría Cahill is not the only person to have claimed she was victimized by the IRA or to have been abused by the civil administration. In the summer of 1997, the Provisionals were a long way from Bobby Sands's dream of hearing 'the laughter of our children'. Peace would be good for their community.

19

ANOTHER SPLIT AND THE GOOD FRIDAY
AGREEMENT (1997–1998)

All sorts of stuff began to creep in, like the political scenario and the agendas, hidden agendas began to sort of manifest.

– Val Lynch[1]

The second ceasefire only set the stage for Sinn Féin's entré into peace negotiations. It was announced that Marjorie 'Mo' Mowlam, Tony Blair's Secretary of State for Northern Ireland, would have to confirm that the ceasefire was 'genuine'.[2] And when Mowlam did make that confirmation, Ian Paisley and his ally, Robert McCartney, announced that the DUP and the UKUP would boycott the negotiations if Sinn Féin were admitted.[3] Tony Blair had been willing to go ahead without Sinn Féin; he was willing to go ahead without the DUP and UKUP.

The withdrawal of Paisley made the continued involvement of David Trimble and the UUP that much more important.[4] Trimble saw the second ceasefire as another sham but was not convinced that walking out was his best option. Incredibly, one of his advisors was Seán O'Callaghan, the informer. O'Callaghan had been released from prison and met Trimble through journalist Ruth Dudley Edwards. O'Callaghan suggested that unionism would be best served if the UUP stayed and fought, that the Provisionals would benefit from a walkout because it would clear out much of their opposition.

The Provisionals' biggest problem was not unionism. The end of the first ceasefire had delayed a day of reckoning over the Mitchell Principles, which required a commitment to disarm. General Order Number 9 of the IRA's Constitution stated that any volunteer 'party to the seizure of arms, ammunition or explosives' controlled by the Army Council was guilty of treachery. If a Sinn Féiner who agreed to the Mitchell Principles was also a member of the IRA, it would violate the standing order. The Principles also required negotiators to 'to abide by the terms' of any agreement. Given the Downing Street Declaration, the principle of unionist consent was probably going to be part of whatever might result from negotiations. That would defer Irish unity until the unionists accepted it, which was never going to happen. It would also be a violation of the IRA Constitution, which pledged members to 'guard the honour and uphold the sovereignty and unity of the Irish Republic as declared by the first Dáil'.[5]

The Army Council had a simple solution to these technicalities: confine the talks to Sinn Féin and have any IRA members involved either resign or receive a special dispensation. The IRA Executive was tired of games being played and turned it down. The implications of the suggestion were clear – the Army Council was willing to set aside 'the sovereignty and unity of the Irish Republic' for a place at a bargaining table where they were going to end up short of a united Ireland. The Council and the Executive agreed that the only way to settle the issue was through another Convention.[6] In the interim, a Sinn Féin delegation of Gerry Adams, Martin McGuinness, Lucilita Bhreatnach, Pat Doherty, Martin Ferris and Caoimhghín Ó Caolain, prepared for talks at Stormont.[7]

On 9 September 1997, Sinn Féin's representatives signed off on the Mitchell Principles and, two days later, in an interview with *AP/RN*, an IRA spokesperson downplayed the significance of the event: 'As to the IRA's attitude to the Mitchell Principles per se, well, the IRA would have problems with sections of the Mitchell Principles. But then the IRA is not a participant in these talks.'[8] The authorities were also tired of games. Tony Blair stated that Sinn Féin and the IRA were 'inextricably' linked and Bertie Ahern said he expected the 'entire Republican Movement' would honour the Mitchell Principles. David Trimble described the Provisionals' leadership as 'scoundrels' and Revd Ian Paisley demanded that Sinn Féin be expelled from the talks.

When the talks resumed, none of the unionist parties were there. The SDLP, the Alliance Party, the Northern Ireland Women's Conference and Sinn Féin debated whether or not Sinn Féin should be expelled. Gerry Adams's position was that Sinn Féin spoke for Sinn Féin and not the IRA and that the party was committed to the Mitchell Principles. George Mitchell describes the discussion as 'inconclusive' and he moved on to discuss the agenda for the talks, their timeline and so on. The next day, a CIRA bomb destroyed the centre of Markethill in County Armagh. The Ulster Unionists immediately demanded that Sinn Féin be expelled from the talks because of the *AP/RN* interview and the Markethill bomb. To press the point, along with the loyalist Progressive Unionist (PUP) and Ulster Democratic (UDP) parties, they re-entered the talks. For the first time, the Ulster Unionists were in a room with Sinn Féin, although the UUP refused to speak with the Sinn Féiners. After much discussion, it was determined that the comments in *AP/RN* were 'vague and obscure' and the Provisional IRA was not responsible for the Markethill bomb. Therefore, Sinn Féin had not violated the Mitchell Principles and the stage was finally set for substantive negotiations on the future of Ireland.[9]

The negotiations were organized around three themes or 'strands': political arrangements in Northern Ireland (Strand One); North–South relations (Strand Two); and the relationship between the Irish and British governments (Strand Three). The key players were the Ulster Unionists, Sinn Féin and the SDLP, plus representatives of the Dublin and London governments. The smaller parties involved included Alliance, the PUP and UDP, and the Northern Ireland Women's Coalition. George Mitchell would later write that Ian Paisley and Robert McCartney's decision to keep the DUP and UKUP out of the talks was probably the best thing that could have happened because, 'Their absence freed the UUP from daily attacks at the negotiating table, and gave the party room to negotiate that it might not otherwise have had.'[10]

The substantive negotiations were underway when the Provisional IRA met in convention that autumn. As presented in Ed Moloney's *A Secret History of the IRA*, Mickey McKevitt, Frank McGuinness and Seamus McGrane led the dissidents.[11] McGrane, the outgoing Chairman of the IRA Executive, argued that the Army Council had misled the Executive:

> [The] Executive expressed fears of a possible ceasefire being called. The Army Council chairman stated: 'There was no case for a ceasefire' and he didn't understand why it was even being discussed. We had only to wait a few weeks to see this commitment flounder. At the next meeting of the Executive the Army Council joined us. We were informed of the decision to call a ceasefire. We were informed that it was to be announced within 48 hours. Pressure was brought to bear on the Executive to support the decision. We were told to 'endorse it or go to a Convention'.[12]

Volunteers were confused and frustrated. There had been too many sacrifices to ignore what was happening. The key questions, then and now, were: was the Army Council intentionally confusing the rank and file so they could end the campaign without a split? And, if the Army Council's approach was intentional, when did they make that decision? McGrane's criticism was damning but the dissidents were outranked, outnumbered and out-manoeuvered.

The leadership of clandestine organizations is always open to speculation and misinformation. James Dingley, in a book entitled *The IRA: The Irish Republican Army*, somehow manages to present Dáithí O'Connell as a 'local figure' in the Belfast IRA and simultaneously a member of the Southern leadership.[13] Others have reported that O'Connell was once Provisional IRA Chief of Staff (C/S); he was, for a time, Chairman of the Army Council but he was never C/S. During the peace process, it was reported that Gerry Kelly was C/S and responsible for ending the 1994 ceasefire and that he was romantically involved with Martha Pope, an aide to George Mitchell.[14] Lawsuits led to apologies and retractions. Ed Moloney's *A Secret History of the IRA* is considered the authoritative account on the Provisional IRA leadership at this time. According to Moloney, the Army Council after the 1997 Convention consisted of Gerry Adams, Martin McGuinness, Pat Doherty, Martin Ferris, Brian Keenan, Tom Murphy and one other person. It appears that the critics' main victim was Kevin McKenna, who observers say was replaced as Chief of Staff by Tom Murphy.[15]

The available evidence suggests that Seamus McGrane, Mickey McKevitt and Frank McGuinness were re-elected to the Executive only to resign in November 1997. They then met with supporters at a location in County Meath and organized the 'Real' IRA – nicknamed the 'Cokes' because they are the real thing. John Mooney and Michael O'Toole, in *Black Operations*, report that the leaders of this third IRA included: Frank McGuinness (Chief of Staff), Mickey McKevitt (Quartermaster), Seamus McGrane (Director of Training), Liam Campbell (Director of Operations for Northern Ireland) and Pascal Burke (Director of Finance). Before long, the press was reporting there had been as many as forty resignations from the Provisional IRA, many of them from the engineering and quartermaster departments.[16]

In 1969 and 1986, the IRA splits were played out in public through Sinn Féin and the same thing happened in 1997. Disenchanted Provisionals organized a conference in Fingal, North County Dublin. Those in attendance are described as sharing 'a common concern regarding the failure of the current peace talks to tackle the key issue of 32 County Sovereignty. Indeed it was felt that the peace-talks, based on the Mitchell and Joint Frameworks documents which guarantee a unionist veto, will ensure an internal Six-County settlement and prohibit the possibility of an end to partition.'[17] The critics re-examined events, trying to figure out what went wrong. Val Lynch joined Dublin Sinn Féin after Bloody Sunday when the Provisionals were at a high point and activists believed they would win. Lynch commented: *'I thought when the campaign got underway that this was going to be the final campaign because we had the support of the people then, particularly in the North – people that were under duress, harassment, all that sort of stuff, and then the loyalist mobs as well.'* The Provisionals did not win. The campaign continued and at some point the Adams–McGuinness leadership changed direction. The result was the Downing Street Declaration, two unilateral ceasefires and the Mitchell Principles. Many activists see the Bobby Sands election as a turning point. Val Lynch again:

So as the war progressed then – then there was all sorts of stuff began to creep in, like the political scenario and the agendas, hidden agendas began to sort of manifest. Maybe not greatly but they did.

Q: What would be the hidden agenda?

A: Well the hidden agenda, in my estimation, would be – when Bobby Sands was fielded as a candidate and the support that was seen then, that amounted from that campaign, I think the Republican Movement in the North of Ireland decided that there was a political scenario here that was going to suit them somewhere along the line. And then Owen Carron follows on from Bobby Sands and I think the same thing occurred then – and that full support. And then there were issues of abstentionism. So the republican leadership was mainly Southern-based then. So, in my estimation then, a lot of the people in the North who were classified as fairly close to the core of things in the North decided that they were going to go down the political trail. Well then, they may have had to get rid of the old rearguard. So, with the result, the question of abstentionism arose. And, knowing that that wouldn't be acceptable by the republican leadership of the South here, it was pressed ahead and pushed ahead. So, with the result, into [the] 1986 Ard Fheis ... it was decided to abolish abstentionism.

Q: Would you have supported that?

A: I was an advocate of refusing to recognize the whole partition of the country. But, with a majority of the vote and that the war was going to carry on, I saw it only as a tool to further the campaign. But that didn't, unfortunately, come about. Ruairí Ó Brádaigh and company, they all walked out, as you know, and formed themselves into what is today called Republican Sinn Féin. Now we didn't really know that the agenda was to get rid of the old rearguard, get rid of the old leadership, then bring the reins of power back to Belfast ...

Q: And would you have supported that up through –

A: Yes, but not knowing that there was something else in mind. Something else in mind being that a political settlement was going to arise out of all that.[18]

With the benefit of hindsight, Adams and McGuinness and company had used dropping abstentionism as a ploy to get rid of Ruairí Ó Brádaigh, Dáithí O'Connell and others who would never settle for less than a British declaration of intent to withdraw. The Fingal Conference created the '32 County Sovereignty Committee', which they said was a pressure group within Sinn Féin dedicated to upholding 'the Declaration of Independence as Proclaimed by Dáil Éireann on January 21st 1919'.

Figure 8 presents the reported founding 'Executive' of the '32 County Sovereignty Committee'.[19] The most prominent member was probably Bernadette Sands, Bobby Sands's sister who would later marry Mickey McKevitt. The senior people included Joe Dillon, a reported founder member of Saor Éire in the 1960s,[20] and Phil O'Donoghue, who was on the Brookeborough Raid in 1957. O'Donoghue was asked about his involvement:

Officers:

Michael Ahern, Chairperson	County Carlow
Bernadette Sands-McKevitt, Vice-Chair	Belfast/Dundalk
Fra Browne, Secretary	Dundalk
Val Lynch, Treasurer	Dublin City
Beatrice Ní Shearbhain, Treasurer	County Kildare
Joe Dillon, Public Relations Officer	County Dublin
Mick Burke, Organizer	Cork

Committee Members:

Rory Dougan	Co. Armagh/Co. Louth
Art O'Shearbheain	County Kildare
Eamonn Flanagan	Tyrone/County Dublin
Pat Farrell	Dundalk
Julie Byrne-Ahern	County Carlow
Gerry McNamara	County Dublin
Pat O'Donnell	Tipperary
Phil O'Donoghue	Dublin/Kilkenny
Francie Mackey	Omagh, Tyrone

FIGURE 8

32 County Sovereignty Committee Executive, November 1997

from day one I couldn't accept this Mitchell Principles. I just couldn't do it. And I was asked to go to a Sinn Féin meeting and at that meeting I couldn't accept what they were talking about. So some of us there went off; we just heard it and that was time to do something about it ... The way I look at it is that, in the twenty-six counties, they fought a very, very bitter civil war on this issue, and then for them to come along and to accept the Crown was just unacceptable. Simple as that.[21]

The Northerners on the committee were Bernadette Sands, Rory Dougan, Eamonn Flanagan and Francie Mackey, although Sands and Dougan lived in Dundalk. Mackey had represented Sinn Féin on the Omagh town council since 1985.

The '32 County Sovereignty Committee' was a direct challenge to the Sinn Féin leadership. In *A Farther Shore*, Gerry Adams writes that those involved were told that it was 'incompatible' with membership in Sinn Féin.[22] Joe Dillon commented on this: *'We were actually given an opportunity to leave Sovereignty or be suspended. And we pointed out that the Sovereignty Movement could not be a threat to Sinn Féin but was singularly a one-issue movement, that the Irish nation was sovereign, right?'*[23] Committee members were suspended and then expelled from Sinn Féin; their view is that they were expelled illegally. They renamed themselves the '32 County Sovereignty Movement' (32 CSM).

When the splits became public, there was speculation that the disenchanted would come together, form a powerful counter to the Provisionals and undermine the peace process. The threat was exaggerated. The political decisions that separated them in 1986 were still important. The Continuity IRA and Republican Sinn Féin were still opposed to 'constitutionalism' and believed that, by refusing to go along with dropping abstentionism, they had remained revolutionary. Des Long, the reported Chief of Staff of the Continuity IRA, and Ruairí Ó Brádaigh, met with members of the 32 CSM.[24] Ruairí Ó Brádaigh had this to say: *'it was not an official delegation. Des Long and I just went to Dundalk to investigate the situation. We did not meet with the leadership, and we just had a conversation. We wanted to find out what they were about. And we laid out our position. Just made it clear.'*[25] Long and Ó Brádaigh were not interested in compromising on abstentionism. On the other side, Real IRA and 32 County Sovereignty activists had their own reservations. Some of them were upset that they had supported the war effort for more than a decade while RSF and the CIRA were, it seemed, missing in action. Others thought Ó Brádaigh and Long had made a mistake in 1986 and that they should have been more flexible. Phil O'Donaghue discussed this:

when we joined up [in the 1950s] we were constantly being told by the leadership, including Ruairí, that unity was the goal, that our strength was in our unity. And this business of breaking up didn't suit, switch me on at all. But it was a bad timing on their part to pull out ... I had known Ruairí a long time. When we set up the Sovereignty Movement a week later I made approaches. And he would have had great influence within the Sovereignty Movement. You know, he could have had – our constitution would have left him room to manoeuvre and he didn't take full advantage of it, which is my criticism. But it was an awful pity because he had plenty of ability. It was just unfortunate that he didn't take advantage of it ... Ruairí had his own views and I didn't necessarily agree with them [laughs] ... I don't mind a person being rigid but, Jesus, you have to size up the situation today and say, whether we like it or not, we have to go down that road there to get to the objective.[26]

The founders of the 32 CSM did not necessarily support taking seats in Leinster House but they did accept the vote in 1986. Ó Brádaigh and the others had participated in the vote but refused to accept the result. Joe Dillon disagreed with the approach: *'I don't like that. I've never liked – I didn't like it in history. I didn't like it when I joined the Movement myself. I don't like it today. In my opinion, if you take part in a vote, you either accept the winning or the losing of the vote. And I think that's where Ruairí made a mistake.*[27] Refusing to accept the legitimacy of the parliaments in Dublin and Belfast was essential for RSF and CIRA supporters. The 32 County Sovereignty activists were more flexible. They were not interested in contesting elections but, by not walking out in 1986, they had gone along with recognizing Dáil Éireann. What was essential for one group was 'rigid' thinking for the other. The four organizations would peacefully co-exist but they would not merge.

In December 1997, a Sinn Féin delegation that included Gerry Adams, Martin McGuinness, Martin Ferris and Michelle Gildernew, met with Tony Blair and Mo Mowlam in London.[28] The previous Sinn Féin delegation to visit Number 10 Downing Street had included Michael Collins and Arthur Griffith. The split had weakened the Provisional IRA but strengthened Sinn Féin. The departure of the disenchanted made it easier to pursue peace. The split also gave Adams and McGuinness some leeway in the negotiations because it showed the two governments that they had to go slowly or there would be more splits. In his memoir, *A Journey: My Political Life*, Tony Blair writes:

> Throughout, the fear of Gerry and Martin was a split, as had happened before to Republicanism, with disastrous consequences. *This meant taking their people step by step, leading them, cajoling them and not always being totally upfront as to what the destination really meant* (emphasis added). It was a tough task and they performed it with immense skill.[29]

Blair also contrasted the negotiating styles of Adams and Sinn Féin and David Trimble and the UUP:

> Here was a strange phenomenon about the difference between the two sides. When you saw the Republicans, you saw unity in motion. They had a line; they took it; they held it. If it appeared to modify in the course of a meeting, it was an illusion – the modification had been pre-built into the line, and the line was sustained. Gerry Adams was the leader. You would no more have had one of the delegation raising eyebrows during his remarks, let alone uttering words of dissent, than you would have had Ian Paisley leading a rousing chorus of 'Danny Boy'. Per contra, the UUP had the most alarming way of conducting meetings. You would think you had them all jolly and sorted and then one of them, usually not the leader, would make a depressing or downbeat comment and helter-skelter they would all follow in leaping off the cliff. Even more alarmingly, it could happen on the most apparently minor issue. As for supporting their leader, they didn't regard that as their job. At all.[30]

The Sinn Féin negotiating team, led by Gerry Adams, included Martin McGuinness, Lucilita Bhreatnach, Bairbre de Brún, Ted Howell, Gerry Kelly, Richard McAuley, Mitchel McLaughlin,

Siobhán O'Hanlon and Joe Reilly. Their ability to work together was probably helped by the fact that the unionists refused to speak with them. Other than a brief exchange in a restroom, David Trimble and Gerry Adams never spoke to each other.[31] Trimble also tried to avoid Mo Mowlam, who he believed was biased in favour of nationalists.

External events also strained the negotiations. At the end of 1997, INLA prisoners in Long Kesh smuggled in pistols and killed Billy Wright, the prominent Mid-Ulster loyalist. Wright's assassination helped fuel an especially violent period when, between the first of the year and the end of March 1998, loyalists, including Wright's Loyalist Volunteer Force, killed seven Catholics. The INLA killed a loyalist, a former member of the RUC and a Protestant civilian. The Provisional IRA killed Brendan Campbell, an alleged drug dealer technically killed by 'Direct Action Against Drugs', and Robert Dougan, a loyalist allegedly involved in killing Catholics. The Continuity IRA and the Real IRA set off car bombs in Enniskillen, Moira and Portadown, and an incendiary device destroyed a factory in Belfast.

Because of the violence, the loyalist UDP was temporarily excluded from the talks in January 1998. After Robert Dougan was killed, Sinn Féin was excluded for seventeen days. Mo Mowlam was essential in holding things together. After Billy Wright was killed, loyalist prisoners in Long Kesh withdrew their support for the peace process. David Trimble met with them but was unable to bring them back on board. A personal visit from Mowlam was more successful and, in George Mitchell's assessment, her intervention 'kept the process intact'.[32] Mowlam also helped convince Tony Blair to set up another inquiry into Bloody Sunday (the Saville Inquiry) and she helped establish an independent Parades Commission to mediate disputes like Drumcree.[33]

Tony Blair writes that the negotiations 'staggered' into early April.[34] Up to the last minute, it appeared they would fail. Then, after a flurry of activity, on Friday 10 April 1998, they concluded with the signing of the 'Good Friday Agreement' (GFA; or, the 'Belfast Agreement'). Under the GFA, there would be significant political changes in the Republic of Ireland, the United Kingdom and Northern Ireland, including:

1. Articles 2 and 3 of the Irish Constitution would be revised so that they no longer claimed the entire island for the Dublin government. A changed Constitution would state, 'It is the firm will of the Irish nation ... to unite all the people who share the territory of the island of Ireland ... recognising that a united Ireland shall be brought about only by peaceful means with the consent of the majority of the people, democratically expressed, in both jurisdictions of the island';

2. The Government of Ireland Act (1949), which guaranteed that Northern Ireland's status could not change without the consent of the Northern Irish parliament, would be replaced with legislation reflecting the 'consent principle'. If a majority of the people of Northern Ireland wanted a united Ireland 'that wish should be given effect';

3. Government would be devolved from London to a 108-member Northern Ireland Assembly that would also establish a North–South Ministerial Council;

4. A British–Irish council would be created that included members of the Northern Ireland assembly and the Dublin government, among others;

5. Prisoners convicted of terrorist offenses would be released within two years;

6. An independent commission would make recommendations on policing in Northern Ireland; and

7. All parties would work to achieve the decommissioning of all paramilitary weapons within two years after the people of Northern Ireland and the Republic of Ireland supported the Good Friday Agreement in separate referenda.

Power sharing was embedded in the Northern Ireland Assembly; elected representatives designate themselves 'nationalist' or 'unionist' and major decisions require cross-community support.[35] Critics argue that the cross-community support requirement reduces the GFA to a sectarian settlement and places an obstacle in the way of class-based politics.[36]

In *Northern Ireland: A Chronology of the Troubles*, Sir Paul Bew and Gordon Gillespie summarize the GFA with:

> Given the conflicting agendas and mutual suspicions of those involved in the talks, it was hardly surprising that the final agreement was characterized by safeguards, vetoes, and some areas of ambiguity. The core of the agreement, however, was unambiguous: the Union of Great Britain and Northern Ireland would continue as long as it was supported by a majority of the people in Northern Ireland. In return for this acceptance by the British and, crucially, the Irish government and other nationalists, unionists were required to accept power-sharing and cross-border co-operation. Perhaps the most difficult area for unionists, however, was that, in return for the ending of the IRA campaign of violence and *de facto* acceptance of the legitimacy of the North's position within the United Kingdom, they had to allow Sinn Féin a 'soft landing'. In practice this soft landing was likely to focus on the contentious issues of the release of prisoners and the decommissioning of weapons.[37]

The SDLP's Seamus Mallon described the GFA as 'Sunningdale for slow learners'. The republican disenchanted described it as 'GFA – Got Fuck All'.

Although there were serious reservations among the Ulster Unionists, David Trimble argued that the Union was safe and that the GFA was proof that the Provisionals had failed. The Ulster Unionist Executive and the Ulster Unionist Council (by a vote of 540 to 210) endorsed the GFA. So did the paramilitary Ulster Defence Association and the Ulster Freedom Fighters. Revd Ian Paisley and the DUP, Robert McCartney and the UKUP, and the Orange Order refused to endorse the GFA.[38]

The vast majority of Irish nationalists supported the Good Friday Agreement but Irish republicans were divided. Republican Sinn Féin rejected the GFA outright and *Saoirse*'s headline declared, 'Provos to enter Stormont'. The accompanying article reminded readers of Martin McGuinness's promise in 1986, 'I can give a commitment on behalf of the leadership that we have no intention of going into Stormont or Westminster.'[39] The 32 CSM also rejected the GFA. Val Lynch commented: *'Again, back to whatever the people in the North thought, I felt the people here in the South could never become part of the Good Friday Agreement because we had attained or achieved nothing – nothing of what we had set out for, and that was a thirty-two-county, independent, Gaelic and free Ireland.* [40]

Joe Dillon drafted an appeal to the United Nations, arguing that Britain's colonial policy, historically and with the GFA, infringed on Irish sovereignty and violated various covenants, including the UN Declaration on the Granting of Independence to Colonial Countries and Peoples. Rory Dougan and Bernadette Sands-McKevitt then travelled to New York and, with the assistance of Martin Galvin, delivered the document to the United Nations. Joe Dillon described the appeal:

> *We felt it was necessary to immediately establish the sovereignty of the nation, lay out the documentation, preparing a file and send a delegation to the United Nations to lodge that before the referendum was held so it would have force. We're not just disenfranchised with Adams now or the Dublin government. We got in touch with the Dublin government on this issue and the Sinn Féin leadership and we made it clear to them, both of them had failed to protect the constitutional position.* [41]

It was a well-crafted argument and, to the surprise of the British and Irish governments, United Nations officials received the document. [42]

On the heels of Sands and Dougan's visit to the United Nations, the Real IRA suffered their first casualty. Gardaí interrupted the robbery of a Securicor van in County Wicklow and Rónán MacLochlain was shot dead. He was the father of three young children. Gerry Adams expressed his 'heartfelt sympathy' for the family and Sinn Féin supported an inquiry into the 'shoot to kill operation'. A Provisional IRA statement, however, claimed that, 'no volunteers in Óglaigh na hÉireann were involved in the incident' and that, 'No one outside our organisation is authorised to use the name of Óglaigh na hÉireann in any attempt to confer legitimacy on their actions.' MacLochlain was given a paramilitary funeral and buried in Glasnevin Cemetery, Dublin. Francie Mackey, who had become Chairman of the 32 CSM, offered the oration. As Mackey described it, Rónán MacLochlain *was* an IRA volunteer: 'As a true republican, Rónán remained loyal and true to the constitution of Óglaigh na hÉireann when others used and usurped that constitution.' [43]

Two days after the funeral, there was a mortar attack on an RUC station in Belleek, County Fermanagh. The Real IRA took responsibility for the attack and formally announced their existence. [44] The Real IRA was just getting started.

There was also opposition to the Good Friday Agreement within Sinn Féin. [45] An Ard Fheis was organized for mid-April but the GFA was so controversial that voting was deferred to an 'Extraordinary' Ard Fheis scheduled for May. At the first Ard Fheis, Gerry Adams and Martin McGuinness offered 'keynote' addresses. Adams echoed Michael Collins and the Treaty debates and argued that the GFA was 'a basis for advancement'. McGuinness admitted that, 'A united Ireland was not attainable in this phase' but argued that, 'The union has undoubtedly been weakened.' More than seventy delegates offered comments. *AP/RN*'s report has Pat Doherty describing the GFA as containing 'manifest dangers'. Joe Cahill is quoted as saying, 'Don't be afraid of change' and 'Whatever changes may come in the future, I guarantee they will not cause us any problems.'[46] A *Sunday Tribune* poll showed that only 42 per cent of those in attendance supported taking seats in a Northern Ireland Assembly and only 44 per cent of those in attendance supported the Good Friday Agreement.[47]

The Extraordinary Ard Fheis in May could have been a disaster. If Sinn Féin rejected the GFA, then the leadership would have been in the awkward position of having to oppose a deal they had negotiated. And if the Irish people, North and South, then endorsed the GFA in the referenda, the peace process would go forward without them. At some point the British would devolve power from London, the Northern Ireland Assembly would be re-established and they would be left out in the cold with nothing to show for years of hard work and compromise. Their positions in the leadership would be damaged beyond repair.

Following the first Ard Fheis, a statement from the Provisional IRA reassured the Sinn Féin membership on the decommissioning issue: 'Let us make it clear that there will be no decommissioning by the IRA.'[48] At the Extraordinary Ard Fheis, Mo Mowlam and the Dublin government gave the leadership an assist. The commanding officers of the prisoners, Padraig Wilson in Long Kesh, Geraldine Ferrity in Maghaberry and Mick O'Brien in Portlaoise, were granted temporary parole so they could attend. And, after almost twenty-three long years in England, the most notorious prisoners of them all, the 'Balcombe Street Gang', were transferred to Portlaoise and released on parole so they could attend. The delegates gave Eddie Butler, Hugh Doherty, Harry Duggan and Joe O'Connell a ten-minute standing ovation when they entered the hall.[49] Unionists were horrified to see the people who had terrorized London given such a reception.[50] The implications were clear – unionists would have to live with the fact that the GFA would release criminal terrorists, Provisional and loyalist. The implications were also clear for the Sinn Féin delegates. The prisoners' freedom was hanging in the balance – they could be free in two years or not.

Two motions were on the agenda. In spite of having promised it would never happen, the first motion would change Sinn Féin's Constitution so that members could take seats in a Northern Ireland Assembly. By this point, the people who would have been most upset by the compromise had left the Provisionals, in 1986 or 1997. The people who were still involved and had reservations believed the leadership had earned the right to compromise. A Limerick delegate commented:

> *I believe most sincerely that Gerry Adams, Martin McGuinness and the rest of the leadership fully believed in what they were doing – a huge commitment. You're not going to find me, like some people – some misguided people do – calling the leadership traitors. I don't believe that. I think it's not really looking at the dynamics that are taking place. Once you set yourself down the road of the peace agreement, and that happened earlier than '98 – once you had gone down that road, the logical conclusion had to be when people had been fighting for thirty years, the war weariness within the communities in the northeastern part of our country was bound to lead to the fact that they wanted peace. Who wouldn't? Who wouldn't want to be able to walk their streets without fear of being shot? Who wouldn't want to be able to send their kids out to play and know that they were going to come back in, in a safe condition? I mean, it was a no-brainer, right?[51]*

The vote on the first motion was not even close. Of 350 delegates, 331 (94 per cent) agreed that Sinn Féin representatives could participate in the Northern Ireland Assembly.[52] Sinn Féin was a fully constitutional political party – albeit with a private army.

The second motion called for a 'Yes' vote in the referenda on the GFA, which in effect would endorse the Agreement and support changing the Irish Constitution. That was the more contested issue since for decades Articles 2 and 3 had frustrated Irish republicans. Because the Dublin government did not enforce its claim to the entire island, the articles were only symbols. They were important symbols, however. The Limerick republican commented:

> *the removal of Articles 2 and 3 from the Constitution, the Free State Constitution, while they didn't mean anything to republicans, basically, what they did do was give solace to people in the South that were nationalists and could view the North as part of our country and looked to as rightfully belonging to a thirty-two county island. By removing that, you gave the unionists, for the first time, their right to remain British – which was never there. … the only thing that we had besides the historical and the actual fact that the North is in Ireland, the only thing that lay claim to that was Articles 2 and 3, and they were given up too easily. They were given up in the referendum.*[53]

Even if they were concerned about the GFA, the delegates trusted the leadership. Davy Hyland was a Sinn Féiner in Newry and when asked if he supported the Good Friday Agreement, he replied, *'I voted against it.'* Hyland also remained active in Sinn Féin:

> *I had misgivings about it and thought long and hard about it. To me, the Good Friday Agreement is built all around the concept of consent. And it was the consent of all the people within this artificially created land of ours, the six-county state. And to me that proved very difficult. The idea that we could consent to something that we were diametrically opposed to in the beginning and from the 1920s onwards. And I know the Sinn Féin leadership foisted this whole idea that we must win over our unionist neighbours and our unionist brothers and sisters. And I had no problems with that but I thought that it was illusionary to think that we were going to convince unionists, who by definition were unionists and wanted to remain part of the union, that their long-term goals and aspirations laid with a united Ireland. However, at the time, and I think many others around me, we were fed a line that this was another step in the road to freedom and we would have to go it bit by bit, and we should have great faith in our leadership. And I have to say, at the time, I would have said, to me Adams and McGuinness did seem very good leaders.*[54]

An Phoblacht/Republican News reports that a majority of the delegates voted 'Yes'. Unfortunately, it appears that the details of the count have never been made public.[55]

The vast majority of the Irish people wanted peace and in separate referenda, on 21 May 1998, they endorsed the Good Friday Agreement. In Northern Ireland, 676,966 people (71.1 per cent) voted 'Yes'. Exit polls showed that 96 per cent of Catholics but only 55 per cent of Protestants supported the Agreement. In the Republic of Ireland, 1,442,583 people (94.4 per cent) voted 'Yes'.[56]

Gerry Adams and Martin McGuinness, with the help of many people, had ended an unwinnable war that was destroying their community. They also transformed Sinn Féin so the party could provide a constitutional political voice for that community in a reformed Northern Ireland and in the Republic of Ireland. And, through it all, the Provisionals had managed to hold onto the weapons that were essential to their identity as defenders and freedom fighters. Even if returning to war was not really an option, those weapons would help them police their community, defend their community from loyalists and provide a symbolic security blanket for all those Provisionals who refused to believe they had lost the war. Those weapons would also keep them out of government.

Understanding the 1997 Split

The splits of 1986 and 1997 were caused by fundamental differences in the beliefs of Irish republicans. In both splits, where people lived (geographic location) was an indicator of shared political beliefs and social interaction among sub-groups of activists.[57]

The Real IRA's founders lived along the east coast of Ireland, in an area that stretched from South Armagh to Dublin. Evidently many of them were involved in a South-to-North munitions operation along the coast. Observers report that Liam Campbell, Seamus McGrane, Mickey McKevitt, Pascal Burke and Frank McGuinness were in the founding IRA leadership. Campbell, McGrane and McKevitt were from County Louth; Burke and McGuinness were Dubliners. The organizational structure of the Provisional IRA reinforced their personal connections. The engineering and quartermaster departments were attached to General Headquarters and, therefore, separate from the top-down structure that ran from the Army Council to the active service units and the civil administration. Within these two departments, activists worked together on a daily basis procuring, manufacturing, hiding and dispensing materials. They had served together for years, had tight social connections and were relatively independent.

It is telling that the 32 County Executive Committee was founded in North Dublin and their story is much the same. Of sixteen people, nine of them lived in or were originally from Counties Louth or Dublin, or Dublin City (see Figure 8). None of them lived in Belfast.

The people who created the Real IRA and the 32 CSM sympathized with the suffering of Northern nationalists. Their goal, however, was a united Ireland and they realized that the Mitchell Principles would lead to a reformed Northern Ireland where most of them did not live. The GFA reduced the Republic of Ireland's claim on a united Ireland where they did live. In 1986, they believed Martin McGuinness when he promised the war would continue 'until freedom is achieved'. Between 1994 and 1997, they came to the conclusion that they were being lied to.[58] Adding to the sense of betrayal was the realization that, while they were taking risks smuggling, making and hiding weapons, the leadership was pursuing peace. They lived relatively near each other and that made it relatively easy for them to meet and reinforce their concerns. In summary, the commitment to a united Ireland among a group of Southern Irish republicans was regularly reinforced by social interaction. When they saw the Provisionals settling for less than that they refused to go along with it.

20

WINNING THE PEACE (1998–2005)

We have won the war, now let us win the peace.

– Joe Cahill (2003)[1]

But like all sensible people who resort to armed struggle because they feel there is no alternative he was prepared to defend, support and promote other options when these were available. Without doubt there would not be a peace process today without Joe Cahill.

– Gerry Adams on the death of Joe Cahill (2004)[2]

Correct me if I am wrong but my understanding of winning a war is when the Victor accepts the symbolic sword of surrender from the defeated who then sits down to be told the conditions they will accept. No ifs or buts if you are the losers. Why then if 'we (Provisionals) won the war' are the Provisional Sinn Fein Party still begging the 'defeated' (Brits I suppose) for more talks, for the re-establishment of the British Assembly at Stormont, for money and, oh yes please, their jobs back! Not my idea of having won a war. Suppose they had lost the war, where would we all be today? Doesn't bear thinking about!

– Dolours Price on the death of Joe Cahill (2004)[3]

The Good Friday Agreement was a triumph for David Trimble. Sinn Féin not only agreed to the principle of unionist consent, but they were also willing to participate in a Northern Ireland Assembly, a British institution they had pledged time and time again they would never enter. And yet, Trimble's unionist critics were outraged that he had negotiated with Sinn Féin, saw power-sharing as a loss and claimed the North–South Ministerial Council was a fast-track to a united Ireland. Worse, more change was on the way, including a review of *their* defenders in the RUC led by Chris Patten. Trimble, understandably, insisted on IRA decommissioning before Sinn Féin could enter the Assembly – 'No guns, no government'.[4] But, over a six-year period, he would be forced to compromise and his standing among unionists would fall. At the same time, Trimble would slowly but surely draw Sinn Féin deeper into constitutional politics, and the deeper they went, the more the Provisional IRA became a liability. David Trimble probably did more to secure the Union than anyone else, though he would lose out to Paisley. It all began with an election to the new Northern Ireland Assembly, on 25 June 1998.

The SDLP topped the poll and won the second-most seats (twenty-four).[5] The Ulster Unionists won the most seats (thirty) and finished second in votes. Under the 'parallel consent formula' David Trimble (DUP) and Seamus Mallon (SDLP) were elected First Minister and Deputy First Minister, respectively, of the Northern Ireland Executive. In both communities, however, the moderates lost ground. In combination, Paisley's DUP (twenty seats) and Robert McCartney's UKUP (five seats) received more votes than the Ulster Unionists of Trimble. In the nationalist community, Sinn Féin (eighteen seats) again increased their vote and the SDLP majority among nationalists was reduced.

The moderates also had to contend with the old habits of the extremists. Mickey Donnelly was one of the 'Hooded Men' and well known among Derry republicans. During the election campaign for the new Northern Ireland Assembly, Donnelly accused Sinn Féin of selling out and it cost them votes. *After* the election, a gang of Provisionals broke his legs.[6] In late June of 1998, the new Parades Commission banned the Orange Order's march down the Garvaghy Road. Another standoff at Drumcree fuelled sectarian tension and a firebomb was tossed into the home of Christine Quinn, a Catholic living in a Protestant estate in Ballymoney. Her three young sons died in the inferno.[7] At the beginning of August, a Real IRA car bomb in Banbridge injured thirty-one people and caused £4 million in damages.[8] Two weeks later, Northern Ireland suffered another atrocity.

On the afternoon of Saturday 15 August 1998, shoppers were out and about in Omagh town when telephone warnings gave vague information about another car bomb.[9] The RUC moved people towards the bomb not away from it, and twenty-nine people were killed – Catholics and Protestants, toddlers, teenagers and the elderly – no one was spared. The casualties included a pregnant mother carrying twins and a Spanish exchange student, his teacher and three of their young Irish hosts. The Real IRA accepted responsibility for the bomb and claimed their warning had been clear: 'Despite media reports it was not our intention at any time to kill civilians. It was a commercial target, part of an ongoing war against the Brits. We offer apologies to the civilians.' It was the deadliest bomb in the history of Northern Ireland and in the immediate aftermath there was no tolerance for anything or anyone associated with paramilitary violence. Gerry Adams was 'horrified' and Martin McGuinness was 'appalled and disgusted'. The INLA announced a complete ceasefire and it became public that Provisionals had visited the homes of 32 CSM activists and threatened that 'action will be taken' if they did not call a ceasefire and quit speaking against the peace process. The Dublin and London governments quickly passed legislation that made it easier to confront terrorists.

The Omagh bomb seriously damaged the Real IRA and 32 CSM, and it effectively destroyed any chance for anti-GFA republicans to mount serious opposition to the Provisionals. But the way the Provisionals distanced themselves from the bomb actually helped with the recruitment of some of the disenchanted. Marian Price was interviewed in 2010:

> *I didn't join the 32s until 1998, actually after Omagh … I was contacted by Francie Mackey and Bernadette McKevitt because I had – there was some public meetings here in Belfast and I had expressed my concern about the road that Sinn Féin were going down. And certainly I was totally opposed to the so-called Good Friday Agreement, which I saw as a total sellout and I was fairly vocal about that, not because I wanted to be any sort of politician or to be out there – but I felt that, as a republican, I had to have it on record that all republicans were not happy with the way things were going. So they contacted me and we went and we had a long talk and we exchanged views and then they asked would I like to be part of the movement that they were embarking upon and I said, 'Yeah, I'd give it a go.' And they seemed like sincere people.*

'Widespread condemnation' does not do justice to the reaction caused by the Omagh bomb. Mickey and Bernadette McKevitt, for example, were forced from their home and had to abandon their printing business in Dundalk. Marian Price commented on joining the 32 CSM:

> *Q: After Omagh, there must have been very few people who were willing to get involved in that organization.*
>
> *A: Oh, absolutely. Yeah. But my view was that Omagh was very much used against republicans who didn't agree with the Sinn Féin line. But my view was that any IRA operation could have ended up in an Omagh and therefore what was the difference? And I didn't see any difference between what happened at Omagh and what happened on Bloody Friday in Belfast or what happened at La Mon or what happened at Enniskillen. Okay, the body count was higher but the actual operations were the same. They were awful tragedies where innocent civilians lost their lives and I wasn't going to be a hypocrite the way Gerry Adams and Martin McGuinness are to come out and condemn Omagh while at the same time being part and parcel of what happened at La Mon, Bloody Friday and Enniskillen and say that's okay because we were in charge then but this isn't okay because we'd taken a different path.[10]*

The Real IRA went on a ceasefire in early September which left only the Continuity IRA in the field.[11] They kept a low profile and, over the next year and a half, They kept a low profile and, over the next year and a half, anti-GFA Republicans were responsible for only two gun attacks on RUC stations.

The Omagh bomb seemingly moved the peace process forward. Gerry Adams stated that Sinn Féin was committed to 'exclusively peaceful and democratic means' and it was announced that Martin McGuinness would be their representative to the Independent International Commission on Decommissioning (IICD). David Trimble and the UUP agreed to meet with Adams and Sinn Féin; the unionist and Sinn Féin leadership had last met in 1923.[12] Unfortunately, the Sinn Féin–UUP relationship went downhill from there. The Northern Ireland Assembly met to select a 'shadow' Executive and develop structures of government so that power could be devolved from London. Instead of progress, as Seamus Mallon described it, there was a 'battle of words'.[13]

The Provisionals refused to move on decommissioning and Trimble and the UUP faced a constant barrage from anti-Agreement Unionists. At the DUP's annual conference, held in Omagh in November 1998, Revd Ian Paisley lashed out at Trimble with, 'Of him who professes to be a dedicated ally but who goes over to the enemy because of personal advantages, no words in any language are adequate to describe. He is a liar, a cheat, a hypocrite, a knave, a thief, a loathsome reptile which needs to be scotched.'[14] This was just after Trimble and John Hume had been awarded the Nobel Peace Prize.

On the other side, the Provisionals kept giving David Trimble good reason to stick with his 'No guns, no government' approach. Eamon Collins was a supergrass who retracted his evidence but later wrote a tell-all book about his experiences, *Killing Rage*. He also offered testimony against Tom 'Slab' Murphy in a libel case.[15] In January 1999, Collins was found lying by the side of a road outside Newry. He had been beaten and stabbed to death. Trimble was not going to create a 'mafia state' with Sinn Féin in government and a fully armed IRA by their side.[16] After Trimble promised the Ulster Unionist Council that Sinn Féin would not be allowed ministerial positions without IRA decommissioning, the Assembly endorsed the basic structures of government.[17] Trimble refused to take the next step and form an Executive.

Early in the summer of 1999, and with the support of Mo Mowlam, the nationalist parties tried to form a government. The unionists refused to go along with it and the result was an SDLP–Sinn Féin Executive that, under the cross-community requirements of the Good Friday Agreement, collapsed.[18] Seamus Mallon resigned as Deputy First Minister designate and called on David Trimble to do the same. Trimble declined but Mowlam adjourned the Assembly and that triggered an automatic review of the GFA, which George Mitchell agreed to direct. Trimble's refusal to let Sinn Féin into government was again vindicated.

The Gardaí and the FBI broke up an IRA gun-smuggling scheme in Florida and Charles Bennett, an alleged informer, was shot dead in Belfast.[19] And yet, from their perspective, the unionists lost more political ground. They demanded that Sinn Féin be excluded from the Assembly and Mo Mowlam turned them down. Then the Patten Commission released its report, *A New Beginning: Policing in Northern Ireland*. The proposals included renaming the Royal Ulster Constabulary the 'Police Service Northern Ireland', recruiting new officers on a 50/50-Catholic/Protestant basis, a Police Ombudsman and a Policing Board with community representation. For unionists, a reformed and renamed RUC was a loss – the RUC had defended them from a terrorist onslaught. David Trimble referred to the report as 'the most shoddy piece of work I have seen in my entire life'. Four hundred thousand people signed a petition requesting the RUC keep its name. [20] Sinn Féin's position was that 'nothing less than disbandment' of the RUC was acceptable. In the autumn of 1999, Tony Blair replaced Mo Mowlam with Peter Mandelson and the unionists were glad to see her go.[21]

In the meantime, George Mitchell had consulted with everyone except the DUP, who refused to participate. Mitchell proposed a 'sequence of events' that linked decommissioning with the devolution of government: a Northern Ireland Executive would be nominated; the Assembly would be instituted; and the Provisional IRA would appoint 'authorised representatives' who would work with John de Chastelain to decommission weapons by the end of January 2000.[22]

If the IRA did not decommission, the British would suspend the Executive and the Assembly. The SDLP, Alliance and Sinn Féin supported the plan. To get the Ulster Unionists on board, Trimble promised to the Ulster Unionist Council that he would resign if the Provisionals did not decommission.

The plan was implemented and Seamus Mallon was reinstated as Deputy First Minister Designate. Ministers for the Executive were selected through a d'Hondt method that allocated seats on a proportional basis – in this case, four ministers to the UUP, three to the SDLP and two each for the DUP and Sinn Féin.[23] The House of Lords and the House of Commons approved the devolution order and a series of political changes were triggered: the North–South Ministerial Council and the British–Irish Ministerial Council were established; the Anglo-Irish Agreement (1985) was replaced by the British–Irish Agreement (1999); and the Irish Constitution was changed to reflect the deletion of Articles 2 and 3. On 2 December 1999, Sinn Féin became a partner in the Northern Ireland Assembly, sited at Stormont.

Martin McGuinness became the Minister for Education and Bairbre de Brún became the Minister for Health. They embraced their roles.[24] McGuinness had left school at the age of fifteen and, as Minister for Education, he argued that the eleven-plus exam promoted 'educational inequality and disadvantage'; he scrapped it. As Minister for Health, de Brún oversaw a rationalization of the Northern Ireland health system that included controversial decisions to cut hospital services in Tyrone and reorganize them in Belfast, including centralizing maternity services at the Royal Victory Hospital and closing a ward at the City Hospital.

In many ways, more interesting than Sinn Féin's participation in the Assembly was the participation of the DUP. Like Sinn Féin, they were making a transition or, as Ed Moloney describes it in *Paisley: From Demagogue to Democrat*, 'the DUP's days of principled and instinctive opposition to power-sharing were over, replaced by the sort of ambition to be found in any normal political party ...'[25] Peter Robinson and Nigel Dodds became Ministers for Regional Development and Social Development, respectively. To calm the concerns of their constituents, they refused to participate in Executive meetings if Sinn Féin representatives were present. They also refused to participate in the North–South Ministerial Council but, in spite of this, twenty-five years after the failure of Sunningdale, it appeared that power sharing would work. Then, on the morning of 1 February 2000, John de Chastelain, Chairman of the Independent International Commission on Decommissioning, reported that the IRA had done nothing about decommissioning.[26]

The Provisionals had assumed that, once the Assembly was up and running, it would be too much of a political disaster to shut it down.[27] Considering the many times the British had accommodated them, it was not an unreasonable assumption. This time, the British were caught between false promises from the Provisionals and the potential resignation of the key unionist politician, David Trimble. They suspended the Assembly. In *Himself Alone: David Trimble and the Ordeal of Unionism,* Dean Godson describes what was probably the high point of Trimble's career: 'the most dramatic political victory won by a Unionist leader in years – the reassertion of British sovereign power at his behest by a Labour Government in the face of the collective opposition of the Irish Government, SDLP and Sinn Féin/IRA and the neutrality of the US Administration ...'[28] The Assembly was suspended but not the peace process. After de

Chastelain's report but prior to the suspension, the Provisional IRA leadership sent a private message to Tony Blair, via Bertie Ahern. They wanted to put their arms 'finally and completely' beyond use but could not at this time. The volunteers weren't ready for it. They also had to worry about defections to the 'dissidents', who had returned with a vengeance. The message led to private meetings between Gerry Adams and Martin McGuinness and Jonathan Powell, Blair's Chief of Staff.[29]

The Continuity IRA and Real IRA had spent the previous year reorganizing. In the autumn of 1999, for example, ten people were arrested at a Real IRA training camp in County Meath.[30] On 21 January 2000, the eighty-first anniversary of the First Dáil Éireann, the Real IRA re-emerged with a statement:

> Once again, Óglaigh na hÉireann declares the right of the Irish people to the ownership of Ireland, and to the unfettered control of Irish destinies to be sovereign and indefeasible. We call on Volunteers loyal to the Irish Republic to unite to uphold the Republic and establish a permanent national parliament representative of all the people. Your allegiance is to the Republic, not to an elite clique, or corrupt, treacherous administrations.[31]

It was the Provisionals who were the 'dissidents' from the republican faith, not them. The statement ended with Patrick Pearse's famous quotation, 'Ireland unfree shall never be at peace.' The next month, the Continuity IRA bombed a hotel in Fermanagh, RSF opened an office in Belfast and the Real IRA bombed a barracks in County Derry.[32]

The presence of former Provisionals among those arrested at the training camp in Meath was not a surprise – Seamus McGrane and Seamus McGreevy were 46 and 47 years old, respectively. What disturbed the authorities, and perhaps the Provisionals, was the presence of younger people, including 19-year-old Alan Ryan and three juveniles. Ryan was a former scout in Na Fianna Éireann, which was closely aligned with RSF. Ryan had moved on to the Real IRA and the police believed he had recruited the juveniles who were arrested. Anti-GFA republicans were attracting the next generation. As always, some people became involved through a family connection. Cáit Trainor was 16 years old when she joined Republican Sinn Féin in 2000. She described her political background:

> I was brought up in a very republican household, in the republican tradition ... I've been birthed in the republican tradition and I've always known that we're under occupation and that the freedom of your country is a noble aspiration. It's not something you should be ashamed of. So that's why I became involved in republicanism because I wanted to see the independence of my country.[33]

In 2000, there would have been thousands of children and grandchildren of former Provisionals who had been raised in families that had actively supported armed struggle between 1969 and 1998. The hypocrisy of the Provisionals also attracted younger people not from republican families. A Republican Sinn Féin recruit from 2001 was asked why he joined the Republican Movement:

I suppose just all my life I've felt that continued British rule in Ireland was unjust and immoral, as well as illegal, and so I suppose, in a sense, it was merely inevitable … I researched them a lot first and I felt that the Provisionals, that their policies were inconsistent with republicanism and that they were recognizing the states that they were claiming to oppose. And to me, it just seemed that they couldn't be considered to be the genuine Republican Movement.[34]

The Provisionals had failed, Ireland was still 'unfree' and other organizations were available.

The Provisionals faced a critique that also included former members who did not want to return to armed struggle but strongly objected to the direction Sinn Féin had taken. Many of them had made deep sacrifices for a united Ireland, not a reformed Stormont. A group of non-aligned republicans had formed the Republican Writers' Group.[35] The most prominent member was Brendan Hughes, who had resigned from the Army Council and left the IRA in the early 1990s. His attitude had soured for a variety of reasons. When he raised concerns about informers, nothing happened and he was suspicious about the 'political direction'. As Hughes described it:

the Army was being run down. I began to get suspicious about the whole political direction, the way things were going. For example, simple things like the West Belfast Festival … I actually was one of the originators of it … The British Army locked the gates of the Falls Park. They wouldn't let us in. And we cut the chain off the Falls Park to let the people in. I mean, there was only a couple hundred people at the start of the West Belfast Festival. Later, it became better organized and it began to get money from Tennant's Lager, for instance, and Guinness paid into it. And people were brought in to manage the West Belfast Festival. And [there were] paid jobs. We done this voluntary for a few years and things started to change. People began to get salaries. And people like myself and [NAMES] were sort of pushed out. That's a simple thing, that this started to change and it became more professional, more organized. And, all that, Gerry had his finger on. He was controlling all this. But I'd seen that, anyway. And I began to get disillusioned because the 'people's festival' turned into an organized, sponsored, systemized type festival. It was no longer a people's festival. Simple things like that.[36]

In the spring of 2000, *Fourthwrite: For a Democratic Socialist Republic*, appeared. The editor was Tommy McKearney. The March 2000 issue carried an interview with Brendan Hughes that was conducted by ex-prisoner Anthony McIntyre. Hughes complained that, 'what we have now we could have had at any time in the last twenty five years'. In an interview for *The Irish Herald*, Hughes complained 'All of my life I spent attempting to bring down Stormont' and now the Provisionals wanted to bring Stormont back.[37] A quip about Sinn Féin's 'Armani suit brigade' cut some people deeply. Up to the spring of 2000, Brendan Hughes was an IRA hero but after that Sinn Féiners questioned his motives and character. There was no direct retaliation, however. Others who were less prominent suffered a worse fate.

Since August of 1969, West Belfast had been at the centre of the Provisionals. They defended their turf from the RUC, the British Army and the Officials, elected Gerry Adams to Westminster and built Sinn Féin into a political party. In March 2000, a member of the 32 CSM in West Belfast was threatened for selling the organization's newspaper, *The Sovereign*

Nation. Joe O'Connor, the Real IRA's Belfast commander, ignored such things and challenged the Provisionals.[38] On 13 October 2000, he was shot dead in the middle of the day and in front of witnesses. Sinn Féin refused to condemn the murder[39] and at O'Connor's funeral, Marian Price argued that he was killed to cover up the Provisionals' sellout:

> Many questions arise as to why, at this particular time, the Provisional leadership chose to sanction such a dastardly act. It cannot be ignored that it comes in the wake of mounting political and internal pressure over decommissioning and Patten issues, all of which the leadership have conceded unbeknownst to their followers. Is the murder of Volunteer Joe O'Connor part of the stepping stone strategy to a United Ireland? Or is this the act of a leadership desperate and bereft of political direction? ... He refused to accept British rule under any guise, irrespective of who administered it, whether it be Peter Mandelson, David Trimble or Martin McGuinness. All are members of the British establishment, all administer it and now we witness how far the Provos are prepared to go to uphold it. They are now reduced to an armed militia of the British State.[40]

Anthony McIntyre and Tommy Gorman, members of the Writers' Group, criticized the murder and their homes were picketed. McIntyre was assaulted.[41] Undaunted, McIntyre and Carrie Twomey went online with *The Blanket: A Journal of Protest and Dissent.*

The anti-GFA activity might have threatened the Provisionals and the peace process but there were too many obstacles. London and Dublin were much more sophisticated and there would not be a repeat of a blunder like internment. Instead, anti-Agreement activists were monitored, questioned and arrested. Whether they were guilty or innocent, they could be denied bail or released with restrictions. If the case went to trial, that took time, energy and money. As an example, a Gardaí raid in Limerick (in December 2001), netted seven people, including Des Long, Republican Sinn Féin's vice President; Paddy Keanelly, their Munster organizer; Joe Lynch, their local spokesperson; and, Matt Conway, a member of the Ard Chomhairle.[42] The police said it was a Continuity IRA meeting; they said it was a Republican Sinn Féin meeting. Eighteen months later, a non-jury court acquitted six of those arrested on the membership charge. The conviction of the seventh person was questionable. The security forces still had informants.[43] David Rupert was a debt-ridden, American-based businessman who first expressed an interest in Republican Sinn Féin. Rupert shifted to the 32 CSM and Real IRA and, along the way, sent information to the FBI, the Garda Special Branch and MI5. Rupert devastated the Real IRA and his information helped convict Liam Campbell, Seamus McGrane and Mickey McKevitt.[44]

Anti-GFA activists also had to contend with the fact that the Provisionals were working with the British.[45] In the spring of 2000, the Provisionals traded weapons for a restored Assembly and a demilitarized South Armagh – step by step. Northern Ireland Secretary of State Peter Mandelson announced there would be a reduction in British soldiers in Northern Ireland *if* the IRA followed through on decommissioning. Cyril Ramaphosa of the African National Congress and Martii Ahtisaari, the former President of Finland, were then allowed to inspect some arms dumps, effectively decommissioning those weapons. Ronnie Flanagan, the Chief Constable, then announced the British would close five Army bases. At the end of May 2000, the British again devolved government to the Northern Ireland Assembly.

It also helped the Provisionals that the vast majority of nationalists were not interested in a return to war. Danny Morrison was released from prison in 1995 and, instead of returning to Sinn Féin, he chose to pursue a career as a writer. His novel, *The Wrong Man*, was published in 1997. Morrison, who kept his close ties to Sinn Féin, also became a political commentator. In the spring of 2001, he was asked about 'people in Armani suits':

> *It's an interesting statement that – people in Armani suits. First of all, people wear suits. That's true, right? In a sense that's a slavish mentality – that approach – that we're not allowed to have cars. We're not allowed to have houses. We're not allowed to have suits. It's a slavish mentality. And it's the type of thing that the Brits have been trying to put us down for years – and make us second-class. And suddenly when Sinn Féin leaders are the equal to any other party leaders, you get this stupid allegation. Which is, by the way, a denial of politics because it means you're not engaging in debate. You're engaging in personality attacks. So I think that is very interesting. I find it indicative of political bankruptcy, if that's your first line of attack. And often it is. The point is this here. I'm not in Sinn Fein, right? I'm not in the IRA. I support Sinn Féin. I support Adams's project. I believe they're still at it. The problem for a lot of these people is that they haven't a clue where they're going, they can't lead anybody anywhere and they're running around chasing their tail, and a lot of them are sitting in arm-chairs. The Good Friday Agreement isn't the end of the project. The Good Friday Agreement is part of the project. Now, there was a necessity to be pragmatic when it was quite clear that the IRA could fight on for another thirty years but without materially changing the situation 'cause a military stalemate had developed. And the IRA and their leadership did something. Fine, they led. They took chances. They engaged with unionism, they have split unionism, divided unionism and the nationalist community in the North's morale is incredibly buoyant in comparison to what it was in 1921. There is a sense that history is on our side … When you fight a war, you have to be a fundamentalist. But, when you fight peace, that's when the challenge comes in, that's when you have to be creative, that's when you have to be pragmatic. And you have to try and outwit and negotiate your enemy and the opposition … the Real IRA or the Continuity IRA are never going to be able to replicate the tempo of that IRA struggle. So they are going to be faced with the same problem somewhere down the road and they're going to have to make a difficult decision. Now, they can opt for just a ceasefire. But they don't represent anybody at this point in time. They do not represent anyone. And it's clear that Sinn Féin represents the bulk of the Republican Movement … It isn't a sell-out, it's part of a process. And the project is a united Ireland.*[46]

Nationalist voters agreed with Morrison. In the June 2001 Westminster election, Sinn Féin finally passed the SDLP in votes and elected four MPs versus three for the SDLP.[47] Gerry Adams and Martin McGuinness were re-elected in West Belfast and Mid-Ulster, Michelle Gildernew was elected in Fermanagh/South Tyrone and Pat Doherty was elected in West Tyrone. If it had been an Assembly election, Sinn Féin would have claimed the Deputy First Minister position. In local elections held the same day, Sinn Féin became the largest party in Belfast. In 1983, the election of Alex Maskey to Belfast City Council set off alarm bells; in 2002, Maskey would become Lord Mayor of Belfast.

There was a parallel change in the unionist community. Ian Paisley's DUP received more votes than David Trimble's UUP and Trimble's position was seriously weakened.[48] He resigned as First Minister and called on Tony Blair to suspend the Assembly and call an election. Blair was not willing to take that gamble. Instead, he organized multi-party talks at Weston, England, and, with an administrative sleight of hand, twice delayed an election by suspending the Assembly for twenty-four hours. In between the suspensions, two events changed the political landscape.

In the first, three Provisionals, Jim Monaghan, Niall Connolly and Martin McCauley, were arrested in Bogota and accused of acting as paid consultants for FARC (Revolutionary Armed Forces of Columbia).[49] It was another ridiculous situation from a group of people supposedly pursuing peace. The Bush Administration was already less friendly than Clinton's and FARC was a major supplier of cocaine to the United States. Sinn Féin was trying to work through the 'Columbia Three' fiasco when suddenly 9/11 united the Western world against terrorism. The Bush Administration declared a 'War on Terror' and the Blair administration would follow the US into Afghanistan and Iraq. In October 2001, the Provisional IRA announced they had decommissioned weapons 'in order to save the peace process'. IICD witnesses confirmed that it was a 'significant' amount.

The Assembly was restored and David Trimble returned as First Minister with Mark Durkan, of the SDLP, as Deputy First Minister.[50] However, decommissioning some weapons was not enough for the unionists, or the British and Irish governments – they wanted *all* weapons decommissioned – and it was too much for anti-GFA republicans. In *Saoirse*, Ruairí Ó Brádaigh described the decommissioning as 'unsurpassed in Irish history'.[51] After previous campaigns, weapons had been kept for future use. Ó Brádaigh had helped organize two IRA campaigns. He commented on decommissioning:

I think that the importance of the fifties campaign is underestimated in all of this and, God help us, the 1940s … it was very important to us in the fifties.

Q: Well, who organized the fifties?

A: Yes. And of course, each time – a very important point – each time we had the arms of the previous generation to start off with.

Q: Really? So, in 1970, you had the arms from the fifties left over?

A: Yes, that's right?

Q: Is that why decommissioning is a betrayal?

A: Ah, that's why it's important. That's why the Brits and the Free Staters wanted this badly. Let's chop the head off this thing for good and glory. They wanted to break the continuity – a clean break from the past and the arms. There'll be no pikes in the thatch or no Fenian guns knockin' around.[52]

The Provisionals had the right to end their armed struggle. Ó Brádaigh and his kind were upset that the Provisionals were trying to end it for everyone.

Sinn Féin's strategy of dragging their feet on anything asked of them while demanding full implementation of the GFA, all the while claiming that everything they did was in the name of peace, was working. To the consternation of unionists, the British implemented the Patten Commission recommendations. The RUC was renamed the Police Service of Northern Ireland (PSNI) and recruitment on a 50/50-Catholic/Protestant basis was initiated. The Northern Ireland Policing Board was established and although *AP/RN* described the PSNI as 'Different name, same bigots', there was a subtle shift from demanding a completely new police force to refusing to sit on the Policing Board until it was made more independent.[53] Sinn Féin was also growing.

Those who had been 'Ceasefire Sinn Féiners' were now recruits to 'New' Sinn Féin.[54] They were often talented, educated and able to contribute right away. Killian Forde was seeking a Master's Degree from Trinity College when he joined Sinn Féin. He described joining the party:

The hunger strikes would have been my own politicization and the effect it had on me would have been that I would have become very interested in social issues. So actually I ended up … as an aid worker. And another reason I became an aid worker was I had an interest in other countries and areas. And I got posted to the Balkans. I suppose, when I came back to Dublin in 2001 to go to college, I was shocked at the level of hostility against Sinn Féin from the press. And given that I was making a comparison between what the political parties were trying to do in the Balkans and the political parties in the North, I thought the progress made is: one, amazing; two, sincere; and three, needed to be applauded. And I suppose there was always a reaction to that. I felt that all my life I had supported Sinn Féin and the IRA, had great admiration for Gerry Adams and Martin McGuinness. And so I decided to join at college … [55]

In the May 2002 Irish general election, Sinn Féin's vote was up and the increase was largely at the expense of Fianna Fáil.[56] Caoimhín Ó Caoláin was re-elected in Cavan-Monaghan and joined by four new TDs: Seán Crowe (Dublin South West), Martin Ferris (Kerry North), Arthur Morgan (Louth) and Aengus Ó Snoddaigh (Dublin South Central). Fianna Fáil did not have quite enough seats to form a government and there was speculation that Bertie Ahern might enter into a coalition with Sinn Féin. Ahern, like David Trimble, was not going to partner with a political party that had a private army. Fianna Fáil formed another coalition government with the Progressive Democrats. However, having grown from one TD in 1998, Sinn Féin was suddenly much more relevant in the South.

The Sinn Féin election manifesto claimed they were the all-Ireland alternative to 'those who have created an unequal and divided Ireland'. The choice was between 'real change and more of the same'. Sinn Féin was a fresh alternative. Seán Crowe's comments reflect this:

The first time I was in Leinster House was the day I got elected … I'd never really particularly wanted it so I'm coming at it with that sort of, you know, I was a republican that didn't agree with the taking of seats in Leinster House and I suppose that sort of guided me when I was in there. I had a sort of healthy … not disrespect. I don't know what word I'd use. But I had a healthy sort of approach to the parliament itself. I'd seen it as a sort of club. I didn't see it as the be-all and end-all of how to move things forward ... [I felt] scepticism, exactly, in relation to it and the workings of it, the formalities of it ... it's dominated by the government parties.

The new TDs built on the foundation laid by Caoimhghín Ó Caoláin, who became the party's parliamentary leader. They also drew on their own experiences as community activists, local councillors and the peace process. Seán Crowe talked about this experience:

The fact that I would have been involved in the Forum for Peace and Reconciliation, that would have helped in relation to working with all the parties ... you were building up a relationship with people you're working with. You were meeting people on a monthly basis in the committee or within the Forum itself. And I suppose you were sort of getting used to working with people that you wouldn't traditionally have worked with ... you try and work with those who will work with you to try and improve conditions and to bring about change in relation to your community.[57]

Younger, energetic, and polished Sinn Féiners like Mary Lou McDonald, Pearse Doherty and Killian Forde would be elected to the European Parliament (McDonald), and Councils in Donegal (Doherty) and Dublin (Forde).[58] Unfortunately, the party of 'change' had members who refused to change.

On St Patrick's Day 2002, PSNI headquarters at Castlereagh were broken into and files and documents stolen. It took months, but eventually the trail led to Denis Donaldson, Sinn Féin's political director at Stormont. The PSNI raided Sinn Féin offices at Stormont as well as Donaldson's home and they discovered that he was gathering intelligence on the other political parties and the names and addresses of PSNI officers, suggesting they were being targeted for assassination. Donaldson was accused of operating a spy-ring and Sinn Féin claimed that 'securocrats' were trying to wreck the peace process. It was a good sound bite but no one in authority believed it. In his memoir, *Great Hatred, Little Room: Making Peace in Northern Ireland*, Jonathan Powell describes David Trimble as 'like the cat that has got the cream'.[59] The Assembly was again suspended and Sinn Féin was again forced to distance itself from its past. Gerry Adams, in a speech that Powell helped write, said that the IRA would never disband in response to an ultimatum but added, 'if you ask me do I envisage a future without an IRA? The answer is obvious. The answer is yes.' Martin McGuinness was more direct with, 'My war is over.'[60]

The problem was that not everyone was willing to admit the war was over. The 2003 Sinn Féin Árd Fheis had the theme 'Building an Ireland of Equals'. A better title might have been, 'Rewrite The Past for the Sake of the Future'. In his report on the peace process, their 'Chief Negotiator', Martin McGuinness blamed the Ulster Unionists and Tony Blair for recent events: 'When the British Government suspended the political institutions 14 October [they were] acting at the behest of the leadership of the Ulster Unionist Party and were in clear breach of the Good Friday Agreement.'[61] The Ard Fheis is best remembered for the contribution of 82-year-old Joe Cahill, Sinn Féin's vice President, described in *AP/RN* as 'a man who personifies the indomitable spirit of Irish Resistance to British rule'. In one sentence, he neatly summarized the leadership's message, 'We have won the war, now let us win the peace.'

Cahill was given a standing ovation. When he died a year later, the Provisionals lionized him.[62] His support, and his comment, softened the reality of the message Gerry Adams delivered in his presidential address, 'Our strategy is about bringing an end to physical force republicanism, by creating an alternative way to achieve democratic and republican objectives.' In other words, there was no longer a need for the IRA.[63]

In a meeting with the press following the Ard Fheis, journalists asked an obvious question: If the IRA had won the war, then why not admit it was over? In his own press conference, Tony Blair asked Gerry Adams the same question and added that he also wanted to know when they were going to get rid of their weapons. Blair did not get a satisfactory reply and postponed the upcoming Assembly election.[64]

The Provisionals were poised to do well and wanted the election. Tony Blair wanted their weapons. In return for a specific election date, the Provisional IRA agreed to allow John de Chastelain and Andrew Sens to witness the decommissioning of a significant amount of weaponry. David Trimble, Tony Blair and Bertie Ahern all endorsed the plan.[65] Unfortunately for him, Trimble did not pay enough attention to detail and the Provisionals pulled a fast one.

With reason, the Provisionals were concerned that unionists would claim that the decommissioning was proof they had lost the war. That would irritate their own people who had been promised the IRA would never decommission and it would also open them up to further criticism from anti-GFA republicans. When the IRA representatives met with de Chastelain and Sens, they refused to go ahead with the decommissioning unless de Chastelain and Sens promised they would not reveal any details. Ambiguity would allow them to fudge the significance of the event. De Chastelain was afraid the deal was falling apart and agreed to the condition and after the fact, de Chastelain and Sens confirmed that a 'substantial' amount had been decommissioned but offered no details. Trimble felt deceived and refused to endorse the Assembly election. Gerry Adams argued that the Provisionals had kept their end of the bargain and called on Trimble and Tony Blair to do the same. The British scheduled the election for 26 November 2003.[66]

As expected, the winners were the DUP and Sinn Féin.[67] The DUP topped the poll and, after forty years as 'Dr No', Ian Paisley replaced David Trimble as the leader of Ulster's unionists. In the nationalist community, Sinn Féin moved further ahead of the SDLP in votes and seats. At first glance, it appeared that extremists had replaced the moderates. It was five years into the Good Friday Agreement and almost a decade since the August 1994 ceasefire, however. Sinn Féin had changed. A former Sinn Féiner who opposed the GFA was interviewed just after the election:

Q: Do you think that Adams will succeed, that the approach that he – the tack that they [Sinn Féin] have taken will succeed?

A: I think it depends on what you mean by succeed. I think they will succeed as politicians, but I do not believe that they will achieve the goal that too many have struggled and died for. Because they're part of the state now. And I think that they are strengthening the institutions, the British institutions, *and they have become constitutional politicians. And I do not believe – I cannot see them achieving the goal of a thirty-two socialist republic.*

Q: *I have a question – what does the peace process mean to you?*

A: *The peace process means to me more of the same. It just means an end to the war. And it means to me strengthening British institutions. It means to me a sectarian settlement. And it means to me strengthening sectarian institutions. It means to me implementing British policies in this part of Ireland. It means to me closing hospitals. It means to me introducing right-wing policies and it means to me heartbreak and fear and disappointment. That so many people struggled for so long and this is what we ended up with. And that it was never necessary to struggle for so long and when we could have had it in 1974. We could have had the same solution ... the peace process means to me a British solution to an Irish problem.[68]*

Sinn Féin had travelled too far to refuse to work with Ian Paisley and the DUP. The question was whether or not Paisley and the DUP would work with them.

Paisley also believed that Sinn Féin had changed. He would later comment, 'they can't be true republicans when they accept the right of Britain to govern this country, and to take part in that government'.[69] As the leader of unionism, Paisley and the DUP had to change, too. Like Sinn Féin, the DUP was on the cusp of political power and to get there, they had to do more than say 'No'. The DUP told the British they would share power with Sinn Féin *if* the Provisional IRA decommissioned weapons and ended all paramilitary activities. In the most recent incident, closed-circuit TV had filmed a dissident being dragged from a Belfast bar, beaten with iron bars and tossed into the back of a van. The PSNI stopped the van and arrested those involved.

There were more multi-party negotiations, including a major conference at Leeds Castle.[70] Sinn Féin insisted that, if there were a deal, the DUP had to commit to entering government. The DUP, upset by Bairbre de Brún's decisions as Minister for Health, wanted ministers to be more accountable to the Executive. The real sticking point, of course, was weapons. Given what had happened to Trimble, the DUP wanted proof of decommissioning. At an annual DUP dinner in the autumn of 2004, Paisley told the faithful, 'The IRA needs to be humiliated. And they need to wear their sackcloth and ashes, not in a backroom but openly. And we have no apology to make for the stand we are taking.' The Provisionals were willing to decommission but they were not going to be humiliated. Eventually another agreement was worked out – decommissioning at the end of 2004 would be followed by restoration of the Assembly in March 2005. Two trusted members of the clergy, Father Alec Reid and Revd Harold Good, were asked to witness and confirm the final decommissioning of IRA weapons. Revd Harold Good commented on the plan: *'Actually I was to have come to the States to a Habitat for Humanity event and then they said, "Decommissioning is going to take place that particular week." So I had to cancel my trip and then we had the Northern Bank robbery.*[71]

Just before Christmas, the families of two officials with the Northern Bank in Belfast were taken hostage. The bank officers spent the next day quietly collecting bags of notes from the vault. When the day ended they tossed rubbish bags worth £25–30 million into a van. It was fundraising par excellence.[72]

321

Only the IRA had the expertise to pull off the raid and it was assumed that it was one last operation to support Sinn Féin's politics. Bertie Ahern broke off all contact with Sinn Féin and the British shut down the negotiations and demanded the IRA 'put itself out of business'. The Provisionals' leaders must have assumed that, at some point, the dust would settle and the British and Irish governments would again come asking for their weapons. What they did not anticipate was an unauthorized IRA operation that would shame Sinn Féin and finally prove once and for all that the Provisional IRA was a liability and had to go.

On Sunday evening, 31 January 2005, Robert McCartney was drinking with his friend, Brendan Devine, in Magennis's bar in central Belfast. There was also a group of Provisionals out for a drink after attending a Bloody Sunday commemoration in Derry. Devine and Jock Davison, a senior figure in the Belfast IRA, got into an argument that escalated. Others became involved and Devine's throat was slashed with a broken bottle. Robert McCartney helped Devine leave the bar, only to be followed by an IRA gang that beat, kicked and stabbed him. McCartney died the next morning; Devine recovered from his injuries. In the bar, customers were warned to say nothing and an IRA forensics team arrived and swept it clean of evidence.[73]

There was nothing political about Robert McCartney's murder. The family lived in the Short Strand, where Billy McKee had led the defense of St Matthew's Church so long ago. Seven years after the GFA, the IRA was covering up a senseless murder of one of the people they had supposedly defended. Mayor Alex Maskey made the situation worse by suggesting the murder was the sad result of a knife fight. Maskey failed to mention that members of his election team and staff, along with other Sinn Féiners, were in the bar. Robert McCartney's sisters mounted a justice campaign that cost Sinn Féin. At St Patrick's Day 2005, for example, the McCartney sisters were invited to the White House. Sinn Féin was not invited and Gerry Adams was denied a fundraising visa.

What Seán Mac Stiofáin, Ruairí Ó Brádaigh, Dáithí O'Connell, Paddy Mulcahy, Seán Treacy, Leo Martin, Joe Cahill and nineteen other middle-aged men started in December 1969 ended on 28 July 2005. Ex-prisoner Seanna Walsh, one of Bobby Sands's closest comrades, read a statement for a video camera: 'The leadership of Óglaigh na hÉireann has formally ordered an end to the armed campaign. This will take effect from 4 pm this afternoon. All IRA units have been ordered to dump arms.' After that, the Provisionals would pursue 'purely political and democratic programmes through exclusively peaceful means'. The path was being cleared for Sinn Féin to take seats in the Assembly once again.[74]

Two months later, Revd Harold Good and Fr Alec Reid witnessed in secret the final decommissioning of Provisional IRA weapons. Dissenters within the ranks had finally accepted the inevitable. Revd Good commented on the attitudes and perspectives of the Provisionals who were there:

I found that very interesting. In fact I, I found myself falling into pastoral mode. If you know what I mean by that. In that, there were people sharing with me their feelings and their thoughts. I wasn't prompting them. There were those who were saying to me that they were thinking of their comrades who had died in this struggle. In a kind of mixture of are we failing them by concluding this struggle before it has achieved what they died for? And that was a very – that was there. That was within the conversations. And I understood that. I'm saying this in as sensitive of a way as I can, because I understood that. Then, on the other hand, there were those who were saying, 'We are doing this for our children and our children's children. We don't want them to have to go through what we went through.' Now here were men, some of whom had spent thirty years of their lives in this cause. They were perhaps thinking, 'What have we to show for all of that? Has it been worth it?' In all those emotions, and in all of those thoughts and feelings, and others who would've probably been saying, 'Well, we had to do what we did, and we did what we did, but we're now glad to find an alternative. We're glad that we're now moving into another way of doing things.' And, 'We want to support this peace process, and this is a part of it, and this is – ' they may not have suggested that they regretted being involved but they would regret the hurt and the pain and the grief that resulted from the conflict, from what they called the 'armed struggle', but they would also say, you know, 'We were put into a situation where we didn't see an alternative.' And, it's easy for me to say there was an alternative but if I were in their position I might not have been able to see an alternative.

The significance of the event was not lost on the Provisionals. Revd Harold Good again:

the very last day, General de Chastelain and his colleagues had done what they must do to the last of the weapons and, as far as the General was concerned, the task was now complete. Done and dusted. When out of this corner, way over there, I can still see it, out of this corner came this young man. And he marched up to the General in military style, clicked his heels, took the gun off his shoulder and presented it to the General. And we all fell silent. And for me, the silence was broken by a whisper from my left, Father Alec saying, 'Harold, there goes the last gun out of Irish politics.' And that was an incredible moment to feel and to realize we were witnessing this moment. And it was very significant and very significant in its symbolism. That one gun was one of many but it wasn't significant in itself, its significance was in the symbolism of this young man. Now, was that orchestrated? Was that planned? I have no idea but it was a very powerful moment.[75]

Finally, the war was over – at least for the Provisionals.

What Gerry Adams and Martin McGuinness had done was unique. Michael Collins, Éamon de Valera and Seán Mac Bride left the IRA and Sinn Féin and created new constitutional political parties. Cathal Goulding and Tomás Mac Giolla had tried to combine the armed struggle of the 'Official' IRA with the constitutional politics of 'Official' Sinn Féin and failed. They morphed into the Workers' Party and then were decimated by another split and defections to Democratic Left in 1992. Adams and McGuinness transformed two revolutionary social movement organizations into a constitutional political party and an unarmed guerrilla army. And when the Provisionals finally did disarm, Sinn Féin was stronger and more relevant than at any time since the 1920s. It was a remarkable achievement.

Something was lost along the way, however. Peter McAleer joined Sinn Féin in the late 1960s and was elected to the Clones Town Council in 1985. He helped build Sinn Féin in County Monaghan and as Sinn Féin became involved in constitutional politics, McAleer watched the party change: *'I found that Sinn Féin then were becoming more like the major political parties ... you know, being crafty and fighting your corner from a party political point of view … the important thing was to have as many seats as possible rather than the actual substance of why you should be there.'* One of the perks of the peace process was access to European Union funds for peace and reconciliation projects. Ex-prisoners received funding to set up Clones Failté, an organization that provides social, educational and employment support for prisoners and ex-prisoners, former combatants and their families. Two employees quit and there was a search to replace them. Peter McAleer commented:

> *I said it was essential that an interview panel should involve somebody of an independent nature which I felt was from any perspective the right thing to do. But I was also making a point because of the kind of internal bickering that had gone on, so nobody could actually come back and say that this was a set up. So, to my amazement, people resented that and the interview panel was totally republicans and the guys that had left had made a prediction about who was going to get the jobs, which came to pass, which to me looked very bad. Not that it looked very bad, it was very bad … that type of recruitment policy and that type of attitude which to me was exactly the same as the Fianna Fáil, Fine Gael type of thing. … This kind of a 'jobs for the boys' attitude and everybody's equal but we're a bit more equal than the rest type of thing. It was, to me as a republican and as a trade unionist, it certainly wasn't acceptable …*

When there was another opening in 2004, McAleer applied for the position:

> *I thought it was very naïve of them after I had made all the objections and the arguments before that they didn't actually come forward with an interviewing panel with an independent person on it; they maintained this thing of three people very closely connected … And it was quite obvious that the decision to employ that person was made before the interviews ever took place. And that was the straw that broke the camel's back.*

McAleer was turned down because of a concern with his IT skills. The job was for a development worker for ex-prisoners and, from McAleer's perspective, such skills were *'neither in the essential or desired criteria. So it was a very flimsy thing to hang the hat on.'* He went on: *'I resigned from Sinn Féin because Sinn Féin were kind of, without actually going out and saying it, were actually backing that type of an operation instead of making the point that that wasn't acceptable to republicans. That was 2005 when I eventually resigned.'*[76] McAleer became an independent on the Clones Town Council.

As Sinn Féin became more constitutional, its members became more interested in the perks associated with political success. That is, they became more and more like members of every other major political party in a Western democracy. David Trimble is responsible for much of that transformation.

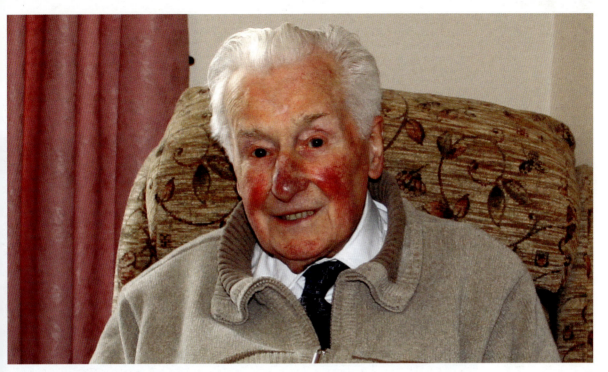

Billy McKee, Belfast, 2014. © Robert White.

Danny Morrison, Belfast, 2014. © Robert White.

Dolours Price, 32 County Sovereignty Movement Easter Commemoration, Arbour Hill, Dublin, 2006. © Robert Whi

Phil O'Donoghue, National Organizer, and Francie Mackey, Chairperson, 32 County Sovereignty Movement. Prior to the funeral of Ruairí Ó Brádaigh. Roscommon, Ireland, 2013. © Robert White.

32 County Sovereignty Movement representation in the 'National 1916 Commemoration Committee' march, Dublin, 28 March 2016. © Robert White.

Joe Dillon, Public Relations Officer, 32 County Sovereignty Movement. Prior to the 'National 1916 Commemoration Committee' march, Dublin, 28 March 2016. © Robert White.

Val Lynch speaking to a large crowd in front of the GPO at the 'National 1916 Commemoration Committee' march in Dublin. The march was open to all Republicans and attracted representatives from a variety of organizations, including the 32 CSM. 28 March 2016. © Robert White.

Republican Sinn Féin Ard Chomhairle, 2009. © Robert White.

Lead member of a colour party of the republican movement, Republican Sinn Féin Annual Wolfe Tone Commemoration, Bodenstown, June 2015. © Robert White.

Na Fianna Éireann scout participating in Republican Sinn Féin's 'Easter Rising Centenary' march, Dublin, 28 March 2016. Sinn Féin suggests that Na Fianna Éireann no longer exists, having been replaced by Young Sinn Féin/Ógra Shinn Féin. © Robert White.

PART 3

Revolution Over the Life Course and Life Over the Course of the Revolution

21

WHO STAYS INVOLVED AND,
IF THEY QUIT, WHAT DO THEY DO?

I think that my experience over the last twenty, twenty-five years has greatly empowered me. I do not see myself as a victim, I see myself a survivor.

– Former Provisional[1]

Between 1969 and 2005, thousands of people joined the Provisional IRA, Sinn Féin or both. John Joe McGirl and Joe Cahill helped create the Provisionals and stayed involved until they died in 1988 and 2004, respectively. The activism of Seán Lynch, Ruairí Ó Brádaigh and Joe O'Neill extended over the entire time period, even if they were in Republican Sinn Féin in 2005. The willingness of Irish republicans to remain active in spite of hardship, repeated failure and limited chance for success given the resources of the British government, is phenomenal. Hardship and limited chance for success, of course, may explain why thousands of people joined the Provisionals for a time and then quit.[2] This chapter addresses the personal consequences of involvement in social movements that embrace political violence.

Why did some people stay involved while others withdrew? In 1984 and 1985, sixty-three Provisionals (members of Sinn Féin, the Provisional IRA or both) were interviewed. The primary question then was why people joined a revolutionary social movement. Approximately a decade later, beginning in 1995, thirty-one of the original sixty-three respondents were reinterviewed. The primary questions addressed the 'biographical consequences' of involvement in a revolutionary movement. Beginning in 2007, seventeen of the respondents who were interviewed in 1984/85 *and* in 1995/96 were reinterviewed, again. In these interviews, respondents were asked to reflect on their activism. The respondents quoted in this chapter include women and men, Northerners and Southerners, activists in Sinn Féin, Republican Sinn Féin and the 32 CSM, and some former Provisionals who 'disengaged'. These oral histories offer insight into why some people stayed involved while others chose to withdraw or 'disengage'.

From Recruitment to a Lifetime of Activism

The oral histories show that being born and raised in an Irish republican environment leads people into the Irish Republican Movement and it also helps to keep them involved.

Approximately a third (eleven) of the thirty-one respondents reinterviewed in the mid-1990s reported that an older family member influenced their involvement – a parent, aunt or uncle, or grandparent. All eleven of them were still actively involved in the mid-1990s, either in Sinn Féin or Republican Sinn Féin. The results were essentially the same in 2005 – of the eight people who were still living and could be located, seven of them were actively involved either in Sinn Féin, Republican Sinn Féin or the 32 CSM. Activists with republican backgrounds may switch organizations but once they are involved in the Republican Movement they tend to stay involved for a long time, if not the rest of their lives. The timing of recruitment also influenced the length of involvement. Nine of the thirty-one respondents joined the Movement prior to 1968 and went with the Provisionals in 1969/70. In the mid-1990s, all of them who were still alive were still involved in a republican organization. The same held in 2005.

These respondents were lifelong republicans. Their willingness to continue was, without question, influenced by the quick growth of the Provisionals' armed campaign, which would have reinforced their belief that they made the right choice and that they were going to win. These are the people who sustained Sinn Féin and the IRA through the lean years and then built

Seán Lynch and Ruairí Ó Brádaigh, Longford Town, 2010. ©Robert White.

the Provisionals, people like Frank Glynn, Seán Keenan, Seán Lynch, John Joe McGirl, Ruairí Ó Brádaigh and J.B. O'Hagan. Several of them were from republican families.

The following is from Seán Lynch, from North County Longford. His account parallels the accounts of several others. Lynch's father and uncles were active in Sinn Féin and the IRA in the 1916–23 era. As he grew up, his elders were pursuing a lifetime of activism. In his words:

> *There was one woman, she was my grandmother. Incidentally, my four grandparents were teachers. But my mother's mother, she was an outstanding republican. When she died in 1969 – she never wavered. As I say, you have people going with Fianna Fáil, with the Free Staters … She never wavered … but at the same time, when I started to get involved she always said to me, 'You have to make up your own mind. I'm not going to do it.' The question there, was you told to do it? I wasn't told to. It was her, 'Come along, and from you're own convictions'.*[3]

The Lynch family have been active Irish republicans in North County Longford for a century. Once people join, family and friends support continued activism. When Joe Cahill was sentenced to death for his involvement in killing Constable Murphy in 1942, his father was the chairman of the reprieve committee, something which Cahill described with a laugh: *'I suppose that's the natural thing to do.'*[4] In the 1950s, his father was the organizer of the Prisoners' Dependents Fund in the North. In 1972, when her son was on hunger strike in Mountjoy Prison with the Ó Brádaigh brothers, Cahill's mother was outside the prison supporting him.

Families often reproduce themselves through children. Irish republican families reproduce themselves in a way that perpetuates a culture of resistance and this observation helps explain the persistence of anti-GFA Irish republicans, 'dissidents'.

Not every long-term Provisional had parents or uncles or a grandmother who was actively involved in the Movement. Whatever a person's background, activism promotes solidarity between comrades and increases commitment to a cause. This 32 CM activist joined the Republican Movement in the early 1970s. In 1984, he commented on his comrades:

> *I found out that … from travelling in the north, the northeast and northwest of Ireland, that there's a hell of a lot of friends, new friends, new comrades, and an opening up of situations that would never have happened if it hadn't of been for the Troubles – where we can go to most parts of this country today and be accepted for what we are, as members of the Republican Movement, with open arms. And it's the comradeship that is within the ranks of the Republican Movement today, that's what takes it all.*

More than twenty years later, he was asked about the 'rewards' of being a republican:

> *The many friends, the people that we met, of every walk of life. Great people – some of the greatest people I've ever met were republicans. And most of it was from a voluntary point of view because nobody got involved in the Republican Movement for any sort of self-gain that I knew of.*[5]

Comrades develop what social movement scholars refer to as a collective identity, a sense of 'we-ness'. Camaraderie and commitment helps keep them involved, even if involvement is high risk.

More than 300 Provisional IRA, Cumann na mBan and Na Fianna Éireann activists died on active service. Loyalists killed more than twenty Sinn Féin activists. Activists and their families, friends and comrades were arrested, had their homes raided, were harassed on the streets by the security forces and so on. The shared threats and the hardship enhanced their attachment to their comrades and communities. One Sinn Féin activist said:

> I've been in prison three times. I was interned twice. And I was on the blanket protest that led to the hunger strike. I had a brother who served three years for possession of a rifle, but he was only fourteen when he was arrested ... they brought [a rifle] up to Belfast and he got caught and he got three years for it ... I had a sister who was interned along with a number of other women from the Divis area.

In an altercation with the RUC, one of the respondent's brothers was killed:

> Q: Did you ever think, 'This is just nuts, I'm getting out of here?'
>
> A: No.
>
> Q: No? Why not? I mean –
>
> A: Well, you see, again it goes back to the commitment that you build up over the years. And, honestly, I've never – I've had my down moments, as I've said to you. When I have my down moments, you know, you go to the graveyard and you talk to your friends who are there. And that brings the sense back to you again. And you set a number of objectives. And that's making a better community for the people that live here but also striving for what your comrades and friends and your brother died for, and that's a united Ireland.[6]

Camaraderie reduces the cost of activism and sustains activism over time, whether it is the women's movement, the labour movement or the Irish Republican Movement.

It is important to note that camaraderie and commitment are reinforced by the belief that continued involvement makes a difference. Another Sinn Féin activist, when asked why she stays involved, said:

> Because I'm a republican. I want to stay just – I want to help them to see the absolute establishment of our goal of the united Ireland ... the fact that people who have been denied any representation, any voice, any even identity of being Irish [are] now represented by Sinn Féin and the strong stand they make on socialism which is – translated of course – is about equality and respect and freedom. I mean that's what republicanism is – liberty, equality, fraternity and I think that there's been a huge amount achieved. And the last push is always the hardest, but I describe myself as a republican.[7]

No single motive keeps people involved in social movements over time. Commitment and camaraderie and a shared belief that involvement is making a contribution work together to sustain activism. That combination helps us understand why the war lasted so long and why some activists were willing to continue to support the leadership through the compromises of the peace process. In spite of commitment and camaraderie, however, not everyone stays involved.

Who Leaves and Why: Exiting Irish Republican Activism

Of the thirty-one respondents who were reinterviewed in the mid-1990s, ten of them had 'disengaged' by the time of the reinterview. Their status when the Provisionals ended armed struggle is complicated by the fact that involvement in social movements is fluid – activists flow into, out of and back into social movement organizations. By 2005, two respondents not active in the mid-1990s had returned to Sinn Féin. In 2005, three people active in Sinn Féin in the mid-1990s had withdrawn.

It is tempting to assume that constant harassment from the security forces finally took its toll and drove people out of the Provisionals. However, it appears that once an activist got past the initial headache, state harassment contributed to the solidarity and commitment that they experienced. In a way, enduring repression became a badge of honour. A Provisional who exited in the mid-1980s was asked if state harassment prompted his exit: *'Oh, no [laughs]. Not in the slightest. To be intimidated by someone who may or may not have politics but certainly has the weight of the apparatus of a police state behind it – the arbitrary placement of law whenever it suits it – would be ultimately to allow everything that you say you believe in to be undermined.'* He left the Provisionals for personal reasons. There was a change in the leadership of a Sinn Féin Office: *'there were a couple of subsequent [directors] – one of whom was then off ill and there was a temporary one and he and I didn't see eye to eye. And that led to me leaving …* [8] A recurring theme is that activists disengage for personal reasons. One activist cut back on his commitment but remained involved:

> *It's because I had to earn money. I came to a period in my life when I had to, basically, because of my life, my lifestyle, and my life with the Republican Movement, I had no house, no financial security, I had no assets and at my time in life, I decided it's about time I got some behind me before I start pulling my pension.* [9]

While they were activists, several of the respondents were unemployed or underemployed. The British counterinsurgency used this to their advantage by providing funds to create social service jobs. These jobs allowed activists to support themselves and their families, engage with their communities in a non-violent way and also pulled them away from activism. [10] For example, one of the respondents was released from prison and became a volunteer at a Sinn Féin Advice Centre. He was unemployed and, in order to receive public assistance, he was required to look for employment. A government-sponsored scheme found him a full-time job and he left the Advice Centre. He said:

> *I've never really left it in as much as that I can always be contacted if needed. But in regards to me actually physically sitting in there, I can no longer because I'm working now, you see? Really, ever since I*

started working, which is five years ago. But up until that there I was always, had some involvement like when I was sitting down with people [unclear]. But I enjoy the work I do now ... working with the young people ... The money isn't spectacular but at least it gets me by and I really enjoy the work.[11]

Another respondent experienced a deep personal change in sexual identity. The respondent came out and became involved in gay rights activism. That conflicted with activism in Sinn Féin:

I'd be out selling An Phoblacht one night and out doing gay stuff the next night and then vice versa. And then the pressures of being gay and the energy that it takes as well, especially when you're in a – what I would perceive as a straight political party, you know, takes actually much more energy. So I finally decided ... that I would ease back. And actually AIDS came along as well. And I was involved with [a support group].

... I went from kind of being a republican to an anti-imperialist, a lesbian, gay, anti-imperialist activist ... I was fucking worn out ... you were just worn out ... being gay, being lesbian, being bisexual, particularly being lesbian and gay means you needed supports and identification with your own community. You don't get that. It's very hard to get that in a straight-dominated environment. And I think that's why a lot of people leave – the same as people leave the country because Ireland is very, very traditional, very straight.[12]

For several activists, when they married and started raising families, their lives changed.

Because of harassment, the threat of assassination and sharing sacrifices in a tight-knit group, many Provisionals married fellow activists. There were benefits to marrying a comrade since a spouse *'would have family, would be from a republican background'*, as one respondent commented:

the people you'd meet would be republicans. But you wouldn't be looking for a republican. But obviously if you were going to be working for the Movement, then it would be handier because they're more understanding and realize your motivation. You know, instead of somebody that didn't come from that sort of background who'd say, 'Why don't you get a job or why don't you do this?' or – [the] next door neighbour, they've got a car and they've got a good life, and 'All you're bringing in the house is raids and harassment.' So you need that sort of tolerance.[13]

This respondent did not disengage, but marrying a fellow activist did not guarantee continued activism and marrying a non-activist did not automatically prompt disengagement. The influence of a spouse and other family members was complex.

There were more sectarian killings in North Belfast than any other area of Northern Ireland.[14] This respondent was active in Sinn Féin and was a target:

What happened was, after my son was killed, my ex-wife had actually said to me that it was my fault that he was dead, and that wrecked me. And five years later I said to her, 'Do you remember you said it was my fault that Seán died?' She said, 'It was your fault.' So it wasn't only her instinct to protect herself that her son was killed. It was she felt it deeply. So I couldn't stand it, so I left.[15]

The following is from a Southern republican who joined Sinn Féin around 1980 when he was single and in his early twenties. By the mid-1990s, he was engaged to be married, had moved to another area and was no longer active in Sinn Féin. He was asked if he was still in the cumann:

Actually no – I'm not actually because when I moved … I discussed it with the people. And I said the fact that my job is bringing me away from here, I'm not going to be able to [take] an active role anymore … and apart from the job moving I knew that myself and [wife's name] were going to get married soon – maybe two or three years ago I knew. We didn't have a date set or anything. I knew we were going to be married. I said we were probably going to be moving away from the town …

Q: Would you join Sinn Féin there?

A: I don't know anybody there. I doubt it, to tell you the truth. I don't know. I'll see what way things go. At the moment, I am in a grade in civil service that prevents anybody from overt political activity.

He did not join Sinn Féin in his new location. In 2010, he commented on the civil service restriction and how that had influenced his activism:

Thirty years ago – indeed, when I joined the civil service, that rule was there then and I was affected by it but I have to say I didn't really – I ignored it and was happy enough to take whatever consequences there might be with that. But nothing ever happened as a result of it … but I suppose things are different now. I've got family and children and everything to look after, a mortgage, like everybody else. So there are other consequences. So I'm happy enough to comply at this stage.[16]

As a young man, he had less to lose and was willing to take a risk. He got married and started raising a family and the risk increased so his behaviour became less risky.

An activist from Limerick was willing to put up with harassment from the police and the negative consequences of being involved when it only affected him. In 1984, he described Special Branch harassment:

Q: Did many of your friends get involved? The kids that you grew up with?

A: No. None.

Q: Can you think of anything – can you think of any reason why you would get involved but they wouldn't?

A: Actually it's the pressure, the pressure from parents. You know, the Special Branch stop them. You see the Special Branch would stop them and say, 'Look, your son is … hanging around with undesirable people, subversives. And they'll brainwash him', and all this. 'The next thing you know he'll have a gun and be up at the border, shooting the British Army'. 'And you'll only bring it on yourself, missus, we'll be raiding your house and wrecking it.' You know, sometimes they just do that – go in and wreck the house and say, 'Your son is – he's involved with subversives.' That usually

333

works. Young people usually get an ultimatum. You either leave or you get out. And most of them stay [at home].

Q: Why wouldn't that work with you?

A: I'm stubborn.[17]

The respondent chose Sinn Féin over his family. He was in his early twenties and went full time with the party but, when he was interviewed in the mid-1990s, he was married and raising a family and no longer actively involved:

I had some personal problems. I was a bit fed up with life. I suppose I was a little depressed with things. I don't want to use the word depressed. I was a bit fed up with life and not having the better things in life. I just wanted to get someone and to – had a hankering to find a woman, settle down and have kids maybe ... Nobody joined it for the money. The one thing that sustained you was that everybody was in the same boat – the comradeship. I've never had friends like it. Sincerely. The sense of togetherness was incredible. It was great. Unbelievable.

In spite of the unbelievable sense of togetherness, he withdrew from Sinn Féin. When asked if having a family influenced the decision, the reply was: *'The only thing that influenced me was my wife's job. Her boss was a virulent anti-republican and if it was found out she would definitely lose her job.'*[18] The respondent supported Sinn Féin but was not actively involved. In 2007, he reflected on the decision to withdraw and was asked if he felt guilty:

I did a bit. It's funny you should say that. I did actually. I felt at the time that I was abandoning the comrades and I always had pains to tell people that although I've gone away, I'm still basically a supporter.

Q: Did they treat you differently?

A: Some did, yeah ... The kind of hardliners would say things like, 'No commitment'. In the main, people were fine ... No, generally I still meet people that were there at the time and, yeah, we chat a bit about the old days and I think we're basically fine.

Q: When you were in the Movement, what was your attitude toward people who would leave?

A: Well, I was exactly the same, wasn't I? I mean I just said that. I would definitely have said, 'No commitment. I knew that fucker had no balls.' [Laughs] Yeah, I would be like that.[19]

Harassment from the security forces or disenchantment with Sinn Féin's policies did not cause him to withdraw from activism. He withdrew because his family was threatened.

Some activists joined, withdrew and then rejoined. This activist joined in the early 1980s. He married in the mid-1980s and, when he was reinterviewed in 1996, described his wife with the comment, *'I think she thought she'd change me and she did.'* That took time, however. They relocated to help Sinn Féin's political development but, with his wife pregnant, they returned home and he withdrew from formal involvement in Sinn Féin:

> it's at that stage when I came back and I settled in Dublin instead of going back in, you know? I said I want some normality, just for a while. Just for once to be able to – we had a baby coming shortly after we came back ... And you know that certainly puts everything into perspective ... So I had to get a job. And we were desperate. We had to pay the rent.

He still supported Sinn Féin and still identified himself as a republican:

> Q: Are you still a republican?
>
> A: Oh yes, of course I am. You don't change your philosophy just because you're not as active as you were.

However, he chose his family over his activism:

> Certainly I'd love to play a far more active role during the whole peace process thing. I'd love to have been involved in the whole evolution of it ... I admire those who are totally involved and totally active. But that's not for everybody. I've got two children. It breaks my heart going away from them for a couple of days.[20]

He was not a formal member of Sinn Féin but he was willing to help out, such as, during the 1997 Dáil election. A few years later, 'they asked me would I do an educational course for new members'. From that point he became increasingly reinvolved. In 2005, he rejoined Sinn Féin:

> I had been involved in a peripheral way, in elections ... a particular friend came home from Dublin that had been an activist ... came back to live in the area and I knew he was back involved and I thought it would be lovely to reinvolve myself with all of my old comrades ... And I suppose I was surprised, I'm going to go back to find that a lot of people who'd been involved with me in the eighties, had gone from the Movement. Some of them had simply pulled away; they didn't agree with the strategy or whatever and simply pulled back and others it was more acrimonious ...
>
> Q: Did getting back involved ... part of the reason you stepped back in the early nineties was family obligations?
>
> A: Absolutely.
>
> Q: Did your family situation change? The kids were old enough that you could get involved again with –
>
> A: Yeah, where there was that and it was very – you remember from the eighties in particular, it was very difficult to be involved. I don't tend to get involved in things without giving it me all and so when I do get involved in a project I give it an awful lot of time. And certainly in the early nineties when [my daughter] and then [my son] came along, you know, there was no debating that that was my

priority. I suppose too there was an element of burn out as well but certainly I was excited by the whole developments in the peace process … I was I suppose a cheerleader from the side for long enough and decided that I would become more involved but certainly not to the level that I had been involved …

Q: Why was it easier to be involved in, say, in 2005?

A: It was easier obviously than the 1980s because that was just horrible in retrospect. We were all living in a pressure cauldron. It was a very strange place to be in and I wouldn't want to go back to that. But the atmosphere had changed greatly by 2005. And I suppose, too, in 2005 it's because … I have a particular friend coming back pursuing me. These are people that I really, really want to be active with again. So it was on that basis. It was as much personal as political … It is easier to be a political activist and a republican activist than it was in the olden days.[21]

Twice, a quarter of a century apart, a social connection with activists helped bring him into Sinn Féin. In between, his availability for activism waxed and waned depending upon his personal circumstances.

Life does not stop when people join social movements. Over time, their activism is confronted by a series of threats – they may clash with a comrade, a spouse or a significant other may question their choices, their health may decline and so on. Biographical changes threaten activism.[22] It would appear that, because the commitment of activists from republican families is reinforced regularly and from a young age, they are relatively immune to these threats. Also, and it may or may not be intentional, some activists find ways to minimize the threat of life's changes, for example by not marrying. Máire Comeford, a republican activist from 1916 to her death in 1982, never married. Alice Paul, a life-long activist in the women's movement in the United States, never married. For some respondents, however, the complexity of life gets in the way and they withdraw.

Life after Activism

One of the more interesting questions is how involvement in social movements affects the lives of former activists. The scholarly literature on involvement in the peaceful US Civil Rights Movement, for example, shows that former activists tend to maintain their progressive politics over time. Also, many of them developed skills through their activism that allowed them to pursue careers consistent with their progressive politics even though they were no longer involved in the Civil Rights Movement. For example, sociologist Doug McAdam interviewed veterans of 'Freedom Summer', a voter registration project in Mississippi in 1964. The respondents were college students in 1964 and, more than twenty years later, McAdam found that they were 'disproportionately concentrated in the so-called "helping professions", principally education, social service, and the law'.[23] The question is, does involvement in a revolutionary social movement that endorses political violence lead to similar outcomes for activists?

In the eighteenth century, Irish republican political philosophy was influenced by the ethos of 'liberty, equality, fraternity'. In the 1960s, Irish republicans declared themselves socialists. The

Provisionals' goal was, and is, a 32-county democratic socialist republic. Republicanism in the eighteenth century and socialism in the twentieth century were progressive political approaches. Respected terrorism scholar Richard English, in *Armed Struggle: A History of the IRA*, writes, 'radical ideas, and specifically socialist ones, have formed a key part of IRA thinking, and analysis of this strand is important to any understanding of the Provisional movement's evolution'.[24] The oral histories show that many former Provisionals chose life courses that were consistent with their progressive politics. And like former civil rights activists in the United States, the oral histories also show that the work lives of former Provisionals were aided by skills that they developed while they were activists.

The development of job-related skills is most clearly evident in accounts from activists who were involved in Sinn Féin's publicity department. Sinn Féin was banned from radio and television in the South; there were broadcasting restrictions in the North. South and North the authorities tried to suppress *An Phoblacht* and *Republican News*. The papers, and then *AP/RN* were important outlets for news and propaganda as one Sinn Féin activist described:

> *the paper was a vital part of the history of the struggle. I mean, people were producing* Republican News *in the backstreets of Belfast and producing different pages in the lounges and the back bedrooms of houses while there were lookouts at the end of the street looking for the British Army because the British Army were raiding places trying to close the paper down. Printers were threatened by the state. Offices were raided. There was that sort of mosquito press operation in homes and people were literally – it was like something out of a Second World War film with maybe the Polish or the French resistance producing a newspaper. It was that sort of thing. That was the history of the paper … Guerrilla press, if you like. And the paper has that history which maybe people don't appreciate now but it was part of the republican struggle because our voice was suppressed. And, in the South, we had censorship. We had Section 31, state censorship for broadcasting which didn't ban just republicans but anyone who was progressive or spoke out and said, 'Oh, hang on mate, the republicans have a point' or 'Actually, I don't agree with the republicans but there's something rotten in the state of the six counties.' That was suppressed. So the paper was very important—so to be asked to work for the paper … was an important part and it was an opportunity which I appreciate.*[25]

Producing *AP/RN* required writers, photographers, editors, copyeditors, layout and design specialists, etc. Another Sinn Féin activist explained:

> *Oh, there's no doubt about it,* An Phoblacht *has been a wonderful training ground for a lot of people. I know of several who have worked on* An Phoblacht *who have gone on to be successful journalists, obviously. Others have gone back – quite a lot of the staff – who came there with very few educational qualifications went back to college and got degrees and got very, very good jobs … it was the education thing. There was a perceived need, even in the Sinn Féin office not simply* An Phoblacht. *But it was just remarkable how many of them decided they wanted to further their education like that and actually did it. And it gave them that opportunity. If it did nothing else, it taught you to live on very little [slight laugh]. You never had money.*[26]

Author and Dublin historian Éamonn Mac Thomáis, writer Danny Morrison and journalist Gerry O'Hare are among the past editors of *An Phoblacht* and *AP/RN*. Belfast mural artist Danny Devenny was in charge of layout and design.[27] Working for the paper allowed some activists to develop specific skills. One former Provisional said:

> *We were very short staffed at the time that I came in and the paper was in bad straits. And we increasingly got more staff allocated to us. In the meantime, I was always interested in photography anyway and I was unhappy with some of the stuff that was being used in the paper and I felt that I could make a contribution in the odd moments of quiet, that I could go out maybe and take some photographs. I was just interested. I [had] never processed my own stuff before and I'd never taken photographs on that professional basis where you go forward to the front and take photographs facing back – if you know what I mean – as a professional does there in a full capacity to take photographs and to produce an end result. I might have been there demonstrating with everybody else and taking some photographs myself but never, never as an observer to try and catch the essence of what was happening and then convey that through a paper so that everybody else understands what was happening. And it was a very, very interesting, very exciting feeling. ...*

> *Q: Would you say that the Movement gave you a career?*

> *A: Well, certainly the Movement gave me an opportunity to do something that I had an innate love of anyway. I mean photography to me is really, really important. It vibrates for me. I get this huge feeling of satisfaction when I produce something that has, to my mind, captured the essence of what has happened. They may not always be creative photographs but they speak of what is going on and they're as true a representation as I can make. And I'm not a biased photographer. I do not do propaganda but I do try and represent what has happened on both sides.*[28]

At its peak during the hunger strikes, more than 50,0000 copies of *AP/RN* were printed and distributed throughout Ireland and internationally on a weekly basis. Papers had to be delivered, printers had to be paid and receipts had to be collected. A respondent from Belfast with a sense of humour described skills that he learned:

> *Q: Did the skills you learned from being a republican influence the job you have now? Help you get the job?*

> *A: Yeah ... I used to work for the finance department of the paper, so I picked up some bookkeeping skills. I took that and I went on to study bookkeeping and accounting. I didn't work there with the idea of getting experience, you know? In bill collecting or something – pay today or we blow you away [laughter]. You pick up some useful tricks. You know, collecting money, you'd wear a balaclava. You'd usually get paid. I'm joking, okay? In case this tape falls into the wrong hands.*[29]

None of the respondents joined the Provisionals hoping to develop job skills for the future. They saw an opening and believed they could make a contribution or they happened to be in the right place at the right time. One Sinn Féin activist was asked how he got his job with the paper:

It's probably like a lot of republicans. I've been in certain places at certain times and certain openings fell into us [laughter]. … 'There's a gap there.' 'Can you do this?' 'Let's try him here. If that doesn't work, we'll move him someplace else.' And they put me in there and I was willing to do it. And maybe I showed some potential for developing. I was totally unskilled in that field. I learned from people like Mick Timothy who was the editor of An Phoblacht. *He taught me huge amounts. One of the best journalists ever … The Movement taught me what I know about journalism and the media. And there's a lot more people who have learned that way as well. A lot of us were self-taught within the paper.*[30]

The development of job-related skills extended beyond those involved with publicity and *AP/ RN*.

Similar to former civil rights activists in the United States, several former Provisionals developed skills that they then used to help their communities. The following is from a former Sinn Féiner who pursued a career in a health-related occupation:

Q: Did skills you learned as a republican help you in your job?

A: Absolutely.

Q: How so?

A: I think that my experience over the last twenty, twenty-five years has greatly empowered me. I do not see myself as a victim, I see myself a survivor. And I think that it has empowered me in terms of dealing with everyday issues when you endure so much and cope with so much; life can throw anything at me now and I have the capacity to cope and deal with it. My life experiences have taught me to have empathy for those who, for example, present to me now with health problems. It doesn't matter which community they come from because I have worked with both and I have worked in London. And I suppose my job has also opened my mind up to all of that. But I think being a republican, and knowing what strife and struggling and suffering is and bereavement and loss and hurt and pain, really empowers me. And I would never see myself as a victim but a survivor of all of that.[31]

Former Provisionals also found work in community centres and helping troubled young people. One talked about this:

My activism on the streets in relation to drugs, in relation to believing communities have the right to organize in relation to working with families with issues, and my belief that all of us are equal has a huge bearing on how I work here and how I influence people here. We have one rule within the centre and it's respect. So I'm not going to shout at any kid. No kid is going to shout at the staff. The other rule is – and here again it's something that I've learned over the years – that … if you want someone to listen, talk to them – not over them, not to their parents, talk to them … It's about me believing that all of us are equal. And in some ways, the kid they bring us has to be given an opportunity to have a say in how their life progresses … From republicanism, we didn't have a media presence for years where we could be heard ... [they] always talked over us, never talked to us. And as an activist I found that when dealing with communities and when you've got to speak to communities on a one-to-one level then people get along with you.[32]

As social service and community workers, their concern for others reflected their progressive politics. Their skill-sets reflected their activist experiences. Another former Provisional described how skills learned as an activist transferred to his work with young people:

My skills are in media, in publicity and that, so in some ways [they apply] to other sectors now. I've worked in the community sector generally for more than a decade, so that did help. I did bring skills from what I learned through Sinn Féin and through An Phoblacht, *the weekly newspaper, to [NAME] Community Centre. I've done public relations for some community groups, anti-drugs campaign groups, for other groups, for women centres, for other projects that work with young people. So, yes, they did in a way, yes.*[33]

The Provisionals attracted some very talented people and put them to work in a variety of ways. Several activists who withdrew took with them skills that they then used to support their communities.

Not every former Provisional found a career in social service[34] and it cannot be denied that some former Provisionals have been arrested for criminal activity. By only highlighting the negative, however, some journalists criminalize the Provisionals and miss the fact that, scattered throughout Ireland, are thousands of former activists who quietly live their lives and contribute to their communities. Ten activists interviewed in the mid-1980s were not actively involved with the Provisionals in the mid-1990s. One of them was too ill for employment or he would still have been an activist. Of the other nine, three were self-employed, including a freelance photographer and a self-employed consultant/researcher, and five were employed in not-for-profits, including two health service workers and three community workers. Of the three activists who withdrew between the mid-1990s and 2005, one returned to teaching and another became a youth community worker. Also, by remaining involved with Sinn Féin, several of the respondents contribute to their communities as elected representatives and political activists.

Oral histories show that long-term involvement in the Irish Republican Movement stems from commitment and camaraderie with fellow activists, a sense of we-ness that is shared. This is especially the case for activists from Irish republican families who are exposed to the Movement at an early age and have their activism repeatedly reinforced by family members. In spite of this commitment, some activists withdraw. They typically withdraw for personal reasons. Similar to activists in the US Civil Rights Movement, those who withdrew took with them skills that allow them to contribute to their communities in a way that is consistent with their progressive politics.

22

WHO WON THE WAR? REFLECTIONS ON
ACTIVISM AND ARMED STRUGGLE

If you say it wasn't justified then you took part in something that was absolutely wrong. If you say it was justified it takes a long time to explain that because when someone slaps you, no one can say you're wrong to slap them back, especially if they're in the wrong. And that's how wars start.

– Former Provisional[1]

People join social protest movements because they want change. In *The Strategy of Social Protest*, William Gamson examines the success that 'challenging' groups have in winning two kinds of outcomes – acceptance and new advantages. Once the dust settles, successful challengers have a voice in political decisions and gain new advantages for their constituents. Unsuccessful challengers collapse with nothing to show for their efforts. There is also a middle ground whereby challengers may be 'co-opted' into the political system so they have a voice but not necessarily new advantages, and they may have their demands 'pre-empted' by established groups.[2]

Since the 1960s, peaceful and violent protest movements in the United States and Western Europe have influenced important social and political changes on issues that include civil rights, ending the Vietnam War, women's rights, the environment and democratization. Involvement in these movements has also affected individuals. Indeed, social movement scholar Charles Tilly commented that sometimes the most important outcome was at the individual level, 'through the transformation of people's lives, co-optation of leaders, or even renewed repression'.

Sometimes revolutionary social movements succeed, like in Cuba. More often, they fail. Gamson's research shows that challenging groups that try to displace their antagonists tend to fail while challengers that seek reform are more likely to gain advantages. The Irish Republican Movement has, for more than two centuries, tried to 'break the connection with England' and failed. For some, a partial victory was won when Irish republicans of the 1919–23 era compromised and settled for the Irish Free State. Over the course of the peace process, the Provisional IRA and Sinn Féin moved from endorsing armed struggle and demanding a British withdrawal from Northern Ireland to embracing peaceful, constitutional politics and seeking a reformed Northern Ireland as one step on the path to a united Ireland. This chapter considers the new advantages won by the Provisionals and how activism influenced activists' lives.

Since 2007, seventeen Provisionals and former Provisionals – first interviewed in the mid-1980s – have been asked to reflect on their activism. When they were reinterviewed, the respondents included activists in Sinn Féin, Republican Sinn Féin and the 32 CSM. Also interviewed were respondents who have disengaged from activism. The respondents represent a variety of political choices and perspectives. They offer their views on who won the war, what the Provisionals may have gained and how activism affected their lives.

Who Won the War?

The Sinn Féin Perspective

From 1969 on, the leadership of the Provisional IRA and Sinn Féin promised their supporters that armed struggle would continue until they won. That promise was reinforced on a regular basis but when the Provisional IRA campaign ended in 2005, a 32-county democratic socialist Irish republic was still a dream. Sinn Féin activists admit that the Provisional IRA did not win in a military sense. Their view, however, is that by surviving, the IRA put Sinn Féin in a position to obtain new advantages through peaceful means. A Sinn Féin activist commented:

> Well, what I can say to you is that the IRA never lost the war. I think there's a realization at that stage, both the British and the IRA had been involved in a long, long campaign. And I think there was a realization that each had fought themselves to a standstill. That there had to be a better way forward. And there had to be a better way of doing things.[3]

One aspect of the Sinn Féin perspective is that by surviving against a much stronger adversary, the Provisionals won. Another activist commented:

> The thing is that the IRA was never going to beat the British Army into submission. Anyone, and some of us in our wildest dreams might have liked to have thought that, in heady days and that ... The whole thing about the IRA is they had to survive and that by surviving the IRA won. That was winning for the IRA because they were fighting one of the most highly professional volunteer armies in the world and one of the most efficient, I might say ruthless, armies at that – one of the best equipped, best resourced, with all the resources of the Western world behind them, because all their allies were supporting them in what they did. The IRA survived, a small guerrilla army, against all the repression and the technology and the surveillance and everything else and the political machinations, the unionist death squads, the paramilitary police, the locally recruited UDR, the SAS, MI5, MI6 – the IRA survived. And that was the thing. That was brilliant for the IRA. The situation changed. The thing is that political movement had to come because the IRA was not going to win militarily and so that's why I think the cessations were correct and that. We reached a stalemate.

In response to 'What is the outcome of the war?', he replied:

Changed political landscape. There are [unclear] all-Ireland institutions. There's a reformed police service in the six counties. It's not all we want at the moment but there are moves afoot. There, I think, is a realization amongst unionists, they are seen as Irish by the British establishment, that their future is in a united Ireland. To what degree someone can gainsay it and that. You see that people are prepared to share power. People are prepared to talk to republicans. People are engaging. It's our job to convince them that we don't want to drive unionists into the sea. And I think nobody really expects that. Their future is in a united Ireland. And we should all unite together and use our resources, acknowledge our talents, to build a better future for the thirty-two counties. It's a changed political landscape.[4]

In addition to a changed political landscape in which Sinn Féin has a voice, they argue that the Provisionals also gained new advantages. In reply to 'What was the outcome of the war?', another activist said:

The outcome was an acceptance from a British government that – implicitly they've accepted that there's going to be an end to British rule in Ireland. And the outcome for the Irish government was forcing them to take responsibility for their own citizens and indeed for an area up until recently they claimed jurisdiction over but never exercised it, and also forcing them to stop accepting what the British decided they could say or do about the North. This consultative role, what bullshit. From the Anglo-Irish Agreement and Sunningdale – consultative role. You know what that meant? What that meant was the Brits decided and then they told the Irish government afterwards – maybe two hours before it was in the media.[5]

Richard English, in *Does Terrorism Work? A History*, notes a potential 'strategic victory' for the Provisionals. He writes, 'If the Provos could prevent the kind of resolution that was anathema to them, and ensure that no settlement was reached which excluded them from the finally arrived-at political structures in the region, then their violence might be seen to have worked in some measure.'[6] This nicely describes the approach of respondents who remained active in Sinn Féin. By surviving the British and Irish counterinsurgency, the Provisionals forced the two governments and the unionists to fully accept Sinn Féin into the political process. Thus, for a documentary by Peter Taylor, former Secretary of State for Northern Ireland James Prior commented, 'Violence probably does work, it may not work quickly and it may not be seen to work quickly, but in the long run, one has to look back and say it did work.'[7]

An Alternative Perspective: Republican Sinn Féin and the 32 County Sovereignty Movement

A very different interpretation of who did or did not win the war is offered by activists who left the Provisionals for Republican Sinn Féin in 1986. In response to the same question, an RSF activist said:

What was the outcome? Now a lot of the people who were deeply republican one time are in taking their big salaries now and hobnobbing with the British and all that, and [unclear] castles and institutions. And

I don't know whether it's any better for the local people up to the North but it seems they have cemented the border for the time being anyway.

Q: Who won the war?

A: [Laughs] Who would I say? I'd say, there's no winner at the moment and is the war over is the other thing.[8]

Another RSF activist was asked, 'Who won the war?' He replied: *'Actually the war, the war isn't over at all yet. The war isn't over at all yet.'*[9] The war is not over and the Provisionals did not win. Instead, the Provisionals' leaders diverted them onto a path of reform that will end in failure. In the words of a third Republican Sinn Féin activist:

The Provisional IRA did not win. They fought the British to a standstill if you like but then they threw the game away ... They stopped the struggle and they went over into the trenches of the enemy and in the last year [2006–07] they have advocated donning the uniform of the enemy. So, one wonders, how long would it be before they used the guns of the enemy against their former comrades and those who continue?[10]

Similar comments were offered by activists who left for the 32 County Sovereignty Movement in 1997:

Q: What was the outcome of the war? ...

A: The outcome of the Provisional IRA campaign was betrayal by the leadership, who, by the way, it's now becoming more and more apparent were in some way influenced by the British intelligence people and misdirected against their own organization's positions.

Q: Okay. The next question. Who won the war? Who won the Provisional IRA campaign?

A: Who won the Provisional IRA campaign? Well, I mean, this business that they didn't win or they didn't lose, that's irrelevant to me – you can't put that question because the Provisional IRA campaign, because of the way they settled and the grounds they called it off on, led to decommissioning. Right? Disarmament. How you can say you won it based on the agreements that they agreed to is beyond me.[11]

A second 32 CSM activist was asked, 'What was the outcome of the war?' He replied:

Well some people say we have peace now but we could have had peace thirty years ago, thirty-five years ago, if we had've accepted partition and worked on it from there, rather than wait for another twenty years and all that went on during that time in the interim. What have we gained? What have we gained? We're still partitioned. As a matter of fact, Articles 2 and 3, they gave us some sort of claim that is gone.

Q: You may have already answered this. Did the IRA win?

A: Again, it wasn't the Irish – The determination of the volunteers on the ground were tainted by a group of people who possibly saw some other agenda. The IRA would never have been beaten, would never have been beaten. There was always volunteers to step into the shoes of people that may have been locked up or may have been lost or whatever. The IRA would never have been beaten whatsoever. But, as I said, terms were dictated behind the scenes which governed the volunteers and that was an agenda that nobody really was aware of.

Q: Did you say the determination of the volunteers?

A: Yeah and the people, the calibre of people that were there. Now admittedly within the ranks, as you do know, there was a lot of informers …

Q: Would you say the IRA lost?

A: I wouldn't say they lost.

Q: Would you say they won?

A: No. Somewhere in the middle there. Again, you're in the middle of a stalemate so where do you go?[12]

From the perspective of those who left the Provisionals for rival organizations, the war is not over. The Provisionals did not win and anything they might have gained does not make up for what was lost through their betrayal.

The Perspective of the 'Disengaged'

Former activists tend to be somewhere in the middle on these issues. Those who disengaged tend to agree that the Provisional IRA did not lose:

Q: Would you say that the Provisionals won?

A: No.

Q: Did they lose?

A: They've been losing. No, no. I think somebody came up with a thing of an honourable draw. But there's no honour in it. It was a dirty war. I mean there's no honour there. I mean they reached impasses. Chess parallels it. It was a stalemate. But they, as I said, they reached some of their objectives, like they have a say in the government of the six counties at the moment. It falls far short of what they originally set out.[13]

Two former Provisionals, one Northern and the other Southern, view the time period from 1969 through to 2005 as a chapter in a longer, ongoing conflict. The first, when asked who won the war, replied:

Well, that's interesting because I would say that they were undefeated ... I don't think they've won. I mean, if they've won we don't need a united Ireland. Okay, so from that aspect – I think, I've got to say this – I think it's a chapter closed and a continuing process. I don't believe in a year's time, fifteen years' time, that we have a united Ireland, now.[14]

The second, when asked who won the war, replied:

Oh. Well, we didn't win it, but we're not beat yet.

Q: Okay. What will it take to win it?

A: Mmm. Brits out. And I think we have to organize again and we have to organize people. And we have to build another alternative movement ... Not necessarily with armed struggle. And certainly not at this point because I think armed struggle at this point is nothing short of blind militarism.[15]

The perspective of those who disengaged from the Provisionals is similar to the perspective of those who left for Republican Sinn Féin and the 32 CSM. They agree that the Provisionals did not win because the British have not withdrawn. At the same time, they do not say that the Provisionals lost. Their reluctance to state that the Provisional IRA lost is complicated by the fact that the Provisionals are part of the larger Irish Republican Movement. Even if the Provisional IRA failed, the Movement continues.

In summary, Sinn Féin supporters focus on the 'new advantages' won and believe the party is in a position to successfully advocate for more change. In contrast, the war is not over for activists who left for RSF and the 32 CSM, and the Provisionals are sell-outs. What is most interesting is that none of the respondents stated that the Provisionals lost the war, which helps explain why it took so long to decommission weapons. Decommissioning was, in part, an admission that the war was over and the Provisionals had lost.

Was the Campaign Justified?

The Provisional IRA killed approximately 1,800 people and injured thousands more. Arguably their most significant political achievement was forcing the British to prorogue Stormont in 1972. That goal was publicly proclaimed in the first issue of *An Phoblacht* but then the Good Friday Agreement brought back the Northern Ireland Assembly sited at Stormont.

The respondents were asked if the Provisional IRA's campaign was justified. It is a complicated question. The Provisional IRA and Sinn Féin were built on the back of state repression and loyalist violence. At the same time, the Provisional IRA was responsible for atrocities. The following is from a person who left Sinn Féin in the 1990s. He was asked if the war was justified:

Well, that's a really difficult question because if you say it wasn't justified then you took part in something that was absolutely wrong. If you say it was justified it takes a long time to explain that because when someone slaps you, no one can say you're wrong to slap them back, especially if they're in the wrong.

And that's how wars start. The loyalists kept our people down. Our people, along with people from other religions, by the way, not just Catholics – Protestants and all were in the Civil Rights Movement – and the police and the loyalists beat them off the streets, burned down their houses and killed them. And people have a right to react to that. But there were a lot of things that happened that were wrong. I mean it's never right, for instance, to put a bomb in a bar that the [loyalist] UVF used and to also know that other people used that bar. It's the same as that we have pubs in our neighbourhood that the IRA would frequent, but other people frequented it as well and people who disagreed with the IRA would frequent it as well. So it's wrong to bomb them bars. Our people did and that was wrong. So you can say there is a justifiability in actions of war but there are other actions that – just because there's a war doesn't mean to say you can just kill for the sake of killing. You can never deliberately target innocent people no matter what happens. You can never do that. There's things like the ten Protestants that were taken off the bus and shot dead … [the Kingsmills massacre]. There had been a numerous amount of Catholics killed in the preceding months and it stopped after that happened. That does not justify it. It was still wrong. The people who did that probably felt justified because the killing stopped but when the next person was killed two or three years later I'm sure their people didn't think it was justified.[16]

A former Sinn Féin activist had another angle on the issue. Asked if the war was justified, she replied:

I think that any country has the right to oppose a foreign occupation by any means possible … I think what you're asking me, was it worth it, and I can't answer that in terms of worth. I cannot answer that because I wasn't part of that military campaign … So for me to say it wasn't worth it would be, could perhaps denigrate someone who did give their life or whatever because they truly believed in what they were doing and they truly believed in their goal and no greater love to give up your life. So I can't say at this point that it was or it wasn't worth it but I know that we didn't win and I know that we're not beat yet.[17]

And for one Sinn Féiner, questions about the war being justified are not fair:

That sort of question irks me in a way because we're constantly being asked to justify the war. Justifying conflicts is always hard if it involves suffering and the thing is that nobody says the same to the British government. Nobody says that to British ministers. Nobody says that to the generals who come over here … Prince Charles is Colonel-in-Chief of the Parachute Regiment. Nobody says to him, 'Was what the Parachute Regiment did on Bloody Sunday justified?'… Nobody asks the British government who created partition, who created an artificial state, who partitioned Ireland on a gerrymandered sectarian headcount, nobody says to them, 'Was that justified?' It's always republicans who are asked to justify the struggle. The IRA's campaign and the republican struggle was a response to the Civil Rights Movement being crushed by the state – by the unionist state – and it was the unionist state for unionist people. Anyone who looks at the footage of the civil rights marches, from Burntollet to Derry, can't help but look at the protests in Alabama, in Montgomery, and say just change the colour of the faces. The same sort of thing that was happening in Montgomery was happening in Derry and Burntollet. That was what happened there. The

347

> *IRA, the armed struggle, the political struggle was a response to the political situation in the six counties. It was a response to that. Nobody asks the folks who perpetuated that were they justified.*[18]

The conflict was not one-sided. The British Army, the RUC, loyalists and the Provisional IRA were responsible for events that are difficult if not impossible to justify.

There was a general consensus among the respondents that the Provisionals were justified in taking up armed struggle. One former Provisional, in response to the question on the justification of the war, said:

> *Yeah, I mean as far as war can be justified. I would certainly be from an anti-war perspective. I think the way things evolved in the North, at some point, it was going to happen, that conditions in the North were going to breed people who would resist and the fact is that when it was resisted in a peaceful manner, that was met with pretty tough violence, pretty tough state violence which allowed a lot of people in uniforms who were pretty nasty people to deal with law and order on the streets and people can argue that the campaign – a lot of innocent people, and all the rest of it – but I think it was unavoidable and yeah, I think certainly it would be [justified]. I would be very hard pressed to say that people that took up arms weren't justified in doing so. I certainly think that there was as much justification for armed struggle in the sixties, seventies, eighties as there was in the beginning of the last century – 1916 and so on. And if you read any of the history books around that time, the editorials in the* Irish Times *and the* Irish Independent *were the same as the editorials you were reading in the seventies and eighties.*[19]

An activist in Sinn Féin offered the following:

> *Q: Given the Belfast Agreement, the Provisionals ended their campaign formally in 2005. Was the war justified?*
>
> *A: Of course.*
>
> *Q: Why?*
>
> *A: Because there was no other way to ensure that there was going to be any change, particularly in the North, but for the whole of Ireland through politics. Because there was no – it was closed off to republicans. There was no way that you could have done it through politics. But to use, I wouldn't use the word justify because it's too sweeping a statement. I'm sure other people would have a totally different viewing. So it's not a word I would use … Was it regrettably necessary at the time? Was it regrettably necessary at the time to fight? Could it have ended much sooner? Yes, that's a big regret of mine. But we started to sue for a peace process, for negotiations in the early eighties and there was no response publicly from anybody. And that certainly could not be laid at Sinn Féin's door … We were up for it, others weren't. Because there was still the idea in both governments that it could be crushed and that you could substitute some fiddling reforms idea for the North and a buying off of the republican sentiment in the South. And they tried over and over again – this nonsense about Sunningdale, you know, the Good Friday Agreement was 'Sunningdale for slow learners'. Well, I'd*

love to see in Sunningdale where there is the massive taking apart of the RUC, the taking apart of the institutionalized sectarianism in the North. The acknowledgement that people have a right to identify themselves as Irish and the acknowledgement from the British government that Irish unity was as legitimate and desirable a political entity as the union with Britain. Where is that in Sunningdale? Nowhere. Sunningdale was an appeasement and it was a platform for the moderate SDLP.[20]

Because the nationalist community in Northern Ireland suffered at the hands of unionist domination and because of state violence, former activists and Sinn Féiners agree that taking up arms against that was justified.

Activists in Republican Sinn Féin and the 32 County Sovereignty Movement also agree that conditions justified starting the campaign. What was not justified was ending it short of a united Ireland. When asked if the war was justified, a Republican Sinn Féiner commented:

Well of course. The people who entered into it, beginning with defense of the nationalist population in the six occupied counties – again, they took their leap in the dark. And one might as well be asked in view of the Treaty of surrender in 1921–22, was the 1916–21 period of resistance justified? And of course it was. But it's not for people like me to justify it. It's for the people who have settled for civil rights under British rule to justify it. How do they justify their participation in all that and then settle for a mere reformed British rule?[21]

An activist in the 32 CSM was asked:

Q: *Given the Belfast Agreement, Good Friday Agreement, and the Provisionals ended their campaign in 2005, would you say the war was justified?*

A: *If it had resulted in the removing of the British presence I would have said yeah. But at the present moment I can't see how it was justified … No. Because to what, for what? What about the sacrifices that people made? What was it for? For Gerry Adams to sit where he is? Martin McGuinness, to guffaw all he likes with Ian Paisley? Travel the corridors of power. Hosted by the best. Tea and brandy in the corridors of power. That's what it was all about?*[22]

Responses to the question of whether or not the war was justified are similar to responses to the question of who won the war. Overall, armed struggle was justified, even if some specific actions, like pub bombings and the Kingsmills massacre, were not. However, the anti-GFA republicans believe that ending the war short of a British withdrawal was not justified.

Regret, Pride and would you do it again?

There is a price to be paid for activism. All of the respondents suffered state harassment and even petty harassment was costly in terms of time and its effect on relationships. One former Provisional spoke about this:

They followed me into a coffee shop once, the Special Task Force, with a girlfriend who wasn't involved and who I hadn't said anything [about being involved]. And they took me, both of us, out of the coffee shop by gunpoint. And this poor woman died on the spot. So that was the end of a potentially beautiful relationship [laughs]. But it happened a few [times]. And they would take great delight in that sort of thing. It's just petty harassment. It could be quite sinister as well. Like on one occasion when they arrested me three [times in succession] – I was just going home with my laundry bag. It was the Special Task Force again. And they took me in and they took all my laundry and they were inspecting my underwear and stuff and throwing it around the station and just totally taking the piss [making fun of me]. But I got out after a couple of hours – straight outside the door and straight back in again. And the same thing – a couple of hours and out and then on the way nearly home, straight back in again. The same. It's just petty.[23]

Sixteen of these seventeen respondents were arrested at one time or another. Several of them were interned and/or convicted of paramilitary offences and spent a significant time in prison.

The respondents were asked if they regretted their involvement. In the words of one respondent, 'in any walk of life' it would be odd 'to look back over thirty years and have no regrets'. There is also the issue of asking someone to analyse and reflect on 'what happened thirty years ago' in the light of current conditions because 'those conditions didn't exist then'.[24] A former Provisional expressed regret at having been involved in some specific incidents:

I suppose I feel that maybe at one early period in the early eighties I probably was somewhat naïve in how I approached one or two particular incidents that had a significant impact on how my involvement would develop in later years. And as such I do have some regrets about those things. I got involved in a couple of incidents around about here and I ended up being locked up for a weekend [unclear] and there was severe hidings, beatings given out by the guards [Gardaí] and it had a significant impact on my own life at the time and some colleagues of mine that were involved ... maybe I would have handled it differently, I would have gone about it differently, and I would have, yeah, I certainly would have handled it differently.

And yet, the respondent also said, '*I have to say that I have been lucky and I haven't paid a high price for my involvement.*' And when he was asked about the 'costs' of involvement he said, '*I gave up what I gave up and I was glad to, and I wouldn't change it now.*'[25]

When asked if they regretted their involvement, the common reply was 'No'. Consider this exchange with a 32 CSM activist:

Q: Do you have any regrets about having been a member of the Republican Movement?

A: No.

Q: No?

A: No.[26]

Of fifteen respondents who addressed the regrets issue, thirteen indicated no personal regrets. Many of them began their response with either 'No' or 'None'.

In several instances, the 'No' or 'None' was qualified. The respondents may not have regretted their personal involvement, but some expressed regret that more had not been achieved. An RSF activist repeatedly stated that he had no regrets about his involvement and then went on to say: *'It's just, that it wouldn't have been more … that it wouldn't have been more successful and that the thing could of – talk about peace. Everybody wants a lasting peace in this country.* [27] Some respondents, when qualifying their response, mentioned the suffering of others. A Sinn Féin activist said:

> *Well, I'm trying to think just in case I do but I can't think of any offhand. As I say, you're meant to do things and regrets get you nowhere anyway but I probably regret – what I do regret, and very much, not doing more to address some of the personal divisions that are all between myself and members of my family, much sooner. Those weren't resolved until after 1999 when I had, I suffered a depression. I suffered a depression in 1999 and I came out of it with a very different way of thinking about – just with dealings with people and that there. So I went and I knocked on doors and said look, 'I want to put all that behind us', and get on with it and not fall out with people. I don't want to fall out with people over politics, especially family. You don't have to be huggy-kissy or that but you can be civil and have normal relations. And that's what it did. It [the conflict] poisoned relationships, you know? … The media was relentless, was relentless. Obviously, republicans did things wrong and some awful events happened but it – you just felt you were not getting a fair hearing … People were allowed to go along tracks of mutual suspicion which developed into mutual antipathy and that I really do regret, yeah.* [28]

A former Provisional commented:

> *I regret that it took so long to reach a resolution, and so many people, in my mind, died needlessly because of – I lay the blame at the door of the British, generally. We could have had these talks way back. I can't understand why it took so long. And I regret that people died because of that, because it was so long and drawn out. That would be one of my main regrets.* [29]

Another former Provisional offered similar comments:

> *the regret that I do have is the number of fantastic people that died – comrades that are no longer with us. And I suppose if anything makes me in any way a bit bitter it is the hunger strikers and the men that died on active service and who died in prisons, the men who have died since coming out of prisons and what they went through. Was that sacrifice worth what we have?* [30]

Yet another former Provisional, in response to the question, 'Do you have any regrets', replied:

> *No. I can't say that I have really. The only thing you can regret, as I've said to you before, the amount of suffering that people – and I'm not talking from my perspective but people's liberty and the way their families suffered and obviously the people that died. But I'd extend that to everybody. I mean the families*

of British soldiers, for instance, that we killed. I mean a lot of the guys that came here as British soldiers – I didn't know any of them but I knew people growing up in Manchester that I went to school with who joined the [British] Army and they were just working class lads. There was nothing else for them, only to join the Army.[31]

All of the respondents paid a price for their activism. In some cases, it was a very high price but, in spite of that cost, the respondents were less concerned about the personal cost of activism than they were about the cost that the conflict inflicted on others.

Fourteen respondents were asked if they were proud to have been a member of the Irish Republican Movement. Each person responded positively. The immediate response from three people was, 'Absolutely'. One Sinn Féin activist said:

Absolutely. Absolutely proud I'm a republican and people I work with now and have worked with know my politics. There's no – I've never hidden that. Even when the war was being prosecuted, people knew my politics. There was no problem there. People sort of respected us for it. They might not have liked us but they respected us. They knew what we were at because it was for the cause, the unification, for a better society. They may not have agreed with us in that but we were quite open about it. I have absolutely no qualms. I'm proud to be a republican and I hope other people feel the same way. There were obviously things that I wish I could have done differently or done better but you look at the lessons. Regret. It's one of those things you can take on but don't let it overwhelm you. If you've done something wrong or you could have done it better then change it.[32]

Activism gave the respondents an opportunity to give service to a worthy cause. This kind of pride was expressed across generations and political perspectives. A Republican Sinn Féin activist was asked if he was proud to have been in the IRA and Sinn Féin:

Yes, yes, both. And I wouldn't – I'm proud to have been in the Republican Movement and in its various aspects. Yes, but I hope it's not an overweening pride or anything like that. It's a confidence and a satisfaction of having given service and having been able to contribute and to make a good contribution.[33]

A Sinn Féin activist, when asked if she was proud to have been involved in the Movement, said:

In a political sense, yeah. I don't think of it as personal pride or anything. I kind of shrink from this sort of personal business because I think the decision you made in terms of politics is about politics. I know you have to also decide how your own personal life can actually cope with it. And for an awful lot of people who are absolutely genuine in support ... it's not that they're false people or anything but their personal circumstances simply wouldn't allow them to do that level of activism or even maybe join the party.[34]

The respondents, regardless of differences in their politics and whether or not they were still actively involved in an Irish republican organization, took pride in having offered service in what they believed was the liberation struggle of their country.

The respondents also reported that activism enhanced their lives. Every person who was asked the question, 'Would you say being a republican gave meaning to your life?' responded positively. Again, a common reply was, 'Absolutely'. A former Provisional was asked to describe how activism gave meaning to her life:

> *I think you have to have your dreams and I think you have to, at the end of the day, you have to make a difference because this is all of our world. This world belongs to all of us and I think every one of us has a big part to play. And I think it's very rewarding when you can do that. And you actually, you can make a difference in many respects. So I think that gives you meaning. I think it would be very, as I say, if I thought that things couldn't change I don't know if I could get up. I don't know how I could survive this world if I thought that things couldn't change. There's meaning for me to try and make things change.*[35]

Another former Provisional was asked, 'Would you say being a republican gave meaning to your life?' He replied: *'Oh, yeah, absolutely, yeah. It made me what I am – for better or for worse. I like to think I have a sense of justice for everybody whether it's in Ireland or South Africa or wherever and that it's just a built-in thing. Equality and justice, to me, that's what it's about.*[36]

The belief that involvement gave meaning to activists' lives extended across the political divide. A Sinn Féin activist commented: *'Being a republican that long has shaped who I am. And that has certainly given meaning to my life.*[37] In one exchange a 32 CSM activist was asked if being a republican had given meaning to his life:

> *Q: Would you say that being a republican gave meaning to your life?*
>
> *A: Well, if I had of spent my life sitting on a wall being a good boy I would feel very disappointed with myself.*
>
> *Q: Sitting on a wall being a good boy?*
>
> *A: Yes.*
>
> *Q: So, were you a bad boy? [Laughing]*
>
> *A: Now why is that? [Laughing] But I go this way What I mean by that is a lot of people now are intimidated into doing nothing. And now it's too late then for to change the mold because the mold has been formed around the nemesis created around them. You meet people like that regularly who say, 'I wish I had of but I didn't', and that's why.*[38]

More than one respondent commented that involvement did not so much give meaning to life as it gave the person a chance to put beliefs into practice. A Sinn Féin activist said:

> *I had meaning to my life anyway. The Republican Movement gave me a means of articulating that, of delivering on my ideals. So I'm not just sitting in the bedsit looking out, dreaming of a new society and that. The Republican Movement gave me the vehicle for achieving that. You had the overall vision and that*

was it. So it's not like I was looking for something to give me meaning. I had a meaning to my life. The Republican Movement was a vehicle for achieving that.[39]

Involvement in the Republican Movement enriched activists' lives. This enrichment, along with camaraderie and commitment to peers and beliefs, outweighed the costs of involvement. An enriched personal life is another outcome of involvement in social movements.

The respondents were asked to consider a hypothetical question, 'If you had the choice, would you join the Republican Movement again?' Because it is a hypothetical, it was not necessarily an easy question to answer. One 32 CSM activist replied:

That's a horse with a different colour now. That's a hard one to answer because, as I said to you earlier, I became a better person in my own estimation because of my involvement. I became more attuned to Ireland's whims and – it's a near enough of an impossible question to answer that. I'm not financially better off by any means because I misdirected my energies. But then again, did I misdirect my energy? What good have I done? Or, how many people would consider that I have done a lot of good? How many people would consider I was a fool for becoming involved? These are things that you have to weigh up, too.

Q: Were you a fool for becoming involved?

A: No, I was never a fool for becoming involved. How could I accept that? Was I a fool? Not at all. Republicanism is about the reunification of Ireland. That remains the goal today. No matter what way you look at it. In my estimation, I'm too late, or too long in the tooth, to change my viewpoints [laughs].[40]

Seventeen respondents were asked if they would 'do it again'. The other sixteen indicated without reservation that they would make the same choice. Twelve of them began their response with 'Yes' or 'Absolutely'.

The positive responses to the hypothetical question of choosing to join again or not extended across the range of activists – people from republican families and not; Northerners and Southerners; people who remained with the Provisionals and those who left for RSF or the 32 CSM, or disengaged. An RSF activist commented:

I think I would. I would, that sort of thing. Wouldn't be worth living if you hadn't … for a stand you take there … There would be nothing to stop me from doing it. I'd do it on account of my own people, too, that went before me, there. And, like we say, all the people that lost their lives, you know?… All the volunteers and everybody that lost their lives down through the years – if you did it for no other reason, you would [so] that they didn't die in vain.[41]

A Sinn Féin activist commented:

It would be easy for me to say no, but I probably would. I would, aye. No doubt about it. But as I say, again, you see all of it's in the circumstances under which, you know? And there was a whole series of circumstances that warranted that I join. But ultimately we were living in a state that had seriously oppressed my community from its inception and before. Whilst politically, I hadn't been clued into that then, when you look back [for me] and for many people like myself, it was almost inevitable that you were headed in this direction.[42]

In some instances, after an initial reply, the respondents added that they would do some things differently. One former Provisional said:

If I knew then what I know now I would do it differently ... [Laughs] Well I'm sure a lot of us would do it differently and we would never have allowed this [outcome] to happen ... But then we didn't know, we didn't know and there were bigger forces, there was stronger forces in terms of how infiltrated the Movement was ... there's also a real learning curve and hopefully people from, you know, future generations can learn from this.[43]

Another former Sinn Féiner commented that he would have reached out more to others:

I would join again. I would join again but I would do things differently ... reach out more ... It would be really important. I mean I, as an individual I was reaching out but one individual can't do it. It takes the Movement to do it ... And then the war would have – in fact, if I reached out well enough we could have stopped the war.[44]

The question is hypothetical. However, none of the respondents indicated they would not join again.

Although none of these activists stated that the Provisionals lost, other activists have. For example, a respondent who was not one of the original sixty-three was asked, 'Who won the war?' The reply was, 'The Brits. Hands down.' However, if these respondents – first interviewed in 1984/85 and reinterviewed in the mid-1990s and after 2005 – are representative of the Provisionals, then it appears that most activists are not willing to say that the Provisionals lost. There was no consensus on who 'won'.

Similarly, there are former activists who regret joining the Provisionals. In his memoir, Seán O'Callaghan describes joining the Provisionals as 'the biggest mistake of my life'.[45] In contrast, among this sample of activists and former activists there was general agreement that involvement affected their lives in a positive way. Some of the respondents expressed regret but it was not regret so much for their own involvement as for the pain that the conflict inflicted on others. The respondents also believe that their lives are better because of their involvement in the Provisionals.

Social movements have helped bring political and social change in the United States and in Western Europe. The same can be said of the Provisionals. Northern Ireland changed between 1969 and 2005 and became more politically inclusive. Although some of their critics deny that the Provisionals were responsible for anything positive, armed struggle did force the British and Irish governments to collaborate on a political solution that had to include Sinn Féin. The Good Friday Agreement formally admitted Sinn Féin and republican politics into the political process in Northern Ireland. By settling for reform, Sinn Féin won new advantages and gained legitimacy. Whether or not that was a sellout depends on one's perspective.

Others have argued that what the Provisionals gained was available years earlier. However, the view that the GFA was 'Sunningdale for Slow Learners' applies as much to the British and Irish governments and unionist politicians as it does to the Provisionals. Even if the Provisionals had settled for Sunningdale, it would not have led to peace. In 1974 and 1975, there was strong opposition among unionist politicians to sharing power with the moderate SDLP, let alone Sinn Féin. The Ulster Workers' Council Strike and the fall of the Northern Ireland Executive in 1974 and the demonization of Sinn Féin into the 1990s – state collusion with loyalist assassinations, state censorship, harassment, the abuse heaped on John Hume simply because he met with Gerry Adams – cannot be ignored. It does not say much for British constitutional politics that it took more than twenty-five years of armed struggle before the British would force unionists to accept power sharing.

Social movements also have outcomes for individuals. Even if activists disagree on whether or not new advantages were won, they may still agree that they personally benefitted from involvement. These personal benefits, including the belief that involvement has meaning, help us understand why people are willing to make sacrifices in the face of incredible odds and past failures.

Since 2005, Sinn Féin has pursued its struggle through peaceful, constitutional politics. Republican Sinn Féin, the 32 County Sovereignty Movement, the Continuity IRA and the Real IRA have also continued. Other movement organizations have joined the 'dissidents'. The Irish Republican Movement continues.

PART 4

The War is Over: The Irish Republican Movement Continues (Activism since 2005)

23

SINN FÉIN: THE WAR IS OVER, THE STRUGGLE CONTINUES

I am a member of the Derry Brigade of the IRA and I am very, very proud of it.

– Martin McGuinness, 1973[1]

Our position is clear, and it will never, never, never change. The war against British rule must continue until freedom is achieved.

– Martin McGuinness, 1986[2]

And of course the relationships we've built with multi-national companies in the United States has seen the New York Stock Exchange come to Belfast and open up offices that employ 500 people ... So, it's about jobs. It's about whether or not I could use the contacts I have, in conjunction with government ministers here, to attract foreign investment so that we put our people back to work.

– Martin McGuinness, 2011[3]

The Provisional IRA's campaign casts a long shadow over Sinn Féin. The party is caught between celebrating the commitment and sacrifices of IRA volunteers and denying embarrassing details of the war. The Sinn Féin response to difficulties is pretty much the same as Gerry Adams's response to reports that he was an IRA commander – deny everything, act like you're the victim, try to deflect the issue and, above all else, move forward. By compromising and distancing themselves from unpleasant parts of their past, Sinn Féin has become a significant all-Ireland political force. The party leadership has even managed to survive the outing of high level informers and allegations that sex-crimes were covered up. It has been a bumpy ride.

In the spring of 2005, Martin Ingram and Greg Harkin's *Stakeknife: Britain's Secret Agents in Ireland* was published. The book provided detailed allegations that Freddie Scappaticci of IRA internal security was an informer, including Scappaticci's role in setting up Danny Morrison. In the fall, and after IRA decommissioning, Denis Donaldson was finally going to be prosecuted for his role in Stormontgate. Out of the blue, the Director of Public Prosecution dropped the charges in the 'public interest' and the move suggested an informer was being protected from having to either commit perjury or reveal himself. A couple of days later, Gerry Adams shocked everyone by announcing that it was Denis Donaldson. In his own press briefing, Donaldson admitted that, since the early 1980s, he had been an agent for British intelligence and the RUC/PSNI Special Branch. Donaldson also denied that he had been involved in a spy ring at Stormont, as if anyone would trust anything he said.[4]

Donaldson's outing revealed the high level at which the Provisionals had been compromised. It also raised questions about the manipulation of people and events. It is reported, for example, that Martin McGuinness stepped down as Chief of Staff because he wanted to be more involved in Sinn Féin politics and that his successor was hard-liner Ivor Bell.[5] Bell was then conveniently removed from the scene by supergrass Robert Lean. Martin McGuinness and Gerry Adams, who would lead the peace movement, were never caught in the supergrass net.

In the old days, Denis Donaldson would have been shot in the head and left in a ditch. Instead, he was expelled to rural Donegal and a cottage with no running water or electricity. In the spring of 2006, a journalist tracked him down for an interview and a photo of the cottage appeared in the *Sunday World*. A few weeks later, Donaldson was killed by a shotgun blast.[6] Why he was killed was obvious but who killed him was not. The Provisionals denied any involvement and condemned the murder.

The embarrassment caused by informers did not end with Denis Donaldson. There was already speculation that the British allowed Freddie Scappaticci to be exposed as an agent because they were protecting someone at a higher level. Some assumed it was Donaldson but others wondered if Donaldson was sacrificed to protect someone even higher. Rumours circulated and activists re-examined their experiences. In the words of a respondent:

> *I was totally committed. I done all that ... I wasn't even getting paid for doing that. I was sitting up in a crap office that had no heating in it, that wasn't even secure in terms of a loyalist attack. I was a sitting duck – quite crazy when I look back [laughs]. But I think all those things speak for themselves. And they were willing to let someone like that go? But the crunch came when ... a certain group of people did everything in their power to prevent me from running as a candidate ... And I found that quite painful at that time because I still believed in the Sinn Féin project at that time ... So when I look now – and it never would have occurred to me at the time – but when I look back now – and now that it has emerged that very high profile people were agents for the British, I'm not surprised that someone like me would be pushed out.*

Asked to comment if the allegations about high-profile agents were true, the respondent replied:

> *Let me make a comment about that. I neither trust the British or the Republican Movement when it comes to if it's true or not true because, when Scappaticci was first ousted as a British agent, the Republican Movement, Gerry Adams and the Republican Movement denied that this was true. So how can you believe anything they say after that? So if they tell me someone's not a British agent, I can't believe them because they tried to cover up for Scappaticci. That is the most absolutely unforgivable – that this man*

Scappaticci was actually in charge of making decisions and who was going to be killed. If I was the relative of someone who was shot and it was alleged that – for informing for example, alleged informing – I would be at Connolly House every day asking them to give me the real evidence. And I would be asking, 'Why?' because I would wonder who really wanted my loved one killed. Was it the British or was it the Republican Movement? Because it was the British who was actually running the 'Nutting Squad' as they called it. And I think for any movement to stand up and try and cover for that man then many more questions have to be asked.

Two years after Denis Donaldson was killed, Roy McShane was exposed as a British agent.[7] For more than a decade he had been one of Gerry Adams's chauffeurs.

Sinn Féin also had internal difficulties. A group of younger activists who believed the party had lost its socialism met in Dublin and formed éirigí (arise).[8] Their inspiration was James Connolly, the executed 1916 leader and socialist who wrote that the 'capitalist and the landlord classes' in Ireland were criminal accomplices with the British government and 'from socialism alone can the salvation of Ireland come'. The Provisionals had settled for much less than a socialist republic. This split was small but important because Sinn Féin presented itself as the alternative to mainstream parties. The éirigí split reinforced the view that Sinn Féin was becoming moderate but, at the same time, moderation increased the party's appeal in some quarters. And in the murky world of Irish republicanism, there are rumours that Sinn Féin created éirigí in order to keep the disaffected from joining dissident organizations.

Sinn Féin denied or ignored the critics, depending upon what worked best, and pushed for restoration of the Northern Ireland Assembly. The curious thing was that their opponents in the DUP were essentially in the same position. Both sides wanted access to political power but neither side could restore the Assembly on their own. Paisley had promised that a deal with Sinn Féin would happen 'over our dead bodies'. Sinn Féin had promised a new police force, not a reformed RUC called the PSNI.[9] If they wanted political power, however, Paisley and the DUP and Adams, McGuinness and Sinn Féin would have to compromise. In the autumn of 2006, the British one more time put together multi-party talks, this time at St Andrew's in Scotland. The key players were Sinn Féin and the DUP, and the key outcome was that, in exchange for Sinn Féin accepting the PSNI as Northern Ireland's police force, the DUP agreed to share power with them in a restored Assembly. The exact composition of the Assembly would be determined by an election in March 2007. And if the Assembly remained in place for two years, the British would devolve the powers of policing and justice from London to Belfast. But, because the Sinn Féin and the DUP leadership were out in front of their respective rank and files, the deal was not quite done. The DUP wanted Sinn Féin to formally accept policing and Sinn Féin, needing to justify yet another compromise, was not quite ready to call an Ard Fheis.

When the peace process hit snags, the Sinn Féin leadership blamed 'securocrats' –securocrats, not Denis Donaldson, were responsible for Stormontgate. Blaming unseen securocrats fit well with the general distrust that Sinn Féin's supporters had for the RUC. The Special Branch, in particular, was seen as a sinister 'force within a force' that had colluded with loyalist death squads. Sinn Féin announced they would not go forward with the plan unless the British agreed to stop 'political policing' and separate MI5 intelligence gathering from PSNI policing.[10] One of the DUP's concerns was that Gerry Kelly, London–bomber in 1973 and Sinn Féin spokesperson on policing thirty plus years later, would become Minister for Justice. Tony Blair and Jonathan Powell stepped in and smoothed things over. At Powell's suggestion, Sinn Féin and the DUP agreed that neither party would claim the justice position in a new Assembly, and that satisfied the DUP. Blair then announced that MI5 would retain control of national security in Northern Ireland but would not have a role in policing. Sinn Féin claimed it was a 'major victory' and an Extraordinary Ard Fheis was scheduled for the end of January 2007.

What Adams claimed was a victory others saw as a broken promise. Independents organized a series of meetings with the theme, 'Policing: A Bridge Too Far'.[11] In a letter to the *Irish News*, Brendan Hughes and John Kelly claimed that Sinn Féin told members to stay away from the meetings and that the party was threatening 'dissenting voices'. It was the same John Kelly who helped found the Provisionals in 1969 and had been implicated in the Fianna Fáil gun-running scandal. Sinn Féin dismissed allegations of intimidation as 'nonsense' and went after internal critics. Davy Hyland, Sinn Féin's MLA for Newry and Armagh, was already sceptical about the party's direction. Hyland commented:

> *My time in Stormont, this sort of reinforced my views, that it was a waste of time being in the place – that very little was to be achieved working within the parameters of British power lines ... and I already had a clear inkling because I knew the way that Sinn Féin works and how people – at that stage, more and more people from the Army, from the IRA, had come over into Sinn Féin – and they were clearly directing how the party operated.*

Hyland was set to defend his seat in the upcoming Assembly election. Because he expressed reservations about policing, the leadership retaliated and he was de-selected, as he explained:

> *Well, the biggest argument used was that I wasn't doing enough work, that I wasn't attending enough meetings, although I never missed a day's work in the whole time I was in Stormont, for any reason. But I believe that it was – I was unhappy, especially with the policing arrangements. I had voiced that opinion to a number of people ... there were a number of people, not only myself, but a few others from different parts of the North were also de-selected and they were also saying they were sceptical about what would happen in relation to policing and felt that it was a step too far and a step too quick. And far too many people had experience in policing that made them very suspicious about the whole idea of accepting a new police force even if it had slightly more Catholics or nationalists in it.*

Hyland was unable to attend the election convention in Newry that would select the candidate for Newry and Armagh. He learned after the fact that delegates were told not to vote for him: *'I know, for instance, at the convention, that I didn't attend myself because I was out of the country, a good friend who attended the conference ... told me in confidence that he had received a phone call on the evening of the convention telling him how to vote by people superior to him.'*[12] Sinn Féin blamed complaints about policing on 'sour grapes' and attacked the character of their critics. The party line on Hyland, for example, was that he left Sinn Féin because he was upset with being de-selected.[13] A letter to the *Irish News* from Jim McAllister, however, said that Hyland 'has been a republican activist and then a good republican elected representative all his adult life and has been shabbily treated'.[14]

At the Extraordinary Ard Fheis, the delegates followed their leaders and supported the compromise on policing 'by a majority of around 90%', according to *AP/RN*. More formally, Sinn Féin endorsed the criminal justice system in Northern Ireland, reiterated their support for An Garda Síochána, agreed to appoint representatives to the Northern Ireland Policing Board and endorsed co-operating with the PSNI *and* the Gardaí to 'solve crime in the community'. Gerry Adams referred to it as a 'truly historic decision' and called on people to cooperate with the police.[15] The critics agreed that the about-face was historic and, for a brief period, a diverse group of republicans came together to challenge Sinn Féin in the Assembly election.[16]

Davy Hyland defended his seat for Newry and Armagh as an Independent. Another independent candidate was Peggy O'Hara, the mother of hunger striker Patsy O'Hara. More than three hundred ex-prisoners, including her son and ex-prisoner Tony O'Hara, signed a letter to the *Derry Journal* supporting her candidacy. Republican Sinn Féin put up six candidates as Independent Republicans, including Geraldine Taylor in Belfast, Mickey McManus in Fermanagh/South Tyrone, Mickey McGonigle in East Derry and Joe O'Neill in West Tyrone. Just before the election, an eclectic pressure group was formed, 'Ex-POWs and Concerned Republicans against RUC/PSNI & MI5'. The group included Brendan Hughes, John Kelly, Anthony McIntyre, the Price sisters, Dermot Gannon in Dublin, former hunger striker John Nixon, Tony O'Hara and two former members of the Sinn Féin Ard Chomhairle, Tony Catney and Gerry McGeough. In a letter to the *Irish News*, Catney complained that the leadership expected people to follow them blindly, 'without question or dissent'.

Gerry McGeough, who is opposed to abortion and quit Sinn Féin because he disagreed with the party's position on the issue, ran as an Independent in Fermanagh/South Tyrone. McGeough commented on the election:

> *When the election was finally called I announced and I made it clear that we just didn't expect to win this thing. It would be ludicrous to think that we could, but what we were doing was making a stand … we had this rollover policy. It was this abomination. It really was the last straw. My argument was that, apart from the fact it was anti-republican recognizing this group, how could you recognize an institution that hadn't been reformed?*[17]

Gerry Adams's greatest strength may be his ability to move the Provisionals forward, compromise by calculated compromise, so that the distance travelled broadens Sinn Féin's appeal enough that it more than compensates for the loss of supporters opposed to change. Anti-policing candidates didn't have a chance.

In the March 2007 election to the Northern Ireland Assembly, Sinn Féin outpolled the SDLP by more than 75,000 votes (180,164 vs 105,064) and elected 28 MLAs (versus 16 for the SDLP).[18] Anti-policing republicans received a total of 8,130 votes and none of them were elected. Two anti-policing candidates, Davy Hyland (2,188 votes) and Peggy O'Hara (1,789 votes) accounted for almost half of that total. The six Independents from Republican Sinn Féin received a total of 2,522 votes. The nationalist community wanted the Assembly up and running and a majority of them wanted Sinn Féin in power.

Unfortunately, the election also showed that political policing was not a thing of the past. Gerry McGeough remembers it as a dirty election, commenting that it 'beggars belief in terms of dirt and nastiness that took place'. He attended the count in Omagh and suspected that his votes were intentionally undercounted. McGeough was considering a protest:

> *I never got any chance to make any protest because I was arrested at the very door on my way out …*
>
> *Q: Did you have any anticipation you'd be arrested?*
>
> *A: None whatsoever. If I had thought I was going to be arrested, I wouldn't have put myself in that position … I'd been up and down for the best part of ten years and living openly and all the rest of it, and called for jury duty, taking part in all kinds of stuff, my kids went to school and all that sort of thing, running in an election as a high profile candidate …*[19]

Gerry McGeough was politically inconvenient and he was charged with several offenses dating from 1981, including attempted murder. That effectively silenced his critique[20] and Sinn Féin moved on without Tony Catney, Davy Hyland, Gerry McGeough, etc.

The Assembly met in May 2007 and, in a scenario that no one would have anticipated given their histories, Revd Ian Paisley and Martin McGuinness were elected First and Deputy First Ministers.[21] Adding to everyone's amazement, Paisley and McGuinness got along so well that they were nicknamed the 'Chuckle Brothers'. And the political institutions of Northern Ireland were solid enough that there was a smooth transition to Peter Robinson as First Minister when Paisley retired (2008), and then to Arlene Foster when Robinson retired (2016). In 2010, as agreed at St Andrew's, the Department of Justice, Northern Ireland, was established. With the support of the DUP, Sinn Féin and some of the smaller parties, David Ford, leader of the Alliance Party, became the Minister for Justice, Northern Ireland.[22]

After their success in the North, Sinn Féin went into the May 2007 Dáil election with high expectations. It turned out that the Southern electorate was less interested in 'New' Sinn Féin sharing power in Northern Ireland than they were in basic issues that affected their lives. It did not help that, in debates, Gerry Adams handled questions about the Southern economy poorly and seemed out of touch on issues in the Republic of Ireland.[23] Adding to the disappointment, young candidates, like Mary Lou McDonald (Dublin Central), Pearse Doherty (Donegal), Lynn Boylan (Kerry South) and Joanne Spain (Dublin Mid-West), were not elected and Seán Crowe lost his seat. Mary Lou McDonald's loss was especially upsetting because she was a sitting MEP and had been selected as a candidate ahead of senior people. Bertie Ahern continued as Taoiseach in a Fianna Fáil/Progressive Democrat/Green Party coalition.

Eoin Ó Broin, who joined Sinn Féin in the mid-1990s and has a master's degree in politics from Queen's University, is seen as an important political theorist for Sinn Féin. In *Sinn Féin and the Politics of Left Republicanism*, he writes of the party's 'failure to articulate a credible alternative economic policy to that of Fianna Fáil and Fine Gael ...' as a key problem in the election. Ó Broin also notes the party's organizational problems. It was the beginning of a tough stretch. Mary Lou McDonald succeeded Pat Doherty as vice President and then promptly lost her seat in the 2009 European election. Christy Burke then left Dublin Sinn Féin and became an Independent on the City Council. John Dwyer, a Councillor in Wexford, followed suit and became an Independent; he would later join éirigí. A couple of months after that, Dublin Councillor Louise Minihan left for éirigí[24] and the defections continued into 2010.

Killian Forde was a rising star in Sinn Féin and a likely candidate in the next Dáil election. He also was Chair of the Dublin City Council's Budget Committee. The recession had wrecked finances everywhere and Forde's committee put together a budget that included a rubbish removal ('bin') charge for low-income families. He described the budget process:

> *I'd been given the job as the Finance Chairperson for Dublin City Council, which is a fairly big – I mean it's a job in itself. Because of the recession, it was never going to be an easy budget to pass and it was never going to be an easy budget to put together. We managed to do it. We managed to protect jobs. We managed to keep swimming pools open. We managed to ensure that there was still some overtime left for people, that services weren't cut and so on and so on. One of the things that was going to happen was that charges for bins was going to go up. Now that's not within our power. This all gets very technical [the City Manager sets fees]. The long and short of it was that I felt that Sinn Féin had asked me to go in and do a job. I did it in good faith ... I got Labour on board in terms of the budget and we broadly agreed that it was the least worst option – broadly. And then, very late in the day, I got an instruction that we were to vote no. And I said, 'Well, I'll vote no but I'll have to resign as the Chairperson of the Finance Committee'. You cannot be effectively a minister of finance, which is sort of what that job is, and then vote against your own budget because I had to introduce the budget legally. It's a statute requirement that the Chairperson actually introduce the budget. So Sinn Féin asked me to introduce the budget and then vote 'no' for it. And I said, 'Well, I'll do that, that's okay, but like, I'll resign after it.' And they said, 'No, you're not to resign either.' And so I talked to the group and I decided I'd vote for it. They'd vote against and I'd vote for it. And I voted for it on the basis that I thought this was the best we could do and so be it. And so I did that and that set off a shit-storm at the end of which I resigned.*[25]

Forde left for the Labour Party and Éoin Ó Broin, on behalf of Sinn Féin, described him as a 'careerist politician' who should resign and let the seat revert to the party.[26]

The press overplayed the defections and suggested there was a crisis in Sinn Féin. Instead of a crisis, the defections showed that the party was still sorting itself out in a post-armed struggle world. More than Dublin's budget was involved in Killian Forde leaving Sinn Féin. A detailed internal memo that he had written became public and helped explain his decision:

> The power and associated decision-making in the party lies with individuals not embedded structures. This means that those seeking to question or contribute to decisions, policies

or strategy have to try and negotiate through a maze of offices, titles, committees, working groups and individuals to try to get their voice heard …

People are routinely appointed to positions in the party with no experience in the role. This must end. In the period preceding the 2009 election we have had the appointment and employment of a Head of Publicity that has no experience in PR … The Director of Elections appointed to oversee Mary Lou's crucial European campaign had never even participated in any form in any election before, anywhere.

….

Sinn Féin and republicans value loyalty and obedience, probably above any other virtue. This was an understandable position when the republican movement was at war. It has now become the greatest hindrance to us developing as a dynamic, interesting, vibrant, creative party. There is little tolerance for dissenting opinions and nowhere for people to take those opinions.[27]

When the Provisional IRA was active, Sinn Féin needed leaders who were loyal and committed in the face of extreme opposition and pressure. Being trustworthy, loyal and sound trumped organizational skills. The war was over. Forde remained on the Dublin Council for another year and then resigned to go and work for a non-profit. Mícheál Mac Donncha, a past editor of *AP/ RN*, was co-opted to fill the vacant seat for Sinn Féin.

External events have a way of compensating for internal difficulties in political organizations. Fianna Fáil was already suffering from the staleness of being in government for too long when the recession hit. The party handled the recession poorly, as did most parties in power. In the 2011 Irish general election, Fianna Fáil's presence in Dáil Éireann fell from seventy-one seats to twenty. Fine Gael, Labour, Sinn Féin and Independents reaped the benefits. Sinn Féin gained 75,000 votes and elected 14 TDs. The successful candidates included Gerry Adams, who had resigned as MP for West Belfast and was elected a TD for Louth, Pearse Doherty in Donegal South West, and Seán Crowe in Dublin.[28] It was an impressive showing but not enough to get into power. Fine Gael and Labour formed a coalition government. In the 2016 Irish general election, Sinn Féin did even better and picked up nine more TDs for a total of twenty-three. Fianna Fáil, however, rebounded nicely and picked up twenty-three TDs. No party won a majority and, at the time of writing, Fine Gael leads a minority government.[29]

At the time of writing, Michelle O'Neill of Tyrone has just succeeded Martin McGuinness as Sinn Féin's leader in Northern Ireland and Gerry Adams continues as the leader of the Sinn Féin parliamentary party in Dáil Éireann. Of the two men, history will be more kind to McGuinness. He is the Chief Negotiator who delivered peace and was willing to serve as Deputy First Minister alongside DUP First Ministers Ian Paisley, Peter Robinson and Arlene Foster, until he resigned in protest over Foster's handling of the RHI scandal and then retired from politics because of poor health.[30] McGuinness has reached out to unionists and shaken the hand of Queen Elizabeth when she toured Northern Ireland; the handshake showed how far the Provisionals, McGuinness and the Queen (whose uncle Lord Mountbatten had died at the hands of the IRA) have travelled. McGuinness has also been more direct about his past, although there remain allegations that he was involved in the execution of informer Frank Hegarty. As part of his testimony to the Saville Inquiry into Bloody Sunday, McGuinness admitted that he was second in command of the Derry IRA that day. The testimony only confirmed what he blurted out in a courtroom in 1973, but the contrast with Adams's continued denial of membership is striking.[31] In 2011, McGuinness was Sinn Féin's candidate for President of the Republic of Ireland and received 240,000 votes, finishing third behind Michael D. Higgins (Labour) and Seán Gallagher (formerly of Fianna Fáil and running as an Independent) and ahead of Gay Mitchell, of Fine Gael.

Gerry Adams will be remembered as a charismatic leader and political genius whose legacy is haunted by the suspicion that he is a manipulative liar with lots of blood on his hands and no conscience. One of the best descriptions of Adams is found in Kieran Conway's memoir, *Southside Provisional: From Freedom Fighter to the Four Courts*. Conway, who at one point in the 1970s was the IRA's Director of Intelligence, describes Adams as 'a mendacious, lying bastard. But what else could he be? For the movement could never have been taken in the direction that he took it without a bit of dissembling.' Conway also writes, 'The "peace process" was, in my view, simply Adams' Plan B, to cover for the eventuality of an IRA failure, but there's no way he could have, or did, *make*, the IRA fail. And he was the only one who even *had* a Plan B.'[32] Complicating 'Plan B' are allegations that Adams has a very bloody past.

The allegations resurfaced when Ed Moloney published *Voices From the Grave: Two Men's War in Ireland*, which drew on oral histories from the 'Boston College Oral History Archive on the Troubles in Northern Ireland', the 'Belfast Project'. The book presented oral histories from two men, David Ervine (1953–2007) and Brendan Hughes (1953–2008). Ervine, a member of the UVF turned loyalist politician, had played an important role in the loyalist ceasefire. Hughes had, at one time, been very close to Adams. His allegation that Adams was involved in the Bloody Friday bombings and the abduction and murder of Jean McConville made the book an immediate and controversial bestseller. Hughes was dead, however, and chances are the controversy would have faded if the *Irish News* had not published articles in which Dolours Price described Adams as the 'mastermind' of McConville's disappearance. Price also revealed that she had driven McConville across the border and that her oral history was lodged with Boston College.[33]

Boston College had promised that the oral histories would be not be used 'until and unless the interviewee consented or had died'.[34] It was a promise they could not keep. The PSNI used subpoenas to obtain several interviews. Sadly, as the controversy continued, Dolours Price passed away at sixty-one years of age, in 2013. Described as 'defiant to the end', she had suffered from post-traumatic stress and addictions caused by her prison experience, including the famous hunger strike and force-feeding of 1973–4.[35] Also, Price's passing made it that much easier for Gerry Adams to defend himself by countering that she and Brendan Hughes told lies.[36] The Boston College oral histories would lead the PSNI to question several people, including Gerry Adams and Ivor Bell. Adams was released but charges have been filed against Bell. In the meantime, Boston College's mishandling of the Belfast Project has seriously damaged scholarship on the conflict in Ireland. In the words of an online commentator on the *Irish Republican Forum*, 'You'd want to be mental to share your story or record it for posterity in this climate.'[37]

Personal issues also damage Adams's reputation. The allegation that Liam Adams was a paedophile became public in 2009. Gerry Adams acknowledged that he had known of the allegation since the 1980s and stated that he believed and supported his niece.[38] However, journalists like Suzanne Breen feasted on Gerry Adams's claim that he had distanced himself from his brother.[39] In *Before the Dawn*, which was published in 1996, Gerry Adams thanks family members for their help on the autobiography – 'our Paddy, my father, brothers and sisters, especially Liam ...'[40] Anyone with old issues of *AP/RN* could see that Liam Adams was prominently involved in Louth Sinn Féin in the mid-1990s. A photograph published in June 1996 shows him at the front of a crowd that was addressed by Martin McGuinness at the opening of a Sinn Féin office in Dundalk. In January 1997, *AP/RN* reviewed a pamphlet entitled, 'Our children, drugs, alcohol and solvents' that was produced by a Dundalk community youth project. According to the review, 'Liam Adams, a voluntary youth worker, introduces the reader to the issues linking youth and drugs and describes the commonest drugs available, from alcohol to heroin, and their likely effects.'[41] Between 1998 and 2006, Liam Adams worked at a youth centre and as a youth development officer in West Belfast.[42] Gerry Adams's credibility was so low that when he revealed that his father had abused some of his siblings, sceptics wondered if it was an attempt to shift the discussion away from him and Sinn Féin.[43] Through all this and his brother's conviction in 2013, he remained the party's President.[44]

Gerry Adams and Martin McGuinness are the public face of Sinn Féin but the party is much bigger than either of them. And there is more to the party's agenda than 'Brits out'. Sinn Féin represents people who were denied full admission to the social, political and economic life of Northern Ireland. Fra McCann grew up in a working-class nationalist family in the Divis area of West Belfast. Today, he is the area's representative to the Northern Ireland Assembly. McCann, joined the Movement in 1971 and, forty years later, he was asked if he had ever expected to be sitting where he was, in the Stormont Parliament Buildings:

> *Oh no, I never – the only time I was ever in Stormont was about 1964. My father had been on the industrial injuries, which is a benefit. And we were here two days before Christmas but there was no money in the house. I was twelve. Ten kids, and I and my da was out trying to get the money. And not far from this building was the offices that eventually dealt with the thing. So that was the only time that I was ever in a place like that. We had to get our benefit or we wouldn't have had our Christmas dinner ...*

McCann did not plan on becoming a politician. He was the first blanketman who was not force-washed and shaved before being released. Because he looked the part, he was asked to speak on their behalf. After the hunger mobilization he helped organize an advice centre in Divis Flats. McCann commented on having been an elected representative for more than twenty years:

> *Twenty odd years, yeah – for my sins [laughs]. Well, I have to say that most of us were reluctant politicians. The Movement at that time in the early eighties was looking about, I was going to say, for 'victims', and anybody they'd seen that may have been involved in community politics, you were a target*

right away for it. And what happened was that you were then groomed. And the way you were groomed was, they just came to you and said, 'There's a council election coming up; you're standing.'

In the autumn of 1987, McCann and Máirtín Ó Muilleoir were elected to Belfast City Council, bringing the Sinn Féin total to nine. They had more councillors than the SDLP, but overall there was still a unionist majority. Staff members were abusive and Sinn Féiners were excluded from committee meetings. McCann described the situation:

Belfast City Council, I have to say, was a very cold house not only for republicans but it was a very cold house for nationalists. I live half a mile, three-quarters of a mile away from the City Hall, and for myself and my family, and the people that I represented, they never felt part of what the City Council had to offer. In fact, the City Hall and those elected to the City Hall and many of the senior officers in the City Hall we would say would have practiced in many ways fairly sectarian politics against my community … my first experience with City Hall, in 1987, was, I think, the first time that I went into it. A cleaner had come over with a collection tin – and it was just after Enniskillen – and shoved a tin under my face and walked on by and spat at me and called me a Fenian bastard. That was my first real introduction to the City Hall. In the aftermath of that things were fairly difficult. And I have to say it became a battle a day to try and work within the confines of it. You know, meetings would be changed to different rooms. Doors would be locked that you had to push or force open to get into meetings.[45]

In court, Sinn Féin argued that its councillors were being denied the opportunity to represent their constituents. They won the case. In response, unionists created sub-committees and excluded Sinn Féin from them.[46] And when Sinn Féiners tried to speak at full meetings of the council, they were disrupted. Fra McCann again:

You never got on subcommittees. You didn't get elected to Chairs, Vice-Chairs. It was very abusive within meetings, but especially full council meetings would have been really abusive. You would have got air freshener sprayed around you. You would have got spat on. You would have been called Fenian bastard. 'Away back to your hovels in West Belfast.' And that was generally the picture … when one of us got up to speak, they would have walked to the bottom of the chamber, the City Hall chamber; they would have just started shouting. So every time one of us got up to speak they would try to drown us out. And that's very – it was very frustrating. And it was nerve wracking trying to work under that atmosphere … it got to the stage where it became almost impossible to do the work.[47]

There were physical confrontations[48] and Alex Maskey was escorted from the chamber more than once. Fra McCann described the conditions further:

It was hard to get involved in normal debate within the City Council. And one night at a full Council meeting, we had decided that we needed to break it and we needed to break that element of the unionist protest … [we decided that] when they walked to the bottom of the chamber and they gathered behind the Lord Mayor's Chair over at the doors and started screaming and shouting, that when our person got up to speak that we would walk down and stand down among them … the unionists were quite shocked at this. And they were screaming at you and shouting at you. And what had happened was that, in the midst of all this, [a unionist] said to Máirtín Ó Muilleoir [a graduate of Queen's University] something about being an educated Fenian scum or something like that – I just cannot recollect the words … and it ended up a huge fight. And I have to say it did break it … our action served its purpose because, after that, we said we have to follow through on it. And from then, whilst it would still remain difficult, things started to change. But it's amazing when you look at a beautiful building in the city centre of Belfast, the City Hall, that for people where I live and represent, those people never went in, never through the doors … their parents might have went in to pay their rent or in to pay their rates or to pay their gas, but they'd have done that in the wee alcove. But generally it was closed gates, closed things. But it's only in later years that you start to realize – while I suppose a cold house for nationalists, many Protestant working class people also were never in the City Hall.[49]

In the autumn of 1992, a judicial review found that the subcommittees were 'invalid and unlawful'.[50] It took years for Sinn Féin to gain full admission to the democratic process of Belfast City Hall. Times have changed. In 1972, Fra McCann was an internee on the *Maidstone* in Belfast Harbour. Thirty years later, he was a member of the Belfast Harbour Commission and worked with unionists and businessmen to help run the port and develop the Titanic Quarter. McCann was elected to the Assembly in 2007 and re-elected in 2011. He commented on this:

the difference between the councils [and the Assembly] is you can physically see what you can get done. I know on the Falls Road, I helped get a leisure centre built for people on the Falls Road. I got a million pound investment for the Dunville Park … we have been involved in a number of housing campaigns. And you can physically see that … Up here you deal with strategy. You deal with longer-term commitments. You build roads. You build – the economics of the place … I'm just out of a meeting with Invest NI to go on and argue for investment in empty sites, pieces of land in West Belfast, and find out what they're doing to try to encourage employment and jobs in what is an economic black spot.[51]

Nationalists are still in the minority in Northern Ireland. Even if Sinn Féin and the SDLP were to join together, they would not be able to bring about a united Ireland. Throughout Northern Ireland, however, Sinn Féin's elected representatives serve a community that was underserved since the foundation of the state. That service includes support for economic development, leisure centres and so on. Another benefit is support for Irish culture and symbols. There is now a mini-Gaeltacht in Belfast and, in Newry, and in spite of unionist opposition, a park has been named after hunger striker Raymond McCreesh.

In the South, Sinn Féin has been effectively representing people at the local level since the mid-1950s. Their significant presence at the national level is relatively new and fresh. Like their counterparts in the North, Sinn Féin representatives in Dáil Éireann did not necessarily plan on careers as politicians. Seán Crowe, who represents Dublin South-West in Dáil Éireann, is an example:

I didn't join to become a member of the Irish Parliament. I didn't join to become one of the leadership within Sinn Féin. It's just – what motivated me was what the conditions were on the ground and what was affecting ordinary people. And I suppose why I stood for election is to continue in the same vein in relation to – I'm still concerned about what's happening to ordinary people and I think there's a need for a strong voice to represent them.[52]

Like many others in Dublin Sinn Féin, Crowe began his political career as a community activist. In response to the recession, Ireland adopted austerity measures, bailed out banks and introduced a 'temporary' Universal Social Charge (USC) that applied to anyone earning more than €4,004. It has been described as 'Ireland's most hated tax' and met with serious opposition. In Dáil Éireann, Pearse Doherty introduced a motion abolishing the USC as 'an unjust and regressive tax, bearing down most heavily on those least able to afford it'. In the debate that followed one of the more strident voices was that of Séan Crowe:

> It is not about bailing out bankers. It is about bailing out people who work for a living. The universal social charge is creating conditions whereby we are creating more and more working poor. That is what is happening right across this city and across the country. That is why people are angry. That is why I am angry ... What the Government is talking about doing is bailing out crooks, fraudsters, speculators and gamblers, but no one is bailing out ordinary working people. That is what is wrong. We need to bring about change. Unguaranteed bondholders in Anglo Irish Bank were given €750 million by this State. That is a scandal. The Government did not have to do it, yet we introduce a new tax which is supposed to be burden sharing. Burden sharing my arse.[53]

Having a voice does not necessarily translate into social change. By a vote of 106 to 27, Doherty's motion was amended so that Dáil Éireann only agreed to review the Universal Social Charge.

Critics argue that Sinn Féin grandstands on issues because they are not in a position to have to act on their rhetoric. As an example, Sinn Féin went along with an austerity budget in the North, where they were in government, but sharply criticized the coalition government in Dublin for adopting austerity measures, where they were not in government.[54] Put another way, Sinn Féin behaves like every other major political party. The full significance of Sinn Féin's involvement in mainstream Irish politics remains to be seen but, in the meantime, Sinn Féin cannot be ignored in Belfast or Dublin.

From one perspective, the transformation of Sinn Féin and Northern Ireland since the Bobby Sands election in Fermanagh/South Tyrone is a remarkable success story. Danny Morrison, Sinn Féin's Director of Publicity during the hunger strike, is currently the Secretary of the Bobby Sands Trust. The convictions against Morrison and his co-accused in the Sandy Lynch affair were later over-turned and, since his release from prison in 1995, he has published novels and works of non-fiction, including a collection of political commentary entitled *Rebel Columns*. Morrison is frequently interviewed by scholars and students seeking his insight on Irish republicanism and the Provisionals. He described the transformation of Northern Ireland:

The fact of the matter is that the state that I live in is not the state that I grew up in.

Q: No?

A: *It's been transformed completely.*

Q: In what way?

A: *There's not an office in the land not open to a nationalist republican. The RUC is gone. And this business of the PSNI is the RUC is bollocks. I know former RUC men. I've met them. They've been devastated by that name change which is why so many of them took the Patten severance pay and took themselves off to Spain. Because they could not stand the dispensation. They saw it as a repudiation of what they and their comrades had suffered and died for. All recent surveys show that nationalist morale is pretty high in comparison to unionist morale, including in working class areas, even though nationalist working class areas still suffer disproportionately higher levels of unemployment and long-term unemployment. But the mood within the nationalist community – there is a confidence there that makes me relaxed. I no longer feel vanquished; I no longer feel second-class. I understand that to win a united Ireland we have to make the case that it makes social, economic and political sense. That means that there has to be a rapprochement with the unionist community. But it also means, incidentally, and this became quite clear during Martin McGuinness's bid for the presidency, the damage that partition has done to the psyche of the people in the twenty-six counties. Devastating. This partitionist thinking. You know, that Ireland, the border, Ireland stops at Dundalk. They're trying to create a nation state out of the twenty-six counties which the electoral rise of Sinn Féin is going to seriously challenge – challenge the Broadcasting Act, challenge the newspapers, challenge the government, challenge even the weather forecast people who think that clouds stop at Dundalk as well. So there's a big lot to be played for. But, you know, if there hadn't been an armed struggle we would still be second-class citizens.[55]*

Sinn Féin is now part of the fabric of Irish constitutional politics. Across Ireland, Sinn Féin has the support of more than 500,000 voters. And Brexit may create some interesting opportunities.

From another perspective, the Sinn Féin leadership is a bunch of hypocrites who sold out the republic for a bit of power and the perks of office. Sinn Féin has simply transformed itself into another treaty party – Fianna Fáil Light.

24

THE WAR CONTINUES:
ANTI-GFA IRISH REPUBLICANS

The British have never left anywhere without the use of force or, in place of that, the threat of force. Where force wasn't used [it] was because there was a massive population there and had they not gone there would have been force. So Ireland's really no different than anywhere else.

— 'Dissident' Irish Republican[1]

Irish Republicans who question Sinn Féin's direction may be grouped into three broad categories: former Provisionals who oppose continued armed struggle; republicans who formed organizations after 2005 in response to Sinn Féin's moderation; and 'dissident' organizations that have not gone away. That is, Republican Sinn Féin and the Continuity IRA, and the 32 CSM and the Real IRA, who reject the dissident label and argue that it is the Provisionals who have dissented from true republicanism. Thus far, the anti-GFA critique is fragmented and has not challenged Sinn Féin.

Former Provisionals who question Sinn Féin's approach and also question continued armed struggle include Tommy McKearney, Anthony McIntyre and Ricky O'Rawe. McKearney's analysis in *From Insurrection to Parliament* nicely describes the radical to moderate transformation of the Provisionals. McIntyre's *Good Friday: The Death of Irish Republicanism* is a compilation of articles, including several that appeared in *The Blanket*, that provide a running critique of events between 1998 and 2007. McIntyre's blog, *The Pensive Quill*, provides a forum for discussion and includes contributions from a variety of sources. O'Rawe's *Blanketmen: An Untold Story of the H-Block Hunger-Strike* and *Afterlives: The Hunger Strikes and the Secret Offer that Changed Irish History* offer compelling evidence to support his assertion that Gerry Adams sacrificed six hunger strikers in order to build electoral support for Sinn Féin.[2]

Éirígí continues to offer a socialist alternative to Sinn Féin but with little success. They failed to elect candidates in the 2014 local elections, North or South. Republican Network for Unity (RNU), which was created out of the pressure group 'Irish Republican Ex-POWs Against the RUC/PSNI & MI5', urges solidarity and values 'the prospect of future unity between disparate republican organisations'.[3] There is, however, very little unity. The long-term influence of new organizations, including the 1916 Societies (founded 2009) and Saoradh ('Liberation'), formed in 2016, remains to be seen.

Anti-GFA Irish republicans agree on two things. First, Sinn Féin has not delivered a united Ireland or much else. The support that the Provisionals received in West Belfast was crucial for both the IRA and Sinn Féin. Gerry Adams was the MP for the area from 1983 to 1992 and from 1997 to 2011 and the MP since 2011 has been Paul Maskey, Alex's brother and another Sinn Féin abstentionist when it comes to Westminster. West Belfast has the second highest level of child poverty in the United Kingdom, behind only the parliamentary constituency of Manchester. Neither Sinn Féin nor the SDLP has delivered for nationalists. A report from the Northern Ireland Statistics Research Agency shows that sixteen of the twenty most deprived wards in Northern Ireland are nationalist.[4]

Second, most anti-GFA republicans agree that the Provisionals are vindictive, petty hypocrites – 'Quisling Sinn Féin' or 'Shame Féin' depending upon the moment. Between the signing of the Good Friday Agreement (1998) and decommissioning (2005), the Provisionals or their friends killed several people, including alleged drug dealers like Charles Bennett, former Provisional and prominent critic Eamon Collins, Joe O'Connor of the Real IRA, and Robert McCartney.[5] The killing did not stop with decommissioning.

Paul Quinn was twenty-one years old and lived in Cullyhanna in South Armagh. After some altercations with local Provisionals he was told to leave the area but he refused. On 20 October 2007, he was lured to a farmhouse and methodically beaten to death with iron bars and nail-studded cudgels.[6] Sinn Féin denied that republicans were involved and suggested Quinn was killed by a criminal gang. Among those supporting the Quinn family was Jim McAllister. McAllister was too prominent for a beating so he was whitewashed from Sinn Féin's history. In the late 1980s, IRA volunteers Brendan Burns and Brendan Moley were killed in an accidental explosion. At the time, McAllister was the local Sinn Féin councillor and offered the oration at Burns's funeral. Twenty-five years after their deaths (2013), South Armagh Sinn Féin put together a commemorative booklet for 'the two Brendans'. McAllister's oration is presented word for word but the speaker is described as a 'local Sinn Féin representative'.[7] Dissatisfaction with Sinn Féin is very personal for some people. The Bobby Sands Trust controls the rights to his writings and its leadership includes several prominent Sinn Féiners. The Sands family has called on the Trust to disband.[8]

In spite of the successes of the peace process, there has never been peace. Compared to the early 1990s, however, Northern Ireland is much more peaceful. Between 1990 and 1993, there were approximately 500 shootings and 280 bombing incidents per year. In those years, sixty-nine members of the security forces were killed. In contrast, between 2006/2007 and 2013/2014, there were around sixty shooting incidents and fifty bombing incidents per year. Between 1998 and 2008, the Continuity IRA and Real IRA did not kill any members of the security forces.[9]

John Horgan, in *Divided We Stand: The Strategy and Psychology of Ireland's Dissident Terrorists*, profiles 199 persons convicted of republican paramilitary activity.[10] The data suggest that the Real IRA is larger and more active than the Continuity IRA and that both organizations are overwhelmingly male. The majority of those convicted were between twenty-one and forty years of age (the youngest was fourteen and the oldest was more than sixty years of age). Dublin

TABLE 5

Northern Ireland Shooting and Bombing Incidents, 1st April 2000–31st March 2014

Year	Shooting Incidents	Bombing Incidents	Total
2000/01	331	177	508
2001/02	358	318	676
2002/03	348	178	526
2003/04	207	71	278
2004/05	167	48	215
2005/06	156	81	237
2006/07	58	20	78
2007/08	42	23	65
2008/09	54	46	100
2009/10	79	50	129
2010/11	72	99	171
2011/12	67	56	123
2012/13	64	44	108
2013/14	54	69	123
Total	2,057	1,280	3,337
Yearly Average	147	91	238

and Louth were 'critical hubs' for personnel, though the centre of activity is Northern Ireland. Horgan's examination of three 'waves' of activity (31 August 1994 to 15 August 1998; 16 August 1998 to 27 January 2007; and 28 January 2007–12) shows that the Continuity IRA and the Real IRA have made a transition. Former Provisionals set up the two organizations and, with time, younger activists have moved into leadership positions. Some recent recruits to republican paramilitary organizations were born after the Good Friday Agreement.

The 'dissidents' have not been able to match the level of violence and disruption of the Provisionals; however, the number of shootings and bombings has recently increased, and, in the spring of 2009, two British soldiers were shot dead while waiting for a pizza delivery at Massereene Barracks in Antrim Town. They were the first British soldiers killed in Northern Ireland for more than a decade. The attack shocked many people who had assumed the violence had ended. The most interesting person to condemn the attack was Martin McGuinness, who said: 'I was a member of the IRA but that war is over now. The people responsible for Saturday night's incident are clearly signaling that they want to restart the war. They do not have the right to do that.' The Real IRA took responsibility for the attack via a phone call to journalist Suzanne Breen. Two days after Massereene, someone threw a brick through a window in the Lismore Manor estate in Craigavon, North Armagh. The PSNI received an emergency call and sent officers to investigate. Officer Stephen Carroll was providing backup when a Continuity IRA sniper shot him dead.[11]

Following the shooting of officer Carroll, Martin McGuinness appeared at a joint press conference with First Minister Peter Robinson and Sir Hugh Orde, the Chief Constable of the PSNI. McGuinness asked people to assist the police services and explained that, as Deputy First Minister, it was his duty and responsibility to lead from the front. He expected people to follow him because, 'These people, they are traitors to the island of Ireland. They have betrayed the political desires, hopes and aspirations of all of the people who live on this island and they don't deserve to be supported by anyone.' It was an incredible statement given his past but it was an appropriate statement given his position as Deputy First Minister. McGuinness caught the attention of Irish republicans of all stripes. Phil O'Donoghue commented: *And for McGuinness to come out and say that we're traitors – this is a British minister saying that we're traitors.*[12] Gerry Adams called the events 'an attack on the Peace Process' and added that those responsible have 'no support and no strategy to achieve a united Ireland'. If it had been a conversation, the likely reply would have been, 'Your strategy failed.'

Whether or not the attacks were part of a concerted strategy, they had an effect. Josephine Hayden, General Secretary of Republican Sinn Féin and a member of Cumann na mBan, placed them in a context:

> Q: *What do you think of the argument that by killing those soldiers and the police officer it's made it even more difficult to achieve a united Ireland?*
>
> A: *No, I don't think so.*
>
> Q: *No?*
>
> A: *No, no. It brings it home to people. People were shocked that two British soldiers were killed but they were just as shocked to discover that there was actually British soldiers still in Ireland. And at one of our pickets against the members of the royal family coming over here, I remember people giving us a lot of abuse, and, 'Why wouldn't the royal family come over?' But they didn't believe that there was about 5,000 British soldiers in the six counties. And I think at that stage there was more British soldiers in the six counties than there was in Iraq because everybody was talking about Iraq and all this. There was nobody speaking about the occupation of Ireland.*[13]

At a press conference in Belfast, Richard Walsh, RSF's Director of Publicity, said the attacks were regrettable 'acts of war' and that 'We have always upheld the rights to the Irish people to use any level of controlled and disciplined force to drive the British out of Ireland. We make no apology for that.' Walsh added that Martin McGuinness and Gerry Adams were guilty of 'severe treachery'. Unionists called for the Chief Constable to investigate Walsh for 'incitement to hatred' and Martin McGuinness complained of 'dissident' journalists.[14]

At the time of the attacks, Ruairí Ó Brádaigh was the most senior of anti-GFA Irish republicans. He was one of only a handful of people who helped found the Provisionals and lived long enough to witness their transformation, from revolution to reform. Of the seven people on the first Army Council, five were deceased: Paddy Mulcahy died in 1990, at 74 years of age; Dáithí O'Connell, who was shot several times in an incident with the RUC in the 1950s and then went forty-seven days without food in the 1970s, died in 1991, at 52 years of age; Seán Treacy, who was killed in a work accident, died in 1998 at 57 years of age; Seán Mac Stiofáin, who survived his own fifty-nine-day hunger strike, died in 2001, at 73 years of age; and Joe Cahill died in 2004, at 84 years of age.[15] The two surviving members from that Council were Leo Martin in Belfast and Ruairí Ó Brádaigh in Roscommon and neither of them supported Sinn Féin.

Ó Brádaigh had been in the public spotlight for half a century, the 'grandfather' of the Republican Movement. He was living proof of how far the Provisionals had strayed and was often sought out for interviews. In the summer of 2009, he commented on the attacks that had killed the soldiers and police officer:

> *Well, I would say having given service for almost three score years, I can't say I was surprised that that happened. In fact, if the truth be known, it would be that I was surprised it didn't happen sooner.*

> *Q: Why?*

> *A: Because all the ingredients remain of British occupation, foreign rule – the presence of the British forces and their attitude towards, particularly, the nationalist people. It's said that everything has changed but the reality is that, on the ground and in these nationalist areas of the six counties, very little has changed. The media, especially in the twenty-six counties, seem to disregard that but those among us who live in the six occupied counties are well aware of the situation and know that this is going to be a recurring situation. So the foreign body has not been removed from the wound. And the wound cannot be bound up and heal until the foreign body is extracted.*

> *Q: Okay. Any comment on the loss of life?*

> *A: Well, all loss of life is regrettable. Of course it is. And it is British policy that needs to be changed. And it's British policy and the British presence that is the root cause. And we have unfortunate sectarian attacks continuing with the loss of life. As I've said, all loss of life is regrettable but this is an ongoing situation and in any war there will be casualties. And Ireland's war of national independence is not over and will not be over until the British government is removed from Ireland. So that's basically it.*[16]

Martin McGuinness had changed but Ruairí Ó Brádaigh had not.

A few weeks after the Massereene and Craigavon attacks, the Real IRA made more dramatic news. Suzanne Breen was given an exclusive interview with a representative of their Army Council along with a copy of their Easter Statement. On Easter morning, 12 April 2009, the *Sunday Tribune* published Breen's articles describing how the Real IRA had killed Denis Donaldson and would threaten Martin McGuinness later that day. McGuinness was a former comrade turned 'traitor':

Let us remind our comrade of the nature and actions of a traitor. Treachery is collaborating with the enemy. Let us give our one-time comrade an example. Denis Donaldson was a traitor and the leadership of the Provisional movement, under guidance from the British government, made provision for Donaldson to escape republican justice in the same manner as Freddie Scappaticci.

It fell to the volunteers of Óglaigh na hÉireann to carry out the sentence and punishment demanded in our Army Orders and by the wider republican family. No traitor will escape justice regardless of time, rank or past actions. The republican movement has a long memory.[17]

It would not be the last time Martin McGuinness was threatened. As for Suzanne Breen, the PSNI threatened her with a court order under the Terrorism Act if she did not provide access to her computer, notes and other materials. She refused to comply and successfully defended journalistic privilege.[18]

It was not Suzanne Breen's fault that anti-GFA republicans had more support than the authorities wanted to admit. Support for a united Ireland among Northern nationalists may have fallen, but the 2007 Assembly election showed that 8,000 nationalist/republicans were tired of Sinn Féin's compromises.[19] A 2010 survey by the Economic and Social Research Council of Northern Ireland found that 14 per cent of nationalist adults in Northern Ireland expressed 'sympathy for the reasons' groups like the Real IRA and Continuity IRA engage in violence. After the 'Staff Report' reorganization, the Provisional IRA probably only needed a couple of hundred volunteers at any given time. The election and the survey showed that there were *thousands* of potential recruits to paramilitary organizations. The survey also found that young working-class Catholics were least likely to support the PSNI. Young, working class and nationalist is the typical background for recruits to republican paramilitary organizations. Sympathy for armed struggle even extended into Sinn Féin. A 'snap survey' by the *Belfast Telegraph* of the 2013 Sinn Féin Ard Fheis found that 26 per cent of respondents believed an armed campaign was justified. Only 12 per cent agreed with Martin McGuinness's statement that the dissidents were 'traitors to Ireland'.[20]

The biggest concern for the authorities is that anti-GFA republicans will unite, though that remains unlikely. Anti-GFA Irish republicans agree on the end goal but the differences that led to different groups splitting at different times are still there. As an example, Des Dalton was asked to comment on the 32 County Sovereignty Movement:

> *at one level there's a commitment to – they would certainly express and I'm not going to get into doubting their sincerity – they'd express their commitment to the project of ending British rule in Ireland ... But I think that on a more fundamental and a more ideological level, if you like, I think there are weaknesses there because they haven't addressed the core reasons why there was a separation between, if you like, those who accepted the Provisional analysis and those who remained committed to the republican position and the republican stance as espoused by people like Ruairí Ó Brádaigh and Dáithí O'Connell and Republican Sinn Fein. And I think what they haven't addressed there is basically they have at best an ambivalent attitude to the twenty-six county state which, in the long term, remains a weakness. Because*

at some point in time that does, fundamentally, if Irish history teaches us anything, that ambivalence has led to all of the major splits in the Republican Movement in the twentieth century. And I think unless that's addressed, and addressed fully, I think that weakness remains and it's the main reason why any cooperation between the two organizations is impossible.[21]

Republican Sinn Féin supporters refused to recognize Leinster House and walked out of the 1986 Ard Fheis. The people who organized the 32 CSM are sincere and committed but they did not walk out of the Ard Fheis when they should have – from this perspective. Activists in the 32 CSM offer parallel comments. Marian Price offered the following on activists in Republican Sinn Féin: *'I would have known people who got involved in it and I would have admired them for the stance they took. And they did get a very difficult time ... a lot of people in Republican Sinn Féin were being threatened by Provisionals and by other people in Sinn Féin and they were suffering in silence.*[22] At the same time, 32 CSM activists lament RSF's unwillingness to moderate its stance. Val Lynch was asked to comment on Republican Sinn Féin:

Republican Sinn Féin, as far as I'm concerned, are stuck in some sort of a cocoon. And they don't want to get on the outside of it whatsoever for some reason – because there have been calls for republican unity throughout the country, whereby a conglomerate of republicans who are totally in opposition to the Good Friday Agreement should come together, irrespective as to what their ideals are and debate the present situation, rather than being isolated into some sort of an elitist group. They were welcomed, they were asked, they were invited to attend some of these meetings but they haven't. They have their own agenda and they're not going to be budged from that. Outside of that, I don't know too much about them at all whatsoever. Some of the greatest people that I knew, Ruairí Ó Brádaigh, I knew Dáithí O'Connell, I knew Peig King – a lot of people, all fine people, finest of people – their ideas are, of course, a united Ireland. But again, as I said last week [at a commemoration], the united Ireland by whatever means.[23]

RSF, the 32 CSM, members of other organizations and independents share the same goal. By marginalizing the internal opposition and compromising bit by bit, Gerry Adams limited the size of the splits and made sure that they happened for different reasons. As a result, what for one group is the correct approach is, for other groups, rigid, impractical, and the wrong approach. This keeps them apart.[24]

Internal difficulties also trouble the anti-GFA organizations. In 2009, 77-year-old Ruairí Ó Brádaigh retired as President of Republican Sinn Féin. In what looked like a smooth transition to the next generation, the Ard Fheis voted overwhelmingly for Des Dalton over Des Long as his successor. Dalton was in his late thirties, Long was in his late sixties.[25] Long also lost a contest for vice President but was elected to the Ard Chomhairle. Ó Brádaigh became the 'Patron' of RSF and also was elected to the Ard Chomhairle, which seemingly would help with the transition.

Appearances were deceiving, however; activists were waiting for Ó Brádaigh to retire so they could take over the Continuity IRA and Republican Sinn Féin. When Des Dalton was elected over Des Long, it only added to their disenchantment. In the spring of 2010, there was an attempted coup in the Continuity IRA.[26] One side claimed that a General Army Convention 'representing 95% of the Volunteers' endorsed a vote of no confidence in the Army Council and the Continuity IRA was under new leadership while the other side claimed the meeting was 'unauthorised', included 'non-members' and was held under false pretences. As such, the 'principal people involved' were dismissed and the Army Council was intact and in control.

There was a parallel split in Republican Sinn Féin. As far as Des Dalton and Republican Sinn Féin were concerned, a small group of activists were expelled. The group, centered in Limerick, has had a troubled history. They started out calling themselves the Limerick Independent Republican Organization and then shifted to 'Real' Sinn Féin. They then claimed that they, not the 'Daltonites', were Republican Sinn Féin. Their officers were: Seamus Ó Suilleabhain (President, County Limerick); Paddy McKenna (vice President, Armagh); Cathleen Knowles McGuirk (Dublin) and Liam Kenny (Dublin), joint General Secretaries; John Sheehy (Kerry) and Joe Morgan (Belfast), joint Treasurers; and Joe Lynch (Limerick), PRO and editor of *Saoirse Nua*. The Ard Chomhairle included Des Long (Limerick City) and Tommy Crossan, an ex-Continuity IRA prisoner from Belfast.[27]

Their grievances were varied. The Ruairí Ó Brádaigh–Des Dalton wing refused to endorse a 'Broad Front' approach and work with groups like Republican Network for Unity. Some of them were upset with a decision that prevented cumainn (local branches) from being named after people who remained with the Provisionals in 1986, including highly-regarded Jim Lynagh.[28] Articles in *Saoirse Nua* attacked Des Dalton's character and pointed to the 'three roles' that Ruairí Ó Brádaigh still held.[29] Two of those roles were public – Patron of RSF and member of the Ard Chomhairle but the third was left to the imagination. Spokespersons for RSF-Limerick reinforced the presentation in *Saoirse Nua*. Joe Lynch, for example, was upset with Dalton's election and Ó Brádaigh's continued involvement:

> *I could see we were wasting our time. That they were going down a cul de sac [unclear]. Then, I was with them up to about eighteen months, two years this May [2011] … Ruairí Ó Brádaigh sat there and told us he was standing down, he was going into retirement. So what does he do at that meeting? Called an Ard Fheis. Put Des Dalton for President, which was rigged. … They had these people picked … He retired as President. There was a couple of dos held around the country, give him a golden hand shake for his service, and what did he do? He took over three positions within the organization – a dictatorship …*[30]

The prominence of several women, many of them also active in Cumann na mBan, was also an issue. A 'Real Sinn Féin' press release described Republican Sinn Féin as a 'band of cronies and old women'. Seamus Ó Suilleabhain offered the following:

> *You see they were control freaks, the old regime. Ninety per cent of their efforts were controlling, maintaining control … Our Ard Chomhairle, the governing body, was dominated by women – about seven women … The organization in the finish was dominated particularly by the two [party] secretaries. … They are very dominating women … The newspaper became meaningless. Nobody read it …*[31]

The attacks on Dalton and Ó Brádaigh would lead to charges of felon setting.

The vast majority of RSF activists supported Dalton and Ó Brádaigh. The Limerick group was also hurt by the deaths from natural causes of Brendan Magill (2011) and Cathleen Knowles McGuirk (2012).[32] They also had their own internal difficulties. Des Long and Tommy Crossan were dismissed for 'anti-republican' activity and Liam Kenny was shot dead.[33] The Gardaí claimed that Kenny was in a dispute with criminals over drug and extortion rackets. *Saoirse Nua* described him as 'Vol. Liam Kenny' and said he was an 'anti-drugs activist' murdered by heroin-dealing gangsters. In retaliation, the 'Limerick-CIRA' shot dead David Darcy in Dublin. *Saoirse Nua* described Darcy as a drug dealer involved in Kenny's murder though everyone else, including the Gardaí, said he was an innocent man, married with children and quietly sitting in his van and getting ready for work early one morning when he was murdered.

Rose Lynch, Joe Lynch's daughter, and Dermot Gannon were arrested in connection with David Darcy's murder. Described as 'besotted' with Gannon, Rose Lynch pleaded guilty and was sentenced to life in prison. The sad story did not end with her conviction and, in court, she expressed no remorse, instead shouting, 'Mná na hÉireann, tiocfaidh ár lá' ('Women of Ireland, our day will come'). Outside the courthouse, her father described her 'as iconic as IRA volunteer Mairéad Farrell'. The media referred to Rose Lynch as a member of the Continuity IRA and Joe Lynch as a member of Republican Sinn Féin. It was a public relations disaster for the Dalton-led organization, who pointed out that Joe Lynch and his daughter were expelled in April 2010. None of it had anything to do with uniting Ireland.

In the spring of 2014, unknown persons murdered Tommy Crossan in Belfast. That autumn, seven members of what is now the 'Continuity' Sinn Féin Ard Chomhairle and five other party members were arrested in a house in Newry, including Joe Lynch and John Sheehy. *Saoirse Nua* reported that they were involved in meetings to discuss the party's new name and to prepare for the centenary of 1916. MI5 monitoring devices in the house had recorded more than seventy hours of conversation and seven people were charged with offenses including membership in a proscribed organization, conspiracy and organizing terrorism.[34] At the time of writing, the case has not yet come to trial.

The Real IRA has also had problems. Beginning in 2009, a group that had split from them and called itself Óglaigh na hÉireann (ONH) was responsible for several shootings and bombings, including an attack that left PSNI officer Peadar Heffron seriously injured.[35] There were also issues with drugs and criminals. Gardaí discovered a marijuana factory on a farm in Donegal and Kieran Doherty, who lived in Derry and was the former O/C of Real IRA prisoners in Portlaoise, rented the farm. Seamus McGreevy, who had been in Portlaoise with Doherty, owned the farm. Any association with drugs was bad for the Real IRA and, even though Doherty was a member of their General Headquarters Staff, he was executed. McGreevy committed suicide. Alan Ryan, who was in Portlaoise with Doherty, McGreevy and Dermot Gannon, was the Real IRA's O/C of Dublin. In 2012, he was shot dead by drug dealers and the police claimed that Ryan was extorting funds from pub owners in a protection racket. His supporters denied the claim and gave him one of the largest paramilitary funerals seen in Dublin in years. Then several people were shot in retaliation for Ryan's death. Journalists feasted on the violence to portray the Real IRA as an out of control criminal gang.[36]

Alan Ryan (far right), at the Garden of Remembrance in Dublin, prior to the 32 CSM's 2006 Easter Commemoration. Phil O'Donoghue is in the centre and Joe Dillon is to O'Donoghue's right. ©Robert White.

In April 2011, 'the IRA', a small group of ex-Provisionals in Tyrone who were upset with Sinn Féin's acceptance of the PSNI, used a car bomb to kill PSNI officer Ronan Kerr.[37] Then, in the summer of 2012, journalist Henry McDonald reported that the Derry-based group Republican Action Against Drugs (RAAD), the Real IRA and a coalition of independents, including the group responsible for Constable Kerr's death, had merged into the 'Irish Republican Army' – the 'New IRA'. According to reports, the group's plan was to 'intensify' their campaign and one of their first acts was killing David Black, a prison warden driving to work in North Armagh.[38] 'New IRA' or not, more violence contributed to the media's portrayal of anti-GFA republicans as criminal gangs. A suspect in the Kieran Doherty killing was shot dead in a car park in County Meath. In March, 2016, Alan Ryan's brother, Vincent, was murdered in Dublin by unknown persons.[39]

In addition to their internal problems, anti-GFA republicans also have to contend with the immense resources of the Dublin and London governments. Internment is not an option, so the authorities use 'internment by remand'. Martin Corey, as an example, was a former Provisional sentenced to life in prison in 1973 for murdering two RUC men.[40] In 1992, he was released on license, went home to Lurgan and put his life back together, and was a supporter of Republican Sinn Féin. In 2010, the Secretary of State for Northern Ireland determined that Corey was a risk to the public and, on the basis of closed material, revoked his license. After two years in custody and with no evidence presented, a judge ruled that Corey's human rights had been breached and released him on unconditional bail. The Secretary of State immediately filed an appeal and Corey was not released. His attorneys were preparing to take the case to the European Court of Human Rights when Corey was finally released in January 2014, with restrictions. He was not charged with anything but spent almost four years in prison.

In May 2011, Queen Elizabeth was scheduled to tour the Republic of Ireland.[41] The visit was at the invitation of Irish President Mary McAleese and was part of the normalization of relations between the two countries. The most recent British monarch to visit Dublin had been King George V, Elizabeth's grandfather, in 1911. As part of their preparations, the authorities focused on dissenters. Marian Price, for example, was an articulate spokesperson for the 32 CSM. From her perspective, the war was justified:

> *Oh, yes, the war was justified. Absolutely. It was a legitimate war and it still is. While the British remain in Ireland armed resistance will always be legitimate. That's not to say that everything done during the war was either legitimate or moral. I mean, certain things like La Mon I would never try to justify to anybody because I thought it was appalling. It was an absolute mistake and that should have been said from day one. It was a mistake. It should never have happened. So, though the war was legitimate I'm not going to, I wouldn't sit and justify everything that took place during the war.*

She also commented on the path taken by Sinn Féin:

> *In the overall picture of things was the sacrifice that was given worth where we are today? No. I think it's totally dishonest for people like Gerry Adams to say that men died on hunger strike or on active service to put Sinn Féin into Stormont. That's nonsense, absolute nonsense. I don't think any sane person would have spent a night in prison in order to get Sinn Féin into Stormont. People went to prison and went out and fought and died or died on hunger strike for the freedom of their country – not to put Sinn Féin into Stormont.*[42]

At Easter 2011, Marian Price spoke at a commemoration in Derry. It was a windy day and she held onto the paper as a Real IRA volunteer dressed in fatigues and wearing a balaclava read out a statement. A few days before the Queen's visit, the PSNI raided her house and she was charged with encouraging terrorism, deemed a security threat and her license was revoked. A few days later, Cáit Trainor and Seán Maloney of RSF were arrested and charged with encouraging terrorism.[43] The charge was based on statements they had made during an interview for a news programme the previous autumn. The charges against Trainor and Maloney were eventually dismissed but Price was in a more difficult situation.[44]

After a year in jail, the case against Marian Price collapsed and the charges were withdrawn but she was not released. Instead, she was charged with providing the mobile phone that was used to claim responsibility for the Massereene attack. Other than a brief parole when her sister Dolours Price passed away, Marian Price remained in isolation. Finally, after two years in prison, her health was so poor that she was released to her family. Six months later, she pleaded guilty to providing the mobile phone for the Massereene attack and to aiding, abetting and encouraging terrorism through the Easter Commemoration speech in Derry. Price was deemed to have 'low-risk of re-offending' and received a suspended sentence.

Another victim of the state's attempt to silence dissent was Stephen Murney, the press officer for éirígí in Newry.[45] Murney's home was raided in November 2012 and the police seized military-style clothing and a computer containing images of police officers. He was charged with publishing, collecting and possessing information that could be of use to terrorists. Murney's defense was that the clothes were band uniforms and that the photographs were part of a case he was building to counter the constant harassment that he and other activists faced. Because of severe restrictions that would have been imposed, including a ban on living in Newry with his partner and child, Murney refused to accept bail. After fourteen months in Maghaberry Prison, he was cleared of all charges – there was no evidence that éirígí supports violence, there was no evidence that his photos could be used to support terrorism and the press officer of a political organization had good reason to have the photos. The most recent victim of internment by remand is Tony Taylor, a member of the RNU Ard Chomhairle from Derry. In March 2016, Taylor's license was revoked because he posed a 'risk' to the public. Without a hearing or a charge, and without legal representation, he was returned to prison.[46]

Activists like Stephen Murney and Tony Taylor are two generations younger than the founders of the Provisionals. Indeed, at the time of writing, the few founding Provisionals still living include Frank Glynn and Des Long, who were members of the Sinn Féin Caretaker Executive in 1970, and Billy McKee, now in his nineties. Leo Martin was 73 years old when he passed away in 2011 and, in the summer of 2013, 80 year old Ruairí Ó Brádaigh was the last member of the first Provisional IRA Army Council to succumb to the inevitable.

Ruairí Ó Brádaigh's funeral marked the end of an era. Republican Sinn Féin and Cumann na mBan were prominently involved and his old comrades Dan Hoban and Seán Lynch offered remarks. The respect that Irish Republicans in general had for Ó Brádaigh was seen in the variety of people attending, including Tony Catney, Colin Duffy, Anthony McIntyre, Tommy McKearney, and Francie Mackey and Phil O'Donoghue of the 32 CSM.[47] It was the end of an era but not the end of resistance to British occupation of Ireland. Ruairí Ó Brádaigh had spent the last decades of his life ensuring that he would not be the last republican. In his words, *'if we were all dead and gone tomorrow … the whole lot, there would be people to carry on'*.[48] Des Dalton also spoke at the funeral and a colour party from Na Fianna Éireann was in attendance.

Cáit Trainor was born sixty plus years after Ruairí Ó Brádaigh. She would, for a time, serve as vice President of Republican Sinn Féin and is now an Independent. Critics argue that she, and others younger than her, are repeating the mistakes of the past but she has a different perspective. Trainor commented on her activism:

> *I believe to do nothing is to be complicit. So if something is wrong and you just sit back and do nothing, you're involved in that wrong. If I drop out tomorrow, there will be someone to take my place. It's the history of Ireland. British occupation will always rear its own generation of Irish republicans and it's just the thing that we can't get away from. It's not that we are doing it out of some sense of it has to be*

Cáit Trainor, Coordinator of the 'Release Martin Corey Campaign', 31st Annual Hunger Strike Commemoration (2012), Bundoran, County Donegal. ©Robert White.

done, its traditional. It's because in this generation we might do something new and different that the last generation didn't or didn't think of.[49]

The belief that Ireland is one country and should be free of British interference provides a foundation that has motivated Irish republicans for more than two centuries. For some activists, their commitment to that belief lasts a remarkable length of time.

Of the many Irish republicans interviewed for this oral history, John Hunt provided the earliest memories. He was born in 1920 and attended his first commemoration, at the Valley of Knockanure, in 1929. Hunt, who was interned in the 1940s, may have left Ireland for the United States in the 1950s but his attitude did not change. In his interview, he commented:

I can't know why at my old age, ninety-four years of age … I still have the same idea as far as Ireland is concerned, as when I was nine or ten years old. If I read a book that said, 'There should be no foreign flag over any part of Ireland', I'll solemnly believe that until the day I die.[50]

Still going strong in 2016, John Hunt addressed the crowd attending Republican Sinn Féin's commemoration of the one hundredth anniversary of the Easter Rising. From in front of the GPO, he told the crowd:

> I am old now. I have learned much. I have forgotten little. As a boy, I read of those heroes. As a young man, in the darkness of my prison cell, I understood that the sacrifices of the republicans before me would inspire generations yet unborn. Forget whoever will the immortal words of Patrick Pearse, 'the fools, the fools, the fools! – they have left us our Fenian dead.'[51]

Irish republican history is filled with people who the authorities considered dangerous because of their unending commitment to the right of Irish people to use physical force in pursuit of the republic – Wolfe Tone, Jeremiah O'Donovan Rossa, Patrick Pearse, Bobby Sands, Mairéad Farrell and Ruairí Ó Brádaigh. Some people, for whatever reason, cannot be co-opted and will not compromise. The authorities can minimize the threat but, as of yet, they cannot eliminate it. In the words of Pearse, 'while Ireland holds these graves, Ireland unfree shall never be at peace'.

PART 5

Conclusion

25

UNDERSTANDING THE PROVISIONALS:
A SOCIOLOGICAL SUMMARY

Ireland is an interesting case history for students of the anti-imperialist, anti-colonial struggles of the twentieth century. It was the Irish with their Easter Rising in 1916 that made the first crack in the British Empire, which at that time covered a quarter of the globe and embraced indeed a quarter of the world's population.

– Ruairí Ó Brádaigh[1]

Individuals are unique. Each of us has a particular history and outlook that is influenced by the specific events we have experienced. In groups, however, individuals often share experiences and social conditions that lead them to react in similar ways to events and conditions – as men or women, as children of the Great Depression or as teenaged nationalists living through August 1969 in Northern Ireland.

Karl Marx, in a famous quotation from the *18th Brumaire of Louis Napoleon*, writes: 'Men make their own history, but they do not make it as they please; they do not make it under self-selected circumstances, but under circumstances existing already, given and transmitted from the past. The tradition of all dead generations weighs like a nightmare on the brains of the living.'[2] Not all tradition weighs like a nightmare, but traditions and interpretations of the past do influence the present. Seán Mac Stiofáin, Ruairí Ó Brádaigh and company were influenced by their interpretation of the Irish Republican Movement's history, especially abstentionism. Gerry Adams, Martin McGuinness and company were influenced by the Movement's history, if only because they broke from it and took seats in Leinster House/Dáil Éireann and then the Northern Ireland Assembly.

The Provisional IRA and 'Provisional' Sinn Féin were unique in their own time and place. They also share similarities with other social movement organizations. The Provisionals were part of a cycle of protest that began in the 1960s. Over the course of that protest cycle, many social movement organizations moderated their demands and settled for reform. Two complementary perspectives from the social movement literature provide insight on the course of Provisional Irish republicanism.

Sidney Tarrow argues that there are phases or cycles of protest that extend across social systems.[3] In the 1960s, the Western world experienced civil rights movements, student movements, women's movements, anti-war movements and so on. In Northern Ireland, there was the Campaign for Social Justice and the Northern Ireland Civil Rights Association. Across these different movements new 'repertoires' of action were developed and shared. The US Civil Rights Movement had the Selma to Montgomery march; Northern Ireland had the Belfast to Derry march.

Because social movements challenge authority and the status quo, counter-movements are organized. As noted in Chapter 1, states and their agents defend themselves and engage in repression. In the United States, the Ku Klux Klan attacked civil rights activists and state troopers attacked the Selma to Montgomery march. Paisleyites, the RUC and the B Specials mobilized against civil rights protesters in Northern Ireland.[4] Theoretically, radicals, usually in the minority, become more confrontational in order to push the agenda and separate themselves from moderates. In the United States, there were the Weathermen and 'Black Power' militants; in Northern Ireland, there was People's Democracy. Shifting tactics, states decide to work with moderates – Martin Luther King and the SDLP – and repress the radicals. In time, moderates are co-opted and either join established organizations or take their new organization into the mainstream. The result is a broader, more inclusive political system. Mobilization and protest decline and elites reassert their authority. The minority radicals are then either repressed out of existence or refuse to quit and turn to violence. Small-group political violence is a 'product of the end of mobilization'.

From this theoretical perspective, a cycle of protest began in the late 1950s and early 1960s, peaked in the mid-to-late 1960s and then went into decline. As the cycle of protest declined, a minority of radical activists formed groups like the Weathermen and the Black Panthers, *Brigate Rosse* (Red Brigades), ETA, the Red Army Faction (Baader–Meinhoff Gang), the PLO, etc. Ireland had the Provisionals, along with other organizations.[5] The Irish case shows that, with enough time, even radicals will choose to become moderates.

Frances Fox Piven and Richard Cloward describe the social processes that cause moderation in radical organizations.[6] Based on case studies, such as the industrial union movement of the 1930s and the civil rights movement in the 1960s, they argue that marginalized people will only gain concessions from elites through mass insurgencies that disrupt the social system. Organizing is counterproductive for two reasons. First, maintaining an organization requires resources that poor people usually don't have. Second, organizing may lead to a more powerful movement but 'power is always conservative'.[7] As relatively disorganized protest escalates, talented people with skills emerge and move into leadership positions and, as the challenging organization grows, the benefits and privileges associated with leadership also increase. Benefits might include the perquisites of leadership (like a chauffeured car), financial support, enhanced status within the group, and media attention. No matter how democratic the radical organization was at the beginning, it will end up being controlled by an undemocratic group of elites – the 'Iron Law of Oligarchy' – concerned about their own position.

At some point, the radical leaders of an organization will realize two things – the cycle of protest and their ability to disrupt has peaked and if they continue to push a radical agenda the opposition will push back so hard that it will threaten not only their organization but also their own privileged position. Negotiation and moderation are attractive alternatives to destruction and loss of privilege. The radical turned moderate can gain some concessions for the cause and, at the same time, maintain her or his position. However, in the words of Piven and Cloward, 'concessions are rarely unencumbered'. Concessions are granted in exchange for moderating demands, bringing the movement into 'normal political channels and to absorb its leaders into stable institutional roles'.

Piven and Cloward's case study of the industrial workers' movement in the US offers an example.[8] In the 1930s, in the midst of the Great Depression, worker unrest threatened economic recovery and political stability. Congress passed the National Labor Relations (Wagner) Act (1935) and workers won the right to organize unions, engage in collective bargaining and strike. In exchange, unionized workers lost some of their ability to disrupt the economy and manufacturers gained a more stable work force. Also, in winning these rights, labour leaders secured a place for their organizations and their own positions in those organizations. As Piven and Cloward note, concessions may be withdrawn once the ability to disrupt has passed. After the Second World War, when the stability of the United States was less threatened by worker unrest, Congress passed the Labor–Management Relations (Taft–Hartley) Act (1947) that placed limits on the right to strike and required union leaders to sign non-communist affidavits.

The Provisionals were not a 'poor people's movement' but they were largely women and men with modest resources.[9] Their capacity for disruption peaked in 1972, when almost 500 people were killed in political conflict in Northern Ireland.[10] It was in 1972 that the Provisionals accomplished two significant achievements – proroguing Stormont and the Mac Stiofáin–Whitelaw meeting.[11] They set out to bring down Stormont and succeeded and meeting with Whitelaw conferred at least some kind of legitimacy on the leadership – even if it was only among their supporters.

As protesters make their own history, they take a leap in the dark. The Provisionals did not know that they peaked in 1972. Piven and Cloward also argue that what protesters gain is limited by conditions beyond their control, '*protesters win, if they win at all, what historical circumstances has already made ready to be conceded*' (emphasis in the original).[12] Unfortunately, activists also do not know the limit of what elites will concede. Other than knowing that they don't want to be forced to concede anything, elites and government officials don't necessarily know their limit either. Hindsight shows that what the British conceded with the Good Friday Agreement – a reformed Northern Ireland with a power-sharing government and North–South political bodies – they were pretty much willing to concede in March 1973. William Whitelaw's White Paper, 'Northern Ireland Constitutional Proposals', included the power-sharing assembly and Council of Ireland that became Sunningdale.

In the face of uncertainty, the Provisionals' leaders relied on their belief that they were pursuing the right course. They split the Movement in 1969/70 because they were convinced that the Officials were destined for reform and failure. Five years later, when the British tried to draw them into the Constitutional Convention, they were still not interested in a reformed Northern Ireland. In 1975, the people who took over from Mac Stiofáin et al. – Gerry Adams, Martin McGuinness and company – agreed with that analysis. It took another twenty plus years of armed struggle but eventually the Adams and McGuinness group were willing to accept that the

Provisionals had peaked and that their best option was to cut a deal with the British. And through the peace process they gained concessions, including a reformed RUC, the release of prisoners and, it would later be revealed, letters that protect 'on the runs' from prosecution. Through the peace process, the Provisionals' leadership was transformed into constitutional politicians who maintained their high status positions. More recently, some concessions won through the GFA have been withdrawn. In 2011, for example, the recruitment of Catholics and Protestants to the PSNI on a 50/50 basis was ended.[13]

The course of Provisional Irish republicanism parallels the course of other social movements and their organizations.[14] At the same time, this oral history offers new insight on social movements and the dynamics of political contention and radicalization.[15]

In Ireland there is a 'permanence of protest' that spans cycles of protest.[16] The Provisionals did not emerge during a period of demobilization.[17] The Irish Republican Movement, in fact, helped create the Northern Ireland Civil Rights Association. In 1969, the IRA and Sinn Féin were already there for the young Northerners – radical social movement organizations in waiting. In terms of the social movement literature, 'outbidding' refers to action-counteraction dynamics that increase the stakes for those involved and may lead to violence.[18] In Ireland, the threat of violence was already there. For more than a century there has been a continuity of activism that extends across cycles of protest in Ireland.

Fenians helped organize the 1916 Rising and were involved in the reorganization of the IRA and Sinn Féin in the 1918–23 era. Veterans of the 1916–23 era like Joe Clarke helped organize the Provisionals. Some of them, like Tom Maguire, were sympathizers into the 1990s. Veteran Provisionals organized the Continuity IRA, Republican Sinn Féin, the Real IRA and the 32 County Sovereignty Movement. Instead of viewing new recruits to these organizations as part of a cycle of violence, it is better to view them as recruits to a long-standing social movement. In most if not all countries, there are groups willing to use armed struggle for political ends. Whether or not those groups attract recruits depends on the state's response to those organizations and the state's response to more general cycles of protest.

Similar to non-violent social movements, the Irish experience has cross-fertilized with other movements.[19] The Easter Rising influenced Indian nationalists and Vladimir Lenin. The Irgun and the Stern Gang drew on the IRA experience of the 1920s. Irish republicans in the 1950s followed anti-colonial struggles and, many of them – Aden, Cyprus, Ireland, Kenya, Malaya and Palestine – were directed against the same imperial power, the United Kingdom. There was more cross-fertilization with the Provisionals. Their early leaders read Franz Fanon's *A Dying Colonialism* and *The Wretched of the Earth* and drew analogies between the 'Colons' of Algeria and the loyalists of Northern Ireland. The Provisionals built connections with the PLO, ETA and FARC. There was also a cross-fertilization in the British response. Frank Kitson was the British Army's Belfast Commander in the early 1970s and his *Low Intensity Operations: Subversion, Insurgency, and Peace-keeping* draws on his service in Malaya and Kenya in the 1950s. The Bush administration drew on the British experience to inform their approach to the War on Terror.

Each of the Irish republican insurgencies in the twentieth century had the same basic motive that was rooted in Irish nationalism and the belief that Irish people have the right to use armed struggle in pursuit of the republic. Activists in organizations like Sinn Féin and the IRA develop a collective identity, a sense of 'we-ness' that embraces this belief.[20] This basic understanding of what it means to be an Irish republican is then passed from one generation of activists to the next and from one cycle of protest to the next through social interaction. Often, but not exclusively, the identity is passed from one generation to the next through family and kin networks, from parents, aunts and uncles to children, nieces and nephews.[21] The passing of the Irish republican identity from one generation to the next helps us understand why the IRA and Sinn Féin already existed in 1969/70, why the Provisionals pursued armed struggle for so long after they had peaked and the persistence of anti-GFA Irish republicans today. This is not unique to Ireland. The transfer of political identity from one generation to the next occurs in many settings, as evidenced by George W. and Jeb Bush.

Each of the republican insurgencies was also unique. In the mid-1970s, the younger Provisionals took what they inherited and began making it their own. The course followed by Gerry Adams and the Provisionals is similar to but also different from that of Éamon de Valera and Fianna Fáil. Like de Valera, the Provisionals held out as long as they could and then compromised. The fact that de Valera and Fianna Fáil were there first influenced the options available to the Provisionals as they compromised. Adams was also able to draw on Official Sinn Féin/The Workers' Party as a model for what to avoid.

Another important finding involves the influence of state violence and repression on activism.[22] The influence of state violence varies across time and space[23] and, in some contexts, state violence served as a 'relational mechanism' that increased interaction among its victims and connected them with already active Irish republicans. Following the Easter Rising, for example, the executions of the 1916 leaders and the heavy response from the British raised the consciousness of Irish nationalists and helped rejuvenate the IRA and Sinn Féin. Between 1919 and 1922, the British counterinsurgency was largely counterproductive, at least in the south and west of Ireland. In response to the disruption caused by the IRA and Sinn Féin, the British were forced to partition the island into two areas – one they could no longer directly control (the Irish Free State) and one that loyal unionists could control for them (Northern Ireland).

Between 1920 and 1970, in a divided Ireland, the ability of the state to repress unrest was transformed. Successive unionist governments in Northern Ireland maintained social, political and economic control over the minority nationalist population and, when necessary, internment was implemented and the RUC and B Specials were mobilized to suppress dissent. The Dublin government used internment and executions in the 1940s, and internment in the 1950s, to control the IRA and Sinn Féin. State repression was effective. *At the same time the repression was counterproductive.* The repression hardened the attitudes of those who remained involved in the IRA and Sinn Féin and heightened their camaraderie. To persist in the face of past failures and constant repression was to succeed.

Conditions changed in the mid-1960s[24] and those changes were part of broader social and political changes that facilitated a cycle of protest in the Western world. Whether it was in Selma or Paris or Derry, the repression of protest was controversial. Mass media contributed to this change. In the 1950s, the RUC attacked peaceful nationalist events in Northern Ireland and it made the headlines of a few newspapers and then faded away. When the RUC attacked the civil rights march in Derry on 5 October 1968, it was broadcast on television and then throughout the world; images and video of the attack are available on the web today.[25] When the Northern Irish and British governments followed standard operating procedure and introduced internment in 1971, they discovered that, in this new environment, repression was less effective and more counterproductive. Compounding the mistaken implementation of state repression was the fact that the Catholic/nationalist population in Northern Ireland had grown significantly in the post-Second World War era. There were thousands of teenagers who were 'biographically' available for activism[26] and, because they were not busy raising families and building careers, they were available for riots and other things.

August 1969, internment and then Bloody Sunday happened in the context of a peaceful civil rights movement that had raised the consciousness of biographically available young people. The state and loyalist violence turned them into defenders and it brought them into contact with the 'permanent protesters' of the Irish Republican Movement. Continued violence confirmed what people like Seán Mac Stiofáin and Joe Cahill were saying – only a united Ireland would bring relief and the path to a united Ireland involved armed struggle. The state violence affected direct victims, their families and friends and entire communities (indirect victims), and it connected them with veteran Irish republicans. State violence made the new generation have something in common with the old generation – as Irish people, they were all victims.[27] Continued state repression generated camaraderie and solidarity and guaranteed future recruits.

The extreme potency of coupling camaraderie and state repression is best seen in the 1981 hunger strike. The mass mobilization did ultimately lay the foundation for Sinn Féin's transformation into a constitutional party but, in the short term, the hunger strike fuelled the Provisionals' insurgency for another decade. Without the hunger strike, the inability of armed struggle to bring about a united Ireland would have been revealed that much earlier. Without the hunger strike, the peace process might have started five years earlier.

This case study also shows that, within social movement organizations, what it means to be an activist varies across subgroups of activists.[28] What a 'collective identity' means is not necessarily entirely agreed upon and the recruitment process influences these differences. There is no single path of recruitment to the Irish Republican Movement. The timing of recruitment and the geography of recruitment influence the interpretation of the Movement that activists join. The people who founded the Provisionals were different in age, outlook and experience from the new recruits of the early 1970s. The recruits from the early 1970s were different from the ceasefire Sinn Féiners of the 1990s. People born and raised in Irish republican families are different from activists who are recruited as adults; they are not necessarily better or worse recruits, just different. The experiences of Southern republicans are different from the experiences of Northern republicans; not everyone is a direct victim of state repression. Everyone involved in the Provisionals experienced a collective identity – solidarity, commitment and camaraderie – but not in the same way. These differences contributed to different courses of activism, factions and splits, and also help us understand why some activists disengaged, others stayed involved and others were willing to compromise. These differences also show that scholars who focus only on

Belfast or Northern Ireland do so at their peril. The Irish Republican Movement is an all-Ireland social movement, as are the Provisionals.

I began this oral history by arguing that our goal as academics should be to try and understand why people choose to endorse and engage in small group political violence rather than simply condemning them as terrorists. Unfortunately, terrorism experts often focus on insurgents and ignore or underplay the important role of state violence in promoting radicalization and insurgency. State violence helped mobilize and sustain the Provisional IRA's campaign and, if the peace process in Northern Ireland is a model for resolving other conflicts, the British response between 1969 and 1972 is a classic example of what governments should not do.[29] Because of people like Frank Glynn, Seán Keenan, Peig King, Seán Lynch, Seán Mac Stiofáin and Ruairí Ó Brádaigh, the Republican Movement was going to split in the late 1960s or early 1970s. Without state violence – which de-legitimated the British and Stormont governments and simultaneously legitimated Irish republican insurgents – young Northerners would never have flocked to the Provisionals.[30] The creation of the Provisional IRA and the Caretaker Executive in 1969/70, the assassination of Lord Mountbatten in 1979 and the attempt on Margaret Thatcher's life in 1984, and Gerry Adams's election to Dáil Éireann in 2016, were 'simply politics'.

Methods

A paucity of data has ... never deterred the academic mind; rather, one suspects, the contrary.

– J. Bowyer Bell[1]

This oral history is an attempt to contribute to the scholarly literature on the causes and consequences of involvement in social movement organizations that endorse political violence. Case studies of social movements are known for their detailed, 'thick' insight.[2] Intensive, 'semi-structured' interviews and oral histories allow for flexibility in asking questions and probing responses. Randomly distributed questionnaires provide a generalizable understanding of social phenomena. While planning this project it seemed that a case study that blended intensive interviews and survey methods would be the best approach to understanding why people joined the Provisionals.

Data Collection

My interests are in motives, more in *why* than what.[3] Instead of asking, 'Why did you join the Provisional IRA?' I asked questions like, 'Why did you join the Republican Movement?' This allowed respondents to discuss recruitment and related issues without incriminating themselves and others.

Other scholars have used oral histories and intensive interviews to collect insightful accounts from Irish republicans, beginning with J. Bowyer Bell's *The Secret Army: A History of the IRA 1916–1970*. My interests combine sociology and history. Understanding the complexity of the Provisionals and their separate but overlapping organizations – the Provisional IRA and Sinn Féin – required interviewing activists throughout Ireland. In what follows (and in the preceding oral history), some information on respondents is intentionally incorrect. This is not to hide illegal activities but rather to make sure that personal information and attitudes remain confidential for those who want them to remain confidential. Only after receiving permission have respondents been identified.

In 1984 and 1985, I interviewed activists in Sinn Féin, The Workers' Party, Fianna Fáil, Fine Gael, the SDLP, one member of the Irish Labour Party and a few activists who had disengaged. Sixty-three of the respondents were actively involved in Sinn Féin; the interviews were often arranged through Sinn Féin and questions and answers were framed around involvement in Sinn Féin. Some of them, events would show, were also members of the Provisional IRA. Based on arrests and reports, perhaps half of the respondents were veterans of or activists in the IRA. Because they had been convicted of membership, some respondents openly discussed their involvement in the IRA. A few people not actively involved in any political organization were interviewed to provide a frame of reference.

The interviews were arranged with the help of Sinn Féin press officers and persons already interviewed who identified potential respondents who fit a quota sampling frame. The geography, gender, date of recruitment into the Movement and the respondents' family political backgrounds were intentionally varied. Respondents were born and raised in Northern Ireland, the Republic of Ireland and England. Respondents from Belfast, Dublin, smaller cities and towns, and rural areas were interviewed. All six counties of Northern Ireland and fourteen of the twenty-six counties of the Republic of Ireland were represented. Fourteen women were interviewed. Most of the respondents joined the Movement after 1969, but included were interviews with recruits from the 1930s on to the 1980s.

In the summer of 1984, a questionnaire was mailed to a random sample of registered voters in West Belfast, South Fermanagh, North Monaghan and the Tallaght area of Dublin. A pre-stamped envelope addressed to an academic office in the United States was provided. If the survey had been successful, it would have provided a general profile of Sinn Féiners and their sympathizers in those areas. Only a few were returned and written on one questionnaire that was returned blank was the comment, 'I consider this questionnaire extremely dubious in origin and probably linked to a terrorist faction.' The failure of the survey confirmed the value of the intensive interviews.

The characteristics of activists in the Provisionals in the mid-1980s cannot be determined with any certainty. Based on available sources, including Bell's *The Secret Army*, Patrick Bishop and Eamon Mallie's *The Provisional IRA* and the pages of *AP/RN*, it appears that the respondents were broadly representative of Sinn Féin activists in the mid-1980s. The respondents included: Sinn Féin officers and past officers; Ard Chomhairle members; elected councillors; office workers; and cumann (local branch) members. Persons wanted in Northern Ireland and living in Southern Ireland – 'on the run' – and/or refugees (not wanted by the authorities but compelled to leave Northern Ireland) were interviewed. These oral histories are probably the most representative data ever collected from activists who endorse and engage in small group political violence while an armed campaign is underway.

Respondents who are not from Irish republican backgrounds may be over-represented. Several early interviews showed that people from republican families have similar political histories, and the following was typical: *'I was involved with the Republican Movement at a very early age because of my father being a member of the Republican Movement as well ... And, I suppose it rubbed off on me. I always had republican ideals.'* 'Theoretical saturation' on this issue was reached early in the research.[4] Beginning with a second research trip in 1984, I consciously sought out respondents from non-republican families and this guaranteed data on the recruitment into republican politics by activists from non-republican backgrounds.

Additional research trips allowed me to follow changes in the Provisionals over time, including the 1986 split. Beginning in 1995, attempts were made to reinterview the 1984/85 respondents as well as new respondents. Five respondents had passed away, four of them from natural causes. The deceased included: a Sinn Féin councillor who was assassinated by loyalists; two pre-1969 recruits who supported the Provisionals until their deaths; a pre-1969 recruit who joined Saor Éire and later joined the Provisionals; and a Northerner recruited during the hunger strikes who had disengaged. Because I never learned the names of several respondents, only forty-four of the original sixty-three respondents were living, known to me and available for reinterviews.

Thirty-one respondents were reinterviewed, including one respondent who was a prisoner in Long Kesh. The reinterviewed respondents included men and women, people from urban and rural areas, Northerners, Southerners, etc. They had been recruited from the 1930s on through to the 1980s. In the mid-1980s, the reinterviewed respondents had held a variety of positions in Sinn Féin: councillors, officers, Ard Chomhairle members, office workers and cumann members. The characteristics of the reinterviewed respondents were consistent with those of the original quota sample.

Since the mid-1990s, additional research trips have allowed me to follow the peace process, the 1997 split and so on. Activists in Republican Sinn Féin, the 32 County Sovereignty Movement, Cumann na mBan and éirigí have been interviewed, along with former Provisionals. In 2007, I began a third wave of interviews with the original 1984/85 respondents.

The Validity and Reliability of Intensive Interview Accounts

Social data are considered valid when they accurately reflect the process that the researcher is investigating. Data are considered reliable when the same collection method yields the same result time after time. Whether they are collected through face-to-face interviews or randomly distributed surveys, the validity and reliability of all social data are subject to threats because people may accidentally or intentionally distort and tailor their responses. Some people tell lies.

It is generally agreed that oral histories and intensive interviews have higher validity than questionnaires.[5] Oral histories and intensive interviews allow for follow-up questions and respondents are given the chance to elaborate on their responses. It is generally agreed that surveys have high reliability. Field research and oral histories are considered less reliable because the same question asked by different interviewers might result in different responses from the same respondent.

Throughout this project I have taken steps to enhance the validity and the reliability of accounts. For example, the initial interviews began with a non-directive, open-ended question, 'Why, in general, did you decide to join the Republican Movement?' This established a common interviewer–respondent understanding of the respondent's recruitment.[6] Questions were often rooted in specific events (such as internment, Bloody Sunday, the hunger strikes) in order to help memory recall and link the account to the historical record. Accounts were routinely probed to clarify potential misunderstanding, errors (purposeful or accidental), and gain a better understanding of the respondent.

None of this eliminated the possibility that activists were intentionally or unintentionally distorting their accounts to make themselves and/or their organization look better or worse. The interview process during the conflict was different from the interview process after 1994. Some respondents might be victims of a kind of groupthink in which they were encouraged to develop personal histories that were tailored to an official interpretation of events that is consistent with the spirit or ethos of the Provisionals, as has happened with respect to religious movements.[7]

It has been entertaining to see scholars question the quality of my interviews with Irish Republicans who then, it would seem, assume that the same validity issues do not threaten their own intensive interviews.[8] In my experience, the more an activist is invested in Sinn Féin, the more likely aspects of the account will be tailored to fit the official interpretation. Examples include blaming the 1975 truce on the 'former leadership'; ignoring Dáithí O'Connell's suggestion that Bobby Sands be a candidate in Fermanagh/South Tyrone; and, claiming that Cumann na mBan no longer exists. Even tailoring has its limits and some people are frank and direct no matter what. This research includes meeting with Irish republicans for more than thirty years. In many instances the meetings were with the same people at different times, in different places and in different contexts. Repeated interaction with respondents limits their opportunities to intentionally distort their attitudes and accounts.[9] It is easier to lie and mislead someone you will meet only once. Interviewing people who left the Provisionals for other organizations, and people who disengaged, allows for a conversation about the 'official' account. My approach to the Provisionals has also been influenced by intensive interviews collected from members of the Palestine Liberation Organization and veterans of Mau Mau.

By chance I began this study while Sinn Féin was making the transition from the Ruairí Ó Brádaigh presidency to the Gerry Adams presidency. With Ruairí Ó Brádaigh as President, Sinn Féin was the political wing of a social movement and it was fairly loosely organized. Gerry Adams led the transformation of Sinn Féin into a constitutional political party and, along the way, the party, and it would seem the Provisionals in general, became much more tightly organized and controlled. In 1984, I was given relatively free access to Sinn Féin members. In 1988, I was asked to route requests for interviews through the Belfast Press Office and was told that what had been done in 1984 was no longer possible. By that point, I knew a variety of activists at different levels across Sinn Féin and in different locations across Ireland, and I also knew activists who had split. In time, others would split or disengage. By not relying solely on Belfast republicans, or Northerners, or ex-prisoners, or post-1969 recruits, etc., a variety of perspectives on the experiences of Provisional Irish republicans have been collected.

Accounts should be treated as working hypotheses that are subject to verification.[10] This is the approach taken and factual information in accounts has been checked against the historical record.[11] The reinterviews in the mid-1990s provided an opportunity for a careful assessment of the validity and reliability of the interviews. A decade apart in time, thirty-one respondents were asked why they joined the Republican Movement. Some accounts were virtually identical across time whilst others were not identical but were, in essence, the same.[12]

The accounts of only two respondents were so different that they raised questions. One respondent, in his second interview, claimed that he had never been involved in the Republican

Movement. It was a curious claim. Another respondent, in his first interview, claimed that, like the Birmingham Six, he had been falsely convicted. The terrible hardship and injustice he suffered, he said, prompted him to join Sinn Féin when he was released from prison. In his second interview, the respondent acknowledged that he was guilty of the paramilitary offenses for which he was convicted. These accounts confirm the value of checking the historical record. For the first respondent, checking *An Phoblacht* confirmed that he had, in fact, been a member of Sinn Féin, if only briefly. Most likely he was protecting his family by minimizing his previous involvement in the Provisionals. For the second respondent, newspaper accounts showed that he had, in fact, pleaded guilty to paramilitary offenses. Evidently he lied in an attempt to build sympathy for himself and enhance the Provisionals' image. In this he was unsuccessful as the account was suspect from the start and had not been presented in publications. For the most part, accounts from activists are valid and reliable and comparing accounts against the historical record further minimizes threats to validity and reliability.

Nothing guarantees the validity or reliability of social data. Activists may remember the same event in different ways, memory plays tricks and attitudes, perspectives and interpretations change over time. It is unlikely that, during an interview, a prominent figure in Sinn Féin (or any other major political party) will openly question the leadership's decisions, let alone say 'We sold out.' Hopefully, by examining the Provisionals as a whole and over time, and through repeated interaction and interviews, threats to the validity and reliability of these oral histories have been minimized.

APPENDIX II: PROVISIONAL REPUBLICAN ROLL OF HONOUR

The primary sources for this appendix are the 'Roll of Honour' as presented in *An Phoblacht/ Republican News* (9 April 1998) and *Tírghrá: Ireland's Patriot Dead*. Additional sources include McKittrick et al.'s *Lost Lives*, Sutton's *Bear in Mind These Dead*, *Ardoyne: The Untold Truth*, and obituaries found in *An Phoblacht*, *Republican News*, and (after their merger) *AP/RN*.

Every attempt has been made to be as accurate as possible. Sometimes information is inconsistent across sources. For example, on the Roll of Honour, the date of death for Francis Rice is 18 May *1973*. It is 18 May *1975* in *Tírghrá*, *Lost Lives* and *Bear in Mind These Dead* and that is what is presented here. In most cases, the information presented on the Roll of Honour and/or *Tírghrá* is presented in Appendix 2, under the assumption that the persons compiling those sources were more likely to have known the person listed. Ages are primarily from *Tírghrá*. The number of children is at the time the person died. However, the spouse or partner of several activists, including Paddy McAdorey, Gerard Fennell, and Gerard McDade, gave birth to a child after they had died.

For some, the cause of death was uncertain and is left blank. In most of these cases, the person probably died of natural causes. In some cases, listing 'natural causes' is misleading because activist-related events and conditions contributed to the person's death. Pat McGeown was on hunger strike for forty-seven days and, because of his fast, McGeown suffered from heart disease and died in 1996 at the age of forty. *Tírghrá* states that Danny McCauley died in 1991 of natural causes 'as a direct result of Active Service'. The year a person joined is often an approximation for when that person became formally involved in a republican organization. For those who joined a youth organization and then graduated to the IRA, the year of joining that organization is recorded. The occupation listed is often based on a report that the person held that job at some time. Several people on the Roll of Honour were on the run and presumably unemployed when they died and others had probably completed their apprenticeships but this was not clear.

Some activists are not found on the Roll of Honour. James Templeton, killed by loyalists on 29 August 1975, is not listed on the Roll of Honour. He is, however, included in *Tírghrá* as a member of Na Fianna Éireann. Patrick Kelly, not listed on the Roll of Honour published 9 April 1998, is listed in later years. Kelly, who suffered from skin cancer, was arrested in England in 1992. As described in *Tírghrá*, there was a reoccurrence of his cancer and yet, 'For almost two years after his cancer reappeared Paddy was not allowed to attend a doctor who was qualified to treat him.' After a transfer to Maghaberry Prison in Northern Ireland and then to Portlaoise Prison, in County Laois, Kelly was released. He died at home in Portarlington, Laois, in June 1997.

Provisional IRA, Cumann na mBan, Sinn Féin, and Na Fianna Éireann Activists as found on the 'Roll of Honour' April 1998

(Note: The Roll of Honour did not include alleged informers executed by the IRA)

Mo	Day	Year	Name	Age	Married	Number of Children Reported	Reported Occupation	Incident	Agent	Year Recruited (approximate)	Organization
AUGUST 1969 WIDESPREAD RIOTING IN NORTHERN IRELAND											
8	15	1969	Gerald McAuley	15			Apprentice Cloth-Cutter	shot	Loyalists		**Fianna Éireann, Belfast**
11	6	1969	Liam McParland	43			Furniture Maker	auto accident		1940s	Belfast, 2nd Battalion
DECEMBER 1969 'PROVISIONAL' IRA FORMED											
1970											
6	26	1970	Thomas McCool	43	yes	2		explosion		1950s	Derry Brigade
6	27	1970	Joseph Coyle	45	yes	9		explosion			Derry Brigade
6	29	1970	Henry McIlhone	32	yes	5	Scaffolder/rigger	shot	Loyalists		Belfast 3rd Battalion
7	8	1970	Thomas Carlin	54				explosion			Derry Brigade
8	9	1970	Jimmy Steele	63	yes		Milkman	natural causes		early 1920s	Belfast 2nd Battalion
9	4	1970	Michael Kane	35			French polisher	explosion		1969	Belfast 3rd Battalion
10	27	1970	Peter Blake	18			Van driver	auto accident		1969	Belfast 2nd Battalion
10	27	1970	Tom McGoldrick	21			Apprentice plumber	auto accident		1966	Belfast 2nd Battalion
1971											
2	6	1971	James Saunders	22			Clerk	shot	British Army	1969/70	Belfast 3rd Battalion
3	8	1971	Charles Hughes	27			Labourer	shot	Official IRA		Belfast 2nd Battalion
4	4	1971	Tony Henderson	21			Apprentice bricklayer	shot accidentally		1969	Belfast 1st Battalion
5	15	1971	Billy Reid	32	yes	4	Joiner	shot	British Army		Belfast 3rd Battalion
AUGUST 1971 INTERNMENT INTRODUCED											
8	9	1971	Patrick McAdorey	24	yes		Wood machinist	shot	British Army	1969	Belfast 3rd Battalion
8	11	1971	Seamus Simpson	21	yes		Apprentice fitter	shot	British Army	1970	Belfast 2nd Battalion
8	18	1971	Eamonn Lafferty	19			Baker	shot	British Army	1968	Derry Brigade
8	19	1971	James O'Hagan	16				shot accidentally			Derry Brigade
10	2	1971	Terence McDermott	18			Apprentice electrician	explosion		1968	Belfast 1st Battalion
10	23	1971	Maura Meehan	31	yes	4		shot	British Army	1971	**Cumann n a mBan, Belfast**

			Name	Age			Occupation	Cause	Force	Joined	Organisation
10	23	1971	**Dorothy Maguire**	19				shot	British Army	1970	**Cumann n a mBan, Belfast**
10	24	1971	Martin Forsythe	19			Labourer	shot	RUC	1970	Belfast 1st Battalion
11	22	1971	Michael Crossey	21			Shop steward	explosion			North Armagh
12	8	1971	Tony Nolan	22			Fruit seller markets	shot accidentally		1971	Belfast 3rd Battalion
12	17	1971	Charles Agnew	36	yes	4				1940s	North Armagh
12	18	1971	John Bateson	20			Motor mechanic	explosion			County Derry
12	18	1971	Martin Lee	17			Bricklayer	explosion			County Derry
12	18	1971	James Sheridan	20			Trainee engineer	explosion			County Derry
12	21	1971	Gerald McDade	21	yes			shot	British Army	1970	Belfast 3rd Battalion
12	30	1971	Jack McCabe	55	yes	2		explosion		1930s	GHQ Staff
1972											
1	7	1972	Danny O'Neill	20			Insurance clerk	shot	British Army	1969	Belfast 2nd Battalion
1	11	1972	Michael Sloan	15			Student	shot accidentally		1972	**Fianna Éireann, Belfast**
1	16	1972	Eamon McCormick	17			Timber yard/unemp	shot	British Army		**Fianna Éireann, Belfast**
1	26	1972	Peter McNulty	46			Farmer	explosion			South Down
1	30	1972	Gerry Donaghy	17			Delivery hand	shot	British Army	1971	**Fianna Éireann, Derry**
BLOODY SUNDAY JANUARY 1972											
2	5	1972	Phelim Grant	32			Farm helper	explosion			North Antrim
2	5	1972	Charles McCann	27			Plasterer	explosion			North Antrim
2	10	1972	Joseph Cunningham	26	yes	2	Docker	shot	RUC	1969	Belfast 3rd Battalion
2	19	1972	David McAuley	15			Student	shot accidentally		1969	**Fianna Éireann, Belfast**
2	21	1972	Gerard Steele	27			Window cleaner	explosion		1971	Belfast 3rd Battalion
2	21	1972	Gerard Bell	18			Apprentice plumber	explosion		1971	Belfast 3rd Battalion
2	21	1972	Joseph Magee	31	yes	3	Steel fixer	explosion		1972	Belfast 3rd Battalion
2	21	1972	Robert Dorrian	28	yes	4	Roofer	explosion		1971	Belfast 3rd Battalion
3	4	1972	Albert Kavanagh	18			Apprentice compositor	shot	RUC	1969	Belfast 2nd Battalion
3	9	1972	Tony Lewis	16			Apprentice butcher	explosion		1969	Belfast 2nd Battalion
3	9	1972	Sean Johnston	19				explosion		1969	Belfast 2nd Battalion
3	9	1972	Gerard Crossan	19	yes	2	Bricklayer	explosion		1969	Belfast 2nd Battalion
3	9	1972	Tom McCann	20			Textile screen printer	explosion		1966	Belfast 2nd Battalion
3	14	1972	Colm Keenan	18			Student	shot	British Army		Derry Brigade

3	14	1972	Eugene McGillan	18			Refrig engr	shot	British Army	1971	Derry Brigade
3	23	1972	Sean O'Riordan	13			Student	shot	British Army		**Fianna Éireann, Belfast**
3	25	1972	Patrick Campbell	16			Bread server	shot accidentally		1970	Belfast 2nd Battalion
4	7	1972	Samuel Hughes	17			Apprentice butcher	explosion		1972	Belfast 3rd Battalion
4	7	1972	Charles McChrystal	17			Milk roundsman	explosion		1972	Belfast 3rd Battalion
4	7	1972	John McErlean	17			Mechanical engineer	explosion		1972	Belfast 3rd Battalion
5	13	1972	Michael Magee	13			Student	shot accidentally			**Fianna Éireann, Belfast**
5	13	1972	John Starrs	19				shot	British Army	1972	Derry Brigade
5	28	1972	Joseph Fitzsimmons	17			Labourer	explosion		1970	Belfast 3rd Battalion
5	28	1972	Jackie McIlhone	17			Apprentice welder	explosion		1971	Belfast 3rd Battalion
5	28	1972	Martin Engelen	18			Appren. motor mechanic	explosion		1971	Belfast 3rd Battalion
5	28	1972	Edward McDonnell	29			Slaughterhouse work	explosion		1971	Belfast 3rd Battalion
6	11	1972	Joseph Campbell	16				shot	British Army	1970	**Fianna Éireann, Belfast**

JUNE-JULY 1972 PROVISIONAL IRA-BRITISH TRUCE

6	28	1972	Tony Jordan	20			Labourer	auto accident		1970	Belfast 1st Battalion
6	28	1972	John Finucane	21	yes	1	Labourer	auto accident		1970	Belfast 1st Battalion
7	3	1972	Denis Quinn	29	yes	1	Unemployed labourer	shot accidentally			Tyrone

TRUCE ENDS

7	8	1972	**Julie Dougan**	26				auto accident			**CmBan, Portadown**
7	9	1972	John Dougal	16			Worked betting shop	shot	British Army		**Na Fianna Éireann**
7	14	1972	James Reid	27			No steady job	shot	British Army	1972	Belfast 3rd Battalion
7	14	1972	Louis Scullion	27				shot	British Army	1970	Belfast 3rd Battalion
7	16	1972	Tobias Molloy	18				Rubber bullet	British Army		**Fianna Éireann**
7	21	1972	Joseph Downey	23			Labourer	shot	British Army	1972	Belfast 3rd Battalion
7	28	1972	Seamus Cassidy	22			Pipe stressor	shot	British Army	1970	Belfast 3rd Battalion
7	31	1972	Seamus Bradley	19			Labourer	shot	British Army		Derry Brigade

31 JULY 1972 'OPERATION MOTORMAN' CLEAR NO-GO AREAS

8	3	1972	Robert McCrudden	19			Barman/labourer	shot	British Army		Belfast 2nd Battalion
8	9	1972	Colm Murtagh	18			Textile worker	explosion		1971	Newry

		Name	Age			Occupation	Cause	Responsible	Joined	Organisation
8	11	1972	**Anne Parker**	18				explosion		1972	**CnB, Belfast**
8	11	1972	Michael Clarke	22				explosion		1972	Belfast 2nd Battalion
8	22	1972	Oliver Rowntree	23				explosion		early 1960s	Newry
8	22	1972	Noel Madden	18			Apprentice painter	explosion			Newry
8	22	1972	Patrick Hughes	34	yes	7	Unemployed	explosion			Newry
8	26	1972	James Carlin	40	yes	4		explosion			South Down
8	26	1972	Martin Curran	21				explosion			South Down
9	17	1972	Michael Quigley	20			Printer	shot	British Army		Derry Brigade
9	20	1972	Joseph McComiskey	18				shot	British Army	1969	**Fianna Éireann, Belfast**
9	29	1972	Jimmy Quigley	18			Student	shot	British Army	1969	Belfast 2nd Battalion
10	6	1972	Daniel McAreavey	21			Chef	shot	British Army	1972	Belfast 2nd Battalion
10	10	1972	John Donaghy	19				explosion		1971	Belfast 2nd Battalion
10	10	1972	Patrick 'Maguire' Pendleton	24			Barman	explosion		1969	Belfast 2nd Battalion
10	10	1972	Joseph McKinney	16			Worked sawyers	explosion		1972	Belfast 2nd Battalion
10	16	1972	Hugh Heron	37	yes	6		shot	British Army		Tyrone
10	16	1972	John Patrick Mullan	37				shot	British Army	1950s	Tyrone
11	13	1972	Stan Carberry	34	yes	6	Heat engineer	shot	British Army	1972	Belfast 2nd Battalion
11	28	1972	John Brady	20			Shoe Factory/Unemp	explosion			Derry Brigade
11	28	1972	James Carr	19			Joiner	explosion			Derry Brigade
12	4	1972	Sean Hughes					unknown			**Na Fianna Éireann**
12	4	1972	Bernard Fox	16				shot	British Army	1970	**Na Fianna Éireann**
12	15	1972	Louis Leonard	26	yes	1	Owned butcher shop	shot	Loyalists		South Fermanagh
12	27	1972	Eugene Devlin	22				shot	British Army		Tyrone
12	29	1972	James McDaid	32	yes	2	Bricklayer	shot	British Army		Derry Brigade
1973											
1	18	1973	Francis Liggett	24	yes		Labourer	shot	British Army	1972	Belfast 2nd Battalion
2	3	1973	James Sloan	19	yes		Chef	shot	Loyalists		Belfast 3rd Battalion
2	4	1973	Tony Campbell	19			Chef	shot	British Army	1970	Belfast 3rd Battalion
2	4	1973	James McCann	17			Apprentice upholsterer	shot	Unknown	1971	Belfast 3rd Battalion
2	10	1973	Leo O'Hanlon	23	yes		Teacher	explosion			South Down
2	10	1973	**Vivien Fitzsimmons**	17			Student	explosion			**CnB, Downpatrick**
3	27	1973	Patrick McCabe	16				shot	British Army	1969	Belfast 3rd Battalion

Mo	Day	Year	Name	Age		No	Occupation	Cause		Joined	Unit / Location
4	12	1973	Edward O'Rawe	27			Docker	shot	British Army	early 1960s	Belfast 2nd Battalion
4	17	1973	Brian Smyth	31			Labourer	shot	British Army		Belfast 3rd Battalion
5	10	1973	Tony Ahern	17			Apprentice gardener	explosion			Cork
5	13	1973	Kevin Kilpatrick	20			Mechanic	shot	British Army		Tyrone
5	17	1973	Thomas O'Donnell	41	yes	8	Building contractor	auto accident		1949	GHQ Staff
5	18	1973	Sean McKee	17			App. ashphalter	shot	British Army	1973	Belfast 3rd Battalion
6	25	1973	Sean Loughran	37	yes	2		explosion		1950s	Tyrone
6	25	1973	Dermot Crowley	18			Apprentice plasterer	explosion		1972	Cork
6	25	1973	Patrick Carty	27				explosion		1969	Tyrone
7	21	1973	**Pauline Kane**	21			Hotel caterer	explosion			**CmB, Newcastle**
7	21	1973	Alphonsus Cunningham	21			Plumbing tradesman	explosion			South Down
8	10	1973	Seamus Harvey	22	yes	1		explosion			Tyrone
8	10	1973	Gerard McGlynn	18			Motor mechanic	explosion			Tyrone
8	16	1973	Patrick Quinn	16			Unemployed	mortar explosion			Tyrone
8	16	1973	Daniel McAnallen	27	yes		Plumber	mortar explosion			Tyrone
8	30	1973	Francis Hall	29	yes	1	Steel erector	explosion		1970	Belfast 1st Battalion
8	31	1973	Patrick Mulvenna	19	yes	1	Apprentice Joiner	shot	British Army	1969	Belfast 2nd Battalion
9	1	1973	**Anne Marie Petticrew**	19			Stitcher	explosion		1971	**Cumann na mBan, Belfast**
9	9	1973	Francis Dodds	31	yes		Prisoner	natural causes			**Long Kesh**
9	22	1973	James Bryson	25	yes	1	Apprentice bricklayer	shot	British Army	1971	Belfast 2nd Battalion
11	15	1973	Michael McVerry	23				shot	British Army	1971	South Armagh
11	24	1973	Michael Marley	17			Apprentice bricklayer	shot	British Army	1973	**Na Fianna Éireann**
11	26	1973	Desmond Morgan	20			Apprentice blumber	shot	British Army	1970	Tyrone
12	3	1973	Joe Walker	18			Apprentice butcher	shot	British Army		Derry Brigade
12	15	1973	Jim McGinn	20				explosion		1971	Tyrone
12	24	1973	Edward Grant	17			Meat factory	explosion			Newry
12	24	1973	Brendan Quinn	18			Meat factory	explosion		1972	Newry
1974											
3	15	1974	Kevin Murray	29	yes	4	Labourer	explosion			Tyrone

3	15	1974	Patrick McDonald	21			Textile worker	explosion			Tyrone
4	9	1974	Daniel Burke	50	yes	7	Bar manager	shot	British Army		Belfast 1st Battalion
4	24	1974	Jim Murphy	42			Garage owner	shot	Loyalists		**Sinn Féin**
5	3	1974	Teddy Campbell	57			Prisoner	natural causes		1930s	**Long Kesh**
5	7	1974	Frederick Leonard	19			Plumber	shot	Loyalists	1971	Belfast 3d Battalion
5	13	1974	Eugene Martin	18			Apprentice draughtsman	explosion			Tyrone
5	13	1974	Sean McKearney	18			Butcher's assistant	explosion			Tyrone
6	3	1974	Michael Gaughan	24				Hunger strike			England
6	24	1974	Gerard Craig	17			Painter	explosion			Derry Brigade
6	24	1974	David Russell	17			Apprentice engineer	explosion			Derry Brigade
7	2	1974	Patrick Teer	20			Window cleaner	nat causes/beating		1972	**Long Kesh**
8	3	1974	Martin Skillen	22			Bricklayer	shot	British Army		Belfast 2d Battalion
8	14	1974	Paul Magorrian	21				shot	British Army		South Down
8	27	1974	Patrick McKeown	29	yes	4	Mental health nurse	explosion			Newry
10	18	1974	Michael Hughes	16			Factory worker	shot	Royal Marine	1972	Newry
10	30	1974	Michael Meenan	16				explosion			Derry Brigade
11	6	1974	Hugh Coney	24			Factory worker	shot	British Army		**Long Kesh**
11	8	1974	Gerard Fennell	28	yes	1	Apprentice engineer	shot	British Army		Belfast 1st Battalion
11	14	1974	James McDade	28	yes	2		explosion		1972	England
11	15	1974	John Rooney	19				hit by car		early 1970s	Belfast 1st Battalion
12	7	1974	**Ethel Lynch**	22			Factory worker	explosion		1972	Derry Brigade
12	7	1974	John McDaid	16			Student	explosion		1973	Derry Brigade
12	21	1974	Brian Fox	27	yes		Eastwoods bookmakers	shot accidentally		early 1960s	England

22 DECEMBER 1974 PROVISIONAL IRA CHRISTMAS CEASEFIRE BEGINS

1975

1	10	1975	John Francis Green	28	yes	3		shot	Loyalists		North Armagh
1	13	1975	James Moyne	27			Dental tech/internee	natural causes		1970	Long Kesh

16 JANUARY 1975 CHRISTMAS/NEW YEAR CEASEFIRE ENDS

1	20	1975	Kevin Coen	21				shot	British Army	1970	Sligo

1	21	1975	John Stone	22			Car sprayer	explosion		1970	Belfast 2nd Battalion
1	21	1975	John Kelly	26	yes		Cabaret singer	explosion			Belfast 2nd Battalion
2	1	1975	Seán Boyle	21	yes	4	Bricklayer	auto accident			South Armagh
10 FEBRUARY 1975 PROVISIONAL IRA-BRITISH TRUCE BEGINS											
2	9	1975	**Bridie Dolan**	63				natural causes		1920s/30s	**Cumann na mBan, Belfast**
3	17	1975	Tom Smith	26			Factory worker	shot	Free St. Army	1969/70	Portlaoise
3	23	1975	Robert Allsopp	15				shot accidentally	Training accident	1969	**Fianna Éireann, Belfast**
5	18	1975	Francis Rice	17			Book-keeper	stabbed	Loyalists		South Down
6	4	1975	Francis Jordan	20			Barman/family farm	shot	British Army		South Armagh
6	5	1975	Sean McKenna	45	yes	8		natural causes			Monaghan
22 SEPTEMBER 1975 TRUCE ENDS											
10	31	1975	Seamus McCusker	40	yes	3	Electrician	shot	Official IRA		Belfast 3rd Battalion
11	6	1975	Kevin McAuley	13				accident			**Na Fianna Éireann**
12	1	1975	Paul Fox	20			Welder	explosion		1970	Belfast 2nd Battalion
12	1	1975	**Laura Crawford**	25			Typist	explosion		1973	**Cumann na mBan, Belfast**
12	5	1975	Terry Brady	54				natural causes		1930s	North Armagh
12	6	1975	James Lochrie	19			Machinist	explosion			South Armagh
12	6	1975	Sean Campbell	20			Tiler	explosion			South Armagh
12	10	1975	David Kennedy	55	yes	12	Laundry worker			1950s	North Armagh
1976											
1	13	1976	Martin McDonagh	23			Mgr, housing executive	explosion			Belfast 3rd Battalion
1	13	1976	**Rosemary Bleakley**	18			Civil servant	explosion		1973	**Cumann na mBan, Belfast**
2	12	1976	Francis Stagg	33	yes		Bus driver	Hunger strike		1972	England
2	12	1976	James O'Neill	17			Apprentice joiner	explosion			**Na Fianna Éireann**
2	13	1976	Sean Bailey	20	yes	1	Factory worker	explosion		1969	Belfast 2nd Battalion
2	15	1976	James McGrillen	24	yes	3	Lorry driver	shot	British Army		Belfast 2nd Battalion
2	18	1976	Paul Best	19			Chef/various jobs	shot	Official IRA	1973	**Sinn Féin**
4	5	1976	Sean McDermott	20				shot	RUC		Belfast 1st Battalion
4	15	1976	Peter Cleary	25				shot	British Army		South Armagh

5	17	1976	Jim Gallagher	20					shot	British Army	1973	Derry Brigade
6	5	1976	Colm Mulgrew	26		yes		Lab technician	shot	Loyalists	1973	**Sinn Féin**
6	30	1976	Brian Coyle	17					explosion			Derry Brigade
7	6	1976	Thomas Kane	28		yes	2	Scrap merchants	auto accident		1971	Belfast 1st Battalion
7	17	1976	Peter McElcar	19					explosion			Donegal
7	17	1976	Patrick Cannon	20				Welder	explosion		1975/76	Dublin
8	10	1976	Danny Lennon	22					shot	British Army	1970	Belfast 1st Battalion
10	9	1976	Noel Jenkinson	47				Prisoner/Leicester Prison	natural causes			**Sinn Féin**
10	16	1976	Paul Marlowe	31		yes	3	Ex-paratrooper	explosion		1969/70	Belfast 2nd Battalion
10	16	1976	Frank Fitzsimons	29		yes	2	Apprentice bricklayer	explosion		1973	Belfast 3rd Battalion
10	16	1976	Joseph Surgenor	24				Various jobs	explosion		1969	Belfast 3rd Battalion
10	28	1976	**Máire Drumm**	57		yes	5		shot	Loyalists	1930s/40s	**Sinn Féin/CmB**

1977 CELL STRUCTURE IN PLACE/LONG WAR BEGINS

1	16	1977	Seamus Harvey	20				Building worker	shot	British Army	1973	South Armagh
4	17	1977	Trevor McKibbin	19				Various	shot	British Army	1976	Belfast 3rd Battalion
4	23	1977	Brendan O'Callaghan	21		yes	2	Lorry driver	shot	British Army	1976	Belfast 1st Battalion
7	27	1977	Tommy Tolan	31		yes			shot	Official IRA	1971	Belfast 2nd Battalion
8	9	1977	Paul McWilliams	15					shot	British Army		**Na Fianna Éireann**
10	1	1977	Seán O'Conaill					Prisoner/Parkhurst Prison	natural causes			**Sinn Féin**

1978

1	18	1978	Jackie McMahon	18				Packer	found deceased	unclear		Belfast 3rd Battalion
2	26	1978	Paul Duffy	20					shot	British Army		Tyrone
6	4	1978	Henry Heaney	65				Prisoner	natural causes		1920s/30s	**Long Kesh**
6	10	1978	Denis Heaney	21				Fitter	shot	British Army		Derry Brigade
6	21	1978	Denis Brown	28		yes	3	Barman	shot	British Army		Belfast 3rd Battalion
6	21	1978	Jackie Mailey	30		yes	3	Apprentice tiler	shot	British Army		Belfast 3rd Battalion
6	21	1978	Jim Mulvenna	28		yes	1	Rent collector	shot	British Army	1969	Belfast 3rd Battalion
11	24	1978	Patrick Duffy	50		yes	6	Fitter	shot	British Army		Derry Brigade

1979

1	5	1979	Frankie Donnelly	24		yes		labourer	explosion			Belfast 3rd Battalion

Month	Day	Year	Name	Age			Occupation	Cause	Agent	Joined	Unit
1	5	1979	Laurence Montgomery	24	yes	2		explosion		1970	Belfast 3rd Battalion
4	25	1979	Billy Carson	32	yes	2	Dock labourer	shot	Loyalists	1970	Belfast 2nd Battalion
6	9	1979	Peadar McElvanna	23				shot	British Army	1971	South Armagh
10	23	1979	Martin McKenna	24				auto accident		1971	Belfast 3rd Battalion
1980											
1	17	1980	Kevin Delaney	26	yes	1		explosion		1966	Belfast 2nd Battalion
4	1	1980	Robert Carr	20	yes	1	Bricklayer	explosion		mid-1970s	Newry
7	1	1980	Terence O'Neill	21	yes	1		shot	RUC	1971	Belfast 2nd Battalion
1981											
2	1	1981	Peadar Mohan	28	yes		Furniture factory	active service			Monaghan
2	2	1981	Liam Hannaway	65	yes	yes		natural causes		1920/30s	Belfast 2nd Battalion
2	23	1981	James Burns	33	wid	3		shot	Loyalists	1963	Belfast 2nd Battalion
1 MARCH 1981 SECOND HUNGER STRIKE BEGINS											
5	5	1981	Bobby Sands	27	yes	1	MP/App coach builder	Hunger strike		1972	**Long Kesh**
5	12	1981	Francis Hughes	31			App paintr/decorator	Hunger strike			**Long Kesh**
5	21	1981	Raymond McCreesh	24			App sheet metal wrkr	Hunger strike		1974	**Long Kesh**
5	**21**	**1981**	**Pastsy O'Hara INLA**	**23**				Hunger strike		**1970**	**Long Kesh**
5	28	1981	Charles Maguire	20	yes	1	Bricklayer	shot	British Army	1977	Derry Brigade
5	28	1981	George McBrearty	24	yes	3	Supermarket worker	shot	British Army	1972	Derry Brigade
7	8	1981	Joe McDonnell	29	yes	2	Upholsterer	Hunger strike		1973	**Long Kesh**
7	8	1981	John Dempsey	16				shot	British Army	1980	**Fianna Éireann, Belfast**
7	13	1981	Martin Hurson	24			App. Fitter/Welder	Hunger strike			**Long Kesh**
8	**1**	**1981**	**Kevin Lynch INLA**	**25**			Labourer	Hunger strike			**Long Kesh**
8	2	1981	Kieran Doherty	25			Tiler	Hunger strike		1971	**Long Kesh**

8	8	1981	Thomas McElwee	23			Appr motor mechanic	Hunger strike			Long Kesh
8	**20**	**1981**	**Mickey Devine INLA**	**27**	**yes**	**2**		**Hunger strike**		**1971**	**Long Kesh**
OCTOBER 1981 SECOND HUNGER STRIKE ENDS											
2	7	1982	Danny McMullan	21			Joiner	auto accident		1977	County Derry
8	25	1982	Eamonn Bradley	23				shot	British Army		Derry Brigade
10	25	1982	Peter Corrigan	47	yes	10	Building trades	shot	Loyalists	1969	Sinn Féin
11	8	1982	Jeff McKenna					hit and run accident			Sinn Féin
11	11	1982	Sean Burns	21			Painter	shot	RUC	1982	North Armagh
11	11	1982	Eugene Toman	21			Apprentice plasterer	shot	RUC	1982	North Armagh
11	11	1982	Gervase McKerr	31	yes	2	Monumental sculpter	shot	RUC	1980	North Armagh
12	24	1982	Phil O'Donnell	50	yes			natural causes		1969	Derry Brigade
1983											
1	15	1983	Colm Daltun					natural causes			Dublin
3	1	1983	Eddie Dynes	37	yes	6	Handyman	auto accident			North Armagh
6	9	1983	Dan Turley	67	wid	9		natural causes		1920s/30s	Belfast 1st Battalion
SEPTEMBER 1983 'GREAT ESCAPE' FROM LONG KESH											
12	4	1983	Brian Campbell	19			Motor mechanic	shot	British Army		Tyrone
12	4	1983	Colm McGirr	23			Bricklayer	shot	British Army	1978	Tyrone
1984											
2	21	1984	Henry Hogan	20				shot	British Army	1981	North Antrim
2	21	1984	Declan Martin	18				shot	British Army	1983	North Antrim
4	21	1984	Richard Quigley	20			Deliveryman	explosion		1980	Derry Brigade
7	13	1984	William Price	28				shot	British Army	1979	Tyrone
8	8	1984	Brendan Watters	24			Unemployed machinist	explosion		1983	Newry
11	16	1984	Paddy Brady	35	yes	2	Milkman	shot	Loyalists		Sinn Féin
12	2	1984	Antoine MacGiolla Bhrighde	27				shot	British Army	1972	County Derry
12	2	1984	Ciaran Fleming	25				drowning on run			Derry Brigade
12	6	1984	Willie Fleming	19			Unemployed barman	shot	British Army	1979	Derry Brigade

12	6	1984	Danny Doherty	23	yes	1	Joiner	shot	British Army	1975	Derry Brigade
12	17	1984	Sean McIlvenna	33	yes	7	Pipe-fitter	shot	RUC	1971	North Armagh
1985											
1	26	1985	Mick Timothy	36	yes	3	Editor, *AP/RN*	natural causes		early 1970s	Dublin
2	23	1985	Charlie Breslin	20			Unemployed	shot	British Army	1979	Tyrone
2	23	1985	Michael Devine	22				shot	British Army	1984	Tyrone
2	23	1985	David Devine	16				shot	British Army	1984	Tyrone
8	4	1985	Tony Campbell	37	yes	yes	Milk deliveryman	natural causes		1968	Belfast 2nd Battalion
8	6	1985	Charles English	21				explosion		1982	Derry Brigade
9	9	1985	Raymond McLaughlin	34	yes	1		drowning accident			Donegal
1986											
2	22	1986	Tony Gough	24			App engr factory	shot	British Army	1980	Derry Brigade
4	26	1986	Seamus McElwain	26				shot	British Army	1974	South Fermanagh
5	31	1986	Philip McFadden	28			Fishing	accidental drowing			Derry Brigade
6	25	1986	Brian Dempsey	25				auto accident		1975	Belfast 2nd Battalion
8	9	1986	Patrick O'Hagan	32	yes	4	Building trades	natural causes			Derry Brigade
9	14	1986	Jim McKernan	29	yes	2		shot	British Army	1971	Belfast 1st Battalion
1987											
3	22	1987	Gerard Logue	26	yes	3		accidental shooting		1978	Derry Brigade
4	2	1987	Laurence Marley	41	yes	6		shot	Loyalists	1969	Belfast 3rd Battalion
5	2	1987	Finbarr McKenna	33				explosion		1968	Belfast 2nd Battalion
MAY 1987 LOUGHALL ATTACK											
5	8	1987	Paddy Kelly	30	yes	3		shot	British Army	1975/76	Tyrone
5	8	1987	Declan Arthurs	21			Agricultural business	shot	British Army	1982	Tyrone
5	8	1987	Seamus Donnelly	19				shot	British Army	1984	Tyrone
5	8	1987	Tony Gormley	24			Engnring sub-contrctor	shot	British Army	1981	Tyrone
5	8	1987	Eugene Kelly	25				shot	British Army	1982	Tyrone
5	8	1987	Jim Lynagh	31				shot	British Army	early 1970s	Tyrone
5	8	1987	Padraig McKearney	32				shot	British Army	early 1970s	Tyrone

5	8	1987	Gerard O'Callaghan	28				shot		1976	Tyrone
POST-LOUGHALL											
6	7	1987	**Margaret McArdle**	29				natural causes			Belfast 1st Battalion
10	28	1987	Paddy Deery	31	yes		3	explosion		1971	Derry Brigade
10	28	1987	Eddie McSheffrey	29	yes		2	explosion		early 1970s	Derry Brigade
12	7	1987	Peter Rodden					auto accident		1981	North Antrim
1988											
2	29	1988	Brendan Burns	30				explosion		1974	South Armagh
2	29	1988	Brendan Moley	30				explosion		1974	South Armagh
3	6	1988	**Mairéad Farrell**	31		Student		shot	British Army	1971	GHQ Staff
3	6	1988	Sean Savage	23				shot	British Army	1982	GHQ Staff
3	6	1988	Dan McCann	30	yes	Butcher	2	shot	British Army	1973	GHQ Staff
3	14	1988	Kevin McCracken	31				shot	British Army	1972	Belfast 1st Battalion
3	16	1988	Caoimhín Mac Brádaigh	30		Taxi driver		shot	Loyalists	1975	Belfast 1st Battalion
5	6	1988	Hugh Hehir	37	yes	Plumber	3	shot	Gardaí	1969	Clare
7	7	1988	Seamus Woods	23		Electrical engineer		explosion		1985	Tyrone
7	25	1988	Brendan Davison	33				shot	Loyalists	1971	Belfast 3rd Battalion
8	30	1988	Gerard Harte	29	yes	Architect	1	shot	British Army	1974	Tyrone
8	30	1988	Martin Harte	21	yes	Joiner	1	shot	British Army	1984	Tyrone
8	30	1988	Brian Mullin	25		Bricklayer		shot	British Army	1981	Tyrone
1989											
2	6	1989	James Joseph Connolly	20		Bricklayer		explosion			Tyrone
2	14	1989	John Davey	61	yes	Councillor		shot	Loyalists	1950s	**Sinn Fein**
4	4	1989	Gerard Casey	29	yes	Joiner	4	shot	Loyalists		North Antrim
9	12	1989	Seamus Twomey	69	yes	Bookmaker		natural causes		1936	GHQ Staff
11	29	1989	Liam Ryan	39	yes	Publican	1	shot	Loyalists		Tyrone
1990											
3	7	1990	Sam Marshall	31				shot	Loyalists		**Sinn Féin**
6	7	1990	Sean Bateson	34		Prisoner		natural causes		early 1970s	**Long Kesh**

			Name	Age			Occupation	Cause	Perpetrator		Area/Unit
10	9	1990	Martin McCaughey	23			Bricklayer	shot	British Army	1983	Tyrone
10	9	1990	Dessie Grew	37				shot	British Army	1970	Tyrone
10	26	1990	Tommy Casey	57	yes	11		shot	Loyalists	1990	**Sinn Féin**
12	30	1990	Fergal Caraher	30			Meat factory worker	shot	British Army	1986	**Sinn Féin**
1991											
1	2	1991	Patrick Sheehy	31			Plasterer	shot	unclear	early 1980s	Limerick
3	3	1991	Noel Wilkinson	23	yes	1	App motor mechanic	unclear	unclear	1985	Tyrone
3	3	1991	John Quinn	22			Various jobs	shot	Loyalists	1987	Tyrone
3	3	1991	Dwayne O'Donnell	17			Student	shot	Loyalists		Tyrone
3	3	1991	Malcolm Nugent	20	yes		Welder	shot	Loyalists	1987	Tyrone
4	10	1991	Colum Marks	29	yes			shot	RUC	1973–75	South Down
5	25	1991	Eddie Fullerton	56	yes	6	Builder	shot	Loyalists	late 1940s	**Sinn Féin**
6	3	1991	Lawrence McNally	39	partner	1	Plasterer	shot	British Army	1968	Tyrone
6	3	1991	Pete Ryan	35			Farm hand/plasterer	shot	British Army	1972	Tyrone
6	3	1991	Tony Doris	22		1	Unemployed	shot	British Army	1986	Tyrone
6	4	1991	Danny McCauley	34	yes			natural causes		1971/72	Tyrone
8	12	1991	Pádraig Ó Seanacháin	33			Driver DoE/family farm	shot	Loyalists	1980	**Sinn Féin**
8	16	1991	Tommy Donaghy	38			Fisherman	shot	Loyalists	early 1970s	**Sinn Féin**
9	16	1991	Bernard O'Hagan	38	yes	3	Lecturer	shot	Loyalists		**Sinn Féin**
11	15	1991	**Patricia Black**	18			Various jobs	explosion		1990	Belfast 1st Battalion
11	15	1991	Frankie Ryan	25				explosion		1985	Belfast 1st Battalion
1992											
1	8	1992	Proinsias Mac Airt	69				natural causes		1930s	Belfast 2nd Battalion
2	4	1992	Pat McBride	39	partner	1	Sinn Féin worker	shot	RUC off duty		**Sinn Féin**
2	4	1992	Paddy Loughran	61	yes	8	Doorman	shot	RUC off duty		**Sinn Féin**
2	5	1992	Joseph McManus	21				shot	UDR	1987	Sligo
2	16	1992	Kevin Barry O'Donnell	21			Student	shot	British Army	1988	Tyrone
2	16	1992	Sean O'Farrell	22			Welder	shot	British Army	1988	Tyrone
2	16	1992	Peter Clancy	21			Fitter/welder	shot	British Army	1988	Tyrone

2	16	1992	Patrick Vincent	20			Crane driver	shot	British Army	1991	Tyrone
2	19	1992	Brendan Seery	43			Prisoner	natural causes			Portlaoise
5	5	1992	Christy Harford	57			Carpenter	natural causes		1970	Dublin
10	16	1992	**Sheena Campbell**	29	div	1	Student	shot	Loyalists		**Sinn Féin**
12	2	1992	Pearse Jordan	22			Family catering bus.	shot	RUC		Belfast 1st Battalion
12	13	1992	Malachy Carey	36			Bricklayer	shot	Loyalists		**Sinn Féin**
1993											
3	24	1993	Peter Gallagher	45	yes	6	Construction worker	shot	Loyalists	early 1980s	**Sinn Féin**
3	25	1993	James Kelly	25			Building worker	shot	Loyalists	1988	County Derry
5	1	1993	Alan Lundy	39	yes	5	Plasterer	shot	Loyalists	1970	**Sinn Féin**
6	12	1993	Michael Motley	35			Various jobs			1981	Laois
10	23	1993	Thomas Begley	22				explosion		1993	Belfast 3rd Battalion
1994											
4	4	1994	John O'Rawe	69	yes			natural causes		1938	Belfast 1st Battalion
5	21	1994	Martin Doherty	35		2	Labourer	shot	Loyalists	1981	Dublin
AUGUST 1994 PROVISIONAL IRA CEASEFIRE											
12	13	1994	Pól Kinsella	31	yes	1	Prisoner	natural causes			**Long Kesh**
1995											
FEBRUARY 1996 PROVISIONAL IRA CAMPAIGN RESUMES											
1996											
2	18	1996	Edward O'Brien	21			Bakery worker	explosion		1992	England
4	8	1996	Eugene Martin	22			Welder	auto accident		1980	South Armagh
8	8	1996	Malachy Watters	22						1991	South Armagh
8	10	1996	Jimmy Roe	68				natural causes		1940s	Belfast 1st Battalion
9	23	1996	Diarmuid O'Neill	27				shot	British police		England
10	1	1996	Pat McGeown	40	yes			natural causes		early 1970s	**Sinn Féin**
JULY 1997 SECOND PROVISIONAL IRA CEASEFIRE											
APRIL 1998 GOOD FRIDAY (BELFAST) AGREEMENT											

ENDNOTES

Chapter 1

1 Derry republican 1 interview, 1984.

2 P. O'Malley, *The Uncivil Wars: Ireland Today* (Boston: Beacon Press, 1983), p. 10; S. Bruce, *The Red Hand: Protestant Paramilitaries in Northern Ireland* (Oxford: OUP, 1992), p. 58.

3 'Grand Orange Lodge of Ireland', http://www.grandorangelodge.co.uk/ (Last accessed: 09/01/2017).

4 C. Anderson, *The Billy Boy: The Life and Death of UVF Leader Billy Wright* (Edinburgh: Mainstream Publishing, 2002), p. 51; *Red Hand*, Issue 53 (2000).

5 Derry republican 1 interview, 1985.

6 R.B. O'Brien (ed.), *The Autobiography of Wolfe Tone, 1763–1798* (Dublin: Maunsel & Co., Ltd, 1914); M. Elliott, *Wolfe Tone: Prophet of Irish Independence* (New Haven: Yale University Press, 1989), pp. 125–6.

7 *Derry* rather than *Londonderry* is used because it is the preferred choice of the respondents. After his arrest, Shane O'Doherty, from Derry, met Belfast IRA prisoners and discovered 'a virtual sectarian war'. S. O'Doherty, *The Volunteer: A Former IRA Man's True Story* (London: Harper Collins, 1993), p. 195; D. McKittrick, S. Kelters, B. Feeney and C. Thornton *Lost Lives: The Stories of the Men, Women and Children who Died as a Result of the Northern Ireland Troubles* (Edinburgh: Mainstream Publishing, 2007), pp. 560–1.

8 Belfast republican 1 interview, 1984; R. English, *Armed Struggle: A History of the IRA* (London: Macmillan, 2003), pp. 120–3.

9 See also J. Ruane and J. Todd's insightful, *The dynamics of conflict in Northern Ireland: Power, Conflict and Emancipation* (Cambridge: Cambridge University Press, 1996).

10 Table 1 is based on but not identical to the classification scheme of M. Sutton, *Bear in Mind these Dead: Index of Deaths from the Conflict in Ireland, 1969–93* (Belfast: Beyond the Pale Publications, 1994) and the CAIN Web Service 'Sutton Index of Deaths' (Conflict Archive on the Internet: http://cain.ulst.

ac.uk/sutton/chron/. Last accessed: 09/01/2017.) There is close agreement across different sources on who killed whom; tables from different sources will yield similar, but not identical conclusions. R.W. White, 'The Irish Republican Army: An assessment of sectarianism', *Terrorism and Political Violence* (*TPV*), 9/1 (1997), pp. 20–54; S. Bruce, 'Victim selection in ethnic conflict: Motives and Attitudes in Irish Republicanism', *TPV*, 9/1 (1997), pp. 56–71; R.W. White, 'The Irish Republican Army and sectarianism: Moving beyond the anecdote', *TPV*, 9/2 (1997), pp. 120–31; J. Dingley, 'A reply to White's non-sectarian thesis of Provisional IRA targeting', *TPV*, 10/2 (1998), pp. 106–17; R.W. White, 'Don't confuse me with the facts: More on the Irish Republican Army and sectarianism', *TPV*, 10/4 (1998), pp. 164–89; H. Patterson, 'Sectarianism revisited: The Provisional IRA in a border region of Northern Ireland', *TPV*, 22/3 (2010), pp. 337–56; R.W. White, 'Provisional IRA attacks on the UDR in Fermanagh and South Tyrone: Implications for the study of political violence and terrorism', *TPV*, 23/3 (2011), pp. 329–49; H. Patterson, 'Response to Robert W. White', *TPV*, 23/3 (2011), pp. 350–3; R.W. White, 'Response to Henry Patterson', *TPV*, 23/3 (2011), pp. 354–6; see also C.J.M. Drake, *Terrorists' Target Selection* (London: Macmillan Press, 1998); G. Maney, M. McCarthy and G. Yukich, 'Explaining political violence against civilians in Northern Ireland: A contention oriented approach', *Mobilization* 17/1, pp. 27–48; G. Ó Faoleán, 'The Ulster Defence Regiment and the Question of Catholic recruitment, 1970–72', *TPV*, 27/5, pp. 838–56.

11 R.W. White, 'Comparing repression on the right and on the left: State repression of pro-state vigilantes and anti-state insurgents', *Mobilization* 4/2 (1999), pp. 189–202.

12 K. Wharton, *Bloody Belfast: An Oral History of the British Army's War Against the IRA* (Port Stroud, Gloucestershire: Spellmount Publishers, 2010), p. 173.

13 *Ibid.*, p. 55–7.

14   B.   McDonald,   'The   "Pitchfork   Murders":
Uncovering the Cover-Up', Newtownbutler: Louise
Leonard Sinn Féin Cumann (2012).

15   A. Cadwallader, *Lethal Allies: British Collusion in
Ireland* (Cork: Mercier Press, 2013).

16   See K. Asmal et al., *Shoot to Kill? International Lawyers'
Inquiry into the Lethal Use of Firearms by the Security
Forces in Northern Ireland* (Dublin: Mercier Press,
1985), pp. 23, 125–50; see also, *Irish Information
Agenda* (London: Irish Information Partnership,
1990), pp. 94–103; R.W. White and T.F. White,
'Repression and the liberal state: The case of
Northern Ireland, 1969-1972', *Journal of Conflict
Resolution* 39 (1995), pp. 330–52.

17   P. Wilkinson, *Terrorism versus Democracy: The Liberal
State Response* (New York: Routledge, 2006, 2nd
edition), pp. 61–2.

18   P. Wilkinson, 'The Provisional IRA: An assessment
in the wake of the 1981 Hunger Strike', *Government
and Opposition*, 17/2 (1982), p. 142.

19   *Terrorist Group Profiles*, report by the US Vice
President's Task Force on Combatting Terrorism
(Washington, D.C.: U.S. Government Printing
Office, 1988), p. 56.

20   See Wilkinson, *Terrorism versus Democracy* (2006),
pp. 15–16; A.P. Schmid and A.J. Jongman et al.,
*Political Terrorism: A New Guide to Actors, Authors,
Concepts, Data Bases, Theories and Literature* (New
York: North-Holland Publishing Company, 1988),
pp. 1–38; A.P. Schmid, 'The response problem as
a definition problem', pp. 7–13 in A.P. Schmid and
R. Crelinsten, *Western Responses to Terrorism* (London:
Frank Cass, 1993); L. Weinberg, A. Pedahzur and S.
Hirsch-Hoefler, 'The challenges of conceptualizing
terrorism', *Terrorism and Political Violence* 16/4
(2004), pp. 777–94; B. Hoffman, *Inside Terrorism*
(New York: Columbia University Press, 2006); R.
English, *Terrorism: How to Respond* (Oxford: OUP,
2009), pp. 1–26; J. Muller, 'Six rather unusual
propositions about terrorism', *TPV*, 17/4 (2005),
pp. 487–505.

21   J. Dingley, *The IRA: The Irish Republican Army* (New
York: Praeger, 2012), pp. 98–9.

22   See Wilkinson, *Terrorism versus Democracy*, p. 94.

23   Two inquiries into Bloody Sunday reached vastly
different conclusions. The Widgery Report (1972)
was condemned by many nationalists as a whitewash.
The Saville Inquiry (2010) found the shootings were
not justified and exonerated the victims. McKittrick
et al., *Lost Lives*, pp. 78–90.

24   W. Manchester and P. Reid, *The Last Lion: Winston
Spencer Churchill Defender of the Realm, 1940-1965*

(New York: Little, Brown and Company, 2012), pp.
216–7.

25   The BBC reported that more than one hundred
people were killed in the attacks on Tripoli and
Benghazi. Danny Morrison interview, 1988. '1986:
US launches air strikes on Libya', *BBC On This Day*,
15 April 1986.

26   '50s Nuclear Target list Offers Chilling Insight',
New York Times, 23 December 2015, p. A10.

27   B. Hoffman, *Inside Terrorism* (New York: Columbia
University Press, 2006), p. 40.

28   J. Goodwin, 'A Theory of Categorical Terrorism',
Social Forces 84 (2006), pp. 2027–46.

29   L. Dugan and E. Chenoweth, 'Beyond Deterrence:
Raising the Expected Utility of Abstaining from
Terrorism in Israel', *American Sociological Review*
77/4 (2012), pp. 597–624. See Global Terrorism
Database: GTD Variables and Inclusion Criteria,
National Consortium for the Study of Terrorism
and   Responses   to   Terrorism.   College   Park:
University of Maryland (2011); D. Rapoport, 'The
four waves of modern terrorism', in John Horgan
and Kurt Braddock, *Terrorism Studies: A Reader*
(Oxfordshire: Routledge, 2012), pp, 41-60; R.
English, *Does Terrorism Work? A History* (Oxford:
Oxford University Press, 2016), pp. 148–55;N.
Chomsky, *Pirates and Emperors: International Terrorism
in the Real World* (New York: Claremont Research
and Publications, 1986).

30   See M. Sageman, 'The stagnation in terrorism
research', *Terrorism and Political Violence* 26/4 (2014),
pp. 565–80; D. Bryan, L. Kelly and S. Templer, 'The
failed paradigm of "terrorism"', *Behavioral Sciences
of Terrorism and Political Aggression*, 3/2 (2011), pp.
80–96.

31   Ruairí Ó Brádaigh interview, 2009. See 'Social
Movements and Terrorism: "And if that's what
a terrorist is I want to be a terrorist"' (2012),
*Mobilizing Ideas: Is Terrorism a Form of Activism? The
Role of Terrorism in Social Change* (University of Notre
Dame, Center for the Study of Social Movements,
blog).

32   C. Tilly, *From Mobilization to Revolution* (New York:
Random House, 1978), p. 176.

33   See Patterson, 'Response to Robert W. White', pp.
350–3.

34   D. della Porta, *Social Movements, Political Violence, and
the State: A Comparative Analysis of Italy and Germany*
(Cambridge: Cambridge University Press, 1995), p.
201; see also, D. McAdam, S. Tarrow and C. Tilly,
Dynamics   of   Contention (Cambridge: Cambridge
University Press, 2001); J. Viterna, *Women in War:*

417

The Micro-Processes of Mobilization in El Salvador (Oxford: OUP, 2013).

35   C. Tilly, L. Tilly and R. Tilly, *The Rebellious Century* (Cambridge: Harvard University Press, 1975), pp. 243, 249.

36   See Tilly, *From Mobilization to Revolution*, p. 175.

37   W. Gamson, *The Strategy of Social Protest* (2nd edition, Belmont, CA: Wadsworth, 1990), pp. 138–9; W. Gamson, B. Fireman and S. Rytina, *Encounters With Unjust Authority* (Chicago: Dorsey Press, 1982), pp. 7–9; McAdam et al., *The Dynamics of Contention*, pp. 4–8; C. Tilly and S. Tarrow, *Contentious Politics* (Oxford: OUP, 2007), pp. 9–11, 69–87, 136–61; B. Klandermans, 'The dynamics of demand', pp. 3–14 in *Dynamics, Mechanisms, and Processes: The Future of Social Movement Research* (Minneapolis: University of Minnesota Press, 2013).

38   Figure 1 courtesy of Michael M. Maitzen and Margaret C. White.

39   J.B. Bell, *The Dynamics of the Armed Struggle* (New York: Routledge, 1995), p. xv; see also, V. Yow, '"Do I like them too much?" Effects of the oral history interview on the interviewer and vice-versa', *Oral History Review* 24/1 (1997), pp. 55–79; J. Horgan, *The Psychology of Terrorism* (New York: Routledge, 2005), pp. 37–9; M. Wieviorka, 'Terrorism in the context of academic research', pp. 597–606 in M. Crenshaw (ed.), *Terrorism in Context* (University Park: Penn State University Press, 1995); L. Bosi, 'Explaining pathways to armed activism in the Provisional Irish Republican Army, 1969–1972', *Social Science History* 36/3 (2012) pp. 347–90.

40   H. Patterson, review of Robert W. White, *Provisional Irish Republicans: An Oral and Interpretive History* (Westport, CT: Greenwood Press, 1989), *Conflict Quarterly* 14/3 (1994), pp. 75–7.

41   L. Coser, *Masters of Sociological Thought: Ideas in Historical and Social Context* (San Diego, CA: Harcourt Brace Jovanovich, 1977), pp. 310–11; C.H. Cooley, 'The Roots of Social Knowledge', *American Journal of Sociology* 32 (1926), pp. 59–79; R.W. White, 'Issues in the study of political violence: Understanding the motives of participants in small group political violence', *TPV*, 12/1 (2000), pp. 95–108; A. Portelli, 'What Makes Oral History Different', Chapter 3 in *The Death of Luigi Trastulli and Other Stories: Form and Meaning in Oral History* (Albany: SUNY Press, 1991), pp. 45–58.

42   E. Herman and G. O'Sullivan, *The Terrorism Industry: The Experts and Institutions that Shape Our View of Terror* (New York: Pantheon Books, 1989).

Chapter 2

1   This chapter is not an exhaustive history of Ireland or Irish Republicanism. It only provides a context for the oral history that follows.

2   'Engels to Marx', 23 May 1856, in *Marx Engels: Ireland and the Irish Question* (Moscow: Progress Publishers, 1978), pp. 93–5.

3   T.W. Moody and F.X. Martin (eds), *The Course of Irish History* (Lanham, MD: Roberts Rinehart, 2001, 4th edition); S. Ellis, *Tudor Ireland: Crown, Community and the Conflict of Culture, 1470–1603* (New York: Longman, 1985); Revd S.A. Cox, 'The Plantation of Ulster', in R.B. O'Brien (ed.), *Studies in Irish History, 1603–1649* (Dublin: Browne and Nolan, Ltd, 1906), pp. 1–68; L. de Paor, *Divided Ulster* (Harmondsworth: Penguin Books, 1970); S. Cronin, *Irish Nationalism* (Dublin: Irish Academic Press, 1980), p. 11.

4   Seán Cronin, *Irish Nationalism: A History of Its Roots and Ideology* (Dublin: The Academy Press, 1980), pp. 40–64. Map 1 Courtesy of Mike Maitzen.

5   See O'Brien, *The Autobiography of Wolfe Tone*, pp. 50–1.

6   See O'Brien, *The Autobiography of Wolfe Tone*.

7   P.M. Geoghegan, *Robert Emmet: A Life* (Dublin: Gill and Macmillan, 2002), pp. 253–4. See also, P.M. Geoghegan, *The Irish Act of Union* (Dublin: Gill and Macmillan, 2001); K. Whelan, 'Robert Emmet: Between History and Memory', *History Ireland*, 11/3 (2003), pp. 50–4.

8   R. Sloan, *William Smith O'Brien and the Young Ireland Rebellion of 1848* (Dublin: Four Courts Press, 2000); Cronin, *Irish Nationalism*, pp. 65–85; F.S.L. Lyons, *Ireland Since the Famine* (London: Fontana, 1973, revised edition), pp. 42–6; John Mitchel, Young Irelanders: J. Mitchel, *Jail Journal* (Dublin: M.H. Gill and Son, 1913); Whelan, 'Robert Emmet: Between History and Memory', *History Ireland*, 11/3 (2003), pp. 50–4; Cronin, *Irish Nationalism*, p. 85.

9   See Lyons, *Ireland Since the Famine*, p. 15.

10   K.R.M. Short, *The Dynamite War: Irish American Bombers in Victorian Britain* (Dublin: Gill and Macmillan, 1979); Revd W. D'Arcy, *The Fenian Movement in the United States: 1858–1886* (Washington: The Catholic University of America Press, 1947); L. O'Broin, *Fenian Fever: An Anglo-American Dilemma* (New York: New York University Press, 1971); and T.W. Moody, 'Fenianism, Home Rule, and the Land War', pp. 228–44, in T.W. Moody and F.X. Martin (eds), *The Course of Irish History.*

11   'Letter from Rossa', pp. 499–501 in *Marx Engels: Ireland and the Irish Question*; O'Donovan Rossa, *Irish*

Rebels in English Prisons (Dingle, Co. Kerry: Brandon, 1991 edition).

12 'Letter from Rossa', pp. 499–501, 399 and 'Marx to Sigfrid Meyer and August Vogt' [1870], pp. 406–9 in *Marx Engels: Ireland and the Irish Question*.

13 O'Donovan Rossa, *Irish Rebels in English Prisons*, pp. 216–8, 237.

14 See Cronin, *Irish Nationalism*, pp. 93–4; P. Bew, *Land and the National Question in Ireland, 1858–1882* (Atlantic Highlands, N.J.: Humanities Press, 1979); Lyons, *Ireland Since the Famine*, pp. 172–5; T.W. Moody, 'Fenianism, Home Rule, and the Land War', pp. 228–44 in T.W. Moody and F.X. Martin (eds), *The Course of Irish History*; A. Boyd, *Holy War in Belfast* (London: Anvil Books, 1987), pp. 119–49; P. Hart, *The I.R.A. at War 1916–1923* (Oxford: OUP, 2005); Lyons, *Ireland Since the Famine*, pp. 178–88, 291–3.

15 G. Lewis, *Carson: The Man Who Divided Ireland* (London: Hambledon Continuum, 2006).

16 See Lyons, *Ireland Since the Famine*, pp. 330–3.

17 See, for example, Des Dalton's oration, 16 June 2013, Republican Sinn Féin Wolfe Tone Commemoration, *Saoirse* July 2013, p. 10.

18 See Lyons, *Ireland Since the Famine*, pp. 329–80; R. Dudley Edwards, *Patrick Pearse: the Triumph of Failure* (Dublin: Irish Academic Press, 2006).

19 P.S. O'Hegarty, *The Victory of Sinn Fein* (Dublin: The Talbot Press, Ltd, 1924), pp. 2–3.

20 See Cronin, *Irish Nationalism*, pp. 6–7, 90–4.

21 M. Caulfield, 'The executions', pp. 259–75 in R. McHugh (ed.), *Dublin: 1916* (Reprinted from M. Caulfied [1964] *The Easter Rebellion* (New York: Hawthorn, 1966)); Lyons, *Ireland Since the Famine*; J.J. Lee, *Ireland: 1912–1985* (Cambridge University Press, 1989), p. 22.

22 See Lyons, *Ireland Since the Famine*, p. 404.

23 See Cronin, *Irish Nationalism*; J. B. Bell, *The Secret Army: The IRA* (Dublin: The Academy Press, 1979); Lyons, *Ireland Since the Famine*, p. 406.

24 D. Ryan, *Sean Treacy and the Third Tipperary Brigade I.R.A.* (Tralee: Anvil Books, 1945); D. Breen, *My Fight for Irish Freedom* (Tralee: Anvil Books, 1993); Lyons, *Ireland Since the Famine*, pp. 413–20; J. Augusteijn, *From Public Defiance to Guerrilla Warfare: The Experience of Ordinary Volunteers in the Irish War of Independence 1916–1921* (Dublin: Irish Academic Press, 1996).

25 T. Barry, *Guerrilla Days in Ireland* (Cork: Mercier Press, 1955), p. 119. Revisionist historian Peter Hart described Tom Barry as a serial killer and argued that the 1920s IRA was engaged in sectarian revenge. These claims are questioned by other scholars. See P. Hart, *The IRA and Its Enemies: Violence and Community in Cork, 1916–1923* (Oxford: OUP, 1998); Hart, *The I.R.A. at War 1916–1923*; M. Ryan, *Tom Barry: IRA Freedom Fighter* (Cork: Mercier Press, 2003); N. Meehan, 'Distorting Irish History, the stubborn facts of Kilmichael: Peter Hart and Irish Historiography', *Spinwatch* (November 2010).

26 See Lyons, *Ireland Since the Famine*, p. 417; Lee, *Ireland: 1912–1985*, p. 47.

27 See, for example: Bell, *The Secret Army*; T. Garvin, *1922: The Birth of Irish Democracy* (Dublin: Gill and Macmillan, 1996); M. Coleman, *County Longford and the Irish Revolution 1910–1923* (Dublin: Irish Academic Press, 2003); M. Farrell, *Northern Ireland: The Orange State* (London: Pluto Press, 1976), e.g. pp. 35–8; M. Farrell, *Arming the Protestants: The Formation of the Ulster Special Constabulary and the Royal Ulster Constabulary, 1920–27* (London: Pluto Press, 1983); P. Buckland, *Ulster Unionism and the Origins of Northern Ireland, 1886–1922* (Dublin: Gill and Macmillan, 1973); Boyd, *Holy War in Belfast*.

28 R.W. White, *Provisional Irish Republicans: An Oral and Interpretive History* (Westport, CT: Greenwood Press, 1993). Map 2 courtesy of Michael Maitzen.

29 See Farrell, *Northern Ireland: The Orange State*, pp. 66–8; Lyons, *Ireland Since the Famine*, pp. 425–8; Cronin, *Irish Nationalism*, p. 131.

30 See Lyons, *Ireland Since the Famine*, pp. 427–38.

31 Treaty debate quotations are taken from Cronin, *Irish Nationalism*, pp. 136–47.

32 See Cronin, *Irish Nationalism*, pp. 132–46; Lyons, *Ireland Since the Famine*, pp. 400–68; Bell, *The Secret Army*, pp. 29–39; R. Ó Brádaigh, *Dílseacht: The Story of Cmdt. General Tom Maguire and the Second (All-Ireland) Dáil* (Dublin: Elo Press, 1997), pp. 13–37.

33 Leinster House is a short walk from the Mansion House. See Lyons, *Ireland Since the Famine*, pp. 456–86; Cronin, *Irish Nationalism*, pp. 133–57; Lee, *Ireland, 1912–1985*, pp. 56–69.

34 *Tírghra: Ireland's Patriot Dead* (Republican Publications, 2002), p. 7; *With the IRA in the Fight for Freedom: 1919 to the Truce* (Cork: Mercier Press, 2010), p. 44.

Chapter 3

1 Ruairí Ó Brádaigh interview, 1984.

2 See Lyons, *Ireland Since the Famine*, pp. 494–7.

3 *Ibid.*, pp. 497–500; Bell, *The Secret Army*, pp. 52–75; Ó Brádaigh, *Dílseacht*, p. 30.

4 John Hunt interview, 2014; National Graves Association, *The Last Post*, p. 137.

5   Bunreacht na hÉireann (Constitution of Ireland), 1937.

6   F. Pakenham (The Earl of Longford) and T.P. O'Neill, *Eamon de Valera: A Biography* (Boston: Houghton-Mifflin, 1971), pp. 289–339; D. Ferriter, *Judging Dev: A Reassessment of the Life and Legacy of Eamon de Valera* (Dublin: Radio Telefís Éireann, 2007), pp. 128–9, 143–6; Bell, *The Secret Army*, pp. 140–1.

7   See Bell, *The Secret Army*, pp. 125–7; B. Hanley, *The IRA: A Documentary History 1916–2005* (Dublin: Gill and Macmillan, 2010).

8   See Farrell, *Northern Ireland: The Orange State*, p. 92, 136–7; R. Munck and B. Rolston, *Belfast in the Thirties: An Oral History* (Dingle: Brandon Books, New York: St. Martin's, 1986); P. Devlin, *Yes, We Have No Bananas: Outdoor Relief in Belfast, 1920–1939* (Belfast: Blackstaff Press, 1981) .

9   Billy McKee interview, 2014.

10   Joe Cahill interview, 1990.

11   Joe Cahill interview, 1996. B. Anderson, *Joe Cahill: A Life in the IRA* (Dublin: O'Brien Press, 2002), pp. 24–7.

12   J.B. (Joe) and Bernadette O'Hagan interview, 1996. The *Argenta* was moored in Belfast Lough between 1920 and 1923. D. Kleinrichter's *Republican Internment and the Prison Ship Argenta* (Dublin: Irish Academic Press, 2001, p. 351) lists Daniel Lynch (J.B. O'Hagan's uncle) among those who participated in a hunger strike.

13   See Bell, *The Secret Army*, p. 47; U. Mac Eoin, *The IRA in the Twilight Years 1923–1948* (Dublin: Argenta Publications, 1997).

14   See Bell, *The Secret Army*, pp. 154–5; Ó Brádaigh, *Dílseacht*, pp. 27–31.

15   On the 1940s IRA campaign see: Bell, *The Secret Army*; T.P. Coogan's *The IRA* (London: Harper Collins, 2000); *The Last Post, Details and Stories of Irish Republican Dead 1916–1985* (Dublin: National Graves Association, 1985), pp. 170–1.

16   Hunt would later emigrate to the United States. John Hunt interview, 2014. Marisa McGlinchey, 'Unbroken Continuity', *The Village*, July 2016, pp. 18–21; J. McPherson, 'A Memory of Prison and Resistance', *Daley Planet*, 13 April 1981, p. 5.

17   See Bell, *The Secret Army*, pp. 17–80; Tim Pat Coogan, *The IRA* (Harper Collins, 2000), pp. 113–217; Mac Eoin, *The IRA in the Twilight Years*; J. Maguire, *IRA Internments and the Irish Government: Subversives and the State 1939–1962* (Dublin: Irish Academic Press, 2008), p. 35.

18   J. McGuffin, *Internment!* (Tralee: Anvil Books, 1973), pp. 69–75, 81–3; J. McVeigh, *Executed: Tom Williams*

and the IRA (Belfast: Beyond the Pale Publications, 1999), pp. 36–9, 43–4, 72–84, 92–5; Mac Eoin, *The IRA In The Twilight Years*, p. 515; Anderson, *Joe Cahill*, pp. 46–72.

19   Ruairí Ó Brádaigh interview, 1984.

20   See Bell, *The Secret Army*, pp. 65, 235; Coogan, *The IRA*, pp. 199–200.

21   See Bell, *The Secret Army*, pp. 241, 246–7.

22   Mac Eoin, *The IRA In The Twilight Years*, pp. 511–2, 537; Bell, *The Secret Army*, pp. 244–7.

23   E. Keane, *Seán Mac Bride: A Life* (Dublin: Gill and Macmillan, 2007); K. Rafter, *The Clann: The Story of Clann na Poblachta* (Cork: Mercier Press, 1996).

24   Pakenham and O'Neill, *Eamon de Valera*, p. 434.

25   Seán Mac Stíofáin interview, 1990.

26   S. Mac Stíofáin, *Revolutionary in Ireland* (London: Gordon, Cremonesi, 1975), pp. 18–40.

27   Seán Mac Stíofáin interview, 1990.

28   Donegal republican interview, 1984.

29   Ruairí Ó Brádaigh interview, 2009.

30   See Bell, *The Secret Army*, pp. 255–88; Coogan, *The IRA*, pp. 297–329; B. Hanley and S. Millar, *The Lost Revolution* (London, Penguin, 2009), p. 10.

31   Ruairí Ó Brádaigh, 'Omagh Raid Electrifies Nation', *Saoirse*, October 2004, p. 14; R. Ó Brádaigh, 'Very successful Prisoners' Collection', *Saoirse*, January 2005, p. 14; B. O'Brien, *The Long War: The IRA and Sinn Féin* (Dublin: O'Brien Press, 1993), p. 356.

32   Ruairí Ó Brádaigh interview, 2008.

33   Phil O'Donoghue interview, 2010.

34   See Farrell, *The Orange State*, pp. 209–11.

35   Seán Lynch interview, 1984.

36   Frank Glynn interview, 1995.

37   Some veterans object to the 'Border Campaign' label because it was not meant to be confined to the border. For them, it was a 'Resistance Campaign'. Joe McGarrity (Seán Cronin), 'Resistance – The story of the struggle in British-Occupied Ireland' (1957). On the campaign, see: Bell, *The Secret Army*; Coogan, *The IRA*; M.L.R. Smith, *Fighting for Ireland: The Military Strategy of the Irish Republican Movement* (New York: Routledge, 1995); and B. Flynn, *Soldiers of Folly: The IRA Border Campaign 1956–1962* (Wilton, Cork: The Collins Press, 2009).

38   Joe Cahill interview, 1996; R.W. White, 'Provisional IRA attacks on the UDR in Fermanagh and South Tyrone', *TPV*, 23 (2011), pp. 329–49; Anderson, *Joe Cahill*, pp. 128–38; A. Bryson (ed.), *The Insider: The Belfast Prison Diaries of Eamonn Boyce 1956–1962* (Dublin: The Lilliput Press, 2007), p. 344.

39   Phil O'Donoghue interview, 2010.

40   See Bell, *The Secret Army*, p. 306.

41   Ruairí Ó Brádaigh interview, 1996.

42   D. Fogarty, *Seán South of Garryowen* (Ennis, Ireland: FX Press, 2006), pp. 31–5.

43   Phil O'Donoghue interview, 2010. Under General Order No. 4 communists could not join the IRA.

44   Seán Mac Stiofáin interview, 1990.

45   J.B. and Bernadette O'Hagan interview, 1996.

46   Ruairí Ó Brádaigh interview, 1995. See also Bell, *The Secret Army*, pp. 326–36; R.W. White, *Ruairí Ó Brádaigh, The Life and Politics of an Irish Revolutionary* (Indianapolis: Indiana University Press, 2010), pp. 102–9.

Chapter 4

1   Seán Mac Stiofáin interview, 1990.

2   Seán Mac Stiofáin interview, 1990.

3   Paddy McLogan also resigned from the IRA. He was later found dead at his home, the apparent victim of an accidental shooting. See Mac Eoin, *The IRA in the Twilight Years*, pp. 875–7; Hanley and Millar, *The Lost Revolution*, pp. 24–5; White, *Ruairí Ó Brádaigh*, pp. 110–6.

4   See Cronin, *Irish Nationalism*, p. 185.

5   C. McCluskey, *Up Off Their Knees* (Southampton: Camelot Press, 1989).

6   Fra McCann interview, 1984.

7   See Hanley and Millar, *The Lost Revolution*, p. 74; Boyd, *Holy War in Belfast*, pp. 220–2.

8   E. Moloney and A. Pollak, *Paisley* (Dublin: Poolbeg, 1986), pp. 39–41, 115–6, 143, 160.

9   R. Johnston, *Century of Endeavour: A Biographical and Autobiographical View of the Twentieth Century in Ireland* (Dublin: Lilliput Press, 2003), pp. 171–86; H. Patterson, *The Politics of Illusion: A Political History of the IRA* (London: Serif, 1997), pp. 96–9; White, *Ruairí Ó Brádaigh*, pp. 119 and 120.

10   Seán Mac Stiofáin interview, 1990.

11   Billy McKee interview, 2014. Others suggest that Goulding found socialism on his own, without Fuchs. See Hanley and Millar, *The Lost Revolution*, p. 30; M. Treacy, *The IRA, 1956–89: Rethinking the Republic* (Manchester: Manchester University Press, 2011), pp. 72–3.

12   G. Adams, *Before the Dawn: An Autobiography* (New York: William and Morrow, 1996), pp. 48–50; Moloney and Pollak, *Paisley*, pp. 120–2.

13   Joe Cahill interview, 1990.

14   Phil O'Donoghue interview, 2010.

15   Seán Mac Stiofáin interview, 1990.

16   See Cronin, *Irish Nationalism*, p. 204.

17   Seán Mac Stiofáin interview, 1990.

18   White, *Ruairí Ó Brádaigh*, pp. 120–3.

19   '20,000 gather at Tyrone centre', *Irish Independent*, 2 April 1966. Tyrone republican 1 interview, 1984.

20   Mitchel McLaughlin interview, 1990.

21   McKittrick et al., *Lost Lives*, pp. 25–9.

22   Mac Stiofáin, *Revolutionary in Ireland*, p. 96; Bell, *The Secret Army*, p. 363.

23   *We Shall Overcome: The History of the Struggle for Civil Rights in Northern Ireland, 1968–1978* (Belfast: NICRA, 1978), p. 20.

24   See *We Shall Overcome*; *Fermanagh Facts*, Fermanagh Civil Rights Association (1969); R. Deutsch and V. Magowan, *Northern Ireland, 1968–1973, Chronology of Events, Volume I* (Belfast: Blackstaff Press, 1973), p. 6.

25   Richard Behal interviews, 1998, 2002. See also, White, *Ruairí Ó Brádaigh*, pp. 130–2.

26   There were two Saor Éire groups. The one based in Cork had several members associated with *An Phoblacht*. The Saor Éire Action Group was based in Dublin. See Treacy, *The IRA, 1956–89*, pp. 135–7; Jim Lane, 'Miscellaneous notes on republicanism and socialism in Cork City, 1954–69', http://irishlabour.com/?p=317 (last accessed 08/11/2013); L. Ó Ruairc, 'A little known republican military group: Saor Éire', *The Blanket*, 13 January 2005; Hanley and Millar, *The Lost Revolution*, pp. 154–55; L. Walsh, *The Final Beat: Gardaí Killed in the Line of Duty* (Dublin: Gill and Macmillan, 2001), pp. 1–22.

27   Peig King quotation; Peig King interview, 2009.

28   See Johnston, *Century of Endeavour*, pp. 235, 258; 'Cumann na mBan Leaflet', dated June 1969, signed by Mrs A. Long, Miss K. O'Sullivan, Miss N. McCarthy and Mrs S. Mulcahy.

29   See Hanley and Millar, *The Lost Revolution*, pp. 86, 88–9; 'Controversial group wants action on housing', *Irish Times*, 17 June 1968; '26 arrested in eviction brawl', *Evening Herald*, 15 January 1968; J.B. and Bernadette O'Hagan interview, 1996; Mac Stiofáin, *Revolutionary in Ireland*, pp. 93–4.

30   Ruairí Ó Brádaigh quotation; Ruairí Ó Brádaigh interview, 1984.

31   J.B. and Bernadette O'Hagan interview, 1996.

32   *The United Irishman*, February 1969, p. 12.

33   Some sources have the Movement formally declaring for socialism in 1967, others have it in 1968. See White, *Ruairí Ó Brádaigh*, p. 137; Cronin, *Irish Nationalism*, pp. 189–90; Treacy, *The IRA, 1956–69*, pp.127–8.

34   A. Currie, *All Hell Will Break Loose* (Dublin: O'Brien Press, 2004), p. 96.

35   Austin Currie estimates there were about 7,000 people on the march (p. 104). See Currie, *All Hell*

Will Break Loose, pp. 89–106; Moloney and Pollak, *Paisley*, p. 155; Farrell, *Northern Ireland*, p. 246; Deutsch and Magowan, *Northern Ireland, Chronology of Events I*, p. 9.

36 P. Taylor, *Behind the Mask: The IRA and Sinn Féin* (New York: TV Books, 1997), p. 40; Farrell, *Northern Ireland*, pp. 246–7; *We Shall Overcome*, p. 13; E. McCann, *War and An Irish Town* (Belfast: Pluto Press, 1981), p. 40–7. See also, S. Prince and G. Warner, *Belfast and Derry in Revolt: A New History of the Start of the Troubles* (Dublin: Irish Academic Press, 2012); N. Ó Dochartaigh, *From Civil Rights to Armalites: Derry and the Birth of the Irish Troubles* (Cork: Cork University Press, 1997). Map 3 of Derry courtesy of Mike Maitzen.

37 Derry republican 1 interview, 1984.

38 CAIN Web Service, 'The Derry March – Chronology of Events Surrounding the March'; McCann, *War and an Irish Town*, p. 48.

39 Seán Mac Stiofáin interview, 1990.

40 See White, *Ruairí Ó Brádaigh*, p. 141; Johnston, *Century of Endeavour*, pp. 235, 258; D. Reinisch, 'Cumann na mBan and the acceptance of women in the Provisional IRA: An Oral history study of Irish Republican women in the early 1970s', *Socheolas: Limerick Student Journal of Sociology* 5/1 (2013), pp. 115–134. In November 1968, after the IRA convention, the Cork group publishing *An Phoblacht* split and created Saor Éire. Lane, 'Miscellaneous notes on republicanism and socialism in Cork City, 1954–69', http://irishlabour.com/?p=317 (last accessed 08/11/2013).

41 B. Egan and V. McCormack, *Burntollet* (London: L.R.S. Publishers, 1969); McCann, *War and an Irish Town*, pp. 49–55; B. Devlin, *The Price of My Soul* (New York: Alfred A. Knopf, 1969), pp. 139–62; 'March for Marian Price on International Women's Day', Indymedia Ireland/saormheáin éireann, 14 February 2014; English, *Armed Struggle*, pp. 96–7.

42 Derry republican 1 interview, 1984. See also McCann, *War and an Irish Town*, pp. 50–3.

43 Tyrone republican 2 interview, 1984. See also R. Rose, *Governing Without Consensus: An Irish Perspective* (London: Faber and Faber, 1971), pp. 194–5, 530.

44 P. Routledge, *John Hume: A Biography* (London: Harper Collins, 1997), pp. 78–9; Hanley and Millar, *The Lost Revolution*, pp. 113–4; White, *Ruairí Ó Brádaigh*, pp. 142–4; Johnston, *A Century of Endeavour*, pp. 262–3; Hanley and Millar, *The Lost Revolution*, p. 125; McKittrick et al., *Lost Lives*, pp. 32–3.

45 Ruairí Ó Brádaigh interview, 1996. Johnston, *Century of Endeavour*, p. 262; P. Bishop and E. Mallie,

Provisional IRA (Aylesbury Bucks, England: Dublin 1989), pp. 92–3.

46 See McKittrick et al., *Lost Lives*, pp. 32–3.

47 Gerry McKerr interview, 2013.

48 P. Taylor, *Behind the Mask*, pp. 60–2; White, *Ruairí Ó Brádaigh*, pp. 144–5.

Chapter 5

1 Seán Mac Stiofáin interview, 1990.

2 See Deutsch and Magowan, *Northern Ireland, Chronology of Events I*, p. 38; Hanley and Millar, *The Lost Revolution*, p. 131; T.R. Dwyer, *Nice Fellow: A Biography of Jack Lynch* (Cork: Mercier Press, 2001), pp. 178–81.

3 Derry republican 1 interview, 1984.

4 See McKittrick et al., *Lost Lives*, pp. 36–8.

5 Armagh republican interview, 1984.

6 Tom Fleming interview, 1984.

7 Fra McCann interview, 1984.

8 'Volunteer Seamus Twomey: Seamus Twomey 1919–'89: A Tribute', Dublin: *AP/RN*, n.d.; McKittrick et al., *Lost Lives*, pp. 34–6; R.J. Quinn, *A Rebel Voice: A History of Belfast Republicanism, 1925–1972* (Belfast: The Belfast Cultural and Local History Group, 1999), p. 144; C. De Baróid, *Ballymurphy and the Irish War* (Baile Atha Cliath/Dublin: Aisling Publishers, 1989), pp. 29–47; McKittrick et al., *Lost Lives*, pp. 34–5. Map 4 courtesy of Mike Maitzen.

9 *Belfast Graves* (Dublin: The National Graves Association, 1985), p. 64; McKittrick et al., *Lost Lives*, pp. 38–9; Government of Northern Ireland, *Violence and Civil Disturbances in Northern Ireland in 1969, Report of Tribunal of Inquiry* (Scarman Report) (Her Majesty's Stationery Office, 1972), pp. 246–9.

10 Joe Cahill interview, 1990.

11 Billy McKee interview, 2014.

12 Joe Cahill interview, 1990.

13 See Hanley and Millar, *The Lost Revolution*, p. 134.

14 Joe Cahill interview, 1990. Cahill's 'I Ran Away' claim is disputed; some argue that the earliest reference to the slogan was in August 1970. There are no known photos of the slogan in 1969. See Hanley and Millar *The Lost Revolution*, p. 136; B. Hanley, '"I ran away"? The I.R.A. and 1969: the evolution of a myth', *Irish Historical Studies* 38 no. 152 (2013), pp. 671–87.

15 Clonard republican interview, 1984. Farrell, *Northern Ireland*, pp. 262–3; Deutsch and Magowan, *Northern Ireland Chronology of Events I*, p. 39.

16 'The Politics of Revolution: The main speeches and debates from the 1986 Sinn Féin Ard-Fheis including the Presidential address of Gerry Adams',

Dublin: Sinn Féin (1986), p. 22; Seán Mac Stiofáin, *Revolutionary in Ireland*, pp. 95, 122–3; P. Bishop and E. Mallie, *Provisional IRA* (Aylesbury Bucks, England: Corgi 1989), p. 115.

17 CAIN Web Service, 'Report of The Advisory Committee on Police in Northern Ireland'; J.B. Bell, *The Irish Troubles* (New York: St. Martin's, 1993), pp. 87–128.

18 See Dwyer, *Nice Fellow*, pp. 185–6; Hanley and Millar, *The Lost Revolution*, p. 137; J. Kelly, *The Thimble Riggers: The Dublin Arms Trial of 1970* (Dublin: James Kelly, 1999), pp. 30–1.

19 See 'Fianna Fáil and the IRA'; Dwyer, *Nice Fellow*, p. 185–96; J. O'Brien, *The Arms Trial* (Dublin: Gill and MacMillan, 2000), pp. 68–78; Bishop and Mallie, *Provisional IRA*, p. 143; Bell, *The Secret Army*, p. 371; Hanley and Millar, *The Lost Revolution*, pp. 137–8.

20 Ruairí Ó Brádaigh interview, 1996.

21 D. Sharrock and M. Devenport, in *Man of War, Man of Peace?: The Unauthorized Biography of Gerry Adams* (London: Macmillan, 1997), p. 77, report that young Gerry Adams was part of the attempted coup. Mac Stiofáin, *Revolutionary in Ireland*, p. 128; Bishop and Mallie, *The Provisionals*, p. 125; White, *Ruairí Ó Brádaigh*, pp. 146–7.

22 Joe Cahill interview, 1990.

23 See Bishop and Mallie, *Provisional IRA*, p. 86; Hanley and Millar, *The Lost Revolution*, pp. 136–7; Mac Stiofáin, *Revolutionary in Ireland*, pp. 127–8.

24 J.B. and Bernadette O'Hagan interview, 1996.

25 See McKittrick et al., p. 42; Moloney and Pollak, *Paisley*, pp. 200–1; 'On This Day: 10 October 1969', BBC Home; Farrell, *Northern Ireland* (1980), p. 266.

26 See Johnston, *Century of Endeavour*, p. 274.

27 Seán Mac Stiofáin acknowledged that Dáithí O'Connell met Neil Blaney. O'Connell asked, 'Can you supply any guns, Mr Blaney?' Blaney replied, 'I'm sorry, I can't.' O'Connell said, 'All right. Goodbye.' See Hanley and Millar, *The Lost Revolution*, pp. 137–40; Johnston, *Century of Endeavour*, p. 276, 282; Mac Stiofáin, *Revolutionary in Ireland*, pp. 139–40; 'Fianna Fáil and the IRA'.

28 See White, *Ruairí Ó Brádaigh*, p. 149.

29 Goulding is quoted in Cronin, *Irish Nationalism*, p. 195.

30 Ruairí Ó Brádaigh interview, 1984.

31 Coogan, *The IRA*, p. 337.

32 Seán Mac Stiofáin interview, 1990.

33 Ruairí Ó Brádaigh interview, 1984.

34 See Mac Stiofáin, *Revolutionary in Ireland*, pp. 133–7; Bell, *The Secret Army*, p. 366; White, *Ruairí Ó Brádaigh*, pp. 150–2. See also, J. Horgan and M.

Taylor, 'Proceedings of the Irish Republican Army Convention, December 1969', *TPV*, 9/4 (2007), pp. 151–8. The official minutes indicate that the vote on the NLF was thirty-three for, eight against, two uncommitted and three abstentions, and that the vote on ending the embargo on parliamentary participation was twenty-seven to twelve. Even if the missing delegates were present both votes had the two-thirds majority required to change the constitution.

35 See Anderson, *Joe Cahill*, pp. 182–4; Ruairí Ó Brádaigh interview, 1996.

36 See Bishop and Mallie, *The Provisionals*, pp. 137–8; Anderson, *Joe Cahill*, pp. 184–5; White, *Ruairí Ó Brádaigh*, pp. 150–2.

37 Seán Mac Stiofáin interview, 1990. See also, Mac Stiofáin, *Revolutionary in Ireland*, pp. 107, 138–9.

38 Ruairí Ó Brádaigh interview, 1996.

39 J.B. and Bernadette O'Hagan interview, 1996.

40 Seán Mac Stiofáin interview, 1990.

41 See Ó Brádaigh, *Dílseacht*, p. 64.

42 See Mac Stiofáin, *Revolutionary in Ireland*, p. 150.

43 See, White, *Ruairí Ó Brádaigh*, pp. 150–8; Hanley and Millar, *The Lost Revolution*, pp. 146–7.

44 Figure 2: White, *Provisional Irish Republicans*, p. 135.

45 Frank Glynn interview, 1995.

46 'On This We Stand,' *An Phoblacht*, February 1970, p. 1.

47 'The IRA in the '70s', *United Irishman* January 1970, p. 8.

48 Gerard Magee, *Tyrone's Struggle: Ar son Saoire na hÉireann*, Tyrone Sinn Féin/Gerard Magee (2011), p. 124.

49 'ATTEMPT TO TAKE OVER REPUBLICAN MOVEMENT: Sinn Fein Statement exposes "master minds" and lists five major reasons for Ard-Fheis walkout', *An Phoblacht*, February 1970, pp. 4–5.

50 See Johnston, *Century of Endeavour*, pp. 279–80, 321–3; 'The IRA in the '70s', *The United Irishman*, January 1970, p. 8; Hanley and Millar, *The Lost Revolution*, pp. 141–3; 149–99 (p. 199 on the fatalities); 'THE REPUBLICAN POSITION,' *An Phoblacht*, July 1970, p. 8.

51 Seán Mac Stiofáin interview, 1990. Mac Stiofáin, *Revolutionary in Ireland*, pp. 134–6.

52 See Cronin, *Irish Nationalism*, p. 292 (note 85).

53 Ruairí Ó Brádaigh interview, 1984. See also, J.F. Morrison, *The Origins and Rise of Dissident Irish Republicanism: The Role and Impact of Organizational Splits* (New York: Bloomsbury, 2013), pp. 39–83.

54 It is alleged that a weapon connected to Fianna Fáil contacts was used to kill Garda Richard Fallon in

April 1970, leading to a cover up. T.R. Dwyer, 'After 39 years, truth about death of brave garda must finally be told', *Irish Examiner*, 18 April 2009. See, Dwyer, *Nice Fellow*, pp. 235–6; Hanley and Millar, *The Lost Revolution*, pp. 138–41; Treacy, *The IRA, 1956–69*, pp. 169–78; 'Fianna Fáil and the I.R.A.', pamphlet.

55 See Bell, *The Secret Army*, p. 370.

56 Ruairí Ó Brádaigh interview, 1996.

Chapter 6

1 Armagh republican interview, 1984.

2 Seán Lynch interview, 1984.

3 Phil O'Donoghue interview, 2010.

4 See Sharrock and Devenport, *Man of War, Man of Peace*, pp. 68–71.

5 Richard Behal interview, 2015.

6 Mitchel McLaughlin interview, 1990.

7 L. Clarke and K. Johnston, *Martin McGuinness: From Guns to Government* (Edinburgh: Mainstream, 2001), pp. 28–34; Bishop and Mallie, *Provisional IRA*, pp. 143–4.

8 Seán Mac Stiofáin interview, 1990; Bishop and Mallie, *Provisional IRA*, pp. 140–2; McCann, *War and An Irish Town*, p. 74; White, *Ruairí Ó Brádaigh*, p. 158.

9 See Mac Stiofáin, *Revolutionary in Ireland*, p. 138.

10 Ruairí Ó Brádaigh interview, 2008.

11 K. Conway, *Southside Provisional: From Freedom Fighter to the Four Courts* (Dublin: Orpen Press, 2014), pp. 32–3, 42.

12 John Paddy Mullan and Gearóid Mac Cárthaigh (or someone similar to Mac Cárthaigh) may be the 'O.C.' and the 'southern training officer from Co. Cork' described in T. McNulty's *Exiled: 40 Years an Exile a Long Time Away from Kith and Kin* (Dublin: Brunswick Press Ltd., 2013), p. 55. See also: Bishop and Mallie, *Provisional IRA*, pp. 143–5, 156; S. Ó Coinn, *The Rising of the Phoenix, Éirí na Fhéinics* (Belfast: Shanway Press, 2013), p. 37; Moloney, *Secret History of the IRA*, p. 87; Mac Stiofáin, *Revolutionary in Ireland*, pp. 147–8; G. Magee, *Tyrone's Struggle: Ar son Saoire na hÉireann* (Tyrone Sinn Féin Commemoration Committee and Gerard Magee, 2011), pp. 124–5; McCann, *War and An Irish Town*, pp. 72–3.

13 See Bishop and Mallie, *Provisional IRA*, p. 145; E. Moloney, *Voices From the Grave: Two Men's War in Ireland* (London: Faber and Faber, 2010), pp. 35–6, 47–9.

14 Brendan Hughes interview, 2001.

15 Seán Mac Stiofáin interview, 1990. See also, Mac Stiofáin, *Revolutionary in Ireland*, pp. 147–8.

16 Ruairí Ó Brádaigh interview, 2008. See J.B. Bell, 'The Thompson Submachine Gun in Ireland', pp. 35–49 in Bell, *The Gun in Politics: An Analysis of Irish Political Conflict, 1916–1986* (New Brunswick, NJ: Transaction Books, 1987); Conway, *Southside Provisional*, pp. 42–3.

17 J.B. Bell, *The Irish Troubles: A Generation of Violence, 1967–92* (New York: St. Martin's, 1993), pp. 179–80; J. Holland, *The American Connection: U.S. Guns, Money, & Influence in Northern Ireland* (New York: Penguin, 1987), pp. 29–33; D. O'Reilly, *Accepting the Challenge: The Memoirs of Michael Flannery* (Dublin: Cló Saoirse/Irish Freedom Press, 2001), pp. 142–3; J. Holland, *Hope Against History: The Course of Conflict in Northern Ireland* (New York: Henry Holt, 1999), p. 31.

18 See Deutsch and Magowan, *Northern Ireland Chronology of Events I*, pp. 59–61; Ó Coinn, *The Rising of the Phoenix*, p. 44.

19 See E. Moloney, *A Secret History of the IRA* (London: W.W. Norton, 2002), p. 88; Deutsch and Magowan, *Northern Ireland Chronology of Events I*, pp. 62–3; Ó Coinn, *The Rising of the Phoenix*, p. 45; Prince and Warner, *Belfast and Derry in Revolt*, p. 229.

20 Fra McCann interview, 1984.

21 Derry republican 1 interview, 1984. See also R.W. White, 'From peaceful protest to guerrilla war', *American Journal of Sociology* 94/6 (1989), pp. 1277–302.

22 Fr Seán McManus, founder of the Irish National Caucus, is another brother of Frank McManus. Bell, *The Irish Troubles* (1993), p. 175; CAIN Web Service, *Northern Ireland Elections*, 'The 1970 Westminster Election in Northern Ireland'.

23 See McKittrick et al., *Lost Lives*, pp. 48–9, 55.

24 See Deutsch and Magowan, *Northern Ireland Chronology of Events I*, pp. 66–8; McKittrick, et al., *Lost Lives*, pp. 48–55; Bell, *The Irish Troubles*, p. 179; Farrell, *Northern Ireland*, pp. 273–4; Hanley and Millar, *Lost Revolution*, pp. 157–8; Ó Coinn, *The Rising of the Phoenix* (2013), pp. 71–6.

25 Paddy Devlin offered to join the Official IRA but Cathal Goulding told him he would be of more service as a politician; some of the Officials suspected Devlin was working for the Dublin government. See Hanley and Millar, *The Lost Revolution*, p. 155; McKittrick et al., *Lost Lives*, pp. 56–7; Bell, *The Secret Army; Belfast Graves*, pp. 57–8; M.A. Murphy, *Gerry Fitt: A Political Chameleon* (Cork: Mercier Press, 2007), pp. 154–5; White, *Ruairí Ó Brádaigh*, p. 160.

26 The average age of nineteen SDLP elected representatives in 1973 was thirty-nine. Eleven

of the nineteen representatives had a university education, or higher, and twelve held professional jobs. I. McAllister, *The Northern Ireland Social Democratic and Labour Party: Political Opposition in a Divided Society* (London: Macmillan, 1977), pp. 67–71. 'Civil Powers Act "Denial of Freedom", No Democracy under Unionism – Fitt', *Irish News*, 22 July 1968, pp. 1, 3.

27 Armagh republican interview, 1984.

28 See Routledge, *John Hume*, pp. 97–9.

29 See, Reinisch, 'Cumann na mBan and the acceptance of women in the Provisional IRA,' *Socheolas* 5/1, p. 121.

30 See Ó Brádaigh, *Dílseacht*, p. 45; White, *Ruairí Ó Brádaigh*, pp. 161–3.

31 See Bell, *The Irish Troubles*, pp. 165–6, 185.

32 Seamus Kelters, 'Violence in the troubles', *BBC History*, February 2013.

33 See Cronin, *Irish Nationalism*, pp. 225–6; Bell, *The Irish Troubles*, pp. 186–7; McKittrick et al., *Lost Lives*, pp. 62–5.

34 Belfast republican 3 interview, 1984.

35 See Bell, *The Irish Troubles*, pp. 194–5.

36 Brendan Hughes interview, 2001.

37 Billy McKee interview, 2014.

38 See McKittrick et al., *Lost Lives*, pp. 70–1; Deutsch and Magown, *Northern Ireland Chronology of Events I*, pp. 97–8.

39 See Bishop and Mallie, *Provisional IRA*, p. 173.

40 See Moloney, *Secret History of the IRA*, pp. 98–9, 106; Moloney, *Voices From the Grave*, pp. 75–6.

41 See Deutsch and Magowan, *Northern Ireland Chronology of Events I*, pp. 103a, 108b–109a; M. McGuire, *To Take Arms: My Year with the IRA Provisionals* (New York: Viking Press, 1973), pp. 95–9; English, *Armed Struggle*, p. 113.

42 See Deutsch and Magowan, *Northern Ireland Chronology of Events I*, pp. 108–114; Bell, *The Irish Troubles*, p. 209; Farrell, *Northern Ireland*, pp. 280–1.

43 See McGuffin, *Internment!*, pp. 118–27; Bell, *The Irish Troubles*, 226–7; Farrell, *Northern Ireland*, pp. 281–2; Bell, *The Secret Army*, p. 383.

44 J.B. and Bernadette O'Hagan interview, 1996.

45 Gerry McKerr interview, 2012.

46 An application from the Republic of Ireland to the European Court found that some internees had been subjected to 'inhuman and degrading treatment' but not torture. The Hooded Men's case alleging they were tortured has recently been reopened. D. Faul and R. Murray, *The Hooded Men: British Torture in Ireland, August, October 1971* (Dublin: Wordwell Books, 2016 [2015 reprint]); S. Elliott and

W.D. Flackes, *Northern Ireland: A Political Directory, 1968–99* (Belfast: Blackstaff Press, 1999), pp. 211, 246; Bell, *The Irish Troubles*, pp. 226–7; McGuffin, *Internment!*, pp. 197–210.

47 See Currie, *All Hell Will Break Loose*, p. 175; Bishop and Mallie, *Provisional IRA*, p. 189; *Irish Times*, 10 August 1971, p. 6.

48 See Bell, *The Secret Army*, pp. 380–3.

49 Armagh republican interview, 1984.

50 See McKittrick et al., *Lost Lives*, pp. 79–87.

51 See Bell, *The Irish Troubles*, pp. 222–3; Anderson, *Joe Cahill*, pp. 228–34; J. Graham, 'Show me the Man': The Official Biography of Martin Meehan* (Belfast: Rushlight Magazine, 2008), pp. 59.

52 See for example, Moloney, *Secret History of the IRA*, pp. 106–7.

53 Figure 3 courtesy of Mike Maitzen. Source: McKittrick et al., *Lost Lives*, pp. 1473–4.

54 Fermanagh republican 1 interview, 1984.

55 Fra McCann interview, 1984.

56 J.B. and Bernadette O'Hagan interview, 1996. The IRA administrator in Monaghan identified as 'J.B.' in McNulty's *Exiled* [(2013), pp. 101, 173)] is presumably J.B. O'Hagan.

57 Seán Mac Stiofáin interview, 1990.

58 See McGuire, *To Take Arms*, pp. 85–6; Cronin, *Irish Nationalism*, pp. 226–7, and esp. note 32, p. 300.

59 See Dingley, *The IRA*, pp. 90–104, esp. pp. 92–3; Wilkinson, *Terrorism versus Democracy* (2006), pp. 27-30, 93–4. There is an interesting argument that Billy McKee lured Protestant vigilantes into attacking St Matthew's Church in June 1970 so that the Provisionals could defend the church and discredit the security forces. See Prince and Warner, *Belfast and Derry in Revolt*, pp. 240–255, esp. pp. 250–2.

60 See R. English, *Terrorism: How to Respond* (Oxford: Oxford University Press, 2009), esp. pp. 128-31.

Chapter 7

1 Derry republican 1 interview, 1985.

2 *An Phoblacht*, January 1972, p. 1.

3 See McGuffin, *Internment!*, pp. 103–5.

4 See McGuire, *To Take Arms*, pp. 89–90; Bell, *The Irish Troubles*, pp. 256, 265–6; J. Graham, 'Show Me The Man': The Official Biography of Martin Meehan* (Belfast: Rushlight Publications, 2008), pp. 83–4.

5 See English, *Armed Struggle*, p. 144 (note 225, p. 410); *Republican News*, 2 January 1972.

6 See, for example, Bell, *The Irish Troubles*; D. Mullen, *Eyewitness Bloody Sunday: The Truth* (Dublin: Merlin Publishing, 2002).

7   P. Pringle and P. Jacobson, *Those are Real Bullets: Bloody Sunday, Derry, 1972* (New York: Grove Press, 2000), pp. 286–7; R.W. White, 'Response to Henry Patterson,' *TPV*, 23/3 (2011), p. 355; Cronin, *Irish Nationalism*, pp. 226–7; M. Tugwell, 'Politics and Propaganda of the Provisional IRA', in P. Wilkinson (ed.), *British Perspectives on Terrorism* (London: Allen and Unwin, 1982), pp. 13–30; R. Clutterbuck, *Protest and the Urban Guerrilla* (London: Casswell, 1973).

8   Derry republican 2 interview, 1984.

9   Lord Widgery's Report of Events in Londonderry, Northern Ireland, on 30 January 1972 (London: The Stationery Office).

10 The respondent could publicly acknowledge past membership in the IRA because of a conviction. Derry republican 1 interview, 1984.

11 See White, *Provisional Irish Republicans*; L. Bosi, 'Explaining pathways to armed activism in the Provisional Irish Republican Army', *Social Science History* 36/3 (2012), pp. 347–90.

12 See McGuire, *To Take Arms*, pp. 97–100; Graham, '*Show me the Man*', pp. 83–4.

13 Val Lynch interview, 1984.

14 Dublin republican 1 interview, 1984.

15 See Appendix 2.

16 Joe Cahill interview, 1990.

17 See McKittrick et al., *Lost Lives*, pp. 172–5; *Tírghrá: Ireland's Patriot Dead* (Dublin: Republican Publications, 2002), pp. 53–5; Appendix 2.

18 Belfast republican 4 interview, 1990. See also R.W. White and T.F. White, 'On the resources of urban guerrillas', *TPV*, 3 (1991), pp. 100–32.

19 See Adams, *Before the Dawn*, pp. 189–96; S. Wright, 'A Multivariate Time-Series Analysis of the Northern Irish Conflict 1969–1976' in Y. Alexander and J. Gleason (eds), *Behavioral and Quantitative Perspectives on Terrorism* (New York: Pergamon Press, 1981), pp. 283–328.

20 See McGuire, *To Take Arms*, p. 110; McKittrick et al., *Lost Lives*, pp. 161–3.

21 Ruairí Ó Brádaigh interview, 1996.

22 D. O'Connell, 'The Wilson-I.R.A. Talks 1972', *Saoirse* January 1989, p. 5; McKittrick et al., *Lost Lives*, pp. 168–73; J. O'Connell, *Doctor John: Crusading Doctor & Politician* (Dublin: Poolbeg, 1989), pp. 127–40.

23 'Events leading to crisis outlined', *Irish Times*, 25 March 1972, p. 8.

24 See Bell, *The Irish Troubles*, pp. 314–30; McKittrick et al., *Lost Lives*, pp. 183–6.

25 See McKittrick et al., *Lost Lives*, pp. 156–7, 189; Bell, *The Irish Troubles*, pp. 288–9.

26 See Bell, *The Irish Troubles*, pp. 338–71.

27 Ruairí Ó Brádaigh interview, 1996.

28 See, J. Dana, 'The Granting of Special Category Status 1972', http://www.hungerstrikes.org/background/special_status.html (last accessed 31/12/2013).

29 See Adams, *Before the Dawn*, pp. 197–9; Moloney, *Voices From the Grave*, pp. 96–7.

30 On the 1972 truce, see also Bell, *The Irish Troubles*, pp. 330–1; Deutsch and Magowan, *Northern Ireland Chronology of Events II*, pp. 185–6; Mac Stiofáin, *Revolutionary in Ireland*, pp. 263–7; M. Dillon, *The Enemy Within: The IRA's War Against the British* (London: Doubleday, 1994), p. 123.

31 O'Connell and Ó Brádaigh were formally unveiling Éire Nua II. Éire Nua I was the Provisionals' social and economic programme, released in 1971.

32 Ruairí Ó Brádaigh interview, 1996.

33 See McKittrick et al., *Lost Lives*, pp. 209–11.

34 Marian Price interview, 2010; see also A. Morris, 'Dolours Price's trauma over IRA disappeared', *Irish News*, 18 February 2010.

35 See Mac Stiofáin, *Revolutionary in Ireland*, pp. 278–9; Seán Mac Stiofáin letter to the author, 7 December 1995.

36 Ruairí Ó Brádaigh interview, 1996.

37 On the IRA-William Whitelaw meeting, see: Mac Stiofáin, *Revolutionary in Ireland*, pp. 278–86; Adams, *Before the Dawn*, pp. 204–6; Bishop and Mallie, *Provisional IRA*, pp. 226–8; McGuire, *To Take Arms*, p. 153; Moloney, *Voices From the Grave*, pp. 99–101; English, *Armed Struggle*, p. 157; T. Craig, 'From Backdoors and Back Lanes to Backchannels: Reappraising British Talks with the Provisional IRA, 1970–1974', *Contemporary British History*, 26/1 (2012), pp. 97–117; Clarke and Johnston, *Martin McGuinness*, pp. 75-7.

38 See Mac Stiofáin, *Revolutionary in Ireland*, p. 281.

39 E. Moloney and B. Mitchell, 'British Cabinet Account of 1972 IRA Ceasefire Talks', *The Broken Elbow*, 21 January 2014.

40 See Adams, *Before the Dawn*, pp. 205–6.

41 Taylor, *Behind the Mask*, pp. 168-70.

42 W. Whitelaw, *The Whitelaw Memoirs* (London: Aurum, 1989), p. 100.

43 See Adams, *Before the Dawn*, p. 206; Bishop and Mallie, *Provisional IRA*, p. 228.

44 See Taylor, *Behind the Mask*, pp. 166–74; see also T. Craig, 'Monitoring the Peace?: Northern Ireland's 1975 Ceasefire Incident Centre and the Politicisation of Sinn Féin', *TPV*, 26/2 (2014), pp. 307–19; Elliott and Flackes, *Northern Ireland: A Political Directory*,

pp. 505–7; Moloney, *Voices From the Grave*, p. 101; McKittrick et al., *Lost Lives*, pp. 214–7; Deutsch and Magowan, *Northern Ireland Chronology of Events II*, pp. 194–5; McGuire, *To Take Arms*, pp. 155–60; Bell, *The Irish Troubles*, pp. 336–7; BBC Home: On This Day, 'Whitelaw's secret meeting with IRA', 10 July 1972.

45 E. Moloney and J.K. White, 'We Can't Take On Both At Once', *The Broken Elbow*, 16 June 2015.

46 S. Winchester and S. Hoggart, '11 Dead, 100 Hurt in an Hour of Bombs', *The Guardian*, 22 July 1972.

47 Seán Mac Stiofáin interview, 1990; Mac Stiofáin, *Revolutionary in Ireland*, pp. 269, 296–7; Moloney, *Voices From the Grave*, pp. 103–6; Deutsch and Magowan, *Northern Ireland A Chronology of Events II*, p. 199; McKittrick et al., *Lost Lives*, pp. 230–3; CAIN Web Service, 'Bloody Friday (21 July 1972) – Northern Ireland Office News-sheet'.

48 See McKittrick et al., *Lost Lives*, pp. 240–2; Elliott and Flackes, *Northern Ireland: A Political Directory*, pp. 380; see also M.L.R. Smith and P.R. Neumann, 'Motorman's long strategy: Changing the strategic setting in Northern Ireland', *Contemporary British History* 19/4 (2005), pp. 413–35.

49 See Elliott and Flackes, *Northern Ireland: A Political Directory*, p. 682 (Table 2).

50 See Bell, *The Irish Troubles*, pp. 347–53.

51 See Mac Stiofáin, *Revolutionary in Ireland*, pp. 235–7, 239–40, 326–8; Deutsch and Magowan, *Northern Ireland Chronology of Events II*, p. 236.

52 See McGuire, *To Take Arms*, pp. 77–8; White, *Ruairí Ó Brádaigh*, pp. 178–9.

53 See Deutsch and Magowan, *Northern Ireland Chronology of Events II*, pp. 244–6; Mac Stiofáin, *Revolutionary in Ireland*, p. 354; 'Dublin I.R.A. Chief Gets Prison Term', *New York Times*, 26 November 1972, pp. 1, 8.

54 J.B. Bell, *In Dubious Battle* (Dublin: Poolbeg, 1999), pp. 13–6; Deutsch and Magowan, *Northern Ireland Chronology of Events II*, p. 246.

55 See Bell, *The Irish Troubles*, pp. 355–6; Ruairí Ó Brádaigh interviews.

56 See Clarke and Johnston, *Martin McGuinness*, pp. 80–3.

Chapter 8

1 Belfast republican 4 interview, 1990.

2 'The undaunted women in Armagh', *Iris* 8 (August 1984), pp. 15–23; E. Brady, E. Patterson, K. McKinney, R. Hamill and P. Jackson (comp.), *In the Footsteps of Anne: Stories of Republican Women Ex-Prisoners* (Belfast: Shanway Press, 2011), pp. 47–9; 53–5.

3 Geraldine Taylor interview, 2009.

4 Non-jury courts were referred to as 'Diplock Courts' after Lord Diplock. Bell, *The Irish Troubles*, pp. 287–8, 347, 362–3, 404; M. Burke, SMA, *Britain's War Machine in Ireland* (New York: Oisin, 1987), pp. 41–2; Coogan, *The IRA*, pp. 382–3.

5 Newry republican interview, 1984.

6 Kevin Heatley's father, Desmond Heatley, suffered from depression after his son's death. He was found dead in Newry Canal and it is believed he committed suicide. See K. Asmal (Chairman), *Shoot to Kill?*, pp. 23–4, 135–42; McKittrick et al., *Lost Lives*, p. 335.

7 Belfast republican 4 interview 1990. R. White and T. Falkenberg White, 'Revolution in the city: On the resources of urban guerrillas', *TPV*, 3 (Winter 1991), pp. 100–32; Bishop and Mallie, *Provisional IRA*, pp. 181–2.

8 Determining who was and was not an informer and why a given person was killed is not always straightforward; informer allegations are often disputed. Thomas McNulty identifies the suspected Tyrone informer as 'Points'. See McNulty, *Exiled*, pp. 60–5; H. Jordan, *Milestone's in Murder: Defining Moments in Ulster's Terror War* (Edinburgh: Mainstream Publishing, 2002), pp. 24–7.

9 See McKittrick et al., *Lost Lives*, pp. 591, 1292–3.

10 It appears that two alleged informers from Tyrone were executed while seventeen were executed by the Belfast IRA. The McConville family rejects the claim that Jean McConville was an informer. *Ibid.*, pp. 274–5, 301–2; Moloney, *Secret History of the IRA*, pp. 118–25; Moloney, *Voices from the Grave*, pp. 119–32; 'Funeral of disappeared victim Kevin McKee ends "43 years of pain" for family', *Belfast Telegraph*, 14 September 2015.

11 A.J. Oppenheimer, *IRA: The Bombs and the Bullets: A History of Deadly Ingenuity* (Dublin: Irish Academic Press, 2009), pp. 59, 200–2; S. O'Callaghan, *The Informer: The Real Life Story of One Man's War Against Terrorism* (London: Bantam Press, 1998), pp. 55–6; Magee, *Tyrone's Struggle*, pp. 232–3.

12 Ethel Lynch joined Cumann na mBan and then moved to the Provisional IRA. A. Quinn, 'Cumann na mBan remembered in new mural', *Derry Journal*, 26 September 2014; Appendix 2; *Tírghrá*, pp. 103, 116, 124, 156.

13 Josephine Hayden interview, 2009.

14 Ó Ruairc, 'A Little Known Republican Military Group', *The Blanket*, 13 January 2005; M. Healey, *Saor Éire Marxist and Republican*, http://theirishrevolution.

wordpress.com/2012/02/14/1289/ (last accessed 1/12/2013).

15 'Dílis go hÉag' and 'Pat Ward', *Saoirse* April 1988, pp. 4–5.

16 John Noonan, *What do I do Now?* (self-published, 2005).

17 See O'Callaghan, *The Informer*, pp. 48–9, 58–60; 63–6, 70–4; Magee, *Tyrone's Struggle*, pp. 146, 214; Appendix 2; *Tírghrá*, pp. 108, 113–4; McKittrick et al., *Lost Lives*, pp. 443, 472–3.

18 See White, *Ruairí Ó Brádaigh*, pp. 209–12, 262; Moloney, *Secret History of the IRA*, pp. 6–10; Anderson, *Joe Cahill*, pp. 262–80; Bishop and Mallie, *Provisional IRA*, pp. 181–2.

19 Richard Behal interview, 1998.

20 See Bishop and Mallie, *Provisional IRA*, pp. 251–3; Taylor, *Behind the Mask*, pp. 182–4; Bell, *The Irish Troubles*, pp. 364–5; S. Breen, 'Marian Price Interview: Old Bailey Bomber Ashamed of Sinn Fein', *The Village*, 7 December 2004.

21 *Brian Keenan 1941–2008 A Republican Legend* (Belfast: An Phoblacht, n.d.), pp. 18–19; G. McKee and R. Franey, *Time Bomb: Irish Bombers, English Justice and the Guildford Four* (London: Bloomsbury, 1988), pp. 1–2; Coogan, *The IRA*, pp. 388–9; Bishop and Mallie, *Provisional IRA*, pp. 254–8; Moloney, *Secret History of the IRA*, pp. 125–7; Moloney, *Voices From the Grave*, pp. 148–50; T. McKearney, *The Provisional IRA: From Insurrection to Parliament* (Belfast: Pluto Press, 2011), pp. 124–7; M. Dillon, *The Enemy Within*, pp. 122–33; Bell, *The Irish Troubles*, p. 393. See also R. O'Donnell, *Special Category: The IRA in English Prisons* [2 volumes] (Dublin: Irish Academic Press, 2015, 2016).

22 See O'Callaghan, *The Informer*, pp. 45–6; Moloney, *Voices from the Grave*, pp. 107–8; Bell, *The Irish Troubles*, pp. 375, 431.

23 See McKittrick et al., *Lost Lives*, pp. 48, 196–7, 576–7. Six members of the Gardaí were killed by the Provisional IRA; hundreds of RUC officers were killed in the North. See 'An Garda Síochána Roll of Honour', http://www.garda.ie/honour/default.aspx (last accessed 18/11/2016). The Provisional IRA killed one prison officer in the Republic of Ireland, Brian Stack, in 1983; David McKittrick, 'The IRA finally admits killing prison officer Brian Stack during the Troubles', *The Independent*, 9 August 2013.

24 Conor Cruise O'Brien, *Memoir: My Life and Themes* (Dublin: Poolbeg Press, 1999), p. 354; D. Whelan, *Conor Cruise O'Brien: Violent Notions* (Dublin: Irish Academic Press, 2009), p. 145; White, *Ruairí Ó Brádaigh*, pp. 202–3.

25 See Deutsch and Magowan, *Northern Ireland Chronology of Events II*, pp. 269–70.

26 See Currie, *All Hell Will Break Loose*, p. 211; Routledge, *John Hume*, pp. 120–3; P. Devlin, *Straight Left: An Autobiography* (Belfast: Blackstaff Press, 1993), pp. 193–6, quotation p. 196; P. Devlin, *The Fall of the N.I. Executive* (Belfast: Paddy Devlin, 1975), p. 4.

27 Ruairí Ó Brádaigh interview, 1996.

28 See *Elections: Northern Ireland Elections*, 'Northern Ireland Assembly Elections 1973', http://www.ark.ac.uk/elections/fa73.htm (last accessed 18/11/2016).

29 See Moloney, *Voices from the Grave*, pp. 151–4; Moloney, *Secret History of the IRA*, p. 133; Adams, *Before the Dawn*, pp. 217–9.

30 Brendan Hughes interview, 2001.

31 See Adams, *Before the Dawn*, pp. 228–32.

32 See Moloney, *Voices From the Grave*, pp. 154–63.

33 J.B. and Bernadette O'Hagan interview, 1996.

34 Seán O'Callaghan writes that Tom Sullivan, from Kerry, was briefly Chief of Staff in late 1973–early 1974. See O'Callaghan, *The Informer*, p. 58.

35 See Bell, *The Irish Troubles*, p. 431.

36 See *Volunteer Seamus Twomey 1919–89 A Tribute* (Dublin: AP/RN print), pp. 9–11; Moloney, *Secret History of the IRA*, Appendix 5, p. 513; Bell, *The Irish Troubles*, pp. 383–5, 427; Ruairí Ó Brádaigh interview, 1996.

37 Brendan Hughes interview, 2001.

38 See Moloney, *Voices From the Grave*, pp. 156–62.

39 Gerry McKerr interview, 2013.

40 S. Farren, *The SDLP: The Struggle for Agreement in Northern Ireland, 1970–2000* (Dublin: Four Courts Press, 2010), p. 87; Routledge, *John Hume*, pp. 120–3.

41 'Marian Price to her family, February 3rd 1974', in Brady, Patterson, McKinney, Hamill and Jackson (comp.), *In the Footsteps of Anne* (Belfast: Shanway Press, 2011), p. 129.

42 Ruairí Ó Brádaigh interview, 1996.

43 See Bell, *The Irish Troubles*, pp. 400, 421–2; CAIN Web Service, 'Westminster General Election (NI) – Thursday 28 February 1974'; Rosa Gilbert, 'The rent and rates strike in the North 1971–1974', paper presented at the conference on Irish Society, History & Culture: 100 Years After 1916, Firenze, October 2016

44 See Currie, *All Hell Will Break Loose*, pp. 256.

45 Tyrone republican 2 interview, 1984.

46 There are allegations that British agents helped the loyalists. See H. McDonald and J. Cusack, *UDA: Inside the Heart of Loyalist Terror* (Dublin: Penguin

Ireland, 2004), p. 21; Bell, *In Dubious Battle*; Bell, *The Irish Troubles*, pp. 372–418;

47 Robert Fisk quotation: R. Fisk, *The Point of No Return: The Strike Which Broke the British in Ulster* (London: Andre Deutsch, 1975), pp. 92–3.

48 Wilson's speech is available in Deutsch and Magowan, *Northern Ireland 1968–74 A Chronology of Events III* (1974), pp. 188–9.

49 See also, J. Newsinger, *British Counterinsurgency: From Palestine to Northern Ireland* (New York: Palgrave Macmillan, 2002), pp. 174–5; P. Devlin, *The Fall of the N.I. Executive* (Belfast: Paddy Devlin, 1975).

50 See McGladdery, *The Provisional IRA in England* (Dublin: Irish Academic Press, 2006), pp. 238–9.

51 *Time*, 17 June 1974; Bell, *The Irish Troubles*, pp. 422–3; McKittrick et al., *Lost Lives*, pp. 457–8.

52 Marian Price interview, 2010. See also, Ian Miller, *A History of Force-Feeding: Hunger Strikes, Prisons, and Medical Ethics*, 1909–1974 (London: Palgrave Macmillan, 2016), pp. 191–236; Bell, *The Irish Troubles*, p. 423.

53 See Bell, *The Irish Troubles*, p. 423.

54 Seán Lynch interview, 1995.

55 'Irish Election Literature', http://irishelectionliterature.wordpress.com/others-project/old-local-election-results/ (last accessed 19/022014); *Irish Identity*, 'A Passion for GAA and politics' (Seán Lynch), http://www.irishidentity.com/extras/people/stories/seanlynch.htm (last accessed 18/11/2016); 'John Joe McGirl: The Unbreakable Fenian', *IRIS the republican magazine*, 22 (Winter 2008), pp. 13–22.

56 'Press Suppressed Editor Arrested', *The Irish People*, 21 September 1974, pp. 1, 3.

57 'The Burning of Long Kesh', *An Phoblacht*, 14 October 2004.

58 Fra McCann interview, 1995.

59 Soldiers claimed they shouted warnings prior to shooting Hugh Coney; others denied this. See McKittrick et al., *Lost Lives*, pp. 488–9.

60 *Tírghrá*, p. 153; Bell, *The Irish Troubles*, 426–33; see also McGladdery, *The Provisional IRA in England*; White, *Ruairí Ó Brádaigh*, pp. 220–1.

61 The reactions of Dáithí O'Connell and Billy McKee to the Birmingham bombs are similar to Ruairí Ó Brádaigh's. An internal inquiry directed by Dáithí O'Connell found the Provisionals were not responsible. Years later, journalistic investigation suggested that O'Connell was lied to. In 1985, Joe Cahill acknowledged that the Provisional IRA was responsible. Ruairí Ó Brádaigh interview, 1984; McGladerry, *The Provisional IRA in England*, pp. 89–

92; C. Mullin, *Error of Judgement: The Truth About the Birmingham Bombings* (Dublin: Poolbeg Press, 1986).

62 Marian Price interview, 2010.

63 P. Maguire, *My Father's Watch* (London: Harper Perennial, 2009), p. 104.

64 See McKee and Franey, *Time Bomb*; Mullin, *Error of Judgement*.

65 M. Mac Donncha, 'Mick Timothy – Revolutionary editor', *AP/RN*, February 2015, p. 20; R. O'Donnell, *Special Category Vol 1 1968–78* (Dublin: Irish Academic Press), p. 440.

66 See White, *Ruairí Ó Brádaigh*, pp. 221–2; Bell, *The Secret Army*, pp. 414–5.

67 Ruairí Ó Brádaigh interview, 1996.

68 J.B. and Bernadette O'Hagan interview, 1996.

69 Ruairí Ó Brádaigh interview, 1996; P. Taylor, Behind the Mask, p. 206.

70 *Irish Times*, 13 December 1974, quoted in Taylor, *Behind the Mask*, p. 205.

71 Revd Harold Good interview, 2014.

72 This count is based on McKittrick et al., *Lost Lives*.

Chapter 9

1 Billy McKee interview, 2014.

2 'Truce' is used here because that was the perspective of the Provisionals. See P. Wilkinson, *Terrorism and the Liberal State* (London: Macmillan, 1986), p. 160.

3 See for example, R. O'Rawe, *Blanketmen: An Untold Story of the H-Block Hunger Strike* (Dublin: New Island Books, 2005), p. 73; Moloney, *Secret History of the IRA*, pp. 177–8; O'Doherty, *The Volunteer*, pp. 170–8; Conway, *Southside Provisional*, pp. 182–4.

4 See White, *Ruairí Ó Brádaigh* (2006), pp. 225–8.

5 M. Cunningham, *British Government Policy in Northern Ireland, 1969–2000* (Manchester: Manchester University Press, 2001), pp. 17–8; M. Rees, *Northern Ireland: A Personal Perspective* (London: Methuen), pp. 151–3; Dillon, *The Enemy Within*, pp. 144–7.

6 Martin Dillon states that Seamus Twomey and Billy McKee, 'the Northern complement on the Council', voted against the ceasefire. Patrick Bishop and Eamon Mallie, record the vote as five to two with 'the two Northern representatives opposing the ceasefire'. See Dillon, *The Enemy Within*, p. 144; Bishop and Mallie, *Provisional IRA*, pp. 269–71; Ricky O'Rawe in *Blanketmen* (p. 72) and Peter Taylor in *Behind the Mask* (p. 209) have Billy McKee in favour of the ceasefire and the subsequent truce.

7 J.B. and Bernadette O'Hagan interview, 1996.

8 Harold Wilson told MI5 not to brief Roy Jenkins and to keep knowledge of the Duddy-Ó Brádaigh

link within Downing Street and the NIO. See Taylor, *Behind the Mask*, pp. 196–216; Brendan Duddy Papers, 'Biographical History', available in the James Hardiman Library, National University of Ireland, Galway: http://archives.library.nuigalway. ie/col_level.php?col=POL35 and http://archives. library.nuigalway.ie/duddy/web (last accessed 11/01/2017); T. Craig, 'From Backdoors and Back Lanes to Backchannels', *Contemporary British History* 26/1 (2012), pp. 97–117; A. Mumford, 'Covert peacemaking: Clandestine negotiations and backchannels with the Provisional IRA during the early "Troubles", 1972–76', *The Journal of Imperial and Commonwealth History* 39/4 (2011), pp. 633–48; T. Craig, 'Monitoring the peace?' *TPV*, 26 (2014), pp. 307–19.

9   Billy McKee interview, 2014. McKee was not asked about and he did not comment on membership in the IRA or the Army Council.

10   P. Taylor, *Talking to Terrorists: A Personal Journey from the IRA to Al Qaeda* (London: HarperPress, 2011), p. 21.

11   Billy McKee interview, 2014; Taylor, *Behind the Mask*, pp. 210–14; White, *Ruairí Ó Brádaigh*, pp. 224–6.

12   Ruairí Ó Brádaigh interview, 1996.

13   'Dílis go hEag', *Saoirse* April 1988, pp. 4–5.

14   The primary victims during the truce were civilians; of 206 people killed in 1975, 174 were civilians. Ruairí Ó Brádaigh papers; English, *Armed Struggle*, pp. 178–9; McKittrick et al., *Lost Lives*, pp. 512–3.

15   J.B. and Bernadette O'Hagan interview, 1996.

16   Billy McKee interview, 2014. Evidently John O'Connell, of the Irish Labour Party, was briefing the British on developments and reported that J.B. O'Hagan was opposed to bringing Seán Mac Bride into the meetings but O'Connell had 'won him over'. See Thomas Hennessey, *The First Northern Ireland Peace Process: Power Sharing, Sunningdale and the IRA Ceasefires 1972–76* (Basingstoke Hampshire: Palgrave Macmillan, 2015), pp. 170–1.

17   See Deutsch and Magowan, *Northern Ireland Chronology of Events III*, p. 37; *Report of a Committee to consider, in the context of civil liberties and human rights, measures to deal with terrorism in Northern Ireland*, http://cain.ulst.ac.uk/hmso/gardiner.htm#2 (last accessed 19/02 2014); Taylor, *Behind the Mask*, p. 217.

18   Ruairí Ó Brádaigh interview, 1996.

19   See Anderson, *Joe Cahill*, pp. 299–307; 'Dílis go hEag', *Saoirse*, April 1988, pp. 4–5.

20   The British did not consider it a truce because that would have involved negotiations. From their perspective, they were presenting a position: If there was a cessation of violence then the 'logical consequences' would be things like troops being withdrawn to barracks. The British terms are described as a 'position paper' in the Brendan Duddy Papers, Pol35/58(i), p. 12.

21   Ruairí Ó Brádaigh interviews, 1996.

22   Ruairí Ó Brádaigh interview, 1996.

23   Billy McKee interview, 2014.

24   Joe McCallion's participation is noted in UK National Archives papers as cited in N. Ó Dochartaigh, 'The longest negotiation: British policy, IRA strategy and the making of the Northern Ireland peace settlement', Political Studies 63/1 (2013). See also Taylor's *Behind the Mask* (1997), Hennessey's *The First Northern Ireland Peace Process* (2015), White's, *Ruairí Ó Brádaigh* (2006), Ruairí Ó Brádaigh's Papers, Brendan Duddy's papers, the UK National Archives; N. Ó Gadhra, *Margdil na Saoirse* [*Bargaining for Freedom*] (Baile Átha Cliath: Cló na Guaidhe, 1988); N. Ó Dochartaigh, '"Everyone Trying", The IRA ceasefire, 1975: a missed opportunity for peace?' *Field Day Review* 7 (2011), pp. 51–60.

25   Clarke and Johnston have Martin McGuinness released from Portlaoise in November 1974 [*Martin McGuinness: From Guns to Government*, pp. 88–9] while others have him released in the spring of 1975. *Tírghrá*, p. 172; Hanley and Millar, *The Lost Revolution*, p. 317; Taylor, *Behind the Mask*, p. 219; Danny Morrison interview, 2001.

26   Danny Morrison interview, 2001. See also P. Fitzgerald, 'From Publicity to the Ballot Box: Danny Morrison and the Provisional Irish Republican Movement', M.A. Thesis in History, School of Humanities, National University of Ireland, Galway, 2013, p. 14; Taylor, *Behind the Mask*, p. 219.

27   T. Craig, 'Monitoring the peace?' *TPV*, 26 (2014), pp. 307–19.

28   Billy McKee interview, 2014. See also O'Rawe, *Blanketmen*, pp. 72.

29   Ruairí Ó Brádaigh interview, 1996. See also O'Rawe, *Blanketmen*, pp. 72–5.

30   The British persuaded General China (Waruhiu Itote) to encourage a Mau Mau surrender. While the 'China Peace Initiative' was underway, the Special Branch collected information in Nairobi. When the peace overture failed tens of thousands of suspects were interned and sent to the reserve. The Land and Freedom Armies never recovered. General Kimathi's reply to the peace overture included the comment, 'Yes, we have seen that it is a Government trap, but we will throw a stick of

ENDNOTES

wood at it and see its reaction'. That, in many ways, summarizes the Provisional leadership's approach in 1975. McKearney, *From Insurrection to Parliament*, pp. 138–40; K. Kyle, *The Politics of the Independence of Kenya* (New York: Palgrave Macmillan, 1999), pp. 60–2; D. Barnett and K. Njama, *Mau Mau From Within* (New York: Monthly Review Press, 1966), pp. 348–52; Newsinger, *British Counterinsurgency*, pp. 72–3; Ó Dochartaigh, '"Everyone Trying"', *Field Day Review* 7 (2011), pp. 51–60.

31 Oatley left the negotiations in March 1975. Taylor, *Behind the Mask*, pp. 196–202, 221; White, *Ruairí Ó Brádaigh*, pp. 219–47.

32 See McKearney, *From Insurrection to Parliament*, pp. 138–40.

33 The British Point 4 stated, 'The only arrests will be arrests of people breaking the law. Interim Custody Order Orders [internment orders] will not be signed if there is no violence'. See O'Doherty, *The Volunteer* (1993), pp. 178–80; McNulty *Exiled*, pp. 152–3; Rees, *Northern Ireland*, pp. 156, 231; S. McDaid, *Template for Peace: Northern Ireland 1972–75* (Manchester: University of Manchester Press, 2013), p. 171; Bruce, *The Red Hand*, pp. 55–6; P. Taylor, *Loyalists* (London: Bloomsbury, 1999), pp. 152–6; Sutton, *Bear in Mind These Dead*; McKittrick et al., *Lost Lives*, pp. 509–21.

34 See Jack Holland and Henry McDonald, *INLA: Deadly Divisions* (Dublin: Torc, 1994).

35 See McKittrick et al., *Lost Lives*, p. 1975.

36 The notes are Ó Brádaigh's minutes of the meetings and summaries of Army Council 'Instructions'. Journalist Peter Taylor summarized the notes with, 'They may be one-sided, but there is no reason to believe they are fantasy' and 'The minutes seemed genuine.' The Brendan Duddy and Ruairí Ó Brádaigh papers are available at the James Hardiman Library of the National University of Ireland, Galway; Taylor, *Behind the Mask*, pp. 211–2.

37 'Formal Meeting 5.3.75 (B).

38 See, 'INSTRUCTIONS 19.2.75' and 'FORMAL MEETING 19.2.75' (A). See also, 'FORMAL MEETING 28.2.75 (A)'; 'FORMAL MEETING, 5.3.75. (B)'; 'FORMAL MEETING 16.3.75 (A)'.

39 'FORMAL MEETING 13.3.75'.

40 Marian Price interview, 2011; see also, 'Price Sisters Sent to Ulster Jail', *The Glasgow Herald*, 19 March 1975.

41 See White, *Ruairí Ó Bradaigh*, pp. 234–5.

42 'FORMAL MEETING 2.4. 75. (b)'.

43 See White, *Ruairí Ó Brádaigh*, p. 235 and accompanying notes.

44 Billy McKee interview, 2014. See also, 'Famous Belfast Stores: The Bank Buildings: Restored Former Bank in the Centre of Belfast', http://www.culturenorthernireland.org/article/767/famous-belfast-stores-the-bank-buildings (last accessed 11/01/2017).

45 'Bloody Truce', *Time*, 28 April 1975; Rees, *Northern Ireland*, pp. 225–6, 235; Elliott and Flackes, *Northern Ireland Political Directory*, p. 307; K. Kelley, *The Longest War: Northern Ireland and the I.R.A.* (London: Zed Books, 1988), pp. 236–7.

46 Ruairí Ó Brádaigh interview, 1996.

47 At the end of May 1975, Revd Arlow stated, 'I have reason to believe that the British government has given a firm commitment to the IRA that they will withdraw the army from Northern Ireland'. Quoted in Kelley, *The Longest War*, pp. 235–6 [see also J.B. Bell, *The Irish Troubles*, p. 442; Merlyn Rees denied Arlow's claim]; G. FitzGerald, *Just Garret, Tales From the Political Front Line* (Dublin: Liberties Press, 2010), pp. 259–61; McDaid, *Template for Peace*, pp. 162–70; Routledge, *John Hume*, pp. 140–2; P. Routlege, *Public Servant, Secret Agent: The Elusive Life and Violent Death of Airey Neave* (London: Fourth Estate), pp. 274–6; Rees, *Northern Ireland*, pp. 227–8; G. FitzGerald, *All in a Life* (London: Macmillan, 1991), pp. 255–65.

48 Danny Morrison interview, 2001.

49 See O'Rawe, *Blanketmen*, p. 71.

50 See McKittrick et al., *Lost Lives*, pp. 523–30.

51 'FORMAL MEETING 17.4.75'.

52 Elections: Northern Ireland Elections, http://www.ark.ac.uk/elections/fc75.htm (last accessed 14/02/2014); D. Godson, *Himself Alone: David Trimble and the Ordeal of Unionism* (London: Harper Collins, 2004), pp. 50–3; Bell, *The Irish Troubles*, pp. 441–3.

53 'INSTRUCTIONS 6.5.75 (A)'. See also, 'REPORT 1.7.75'; 'REPORT 3.7.75'.

54 Constable Gray's father was a prison warder; his colleagues attacked O'Doherty in retaliation. Loyalists in County Down stabbed to death Francis Rice and claimed it was retaliation for Paul Gray; it later emerged that Rice was a member of the IRA. See O'Doherty, *The Volunteer*, pp. 138–48, 178–86; McKittrick et al., *Lost Lives*, pp. 540–1.

55 'Formal Meeting 14.5.75'. See also, 'FORMAL MEETING 4.6.75'; McKittrick et al., *Lost Lives*, pp. 544–5.

56 See for example, 'INSTRUCTIONS 5.6.75'; 'FORMAL MEETING 11.6.75'; 'NOTE 19th June 1975'; 'REPORT 1.7.75' '"Note" 7th July, 1975'.

57 See 'S. to M. REPORT 1.7.75 (B)'.

ENDNOTES

58 See Bell, *The Irish Troubles*, p. 449; Elliott and Flackes, *Northern Ireland: A Political Directory*, pp. 214–5; Ó Brádaigh Notes, 'Reply to Communication of July 7th, 1975'.

59 See White, *Ruairí Ó Brádaigh*, pp. 240–1.

60 See 4 July 1975 issue of *An Phoblacht*.

61 Danny Morrison interview, 2001. See also Fitzgerald, 'From Publicity to the Ballot Box', pp. 15–6.

62 C. Keena, *A Biography of Gerry Adams* (Cork: Mercier Press,1990), pp. 64, 70–4; 'Inside Story', *Republican News*, 16 August 1975, p. 6.

63 Dáithí O'Connell was arrested 9 July 1975. The placement of Ruairí Ó Brádaigh on the Army Council at this time and up to 1 January 1984 is based on the reports of others. See 'Brian Keenan 1941–2008: A Republican Legend', *An Phoblacht*, n.d., pp. 37–8; 'Dublin Head Office opened on New Year's Day', *Saoirse*, January 1996, p. 8; Anderson, *Joe Cahill*, p. 303; Moloney, *Secret History of the IRA*, pp. 157–9, 164; Conway, *Southside Provisional*, pp. 189–90.

64 A fourth soldier injured in the South Armagh attack died later: '"We'll continue to keep low profile" – Derry I.R.A.', *An Phoblacht*, 18 July 1975; McKittrick et al., *Lost Lives*, p. 553.

65 'Notes for Meeting – 22nd July 1975'; 'FORMAL MEETING 22nd July 1975'; 'FORMAL MEETING 31.7.'75'.

66 See Bell, *Irish Troubles*, p. 452; McKittrick et al., *Lost Lives*, pp. 555–7; S. Travers and N. Fetherstonhaugh, *The Miami Showband Massacre: A Survivor's Search for the Truth* (Dublin: Hodder Headline, 2007); Taylor, *Loyalists* , pp. 147–8.

67 'FORMAL MEETING 13.8.'75'.

68 During this time, the Provisionals also met with Glenn Barr and Andy Tyrie of the UDA but it did not stop the sectarian killings. See: 'FORMAL MEETING 25th August 1975'; O'Rawe, *Blanketmen*, p. 73; McKittrick et al., *Lost Lives*, pp. 560–1.

69 '"We Stay" No Matter What – Rees', *Belfast Newsletter*, 27 August 1975; McKittrick et al., *Lost Lives*, pp. 566–8, 571–2; White, *Ruairí Ó Brádaigh*, p. 242; Brendan Duddy Papers, Pol35/62, James Hardiman Library, National University of Ireland, Galway, htttp://archives.library.nuigalway.ie/duddy/web/ (last accessed 11/01/2017).

70 Ruairí Ó Brádaigh interview, 1996.

71 See Smith, *Fighting for Ireland*, pp. 128–33; Ó Dochartaigh, '"Everyone Trying"', *Field Day Review* 7, pp. 51–60; White, *Ruairí Ó Brádaigh*, p. 242; McKittrick et al., *Lost Lives*, p. 579.

72 '26.9. '75 Message received per sub-intermediary', 6.30 p.m. Thursday, 25.9.75; 'S. to L.', 30th September 1975'; no title, 2nd October '75.

73 See FitzGerald, *Just Garret*, p. 265; Merlyn Rees, 'Troops out, loyalists in', *The Guardian: Letters*, 19 July 1983; Ben Fenton, '"Doomsday scenario" for pulling troops out of Ulster', *The Telegraph*, 1 January 2005; Routledge, *John Hume*, p. 140; FitzGerald, *All in a Life*, pp. 264–72.

74 'FORMAL MEETING FEBRUARY 10TH OR 11TH, 1976'. See also, 'RM - HMG Dec '75, Jan & Feb, '76 Notes September 1996'; N. Ó Dochartaigh, 'The longest negotiation: British policy, IRA strategy and the making of the Northern Ireland peace settlement', *Political Studies* 63/1 (2013), p. 4.

75 See McKittrick et al., *Lost Lives*, p. 626; Coogan, *The IRA*, pp. 415–8.

Chapter 10

1 Tyrone republican 3 interview, 1984..

2 See *Tírghrá*, pp. 34, 51; McKittrick et al., *Lost Lives*, pp. 1554, 142–3, 169–70; Appendix 2.

3 See Hanley and Millar, *Lost Revolution*, pp. 311–35; McKittrick et al., *Lost Lives*, pp. 590–5, 684.

4 See Bell, *The Irish Troubles*, pp. 462–4.

5 *Ibid.*, pp. 457, 465; McKee and Franey, *Time Bomb*, pp. 370–413, Joe O'Connell quotation, pp. 384–6; S.P. Moysey, *The Road to Balcombe Street: The Reign of IRA Terror in London* (New York: Routledge, 2009).

6 See Coogan, *The IRA*, p. 443; McKittrick et al., pp. 609–14.

7 See McKittrick et al., *Lost Lives*, p. 598, 684–5; M. Dillon, *The Shankill Butchers: A Case Study of Mass Murder* (London: Arrow Books, 1990).

8 Danny Morrison interview, 2001.

9 Brendan Hughes interview, 2001.

10 See for example Taylor, *Behind the Mask*, p. 232.

11 Joe Cahill interview, 1990.

12 See O'Rawe, *Blanketmen*, p. 71.

13 Billy McKee interview, 2014. See also Taylor, *Behind the Mask*, pp. 232–3.

14 Seán Mac Stiofáin interview, 1990.

15 T. Craig, 'Monitoring the Peace?' *TPV*, 26/2 (2014), pp. 307–19.

16 See *Tírghrá*, p. 191; McKittrick et al., *Lost Lives*, pp. 637–8.

17 D. O'Hearn, *Nothing But an Unfinished Song* (New York: Nation Books, 2006), pp. 113–25.

18 See Appendix 2; McKittrick et al., *Lost Lives*, pp. 682–3; *Belfast Graves*, pp. 146–8; *Tírghrá*, pp. 202–4; Ardoyne Commemoration Project, *Ardoyne: The*

Untold Story (Belfast: Beyond the Pale Publications, 2002), pp. 266–9.

19 Derry republican 3 interview, 1984.

20 See for example, Moxon-Browne, *Nation, Class and Creed in Northern Ireland* (Aldershot: Gower, 1978), pp. 29–31.

21 Seán Crowe interview, 1995.

22 See Coogan, *The IRA*, pp. 524, 530. The most prominent victim of the 'Heavy Gang' was probably Nicky Kelly, an IRSP member arrested in association with a train robbery. Alleged confessions were the primary evidence that convicted Kelly, Osgur Breatnach, and Brian McNally. Kelly fled the country; in 1980, Breatnach and McNally had their convictions quashed on appeal. Kelly returned, was arrested, and was sent to prison to serve out his twelve-year sentence, even though the IRA had accepted responsibility for the robbery. Kelly was finally released in 1984. D. Dunne and G. Kerrigan, *Round Up the Usual Suspects* (Dublin: Magill Publications, 1984), pp. 24, 141–3, 204, 210, 216–18.

23 See for example, White, *Ruairí Ó Brádaigh*, p. 253.

24 Seán Crowe interview, 1995.

25 See Bishop and Mallie, *Provisional IRA*, pp. 350–1; Bell, *The Irish Troubles*, pp. 498, 547–8.

26 Gerry Hodgins interview, 1988. See also Taylor, *Behind the Mask*, pp. 238–9.

27 See Taylor, *Behind the Mask*, pp. 255–6; Brady et al., *In the Footsteps of Anne*, p. 182.

28 Mason also pledged that loyalists would be 'subject to the full rigour of the law'. In the spring of 1977, Revd Ian Paisley and other hard-liners tried to organise another general strike. Mason used the British Army and the RUC to stop it. Paisley and the DUP and Harry West and the UUP took opposite sides on the strike and it split the UUUC. R. Mason, *Paying the Price* (London: Robert Hale, Ltd., 1999), pp. 161; Bell, *The Irish Troubles*, pp. 498–9, 505–7.

29 See McKearney, *From Insurrection to Parliament* , pp. 34, 137–40; P. Taylor, *Beating the Terrorists? Interrogation in Omagh, Gough, and Castlereagh* (London: Penguin, 1980), pp. 36–7, 59–63, 80–1.

30 See O'Hearn, *Nothing But an Unfinished Song*, pp. 136, 158.

31 The quotations are from Taylor's, *Behind the Mask*, pp. 242–3. See also, Taylor, *Beating the Terrorists*, pp. 217–9.

32 Gerry McGeough interview, 2014.

33 Kevin Boyle, T. Hadden and P. Hillary, *Ten Years on in Northern Ireland: The Legal Control of Political Violence* (London: Cobden Trust, 1980), p. 60; Ian Cobain,

'Hundreds of Northern Ireland "terrorists" allege police torture', *The Guardian*, 11 October 2010.

34 See Bell, *The Irish Troubles*, p. 531.

35 Tyrone republican 3 interview, 1984.

36 See Farren, *The SDLP*, p. 134; F.S. Ross, *Smashing H-Block* (Liverpool: Liverpool University Press, 2011), p. 32; Taylor, *Beating the Terrorists*, pp. 188–92.

37 In retaliation for Dr Irwin making his concerns public a false story questioning his motives was leaked to the *Belfast Telegraph*. Gerry Fitt referred to it as a 'vicious smear'. Taylor, *Beating the Terrorists?* pp. 286–97, 318–26; CAIN Web Service, 'Report of an Amnesty International Mission to Northern Ireland, 28 Nov–6 Dec 1977'; Murphy, *Gerry Fitt*, pp. 267–8; C. Ryder, *The RUC: A Force Under Fire* (London: Mandarin Paperbacks, 1992), pp. 197–8; CAIN Web Service, 'Report of the Committee of Inquiry into Police Interrogation Procedures in Northern Ireland'; Coogan, *The IRA*, pp. 440, 528; Ryder, *The RUC*, pp. 187–99; Hansard Reports, 'NORTHERN IRELAND (BENNETT REPORT) HC Deb 16 March 1979 vol. 964 cc961–84'; Mason, *Paying the Price*, pp. 211–17; Elliott and Flackes, *Northern Ireland: A Political Directory*, pp. 177–8.

38 The *Sinn Féin Bulletin* of North Belfast suggests that Fleming joined Sinn Féin in 1975. Tom Fleming interview, 1984; see also Gerard Magee, 'Propelled to take on unjust state', *Sinn Féin Bulletin*, North Belfast edition, December (2007), pp. 10–11.

39 Brendan Hughes interview, 2001.

40 See Moloney, *Secret History of the IRA*, pp. 148–9, 156–7; Bishop and Mallie, *Provisional IRA*, pp. 321–3; Moloney, *Voices From the Grave*, pp. 196–205.

41 See Taylor, *Beating the Terrorists?*, p. 345; Coogan, *The IRA*, p. 465–7.

42 See Coogan, *The IRA*, p. 564, emphasis in the original.

43 *Ibid.*, pp. 465–7; Taylor, *Beating the Terrorists?*, pp. 345–7.

44 See McKearney, *From Insurrection to Parliament*, pp. 141–3; G. Bradley and B. Feeney, *Insider: Gerry Bradley's Life in the IRA* (Dublin: O'Brien Press, 2009), pp. 196–9.

45 See Bradley and Feeney, *Insider*, pp. 207–25.

46 See Bishop and Mallie, *Provisional IRA*, pp. 311–12; O'Brien, *The Long War*, pp. 107–11; McKearney, *From Insurrection to Parliament*, p. 142; Moloney, *Secret History of the IRA*, p. 160.

47 See Moloney, *Secret History of the IRA*, p. 166; Clarke and Johnston, *Martin McGuinness*, pp. 85–90; Elliott and Flackes, *Northern Ireland Political Directory*, pp. 330–2; Moloney, *Secret History of the IRA*, p. 157.

48 See Moloney, *Secret History of the IRA*, pp. 163–4; White, *Ruairí Ó Brádaigh*, pp. 98–9.

49 Dáithí O'Connell was released in April 1976 and rearrested in July 1976. The Portlaoise prisoners believed they had been promised an inquiry that would lead to improved conditions but did not obtain any direct concessions. See RM – HMG Dec '75, Jan & Feb. '76, Notes. N.d.; Coogan, *The IRA*, pp. 418–19; J.J. Barrett, *Martin Ferris: Man of Kerry* (Dingle, Co. Kerry: Brandon, 2005), pp. 97–112; 'Portlaoise Pledges Must be Honoured,' *An Phoblacht*, 26 April 1977, pp. 1, 3; Dieter Reinisch, '"The Pinochet-style regime" Portlaoise Prison Protests, 1973–7: Prologue to the H-Blocks Struggle', *studi irlandesi* 7, June 2017.

50 Membership on the Army Council in 1976–77 is based on various reports, including Moloney, *Voices From the Grave*, pp. 105–10; Bell, *The Irish Troubles*, p. 495; Moloney, *Secret History of the IRA*, pp. 163–4; 'Dílis go hÉag', *Saoirse*, April 1988, pp. 4–5.

51 See Bell, *The Irish Troubles*, pp. 503–4; Hanley and Millar, *The Lost Revolution*, pp. 378–80.

52 See Moloney, *Secret History of the IRA*, pp. 166–8.

53 The Gardaí found with Twomey a copy of the 'Staff Report' tucked inside a pencil case. See Taylor, *Beating the Terrorists?*, p. 345.

54 See Moloney, *Secret History of the IRA*, pp. 171–2.

55 *Ibid.*, pp. 157–64; Bishop and Mallie, *Provisional IRA*, p. 311.

56 See Coogan, *The IRA*, p. 467. See also Líta Ní Chathmhaoil and Dieter Reinisch, *Cumann na mBan: 100 Years of Defending the Republic* (Dublin: Irish Freedom Press, 2014).

57 Líta Ní Chathmhaoil interview, 2009.

58 The lone Provisional IRA woman killed on active service prior to the reorganization, Ethel Lynch, died in a premature explosion at a bomb factory, on 7 December 1974. The first Cumann na mBan volunteers killed in the conflict were Maura Meehan and Dorothy Maguire, 23 October 1971. They were shot while trying to warn people that British soldiers were nearby. Appendix 2; D. Reinisch, 'Cumann na mBan & Women in Irish Republican Paramilitary Organisations, 1969–1986', *Estudios Irlandeses* 11(2016), pp. 149–62; E. McDonald, *Shoot the Women First* (New York: Random House, 1991), p. 142; Viterna, *Women in War*, pp. 117–50.

59 Different sources provide different counts of events and deaths from political violence, and in some instances there is disagreement over the perpetrator and the classification of the victim of an event. For information on Tables 2 and 3, see Sutton,

Bear in Mind These Dead… , p. 206, and the CAIN Web Service http://cain.ulst.ac.uk/sutton/index. html (last accessed 11/01/2017); Elliott and Flackes, *Northern Ireland Political Directory*, p. 681 (Table 1), p. 685 (Table 5); McKittrick et al., *Lost Lives*, p. 1475; White, 'The Provisional Irish Republican Army,' *TPV*, 9/1 (Spring 1997), pp. 20–55; R.W. White, 'The 1975 British-Provisional IRA Truce in Perspective', *Éire-Ireland*, 45 (3&4; Autumn/Winter, 2010), pp. 211–44; and, White and White, 'Revolution in the city', *TPV*, 3/4 (1991), pp. 100–32.

60 See also, White and White, 'Revolution in the city', *TPV*, 3/4 (1991), pp. 100–32;

61 See Cronin, *Irish Nationalism*, pp. 339–57 (Appendix XVIII, pp. 342, 356).

Chapter 11

1   Gerry Hodgins interview, 1988.

2   See Taylor, *Beating the Terrorists?*, p. 347.

3   G. Adams, *Cage Eleven* (Dingle: Co. Kerry, 1990), pp. 72–7.

4   *Ibid.*, pp. 134–7.

5   See Bell, *The Irish Troubles*, pp. 482–9, 520–2; White, *Ruairí Ó Brádaigh*, pp. 251–2; McKittrick et al., *Lost Lives*, pp. 670–2.

6   Several of the Brownie columns were published in *Cage Eleven*, but this column was left out. In the foreword, Adams claims he was one 'of a small number of Long Kesh POWs' who wrote the Brownie column. The *Cage Eleven* columns are edited versions of what appeared *Republican News*. See Adams, *Cage Eleven*; Taylor, *Behind the Mask*, pp. 235–6; Sharrock and Devenport, *Man of War, Man of Peace*, pp. 131–4; Moloney, *Voices From the Grave*, pp. 202–3; L. Whalen, *Contemporary Irish Republican Prison Writing* (New York: Palgrave Macmillan, 2007), pp. 10–11, 30–4; C. Thornton, 'Adams' IRA sham', *Belfast Telegraph*, 19 March 2004.

7   'Annual Commemoration, Wolfe Tone, Bodenstown', *Republican News*, 18 June 1977, pp. 6–7; Adams, *Before the Dawn*, pp. 263-5; 'SOLIDARITY WITH HUNGER STRIKERS', *An Phoblacht*, 5 April 1977, p. 3.

8   'Editorial', *Belfast Telegraph*, 14 June 1977.

9   K. Bean and M. Hayes (eds), *Republican Voices* (Monaghan, Co. Monaghan: Seesyu Press, 2001), p. 71.

10 Ardoyne Commemoration Project, *Ardoyne: The Untold Story* (2002), p. 267.

11 E. Moxon-Browne, *Nation, Class and Creed in Northern Ireland* (Aldershot: Gower, 1978), p. 24; E. Davis and R. Sinnott, *Attitudes in the Republic of*

Ireland Relevant to the Northern Ireland Problem: Vol. 1 (Dublin: Economic and Social Research Institute, 1979), p. 33.

12 See Moxon-Browne, *Nation, Class and Creed in Northern Ireland*, pp. 29–30.

13 See Dwyer, *Nice Fellow*, pp. 314–7, 336–7; 354–5; Bell, *The Irish Troubles*, p. 507.

14 See White, *Ruairí Ó Brádaigh*, pp. 250–1.

15 See McKittrick et al., *Lost Lives*, pp. 745–9; Bell, *The Irish Troubles*, pp. 536–7.

16 See Keena, *Gerry Adams*, pp. 81–4; Sharrock and Devenport, *Man of War, Man of Peace*, pp. 156–63; Moloney, *Secret History of the IRA*, p. 173; Adams, *Before the Dawn*, pp. 274–5.

17 'Danny Morrison: Writer. "Biography"'; *'an phoblacht'*, https://www.anphoblacht.com/about (last accessed 30/04/2014); 'Interview: Author Danny Morrison', 14 December 2006, *AP/RN*.

18 Danny Morrison interview, 2001.

19 L. McKeown, *Out of Time: Irish Republican Prisoners Long Kesh, 1972–2000* (Belfast: Beyond the Pale Publications, 2001), pp. 56–7; Moloney, *Voices From the Grave*, pp. 213–9; McKeown, *Out of Time*, p. 57; O'Hearn, *Nothing But an Unfinished Song*, p. 180.

20 See O'Hearn, *Nothing But An Unfinished Song*, pp. 171–4.

21 See McKeown, *Out of Time*, pp. 56–7; Moloney, *Voices From the Grave*, pp. 213–9; McKeown, *Out of Time*, p. 57; O'Hearn, *Nothing But an Unfinished Song*, p. 180.

22 See B. Campbell, L. McKeown and F. O'Hagan (compiled by Brian Campbell), *Nor Meekly Serve My Time: The H-Block Struggle 1976–1981* (Belfast: Beyond the Pale Publications, 1994); McKeown, *Out of Time*, pp. 57–8; 88–92; Moloney, *Voices From the Grave*, pp. 222–5.

23 *Ibid.*, pp. 212–4; P. O'Malley, *Biting at the Grave: The Irish Hunger Strikes and the Politics of Despair* (Boston: Beacon Press, 1990), pp. 45–6; McKeown, *Out of Time*, pp. 64–5; 'Bobby Sands, MP' (Bobby Sands Trust), http://www.bobbysandstrust.com/bobbysands (last accessed 11/01/2017).

24 See Campbell, McKeown and O'Hagan, *Nor Meekly Serve My Time*, pp. 45–6; O'Hearn, *Nothing But An Unfinished Song*, pp. 200–1; 'Four years on the blanket', *Iris: The Republican Magazine* 1/2 (1981), p. 6.

25 R. Mooney, 'We need a forward thinking leadership', *The Sunday Journal* – reprinted in *The Pensive Quill*, 9 November 2011.

26 See McKittrick et al., *Lost Lives*, pp. 771, 782–3.

27 See Bell, *The Irish Troubles*, p. 538; Moloney, *Secret History of the IRA*, pp. 241–2, 613; Clarke and Johnston, *Martin McGuinness*, pp. 110–2.

28 Danny Morrison interview, 2001.

29 Danny Morrison interview, 2001. See also, White, *Ruairí Ó Brádaigh*, pp. 268–71.

30 Ruairí Ó Brádaigh interviews, 1996; Danny Morrison interview, 2001.

31 See Moloney, *Secret History of the IRA*, pp. 190–5; Ruairí Ó Brádaigh interviews.

32 Belfast republican 1 interview, 1996.

33 Derry republican 4 interview, 1984.

34 See McKeown, *Out of Time* (2001), pp. 63–6, 86. See also O'Rawe, *Blanketmen*, pp. 45–9; O'Hearn, *Nothing But An Unfinished Song*, p. 214; Moloney, *Voices From the Grave*, pp. 228–30; C. McCauley and S. Moskaleno, *Friction: How Radicalization Happens to Them and Us* (Oxford: OUP, 2011), pp. 106–8.

35 See O'Hearn, *Nothing But An Unfinished Song*, p. 229; Routledge, *John Hume*, p. 157; Mason, *Paying the Price*, pp. 222–7.

36 M. Thatcher, *The Path to Power* (London: Harper Collins, 1995), p. 434; Routledge, *Public Servant Secret Agent*, pp. 316–7.

37 See O'Hearn, *Nothing But An Unfinished Song*, pp. 229–30; Murphy, *Gerry Fitt*, pp. 266–71; Campbell, McKeown and O'Hagan, *Nor Meekly Serve My Time*, pp. 92–3; 'Westminster General Election (NI) – Thursday 3 May 1979', CAIN Web Service, 'Westminster General Election (NI) – Thursday 3 May 1979'.

38 See McKittrick et al., *Lost Lives*, pp. 793–6.

39 'Homily of His Holiness John Paul II', 29 September 1979.

40 See Bell, *The Irish Troubles*, pp. 569–76; 'Irish Republican Army Statement' and 'Statement to the World's Press', *The Irish People*, 20 October 1979, p. 8.

41 See O'Callaghan, *The Informer*, pp. 82–5, 92–7.

42 Seán O'Callaghan interview, 2008.

43 Ruairí Ó Brádaigh interviews, 1996.

44 John Taylor of the Ulster Unionist Party won the third seat with 77,000 votes. Lee, *Ireland 1912–1985*, pp. 464–5; The Referenda of 1973 and 1975, Northern Ireland Elections, http://www.ark.ac.uk/elections/fref70s.htm and http://www.ark.ac.uk/elections/fe79.htm (last accessed 26/07 2016); White, *Ruairí Ó Brádaigh*, p. 282.

45 See Murphy, *Gerry Fitt*, pp. 272–6; Routledge, *John Hume*, pp. 152–60; Devlin, *Straight Left*, pp. 278–83; Farren, *The SDLP*, pp. 137–9, 148–55.

46 Derry republican 4 interview, 1984.

47 'Kieran Nugent Seized', *The Irish People*, 18 August 1979; CAIN Web Service, 'Abstracts on Organizations'; 'H-Block is torture and before long

it will be murder – the Blanketmen', *The Irish People*, 3 November 1979, pp. 8–9; Ross, *Smashing H-Block*, pp. 60–4; Martin Galvin interview, 2013.

48   Gerry Hodgins interview, 1988.

49   Fra McCann interview, 2011.

50   See McKittrick et al., *Lost Lives*, pp. 818–9, 830–1.

51   Brian McDonald interview, 1984.

52   See Bradyet al., *In the Footsteps of Anne*, p. 221; S. Darragh, '*John Lennon's Dead': Stories of Protest, Hunger Strikes, and Resistance* (Belfast: Beyond the Pale Publications, 2011), pp. 60–9.

53   Gerry Hodgins interview, 1988.

54   See Moloney, *Voices From the Grave*, p. 229; O'Rawe, *Blanketmen*, p. 91.

55   See Bean and Hayes, *Republican Voices*, p. 79.

56   Gerry Hodgins interview, 1988.

57   For ten years Seán Ó Brádaigh was employed full-time by Irish Rail and served as Director of Publicity. He saw that Sinn Féin needed a full time Director and also was not interested in a repeat of the negativity of the 1960s and stepped down in 1980. D. Morrison, *Then The Walls Came Down: A Prison Journal* (Cork: Mercier Press, 1999), p. 59; O'Hearn, *Nothing But An Unfinished Song*, pp. 260–2, 271–2.

58   See Moloney, *Voices From the Grave*, pp. 230–5;

59   Brian McDonald interview, 1984.

Chapter 12

1   Belfast republican 4 interview, 1985.

2   See O'Hearn, *Nothing But an Unfinished Song*, pp. 276, 281–2, 290–6; The 14 Hooded Men, 'Seán McKenna'; O'Hearn, *Nothing but an Unfinished Song*, pp. 276, 281; Darragh, '*John Lennon's Dead*', pp. 99–102; 'Tommy McKearney ex hunger striker … on "Bobby Sands 66 Days"', Connolly Media Group, 2016.

3   There was an added complexity in that their conditions were not identical; the women prisoners in Armagh were allowed to wear their own clothes while the men in the H-Blocks were not.

4   Some have claimed that Mary Doyle was a member of Cumann na mBan. See also Ní Chathmhaoil and Reinisch, *Cumann na mBan* (2014).

5   See Holland and McDonald, *INLA: Deadly Divisions*, pp. 173–5; Tony O'Hara comment, 'Sorry Initiatives and Prime Time Apologies', *The Pensive Quill* (Martin Galvin letter), 5 May 2013; O'Hearn, *Nothing But an Unfinished Song*, p. 277; Moloney, *Voices From the Grave*, p. 236.

6   See O'Rawe, *Blanketmen*, p. 103; O'Hearn, *Nothing But an Unfinished Song*, pp. 275–6; D. Beresford, *Ten*

Men Dead: The Story of the 1981 Irish Hunger Strike (London: Grafton, 1987), p. 337.

7   See O'Hearn, *Nothing But An Unfinished Song*, pp. 278–9, 282–3; O'Rawe, *Blanketmen*, pp. 108–11.

8   See O'Rawe, *Blanketmen*, pp. 103–5.

9   Caoimhghín Ó Caoláin interview, 1996.

10   Brian McDonald interview, 1984.

11   See the *Irish Times*, 20 July 1981, p. 6.

12   See Darragh, '*John Lennon's Dead*', pp. 104–5.

13   See O'Malley, *Biting at the Grave*, p. xi.

14   See Farren, *The SDLP*, pp. 160–5; Bell, *The Irish Troubles*, pp. 600–3; M. Thatcher, *The Downing Street Years, 1979–90* (New York: Harper Collins, 1993), pp. 390–1; CAIN Web Service, 'A Chronology of the Conflict – 1980'.

15   See O'Hearn, *Nothing But an Unfinished Song*, pp. 292–7; O'Rawe, *Blanketmen*, p. 108; O'Rawe, *Afterlives*, p. 106.

16   See O'Hearn, *Nothing But An Unfinished Song*, pp. 296–7; O'Rawe, *Blanketmen*, pp. 106–11.

17   See Taylor, *Behind the Mask*, p. 272.

18   B. Hughes, 'Risking the Lives of Volunteers is not the IRA Way', letter to *Irish News*, 13 July 2006; Taylor, *Behind the Mask*, p. 273; O'Hearn, *Nothing But an Unfinished Song*, pp. 297–8; Moloney, *Voices from the Grave*, pp. 237–40; 'Tommy McKearney ex hunger striker … on "Bobby Sands 66 Days"', Connolly Media Group, 2016.

19   See O'Hearn, *Nothing But an Unfinished Song*, pp. 300–1; Taylor, *Behind the Mask*, p. 274; O'Rawe, *Blanketmen*, pp. 106–11; O'Rawe, *Afterlives*, pp. 106–7; Beresford, *Ten Men Dead*, pp. 44–5.

20   See Darragh, '*John Lennon is Dead*', pp. 109–13.

21   See Ross, *Smashing H-Block*, p. 103; O'Rawe, *Blanketmen*, p. 122; O'Hearn, *Nothing But an Unfinished Song*, pp. 300–2.

22   The McAliskey attack fit a pattern suggesting past or current IRSP and INLA activists were targeted, including Miriam Daly, Ronnie Bunting, and Noel Lyttle. There was speculation that the security forces were colluding with loyalists and seeking retribution for Airey Neave. See Holland and McDonald, *INLA Deadly Divisions*, pp. 155–60; Routledge, *Public Servant Secret Agent*, pp. 339–47; Ross, *Smashing H-Block*, pp. 111–12; R. Murray, *The SAS in Ireland* (Cork: Mercier Press, 1990), pp. 259–64; McKittrick et al., *Lost Lives*, pp. 849–50; Beresford, *Ten Men Dead*, pp. 48–50.

23   See O'Rawe, *Blanketmen*, pp. 115–16.

24   Early in 1973, Ruairí Ó Brádaigh was convicted of IRA membership. As such, he was willing to discuss his involvement up to 1972. To the author's

knowledge, Ó Brádaigh did not comment on post-1972 IRA membership and never confirmed nor denied post-1972 membership on the Army Council. See O'Rawe, *Afterlives*, pp. 75–81; Moloney, *Secret History of the IRA*, pp. 194, 200–1, 214; Clarke and Johnston, *Martin McGuinness*, p. 127.

25 'Seán McKenna – Autobiography – Voice from the Grave', *The Irish Observer*, 4 August 2013; Ross, *Smashing H-Block*, pp. 113–14; Adams, *Before the Dawn*, p. 285.

26 Ruairí Ó Brádaigh interviews, 1996.

27 O'Rawe, *Blanketmen*, pp. 116–9.

28 As described by Danny Morrison, when Bobby Sands went on hunger strike, 'he made a will. Which Pat Finucane signed. And Bobby signed. And basically he bequeathed all his writings to the Republican Movement.' The 'Bobby Sands Trust' holds the copyright on Sands's writings and several photographs. According to the Trust's web site (http://www.bobbysandstrust.com/ (last accessed 12/01/2017), the initial members were Gerry Adams, Tom Cahill (Joe's brother), Danny Devenny, Tom Hartley, Danny Morrison and Marie Moore. The members at the time of writing are: Adams, Síle Darragh, Jim Gibney, Hartley, Bik McFarlane, Peter Madden (of the law firm Madden & Finucane), Morrison and Caral Ní Chulilinn. Morrison is the Trust's Secretary. Bobby Sands's sisters Marcella and Bernadette were, at one time, members of the Trust. The Sands family is no longer involved and has called on the Trust 'to disband and desist from using Bobby's memory as a commercial enterprise'. Danny Morrison interview, 2014; 'Sands Family Responds to Publication of Book – "Bobby Sands Freedom Fighter"', *The Pensive Quill*, 25 February 2016. See also Danny Morrison's web site ('Danny Morrison: Writer. "Biography"').

29 See O'Hearn, *Nothing But An Unfinished Song*, p. 321.

30 Tony O'Hara comment, 'Sorry Initiatives and Prime Time Apologies', *The Pensive Quill*, 14 May 2013.

31 See O'Rawe, *Afterlives*, pp. 62–7; O'Rawe, *Blanketmen*, pp. 109–11, 121–2, 128, 158–60; Beresford, *Ten Men Dead*, pp. 143–60.

32 'Four years on the Blanket', *Iris: IRA salute martyred dead* 1/2 (1981), p. 7; O'Rawe, *Blanketmen*, pp. 122–4.

33 See O'Rawe, *Blanketmen*, pp. 125–6.

34 See Adams, *Before the Dawn*, p. 292.

35 Cathleen Knowles interview, 2009. Unfortunately, I have been unable to interview Gerry Adams and discuss this issue. Others place the idea with Bernadette Devlin McAliskey. David Beresford states that Adams 'floated the idea'. Several people may have come up with the idea independently, but compelling evidence suggests Dáithí O'Connell was the first of the republicans to suggest running Sands. See also, White, *Ruairí Ó Brádaigh*, p. 393; O'Rawe, *Blanketmen*, p. 130; Beresford, *Ten Men Dead*, pp. 96–7; B. Feeney, *Sinn Féin: A Hundred Turbulent Years* (Dublin: O'Brien Press, 2002), p. 288; Ross, *Smashing H-Block*, pp. 118–19.

36 Ruairí Ó Brádaigh interview, 1996.

37 Tony O'Hara comment on Martin Galvin, 'Sorry Initiatives and Prime Time Apologies', *The Pensive Quill*, 15 May 2013.

38 See O'Rawe, *Blanketmen*, p. 128; Beresford, *Ten Men Dead*, pp. 209–10.

39 See Beresford, *Ten Men Dead*, pp. 95–8.

40 Owen Carron interview, 1996.

41 Gerry McGeough interview, 2014.

42 Owen Carron interview, 1996.

43 Owen Carron interview, 1996. See Beresford, *Ten Men Dead*, pp. 102–5, 109–10.

44 Cathleen Knowles interview, 2009; D. Beresford, *Ten Men Dead*, p. 98.

45 See Currie, *All Hell Will Break Loose*, p. 320; CAIN Web Service, 'The Hunger Strike of 1981'.

46 See McKittrick et al., *Lost Lives*, p. 854; 'Husband recalls horrific murder', *Londonderry Sentinel*, 17 March 2011.

47 See Bell, *The Irish Troubles*, p. 611.

48 See 'Margaret Thatcher: A Crime is a Crime', YouTube, http://www.youtube.com/watch?v=D7bTsRZh5bk (last accessed 14/07/2014).

49 See O'Hearn, *Nothing But An Unfinished Song*, pp. 366–70; O'Rawe *Blanketmen*, pp. 121–2; Beresford, *Ten Men Dead*, p. 404.

50 'A deep-thinking republican with a great sense of humour', *Iris*, 1/2 (1981), pp. 35–6

51 Derry republican 1 interview, 1985.

52 See McKittrick et al., *Lost Lives*, pp. 861–5.

53 Belfast republican 4 interview, 1985.

54 See *Irish Information: Agenda*.

55 See Adams, *Before the Dawn*, p. 299; CAIN Web Service, Local Government Election (NI) – Wednesday 20 May 1981.

56 Tony O'Hara has commented, 'Whoever in the IRA leadership decided that should hang their head in shame as it resulted in Patsy and Ray dying within hours of each other on the same day. To this day I have never got an answer as to why this needless sacrifice happened'. See, 'Sorry Initiatives and Prime Time Apologies', *The Pensive Quill*, 15 May 2013; McKittrick et al., *Lost Lives*, p. 864; 'Patsy O'Hara:

"A determined and courageous Derryman'", *Iris*, 1/2 (1981), p. 33.

57 T. Collins, *The Irish Hunger Strike* (Dublin: White Island, 1986), p. 249.

58 See O'Rawe, *Blanketmen*, pp. 152–3; 'Why we ended the hunger-strike', *Iris*, 1/2 (1981), pp. 23–6.

59 Ruairí Ó Brádaigh interviews, 1996. Richard Behal confirms that the Northerners were still cautious about elections. Richard Behal interview, 2015.

60 'Meeting in Head Office', 29 May 1981 (personal copy). See also, Beresford, *Ten Men Dead*, p. 239; Ross, *Smashing H-Block*, pp. 135–6.

61 See 'Joe McDonnell: "A deep-thinking republican with a great sense of humour'", *Iris*, 1/2 (1981), p. 36; Seán Lynch interview, 2008; Magee, *Tyrone's Struggle* (2011), pp. 270–1; T. Hennessey, *Hunger Strike: Margaret Thatcher's Battle with the IRA 1980–1981* (Dublin: Irish Academic Press, 2014), pp. 268–9.

62 See Hanley and Millar, *The Lost Revolution*, pp. 425–31.

63 Kerry republican, 1984 interview.

64 Sligo republican, 1984 interview.

65 Dublin republican 3 interview, 1984.

66 Sligo republican interview, 1984.

67 Fermanagh republican 2, 1984 interview.

68 'Irish Commission for Justice and Peace', *Iris: IRA salute martyred dead*, 1/2 (1981), p. 14; O'Malley, *Biting at the Grave*, pp. 87–98.

69 Representation of the People Act (1981), http://www.legislation.gov.uk/ukpga/1981/34/introduction/enacted (last accessed 18/07/2014).

70 Mitchel McLaughlin interview, 1990.

71 See O'Malley, *Biting at the Grave*, pp. 91–2.

72 See O'Rawe, *Blanketmen*, pp. 156–71 (esp. pp. 167–71); Beresford, *Ten Men Dead*, pp. 274–5, 292–303.

73 See O'Rawe, *Blanketmen*, pp. 172–83; Hennessey, *Hunger Strike* (2014), pp. 309–14.

74 Morrison states that several of the hunger strikers were present, including Kieran Doherty, Tom McElwee, Kevin Lynch and Mickey Devine. 'Danny Morrison on Richard O'Rawe', *Daily Ireland*, 2 March 2005; D. Beresford, *Ten Men Dead*, p. 294.

75 See O'Malley, *Biting at the Grave*, pp. 96–8.

76 See O'Rawe, *Blanketmen*, pp. 174–83; Beresford, *Ten Men Dead*, pp. 290–2, 296–9.

77 See Adams, *Before the Dawn*, pp. 300–1. Ricky O'Rawe writes that, 'After Joe's death, the line of communication with the British government went dead'. See O'Rawe, *Blanketmen*, p. 191.

78 See McKittrick et al., *Lost Lives*, pp. 869–71; Beresford, *Ten Men Dead*, pp. 307–10; Adams, *Before the Dawn*, pp. 303–4; *Irish Times*, 11 July 1981, p. 7.

79 See O'Rawe, *Blanketmen*, pp. 158–60; Beresford, *Ten Men Dead*, pp. 338–44, 416–7.

80 Kerry republican interview, 1984.

81 Dublin republican 2 interview, 1984.

82 '1981: Violence erupts at Irish hunger strike protest', *BBC on This Day*, 18 July 1981; CAIN Chronology, '1981'.

83 Brendan Duddy Archive, Pol35/166 (19), James Hardiman Library, National University of Ireland, Galway, htttp://archives.library.nuigalway.ie/duddy/web/ (last accessed 12/01/2017).

84 See O'Rawe, *Blanketmen*, pp. 210–6.

85 Adams and the others visited Kieran Doherty but Kevin Lynch was too ill for visitors. They saw Lynch's father in a waiting room. He asked, 'You are responsible my son is dying there ... Why don't you take them off it? Adams replied, 'I can't take him off, but you can.' Mr Lynch then said, 'To raise a son and see him die like this!' Adams did not pursue the exchange. See Beresford, *Ten Men Dead*, pp. 344–7; O'Rawe, *Blanketmen*, pp. 226–30; Campbell, McKeown and O'Hagan, *Nor Meekly Serve My Time*, pp. 235–6.

86 See O'Rawe, *Blanketmen*, p. 231.

87 *Ibid.*, pp. 195–230; Beresford, *Ten Men Dead*, pp. 407–22; Ross, *Smashing H-Block*, p. 145; 'Why we ended the hunger-strike', *Iris*, 1/2 (1981), pp. 23–6.

88 'Owen Carron: MP Denied Visa', *The Irish People*, 4 October 1981, p. 1; A. Hegarty, *Kevin Lynch and the Irish Hunger Strike* (Camlane Press, 2006), p. 141.

89 'Seán McKenna – Autobiography – Voice from the Grave', *The Irish Observer*, 4 August 2013; Beresford, *Ten Men Dead*, pp. 417–22; 'Why we ended the hunger-strike', *Iris*, 1/2 (1981), pp. 23–6; O'Rawe, *Blanketmen*, p. 239.

90 Gerry Hodgins interview, 1988.

91 Raymond McCreesh (arrested in 1976 and sentenced to fourteen years), with remission, would have been released in 1983. A. Sanders, *Inside the IRA: Dissident Republicans and the War for Legitimacy* (University of Edinburgh Press, 2011), p. 152.

92 Gerry Hodgins interview, 1988.

93 Another volunteer on the operation with Doherty and Farrell was Seán McDermott, who was killed that day. See White, 'Commitment, efficacy, and personal sacrifice among Irish Republicans', *Journal of Political and Military Sociology* 16 (1988), pp. 77–90; Hegarty, *Kevin Lynch and the Irish Hunger Strike*, pp. 56, 80, 85, 135; Beresford, *Ten Men Dead*; Collins, *The Irish Hunger Strike*, pp. 506–7.

94 Darragh, *'John Lennon's Dead'*, pp. 21–2.

95 Gerry Hodgins interview, 1988.

96   See Ross, *Smashing H-Block*, p. 164.

97   Laurence McKeown's account of the 29 July meeting in *Nor Meekly Serve My Time* is contradicted in David Beresford's *Ten Men Dead*. According to McKeown, Gerry Adams told Kieran Doherty's parents, 'there was no deal on the table from the Brits, no movement of any sort' (p. 236). Beresford writes of Adams at the meeting, 'He spelt out in detail – based on his direct contacts with the Mountain Climber – what was on offer from the Government' (p. 345). Carrie Twomey has compiled two comprehensive resources on the issue: 'July 1981 Uncovering the Truth About the 1981 Hunger Strike', http://www.longkesh.info/ (last accessed 12/01/2017) and '55 Hours', http://thepensivequill.am/p/55-hours-day-by-day-account-of-events.html (last accessed 12/01/2017). See O'Rawe, *Blanketmen*, pp. 174–84, 188, 250–9; O'Rawe, *Afterlives*, pp. 16–24, 78–87, 183–8, 194; Beresford, *Ten Men Dead*, pp. 293–302, 344–7; Campbell, McKeown and O'Hagan, *Nor Meekly Serve My Time*, pp. 235–6.

98   'Danny Morrison on Richard O'Rawe', 2 March 2005, *Daily Ireland*.

99   Steven McCaffrey, 'Former comrades war of words over hunger-strike', 12 March 2005, *Irish News*; O'Rawe, *Afterlives*, pp. 38–40.

100   See Beresford, *Ten Men Dead*, p. 295.

101   See Hennessey, *Hunger Strike*, pp. 463–4; G. Hodgins, 'All Evidence Points to Dark Dealings: The Hunger Strike', *Irish News*, 29 September 2009.

102   See O'Rawe, *Afterlives*, pp. 3, 75–82, 103–17, 194.

Chapter 13

1   Tyrone republican 4 interview, 1996.

2   See Ross, *Smashing H-Block*, pp. 180–1.

3   *Sinn Féin: A Century of Struggle Céad Bliain ar son na saoirse* (Dublin: Sinn Féin, 2005), p. 185.

4   See White, *Ruairí Ó Brádaigh*, p. 284.

5   Ruairí Ó Brádaigh interviews, 1996; Seán Mac Stiofáin interview, 1997; M. Devine, 'MacStiofain leaves Sinn Fein', *Belfast Telegraph*, 25 November 1981.

6   '2 I.R.A. leaders arrested while trying to enter U.S. illegally', *New York Times*, 22 January 1982; Martin Galvin interview, 2012.

7   See Lee, *Ireland, 1912–1985*, pp. 507–8.

8   Ruairí Ó Brádaigh interview, 1996.

9   See Feeney, *Sinn Féin*, pp. 304–6.

10   Tony Gregory went with 'Official' Sinn Féin in 1970 and flirted with the IRSP before becoming an independent. Hanley and Millar, *The Lost Revolution*, pp. 435–7; R. Gilligan, *Tony Gregory* (Dublin: The O'Brien Press, 2011), pp. 34–6, 38, 73–90; Lee, *Ireland*, pp. 506–10.

11   Ruairí Ó Brádaigh interview, 1996.

12   See Bew and Gillespie, *Northern Ireland: A Chronology of the Troubles*, pp. 164–5; Thatcher, *The Downing Street Years*, pp. 173–235 225–6, quotation pp. 393–4; White, *Ruairí Ó Brádaigh*, p. 286 and references within; FitzGerald, *All in a Life*, p. 460.

13   See Lee, *Ireland: 1912–1985*, pp. 509–10; Hanley and Millar, *The Lost Revolution*, pp. 450–51; Gilligan, *Tony Gregory*, pp. 100–1.

14   Tyrone republican 4 interview, 1996.

15   Bradley and Feeney, *Insider: Gerry Bradley's Life in the IRA* (Dublin: O'Brien Press, 2008), pp. 209–10.

16   Andrew Boyd states that thirty-five people were convicted on the word of Christopher Black. A. Boyd, *The Informers: A Chilling Account of the Supergrasses in Northern Ireland* (Cork: Mercier Press, 1984), p. 56. See also, Bradley and Feeney, *Insider*, pp. 209–10; O'Callaghan, *The Informer*, p. 128; T. Gifford, *Supergrasses, the use of accomplice evidence in Northern Ireland: a report* (London: Cobden Trust 1984), p. 29; 'Interview: Jim Gibney, Frontline: THE IRA AND SINN FEIN'; Danny Morrison, 'Happy Birthday, Jim'.

17   See Thatcher, *The Downing Street Years*, p. 151; Bew and Gillespie, *Northern Ireland A Chronology of the Troubles*, p. 164; 'Sinn Féin and the Assembly elections,' *Iris*, 4 (November 1982), pp. 6–9.

18   See Clarke and Johnston, *Martin McGuinness*, pp. 133–4; Moloney, *Secret History of the IRA*, pp. 242–3; O'Callaghan, *The Informer*, pp. 128–9.

19   Mitchel McLaughlin interview, 1990.

20   See Feeney, *Sinn Féin*, p. 310; Northern Ireland Elections, http://www.ark.ac.uk/elections/fa82.htm (last accessed 01/09/ 2014).

21   See Feeney, *Sinn Féin*, p. 312.

22   Mitchel McLaughlin interview, 1990.

23   Derry republican 3 interview, 1984.

24   'Peter Corrigan: 1934–1982,' Armagh Comhairle Ceantair and Armagh Sinn Féin Republican Youth, n.d.; McKittrick et al., *Lost Lives*, p. 918.

25   'They were our volunteers – IRA,' *AP/RN*, 18 November 1982, p. 12; McKittrick et al., *Lost Lives*, pp. 918–21; J. Stalker, *The Stalker Affair: The Shocking True Story of Six Deaths and a Notorious Cover-Up* (New York: Viking, 1988), pp. 65–70; McKittrick et al., *Lost Lives*, pp. 920–31; CAIN Web Service, B. Rolston, 'Unfinished Business: State Killings and the Quest for Truth'.

26   In 1971, Tom McNulty (see Chapter 6) suspected there was an informer problem but the issue was

not pursued. It was a serious mistake, as shown by the losses in Tyrone. See Appendix 2; McNulty, *Exiled*, pp. 63–4; Jordan, *Milestones in Murder*, pp. 25–7;

27 M. Mac Donncha, 'Mick Timothy,' *AP/RN*, February 2015, p. 20.

28 'The ballot bomb' and 'Sinn Féin and the Assembly, elections,' *Iris*, 4, November 1982, pp. 3–5, 6–9; 'Visiting Belfast,' *AP/RN*, 3 March 1983, p. 1; M. Armstrong, 'Belfast welcome for GLC leader,' *AP/RN*, 3 March 1983, pp. 2–3.

29 Caoimhghín Ó Caoláin interview, 1996.

30 Seán Crowe interview, 1996.

31 Sligo republican interview, 1984.

32 See for example Feeney, *Sinn Féin*, pp. 322–3.

33 Ruairí Ó Brádaigh interview, 1996.

34 See White, *Ruairí Ó Brádaigh*, p. 286–90, and the references therein.

35 'KERR TAKES SEAT: Historic Occasion in Omagh,' *AP/RN*, 7 April 1983, p. 2; 'Another first for Sinn Féin,' *AP/RN*, 7 July 1983, p. 3; Murphy, *Gerry Fitt*, pp. 312–7; CAIN Web Service, 'Westminster General Election (NI) Thursday 9 June 1983'.

36 Kevin Burke, 'Sinn Fein in London', *AP/RN*, 28 July 1983, pp. 6–7.

37 B. McCaffrey, *Alex Maskey: Man and Mayor* (Belfast: The Brehon Press, 2003), pp. 55–6.

38 See FitzGerald, *All in a Life*, pp. 496–7.

39 *Ibid.*, p. 463; Bell, *The Irish Troubles*, pp. 668–72; CAIN Web Service, 'New Ireland Forum Report,' 2 May 1984.

40 See FitzGerald, *All in a Life*, pp. 463 (quotation), 470, 493, 500.

41 McKittrick et al., *Lost Lives*, pp. 948-9; Asmal et al., *Shoot to Kill?*, p. 150.

42 Derry republican 1 interview, 1985.

43 At the time of Thain's conviction, there were an estimated 400 Irish republican prisoners serving life sentences. In 1989, the average time served by life prisoners was more than thirteen years. *Irish Information: Agenda* (1989), pp. 94–103; Asmal et al., *Shoot to Kill*, pp. 135–50; McKittrick et al., *Lost Lives*, pp. 948–9; 'Life Sentence and SOSP Prisoners in Northern Ireland', The Committee on the Administration of Justice, Pamphlet No. 12, February 1989, http://www.caj.org.uk/files/2011/02/01/Life_sentence_and_SOSP_prisoners_in_NI_1989.pdf (last accessed 29/08/2014); McKittrick et al., *Lost Lives*, p. 335.

44 Tyrone republican 4 interview, 1996.

45 Thirty-eight prisoners were on the escape. Of the nineteen successful escapees, several were

rearrested, three died on active service (Pádraig McKearney, Seamus McElwaine and Kieran Fleming) and others fled the country (at least two surfaced in the United States). G. Kelly, *the escape: The Inside Story of the 1983 Escape from Long Kesh Prison* (M&G Publications, 2013), see pp. 281–308; Bell, *The Irish Troubles*, p. 675; M. Armstrong, 'TWO IRISH HEROES LAID TO REST,' *AP/RN*, 8 December 1983, pp. 8–9.

46 See Moloney, *Secret History of the IRA*, pp. 242–3.

47 Ruairí Ó Brádaigh interview, 1984.

48 See Moloney, *Secret History of the IRA*, p. 243; O'Callaghan, *The Informer*, pp. 161, 183–4.

49 See Conway, *Southside Provisional*, p. 172.

50 See Moloney, *Secret History of the IRA*, p. 242; Don Tidey kidnapping: McKittrick et al., *Lost Lives*, pp. 968–9; 'Tidey tells court of kidnap ordeal in McFarlane trial', breakingnews.ie, 6 December 2008.

51 'Sinn Féin – the most progressive political force on this island', *AP/RN*, 17 November 1983, p. 11.

52 'New Ard Chomhairle', *AP/RN*, 17 November 1983, p. 7.

53 The Ard Fheis also passed a motion that, 'no aspect of the constitution and rules be closed to discussion'. Feeney, *Sinn Féin*, p. 326; 'Presidential Address', *AP/RN*, 17 November 1983, pp. 8–9; 'Gerry Adams' Address to Ard Fheis 1983', author's photocopy.

Chapter 14

1 Derry republican 1 interview, 1985.

2 See O'Callaghan, *The Informer*, pp. 172–3; 'Paddy Ryan', *Saoirse*, February 2010, p. 12; Moloney, *Secret History of the IRA*, p. 243; Conway, *Southside Provisional*, p. 190.

3 '1984: Sinn Fein leader shot in street attack', *BBC On This Day*, 14 March 1984; Adams, *Before the Dawn*, p. 319.

4 'Harmonising political and military strategies', *Iris*, 8 (August) 1984, pp. 2–5; J. McHugh, 'Sinn Féin Alone', *Politico: Social and Political Issues*, 1 September 1984 (first published in *Magill Magazine*).

5 CAIN Web Service, 'New Ireland Forum Report', 2 May 1984.

6 See Farren, *The SDLP*, p. 192.

7 See FitzGerald, *All in a Life*, p. 492.

8 See Stalker, *The Stalker Affair*, pp. 22–6, 33, 65–70, 84–6.

9 Justice Gibson also acquitted the British soldier who shot 12-year-old Majella O'Hare. CAIN Web Service, Rolston, 'Unfinished Business: State

Killings and the Quest for Truth'; Stalker, *The Stalker Affair*, pp. 1–38, quotation p. 33; 'Ministry of Defence says sorry for killing of Majella O'Hare', *The Guardian*, 27 March 2011; FitzGerald, *Just Garret*, pp. 355–65; FitzGerald, *All in a Life*, pp. 460–527 (p. 506 on Lord Justice Gibson); McKittrick et al., *Lost Lives*, pp. 920–1, 1075–6.

10   '"Steady progress … and an injection of reality" – Adams', *AP/RN*, 21 June 1984, pp. 2–3; CAIN Web Service, 'European Election (NI): Thursday 14 June 1984'.

11   J. Holland, *The American Connection: U.S. Guns, Money, & Influence in Northern Ireland* (New York: Viking Penguin, 1988), pp. 46–7, 93-107; Oppenheimer, *IRA: The Bombs and the Bullets*, pp. 155-7; D. O'Reilly (ed.), *Accepting the Challenge: The Memoirs of Michael Flannery* (Dublin: Cló Saoirse/Irish Freedom Press, 2001), pp. 154–85; Robert McFadden, '5 are acquitted in Brooklyn of plot to run guns to I.R.A.', *New York Times*, 6 November 1982; Moloney, *Secret History of the IRA*, p. 16; Bell, *The Irish Troubles*, pp. 179–80, 324–7.

12   Martin Galvin interview, 2012; 'Tirade Against Noraid', *The Irish People*, 20 August 1983, p. 1; 'Seeing it first hand', *The Irish People*, 20 August 1983, pp. 1, 7; 'Noraid Tour Nationalist Areas of Belfast', *The Irish People*, 27 August 1983, p. 1; 'Noraid group stopped at IRA checkpoint', *The Irish People*, 27 August 1983, p. 8.

13   'The Slaying of John Downes' (Dublin: Republican Publications/Sinn Fein Publicity Department, September 1984), pp. 3–6;

14   Martin Galvin interview, 2012. See also, 'Martin Galvin interviews Gerard Hodgins', *The Pensive Quill*, 20 August 2014.

15   The Downes family was later awarded damages. 'The Slaying of John Downes', pp. 3–6; *Irish Information Agenda*, pp. 120–8; McKittrick et al., *Lost Lives*, pp. 993–4; 'Martin Galvin interviews Gerry Hodgins', *The Pensive Quill*, 20 August 2014; CAIN Web Service, 'Violence – List of People Killed by "Rubber" and "Plastic" Bullets'.

16   Seán O'Callaghan interview, 2008.

17   US Customs found the *Valhalla* in Boston Harbour. The Provisionals' concerns were probably calmed because Bulger's group killed John McIntyre, a suspected informer. 'Trawler's seizure called major setback for I.R.A.', *New York Times*, 30 September 1984; P. Nee (with R. Farrell and M. Blyth), *A Criminal & An Irishman: The Inside Story of the Boston Mob-IRA Connection* (Hanover, New Hampshire: Steerforth Press, 2006), pp. 166–215, esp. pp. 204–5;

O'Callaghan, *The Informer*, pp. 176–85; Barrett, *Man of Kerry*, pp. 129–60.

18   See Oppenheimer, *The IRA: The Bullets and the Bombs*, p. 119.

19   See Thatcher, *The Downing Street Years*, pp. 379–83; McKittrick et al., *Lost Lives*, pp. 995–8; McGladdery, *The Provisional IRA in England*, pp. 126–7; Taylor, *Behind the Mask*, pp. 182–4; Ruán O'Donnell, *Special Category, Vol. 1*, p. 88.

20   'IRA bomb blasts British cabinet', *AP/RN*, 18 October 1984, p. 2.

21   Danny Morrison interview, 1988; Bishop and Mallie, *Provisional IRA*, pp. 426–30.

22   See Thatcher, *The Downing Street Years*, p. 382.

23   *Ibid.*, p. 383.

24   Margaret Thatcher Foundation, '1984 Nov 19 Mo, Margaret Thatcher, Press Conference following Anglo-Irish Summit ("out … out … out")'; Thatcher, *The Downing Street Years*, pp. 396, 400; FitzGerald, *All in A Life*, pp. 460–575; FitzGerald, *Just Garret*, pp. 355–72.

25   See O'Callaghan, *The Informer*, pp. 210–11; Brendan O'Brien, *The Long War*, pp. 128–38; Clarke and Johnston, *Martin McGuinness*, pp. 151–2; L. Clarke, *Broadening the Battlefied: The H-Blocks and the Rise of Sinn Féin* (Dublin: Gill and Macmillan, 1987), pp. 229–31.

26   See O'Callaghan, *The Informer*, pp. 190–1, 214–32; Feeney, *Sinn Féin*, pp. 326–8; Moloney, *Secret History of the IRA*, pp. 243–5. In February 1985, John Hume outmaneuvered Gerry Adams. Adams and Hume were in a radio discussion when Adams asked Hume to meet with Sinn Féin. Hume replied that he would prefer meeting with the IRA, 'Sinn Féin's masters'. It was a bold move. Unionists threatened to boycott the SDLP if Hume met with the Provisional IRA. Dick Spring said the Provisionals should end violence prior to such a meeting. Douglas Hurd complained that meeting with the IRA would give them credibility. Hume was supported by the SDLP and went ahead with the meeting but it was a 'non-event'. The Provisionals insisted on video recording the meeting. Hume refused because the video would be out of his control and might be edited. The episode buttressed Hume's claim that Sinn Féin was controlled by the Provisional IRA. See Farren, *The SDLP*, pp. 201–2, 229.

27   'Electoral goal achieved: Successful intervention', *Iris*, 10 (July 1985), pp. 10–15; 'RELUCTANT RULING', *AP/RN*, 4 July 1983, p. 3; 'Belfast council walk-out', *AP/RN*, 7 November 1985, p. 2.

28   J. Noonan, *What Do I Do Now?* (Dublin: Self Published, 2005), pp. 44–52, 54, 94–8, 115, 121–2.

29   Sligo republican interview, 1984. See also Feeney, *Sinn Féin*, pp. 322–3.

30   'Sinn Féin moving forward', *AP/RN*, 13 June 1985, p. 1; 'For effective local leadership', *AP/RN*, 30 May 1985, pp. 8–9; 'Election '85', *AP/RN*, 6 June 1985, pp. 10–11; Clarke and Johnston, *Martin McGuinness*, p. 152; 'Irish Identity: A Passion for GAA and politics', 8 April 2005.

31   Christy Burke interview, 1996. See also Geróid Phelan, '"The big bluff or double bluff?" Concerned parents against drugs and the Provisional IRA', *History Studies*, 11 (2010), pp. 68–77

32   'Ex-IRA man, anti-drugs campaigner, occasional Joe Dolan impersonator: Meet the Lord Mayor', *the journal.ie*, 21 June 2015; Gilligan, *Tony Gregory*, pp. 147–8; 'Irish Election Literature, 1985 Dublin City Council Results'.

33   *AP/RN*, 19 May 1994; 'MAJORITY EXCLUDED', *AP/RN*, 4 July 1985, p. 6.

34   Peter McAleer interview, 2009.

35   CAIN Web Service, 'Anglo-Irish Agreement – Document'; FitzGerald, *Just Garrett*, pp. 365–72; Garret FitzGerald, *All in a Life*, pp. 494–575; Bell, *The Irish Troubles–*, pp. 696, 708–9.

36   See Bell, *The Irish Troubles*, pp. 710–1; Bew and Gillespie, *Northern Ireland: A Chronology of the Troubles*, pp. 193–4; E. Moloney, *Paisley: From Demagogue to Democrat* (Dublin: Poolbeg Press, 2008), pp. 336–7.

37   See Bew and Gillespie, *Northern Ireland A Chronology of the Troubles*, p. 197; Bell, *The Irish Troubles*, pp. 709–18; 'Elections: Northern Ireland Elections, North Antrim', http://www.ark.ac.uk/elections/ (last accessed 12/01/2017).

38   Sligo republican interview, 1985.

39   Derry republican 1 interview, 1985.

40   See Bell, *The Irish Troubles*, p. 720; Rebecca Black, 'Ian Paisley and Peter Robinson: A very public falling out', *Belfast Telegraph*, 11 January 2014.

41   Martin McGuinness interview, 1991.

42   Mitchel McLaughlin interview, 1990.

43   Danny Morrison interview, 1988.

44   'Electoral Strategy', *AP/RN* 7 November 1985, p. 13; White, *Ruairí Ó Brádaigh*, pp. 297–8.

45   Figure 4 is a reconstruction of the 1985 Sinn Fein Ard Chomhairle based on information found in *AP/RN*, *The Politics of Revolution*, and personal information.

46   The leadership authorized Owen Carron jumping bail. Owen Carron interview, 1996; Angelique Chrisafis, 'IRA fugitives will be free to return home under amnesty scheme', *The Guardian*, 10 November 2005.

47   Derry republican 1 interview, 1985.

Chapter 15

1   Pat Doherty interview, 1992.

2   'Paddy Ryan', *Saoirse*, February 2010, p. 12.

3   The abstentionists also argued that changing the IRA constitution required two conventions. At the first, embargoes on entering Leinster House had to be removed and then, at a second convention, there could be a motion on taking seats in Leinster House. See White, *Ruairí Ó Brádaigh*, pp. 298–302, 309–10.

4   The author assumes that Ó Brádaigh attended the 1986 IRA Convention; if he attended, he would have again made this argument. Ruairí Ó Brádaigh interview, 1984; White, *Ruairí Ó Brádaigh*, pp. 298–9.

5   See Moloney, *Secret History of the IRA*, p. 19; Bell, *The Irish Troubles*, pp. 728–31; Oppenheimer, *IRA: The Bombs and the Bullets*, pp. 137–40, 191–2, 240–3.

6   Tom Murphy has denied IRA membership. W.J. Duiker, *Ho Chi Minh* (New York: Hyperion, 2000), pp. 557–60; Clarke and Johnston, *Martin McGuinness*, pp. 159–66; Moloney, *Secret History of the IRA*, pp. 20–4, 387–9; E. Mallie and D. McKittrick, *The Fight For Peace: The Secret Story Behind The Irish Peace Process* (London: Heineman, 1996), pp. 44-53; Taylor, *Behind the Mask*, pp. 320-2; Maddock, John, 'Informer Identifies Top IRA Personnel', Independent 30 April 1998.

7   See 'Volunteer Seamus Twomey 1919–89: A Tribute', *AP/RN*, n.d.; J.B. Bell, *The Secret Army: The IRA* (Dublin: Poolbeg, 1997 [revised]), p. 576.

8   See 'Historic IRA Convention', *AP/RN*, 16 October 1986, p. 1.

9   Brendan Hughes interview, 2001; Ruairí Ó Brádaigh interview, 1996; Moloney, *Voices From the Grave*, pp. 262–5.

10   Ruairí Ó Brádaigh interview, 2010.

11   'Entering Leinster House: A Veteran Speaks', Republican Sinn Féin literature, n.d.; Ó Brádaigh, *Dílseacht*, p. 65.

12   See White, *Ruairí Ó Brádaigh*, pp. 298–9.

13   Supporters of abstentionism argued that the embargo on discussing Leinster House had to be dropped at one Ard Fheis and then at a second Ard Fheis there could be a motion on whether or not to enter Leinster House. Several sources present speeches from the 1986 Ard Fheis: Linen Hall Library, Political Collection, audio tape; *The Politics of Revolution; 1986 Split: The Provo Desertion* (Dublin: Republican Sinn Féin, 2000); 'Ruairí O Bradaigh: "Never, I say to you,

never'", *Magill*, 13 November 1986, p. 12; CAIN Web Service, 'Abstentionism: Sinn Féin Ard Fheis, 1–2 November 1986 – Details of Source Material'.

14   Frank Glynn interview, 1995.

15   *Ibid.*

16   Mitchel McLaughlin interview, 1990; Bell, *The Irish Troubles*, p. 731-2.

17   See Moloney, *Secret History of the IRA*, p. 296; White, *Ruairí Ó Brádaigh*, p. 397.

18   Karl Mannheim writes that people in the same generation or age group share 'a common location' in the historical social process. This limits them 'to a specific range of potential experience, predisposing them for a certain characteristic mode of thought and experience' (p. 291). A 'generation-unit' develops when differentiated groups of individuals share 'an identity of responses, a certain affinity in the way in which all move with and are formed by their common experiences' (p. 306). Karl Mannheim, 'The Problem of Generations', in *Essays on the Sociology of Knowledge* (London: Routledge & Kegan Paul, 1952 [1928]), pp. 276–322.

19   Figure 5: Sinn Féin Head Office fax, 9 December 1991; personal information.

20   Sharrock and Devenport, *Man of War, Man of Peace*, pp. 68-9; Clarke and Johnston, *Martin McGuinness*, pp. 29-34.

21   Mitchel McLaughlin interview, 1990.

22   Danny Morrison interview, 1988.

23   Pat Doherty interview, 1992.

24   Brian McDonald interview, 1996.

25   Tipperary republican interview, 1996.

26   Dublin republican 5 interview, 1995.

27   J.B. and Bernadette O'Hagan interview, 1996. It would appear that O'Hagan's decision to support taking seats was a last minute one; see Moloney, *A Secret History*, p. 312; McKearney, *From Insurrection to Parliament*, pp. 156–7.

28   Joe Cahill interview, 1990. At an Ard Chomhairle meeting in 1980, Cahill stated, 'I never believed in Federalism. This may come as a surprise to many of you.' Moloney, *Secret History of the IRA*, p. 493–7.

29   See Conway, *Southside Provisional*, pp. 190–1. A respondent who knew Cahill very well (paraphrasing) once commented, 'If there was a new leadership tomorrow, Cahill would be with them'.

30   Figure 6: White, *Provisional Irish Republicans*, pp. 159–60.

31   Frank Glynn interview, 1995.

32   See Cronin, *Irish Nationalism*, p. 292 (note 85).

33   Seán Lynch interview, 1995.

34   A careful analysis suggests that around 130 people assembled at the West County Hotel; 100 or so of them were delegates and the rest were visitors. There were also forty or so reporters. See White, *Ruairí Ó Brádaigh*, p. 308 and accompanying notes; 'The Politics of Revolution', p. 34; Mitchel McLaughlin interview, 1990.

35   Joe Cahill interview, 1990.

36   Mitchel McLaughlin interview, 1990.

37   See Feeney, *Sinn Féin: A Hundred Turbulent Years*, pp. 274–5.

38   Jonathan Powell, *Great Hatred, Little Room: Making Peace in Northern Ireland* (New York: Vintage Books, 2008), p. 47.

39   T. O'Keefe, *Feminist Identity Development and Activism in Revolutionary Movements* (London: Palgrave Macmillan, 2013), p. 17.

40   See also, Ed Moloney's 'Foreword', in White, *Ruairí Ó Brádaigh*; Hanley and Millar, *The Lost Revolution*, pp. 371–4, 429–30, 484–6.

41   O'Hearn, *Nothing But An Unfinished Song*, p. 383. See also McKeown, *Out of Time* (2001), pp. 160–2; A McIntyre, 'Provisional Irish Republicanism: Internal politics, inequities, and modes of repression', in Fearghal McGarry (ed.), *Republicanism in Modern Ireland* (Dublin: University College Dublin Press, 2003), pp. 178–98.

42   'Remembering The Past', *AP/RN*, 1 April 1993, p. 13; Ní Chathmhaoil and Reinisch, *Cumann na mBan*, pp. 102–3; Coogan, *The IRA*, p. 467.

43   *Na Fianna Éireann 1909–2009: Centenary Commemorative Booklet* (Irish Freedom Press, n.d. [probably 2009]), pp. 12–15.

44   See 'About Ogra Shinn Fein' (http://www.sebelfastsinnfein.com/elections, last accessed 4 February 2017).

45   Tipperary republican interview, 1996.

46   Geraldine Taylor interview, 2009.

47   Martin Galvin interview, 2013. See also O'Reilly, *Accepting the Challenge*, pp. 187–8.

48   See the NIFC web pages, http://irishfreedom.net/ (last accessed 22/11/ 2016).

49   The Tom Murphy quotation is from an interview with Des Long presented in Morrison's, *The Origins and Rise of Dissident Irish Republicanism* (pp. 141–3). See also, 'CIRA Bomb Adds to Growing Crisis in the Peace Process, Others say', *Irish Examiner.com*, 2 July 2000; White, *Ruairí Ó Brádaigh*, pp. 309–10.

Chapter 16

1   Danny Morrison interview, 1998.

2   L. Bosi, 'Contextualizing the biographical outcomes of Provisional IRA former activists: A structure-

agency dynamic', forthcoming, in O. Fillieule and E. Neveu (eds), *Activists Forever? The Long-Term Impacts of Political Activism in Various Contexts* (Minneapolis: University of Minnesota Press).

3   See Oppenheimer, *IRA: The Bombs and the Bullets*, pp. 137–44, 169-71, 191–2, 240–3; E. Moloney and A. McIntyre, 'THE SECURITY DEPARTMENT: IRA DEFENSIVE COUNTERINTELLIGENCE IN A 30-YEAR WAR AGAINST THE BRITISH', April 2006.

4   See McKearney, *From Insurrection to Parliament*, pp. 156–7; Moloney, *Voices From the Grave*, pp. 270–88, 294–5; M. Ingram and G. Harkin, *Stakeknife: Britain's Secret Agent in Ireland* (Dublin: O'Brien Press, 2004); Moloney and McIntyre, 'THE SECURITY DEPARTMENT', April 2006, pp. 14–5. Scappaticci denies the allegation.

5   See O'Rawe, *Afterlives*, pp. 64–5.

6   See Bradley and Feeney, *Insider*, pp. 196–9, 201–2.

7   'Presidential Address', *The Politics of Revolution*, p. 13.

8   The Workers' Party had its best showing to date with 67,273 first preference votes (3.8 per cent) and four TDs elected. 'No short-cuts', *AP/RN*, 19 February 1987, p. 1; 'Your 27 Candidates', *AP/RN*, 12 February 1987, p. 6 ; 'Irish General Election 1987', Irish Political Maps, http://irishpoliticalmaps.blogspot.com/2011/06/irish-general-election-1987.html; 'ElectionsIreland.org 1987 25th Dáil 1987' (last accessed 14/01/2017).

9   *A Scenario for Peace*, Sinn Féin, p. 1.

10   See Feeney, *Sinn Féin*, p. 5; *A Scenario for Peace*.

11   See Moloney, *Secret History of the IRA*, pp. 312–5; Clarke and Johnston, *Martin McGuinness*, pp. 163–4; M. Urban, *Big Boys' Rules: The SAS and the Secret Struggle Against the IRA* (London: Faber and Faber, 1992) pp. 220–6; P. Antoine, '*Brigades of the IRA: The East Tyrone Brigade*', 23 April 2014.

12   Appendix 2; McKee and Franey, *Time Bomb*, pp. 192–6, 198–9, 225, 399.

13   Danny Morrison interview, 1988.

14   Rejecting the proposal may have also reflected concerns about Lynagh and McKearney and their opposition to taking seats in Leinster House. See Moloney, *Secret History of the IRA*, pp. 292, 304–14; McKearney, *From Insurrection to Parliament*, pp. 142–5.

15   See S. Hartnett, *Charlie One: The True Story of an Irishman in the British Army and His Role in Covert Counter-Terrorism Operations in Northern Ireland* (Newbrige, Co. Kildare: Merrion Press, 2016), pp. 115–9; Moloney, *Secret History of the IRA*, pp. 315–16; Taylor, *Behind the Mask*, pp. 317–22; Urban, *Big Boys' Rules*, pp. 227–37.

16   See McKittrick et al., *Lost Lives*, pp. 1077–80; Magee, *Tyrone's Struggle*, pp. 344–79.

17   See also *Lost Lives* (pp. 1077-80). Paddy Kelly's wife was pregnant at the time of his death. Appendix 2; 'Vol Declan Arthurs', *AP/RN*, 14 May 1987, p. 10; Magee, *Tyrone's Struggle*, pp. 352, 364; 'Loughall Martyrs', *AP/RN*, 14 May 1987; Moloney, *Secret History of the IRA*, pp. 311–8.

18   Tipperary republican interview, 1996.

19   Paddy Kelly, was born in Carrickfergus and moved to Dungannon at 16, and joined in the 1975-76. If included, there would be 15 who joined the IRA in 1975 or earlier. McKittrick et al, *Lost Lives* (p. 1077-80) show Jim Lynagh from Church Street, Monaghan and Eugene Kelly from Cappagh, Co. Tyrone. Appendix 2; 'Loughall Martyrs, *AP/RN* 14 May 1987, pp. 1, 6-13.

20   Magee, *Tyrone's Struggle*, p. 378.

21   'Heroic Freedom Fighter', *AP/RN*, 14 May 1987, p. 13.

22   Archbishop (now Cardinal) Joseph Tobin interview, 2014;   http://theredemptorists.blogspot.com/p/faqs.html (last accessed 25/12/ 2016).

23   See Moloney, *Secret History of the IRA*, pp. 269–77; Feeney, *Sinn Féin*, pp. 346–8; Seán Farren, *The SDLP*, pp. 229–30; Gerry Adams, *A Farther Shore: Ireland's Long Road to Peace* (New York: Random House, 2003), pp. 43–50, 59–60, 80–2; Archbishop Joseph Tobin interview, 2014.

24   The Ulster Unionists, led by James Molyneaux, won nine seats (276,230 votes; 37.8 per cent), the DUP, led by Revd Ian Paisley, won three seats (85,642 votes; 11.7 per cent) and the Ulster Popular Unionist Party (18,420) won one seat. The Alliance party received 72,761 (10 per cent) and the Workers' Party received 19,294 (2.6 per cent) of the votes. See CAIN Web Service, 'Elections in Northern Ireland'.

25   See Moloney, *Secret History of the IRA*, pp. 8–23, 386–8; Brendan O'Brien, *The Long War*, pp. 143–50; Oppenheimer, *IRA: The Bombs and the Bullets*, pp. 165–9, 297–8; Mallie and McKittrick, *The Fight For Peace*, pp. 49-53.

26   See Patterson, 'Sectarianism Revisited', *TPV*, 22/3, pp. 337–56; White, 'Provisional IRA attacks on the UDR in Fermanagh and South Tyrone', *TPV*, *23/3*, pp. 329–49 and 'Response to Henry Patterson', *TPV*, 23/3, pp. 354–6.

27   Consolatio, 'Gordon Wilson: I have lost my daughter … I shall pray for those people every night'; McKittrick et al., *Lost Lives*, pp. 1095–9; Bew and Gillespie, *Northern Ireland: A Chronology of the Troubles*, p. 210.

28 See Routledge, *John Hume*, p. 216.
29 See Farren, *The SDLP*, pp. 230–2 (note 31, p. 378).
30 See Bew and Gillespie, *Northern Ireland*, p. 214.
31 See: McKittrick et al., *Lost Lives*, pp. 615–6, 1112–6, 1121–3, 1164; Taylor, *Beating the Terrorists*, pp. 318–9; J.B. Bell, 'Career moves: Reflections on the Irish gunman', *Studies in Conflict and Terrorism* 15 (1992), pp. 69–88; N. Eckert, *Fatal Encounter: The Story of the Gibraltar Killings* (Belfast: Poolbeg Press, 1999), pp. 9–22, 56–8, 86–7; O'Brien, *Killing Finucane*, pp. 57–65; Rachel Oppenheimer, '"Inhuman conditions prevailing": The significance of the dirty protest in the Irish Republican prison war', 1978–81, *Éire-Ireland*, 49, 1/2 (2014), pp. 142–63; B. Rolston with M. Gilmartin, *Unfinished Business: State Killings and the Quest for Truth* (Belfast: Beyond the Pale, 2000), pp. 155–74; 'Volunteer Dan McCann', *AP/RN*, 10 March 1988.
32 Brendan Hughes interview, 2001. See R. Alonso, *The IRA and Armed Struggle* (London: Routledge, 2007), pp. 124–5; Moloney, *Secret History of the IRA*, pp. 243–4.
33 D. McKittrick, 'Mary Holland: Campaigning Anglo-Irish Journalist', *The Independent* 10 June 2004.
34 See McKittrick et al., *Lost Lives*, p. 1122.
35 E. Moloney, 'Fr. Alec Reid & The Two Corporals: The Day The RUC Turned A Blind Eye', *The Broken Elbow*, 22 November 2013; O'Brien, *Killing Finucane*, p. 69.
36 See Farren, *The SDLP*, pp. 230–2, 378 (note 31); Feeney, *Sinn Féin*, pp. 348–51.
37 The Martin Mansergh interview was not tape recorded. Extensive notes were taken and then verified via e-mail. Martin Mansergh interview, 2012. See also Adams, *A Farther Shore*, pp. 81–2.
38 Danny Morrison interview, 1988.
39 See McKittrick et al., *Lost Lives*, pp. 1130–1, 1141–3.
40 Danny Morrison interview, 1988. David Halberstam records instances where US military and political leaders assumed the North Vietnamese could not win. D. Halberstam, *The Best and the Brightest* (New York: Random House, 1972), pp. 772–4. See also Bell, *On Revolt*, pp. 119, 260–1.
41 See Adams, *A Farther Shore*, pp. 81–2, 94; Routledge, *John Hume*, p. 230.
42 See O'Callaghan, *The Informer*, pp. 198–224, 228–34.
43 See Thatcher, *The Downing Street Years*, p. 412; D. Miller, *Don't Mention the War: Northern Ireland, Propaganda, and the Media* (Belfast: Pluto Press, 1994), pp. 54–66; Alonso, *The IRA and Armed Struggle*, p. 177; 'Speak No Evil: The Story of the Sinn Féin Broadcast Ban', *BBC Four*, 2005.
44 See O'Brien, *Killing Finucane*, pp. 8–12, 56, 74–5, 78–9, 82–4; Adams, *A Farther Shore*, p. 89; McKittrick et al., *Lost Lives*, p. 1162.
45 See Adams, *A Farther Shore*, p. 89.
46 See McKittrick et al., *Lost Lives*, pp. 1167–8; 'Smithwick Tribunal Key Points', *BBC News*, 4 December 2013.
47 Elected Authorities (Northern Ireland) Act 1989 (http://www.legislation.gov.uk/ukpga/1989/3/contents (last accessed 12/10/2014); 'Sinn Féin Election Challenge', *AP/RN*, 27 April 1989, pp. 8–9.
48 'Elections and abstentionism – 2000', Republican Sinn Fein (2000); 'THE OATH: Candidates Debarred', *Saoirse*, May 1989, p. 1.
49 CAIN Web Service, 'Local Government Election (NI), Wednesday 15 May 1985'; CAIN Web Service, 'Local Government Election (NI), 17 May 1989'.
50 Des Dalton interview, 2009.
51 Brian McDonald interview, 2009. See A.J. Wilson, 'The Conflict between Noraid and the Friends of Irish Freedom', *The Irish Review*, 15 (Spring 1994), pp. 40–50.
52 'Prison Walls Cannot Conquer The Republican Spirit', *An Phoblacht*, 29 October 1972, p. 5.
53 Martin Galvin interview, 2012. See also 'FBI RAID INA NATIONAL OFFICE', 25 May 1991, p. 1.
54 See Oppenheimer, *IRA: The Bombs and the Bullets*, p. 85; McKittrick et al., *Lost Lives*, pp. 908–10, 1179–80.
55 See Bell, *The Irish Troubles*, pp. 770–1; Sister Sarah Clarke, *No Faith in the System: A Search For Justice* (Dublin: Mercier Press, 1995).
56 'Spotlight on British strategy', *AP/RN*, 9 November 1989, p. 9; E. Mallie and D. McKittrick, *The Fight for Peace*, pp. 98–101.

Chapter 17

1 Mitchel McLaughlin interview, 1990.
2 'No thaw in sight' and 'The Four-corner game', *AP/RN*, 25 January 1990, pp. 1, 3; Adams, *A Farther Shore*, p. 94; Powell, *Great Hatred, Little Room*, p. 63; CAIN Events, 'Brooke Mayhew Talks (April 1991 to November 1992).
3 See Moloney, *Secret History of the IRA*, pp. 396–8.
4 On 9 November 1989, undercover RUC officer Ian Johnston was killed by the RUC in North Belfast. Sinn Féin suggested it was a shoot to kill operation that backfired. See McKittrick et al., *Lost Lives*, pp. 1184–5; 'Shoot to Kill Backfires', *AP/RN*, 18 November 1989, p. 4.
5 Danny Morrison interview, 2014.

6   On Easter Sunday, 1990, Eoin Morley was shot dead by the Provisional IRA, an alleged informer. In 2007, the Provisional IRA apologized and admitted the allegation was 'incorrect and totally inaccurate'. See McKittrick et al., *Lost Lives*, pp. 1196–7; 'Morley Family Respond to IRA Statement', *AP/RN*, 12 April 2007; Danny Morrison, *Then the Walls Came Down: A Prison Journal* (Cork: Mercier Press, 1999), p. 11; 'RUC web of deceit: Lynch "Victim of Blackmail" says Family', *AP/RN*, 11 January 1990; Ingram and Harkin, *Stakeknife*, pp. 136–59.

7   See O'Callaghan, *The Informer*, pp. 246–7, 252–3, 259–66.

8   Danny Morrison interview, 2014.

9   Danny Morrison interview, 2014; Morrison, *Then the Walls Came Down*, pp. 188–9.

10 Mitchel McLaughlin interview, 1990.

11 See Brendan Duddy Archive, Éamonn Downey Memorandum, Pol35/227, James Hardiman Library, National University of Ireland, Galway, http:// archives.library.nuigalway.ie/duddy/web/ (last accessed 14/01/2017); Adams, *A Farther Shore*, pp. 94–6; Mallie and McKittrick, *The Fight for Peace*, pp. 102–7; Powell, *Great Hatred, Little Room*, p. 70; 'SETTING THE RECORD STRAIGHT' (Dublin: Sinn Féin, 1994), p. 16.

12 Adams's quote of an IRA spokesperson in *A Farther Shore* (p. 96) is not identical to the *AP/RN* quotation but is essentially the same as that given to journalist David McKittrick about a month later. '"We will win and are set firmly to the task of achieving victory" – IRA', *AP/RN*, 28 June 1990, pp. 2–3; D. McKittrick, 'Long Night's Journey into Day', *The Independent*, 1 September 1994 'Life & Style'.

13 See Adams, *A Farther Shore*, pp. 94–6; 'SETTING THE RECORD STRAIGHT', p. 12..

14 'The British Military Garrison in Ireland', *AP/ RN*, 58 Parnell Square, 1994; T. Harndon, *'Bandit Country': The IRA & South Armagh* (London: Hodder & Stoughton, 2000).

15 Belfast republican 5 interview, 1996.

16 See McKittrick et al., *Lost Lives*, pp. 1207–10.

17 'Bishop rebukes I.R.A. for car bomb attacks', *New York Times* Archives, 28 October 1990; Taylor, *Behind the Mask*, pp. 366–7; Moloney, *Secret History of the IRA*, pp. 347–8; McKittrick et al., *Lost Lives*, pp. 1214–6; S. Pogatchnik, 'IRA Proxy Bombings Kill 6 Troops, Civilian: Northern Ireland', *Los Angeles Times*, 25 October 1990.

18 Taylor (*Talking to Terrorists*, pp. 33-4) and Powell (*Great Hatred, Little Room*, pp. 71-2) have the meeting in early 1991, after Thatcher left office, but McGuinness ('SETTING THE RECORD STRAIGHT', pp. 12, 17) has it in October 1990, before she left office. See also, N. Ó Dochartaigh, 'The Longest Negotiation', *Political Studies* 63 (2015), pp. 202–20.

19 See Adams, *A Farther Shore*, p. 98; 'SETTING THE RECORD STRAIGHT', pp. 11–2, 17; Brendan Duddy Archive, Éamonn Downey Memorandum, Pol35/227, James Hardiman Library, National University of Ireland, Galway, http://archives. library.nuigalway.ie/duddy/web/ (last accessed 14/- 1/2017); Powell, *Great Hatred, Little Room*, pp. 70–1.

20 Martin McGuinness interview, 1991; see also Taylor, *Talking to Terrorists*, 33-4;.

21 See Adams, *A Farther Shore*, p. 98; see also *AP/RN*, 14 March 1991, p. 6.

22 Brendan Duddy Archive, Éamonn Downey Memorandum, Pol35/231(1), James Hardiman Library, National University of Ireland, Galway, http://archives.library.nuigalway.ie/duddy/web/ (last accessed 14/01/2017); Mallie and McKittrick, *The Fight for Peace*, pp. 134–8, 150–1.

23 Because of a mix-up Major did not receive the letter until February 1991. See Adams, *A Farther Shore*, p. 100.

24 *AP/RN*, 14 February 1991, p. 9; Bell, *The Irish Troubles*, pp. 784–6; McGladdery, *The Provisional IRA in England*, p. 229.

25 Sinn Féin interview, 1991.

26 See Adams, *A Farther Shore*, p. 107.

27 See McKittrick et al., *Lost Lives*, pp. 588–9, 1236– 7, 1249, 1263, 1267, 1296; English, *Does Terrorism Work?*, p. 112.

28 See Mallie and McKittrick, *The Fight for Peace*, pp. 151–2; McKittrick et al., *Lost Lives*, pp. 1268–71, 1277–80.

29 See 'SETTING THE RECORD STRAIGHT', p. 17; Adams, *A Farther Shore*, pp. 102–3.

30 See *Towards a lasting peace in Ireland*, Sinn Féin (1992), pp. 2, 9, 11 (an amended version (1994) is on the Sinn Féin web site); Mallie and McKittrick, *The Fight for Peace*, pp. 138–46; Adams, *A Farther Shore*, p. 108; Feeney, *Sinn Féin*, pp. 378–80.

31 See Reynolds, *Albert Reynolds*, p. 198 (see also pp. 142–7, 150); Mallie and McKittrick, *The Fight for Peace*, p. 181; Adams, *A Farther Shore*, p. 129.

32 B. O'Leary and J. McGarry, *The Politics of Antagonism* (Atlantic Highland, NJ, 1993), pp. 320, 326 note 16; Mallie and McKittrick, *The Fight for Peace*, pp. 152–3.

33 See Bew and Gillespie, *Northern Ireland: A Chronology of the Troubles*, p. 258.

34 See Morrison, *Then the Walls Came Down*, pp. 288–93.

35   Martin Galvin interview, 2012; 'Clinton-Brown at Irish Forum', *The Irish People*, 11 April 1992, pp. 1–14.

36   See Adams, *A Farther Shore*, p. 150; Bill Clinton, *My Life* (New York: Alfred A. Knopf, 2004), pp. 433, 578–80; Powell, *Great Hatred, Little Room*, p. 78.

37   *Operation Banner: An Analysis of Military Operations in Northern Ireland*, prepared under the direction of the Chief of the General Staff, British Ministry of Defence, 'ATTACK ON PERMANENT VEHICLE CHECK POINT R15' (2006), p. 5–2; McKittrick et al., *Lost Lives*, p. 1992.

38   See Farren, *The SDLP*, p. 283; Albert Reynolds, *My Autobiography* (Dublin: Transworld Ireland, 2009), pp. 201–5; Mallie and McKittrick, *The Fight for Peace*, pp. 150–1, 375–7; Moloney, *Secret History of the IRA*, p. 410.

39   Gerard Murray and Jonathan Tonge, *Sinn Féin and the SDLP: From Alienation to Participation* (London: Palgrave Macmillan, 2005), p. 181.

40   See 'It is our job to develop the struggle for freedom', *AP/RN*, 25 June 1992, pp. 8–9; Mallie and McKittrick, *The Fight for Peace*, p. 145; G. Murray and J. Tonge, *Sinn Féin and the SDLP: From Alienation to Participation* (London: Palgrave Macmillan, 2005), p. 281; White, *Ruairí Ó Brádaigh*, pp. 274–5.

41   Elliott and Flackes, *Northern Ireland: A Political Directory*, p. 656–7.

42   Reynolds, *My Autobiography*, pp. 200–5.

43   Martin Mansergh interview, 2012.

44   See 'SETTING THE RECORD STRAIGHT', p. 21; Adams, *A Farther Shore*, pp. 99, 104–5; G. Kelly, *The Escape* (M&G Publications, 2013), pp. 290–1, 297–8.

45   H. McDonald and J. Cussack, *UVF* (Dublin: Poolbeg Press, 1997), pp. 292–9, 332–3.

46   See Reynolds, *Albert Reynolds*, pp. 195–203; Mallie and McKittrick, *The Fight for Peace*, pp. 156–66; ElectionsIreland.org, '27th Dail 1992'; 'Sinn Féin General Election 1992', *AP/RN*, 19 November 1992, pp. 6–7.

47   See Powell, *Great Hatred, Little Room*, pp. 71–3; Taylor, *Behind the Mask*, p. 379.

48   It remains unclear who sent this message. One suggestion is it was an attempt by Denis Bradley to help move things forward. See Powell, *Great Hatred, Little Room*, pp. 72–3; O. Bennett-Jones, 'What Fred Did', *London Review of Books*, 37/2, 22 January 2015, pp. 3–6.

49   See for example, McKittrick et al., *Lost Lives*, pp. 1314–7; Mallie and McKittrick, *The Fight for Peace*, pp. 166–8.

50   D. McKittrick, '"40 more years of violence": Unionists condemn secret IRA meeting that leaves

Gordon Wilson with somber message for Northern Ireland', *Independent*, 23 October 2011; Mallie and McKittrick, *The Fight for Peace*, pp. 168–9; 'IRA Meets Gordon Wilson', *AP/RN*, 8 April 1993, p. 1.

51   Revd Harold Good interview, 2014.

52   See 'SETTING THE RECORD STRAIGHT'; Jonathan Powell, *Great Hatred, Little Room*, p. 72; Mallie and McKittrick, *The Fight for Peace*, pp. 238–44.

53   See Routledge, *John Hume*, p. 245; Holland, *Hope Against History*, p. 183; Moloney, *Secret History of the IRA*, p. 411; Mallie and McKittrick, *The Fight for Peace*, pp. 6–7, 172–3.

54   See 'SETTING THE RECORD STRAIGHT', pp. 31–4.

55   See Clinton, *My Life*, p. 401; Mallie and McKittrick, *The Fight for Peace*, pp. 279–82; Adams, *A Farther Shore*, p. 150.

56   See McKittrick et al., *Lost Lives* , pp. 1304, 1323, 1328–35; Moloney, *Secret History of the IRA*, p. 415; Mallie and McKittrick, *The Fight for Peace*, pp. 201–3, 212.

57   See 'SETTING THE RECORD STRAIGHT', pp. 1, 11; Mallie and McKittrick, *The Fight for Peace*, pp. 203, 234–8, 258–65, 272; Adams, *A Farther Shore*, pp. 138–9; Powell, *Great Hatred, Little Room*, pp. 72–3; Taylor, *Behind the Mask*, pp. 393–5; Bew and Gillespie, *Northern Ireland A Chronology of the Troubles*, p. 281.

58   CAIN Web Service, 'Joint Declaration on Peace: The Downing Street Declaration, Wednesday 15 December 1993'.

59   See Moloney, *Paisley*, pp. 339–40.

60   See Moloney, *Secret History of the IRA*, pp. 416–8; Powell, *Great Hatred, Little Room*, pp. 76–7; 'Disappointment among nationalists over declaration', *AP/RN*, 16 December 1993, p. 3.

61   *Saoirse*, January 1994, p. 16.

62   'Final Salute to Comdt General Tom Maguire', *Saoirse*, February 1994, p. 2; White, *Ruairí Ó Brádaigh*, pp. 323–4.

63   See Mallie and McKittrick, *The Fight for Peace*, p. 277; Adams, *A Farther Shore*, pp. 144, 158–9, 163–4.

64   Henry McDonald, *Gunsmoke and Mirrors* (Dublin: Gill and Macmillan, 2008), pp. 94–5; Mallie and McKittrick, *The Fight for Peace*, pp. 296–7; McKittrick et al., *Lost Lives*, pp. 1363–8.

65   Belfast republican 6 interview; names are psuedonyms.

66   'Irish Political Prisoners Information Package', Irish Northern Aid, May 1993.

67   See Moloney, *Secret History of the IRA*, p. 431; 'Negative and contradictory elements', 'Declaration

was stage in the process – now time to advance', 28 *AP/RN*, July 1998, pp. 8–9; 'IRA given Sinn Féin view', *AP/RN*, 4 August 1994, p. 1.

68 See Adams, *A Farther Shore*, pp. 163, 171–2; Mallie and McKittrick, *The Fight for Peace*, pp. 381–2; Moloney, *Secret History of the IRA*, pp. 423–5, 498.

69 See Moloney, *Secret History of the IRA*, pp. 426–7; J. Holland and S. Phoenix, *Phoenix: Policing the Shadows* (London: Hodder and Stoughton, 1996), pp. 205–6.

70 See McKittrick et al., *Lost Lives*, pp. 1362, 1377–8.

71 See Adams, *A Farther Shore*, pp. 177–8.

Chapter 18

1 Anthony McIntyre, 'The Imperfect Peace: Terence O'Neill's Day has Come', *The Blanket (Belfast Telegraph)*, 18 August 2004.

2 See Adams, *A Farther Shore*, pp. 179–80; Bew and Gillespie, *Northern Ireland Chronology*, p. 293.

3 Henry McDonald, *Trimble* (London: Bloomsbury, 2000), p. 136; Andrew Roth, '"David Trimble": Andrew Roth's Parliament Profiles', *The Guardian*, 25 March 2001.

4 See Cusack and McDonald, *UVF*, p. 315.

5 'Tony Catney Sharing his Political Thoughts', *The Pensive Quill*, 13 August 2014; E. Moloney, 'Tony Catney: Some Musings on the Irish Peace Process', *The Broken Elbow*, 20 August 2014.

6 Belfast republican 6 interview, 1996.

7 Joe Lynch interview, 2011.

8 See Adams, *A Farther Shore*, pp. 181–2.

9 R. Cornwell, 'Irish debate fails to demolish barriers', *The Independent*, 6 October 1994; Adams, *A Farther Shore*, pp. 184–8; Moloney, *Secret History of the IRA*, p. 460.

10 See Adams, *A Farther Shore*, p. 190; H. Sinnerton, *David Ervine: Unchartered Waters* (Dingle, Co. Kerry: Brandon 2002), p. 171.

11 Belfast republican 7 interview, 1996; Elliott and Flackes, *Northern Ireland*, pp. 324-5.

12 See Bew and Gillespie, *Northern Ireland Chronology*, p. 300; McKittrick et al., *Lost Lives*, pp. 1382–3.

13 Proinsias de Rossa, an internee in the 1950s, became Minister for Social Welfare. Democrat Left split from the Workers' Party in 1992 and was absorbed into the Irish Labour Party in 1999. The split effectively wiped out the Workers' Party. See Mallie and McKittrick, *The Fight for Peace*, p. 343.

14 See Bew and Gillespie, *Northern Ireland Chronology*, p. 303; G. Mitchell, *Making Peace* (New York: Alfred A. Knopf, 1999), p. 10.

15 CAIN Web Service, 'The Framework Documents'; Bew and Gillespie, *Northern Ireland Chronology*, pp. 304–5.

16 Figure 7: Co-options after the Ard Fheis ensured a wider geographic spread and no less than 25 per cent women. Sinn Féin Head Office fax, 03/04/1995; Owen Carron interview, 1996.

17 See Mitchell, *Making Peace*, p. 25.

18 See Adams, *A Farther Shore*, pp. 197–9; Mallie and McKittrick, *The Fight for Peace*, p. 352.

19 Seán Lynch interview, 1995.

20 See Mallie and McKittrick, *The Fight for Peace*, p. 352–5.

21 In November 1995, special legislation increased remission of prison sentences and eighty-three prisoners were released. The change did not apply to those serving life sentences. Lee Clegg's conviction was later quashed and, in a second trial, he was cleared of murdering Karen Reilly but was convicted of attempting to wound Martin Peake. See McKittrick et al., *Lost Lives*, pp. 1209–10; 'Clegg Out All Out!' *AP/RN*, 6 July 1995, p. 1; Bew and Gillespie, *Northern Ireland Chronology*, p. 314.

22 It is part of nationalist folklore that Paisley and Trimble came together and danced a triumphant jig. See C. Ryder and V. Kearney, *Drumcree: The Orange Order's Last Stand* (London: Methuen, 2001), pp. 104–23; Garvaghy Residents, *Garvaghy: A Community Under Seige* (Belfast: Beyond the Pale Publications, 1999), pp. 111–48; D. Godson, *Himself Alone: David Trimble and the Ordeal of Unionism* (London: Harper Collins Publishers, 2004), pp. 129–40; H. McDonald, *Trimble* (London: Bloomsbury, 2004), pp. 142–57.

23 Fra McCann interview, 1995.

24 P. Ó Muirigh, 'RUC Brutality at City Hall Protest: Demos Across the Six Counties', *AP/RN*, 27 July 1995, p. 3.

25 Fra McCann interview, 1995.

26 Seán Crowe interview, 1995.

27 See Bew and Gillespie, *Northern Ireland Chronology*, p. 310.

28 See Mallie and McKittrick, *The Fight for Peace*, pp. 349–57; J.F. Clarity, 'New Plan Drawn to Support Irish Peace Effort', *New York Times* 25 July 1995.

29 Videotaped by the author.

30 Bew and Gillespie, *Northern Ireland Chronology*, p. 310–1; CAIN Web Service, Chronology, 1995.

31 See Mitchell, *Making Peace*, pp. 22–9; Adams, *A Farther Shore*, pp. 219–20.

32 See Clinton, *My Life*, pp. 685–88.

33 'Revolutionary IRA Emerges', and 'Statement of recognition by Comdt General Tom Maguire', *Saoirse*, February 1996, p. 9.

34 See Mitchell, *Making Peace*, pp. 35–6; Moloney, *Secret History of the IRA*, Appendix 6.

35 See Mitchell, *Making Peace*, pp. 35–6.

36 See Farren, *The SDLP*, pp. 320–2; Mitchell, *Making Peace*, pp. 37–9.

37 Belfast republican 6 interview, 1996.

38 Harold Good interview, 2014.

39 See Moloney, *Secret History of the IRA*, pp. 440–4; Adams, *A Farther Shore*, p. 230.

40 See McKittrick et al., *Lost Lives*, pp. 1390–1.

41 See Mitchell, *Making Peace*, pp. 42–3.

42 'No Return to Stormont – IRA', *AP/RN*, 4 April 1996, p. 1; H. Mac Thomais and M. Mac Donncha, 'Sinn Féin will defend its mandate', *AP/RN*, 28 March 1996, p. 9.

43 The results for other parties were: United Kingdom Unionist Party, three seats; Northern Ireland Women's Coalition, two seats; and Labour, two seats. See Mitchell, *Making Peace*, pp. 44–5; CAIN Web Service, 'Forum Election (NI) Thursday 30 May 1996'.

44 See McKittrick et al., *Lost Lives*, pp. 1303–94; 'Sinn Féin mandate to be spurned: No real talks on 10 June', H. Mac Thomais and M. Mac Donnacha, *AP/RN*, 6 June 1996, p. 3.

45 See Sinnerton, *David Ervine*; Mitchell, *Making Peace*, pp. 45–56.

46 There is some dispute that Billy Wright sanctioned Michael McGoldrick's murder. See McKittrick et al., *Lost Lives*, pp. 1395–6; Mitchell, *Making Peace*, pp. 59–60; Anderson, *The Billy Boy*, pp. 50–2.

47 See Ryder and Kearney, *Drumcree*, pp. 128–75, quotation p. 143.

48 See McKittrick et al., *Lost Lives*, pp. 1396–7.

49 CAIN Chronology, 13 July 1997.

50 '"Republican IRA" a significant threat to British rule', *Saoirse*, September 1996, p. 1; 'Republican IRA: An Emerging Secret Army', *Saoirse*, September 1996, pp. 2–3.

51 Ruairí Ó Brádaigh interview, October 1996.

52 Joe Cahill interview, September 1996.

53 J.B. and Bernadette O'Hagan interview, 1996.

54 See McKittrick et al., *Lost Lives*, p. 1399.

55 Suzanne Breen, 'Down Through History, the Working Class has been Cannon-Fodder in Wars', *Belfast Telegraph*, 30 September 1996.

56 See Moloney, *Secret History of the IRA*, p. 444.

57 *Ibid.*, pp. 438–54, 476–7; Mooney and O'Toole, *Black Operations*, pp. 21–53; J. Morrison, *The Origins and Rise of Dissident Irish Republicanism: The Role and Impact of Organizational Splits* (New York: Bloomsbury, 2013), pp. 155–67; Barrett, *Martin Ferris*, pp. 194–6, 200;

Brian Keenan 1941–2008 (Dublin: *An Phoblacht*/Sinn Féin, n.d).

58 Belfast Provisional 6 interview, 1996.

59 See Mitchell, *Making Peace*, pp. 90–1; CAIN Web Service, 'Westminster General Election (NI) Thursday 1 May 1997'.

60 CAIN Web Service, 'Address by Prime Minister Tony Blair at the Royal Agricultural Society Belfast', 16 May 1997'; T. Blair, *A Journey: My Political Life* (London: Vintage Books, 2011), pp. 153–65; Mitchell, *Making Peace*, p. 103.

61 Bertie Ahern: Moloney, *Secret History of the IRA*, pp. 462–3; Adams, *A Farther Shore*, p. 279.

62 Caoimhghín Ó Caoláin interview, September 1996.

63 See Mitchell, *Making Peace*, p. 104.

64 See Moloney, *Secret History of the IRA*, pp. 467–72.

65 J. Mooney and M. O'Toole, *Black Operations: The Secret War Against the Real IRA* (Dublin: Maverick House, 2003), p. 24.

66 See the CAIN Web Service, 'Irish Republican Army (IRA) Ceasefire Statement, 19 July 1997'.

67 See Maguire, *To Take Arms*, in which she discusses the attitudes toward Mac Stiofáin and her alleged affair with O'Connell.

68 See Clarke and Johnston, *Martin McGuinness*, p. 111.

69 'Gerry Adams and niece Áine Tyrell row over abuse claims', *BBC News*, 25 January 2010; P. Baker, 'In the end I realised it was all about PR and protecting his own image', Slugger O'Toole, 24 January 2010; S. Breen, 'Exposed: Gerry Adams' lies over brother's Sinn Féin role', *Tribune*, 27 December 2009, see *Saoirse* 32, 28 December 2009; 'Child abuse scandal rocks Irish republican leader Gerry Adams', *Christian Science Monitor*, 23 December 2009; 'Boost for Sinn Féin in Dundalk', *AP/RN*, 6 June 1996, p. 17; 'Raising Awareness', *AP/RN*, January 1997.

70 '"They may smear me as a traitor. But the IRA will never stop me telling of how I was raped at 16"', *The Observer: Northern Ireland*, 15 November 2014.

Chapter 19

1 Val Lynch interview, 2007.

2 See Mitchell, *Making Peace*, p. 110; Adams, *A Farther Shore*, p. 295; Blair, *A Journey*, pp. 164–7; S. Pogatchnik, 'Sinn Fein delegates arrive at site of talks', *The Day*, 22 July 1997.

3 See Mitchell, *Making Peace*, p. 111.

4 See McDonald, *Trimble*, pp. 179–85.

5 See O'Brien, *The Long War*, p. 357; Moloney, *Secret History of the IRA*, pp. 473-4, 502, Appendix 6.

6   See Moloney, *Secret History of the IRA*, pp. 473–5, 502–12.

7   'Sinn Féin enter talks', L. Friel, *AP/RN*, 11 September 1997, p. 3.

8   See Mitchell, *Making Peace*, pp. 114–5; '"Rise to the challenge" IRA tells parties', *AP/RN*, 11 September 1997, p. 5.

9   See Blair, *A Journey*, p. 165, 196–7; Mitchell, *Making Peace*, pp. 111–8; Adams, *A Farther Shore*, p. 297; Moloney, *Paisley*, pp. 352–4; CAIN Web Service Chronology, 1997.

10 See Mitchell, *Making Peace*, p. 110, 120–1; Moloney, *Paisley*, p. 355.

11 See Moloney, *Secret History of the IRA*, pp. 478–9. See also Mooney and O'Toole, *Black Operations*, pp. 4–28.

12 See 'Appendix 4: IRA Executive Seamus McGrane's Speeech at the 1997 Convention', in Moloney, *Secret History of the IRA*, p. 511.

13 All of us make the occasional mistake, the author included. In the author's opinion, Dingley's scholarship has many factual errors and conceptual problems. See Dingley, *The IRA*, pp. 95-6, 101-2; White, 'Don't confuse me with the facts', *TPV*, 10/4 (1998), pp. 164–89.

14 See Mitchell, *Making Peace*, pp. 89–95; '*Sunday World* defames Gerry Kelly over "Chief of Staff" article', *BBC News Northern Ireland*, 10 November 2011.

15 It appears that media reports that McKenna was in ill-health helped him step aside gracefully. See Moloney, *Secret History of the IRA*, p. 479; James O'Shea, 'Conviction of Thomas "Slab" Murphy, former IRA Chief of Staff, a blow for peace process', *Irish Central*, 24 December 2015.

16 See Mooney and O'Toole, *Black Operations*, pp. 31–5; 'Update on Resignations', *The Dissenter: The Voice of Traditional Irish Republicanism*, 9 November 1997; Moloney, *Secret History of the IRA*, p. 479.

17 32 County Sovereignty Committee 'Policy Document', 4 January 1998.

18 Val Lynch interview, 2007. 32 County Sovereignty Committee supporters made similar comments at the time of the split. See 'Dissidents back step for the moment', *The Dissenter: The Voice of 'Traditional' Irish Republicanism*, 30 November 1997; J. Hannigan, 'The Armalite and the Ballot Box: Dilemmas of Strategy and Ideology in the Provisional IRA', *Social Problems*, 33 (1985), pp. 31–40.

19 Figure 8 also relies on personal information. Martina Purdy, 'Who is behind the hardline grouping?' *Belfast Telegraph*, 21 August 1998; Mooney and O'Toole, *Black Operations*, pp. 31–5; Moloney, *Secret History of the IRA*, pp. 472–9.

20 See Walsh, *The Final Beat: Gardaí Killed in the Line of Duty*, , pp. xi–22; Treacy, *The IRA, 1956–69*, pp. 136–7.

21 Phil O'Donoghue interview, 2010.

22 See Adams, *A Farther Shore*, p. 308.

23 Joe Dillon interview, 2007.

24 See for example, Mooney and O'Toole, *Black Operations*, pp. 50–1, 220. John Morrison, in *The Origins and Rise of Dissident Irish Republicanism*, pp. 160–1, reports an interview in which Des Long states that Mickey McKevitt refused to meet with Ó Brádaigh and him.

25 Ruairí Ó Brádaigh interview notes, 2003.

26 Phil O'Donoghue interview, 2010.

27 Joe Dillon interview, 1996.

28 See Barrett, *Martin Ferris*, pp. 201–2.

29 See Blair, *A Journey,*, p. 197 (emphasis added).

30 *Ibid.*, p. 169; McDonald, *Trimble*, pp. 191–2.

31 See Adams, *A Farther Shore*, pp. 53, 363.

32 See Mitchell, *Making Peace*, pp. 131–2; McKittrick et al., *Lost Lives*, pp. 1419–20; Anderson, *The Billy Boy*, pp. 63–80; McDonald, *Trimble*, pp. 191–4; McKittrick et al., *Lost Lives*, pp. 1427–31; M. Frampton, *Legion of the Rearguard* (Dublin: Irish Academic Press, 2011), pp. 290–1; Adams, *A Farther Shore*, pp. 353, 363.

33 See Blair, *A Journey*, p. 166; 'The Bloody Sunday Inquiry' and 'Public Processions Act (Northern Ireland) 1998', http://www.bloody-sunday-inquiry. org.uk/ (last accessed 14/01/2017); Powell, *Great Hatred Little Room*, pp. 26–7, 45–6, 114–5.

34 See Blair, *A Journey*, p. 166.

35 The GFA may be found via the CAIN Web Service, http://cain.ulst.ac.uk/events/peace/docs/ agreement.htm (last accessed 14/01/2017). 'Cross-community' support requires either a majority of representatives in both communities or a weighted majority (60 per cent) with at least 40 per cent of nationalist and unionist support. See Bew and Gillespie, *Northern Ireland Chronology*, p. 360; Adams, *A Farther Shore*, p. 342; Mitchell, *Making Peace*, p. 176.

36 See McKearney, *From Insurrection to Parliament*, p. 190.

37 See Bew and Gillespie, *Northern Ireland Chronology*, pp. 359–60.

38 See Godson, *Himself Alone*, pp. 362–4; Moloney, *Paisley*, pp. 356–9; Bew and Gillespie, *Northern Ireland Chronology*, p. 362.

39 *Saoirse*, May 1998, p. 1.

40 Val Lynch interview, 2007.

41 Joe Dillon interview, 2007.

42 R. Dudley Edwards, *Aftermath: The Omagh Bombing and the Families' Pursuit of Justice* (London: Random

House, 2010), p. 36; '32 CSM Policy Documents'; R. O'Hanlon, 'Irish American News Briefs, Ahern to Speak in Boston', *The Irish Echo*, 10-16 (presumably the incorrect date) September 1997; E. Moloney, 'The Hypocrisy of Peter King', *CounterPunch*, 2 December 2010.

43   See Mooney and O'Toole, *Black Operations*, pp. 86–93; McKittrick et al., *Lost Lives*, pp. 1432–33; 'For The Record', *Saoirse*, June 1998, p. 4.

44   See Frampton, *Legion of the Rearguard*, p. 291.

45   See Adams, *A Farther Shore*, p. 357; 'Preparing for a new phase of struggle', 'Presidential Address of Gerry Adams', *AP/RN*, 23 April 1998, p. 18; 'Negotiating an agenda for change', *AP/RN*, 23 April 1998, p. 19.

46   'Debating the future', *AP/RN*, 23 April 1998, p. 9.

47   See Moloney, *Secret History of the IRA*, p. 482.

48   'The IRA's Response', *AP/RN*, 30 April 1998, p. 1.

49   See Moloney, *Secret History of the IRA*, pp. 482–3. Clarke and Johnston, *Martin McGuinness*, pp. 230–4. See also the 7 and 14 May issues of *AP/RN*.

50   Unionists were also shocked when loyalist Michael Stone was released to speak to an Ulster Democratic Party/Ulster Defence Association rally. See Godson, *Himself Alone*, pp. 364, 366–7;

51   Limerick republican interview, 2012.

52   'The Struggle Continues', *AP/RN*, 14 May 1998, p. 1.

53   Limerick republican interview, 2012.

54   Davy Hyland interview, 2014.

55   Unless the author missed it, a careful reading of *AP/RN* following the May 1998 Ard Fheis does not show the vote tally. Gerry Adams, in *A Farther Shore*, does not present a vote tally. Liam Clarke and Kathryn Johnston only state that the Ard Fheis 'recommended a "yes" vote in the referenda'. See Adams, *A Farther Shore*, pp. 361–2; Clarke and Johnston, *Martin McGuinness*, p. 233; 'Focused and imaginative debate', *AP/RN*, 14 May 1998, p. 10; 'United we stand', *AP/RN*, 7 May 1998, p. 1.

56   See Bew and Gillespie, *Northern Ireland Chronology*, p. 365.

57   The geographic distribution of those directing the splits in 1969/70, 1986 and 1997 reflect social interaction among people with similar perspectives. In each split, there were exceptions to the geographic tendency. In 1969/70, Joe Cahill and Leo Martin were from Belfast and sided with Southern republicans like Ruairí Ó Brádaigh and Seán Mac Stiofáin. In 1986, Cahill sided with Adams while Martin was sympathetic to Ó Brádaigh et al. With each split, and with time, others from different

areas would conclude that those directing the split were right. Hence, the Provisionals, RSF and the Continuity IRA, and the 32 CSM and Real IRA grew.

58   As Tony Blair comments, Adams and McGuinness were 'not always being totally upfront as to what the destination really meant'. See Blair, *A Journey*, p. 197.

Chapter 20

1   See A. McIntyre ('Joe Cahill – Provisional Republican Veteran'), *Good Friday: The Death of Irish Republicanism* (New York: Asubo Press, 2008), pp. 37–8.

2   'Gerry Adams oration at the funeral of Joe Cahill today', Sinn Féin online, 27 July 2004.

3   D. Price, 'The UnHung Hero', *The Blanket*, 3 August 2004.

4   See Godson, *Himself Alone*, pp. 816–7; 804–6.

5   The SDLP won 24 seats with 177,963 votes (21.97 per cent); the UUP won 30 seats with 172,225 votes (21.25 per cent); the DUP won 20 seats with 146,989 votes (18.14 per cent); and the UKUP won 5 seats with 36,541 votes (4.51 per cent). Sinn Féin won 18 seats with 142,848 votes. See Bew and Gillespie, *Northern Ireland Chronology*, pp. 369–70; 'History of the Northern Ireland Assembly', Northern Ireland Assembly.

6   See Clarke and Johnston, *Martin McGuinness*, pp. 233–5.

7   See Ryder and Kearney, *Drumcree*, pp. 265–7, 270–314; McKittrick et al., *Lost Lives*, pp. 1434–6.

8   See Frampton, *Legion of the Rearguard*, p. 292.

9   The CIRA deny reports that the Omagh bomb was a joint Real IRA-Continuity IRA operation. See McKittrick et al., *Lost Lives*, pp. 1437–60; Bew and Gillespie, *Northern Ireland Chronology*, p. 374; Moloney, *Secret History of the IRA*, p. 508; Dudley Edwards, *Aftermath*, pp. 41–2; Mooney and O'Toole, *Black Operations*, pp. 151–60.

10   Marian Price interview, 2010.

11   See Bew and Gillespie, *Northern Ireland Chronology*, p. 374; Frampton, *Legion of the Rearguard*, pp. 292–3; CAIN Web Service, Chronology online.

12   See McDonald, *Trimble*, pp. 264–7; Bew and Gillespie, *Northern Ireland Chronology*, pp. 373–6; Godson, *Himself Alone*, p. 393.

13   See Bew and Gillespie, *Northern Ireland Chronology*, pp. 373–8, 383.

14   See Moloney, *Paisley*, pp. 367.

15   Eamon Collins, *Killing Rage* (London: Granta Books, 1998); McKittrick et al., *Lost Lives*, pp. 1466–7; E. Moloney, 'Why Collins died', *Sunday Tribune*, n.d.

16 See Godson, *Himself Alone*, p. 452; Farren, *The SDLP*, p. 356.

17 See Godson, *Himself Alone*, pp. 413, 426–7; Moloney, *Paisley*, pp. 370, 388.

18 See Farren, *The SDLP*, p. 356; CAIN Web Service, 'Chronology, 1999'; Godson, *Himself Alone*, pp. 462–3.

19 CAIN Web Service, 'Chronology 1999'; Godson, *Himself Alone*, pp. 468–70.

20 The Patten Commission report is available at http://cain.ulst.ac.uk/issues/police/patten/patten99.pdf (last accessed 14/01/2017); Farren, *The SDLP*, p. 357; Agnés Maillot, *New Sinn Féin: Irish republicanism in the twenty-first century* (2005), pp. 67–9; L. Friel, 'Patten meets mixed response', *AP/RN*, 16 September 1999, pp. 10–1; 'RUC Name Traded in "Shameful" Bargain', *BBC News*, 13 June 2000; CAIN Web Service, 'Chronology 1999'.

21 See Godson, *Himself Alone*, pp. 498–500.

22 Brian Rowan, *How the Peace Was Won* (Dublin: Gill and Macmillan, 2008), pp. 76, 83–6; Powell, *Great Hatred, Little Room*, p. 165; P. Wintour, M. Holland and J. O'Farrell, 'We've done our bit Mr. Adams, now it's over to you', *The Observer*, 27 November 1999; Moloney, *Paisley*, pp. 370–1.

23 See Farren, *The SDLP*, pp. 361–2; CAIN Chronology 1999; Powell, *Great Hatred, Little Room*, pp. 165–6; Godson, *Himself Alone*, p. 563.

24 'McGuinness – 11 plus will not return', 14 October 2006; Maillot, *New Sinn Féin*, pp. 54–7; T. McKearney, 'The helot has responsibility but not power', 20 August 2000, rwg web; Godson, *Himself Alone*, pp. 547–9; Murray and Tonge, *Sinn Féin and the SDLP*, pp. 245–6.

25 The decision to participate in the Assembly also sealed a break between Ian Paisley and Robert McCartney of the UKUP. See Moloney, *Paisley*, p. 382; see pp. 379–83.

26 See the CAIN Chronology '2000'.

27 See Godson, *Himself Alone*, pp. 522–3; W. Hoge, 'New Obstacle Seen as Ulster is Given Date of Home Rule', *New York Times*, 21 November 1999.

28 See Godson, *Himself Alone*, p. 579.

29 See Powell, *Great Hatred, Little Room*, pp. 168–73

30 'Six given jail for taking part in Real IRA Training Camp', *Drogheda Independent*, 30 March 2001; H. McDonald, 'Terrorists Recruit Teenage Soldiers', *The Observer*, 23 October 1999; Powell, *Great Hatred, Little Room*, pp. 170, 176, 181.

31 'There Is Only One Enemy', *The Sovereign Nation*, Jan/Feb 2000, p. 1.

32 See Frampton, *Legion of the Rearguard*, p. 293.

33 Cáit Trainor interview, May 2012.

34 Republican Sinn Féin recruit interview, 2009.

35 See McIntyre, *Good Friday*, pp. 197–8.

36 Brendan Hughes interview, 2001.

37 See McIntyre ('A Dark View of the Process'), *Good Friday*, pp. 199–200; 'Interview with Brendan [Darkie] Hughes', *The Herald*, 24 November 2000; reprinted in *The Blanket*; N. Strange, 'Hughes no longer toes the party line', *Sunday Tribune*, 17 December 2000.

38 See Frampton, *Legion of the Rearguard*, p. 136–7; Mooney and O'Toole, *Black Operations*, p. 268.

39 S. Breen, 'SF Refuses to Condemn Killing of "Real" IRA Man', *Irish Times*, 17 October 2000.

40 M. Price, 'Vol Joe O Connor: Graveside Oration for Vol Joe O'Connor', https://tenyearson.wordpress.com/ (last accessed 25/11/2016).

41 See, 'Vol. Joe O'Connor' and accompanying articles, https://tenyearson.wordpress.com/ (last accessed 25/11/2016).

42 'Membership charges amount to internment' and 'Eight are members of Republican Sinn Féin', *Saoirse*, January 2002, p. 2; 'Limerick Eight – Political Trial', *Saoirse*, January 2003, p. 1; 'A travesty of justice', *Saoirse*, June 2003, pp. 1, 3.

43 See Mooney and O'Toole, *Black Operations*, p. 278; Frampton, *Legion of the Rearguard*, pp. 141–2; Dudley Edwards, *Aftermath*; 'Michael McKevitt: Real IRA leader's appeal bid fails', *BBC News Northern Ireland*, 20 May 2014; H. McDonald, 'Real IRA's days look numbered as police close in', *The Observer*, 9 August 2003.

44 Mickey McKevitt was released in 2016. See E. Moloney, 'Michael McKevitt, "The British only take notice of armed struggle"', 28 March 2016, The Broken Elbow.

45 See Powell, *Great Hatred, Little Room*, pp. 172–81; 'Noose tightens on Trimble', *Saoirse*, June 2000, p. 1.

46 Danny Morrison interview, 2001.

47 Sinn Féin received 175,392 votes (21.7 per cent) the SDLP received 169,865 votes (21 per cent). See Murray and Tonge, *Sinn Féin and the SDLP*, pp. 208–12, 227–33; McCaffrey, *Alex Maskey*, pp. 143–9.

48 See Powell, *Great Hatred, Little Room*,, pp. 195–201; CAIN Web Service, Implementation Plan issued by the British and Irish Governments on 1 August 2001; Maillot, *New Sinn Féin*, pp. 68–9; CAIN Web Service, 'Chronology 2001'.

49 See O'Callaghan, *The Informer*, pp. 52–6; D. Morrison, 'Injustice and Farce in Columbia'; M. Hodgson, H. McDonald and P. Beaumont, 'IRA blunder in the jungle sparks US rage', *The Observer*, 18 August

2005; A. Ruddock, 'How America had the IRA over a barrel', *The Observer*, 28 October 2001; Moloney, *Secret History of the IRA*, pp. 490–1; 'IRA Statement', and 'IICD Statement', *AP/RN*, 25 October 2001, p. 3.

50 John Hume and Seamus Mallon had retired; Durkan also became Leader of the SDLP.

51 'Stormont saved – arms destroyed', *Saoirse*, November 2001, p. 1.

52 Ruairí Ó Brádaigh interview, 2008.

53 'Sinn Fein will not sit on flawed Policing Board', press release, 7 November 2001; 'Different Name, Same Bigots', *AP/RN*, 8 November 2001, p. 4; Maillot, *New Sinn Féin*, pp. 67–70; Murray and Tonge, *Sinn Féin and the SDLP*, pp. 215–7.

54 K. Bean, *The New Politics of Sinn Féin* (Liverpool: Liverpool University Press, 2007), pp. 98–9.

55 Killian Forde interview, 2010.

56 'Irish General Election, 2002', Irish Political Maps; 'Sinn Féin Election Manifesto' (2002).

57 Seán Crowe interview, 2011.

58 See also D. de Bréadún, *Power Play: The Rise of Modern Sinn Féin* (Sallins: Merrion Press, 2015), pp. 26–46, 165–9.

59 See Powell, *Great Hatred, Little Room*, p. 209; pp. 206–13; 'Stormont spying case collapses', *BBC News*, 8 December 2005.

60 See Powell, *Great Hatred, Little Room*, p. 213.

61 Joe Cahill: 'Negotiating for Democratic Rights: Sinn Féin Chief Negotiator Reports to Ard Fheis', *AP/RN*, Thursday, 3 April 2003, pp. 10–11; 'Joe Cahill points up Assembly elections', *AP/RN*, Thursday 3 April 2003, p. 17; 'Building an Ireland of Equals: Gerry Adams Presidential Address – Sinn Féin Ard Fheis 2003', *AP/RN*, Thursday 3 April, 2003, pp. 12–5.

62 See also Dolours Price, 'The Unhung Hero', *The Blanket*, 3 August 2004.

63 'Building an Ireland of Equals: Gerry Adams Presidential Address – Sinn Féin Ard Fheis 2003', *AP/RN*, Thursday 3 April 2003, pp. 12–15.

64 Anthony McIntyre, 'Joe Cahill—Provisional Republican Veteran', *The Death of Irish Republicanism* (2008), pp. 36–8; Powell, *Great Hatred, Little Room*, pp. 221, 225–6; Godson, *Himself Alone*, p. 755; Dolours Price, 'The Unhung Hero', *The Blanket*, 3 August 2004; Anthony McIntyre, 'St Joseph Patron Saint of the Peace Process', *The Blanket*, 14 December 2004.

65 See Godson, *Himself Alone*, pp. 778–80.

66 'Trimble rejects IRA weapons move', *The Telegraph*, 21 October 2003; T. Harding, 'De Chastelain wrong over "secrecy" for IRA weapons', *The Telegraph*, 30 October 2003; Powell, *Great Hatred, Little Room*, pp. 229–35; Moloney, *Secret History of the IRA*, pp. 220–34.

67 In the election, 26 November 2003, the DUP won thirty seats. Sinn Féin passed the SDLP in votes (162,758 vs 117,547) and seats (24 vs 18). See Moloney, *Paisley*, p. 401; Godson, *Himself Alone*, pp. 816–7.

68 Former Sinn Féiner interview, 2003.

69 See Andrew Marr interview, 'Paisley: Time for a new generation', *BBC News*, 9 March 2008.

70 See Moloney, *Paisley*, pp. 398–401, 416–20; Powell, *Great Hatred, Little Room*, pp. 217–8, 236–41, 251–9

71 Revd Harold Good interview, 2014.

72 See Moloney, *Secret History of the IRA* (2007, 2nd edition), pp. 536–9; Moloney, *Paisley*, p. 424; Powell, *Great Hatred, Little Room*, pp. 263–4.

73 See Moloney, *Secret History of the IRA* (2007, 2nd edition), pp. 548–58; C. McCartney, *Walls of Silence* (Dublin: Gill and Macmillan, 2007), pp. 13–14; C. Thornton, 'Gerard "Jock" Davison', *Belfast Telegraph*, 3 March 2005; S. Pogatchnik, 'Irish Police Arrest 7 in Belfast Bank Robbery', *Washington Post World*, A21, 18 February 2005.

74 'Irish Republican Army orders end to armed campaign' and 'Historic Statement read by Séanna Walsh', *AP/RN*, 28 July 2005, p. 3.

75 Revd Harold Good interview, 2014.

76 Peter McAleer interview, 2010.

Chapter 21

1 Former Provisional 8 interview, 2003. For consistency and to protect confidentiality respondents are not identified (other than Joe Cahill and Seán Lynch, as noted). In a few instances, misleading information is provided. The status of the respondents is in 2005. This chapter draws on, White, 'Structural Identity Theory and the Post-Recruitment Activism of Irish Republicans: Persistence, Disengagement, Splits and Dissidents in Social Movement Organizations', *Social Problems*, 57 (2010), pp. 341–70.

2 There is a developing literature on disengagement from activism, including: J. Horgan, *Walking Away from Terrorism: Accounts of Disengagement from Radical and Extremist Movements* (New York: Routledge, 2009); White, 'Structural Identity Theory and the Post-Recruitment Activism of Irish Republicans', *Social Problems*, 57 (2010), pp. 341–70; O. Fillieule, 'Some elements of an interactionist approach to political disengagement', *Social Movement Studies*, 9/1 (2010) , pp. 9–15; Bosi,

'Contextualizing the biographical outcomes of Provisional IRA former activists', forthcoming in O. Filleule and E. Neveu, *Activists forever? The Long-Term Impacts of Political Activism in Various Contexts* (Minneapolis: University Minnesota Press); Viterna, *Women in War*, pp. 183–4.

3   Seán Lynch interview, 1984. See also, M. Coleman, *County Longford and the Irish Revolution: 1910–1923* (Dublin: Irish Academic Press, 2003), especially pp. 149–50.

4   Joe Cahill interview, 1996. 'A Proud Mother & A Great Irish Lady', *An Phoblacht*, 29 June 1973, p. 8.

5   32 CSM activist 1 interviews, 1984, 2007.

6   Sinn Féin activist 1 interview, 2011.

7   Sinn Féin activist 2 interview, 2007.

8   Former Provisional 1 interview, 1996.

9   Former Provisional 2 interview, 1995. Bishop and Mallie quote an IRA volunteer who describes peers who joined 'based on emotionalism' and then discovered that after shooting someone dead 'They couldn't stomach it.' This, too, would be disengagement for a personal reason. See Bishop and Mallie, *Provisional IRA*, p. 195.

10   The Fianna Fáil government did the same thing in the 1930s. In this way, activists can directly serve their communities while also supporting the status quo. See Bell, *The Secret Army*, pp. 110–12, 99–141; Bosi, 'Contextualizing the biographical outcomes of Provisional IRA former activists', forthcoming in Filleule and Neveu, *Activists forever?*; Viterna, *Women in War*, pp. 183–4.

11   Former Provisional 3 interview, 1996.

12   Former Provisional 4 interview, 1996.

13   Sinn Féin activist 3 interview, 1996.

14   See White, 'The Irish Republican Army', *TPV*, 9/1 (1997), pp. 20–55.

15   Former Provisional 5 interview, 2007.

16   Former Provisional 6 interview, 2010.

17   Former Provisional 7 interview, 1984.

18   Former Provisional 7 interview, 1995.

19   Former Provisional 7 interview, 2007.

20   Sinn Féin activist 4 interview, 1996.

21   Sinn Féin activist 4 interview, 2009.

22   D. Snow, L. Zurcher and S. Ekland-Olson, 'Social networks and social movements: A microstructural approach to differential recruitment', *American Sociological Review*, 45 (1980), pp. 787–801.

23   J.M. Fendrich and A.T. Tarleau, 'Marching to a different drummer: Occupational and political correlates of former student activists', *Social Forces*, 52 (1973), pp. 245–53; J.M. Fendrich, 'Black and White activists ten years later: Political socialization and adult left-wing politics', *Youth and Society*, 8 (1976), pp. 81–104; J.M. Fendrich, 'Keeping the faith or pursuing the good life: A study of the consequences of participation in the civil rights movement', *American Sociological Review*, 42 (1977), pp. 144–57; R.G. Braungart and M.M. Braungart, 'Political career patterns of radical activists in the 1960s and 1970s: Some historical comparisons', *Sociological Focus*, 13 (1980), pp. 237–54; D. McAdam, *Freedom Summer* (Oxford: OUP, 1988), p. 225. See also J.B. Bell, 'Career Moves: Reflections on the Irish gunman', *Studies in Conflict and Terrorism*, 15/1 (1992), pp. 69–88; N. Van Dyke and M. Dixon, 'Activist human capital: Skills acquisition and the development of commitment to social movement activism', *Mobilization*, 18(2), pp. 197–212; Viterna, *Women in War*, pp. 172–202.

24   See English, *Armed Struggle*, p. 369.

25   Sinn Féin activist interview, 2007.

26   Sinn Féin activist 4 interview, 1996.

27   P. Whelan, 'Art as Struggle: The Murals of West Belfast: The Draw of Politics', *AP/RN*, 16 June 2011.

28   Former Provisional interview, 1996.

29   Former Provisional interview, 1996.

30   Sinn Féin activist interview, 2007.

31   Former Provisional 8 interview, 2003.

32   Former Provisional 9 interview, 2010.

33   Former Provisional interview, 2007.

34   See for example McNulty, *Exiled*; S. McKay, 'Tom McFeely: From IRA hunger striker to bankrupt millionaire property developer', *The Guardian*, 10 August 2012; 'Simon Cowell's bodyguard at Britain's Got Talent auditions is ex-IRA gunman Brendan Curran', *Belfast Telegraph*, 27 January 2014; A. Cullen and J. Cusack, 'Crackdown on Provo border rackets after Garda killing', *Irish News*, 19 October 2015.

Chapter 22

1   Former Provisional 4 interview, 2008. For consistency and to protect confidentiality respondents are not identified. In a few instances, misleading information is provided. Identifiers in Chapter 22 are independent of identifiers in Chapter 21 – 'Former Provisional 1' here is not necessarily 'Former Provisional 1' in Chapter 21. The status of the respondents is in 2005. This chapter draws on, White, 'Structural Identity Theory and the Post-Recruitment Activism of Irish Republicans: Persistence, Disengagement, Splits and Dissidents in Social Movement Organizations', *Social Problems*, 57 (2010), pp. 341–70.

2   See Gamson, *The Strategy of Social Protest*, pp. 28–37, 41–4, 72–88; P. Burstein, R. Einwohner and J.A. Hollender, 'The success of political movements: A bargaining perspective', pp. 275–95 in J.C. Jenkins and B. Klandermans (eds), *The Politics of Social Protest* (Minneapolis: University of Minnesota Press, 1995); W. Gamson, 'Social movements and cultural change', pp. 57–77 in M. Guigni, D. McAdam and C. Tilly (eds), *From Contention to Democracy* (Lanham, MD: Rowman & Littlefield, 1998); D. della Porta and M. Diani, *Social Movements: An Introduction* (Malden, MS: Blackwell, 1999), pp. 226–54; S. Staggenborg, *Social Movements* (Oxford: OUP, 2011), pp. 42–5; 'Introduction', pp. xiii–xxxiii in M. Guigni, D. McAdam and Charles Tilly (eds), *How Social Movements Matter* (Minneapolis: University of Minnesota Press, 1999); C. Tilly, 'Conclusion: From Interactions to Outcomes in Social Movement Research', pp. 253–70 in Guigni et al., *How Social Movements Matter*.

3   Sinn Féin activist 1 interview, 2011.

4   Sinn Féin activist 2 interview, 2007.

5   Sinn Féin activist 3 interview, 2007.

6   English, *Does Terrorism Work?* p. 110.

7   Prior also said, 'I know we did not win but I am not certain the other side won'. 'Lord Prior: Former NI Secretary says violence "did work"', *BBC News* 26 September 2014.

8   Republican Sinn Féin activist 1 interview, 2008.

9   Republican Sinn Féin activist 2 interview, 2008.

10 Republican Sinn Féin activist 3 interview, 2007.

11 32 CSM activist 1 interview, 2008.

12 32 CSM activist 2 interview, 2007.

13 Former Provisional 1 interview, 2007.

14 Former Provisional 2 interview, 2011.

15 Former Provisional 3 interview, 2009.

16 Former Provisional 4 interview, 2008.

17 Former Provisional 3 interview, 2008. Another respondent was asked, 'Was it worth it?' The reply was, 'No'. In response to 'No?' the reply was, 'No, no. Not for what you got at the end of the day. It definitely wasn't, you know? I joined the Movement to get a united Ireland. And we didn't get that.' Former Provisional interview, 2011.

18 Sinn Féin activist 2 interview, 2007. See also O'Doherty, *The Volunteer*, pp. 214–6.

19 Former Provisional 5 interview, 2009.

20 Sinn Féin activist 3 interview, 2007.

21 Republican Sinn Féin activist 3 interview, 2007.

22 32 CSM interview, 2007.

23 Former Provisional 1 interview, 2007.

24 Sinn Féin activist interview, 2007.

25 Former Provisional interview, 2010.

26 32 CSM activist 2 interview, 2007.

27 Republican Sinn Féin activist 2 interview, 2008.

28 Sinn Féin activist 4 interview, 2009.

29 Former Provisional 1 interview, 2007.

30 Former Provisional 2 interview, 2011.

31 Former Provisional 5 interview, 2010.

32 Sinn Féin activist 2 interview, 2007.

33 Republican Sinn Féin activist 3 interview, 2007.

34 Sinn Féin activist 3 interview, 2007.

35 Former Provisional 3 interview, 2008.

36 Former Provisional 5 interview, 2010.

37 Sinn Féin activist 1 interview, 2011.

38 32 CSM activist 1 interview, 2008.

39 Sinn Féin activist interview 2, 2007.

40 32 CSM activist 2 interview, 2007.

41 Republican Sinn Féin activist 2 interview, 2008.

42 Sinn Féin activist 1 interview, 2011.

43 Former Provisional 3 interview, 2008.

44 Former Provisional 4 interview, 2008.

45 See O'Callaghan, *The Informer*, p. 85.

Chapter 23

1   See Clarke and Johnston, *Martin McGuinness*, pp. 80–3.

2   See 'The Politics of Revolution', p. 26.

3   Response of Martin McGuinness to a journalist's question while campaigning for the Irish Presidency, 2011.

4   Laura Friel, 'Donaldson Admits Role as British Agent', *AP/RN*, 5 January 2006; 'Denis Donaldson Press Briefing', 21 December 2005; Seán O'Driscoll and Seán O'Neill, 'Outrage at payout for IRA gang as victims suffer', *The Times* (London), 30 January 2016.

5   See for example, Moloney, *Secret History of the IRA* (2007, 2nd edition), pp. 242–3.

6   D. McKittrick, 'The Execution: How an IRA man turned British spy met his brutal end', *The Independent*, 5 April 2006.

7   H. McDonald, 'The leader, his driver, and the driver's handler: chauffer revealed as MI5 agent', *The Guardian*, 8 February 2008; T. Peterkin, 'Gerry Adams's chauffer outed as informer', *The Telegraph*, 9 February 2008; D. Young, 'Former Friend: I always knew that he was a slimy bastard', *The Irish News*, 2 February 2008.

8   The quotation, often attributed to Connolly's *The Re-Conquest of Ireland*, is from *The Harp* (1909); P. Beresford Ellis, *James Connolly: Selected Writings* (Belfast: Pluto Press, 1988), p. 17; D.R. O'Connor

Lysaght, 'Connolly, syndicalism & Irish Labour', *Arguments for a Workers Republic*, http://www.workersrepublic.org/Pages/Ireland/Connolly/workshoptalks1.html (last accessed 18/02/2015). éirígí activist interview, 2008; éirígí website, http://www.eirigi.org/ (last accessed 15/01/2017); de Bréadún, *Power Play*, pp. 162–5.

9   See Moloney, *Secret History of the IRA*, p. 587; Adams, 'All of the outstanding issues can be resolved', *AP/RN*, 30 November 2006, p. 3; Moloney, *Paisley*, pp. 460–76.

10   'Sinn Féin secures major victory on issue of MI5', *AP/RN*, 11 January 2007, p. 3; see also Powell, *Great Hatred, Little Room*, pp. 278–95.

11   John Kelly, an MLA, was de-selected in 2003 and left Sinn Féin complaining of a 'control dictatorship'. W. Gallagher, 'Ireland: Policing, A Bridge Too Far for Republicans', speech on 27 November 2006, *Fightback: The Marxist Voice of Labour and Youth*; H. Patterson, 'Beyond the "Micro-group": The Dissident Republican Challenge', pp. 65–95 in P.M. Currie and M. Taylor (eds), *Dissident Irish Republicanism* (London: The Continuum International Publishing Group, 2011); J. McAllister, 'This isn't just about policing', *Irish News*, 22 January 2007; C. Thornton and M. McCreary, 'SF bid to silence policing rebels', *Belfast Telegraph*, 4 January 2007; B. Hughes and J. Kelly, 'Sinn Fein Trying to Smear "Dissenters"', *Irish News*, 3 January 2007, posted in *The Blanket*; Bimpe Fatogun, 'Dougan follows through on resignation threat', *Irish News*, 19 January 2007; 'De-selected Sinn Féin man resigns', *BBC News*, 3 January 2007.

12   Davy Hyland interview, 2014.

13   A post on the Slugger O'Toole blog confirms that delegates were told not to vote for Hyland (Slugger O'Toole, 'Stephen Murney' post, 21 March 2015).

14   McAllister left Sinn Féin in the early 1990s. See Jim McAllister, 'This isn't just about policing', *Irish News*, 22 January 2007; 'Councilor quits Sinn Féin amid "serious fractures"', *BBC News Northern Ireland*, 12 November 2013; 'Curran unleashes during final council meeting', *Newry Democrat*, 24 March 2015.

15   Caoilfhionn Ní Dhonnabháin, 'Motion passed by huge majority', *AP/RN*, 1 February 2007, p. 14; 'Extraordinary Ard Fheis: Political Pressure falls on Paisley', *AP/RN*, 1 February 2007, p. 3; 'Policing Motion passed at the Special Ard Fheis', Sinn Féin, 28 January 2007, http://www.sinnfein.ie/contents/16461 (last accessed 30/11/2016).

16   A. McIntyre, 'Felon Setting', *The Pensive Quill*, 25 July 2009; T. Catney, 'Always Tell the Truth', Letter to the *Irish News*, 2 December 2006; '330 Ex-POWs enter the fray', *Derry Journal*, n.d.; S. Breen, 'Provos move to smash dissent', *Sunday Tribune*, 3 December 2006; 'Irish Republican Ex-Pows Against the RUC PSNI & MI5', *The Blanket*, 6 March 2007; H. McDonald, 'IRA bomber attacks Sinn Féin on abortion', *The Guardian*, 27 December 2003.

17   Gerry McGeough interview, 2014.

18   CAIN Web Service, 'Assembly Election NI Wednesday 7 March 2007'.

19   Gerry McGeough interview, 2014.

20   McGeough was convicted of attempted murder. Under the terms of the GFA, he served two years of a twenty-year sentence. 'Gerry McGeough to appeal IRA murder bid conviction', *BBC News Northern Ireland*, 14 April 2014.

21   Paisley's compromise upset many people within his Free Presbyterian Church. He retired as Moderator in January 2008. See Moloney, *Paisley*, pp. 489–511.

22   'About the Department of Justice', Department of Justice: NI.

23   L. Clarke, '"Magician" Gerry Adams still fails to impress in TV debate', *Belfast Telegraph*, 15 February 2011; H. McDonald, 'Gerry Adams and Micheál Martin Class in Irish TV Debate', *The Guardian*, 15 February 2011; 'Election 2007: Leaders clash in debate', RTÉ News, 16 May 2007; McDonald, *Gunsmoke and Mirrors*, pp. 172–4; de Bréadún, *Power Play*, pp. 48–50; '30th DÁIL GENERAL ELECTION May, 2007 Election Results and Transfer of Votes'.

24   E. Ó Broin, *Sinn Féin and the Politics of Left Republicanism* (London: Pluto Press, 2009), pp. 281–3; 'Cllr Louise Minihan resigns from Sinn Féin', *Indymedia Ireland*, 17 July 2009, Press Release; S. Millar, 'SF lose another council seat', *Irish Examiner*, 21 July 2009; 'Independent New Ross councilor John Dwyer has joined éirígí', *Political World*, 1 October 2010; P. Barker, 'Second Sinn Féin councilor resigns from party in election aftermath', Slugger O'Toole, 16 June 2009.

25   Killian Forde interview, 2010. See also, de Bréadún, *Power Play*, pp. 165–9.

26   K. Forde, 'My resignation', 9 January 2010; 'Dumping SF for Labour: Killian Forde', *The Village*, 14 April 2010; 'Sinn Féin comment on resignation of Councilor Killian Forde', 9 January 2010.

27   'Killian Forde's analysis of the problems faced by Dublin Sinn Féin made in June '09', *Sinn Féin: Keep*

Left, 10 January 2010; K. Forde, 'Submission in relation to the 2009 local and European election in Dublin', June 2009.

28 Pearse Doherty was elected to Dáil Éireann in a 2010 by-election and then re-elected in 2011. '31st Dáil February, 2011 General Election, Election Results and Transfer of Votes', Houses of the Oireachtas 2011.

29 *Irish Times*' 'Results Hub': http://www.irishtimes.com/election-2016/results-hub (last accessed 30/11/2016).

30 Timeline: Renewable Heat Incentive Scandal, *BBC News* 25 January 2017.

31 McGuinness told the Saville Inquiry that he resigned from the IRA in 1974. During a presidential debate journalist Miriam O'Callaghan suggested McGuinness had been involved in several murders which led to a contentious confrontation. See Clarke and Johnston, *Martin McGuinness*, pp. 160–6; S. Breen, 'A Path Paved With Blood', *Mail Online*, 25 September 2011; F. Sheahan, K. Sweeney and C. Kelpie, 'O'Callaghan left Shaken after McGuinness row', *Irish Independent*, 14 October 2011.

32 See Conway, *Southside Provisional*, pp. 173–6, 204, 208.

33 'The Belfast Project, Boston College, and a Sealed Subpoena'. https://bostoncollegesubpoena. wordpress.com/ (last accessed 15/01/2017). In particular, see C. Barnes, 'Jean McConville's daughter says republican chief was behind mum's murder', *Sunday Life*, 21 February 2010.

34 T. Hachey and R.K. O'Neill, 'Preface', pp. 1–4 in Moloney, *Voices From the Grave*.

35 'Dolours Price: Defiant IRA Bomber, Dies at 61', *New York Times*, 25 January 2013.

36 L. Hogan and F. Sheahan, 'IRA recordings on McConville death may bring about Adams' downfall', *Irish Independent*, 2 May 2013.

37 Forum posting by 'AnClar', 10 February 2015, Irish Republican Forum.

38 'Gerry Adams and niece Áine Tyrell row over abuse claims', *BBC News*, 25 January 2010; P. Baker, 'In the end I realised it was all about PR and protecting his own image', Slugger O'Toole, 24 January 2010; 'Child abuse scandal rocks Irish republican leader Gerry Adams', *Christian Science Monitor*, 23 December 2009; 'Gerry Adams responds to *Sunday Tribune* article', 17 January 2010, West Belfast Sinn Féin; 'Response to *Sunday Tribune*', Léargas, by Gerry Adams, 17 January 2010; 'Liam Adams appears in court to face abuse charges', *BBC News Northern Ireland*, 3 November 2011; 'Child abuser

Liam Adams sentenced to 16 Years in Prison', *Belfast Telegraph*, 27 November 2013.

39 S. Breen, 'Exposed: Gerry Adams' lies over brother's Sinn Féin role', *Sunday Tribune*, see *Saoirse*, 32, 28 December 2009.

40 See Adams, *Before the Dawn*, p. 2.

41 'Boost for Sinn Féin in Dundalk' *AP/RN*, 6 June 1996, p. 17; 'Raising Awareness', *AP/RN*, January 1997; 'Sinn Féin did not know about Liam Adams allegation', *AP/RN*, 15 January 2010, p. 19;

42 'Liam Adams' employers hit out over vetting', *BBC News*, 12 December 2009.

43 'Gerry Adams: My father was a child sex abuser', *The Guardian*, 20 December 2009.

44 See S. Breen, 'The nine year silence that should have cost Gerry his political career', *Belfast Telegraph*, 6 May 2015.

45 Fra McCann interview, 2011. See also McCafferty, *Alex Maskey*, pp. 71–3.

46 See McCaffrey, *Alex Maskey*, p. 106.

47 Fra McCann interview, 2011.

48 See McCafferty, *Alex Maskey*, pp. 110–1; Máirtín Ó Muilleoir, *Belfast's Dome of Delight: City Hall Politics 1981–2000* (Belfast: Beyond the Pale Publications, 1999), pp. 35–7, 64–5, 72.

49 Fra McCann interview, 2011.

50 See Ó Muilleoir, *Belfast's Dome of Delight*, pp. 89–94.

51 Sinn Féin policy is that representatives cannot hold two elected positions. Upon being elected an MLA, McCann gave up his seat on Belfast City Council. Fra McCann interview, 2011. See also 'Sinn Féin delivers for West Belfast', *AP/RN*, April 2016, p. 23.

52 Seán Crowe interview, 2011.

53 'Houses of the Oireachtas, Universal Social Charge Motion (resumed)', 30 March 2011.

54 See K. Allen, *1916: Ireland's Revolutionary Tradition* (London: Pluto Press, 2016), p. 175-6.

55 Danny Morrison interview, 2014. See also, 'Outrage at payout for IRA gang as victims suffer', *The Times* (London), 29 January 2016.

Chapter 24

1 'Dissident' Irish republican interview, 2009.

2 See Stephen Hopkins, 'Hunger strikes and politics of republican memory: complex and contested legacies', *Irish Times*, 5 July 2016.

3 'Who we are', RNU web site (last accessed 23/02/2015; no longer available; hard copy available from the author).

4 'West Belfast "second highest in UK for child poverty"', *BBC News Northern Ireland*, 20 February

2013; S. McCaffery, 'Deprivation and religion in Northern Ireland', *Investigations and Analyses Northern Ireland*, 20 October 2013. See also, 'Sinn Féin delivers for West Belfast', *AP/RN*, April 2016, p. 23.

5   It is not always clear who was responsible, but it appears that the Provisionals or their friends killed a dozen people between 1998 and 2005. Another victim was Ronnie Hill who, after thirteen years in a coma, finally succumbed to injuries from the Enniskillen bomb. See McKittrick et al., *Lost Lives*, pp. 1488-9.

6   J. Cusack, 'Sinn Féin leader's slur on our murdered boy', *Independent.ie*, 26 October 2014; 'Legends in Their Time: 25 Years On…', South Armagh Sinn Féin (2013), p. 49; P. McNamee, 'At the graveside of Jim McAllister', *The Pensive Quill*, 12 April 2013; J. Hedges and P. Whelan, 'Stand up to criminal gangs – Gerry Adams at Burns/Moley Commemoration in South Armagh', *AP/RN*, 1 March 2015; S. Breen, 'Fatal attack on Paul Quinn was "ordered by Provisional IRA"', *Sunday Tribune*, 28 October 2007.

7   'The funeral of Volunteer Brendan Burns', *AP/RN* 10 March 1988, pp. 8-9; 'Legends In Their Time: 25 years on…' South Armagh Sinn Féin (2013), p. 49. See also, 'Airbrushing Out Alan Lundy Would be Vindictive', *The Pensive Quill*, 3 September 2012; McCaffery, *Alex Maskey*, pp. 118–21.

8   See Henry McDonald, 'Family of Bobby Sands attack graphic novel about IRA hunger striker', *The Guardian*, 25 February 2016; Rebecca Black, 'Hunger Striker's family blasts Sinn Féin for turning commemoration into an "electioneering stunt"', *Belfast Telegraph*, 5 May 2016.

9   'PSNI Annual Statistical Report: Report No. 5, Statistics Related to the Security Situation, 1st April 2009 – 31st March 2010', p. 5; 'Police Recorded Security Statistics: Annual Report covering the period 1st April 2013 – 31st March 2014' (2014), p. 4; CAIN Web Service, 'Sutton Index of Deaths'; CAIN Web Service, 'Table NI-SEC-06: Security Related Incidents (number) in Northern Ireland (only), shootings, bombings, and incendiaries, 1969 to 2003'.

10   J. Horgan, *Divided We Stand: The Strategy and Psychology of Ireland's Dissident Terrorists* (Oxford: OUP, 2012), pp. 77–103.

11   See: M. Jordan, 'IRA Splinter Group Says It Killed Troops', *Washington Post*, 9 March 2009; McKittrick et al., *Lost Lives*, pp. 1404–5; L. Friel, 'Peace Process under attack', *AP/RN*, 12 March 2009, p. 6; 'Real IRA's Easter Message to McGuinness: "traitors die"', *The Independent*, 13 April 2009.

12   Phil O'Donoghue interview, 2010.

13   Josephine Hayden interview, 2009.

14   M. Devenport, 'Dissidents defend use of violence', *BBC News Channel*, 26 March 2009; 'Outrage at Derry republican's remarks over dissident murders', *Derry Journal*, 30 March 2009; 'First Ministers take a swing at the media', *Belfast Telegraph*, 9 April 2009.

15   See for example, 'Fógrai bháis: Sean Treacy', *AP/RN*, 3 July 1998, p. 17.

16   Ruairí Ó Brádaigh interview, 2009.

17   S. Breen, 'We will take campaign to Britain', *Sunday Tribune*, 12 April 2009.

18   S. Breen, 'I'm not going to put my life in danger to do the PSNI's job', *Sunday Tribune*, 3 May 2009; H. McDonald, 'Judge upholds journalist Suzanne Breen's right to withhold IRA details', *The Guardian*, 18 June 2009; A. McIntyre, 'Suzanne Breen: Give them absolutely nothing', *X Index: The Voice of Free Expression*, 6 May 2009.

19   L. Clarke, 'Survey: Most Northern Irish Catholics Want to Remain in UK', *Belfast Telegraph*, 17 June 2011.

20   J. Evans and J. Tonge, 'Menace without mandate: Is there any sympathy for "Dissident" Irish republicanism in Northern Ireland', *TPV*, 24/1 (2012), pp. 61–78; H. McDonald, 'One in seven nationalists sympathize with dissident terrorists', *The Guardian*, 6 October 2010; L. Clarke, 'Poll: Quarter of Sinn Féin Supports still back armed struggle', *Belfast Telegraph*, 15 April 2013.

21   Des Dalton interview, 2009.

22   Marian Price interview, 2010.

23   Val Lynch interview, 2008.

24   See, however, 'Chairman's Address', 32 County Sovereignty Movement Ard Fheis, 2013, *The Sovereign Nation*, February/March 2014, pp. 6–7.

25   The vote was 68 per cent for Dalton, 32 per cent for Long. D. Dalton, 'Presidential Address', November 2010.

26   This was at least the second split in the CIRA (Horgan, *Divided We Stand*, p. 27). 'RSF Will Not Yield to Threats', *Saoirse*, June 2010, p. 1; 'New Army Leadership elected by Continuity IRA', *Saoirse Nua*, October/November 2010, p. 1; 'Army Council intact and in control', *Saoirse*, June 2010, p. 1.

27   'RSF condemns breakaway Limerick group', *Irish Republican News* 23 August 2010; 'New leadership elected', *Saoirse Nua*, March 2011/April 2011, p. 2.

28   'IRA speaks', *Saoirse*, June 2010, p.1 ; J. Lynch, 'Daltonites Tell Lies to Hide the Truth of Real Reasons', *Saoirse Nua*, December 2010/January 2011, p. 2; D. Dalton, 'Presidential Address', *Saoirse*,

December 2010, pp. 10-11; Morrison, *The Origins and Rise of Dissident Irish Republicanism*, pp. 197–9.

29   'Daltonites tell lies to hide the truth of real reasons for split', *Saoirse Nua*, December 2010/January 2011, p. 2; 'USA visits allowed by State Department', *Saoirse Nua*, June–July 2011, p. 2; 'Felon-setting by splinter', *Saoirse*, June 2011, p. 2.

30   Joe Lynch interview, 2011.

31   Seamus Ó Suilleabhain interview, 2011. See also Morrison, *The Origins and Rise of Dissident Irish Republicanism*, pp. 197–9; Horgan, *Divided We Stand*, p. 89.

32   See various issues of *Saoirse Nua*, 'RSF Dismiss Members Including Vice-President', *Saoirse Nua*, December 2012/January 2013, p. 3.

33   See 'Dublin man convicted of Continuity IRA membership', *RTÉ News*, 31 May 2001; 'Clarification from Republican Sinn Féin', 10 April 2013; 'Murder victim was suspected of key role in Continuity IRA', *Irish News Independent*, 11 June 2011; 'Vol. Liam Kenny, 1958–2011', *Saoirse Nua*, June/July 2011, p. 4; 'Female assassin pleads guilty to IRA killing in Dublin', *Irish Times*, 9 April 2013; 'IRA assassin planned five more hits – "deluded" father in court sees Rose Lynch as hero', *Irish Central.com*, 11 April 2013.

34   'Free the Newry Seven', *Saoirse Nua*, December 2014/January 2015, p. 1; D. Young, 'Seven charged over dissident republican activity', *The Irish Examiner*, 18 November 2014; D. Young, 'MI5 uncovers plot to "target" judges and police in the North', *Irish Independent*, 18 November 2014.

35   See Horgan, *Divided We Stand*, pp. 123–4; H. McDonald, 'Northern Ireland dissidents use remote control bomb in attack on PSNI officer', *The Observer*, 16 January 2010.

36   'Dissident show of strength for Alan Ryan funeral', *Belfast Telegraph*, 9 September 2012; 'Priest's plea as veteran crimelord laid to rest', S. Murphy, *The Irish Daily Star*, 14 December 2012; 'RIRA gang kidnap and then shoot man', *Herald.ie*, 9 May 2013.

37   Morrison, *The Origins and Rise of Dissident Irish Republicanism*, pp. 190–1.

38   H. McDonald, 'Republican dissidents join forces to form a new IRA', *The Guardian*, 26 July 2012; H. McDonald, 'Irish Republican Colin Duffy freed after questioning over prison officer murder', *The Guardian*, 5 November 2012; Morrison, *The Origins and Rise of Dissident Irish Republicanism*, pp. 175–6, 196.

39   'Kieran Doherty murder: Main suspect Peter Butterly murdered last year', *BBC News Foyle and West*, 13 May 2014; T. Brady, 'Armagh leader of "New IRA" ordered Co Meath murder in row over cash', *Belfast Telegraph*, 8 March 2013; 'Deirdre Quinn, 'Dirty Money And A River of Blood', *The Pensive Quill*, 13 March 2016.

40   Vincent Kearney, 'Martin Corey lawyers compare his imprisonment to internment', *BBC News Northern Ireland*, 17 May 2013; 'Arrests political attack on Republican Sinn Féin', *Saoirse*, August 2011; 'The real face of British rule', *Saoirse*, August 2011, p. 1; 'Martin Corey released from prison', *BBC News Northern Ireland*, 16 January 2014.

41   'Queen Lays Wreath on Republic of Ireland State Visit', *BBC News*, 17 May 2011.

42   Marian Price interview, 2010.

43   Suzanne Breen, 'Heavy police presence for Price court appearance', *Belfast Telegraph*, 17 May 2011; 'Cait Trainor, Seán Maloney face terror charges', *BBC News*, 16 May 2011; Terrorism Act 2006, http://www.legislation.gov.uk/ukpga/2006/11/section/2 (last accessed 04/03/ 2015.

44   See 'Marian Price "refuses to meet Sinn Féin" during prison visit', *BBC News Northern Ireland*, 14 March 2012; 'Marian Price case collapses', *Irish Republican News*, 11 May 2012; S. Breen, 'Marian Price leaves hospital for sister's wake', *Belfast Telegraph*, 29 January 2013; 'Marian Price released from custody', *BBC News Northern Ireland*, 30 May 2013; Horgan, *Divided We Stand*, pp. 89–90; H. McDonald, 'Old Bailey Bomber Charged Over Murder of British Soldiers', *The Guardian*, 22 July 2011; 'Old Bailey bomber Marian Price guilty of providing phone used to claim the murders at Masserene Army Barracks', *Belfast Telegraph*, 22 November 2013; 'Massereene murders: Marian Price handed suspended sentence for terrorist offences', *Belfast Newsletter*, 7 January 2014.

45   P. Malone, 'Éirígí and RNU demand release of Newry republican Stephen Murney', *Newry Times*, 3 December 2012; 'Éirígí press officer Stephen Murney cleared of terrorism charges', *BBC News Northern Ireland*, 24 February 2014; 'Stephen Murney in his own words', 16 March 2014.

46   Seamus McKinney, 'Leading republican Tony Taylor returned to prison after licence revoked', *Irish News*, 12 March 2016; see also the 'Free Tony Taylor' Facebook page.

47   Prominently missing were the Provisionals, who were told to stay away, and the RSF-Limerick group. Those paying their respects included the local Fine Gael TD. Grainne Cunningham, 'TD stands by decision to attend funeral of dissident republican leader Ó Brádaigh', *Independent*, 10 June 2013.

48 Ruairí Ó Brádaigh interview, 1996.

49 Cáit Trainor interview, 2012.

50 John Hunt interview, 2014.

51 John Hunt oration, 'A Dream Deferred', 23 April 2016, Dublin GPO. See also, '1916: "A Dream Deferred"', *Saoirse*, May 2016, p. 3.

Chapter 25

1 Ruairí Ó Brádaigh interview, 2009.

2 K. Marx, *The 18th Brumaire of Louis Bonaparte* (New York: International Publishers, 1984 edition), p. 15. See also McKearney, *From Insurrection to Parliament*, pp. 90–100.

3 S. Tarrow, *Democracy and Disorder* (Oxford: OUP, 1989), pp. 3–9, 163–4, 307–9, 345; S. Tarrow, *Power in Movement: Social Movements, Collective Action, and Politics* (Cambridge: Cambridge University Press, 1998). See also, D. della Porta and M. Diani, *Social Movements: An Introduction* (Oxford: Blackwell, 1999), pp. 188–92, 231–2; McAdam et al., *Dynamics of Contention*, pp. 28–32; Tilly and Tarrow, *Contentious Politics*, pp. 89–109.

4 See for example, L. Bosi, 'Incorporation and democratization: The long-term process of institutionalization of the Northern Ireland Civil Rights Movement', pp. 338–60 in L. Bosi, M. Giugni and K. Uba (eds) *The Consequences of Social Movements: Policies, People and Institutions* (Cambridge: Cambridge University Press, 2015).

5 Several of the 1960s social movements were linked, including the civil rights movement, the environmental movement, the new American right movement and the global justice movement. See Staggenborg, *Social Movements*; on Northern Ireland, see L. Bosi and S. Prince, 'Writing the Sixties into Northern Ireland and Northern Ireland into the Sixties', *The Sixties: A Journal of History, Politics, and Culture*, 2/2 (2009), pp. 145–61.

6 F.F. Piven and R. Cloward, *Poor People's Movements: Why They Succeed, How They Fail* (New York: Vintage, 1977) (quotation pp. xxi, 32).

7 Piven and Cloward (p. xvi) build on R. Michels, *Political Parties: A Sociological Study of the Oligarchical Tendencies of Modern Democracy* (New York: The Free Press, 1962 [1911]), pp. 333–56, quotations, pp. 333, 342;.

8 See Piven and Cloward, *Poor People's Movements*, pp. 96–180.

9 See Bell, *The Gun in Politics*, pp. 181–5.

10 McKittrick et al.'s *Lost Lives* (p. 138) records 496 fatalities in 1972; Elliott and Flackes, *Northern Ireland Political Directory* (p. 681) have the total as 470; Sutton, *An Index of Deaths from the Northern Ireland Conflict* (p. 206), has the total as 472.

11 See Gamson, *The Strategy of Social Protest*, pp. 31–4.

12 See Piven and Cloward, *Poor People's Movements*, p. 36.

13 K. Mullan, '50/50 recruitment not on', *Londonderry Sentinel*, 8 November 2015.

14 See S.G. Jones and M.C. Libicki, *How Terrorist Groups End* (Santa Monica, CA: RAND Corporation, 2008), pp. 20–6.

15 See Tilly, *From Mobilization to Revolution*; McAdam, Tarrow and Tilly, *Dynamics of Contention*; Tarrow and Tilly, *The Politics of Contention*.

16 R.W. White and M. Fraser, 'Personal and Collective Identities and Long Term Movement Activism', pp. 324–46 in Stryker et al. (eds), *Self, Identity, and Social Movements* (Minneapolis: University of Minnesota Press, 2000); V. Taylor, 'Social movement continuity', *American Sociological Review*, 54 (1989), pp. 761–75; N. Whittier, *Feminist Generations: The Persistence of the Radical Women's Movement* (Philadelphia: Temple University Press, 1995).

17 See Cronin, *Irish Nationalism*, p. 202; T. Demeril-Pegg, 'From the streets to the mountains: The dynamics of transition from a protest wave to an insurgency in Kashmir', *Mobilization*, 19/3, pp. 309–27.

18 For an insightful analysis of 'outbidding' and radicalization in general, see E. Alimi, C. Demetriou, and L. Bosi, *The Dynamics of Radicalization* (Oxford: OUP, 2015).

19 V.I. Lenin, 'The Discussion on Self-Determination Summed Up' (1916); Cronin, *Irish Nationalism*, pp. 38–9, 227–8; Bell, *On Revolt*; Bell, *The Secret Army*, p. 149; E. Moloney, 'Fascinating links between the Irgun and IRA', *The Broken Elbow*; Ruairí Ó Brádaigh interviews; Kitson, *Low Intensity Operations* (1971).

20 V. Taylor and N. Whittier, 'Collective identity in social movement communities: Lesbian feminist mobilization', pp. 104–29 in A. Morris and C. Mueller, *Frontiers in Social Movement Theory* (1992); Gamson, *Encounters With Unjust Authority*, p. 60; D. Snow and D. McAdam, 'Identity work processes in the context of social movements', pp. 41–67 in Stryker et al. (eds), *Self, Identity, and Social Movements*; P. Thoits and L.K. Virshup, 'Me's and we's: Forms and functions of social identities', pp. 106–33 in R. Ashmore and L. Jussim (eds), *Self and Identity: Fundamental Issues* (Oxford: OUP,1997); J. Veugelers, 'Dissenting families and social movement abeyance: the transmission of neo-fascist frames in postwar Italy', *British Journal of Sociology*, 62 (2011), pp. 241–61.

21   See K. Blee, *Women of the Klan: Racism and Gender in the 1920s* (Berkeley: University of California Press, 1991); L. Bosi and D. della Porta, 'Micro-mobilization into armed groups: Ideological, instrumental and solidaristic paths,' *Qualitative Sociology*, 35 (2012), pp. 361–83; D. della Porta, 'Recruitment Processes in Clandestine Political Organizations: Italian Left-Wing Terrorism,' pp. 155–72 in B. Klandermans, H.P. Kriesi and S. Tarrow (eds), *International Social Movement Research*. (Vol. 1) (Greenwich, CT: JAI Press, 1988); J. Veugelers, 'Dissenting families and social movement abeyance: the transmission of neo-fascist frames in postwar Italy', *British Journal of Sociology*, 62/2 (2012), 241–61.

22   See for example, C. Tilly, 'Repression, mobilization, and explanation', pp. 211–26 in C. Davenport, H. Johnston and C. Mueller (eds), *Repression and Mobilization* (2005); D. della Porta, *Social Movements, Political Violence, and the State* (Cambridge: Cambridge University Press, 1995); R.A. Francisco, 'The relationship between coercion and protest: An empirical evaluation in three coercive states', *The Journal of Conflict Resolution*, 39 (1995), pp. 263–82; K. Rasler, 'Concessions, repression, and political protest in the Iranian revolution', *American Sociological Review*, 61 (1996), pp. 132–52.

23   For a description of the influence that state repression had on Irish republicans from 1916–79, see Bell, *The Secret Army*.

24   See Bell, *The Irish Troubles*, pp. 25–86; B. Probert, *Beyond Orange and Green: The Political Economy of the Northern Ireland Conflict* (London: Zed Books, 1978).

25   See White, *Ruairí Ó Brádaigh*, pp. 80–1; Bosi and Prince, 'Writing the Sixties into Northern Ireland and Northern Ireland into the Sixties', *The Sixties: A Journal of History, Politics, and Culture*, 2:2 (2009), pp. 145–61; L. Bosi, 'The dynamics of social movement development: Northern Ireland's civil rights movement in the 1960s', *Mobilization*, 11/1 (2011), pp. 81–100.

26   See Snow et al., 'Social networks and social movements', *American Sociological Review*, 45, pp. 787–801; D. McAdam, J. McCarthy and M. Zald, 'Social Movements', in N.J. Smelser (ed.), *Handbook of Sociology* (London: Sage, 1988), pp. 695–737.

27   Processes that bring together previously unconnected groups are referred to as 'brokerage'. See Tilly and Tarrow, *Contentious Politics*, p. 215; T. Demirel-Pegg and Scott Pegg, 'Razed, repressed and bought off: The demobilization of the Ogoni protest campaign in the Niger Delta', *Extractive Industries and Society*, 2 (2015), pp. 654–63.

28   Viterna (*Women in War*, p. 214) shows that there was no 'typical' path for recruitment to the FMLN. See White, 'Structural Identity Theory and the post-recruitment activism of Irish Republicans', *Social Problems*, 57/3 (2010), pp. 341–70; H. Johnston, *What is a Social Movement?* (Malden, MA: Polity Press, 2014); J. Weinstein, *Inside Rebellion: The Politics of Insurgent Violence* (Cambridge: Cambridge University Press, 2007).

29   On the Irish peace process, see T. White, *Lessons from the Northern Ireland Peace Process* (Madison: University of Wisconsin Press, 2013).

30   See White, 'From Peaceful Protest to Guerrilla War', *American Journal of Sociology*, 94/6 (1989), pp. 1277–302; English, *Terrorism: How to Respond*, pp. 118–43.

Appendix I

1   J.B. Bell, 'Terror: An Overview,' pp. 36–43 in M.H. Livingston, L.B. Kress and M.G. Wanek (eds.), *International Terrorism in the Contemporary World* (Westport, CT: Greenwood Press, 1978).

2   D. Snow and D. Trom, 'The Case Study and the Study of Social Movements,' pp. 146–72 in B. Klandermans and S. Staggenborg, *Methods of Social Movement Research* (Minneapolis: University of Minnesota Press, 2002); D. della Porta, 'Biographies of social movement activists: State of the art and methodological problems', pp. 168–93 in M. Diani and R. Eyerman (eds), *Studying Collective Action* (Newbury Park: Sage Publications, 1992); B. Klandermans, S. Staggenborg and S. Tarrow, 'Conclusion: Blending Methods and Building Theories in Social Movement Research', pp. 314–49 in Klandermans and Staggenborg (eds), *Methods of Social Movement Research* (Minneapolis: University of Minnesota Press, 2002); B. Klandermans, 'The Case for Longitudinal Research on Movement Participation', pp. 55–75 in Diani and Eyerman (eds), *Studying Collective Action* (Newbury Park: Sage Publications, 1992). For an insightful description of qualitative interviewing of activists in armed struggle, see Viterna, *Women at War* (2013), pp. 221–55.

3   This section draws on White, *Provisional Irish Republicans* (1993) and White, 'Structural Identity Theory and the Post-Recruitment Activism of Irish Republicans', *Social Problems*, 57/3 (2010), pp. 341–70.

4   B. Glaser and A. Strauss, *The Discovery of Grounded Theory: Strategies for Qualitative Research* (New York: Aldine, 1967).

ENDNOTES

5   E. Babbie, *The Practice of Social Research* (Belmont, CA: Wadsworth, 1983), pp. 286–7; K. Blee and V. Taylor, 'Semi-structured interviewing in social movement research', pp. 92–117 in Klandermans and Staggenborg (eds), *Methods of Social Movement Research*; M. Brenner, 'Intensive Interviewing', pp. 147–62 in M. Brenner, J. Brown and D. Canter (eds), *The Research Interview* (New York: Academic Press, 1985); W. Cutler, 'Accuracy in oral history interviewing', *Historical Methods Newsletter*, 3 (1970), pp. 1–7.

6   See A. Bryson and S. McConville (assisted by M. McClean), *The Routledge Guide to Interviewing: Oral History, social enquiry and investigation* (New York: Routledge, 2014).

7   See D. Snow and R. Machalek, 'The sociology of conversion', *Annual Review of Sociology*, 10 (1984), pp. 787–801.

8   See Bruce, 'Victim selection in ethnic conflict: Motives and Attitudes in Irish Republicanism', *TPV*, 9/1 (1997), pp. 56–71; R. Alonso, *The IRA and Armed Struggle* (New York: Routledge, 2003), pp. 8, 67–101.

9   H. Becker, *Sociological Work: Method and Substance* (New Brunswick, NJ: Transaction Books, 1970), pp. 39–62.

10 R. Wallis and S. Bruce, 'Accounting for action: Defending the common sense heresy', *Sociology*, 17 (1983), pp. 97–111.

11 J. Brown and J. Sime, 'A methodology for accounts', in M. Brenner (ed.), *Social Method and Social Life* (New York: Academic Press, 1981).

12 R.W. White, '"I'm not too sure what I told you the last time": A methodological note on the consistency of the accounts of activists in political violence', *Mobilization*, 12 (2007), pp. 287–306.

SOURCES AND BIBLIOGRAPHY

This oral history is the result of more than thirty years of visits to Ireland, formal interviews and informal conversations with activists and interested parties, time spent in libraries tracking down sources and reading newspapers, consideration of the scholarly literature and reflection on the causes and consequences of political violence. While trying to gather as much information on the Irish conflict as possible, I have also tried to follow the lead of the late J. Bowyer Bell by drawing on primary sources as much as possible.

Some respondents graciously agreed to allow me to identify them and quote from their interviews. Other respondents, for various reasons, preferred to not be quoted. Some asked that the conversation not be recorded and I never learned the names of some respondents. Every attempt has been made to be as rigorous, systematic, and factual as possible, especially in transcribing interviews. The quotations are as accurate as possible, with the caveat that the occasional 'you know', 'eh', and such has been left out to help with clarity. Because of accents and poor recordings, every now and then a word or phrase was unclear. If anyone has been misquoted or misinterpreted, it has been an accident.

The following is a list of respondents (from left to right) based on their order of appearance:

Derry republican 1
Ruairí Ó Brádaigh
Joe Cahill
Donegal republican
Frank Glynn
Mitchel McLaughlin
Gerry McKerr
Clonard republican
Fermanagh republican 1
Dublin republican 1
Geraldine Taylor
Richard Behal
Seán Crowe
Tyrone republican 3
Seán O'Callaghan
Cathleen Knowles McGuirk
Kerry republican

Belfast republican 1
John Hunt
Joe B. O'Hagan
Phil O'Donoghue
Fra McCann
Peig King
Armagh republican
Brendan Hughes
Derry Republican 2
Belfast IRA veteran
Newry republican
Revd Harold Good
Gerry Hodgins
Líta Ní Chathmhaoil
Brian McDonald
Owen Carron
Sligo republican

Danny Morrison
Billy McKee
Seán Mac Stiofáin
Seán Lynch
Tyrone republican 1
Tyrone republican 2
Tom Fleming
Bernadette O'Hagan
Val Lynch
Marian Price
Josephine Hayden
Derry republican 3
Gerry McGeough
Derry republican 4
Caoimhghín Ó Caoláin
Belfast republican 4
Dublin republican 2

Fermanagh republican 2
Christy Burke
Pat Doherty
Belfast republican 5
Belfast republican 6
Joe Dillon
Cáit Trainor
Seamus Ó Suilleabhain

Tyrone republican 4
Peter McAleer
Tipperary republican
Martin Mansergh
Joe Lynch
Davy Hyland
RSF activist

Martin Galvin
Martin McGuinness
Dublin Republican 5
Des Dalton
Belfast republican 7
Limerick republican
Killian Forde

Newspapers and News Magazines Consulted

In reporting on people and events, several journalists have provided critical insight that otherwise would have been lost, especially Ed Moloney, Suzanne Breen, Peter Taylor, David McKittrick, Liam Clarke, Eamonn Mallie, Mary Holland, Eamon McCann, Henry McDonald, and Anne Cadwallader. *Lost Lives*, by David McKittrick, Seamus Kelters, Brian Feeney and Chris Thornton is an incredible resource. In the end notes, and in order to minimise length, some articles and other sources that do not have page numbers are from web sources but the link has not been included.

An Phoblacht
An Phoblacht/Republican News
Belfast Telegraph
Christian Science Monitor
Danny Morrison blog www.dannymorrison.com
Evening Herald
Fourthwrite: For a Democratic Socialist Republic (several issues are archived: http://www2.ulib.iupui.edu/digitalscholarship/collections/Fourthwrite)
Iris: The Republican Magazine
Irish Examiner
Irish News
Irish Post
Irish Press
Irish Times
Magill
Republican News
Saoirse (archived: http://www.ulib.iupui.edu/collections/IrishNews)
Sunday Tribune
The Guardian
The New York Times
The Sovereign Nation (several issues are archived: http://www2.ulib.iupui.edu/digitalscholarship/collections/SNation)

The United Irishman
The Village

Web-based Sources

"55 Hours" (Carrie Twomey: detailed information on the British offer to end the hunger strike in July 1981; http://thepensivequill.am/p/55-hours-day-by-day-account-of-events.html).

CAIN Web Service – Conflict Archive on the INternet; http://cain.ulst.ac.uk/ (words cannot describe the value of the CAIN Web Service).

Danny Morrison: Writer (http://www.dannymorrison.com/).

Irish Republican Education Forum, Facebook (http://www.republican.ie/forum/).

Irish Republican Forum (http://www.republican.ie/forum/).

Saoirse32 (https://saoirse32.dreamwidth.org/).

Slugger O'Toole (http://sluggerotoole.com/).

The Belfast Project, Boston College and a Sealed Subpoena (Carrie Twomey: https://bostoncollegesubpoena.wordpress.com).

The Blanket: A Journal of Protest and Dissent (archived: http://www2.ulib.iupui.edu/digitalscholarship/collections/blanket).

The Broken Elbow (Ed Moloney: http://thebrokenelbow.com/).

The Pensive Quill (Anthony McIntyre: http://thepensivequill.am/)

Slugger O'Toole (http://sluggerotoole.com/).

Vol. Joe O'Connor, https://tenyearson.wordpress.com/.

Archives/Library Resources

Brendan Duddy Papers, Hardiman Library, National University of Ireland, Galway.

Irish Republican Movement Collection, University Library, IUPUI (http://www.ulib.iupui.edu/collections/IrishRepublicanMovement).

Linenhall Library, Northern Ireland Political Collection, Belfast.

Ruairí Ó Brádaigh Papers, Hardiman Library, National University of Ireland, Galway.

Bibliography: Books

Adams, Gerry, *Cage Eleven* (Dingle: Co. Kerry, 1990).

Adams, Gerry, *Before the Dawn: An Autobiography* (New York: William and Morrow, 1996).

Adams, Gerry, *A Farther Shore: Ireland's Long Road to Peace* (New York: Random House, 2003).

Allen, Kieran, *1916: Ireland's Revolutionary Tradition* (London: Pluto Press, 2016),

Alimi, Eitan, Chares Demetriou and Lorenzo Bosi, *The Dynamics of Radicalization* (Oxford: Oxford University Press, 2015).

Alonso, Rogelio, *The IRA and Armed Struggle* (London: Routledge, 2007).

Anderson, Brendan, *Joe Cahill: A Life in the IRA* (Dublin: O'Brien Press, 2005).

Anderson, Chris, *The Billy Boy: The Life and Death of UVF Leader Billy Wright* (Edinburgh: Mainstream Publishing, 2002).

Ardoyne Commemoration Project, *Ardoyne: The Untold Story* (Belfast: Beyond the Pale Publications, 2002).

Ashmore, Richard and Lee Jussim (eds), *Self and Identity; Fundamental Issues* (Oxford: Oxford University Press,1997).

Asmal, Kader Asmal (Chairman), *Shoot to Kill? International Lawyers' Inquiry into the Lethal Use of Firearms by the Security Forces in Northern Ireland* (Dublin: Mercier Press, 1985).

SOURCES AND BIBLIOGRAPHY

Augusteijn, Joost, *From Public Defiance to Guerrilla Warfare: The Experience of Ordinary Volunteers in the Irish War of Independence 1916–1921* (Dublin: Irish Academic Press, 1996).

Babbie, Earle, *The Practice of Social Research* (Belmont, CA: Wadsworth, 1983).

Barnett, Donald and Karari Njama, *Mau Mau From Within* (New York: Monthly Review Press, 1966).

Barrett, J.J., *Martin Ferris: Man of Kerry* (Dingle, Co. Kerry: Brandon, 2005).

Barry, Tom, *Guerrilla Days in Ireland* (Cork: Mercier Press, 1955).

Bean, Kevin, *The New Politics of Sinn Féin* (Liverpool, Liverpool University Press, 2007).

Bean, Kevin and Mark Hayes (eds), *Republican Voices* (Monaghan, Co. Monaghan: Seesyu Press, 2001).

Becker, Howard Becker, *Sociological Work: Method and Substance* (New Brunswick, NJ: Transaction Books, 1970).

Belfast Graves (Dublin: The National Graves Association, 1985).

Boyle, Kevin, T. Hadden and P. Hillary, *Ten Years on in Northern Ireland: The Legal Control of Political Violence* (London: Cobden Trust, 1980).

Bradley, Gerry and Brian Feeney, *Insider: Gerry Bradley's Life in the IRA* (Dublin: O'Brien Press, 2009).

Brenner, Michael (ed.), *Social Method and Social Life* (New York: Academic Press, 1981).

Bell, J. Bowyer, *On Revolt* (Cambridge: Harvard University Press, 1976).

Bell, J. Bowyer, *The Secret Army: The IRA 1916 –* (Dublin: The Academy Press, 1979).

Bell, J. Bowyer, *The Gun in Politics* (New Brunswick, NJ: Transaction Publishers, 1986).

Bell, J. Bowyer, *The Irish Troubles: A Generation of Conflict* (New York: St. Martin's, 1993).

Bell, J. Bowyer, *The Dynamics of the Armed Struggle* (New York: Routledge, 1995).

Bell, J. Bowyer, *The Secret Army: The IRA* (Dublin: Poolbeg, 1997).

Bell, J. Bowyer, *In Dubious Battle* (Dublin: Poolbeg, 1999).

Beresford, David, *Ten Men Dead: The Story of the 1981 Irish Hunger Strike* (London: Grafton, 1987).

Bew, Paul, *Land and the National Question in Ireland, 1858–1882* (Atlantic Highlands, N.J.: Humanities Press, 1979).

Bew, Paul and Gordon Gillespie, *Northern Ireland: A Chronology of the Troubles, 1968–1999* (Dublin: Gill and Macmillan, 1999).

Bishop, Patrick and Eamon Mallie, *The Provisional IRA* (Aylesbury Bucks, England: 1989).

Blair, Tony, *A Journey: My Political Life* (London: Vintage Books, 2011).

K. Blee, *Women of the Klan: Racism and Gender in the 1920s* (Berkeley: University of California Press, 1991).

Brady, Evelyn, Eva Patterson, Kate McKinney, Rosie Hamill and Pauline Jackson (comp.), *In the Footsteps of Anne: Stories of Republican Women Ex-Prisoners* (Belfast: Shanway Press, 2011).

Brenner, Michael, Jennifer Brown and David Canter (eds), *The Research Interview* (New York: Academic Press, 1985).

Boyd, Andrew, *The Informers: A Chilling Account of the Supergrasses in Northern Ireland*(Cork: Mercier Press, 1984).

Boyd, Andrew, *Holy War in Belfast* (London: Anvil Books, 1987).

Breen, Dan, *My Fight for Irish Freedom* (Tralee: Anvil Books, 1993).

Bruce, Steve, *The Red Hand: Protestant Paramilitaries in Northern Ireland* (1992).

Bryson, Anna (ed.), *The Insider: The Belfast Prison Diaries of Eamonn Boyce 1956–1962* (Dublin: The Lilliput Press, 2007).

Bryson, Anna and Seán McConville (assisted by Mairead McClean), *The Routledge Guide to Interviewing: Oral History, social enquiry and investigation* (New York: Routlege, 2014).

Buckland, Patrick, *Ulster Unionism and the Origins of Northern Ireland, 1886–1922* (Dublin: Gill and Macmillan, 1973).

Burke, Maurice, SMA, *Britain's War Machine in Ireland* (New York: Oisin, 1987).

Burton, Frank, *The Politics of Legitimacy – Struggles in a Belfast Community* (London: UK, Routledge and Kegan Paul, 1978).

Cadwallader, Anne, *Lethal Allies: British Collusion in Ireland* (Cork: Mercier Press, 2013).

Campbell, Brian, Lawrence McKeown and Felim O'Hagan (eds) (compiled by Brian Campbell), *Nor Meekly Serve My Time: The H-Block Struggle 1976–1981* (Belfast: Beyond the Pale Publications, 1994).

Chomsky, Noam, *Pirates and Emperors: International Terrorism in the Real World* (New York: Claremont Research and Publications, 1986).

Cicourel, Aaron V. *Method and Measurement in Sociology* (New York: The Free Press, 1964).

Clarke, Liam, *Broadening the Battlefield: The H-Blocks and the Rise of Sinn Féin* (Dublin: Gill and Macmillan, 1987).

Clarke, Liam and Kathryn Johnston, *Martin McGuinness: From Guns to Government* (Edinburgh: Mainstream, 2001).

Clarke, Sister Sarah, *No Faith in the System: A Search for Justice* (Dublin: Mercier Press, 1995).

Clinton, Bill, *My Life* (New York: Alfred A. Knopf, 2004).

Clutterbuck, Richard, *Protest and the Urban Guerrilla* (London: Casswell, 1973).

Coleman, Marie, *County Longford and the Irish Revolution 1910–1923* (Dublin: Irish Academic Press, 2003).

Collins, Eamon, *Killing Rage* (London: Granta Books, 1998).

Collins, Lorcan, *James Connolly: 16 Lives* (Dublin: The O'Brien Press, 2012).

Collins, Tom, *The Irish Hunger Strike* (Dublin: White Island, 1986).

Conway, Kieran, *Southside Provisional: From Freedom Fighter to the Four Courts* (Dublin: Orpen Press, 2014).

Coogan, Tim Pat, *The I.R.A.* (London: Harper Collins, 2000).

Coser, Lewis, *Masters of Sociological Thought: Ideas in Historical and Social Context* (San Diego, CA: Harcourt Brace Jovanovich, 1977).

Cronin, Seán, *Irish Nationalism* (Dublin: Irish Academic Press, 1980).

Cruise O'Brien, Conor, *Memoir: My Life and Themes* (Dublin: Poolbeg Press, 1999).

Cunningham, Michael, *British Government Policy in Northern Ireland, 1969–2000* (Manchester: Manchester University Press, 2001).

Currie, Austin, *All Hell Will Break Loose* (Dublin: O'Brien Press, 2004).

D'Arcy, Revd William, *The Fenian Movement in the United States: 1858–1886* (Washington: The Catholic University of America Press, 1947).

Darragh, Síle, *'John Lennon's Dead': Stories of Protest, Hunger Strikes, and Resistance* (Belfast: Beyond the Pale Publications: 2011).

David, Earle and Richard Sinnott, *Attitudes in the Republic of Ireland Relevant to the Northern Ireland Problem: Vol. 1.* (Dublin, Economic and Social Research Institute, 1979).

De Baróid, Ciarán, *Ballymurphy and the Irish War* (Baile Atha Cliath–Dublin: Aisling Publishers, 1989).

della Porta, Donatella, *Social Movements, Political Violence, and the State: A Comparative Analysis of Italy and Germany* (Cambridge: Cambridge University Press, 1995).

della Porta, Donatella and Mario Diani, *Social Movements: An Introduction* (Oxford: Blackwell, 1999).

de Paor, Liam, *Divided Ulster* (Harmondsworth: Penguin Books, 1970).

Deutsch Richard and Vivien Magowan, *Northern Ireland, 1968–1972, Chronology of Events, Volume I* (Belfast: Blackstaff Press, 1973).

Deutsch, Richard and Vivien Magowan, *Northern Ireland: A Chronology II*, 1973 (Belfast: Blackstaff Press, 1975).

Deutsch, Richard and Vivien Magowan, *Northern Ireland Chronology III*, 1975 (Belfast: Blackstaff Press, 1975).

Devlin, Bernadette, *The Price of My Soul* (New York: Alfred A. Knopf, 1969).

Devlin, Paddy, *The Fall of the N.I. Executive* (Belfast: Paddy Devlin, 1975).

Devlin, Paddy, *Yes, We Have No Bananas: Outdoor Relief in Belfast, 1920–1939* (Belfast: Blackstaff Press, 1981).

Devlin, Paddy, *Straight Left: An Autobiography* (Belfast: Blackstaff Press, 1993).

Diani, Mario and Ron Eyerman (eds), *Studying Collective Action* (Newbury Park: Sage Publications, 1992).

Dillon, Martin, *The Shankill Butchers: A Case Study of Mass Murder* (London: Arrow Books, 1990).

Dillon, Martin, *The Enemy Within: The IRA's War Against the British* (London: Doubleday, 1994).

Dingley, James, *The IRA: The Irish Republican Army* (New York: Praeger, 2012).

Drake, C.J.M., *Terrorists' Target Selection* (London: Macmillan Press, 1998).

Dudley Edwards, Ruth, *Patrick Pearse: The Triumph of Failure* (Dublin: Irish Academic Press, 2006).

Dudley Edwards, Ruth, *Aftermath: The Omagh Bombing and the Families' Pursuit of Justice* (London: Random House, 2010).

Duiker, William J., *Ho Chi Minh* (New York: Hyperion, 2000).

Dunne, Derek and Gene Kerrigan, *Round Up the Usual Suspects* (Dublin: Magill Publications, 1984).

Dwyer, T. Ryle, *Nice Fellow: A Biography of Jack Lynch* (Cork: Mercier Press, 2001). Eckert, Nicholas, *Fatal Encounter: The Story of the Gibraltar Killings* (Belfast: Poolbeg Press, 1999).

Edwards, Aaron and Cillian McGrattan, *The Northern Ireland Conflict: A Beginner's Guide* (London: OneWorld Publications, 2010).

Egan, Bowes and Vincent McCormack, *Burntollet* (London: L.R.S. Publishers, 1969).

Elliott, Sydney and W.D. Flackes, *Northern Ireland: A Political Directory, 1968–99* (Belfast: Blackstaff Press, 1999).

Ellis, P. Beresford, *James Connolly: Selected Writings* (Belfast: Pluto Press, 1988).

Ellis, Steven, *Tudor Ireland: Crown, Community and the Conflict of Culture, 1470–1603* (New York: Longman, 1985).

English, Richard, *Armed Struggle: A History of the IRA* (London: Macmillan, 2003).

English, Richard, *Terrorism: How to Respond* (Oxford: OUP, 2009).

English, Richard, *Does Terrorism Work? A History* (Oxford: Oxford University Press, 2016).

Farrell, Michael, *Northern Ireland: The Orange State* (London: Pluto Press, 1980).

Farrell, Michael, *Arming the Protestants: The Formation of the Ulster Special Constabulary and the Royal Ulster Constabulary, 1920–7* (London: Pluto Press, 1983).

Farren, Seán, *The SDLP: The Struggle for Agreement for Agreement in Northern Ireland, 1970–2000* (Dublin: Four Courts Press, 2010).

Feeney, Brian, *Sinn Féin: A Hundred Turbulent Years* (Dublin: O'Brien Press, 2002).

'Fermanagh Facts' (Fermanagh Civil Rights Association, 1969).

Ferriter, Diarmuid, *Judging Dev: A Reassessment of the Life and Legacy of Eamon de Valera* (Dublin: Radio Telefís Éireann, 2007).

Fisk, Robert, *The Point of No Return: The Strike Which Broke the British in Ulster* (London: Andre Deutsch, 1975).

FitzGerald, Garret, *All in a Life* (Dublin: Gill and Macmillan, 1991).

FitzGerald, Garret, *Just Garret: Tales From the Political Front Line* (Dublin: Liberties Press, 2010).

Flynn, Barry, *Soldiers of Folly: The IRA Border Campaign 1956–1962* (Wilton, Cork: The Collins Press, 2009).

Fogarty, Des, *Seán South of Garryowen* (Ennis, Ireland: FX Press, 2006).

Frampton, Martyn, *Legion of the Rearguard* (Dublin: Irish Academic Press, 2011).

Gamson, William, *The Strategy of Social Protest* (Belmont, CA: Wadsworth, 1990).

Gamson, William, Bruce Fireman and Steve Rytina, *Encounters With Unjust Authority* (Chicago: Dorsey Press, 1982).

Garvaghy Residents, *Garvaghy: A Community Under Siege* (Belfast: Beyond the Pale Publications, 1999).

Garvin, Tom, *1922: The Birth of Irish Democracy* (Dublin: Gill and Macmillan, 1996).

Geoghegan, Patrick M., *The Irish Act of Union* (Dublin: Gill and Macmillan, 2001).

Geoghegan, Patrick M., *Robert Emmet: A Life* (Dublin: Gill and Macmillan, 2002).

Gifford, Tony, *Supergrasses, the use of accomplice evidence in Northern Ireland: a report* (London: Cobden Trust 1984).

Gilligan, Robbie, *Tony Gregory* (Dublin: The O'Brien Press, 2011).

Glaser, Barney and Anselm Strauss, *The Discovery of Grounded Theory: Strategies for Qualitative Research* (New York: Aldine, 1967).

Godson, Dean, *Himself Alone: David Trimble and the Ordeal of Unionism* (London: Harper Collins, 2004).

Gorden, Robert L., *Interviewing: Strategy, Techniques and Tactics* (Homewood, IL: Dorsey Press, 1975).

Government of Northern Ireland, Violence and Civil Disturbances in Northern Ireland in 1969, Report of Tribunal of Inquiry (Scarman Report) (Her Majesty's Stationery Office, 1972).

Graham, Joe, *"Show Me The Man": The Official Biography of Martin Meehan* (Belfast: Rushlight Publications, 2008).

Guigni, Marco, Doug McAdams and Charles Tilly, *From Contention to Democracy* (Lanham, MD: Rowman & Littlefield, 1998).

Guigni, Marco, Doug McAdam, and Charles Tilly, *How Social Movements Matter* (Minneapolis: University of Minnesota Press, 1999).

Halberstam, David, *The Best and the Brightest* (New York: Random House, 1972).

Hanley, Brian, *The IRA: A Documentary History 1916–2005* (Dublin: Gill and Macmillan, 2010).

Hanley, Brian and Scott Millar, *The Lost Revolution* (London, Penguin, 2009).

Harndon, Toby, *'Bandit Country': The IRA & South Armagh* (London: Hodder & Stoughton, 2000).

Hart, Peter, *The I.R.A. at War 1916–1923* (Oxford: Oxford University Press, 2003).

Hart, Peter, *The I.R.A. at War 1916–1923* (Oxford: Oxford University Press, 2005).

Hegarty, Aidan, *Kevin Lynch and the Irish Hunger Strike* (Camlane Press, 2006).

Hennessey, Thomas, *Hunger Strike: Margaret Thatcher's Battle with the IRA 1980–1981* (Dublin: Irish Academic Press, 2014).

Hennessey, Thomas, *The First Northern Ireland Peace Process: Power Sharing, Sunningdale and the IRA Ceasefires 1972–76* (Basingstoke Hampshire: Palgrave Macmillan, 2015).

Herman, Edward S. and Gerry O'Sullivan, *The Terrorism Industry: The Experts and Institutions that Shape Our View of Terror* (New York: Pantheon Books, 1989).

Hoffman, Bruce, *Inside Terrorism* (New York: Columbia University Press, 2006).

Holland, Jack, *The American Connection: U.S. Guns, Money, & Influence in Northern Ireland* (New York: Penguin, 1987).

Holland, Jack, *Hope Against History: The Course of Conflict in Northern Ireland* (New York: Henry Holt, 1999).

Holland, Jack and Henry McDonald, *INLA: Deadly Divisions* (Dublin: Torc, 1994).

Holland, Jack and Susan Phoenix, *Phoenix: Policing the Shadows* (London: Hodder and Stoughton, 1996).

Horgan, John, *The Psychology of Terrorism* (New York: Routledge, 2005).

Horgan, John, *Walking Away from Terrorism: Accounts of Disengagement from Radical and Extremist Movements* (New York: Routledge, 2009).

Horgan, John, *Divided We Stand: The Strategy and Psychology of Ireland's Dissident Terrorists* (Oxford: Oxford University Press, 2012).

Horgan, John and Kurt Braddock, *Terrorism Studies: A Reader* (Oxfordshire: Routledge, 2012).

Ingram, Martin and Greg Hakin, *Stakeknife: Britain's Secret Agent in Ireland* (Dublin: O'Brien Press, 2004).

Irish Information: Agenda: A Database of Facts and Information on the Northern Ireland Conflict and Anglo-Irish Affairs (London: Irish Information Partnership, 1987).

Irish Information: Agenda: A Database of Facts and Information on the Northern Ireland Conflict and Anglo-Irish Affairs (London: Irish Information Partnership, 1990 Update).

Jenkins, J. Craig and Bert Klandermans (eds), *The Politics of Social Protest* (Minneapolis: University of Minnesota Press, 1995).

Johnston, Hank, *What is a Social Movement?* (Malden, MA: Polity Press, 2014).

Johnston, Roy, *Century of Endeavour: A Biographical and Autobiographical View of the Twentieth Century in Ireland* (Dublin: Lilliput Press, 2003).

Jones, Seth G. and Martin C. Libicki, *How Terrorist Groups End: Lessons for Countering al Qa'ida* (Santa Monica, CA: Rand, 2008).

Jordan, Hugh, *Milestone's in Murder: Defining Moments in Ulster's Terror War* (Edinburgh: Mainstream Publishing, 2002).

Keane, Elizabeth, *Seán Mac Bride: A Life* (Dublin: Gill and Macmillan, 2007).

Kelley, Kevin, *The Longest War: Northern Ireland and the I.R.A.* (London: Zed Books, 1988).

Kelly, Gerry, *The Escape: The Inside Story of the 1983 Escape from Long Kesh Prison* (M&G Publications, 2013).

Kelly, James, *The Thimble Riggers: The Dublin Arms Trial of 1970* (Dublin: James Kelly, 1999).

Kitson, Frank, *Low Intensity Operations: Subversion, Insurgency, and Peace-keeping* (Harriburg, PA: Stackpole Books, 1971).

Klandermans, Bert and Suzanne Staggenborg, *Methods of Social Movement Research* (Minneapolis: University of Minnesota Press, 2002).

Kleinrichter, Denise, *Republican Internment and the Prison Ship Argenta* (Dublin: Irish Academic Press, 2001).

Kyle, Keith, *The Politics of the Independence of Kenya* (New York: Palgrave Macmillan, 1999).

Lewis, Geoffrey, *Carson: The Man Who Divided Ireland* (London: Hambledon Continuum, 2006).

Livingstone, Marius H., Lee Bruce Kress, and Marie G. Wanek (eds), *International Terrorism in the Contemporary World*, (Westport, CT: Greenwood Press, 1978).

Lyons, F.S.L., *Ireland Since the Famine* (Rev. Ed.) (London: Fontana, 1973).

SOURCES AND BIBLIOGRAPHY

Mac Eoin, Uinsean, *The IRA in the Twilight Years 1923–1948* (Dublin: Argenta Publications, 1997).

Mac Stiofáin, Seán, *Revolutionary in Ireland* (London: Gordon Cremonesi,1975).

Magee, Gerard, *Tyrone's Struggle: Ar son Saoire na hÉireann* (Tyrone Sinn Féin/Gerard Magee, 2011).

Maguire, Patrick, *My Father's Watch* (London: Harper Perennial, 2009).

Maillot, Agnés, *New Sinn Féin: Irish republicanism in the twenty-first century* (London: Routledge, 2005).

Mallie, Eamonn and David McKittrick, *The Fight for Peace: The Secret Story Behind the Irish Peace Process* (London: William Heinemann, 1996).

Manchester, William and Paul Reid, *The Last Lion: Winston Spencer Churchill Defender of the Realm, 1940–1965* (New York: Little, Brown and Company, 2012).

Mannheim, Karl, *Essays on the Sociology of Knowledge* (London: Routledge & Kegan Paul, 1952 [1928]).

Marx, Karl, *The 18th Brumaire of Louis Bonaparte* (New York: International Publishers, 1984 [1852]).

Mason, Roy, *Paying the Price* (London: Robert Hale, Ltd., 1999).

McAdam, Doug, *Political Process and the Development of Black Insurgency, 1930–1970* (Chicago: University of Chicago Press, 1982).

McAdam, Doug, *Freedom Summer* (Oxford: Oxford University Press, 1988).

McAdam, Doug, Sidney Tarrow and Charles Tilly, *Dynamics of Contention* (Cambridge: Cambridge University Press, 2001).

McAllister, Ian, *The Northern Ireland Social Democratic and Labour Party: Political Opposition in a Divided Society* (London: Macmillan, 1977).

McCaffrey, Barry, *Alex Maskey: Man and Mayor* (Belfast: The Brehon Press, 2003).

McCartney, Catherine, *Walls of Silence* (Dublin: Gill and Macmillan, 2007).

McCauley, Clark and Sophia Moskalenko, *Friction: How Radicalization Happens to Them and Us* (Oxford: OUP, 2011).

McCluskey, Conn, *Up Off Their Knees* (Southampton: Camelot Press, 1989).

McDaid, Shaun, *Template for Peace: Northern Ireland 1972–75* (Manchester: University of Manchester Press, 2013).

McDonald, Eileen, *Shoot the Women First* (New York: Random House, 1991).

McDonald, Henry, *Trimble* (London: Bloomsbury, 2004).

McDonald, Henry, *Gunsmoke and Mirrors* (Dublin: Gill and Macmillan, 2008).

McDonald, Henry and Jim Cusack, *UDA: Inside the Heart of Loyalist Terror* (Penguin Ireland, 2004).

McGarrity, Joe (Seán Cronin), 'Resistance – The story of the struggle in British-Occupied Ireland' (Dublin, 1957).

McGladdery, Gerry, *The Provisional IRA in England: The Bombing Campaign, 1973–1997* (Dublin: Irish Academic Press, 2006).

McGuffin, John, *Internment!* (Tralee: Anvil Books, 1973).

McGuire, Maria, *To Take Arms: My Year with the IRA Provisionals* (New York: Viking Press, 1973).

McIntyre, Anthony, *Good Friday: The Death of Irish Republicanism* (New York: Asubo Press, 2008).

McKearney, Tommy, *The Provisional IRA: From Insurrection to Parliament* (Belfast: Pluto Press, 2011).

McKee Grant and Ros Franey, *Time Bomb: Irish Bombers, English Justice and the Guildford Four* (London: Bloomsbury, 1988).

McKeown, Lawrence, *Out of Time: Irish Republican Prisoners Long Kesh, 1972–2000* (Belfast: Beyond the Pale Publications, 2001).

McKittrick, David, Seamus Kelters, Brian Feeney, Chris Thornton and David McVea, *Lost Lives: The Stories of the Men, Women and Children who Died as a Result of the Northern Ireland Troubles* (Edinburgh: Mainstream Publishing, 2007).

McNulty, Thomas, *Exiled: 40 Years an Exile A Long Time Away from Kith and Kin* (Dublin: Brunswick Press Ltd., 2013).

McVeigh, Jim, *Executed: Tom Williams and the IRA* (Belfast: Beyond the Pale Publications, 1999).

Michels, Robert, *Political Parties: A Sociological Study of the Oligarchical Tendencies of Modern Democracy* (New York: The Free Press, 1962 [1911]).

Miller, David, *Don't Mention the War: Northern Ireland, Propaganda, and the Media* (Belfast: Pluto Press, 1994).

Miller, I. *A History of Force-Feeding: Hunger Strikes, Prisons, and Medical Ethics, 1909–1974* (London: Palgrave Macmillan, 2016), pp. 191–236.

Mitchel, John Mitchel, *Jail Journal* (Dublin: M.H. Gill and Son, 1913).

Mitchell, George, *Making Peace* (New York: Alfred A. Knopf, 1999).

Moloney, Ed, *A Secret History of the IRA* (New York: Norton, 2002).

Moloney, Ed, *A Secret History of the IRA* (London: Penguin Books, 2007).

Moloney, Ed, *Voices From the Grave: Two Men's War in Ireland* (London: Faber and Faber, 2010).

Moloney, Ed and Andy Pollak, *Paisley* (Dublin: Poolbeg, 1986).

Moloney, Ed *Paisley: From Demagogue to Democrat* (Dublin: Poolbeg, 2008.

Moody, T.W. and F.X. Martin, *The Course of Irish History* (Lanham, MD: Roberts Rinehart, 2001, 4th ed.).

Mooney, John and Michael O'Toole, *Black Operations: The Secret War Against the Real IRA* (Dublin: Maverick House, 2003).

Morris, Aldon and Carol Mueller, *Frontiers in Social Movement Theory* (New Haven, CT, 1992).

Morrison, Danny, *Then The Walls Came Down* (Cork: Mercier Press, 1999).

Morrison, John F., *The Origins and Rise of Dissident Irish Republicanism: The Role and Impact of Organizational Splits* (New York: Bloomsbury, 2013).

Moxon-Browne, Edward, *Nation, Class and Creed in Northern Ireland* (Aldershot: Gower, 1978).

Moysey, Steven P., *The Road to Balcombe Street: The Reign of IRA Terror in London* (New York: Routledge, 2009).

Mullen, Don, *Eyewitness Bloody Sunday: The Truth* (Dublin: Merlin Publishing, 2002).

Mullin, Chris, *Error of Judgement: The Truth About the Birmingham Bombings* (Dublin: Poolbeg Press, 1986).

Munck, Ronnie and Bill Rolston, *Belfast in the Thirties: An Oral History* (Dingle: Brandon Books, New York: St. Martin's, 1986).

Murphy, Michael A., *Gerry Fitt: A Political Chameleon* (Cork: Mercier Press, 2007).

Murray, Gerry and Jonathan Tonge, *Sinn Féin and the SDLP: From Alienation to Participation* (London: Palgrave Macmillan, 2005).

Murray, Raymond, *The SAS in Ireland* (Cork: Mercier Press, 1990).

Na Fianna Éireann 1909–2009: Centenary Commemorative Booklet (Irish Freedom Press, n.d. [probably 2009]).

Nee, Patrick with Richard Farrell and Michael Blyth, *A Criminal & An Irishman: The Inside Story of the Boston Mob-IRA Connection* (Hanover, New Hampshire: Steerforth Press, 2006).

Newsinger, John, *British Counterinsurgency: From Palestine to Northern Ireland* (New York: Palgrave Macmillan, 2002).

Ní Chathmhaoil, Líta and Dieter Reinisch, *Cumann na mBan: 100 Years of Defending the Republic* (Dublin: Clo-Saoirse Press, 2014).

Ó Brádaigh, Ruairí, *Dílseacht: The Story of Cmdt. General Tom Maguire and the Second (All-Ireland) Dáil* (Dublin: Elo Press, 1997).

O'Brien, Brendan, *The Long War: The IRA & Sinn Féin from Armed Struggle to Peace Talks* (Dublin: O'Brien Press, 1995).

O'Brien, Justin, *Killing Finucane: Murder in Defence of the Realm* (Dublin: Gill and Macmillan, 2005).

O'Brien, R. Barry (ed.), *The Autobiography of Wolfe Tone, 1763–1798* (Dublin: Maunsel & Co., Ltd, 1914).

O'Broin, Leon, *Fenian Fever: An Anglo-American Dilemma* (New York: NYU Press, 1971).

O'Callaghan, Seán, *The Informer: The Real Life Story of One Man's War Against Terrorism* (London: Bantam Press, 1998).

Ó Coinn, Seán, *The Rising of the Phoenix, Éirí na Fhéinics* (Belfast: Shanway Press, 2013).

O'Connell, John, *Doctor John: Crusading Doctor & Politician* (Dublin: Poolbeg, 1989).

Ó Dochartaigh, Niall, *From Civil Rights to Armalites: Derry and the British of the Irish Troubles* (Cork: Cork University Press, 1997).

O'Doherty, Shane Paul, *The Volunteer: A Former IRA Man's True Story* (London: Harper Collins, 1993).

O'Donnell, Ruán, *Special Category: The IRA in English Prisons*, Vols 1 and 2 (Dublin: Irish Academic Press, 2012; 2015).

Ó Gadhra, Nollaig, *Margdil na Saoirse [Bargaining for Freedom]* (Baile Átha Cliath: Cló na Guaidhe, 1988)

O'Hearn, Denis, *Nothing But an Unfinished Song* (New York: Nation Books, 2006). O'Hegarty, P.S., *The Victory of Sinn Fein* (Dublin: The Talbot Press, Ltd., 1924).

O'Leary, Brendan and John McGarry, *The Politics of Antagonism* (Atlantic Highland, NJ, 1993).

O'Malley, Padraig, *The Uncivil Wars: Ireland Today* (Boston: Beacon Press, 1983).

O'Malley, Padraig, *Biting at the Grave: The Irish Hunger Strikes and the Politics of Despair* (Boston: Beacon Press, 1990).

SOURCES AND BIBLIOGRAPHY

Ó Muilleoir, Máirtín, *Belfast's Dome of Delight: City Hall Politics 1981–2000* (Belfast: Beyond the Pale Publications, 1999).

Operation Banner: An Analysis of Military Operations in Northern Ireland (Chief of the General Staff, British Ministry of Defence, 2006).

Oppenheimer, A.J., *IRA: The Bombs and the Bullets: A History of Deadly Ingenuity* (Dublin: Irish Academic Press, 2009).

O'Rawe, Richard, *Blanketmen: An Untold Story of the H-Block Hunger Strike* (Dublin: New Island Books, 2005).

O'Reilly, Dermot, *Accepting the Challenge: The Memoirs of Michael Flannery* (Dublin: Cló Saoirse/Irish Freedom Press, 2001).

Pakenham, Frank (The Earl of Longford) and Thomas P. O'Neill, *Eamon de Valera: A Biography* (Boston: Houghton-Mifflin, 1971).

Patterson, Henry, *The Politics of Illusion: Republicanism and Socialism in Modern Ireland* (London: Hutchinson Radius, 1989).

Piven, Frances Fox and Richard Cloward and *Poor People's Movements: Why They Succeed, How They Fail* (New York, Vintage, 1977).

Portelli, Alessandro, *The Death of Luigi Trastulli and Other Stories: Form and Meaning in Oral History* (Albany: SUNY Press, 1991).

Powell, Jonathan Powell, *Great Hatred, Little Room: Making Peace in Northern Ireland* (New York: Vintage Books, 2008).

Prince, Simon and Geoffrey Warner, *Belfast and Derry in Revolt: A New History of the Start of the Troubles* (Dublin: Irish Academic Press, 2012).

Pringle, Peter and Philip Jacobson, *Those are Real Bullets: Bloody Sunday, Derry, 1972* (New York: Grove Press, 2000).

Probert, Belinda, *Beyond Orange and Green: The Political Economy of the Northern Ireland Conflict* (London: Zed Books, 1978).

Quinn, Raymond, *A Rebel Voice: A History of Belfast Republicanism, 1925–1972* (Belfast: The Belfast Cultural and Local History Group, 1999).

Rafter, Kevin, *The Clann: The Story of Clann na Poblachta* (Cork: Mercier Press, 1996).

Rees, Merlyn, *Northern Ireland: A Personal Perspective* (London: Methuen, 1985).

Reynolds, Albert, *Albert Reynolds: My Autobiography* (Dublin: Transworld Ireland, 2009).

B. Rolston with M. Gilmartin, *Unfinished Business: State Killings and the Quest for Truth* (Belfast: Beyond the Pale, 2000).

Rose, Richard, *Governing Without Consensus: An Irish Perspective* (London: Faber and Faber, 1971).

Ross, F. Stuart, *Smashing H-Block* (Liverpool: Liverpool University Press, 2011).

Rossa, O'Donovan, *Irish Rebels in English Prisons* (Dingle, Co. Kerry: Brandon, 1991 edition).

Routledge, Paul, *John Hume: A Biography* (London: Harper Collins, 1997).

Routledge, Paul, *Public Servant, Secret Agent: The Elusive Life and Violent Death of Airey Neave* (London: Fourth Estate, 2002).

Rowan, Brian, *How the Peace Was Won* (Dublin: Gill and Macmillan, 2008).

Ruane, Joseph and Jennifer Todd, *The Dynamics of Conflict in Northern Ireland: Power, Conflict and Emancipation* (Cambridge: Cambridge University Press, 1996).Ryan, Desmond, *Sean Treacy and the Third Tipperary Brigade I.R.A.* (Tralee: Anvil Books, 1945).

Ryan, Meda, *Tom Barry: IRA Freedom Fighter* (Cork: Mercier Press, 2003).

Ryder, Chris, *The RUC: A Force Under Fire* (London: Mandarin Paperbacks, 1992).

Ryder, Chris and Vincent Kearney, *Drumcree: The Orange Order's Last Stand* (London: Methuen, 2001).

Sanders, Andrew, *Inside the IRA: Dissident Republicans and the War for Legitimacy* (University of Edinburgh Press, 2011).

Schmid, Alex P. and Albert J. Jongman, *Political Terrorism: A New Guide to Actors, Authors, Concepts, Data Bases, Theories and Literature* (New York: North-Holland Publishing Company, 1988).

Setting The Record Straight (Dublin: Sinn Féin, 1993).

Sharrock, David and Mark Devenport, *Man of War Man of Peace: The Unauthorized Biography of Gerry Adams* (London: Macmillan, 1997).

Short, K.R.M., *The Dynamite War: Irish American Bombers in Victorian Britain* (Dublin: Gill and Macmillan, 1979).

Sinnerton, Henry, *David Ervine: Unchartered Waters* (Dingle, Co. Kerry: Brandon, 2002).

Sinn Féin: A Century of Struggle Céad Bliain ar son na saoirse (Dublin: Sinn Féin, 2005).

Sloan, Robert, *William Smith O'Brien and the Young Ireland Rebellion of 1848* (Dublin: Four Courts Press, 2000).

Sluka, Jeffrey, *Hearts and Mind, Water and Fish: Support for the IRA and INLA in a Northern Irish Ghetto* (Bingley, West Yorkshire, UK: Emerald Group Publishing, 1990).

Smelser, Neil J. (ed.), *Handbook of Sociology* (London: Sage, 1988).

Smith, M.L.R., *Fighting for Ireland: The Military Strategy of the Irish Republican Movement* (New York: Routledge, 1995).

Staggenborg, Suzanne, *Social Movements* (Oxford: OUP, 2011).

Stalker, John, *The Stalker Affair: The Shocking True Story of Six Deaths and a Notorious Cover-Up* (New York: Viking, 1988).

Stryker, Sheldon, Timothy J. Owens and Robert W. White (eds), *Self, Identity, and Social Movements* (Minneapolis: University of Minnesota Press, 2000).

Sutton, Malcolm, *Bear in Mind these Dead: Index of Deaths from the Conflict in Ireland, 1969–93* (Belfast: Beyond the Pale Publications, 1994).

Tarrow, Sidney, *Democracy and Disorder* (Oxford: OUP, 1989).

Tarrow, Sidney, *Power in Movement: Social Movements, Collective Action, and Politics* (Cambridge: Cambridge University Press, 1998).

Taylor, Peter, *Beating the Terrorists? Interrogation in Omagh, Gough, and Castlereagh* (London: Penguin, 1980).

Taylor, Peter, *Behind the Mask: The IRA and Sinn Féin* (New York: TV Books, 1997).

Taylor, Peter, *Loyalists* (London: Bloomsbury Publishing, 1999).

Taylor, Peter, *Talking to Terrorists: A Personal Journey from the IRA to Al Qaeda* (London: HarperPress, 2011).

Terrorist Group Profiles, report by the US Vice President's Task Force on Combatting Terrorism (led by George H.W. Bush) (Washington, D.C.: U.S. Government Printing Office, 1988).

Thatcher, Margaret, *The Downing Street Years, 1979–90* (New York: Harper Collins, 1993).

The Last Post, Details and Stories of Irish Republican Dead 1916–1985 (Dublin: National Graves Association, 1985).

Tilly, Charles, *From Mobilization to Revolution* (New York: Random House, 1978).

Tilly, Charles, Louise Tilly, and Richard Tilly, *The Rebellious Century* (Cambridge: Harvard University Press, 1975).

Tírghrá: Ireland's Patriot Dead (Republican Publications, 2002).

Travers, Stephen and Neil Fetherstonhaugh, *The Miami Showband Massacre: A Survivor's Search for the Truth* (Dublin: Hodder Headline, 2007).

Treacy, Matt, *The IRA, 1956–69: Rethinking the Republic* (Manchester: Manchester University Press, 2011).

Urban, Mark, *Big Boys' Rules: The SAS and the Secret Struggle Against the IRA* (London: Faber and Faber, 1992).

Viterna, Jocelyn, *Women in War: The Micro-Processes of Mobilization in El Salvador* (Oxford: OUP, 2013).

Walsh, Liz, *The Final Beat: Gardaí Killed in the Line of Duty* (Dublin: Gill and Macmillan, 2001).

Weinstein, Jeremy, *Inside Rebellion: The Politics of Insurgent Violence* (Cambridge: Cambridge University Press, 2007).

We Shall Overcome: The History of the Struggle for Civil Rights in Northern Ireland, 1968–1978 (Belfast: NICRA, 1978).

Whalen, Lachlan, *Contemporary Irish Republican Prison Writing* (New York: Palgrave Macmillan, 2007).

Wharton, Ken, *Bloody Belfast: An Oral History of the British Army's War Against the IRA* (Port Stroud, Gloucestershire: Spellmount Publishers, 2010).

Whelan, Diarmuid, *Conor Cruise O'Brien: Violent Nations* (Dublin: Irish Academic Press, 2009).

White, Robert W., *Provisional Irish Republicans: An Oral and Interpretive History* (Westport, CT: Greenwood Press, 1993).

White, Robert W., *Ruairí Ó Brádaigh: The Life and Politics of an Irish Revolutionary* (Indianapolis: Indiana University Press, 2006).

White, Timothy, *Lessons from the Northern Ireland Peace Process* (Madison: University of Wisconsin Press, 2013).

Whittier, Nancy, *Feminist Generations: The Persistence of the Radical Women's Movement* (Philadelphia: Temple University Press, 1995).

Widgery Report: Lord Widgery's Report of Events in Londonderry, Northern Ireland, on 30 January 1972 (London: The Stationery Office, 1972);

Wilkinson, Paul, *Terrorism and the Liberal State* (London: Macmillan, 1986, 2nd ed.).

Wilkinson, Paul, *Terrorism versus Democracy: The Liberal State response* (New York: Routledge, 2006, 2nd ed.).

With the IRA in the Fight for Freedom: 1919 to the Truce (Cork: Mercier Press, 2010).

INDEX

INDEX

INDEX